CONSTITUTIONAL HISTORY
OF ENGLAND

STUBBS

VOL. II.

THE CONSTITUTIONAL HISTORY OF ENGLAND

IN ITS ORIGIN AND DEVELOPMENT

BY

WILLIAM STUBBS, D.D., Hon. LL.D.

Bishop of Oxford and Honorary Student of Christ Church
Late Regius Professor of Modern History

VOL. II

FOURTH EDITION

BARNES & NOBLE, Inc.
NEW YORK
PUBLISHERS & BOOKSELLERS SINCE 1873

First published by The Clarendon Press, 1897

Reprinted, 1967
by Barnes & Noble, Inc.
through special arrangement
with The Clarendon Press

Printed in the United States of America

CONTENTS.

CHAPTER XIV.

THE STRUGGLE FOR THE CHARTERS.

CHAPTER XV.

THE SYSTEM OF ESTATES, AND THE CONSTITUTION UNDER EDWARD I.

CHAPTER XVI.

EDWARD II, EDWARD III, AND RICHARD II.

CHAPTER XVII.

ROYAL PREROGATIVE AND PARLIAMENTARY AUTHORITY.

CHAPTER XIV.

THE STRUGGLE FOR THE CHARTERS.

168. Outline of the period.—169. Sketch of the political history of 1215 and 1216.—170. Administration of William Marshall.—171. Joint administration of Peter des Roches and Hubert de Burgh, 1219–1227.—172. Administration of Hubert, 1227–1232.—173. His downfall.—174. Henry's own administration.—175. Beginning of the Constitutional struggle.—176. The Provisions of Oxford, and government under them.—177. The Barons' war.—178. The close of the Reign.—179. Legislative period of Edward I.—180. Constitutional struggle.—181. Close of the Reign.—182. Summary.

168. THE Great Charter closes one epoch and begins another. On the one hand it is the united act of a nation that has been learning union; the enunciation of rights and liberties, the needs and uses of which have been taught by long years of training and by a short but bitter struggle: on the other hand it is the watchword of a new political party, the starting-point of a new contest. For eighty years from the 'parliament of Runnymede,' the history of England is the narrative of a struggle of the nation with the king, for the real enjoyment of the rights and liberties enunciated in the Charter, or for the safeguards which experience showed to be necessary for the maintenance of those rights. The struggle is continuous; the fortunes of parties alternate; the immediate object of contention varies from time to time; the wave of progress now advances far beyond the point at which it is to be finally arrested, now retires far below the point at which a new flow seems to be possible. And yet at each distinct epoch something is seen to be gained, something consolidated, something defined, something

Importance of the Great Charter as an era in Constitutional History.

Permanence of the fundamental principles of national life, as contrasted with the schemes of statesmen.

reorganised on a better principle. Of the many contrivances adopted on either side, some are cast away as soon as they have been tried, notwithstanding their effectiveness; some have become part of the permanent mechanism of the constitution, notwithstanding their uselessness. The prolific luxuriance of the age furnishes in politics, just as in architecture and in science, inventions which the rapidity of its movements and the involution of its many interests will not allow it to test. Hence the political ideas of the time produce on the fabric of society less effect than might reasonably be looked for, and the strong and ancient groundwork on which the edifice has already been begun outlasts the many graceful but temporary superstructures which are now and again raised upon it. There are great men abroad, and great schemes; but the determination of the great struggles often turns on points of momentary interest. The life which the heroes of the age breathe into the constitutional body tends to invigorate the whole: their spirit remains whilst their designs perish. Slowly and steadily the old machinery gains strength and works out its own completeness. It shakes off the premature accretions which would anticipate the forms towards which it is ultimately tending. Hence the political and the mechanical sides of the story must be looked at separately; the growth of the spirit of liberty apart from the expansion of the machinery; for the spirit works in forms which it has soon to discard, the machinery grows in its own proper form in spite of the neglect or contempt of the men by whose force it subsists. Their genius lives, but with a life which runs in other channels than those which it might itself have chosen.

The Charter a treaty between two parties largely affected by momentary circumstances.

The eighty years' struggle sprang directly out of the circumstances under which the Charter was drawn up. The Charter was a treaty between two powers neither of which trusted or even pretended to trust the other. The king, on his side, was by his personal fault encumbered with difficulties and entangled in combinations which were no necessary part of his constitutional position; while the national party comprised elements which needed the pressure of such a king to bring them together, and which, when released from that particular pressure, had little

A change of circumstances would alter the relation of the parties.

The union of the national party was itself the result of compromise.

sympathy or desire of union. The removal of John might bring back to the side of the crown all whom personal hatred had arrayed against him; the suspension or silencing of Langton might in an instant reverse the judgments that had been drawn from his arguments; and, if the mere rivalries of the leaders who had won the victory carried within them the seeds of future contests, the difference of the principles which had actuated them in the compromise were the beginnings of still deeper party distinctions. Some had struggled for national freedom, some for class privilege, some for personal revenge, against a king whose tyranny had infringed the rights of nation, class, and individual. When that king was gone, nation, class and individual, the country, the estate, and the personal interest, would stand marshalled against each other, all stronger for the common victory, each more exacting because of the share which it had in the winning of it. The victory won by such a coalition was in itself a premature triumph, an enunciation of principles which could not attain their full working until for coalition was substituted organic union; until the parties had renounced or forgotten the often conflicting motives which they now only suppressed in the presence of a common antagonist.

The national party was broken up by the concession of the Charter,

but was reunited by John's renewed tyranny.

The granting of the Charter at once disarmed a considerable portion of the barons, and drew others to the king's side. The clauses which directed the compulsory execution of the compact opened the way for jealousies amongst those who had won them; and the pope's interference neutralised the force which had brought them together and might have kept them in concert. The king in renewed strength might now crush in detail the various components of the force that had threatened to overwhelm him. The risk of such a result drew them again together, but not now under the guidance of constitutional leaders: they sought a violent release from the difficulty by renouncing the house of Anjou and by bringing in a new Conqueror. John's power owed its continued existence to the support of the papacy, the introduction of foreign mercenaries, and the faithfulness of his personal servants. His death saved the kingdom for his descendants. It removed the great stumbling-block

The work of William Marshall to reunite the nation.

and reversed the papal policy as regarded the Charter. The sagacious and honest policy of the earl of Pembroke drew to him all save those who were hopelessly committed to the invader. He placed the country under a government which included all elements, and which, whilst it could not suppress all jealousies, found room for all energies. Next, under Hubert de Burgh, a minister who had been taught in the school of Henry II, England was reclaimed for the English: the papal influence was eliminated or restricted; the foreign adventurers, who had traded on the fact that they were the king's friends, were humbled and banished; and the renewed growth of feudal ideas which had sprung up in the recent anarchy was steadily and sternly repressed. With the maturity of Henry a new phase of the struggle begins. The forces that Hubert had kept down, the Poictevin favourites, the feudal aspirants, the papal negotiators, the unconstitutional advisers, rise when he falls, and, alternately or in concert, urge the weak unsteady king forward in a course which has no consistent direction save that of opposition to the wishes of his people. For a long time the political parties are without great leaders. Henry acts as his own minister: until he has summed up the series of his follies and falsehoods, he disarms opposition by alternate concession and compulsion. When at length he has accumulated an irresistible weight of national indignation, he finds that he has also raised up within his own house a leader not unequal to the national demand. A seven years' struggle follows, in which the royal power is practically superseded by an aristocratic oligarchy resting on popular sympathies. At the end of that struggle the king triumphs; the aristocratic oligarchy vanishes, but the popular desire on which it rested has been satisfied: the constitutional reforms which were the pretext of aggression are secured, and more is gained from the perishing of the new polity than could have been gained from its permanence. The old life has drawn in a new inspiration for its own growth. The liberties of the nation are not yet vindicated, but the domination of the aliens is at an end for ever.

The work of Hubert de Burgh to expel the foreign influences.

Revival of the evil influences under the personal rule of Henry III.

These accumulate until a struggle is inevitable.

In the struggle the cause of the people is won, although the king triumphs.

With a new reign the old antipathies vanish, and the nation

rises to its full growth, in accord, for the most part, with the genius of its ruler. Edward earns its confidence by his activity in legislating and organising: and his peculiar policy, like that of Henry II, creates and trains the force which is to serve as its corrective. The great crisis, when it comes, turns on the main constitutional principles, not now encumbered with matters of personal or selfish interest. The struggle is decided permanently for a nation sufficiently well grown to realise its own part in it, and sufficiently compacted, under its new training, to feel its own strength. The 'Confirmatio Cartarum' did not need the executory provisions of the charter of John. It rested not only on the word of a king who might be trusted to keep his oath, but on the full resolve of a nation awake to its own determination. The king has taught in the plainest terms the principle by which the nation binds him: 'that which touches all shall be allowed of all'—the law that binds all, the tax that is paid by all, the policy that affects the interest of all, shall be authorised by the consent of all. From the date of that great pacification party politics take new forms.

Edward I trains the nation for a final vindication of constitutional right.

Edward's main principle.

In the history of these eighty years the growth of the constitutional mechanism is distinct from the growth of political ideas, and must be examined apart from it. Certain very marked results may be noted. The completion and definition of the system of the Three Estates: the completion of the representative system as based on local institutions and divisions, and as made possible by Edward's policy of placing the whole administration in direct relation with the crown: the clear definition of functions, powers, and spheres of action, in church and state, in court and council, in parliament and convocation, in legislature and judicature;—these are the work of the century. Their progress can be traced step by step, only at particular moments crossing the orbits of the political forces, although vivified and stimulated by the electric state of the political atmosphere. So much of this progress towards completion and definition as belongs to our subject must be treated in separate detail. We have now to trace somewhat more fully the process and variations, and to determine the personal agencies, in the political struggle of which we have here drawn the outline.

Division of the subject.

Constitutional results, to be stated in Chapter XV.

Historical narrative in the following chapter.

Measures for carrying out the pacification, June, 1215.

169. The Great Charter was granted on the 15th of June, 1215. The rest of the month was devoted to the measures by which the pacification was to be completed. On the 18th the king directed his partisans to abstain from hostilities [1]; on the 19th the writs were issued for the inquest into the evil customs [2]; on the 23rd Hugh de Boves was ordered to dismiss the mercenaries assembled at Dover [3]; on the 27th directions were given for a general enforcement of the oath of obedience to the twenty-five executors of the Charter [4]; writ after writ went forth for the restoration of hostages and castles, and for the liberation of prisoners [5]. The 16th of August was fixed as the day for general restitution and complete reconciliation [6]; in the meantime the city of London was left in the hands of the twenty-five, and the Tower was intrusted to the archbishop as umpire [7] of conflicting claims. Under this superficial appearance of peace both parties were arming. The surrender of castles and prisoners was little more than an exchange of military positions: the earl of Winchester recovered Mountsorel, the earl of Essex Colchester, and William of Aumâle Rockingham [8]. Whilst they transferred their garrisons from the king's castles to their own, he was fortifying and victualling his strongholds [9], borrowing money on all sides, placing the county administration in the hands of his servants as 'vicecomites pacis' [10] in order to defeat the measures of the twenty-five,

Both parties prepare to continue the contest.

[1] Foedera, i. 133; Rot. Pat. i. 143. I must content myself with a general reference to the works of Brady, Carte, Prynne, and Hume, as well as to the more recent labours of Mr. Pearson, and to the invaluable history of Dr. Pauli.

[2] Foedera, i. 134; Rot. Pat. i. 145, 180; Select Charters, p. 306.

[3] Foedera, i. 134; Rot. Pat. i. 144.

[4] Foedera, i. 134.

[5] See Rot. Claus. i. pp. 216 sq.

[6] 'Ad jura restituenda;' R. Coggeshall, ed. Stevenson, p. 172; Foedera, i. 133.

[7] 'Tanquam mediator ac sequester,' R. Coggeshall, p. 173; 'tanquam in sequestro,' W. Cov. ii. 221.

[8] W. Cov. ii. 221; Rot. Pat. i. 143, 144.

[9] M. Paris, ii. 612.

[10] W. Cov. ii. 222. The appointments made in June will be found in the Patent Rolls, i. 144, 145. None of these 'vicecomites pacis' were the regular sheriffs; and, as the barons soon after divided the counties among themselves, there must have been three rival and conflicting authorities in each. But the king made further changes in July (Rot. Pat. i. 150); and within a few months some of those nominated in June are found in arms against him.

mustering new forces at sea, and writing to Innocent and Philip to ask for aid against the bold men who, in extorting the terms of the charter, had degraded royalty and set at nought the claims of the pope [1]. The more extreme men on the baronial side, who had committed themselves too deeply to trust John, had retired to their estates, where they complained that the peace had been made without their participation [2]. The north was already full of the rumours of war [3]; and as early as the beginning of July Robert Fitz-Walter was afraid to let the barons leave the neighbourhood of London [4]. On the 15th John avoided an intended meeting with the barons at Oxford [5].

John appeals to Rome.

Mutual alarms.

The 16th of August came: the bishops met at Oxford, the barons at Brackley; the king failed to appear. He had, he said, performed his part of the covenant, the barons had neglected theirs; it was not safe for him to trust himself within reach of their armed host. A papal letter was laid before the prelates, in which the archbishop was charged to excommunicate the king's enemies and the disturbers of the peace; and Pandulf, with the bishop of Winchester and the abbot of Reading, was empowered to compel obedience [6]. After three days' discussion, the bishops determined to make another appeal to the king, and try to induce him to meet the barons. But their mediation failed, and on the 26th of August, at Staines, they published the sentence in the presence of the baronial army, each party interpreting it in their own way, and the majority regarding John as his own worst enemy, the great disturber of the peace, on whom sooner or later the curse would fall [7].

Meeting of the bishops at Oxford, August, 1215

Letter of excommunication produced,

and published, Aug. 26, at Staines.

[1] M. Paris, ii. 613, 615. John's letters to the pope are in the Rot. Pat. i. 182.

[2] W. Cov. ii. 222. The barons generally refused to take the oath of fealty in the terms prescribed by John, who obtained a declaration from the bishops that they had refused: but the date of the negotiation is not given; Rot. Pat. i. 181; Foed. i. 134.

[3] See Rot. Pat. i. 150.

[4] Foed. i. 134. He had to change the place fixed for a tournament on the 4th of July from Stamford to a spot between Staines and Hounslow.

[5] Rot. Pat. i. 149.

[6] W. Cov. ii. 223. The names of the executors of this first sentence enable us to identify the papal letter produced on Aug. 16 with that given by Matthew Paris (ii. 627) without date; 'Miramur.' The bull by which the Charter was quashed was not issued until August 25; Foed. i. 136.

[7] W. Cov. ii. 223, 224; R. Coggesh. p. 173.

Mutual defiance.

This act broke up the temporary peace. John now made no secret that he was collecting forces[1]; the twenty-five allotted amongst themselves[2] the counties that were to be secured, and summoned a council to take into consideration the election of a new king: Pandulf and his colleagues proceeded to a personal excommunication of the more eminent leaders, who in reply appealed to the general council summoned to the Lateran for the following November[3]. Langton, seeing himself powerless, determined to go to Rome. John was at first inclined to forbid his departure, not wishing perhaps to lose so important a hostage or to risk a second interdict: but from all fear of the latter danger he was delivered by Pandulf, who took upon himself to suspend the archbishop at the moment of his embarkation[4]. The king laid hold on the archiepiscopal estates on the plea of insuring their indemnity, but failed in securing the castle of Rochester, which was occupied by William of Albini and Reginald of Cornhill for the baronial party[5].

Langton goes to Rome.

War begins, Sept. 1215.

The departure of Langton and the end of harvest gave the signal for war. This was early in September[6]. Two parties were immediately formed: many of the great nobles, protesting their belief in the good intentions of John, had refused, notwithstanding their oath, to obey the summons of the twenty-five.

[1] On the 28th of August he had come to Sandwich to meet the mercenaries, Rot. Pat. i. 155; but as early as the 12th he had summoned the count of Brittany, ibid. 152.

[2] Geoffrey de Mandeville took Essex; Robert Fitz-Walter, Northampton; Roger de Cresci, Norfolk and Suffolk; Saer de Quincy, Cambridge and Huntingdon; William of Albini, Lincoln; John de Lacy, York and Nottingham; Robert de Ros, Northumberland; W. Cov. ii. 224. On the 17th of September Robert Fitz-Walter's lands in Cornwall were granted by the king to his son Henry; Rot. Claus. i. 228: and early in October the king bestowed the estates of Geoffrey de Mandeville and Saer de Quincy on his servants; ibid. 230. On the 31st the earls of Chester and Derby and others had the grant of the lands held of them by the king's enemies; ibid. 233.

[3] W. Cov. ii. 224. London was put under interdict, but the sentence was not observed.

[4] W. Cov. ii. 225; M. Paris, ii. 630; R. Coggesh. p. 174. The sentence of suspension was confirmed by the pope, Nov. 4, 1215; Foed. i. 139; M. Paris, ii. 634: and the confirmation reached the king on the Sunday before Christmas, Rot. Claus. i. 269.

[5] R. Coggesh. pp. 173, 176; W. Cov. ii. 226.

[6] W. Cov. ii. 222.

Of the great earls, those of Pembroke, Salisbury, Chester, Warenne, Ferrers, Arundel, and Warwick were for the king: on the side of the barons were those of Gloucester, Winchester, Hertford, Hereford, Oxford, Norfolk, and Huntingdon. One bishop, Giles de Braiose, took part with the barons, and one of the twenty-five, William of Aumâle, placed himself on the side of the king[1]. The younger William Marshall opposed his father. The Northern lords were faithful to the cause of freedom; the clergy, although they sympathised with the barons, were paralysed by the weight of ecclesiastical authority arrayed on behalf of John, and, having lost their leader, could show their sympathy only by contemning the papal threats. The leading spirits of the opposition were Robert Fitz-Walter and Eustace de Vescy, who, relieved from the wiser influence of Langton, despairing of safety under John, and already perhaps committed to France, were eager, as they had been in 1213, to advocate extreme counsels; and their arguments prevailed.

Division of parties.

At first the barons mistrusted their own strength. The abstention of the bishops, the strong measures of the pope, who on the 24th of August annulled the charter[2], forbade John to keep his oath, and summoned the barons to account for their audacious designs; the return of the most powerful earls to the king's side, and John's own unexpected readiness and energy, seem to have thoroughly disheartened them. Foreign aid must be obtained, and it could be obtained only on one condition—they must renounce their allegiance to John, and choose a new king. Saer de Quincy was sent to offer the crown to Lewis, the son of Philip of France[3]. The act, although technically justified by John's conduct and by ancient precedent, was a degrading one, and morally has no excuse but the plea of necessity. Like the Normans in 1204, the barons saw no choice but between

The baronial party seek foreign aid.

[1] See W. Cov. ii. 225. The bishop made his peace in October, Rot. Pat. i. 157; and died a month after.

[2] Foed. i. 135, 136; M. Paris ii. 616, 619.

[3] W. Cov. ii. 225, 226; R. Coggesh. p. 176; M. Paris, ii. 647, 648. The abjuration of John must have been a formal act and notified to the king, who excepts from his promises of pardon 'illis qui nos abjuraverunt;' Rot. Claus. i. 270. The election of Lewis was made unanimously by the baronage, but no dates are given; Ann. Waverley, p. 283; Foed. i. 140.

The act not without justification: John and Philip, their own extinction and a foreign ruler. Yet it is not at all necessary to suppose that the moral and political problem would take in their minds the formidable shape which it would have taken two centuries later, when the idea of loyalty was full grown, and when the legislation respecting treason had impressed the iniquity of rebellion in burning marks on men's consciences. (in the circumstances,) John was a tyrant, and no one doubted that the due reward of tyranny was death[1]: death should not indeed be inflicted by his liege servants, but his own oath taken to the Charter had put them in the position of belligerents rather than liegemen; nor did they seek his death, but his banishment. (in the theory of election and homage,) They used the power which the theory of election gave them, of setting aside one who had proved himself unworthy; the theory also of feudal relation compelled them to maintain his right only so long as he maintained theirs[2]. (and as a politic measure) Some few of them perhaps regarded the election of Lewis as a mere stratagem, by which, without declaration of war, Philip might be induced to withdraw from John's side the French mercenaries whom he had been allowed to enlist. The French soldiers could not fight against a French king, John would be left alone and would be again at their mercy.

Langton's complicity questionable. The offer to Lewis must have been made some time after Langton's departure, and it may never be clearly known how far he was cognisant of it. He was not likely to give it his open approval; it is not to be believed that, whilst patiently acquiescing in the papal suspension, he secretly supported the proposal. The appointment of his brother Simon as chancellor to the invader was rather a bribe to attract or a contrivance to implicate the archbishop, than an evidence of his complicity. He may be credited with neutrality; for otherwise some proof would have been forthcoming when the one party was as eager to claim him for an ally, as the other was to incriminate him as a traitor.

The military details of the struggle are simple. On the 11th

[1] Joh. Salisb. Polycr. viii. c. 20: 'Non quod tyrannos de medio tollendos non esse credam, sed sine religionis honestatisque dispendio.'

[2] 'Est itaque tanta et talis connexio per homagium inter dominum et tenentem suum, quod tantum debet dominus tenenti quantum tenens domino, praeter solam reverentiam;' Bracton, lib. ii. c. 35.

of October the king's forces besieged the castle of Rochester[1], and at the same time measures were taken for the relief of Northampton and Oxford, which were threatened by the barons. Their attempt to save Rochester failed, and it was taken on the 30th of November[2]. John, acting under the advice of his veterans, exercised only petty cruelties on the defenders. He then marched northwards as far as Berwick[3], reducing the castles of his enemies, and ravaging their estates, while at the same time he endeavoured to secure the frontier against the Scots, who had besieged Norham and overrun Northumberland. Having brought the Northern counties to his feet, and received proposals for submission from some of his most pertinacious foes, he returned to the South, where he had left half his army under Savaric de Mauleon and Falkes de Breauté, and joined the force which was besieging Colchester. Colchester surrendered in March, 1216[4]. This was the highest point that John's fortunes ever reached. The papal excommunication, issued on the 16th of December[5] and directed against the several rebels by name, had reduced them to the last extremity. The earl of Hertford and even Robert de Ros and Eustace de Vescy were petitioning for safe conduct in order to negotiate; on the 1st of January[6] the Constable of Chester and Roger of Mont Begon

After taking Rochester,

John reduces the North,

and returning southwards takes Colchester, March, 1216.

Despair of the barons.

[1] See W. Cov. ii. 226. William of Albini had got into the castle three days before. John arrived in person on the 13th. See M. Paris, ii. 621-625; R. Coggesh. p. 175; and the Itinerary of John.

[2] M. Paris, ii. 625.

[3] Every step of his progress may be traced by help of Sir T. D. Hardy's Itinerary. He left Rochester Dec. 6, and moved north from Windsor on the 16th. On the 14th of January he reached Berwick, and there stayed until the 22nd. Moving down slowly he was at York on Feb. 15, at Lincoln on the 23rd, and he reached Colchester on the 14th of March.

[4] R. Coggesh. p. 179.

[5] Foed. i. 139; M. Paris, ii. 642, 644. There are two lists of persons to be excommunicated. The first contains thirty-one names, eighteen out of the twenty-five executors, five sons or heirs of barons, and in addition, Peter de Brus, Roger de Cressi, Fulk Fitz-Warin, W. de Montacute, W. de Beauchamp, Simon de Kyme and Nicholas de Stuteville. The second contains twenty-nine names of secondary importance; and both lists end with Master Gervase the Chancellor of S. Paul's, the king's 'manifestissimus persecutor.'

[6] Rot. Claus. i. 245; cf. Foed. i. 137. Negotiations for peace were on foot as early as Oct. 22, 1215; Rot. Pat. i. 157. On the 9th of November the earl of Hertford, Robert Fitz-Walter, and the citizens of London had

made their peace. Although French forces had already landed, the efforts of the cardinal Gualo, who was now at Philip's court, and the intrigues of John's agents there, were impeding the action of Lewis. The king used his opportunity, and by unsparing confiscations placed the great estates of his enemies in the hands of his unscrupulous servants. His chief strength lay in such men as Falkes de Breauté, Savaric de Mauleon, Peter de Mauley and others who gain an unenviable eminence in the next reign, many of them Poictevin adventurers, who had learned the use of arms in rebellion against Henry and Richard, or who had taken service under those kings during the constant border-warfare in the French provinces. Notwithstanding his temporary triumph, these were the only men in whom he could really trust. Hubert de Burgh, who had been made justiciar in June 1215 [1], and William Marshall, the great earl of Pembroke, who never wavered in his faith, were second to such men in the king's confidence, and his undisguised dependence on them disgusted and repelled all others.

John uses his advantages.

Justification of the action of Lewis.

Medieval morality did not recognise political expediency as a justifiable cause of war: it required some claim of right or some plea of provocation before it would acknowledge the aggressor as better than a robber or a pirate. The great international tribunal at Rome was scarcely likely to admit such a plea as might reasonably have been alleged for Lewis's interference, the appeal of the perishing kingdom [2]. Philip and John were at

safe conduct for a conference; ibid. 158. John de Lacy had safe conduct to make his own peace Dec. 31, and several others at the same time, ibid. 162; and every step of the journey northwards is marked by the like submissions. After the capture of Colchester, the earl of Oxford had safe conduct, March 23; the earl of Hertford, March 27; Robert de Ros, Eustace de Vescy, and Peter de Brus, April 12; ibid. 176. The correspondence was going on as late as the 7th of May; ibid. 180. The Close Rolls for March are full of writs stating the submission and reconciliation of the king's enemies.

[1] He first appears as justiciar on the 24th of June; Rot. Pat. i. 143.

[2] 'Rex autem habet superiorem, Deum scilicet; item legem per quam factus est rex; item curiam suam, videlicet comites, barones, quia comites dicuntur quasi socii regis, et qui habet socium habet magistrum; et ideo si rex fuerit sine fraeno, id est, sine lege, debent ei fraenum ponere, nisi ipsimet fuerint cum rege sine fraeno; et tunc clamabunt subditi et dicent, Domine Jesu Christe, in chamo et fraeno maxillas eorum constringe. Ad quos Dominus, "vocabo super eos gentem robustam et longinquam et ignotam

peace; the five years' truce, concluded at Chinon in October 1214, was to last until Easter 1220 [1]. But neither conscientious scruples nor public law fetter men who are determined to take their own way. The truce served Philip as an excuse for holding back his son from overt action until a fair chance of success was secured, and the earls of Gloucester and Hereford were placed as hostages in his hands [2]. A threefold statement of reasons was drawn up. The legate was told [3] that John's gift to the pope was void; he had been condemned for treason to Richard, and was never really a king. If he were, however, then king, he was so no more, he had forfeited his crown when he was sentenced as Arthur's murderer. If that sentence were invalid, he had resigned his crown by submitting to the pope: it was clear that he might resign the crown, but without the consent of the barons he could not transfer it. The barons, regarding the throne as vacant, had elected to it Lewis, the husband of Blanche of Castille, the daughter of the eldest sister who had survived Richard [4]. In reply to the legate's assertion, that John was a crusader and that his dominions were for four years under papal guardianship, Lewis declared that John was the aggressor, having attacked his French dominions both before and after he took the cross.

Policy of Philip.

Formal arguments: (1) Between Philip and Gualo, April, 1216.

A like discussion took place at Rome, Innocent himself pleading the cause of John [5]. The sentence of forfeiture for Arthur's murder the pope set aside at once. A second argument, that John had incurred the sentence by contumacy and that his rights had devolved on Blanche, he refuted in detail. John's

(2) Between the pope and the French agents. May 8, 1216.

cujus linguam ignorabunt, quae destruet eos et evellet radices eorum de terra, et a talibus judicabuntur quia subditos noluerunt juste judicare, et in fine ligatis manibus eorum mittet eos in caminum ignis et tenebras exteriores, ubi erit fletus et stridor dentium;"' Bracton, lib. ii. c. 16. § 3.

[1] Foed. i. 125.

[2] R. Coggesh. p. 175. Matthew Paris, ii. 648, states that twenty-four hostages were demanded. John sent forged letters from the barons to Philip dissuading him from the invasion; R. Coggesh. p. 176.

[3] M. Paris, ii. 650–653. The argument was held fifteen days after Easter; according to M. Paris at Lyons, more probably at Laon.

[4] Eleanor of Castille died Oct. 21, 1214. She had thus survived John's act of defeasance; she was the elder surviving sister at the time of Richard's death; Johanna died in September 1199.

[5] A month after Easter; M. Paris, ii. 657–663.

Papal argument for John.

contumacy did not affect the rights of his children, and even if they did, Eleanor of Brittany, the Saxon dukes, the emperor Otto, and the king of Castille, stood nearer to the succession than Blanche. Her right could be maintained only by proving that her brother and mother had resigned their claims to her, that Eleanor of Brittany was excluded as being in the ascending line of succession, and that the living younger sister shut out the pretensions of the children of the elder. The charge that John was the aggressor was sustained only by similar special pleading.

(3) Lewis's argument addressed to the English.

The argument addressed to the English took a slightly different form. It is contained in a manifesto directed to the monks of S. Augustine's[1]; John had been condemned as a traitor for his conduct during Richard's captivity, and had thus lost his right to inherit, which had passed on to the queen of Castille. His coronation had been a violent infraction of her right, as was proved by the argument used by archbishop Hubert on the elective title to the crown. When John, still a childless man, was condemned for Arthur's murder, her rights revived in full force, and ever since then Lewis had been at war with him and unfettered by his father's truces. Finally, having at his coronation sworn to maintain the liberties of his kingdom, he had broken his oath by making it tributary; Lewis had been chosen into his place, with the common counsel of the realm, by the barons who, under the terms of the Great Charter which John had sworn and broken, were fully justified in doing so. On these grounds he demanded the support of the nation. His legal claim may be regarded as midway between the claim of William the Conqueror, as heir of Edward, to the crown of England, and that of Edward III, as representative of Charles IV, to the crown of France.

Arrival of the French, in Autumn, 1215.

The warlike preparations were not made to wait for the proof of the claim: John's fleet under Hugh de Boves perished in a great storm on the 26th of September; a misfortune which made the French invasion possible. A force

[1] Foed. i. 140.

of seven thousand Frenchmen landed in Suffolk[1] in November 1215; Saer de Quincy with forty-one transports reached London on the 9th of January[2]; on the 27th of February a large body of French nobles arrived in the Thames[3], and the marshal of France took the command of a garrison of his countrymen in the city[4]. On the 21st of May Lewis himself landed at Stonor[5], and John, who since the capture of Colchester had been waiting on the coast to intercept him, immediately retired to Winchester. This retreat was no doubt forced on him by a panic among his followers; the French soldiers could not be trusted to fight against the son of their king, and the more politic of the barons who were still on John's side were inclining to cast in their lot with their brethren. Lewis, without stopping, as his father advised him, to secure Dover, pressed on by Canterbury and Rochester to London, where he received the homage and fealty of the barons on the 2nd of June[6]. He is said to have made promises of good laws and of the restoration of lost heritages[7], but he does not seem to have bound himself by any formal constitutional engagements, or promised to observe the Charter; such undertakings were probably left for the day of coronation, before which John must be finally humbled. Eager to decide the contest Lewis pressed on to Winchester, taking Reigate, Guildford and Farnham on the way. On the 14th of June Winchester was surrendered; John, who had quitted it on the 5th, retiring by Wilton and Wareham to his stronghold at Corfe. The capture of Winchester decided the choice of the hesitating earls: within a few weeks William of Salisbury, the son of Henry II, William of Aumâle, the earls of Oxford, Arundel and Warenne, had declared for the winning side[8]. The castle of Marlborough was surrendered. The city

Arrival of Lewis, May, 1216.

Progress of Lewis, 1216.

He is received in London.

His early success.

The earls desert John.

[1] R. Coggesh. p. 176; Chr. Mailros, p. 188; M. Paris, ii. 623.
[2] R. Coggesh. p. 178. [3] M. Paris, ii. 648. [4] W. Cov. ii. 228.
[5] M. Paris, ii. 653; Ann. Waverl. p. 285. The day is given as May 14 by W. Cov. ii. 228; May 19, R. Coggesh. p. 181. See Pauli, Gesch. v. Eng. iii. 458.
[6] Liber de Antt. Legg. p. 202. 'Factae sunt ei fidelitates et hominia;' W. Cov. ii. 230; R. Coggesh. p. 181; M. Paris, ii. 654.
[7] 'Ille vero tactis sacrosanctis evangeliis juravit quod singulis eorum bonas leges redderet, simul et amissas hereditates;' M. Paris, ii. 654.
[8] W. Cov. ii. 231. The earl of Salisbury was with the king on the 13th

Success of Lewis against John, 1216.

of Worcester placed itself in the hands of the younger William Marshall [1]. In vain Gualo, who had followed Lewis to England and had excommunicated him and his supporters at Whitsuntide, placed an interdict on the lands of the barons and on the city of London: in vain the king denounced the forfeiture of the estates and decreed the demolition of the castles of the rebels. The Northern lords set out to join Lewis, and the king of Scots arrived at Dover to perform the customary homage, having captured the city of Carlisle on his way. Lewis was now certified of John's helplessness or incapacity, and was attempting to secure the royal fortresses, Dover which held out under Hubert de Burgh, Windsor, and Lincoln [2]. The king finding his adversaries so employed, left Corfe and proceeded through the marches to Shrewsbury: he then returned to Worcester, which had been recovered in July, and by Bristol into Dorsetshire, whence he started again at the end of August by Oxford and Reading, intending to raise the sieges of Windsor and Lincoln and to cut off the return of the king of Scots. His march was a continuous devastation. Indiscriminately the lands of friends and enemies were ravaged. As if his cause seemed to himself to be desperate, he acted as one bent on involving the whole nation in his own destruction [3]. Yet although his fortunes and his moral position had now sunk even lower than on the day of Runnymede, he still retained the service and allegiance of some of the most powerful lords, whose adhesion was unquestionably dictated in some measure by national feeling. Ranulf of Chester never flinched: the earl Marshall was now as ever faithful: the earl Ferrers and Henry of Warwick, the last almost of the faithful Beaumonts,

Homage of the king of Scots.

John's wanderings and devastations.

His remaining elements of strength.

of June, but had joined the enemy before the 17th of August; Rot. Claus. i. 282: the Constable of Chester had returned to the barons before Sept. 23; ibid. 289. The desertion of the earls immediately followed the capture of Winchester; R. Coggesh. p. 181; Chron. Mailros, p. 191.

[1] Worcester surrendered to the younger William Marshall, but was recovered by the earl of Chester and Falkes de Breauté on the 17th of July; Ann. Wigorn. p. 406; Ann. Theokesb. p. 62.

[2] Dover was besieged from July 22 to October 14; R. Coggesh. p. 182. Cf. Ann. Waverley, p. 285. The siege of Windsor had lasted two months when it was broken up on account of John's march on Lincoln; ibid.

[3] R. Coggesh. p. 183; W. Cov. ii. 231.

remained with him. Hubert de Burgh, William Briwere and Peter des Roches, even the foreign servants, whatever were their demerits, justified his confidence. But the end was close at hand. His march by Oxford had drawn away the besiegers from Windsor; he had dispersed the leaguer at Lincoln and put to flight the remnant at Lynn, when he was seized with a fatal illness at Sleaford on the 14th of October, and died at Newark on the 19th[1]. We need not ask whether poison, excess, or vexation hastened his death. He was the very worst of all our kings: a man whom no oaths could bind, no pressure of conscience, no consideration of policy, restrain from evil; a faithless son, a treacherous brother, an ungrateful master; to his people a hated tyrant. Polluted with every crime that could disgrace a man, false to every obligation that should bind a king, he had lost half his inheritance by sloth, and ruined and desolated the rest. Not devoid of natural ability, craft or energy, with his full share of the personal valour and accomplishments of his house, he yet failed in every design he undertook, and had to bear humiliations which, although not without parallel, never fell on one who deserved them more thoroughly or received less sympathy under them. In the whole view there is no redeeming trait; John seems as incapable of receiving a good impression as of carrying into effect a wise resolution.

Death of John, Oct. 19, 1216.

His vices,

and humiliations.

A few months before him, on the 16th of July, died Innocent III, just as he must have been convinced of the folly of his determination to support John at all hazards, and of the impossibility of reconciling his present policy with that moral government which he aspired to exercise over the Christian world. In England the news of the pope's death was received with thanksgiving. Great and wise as he was, his name had here been always coupled with calamity. He had pronounced the interdict, he had condemned the champions of liberty and the form of sound government; he had suspended the arch-

Death of Innocent III, July 16, 1216.

A relief to England.

[1] W. Cov. ii. 231. The executors named in his will are—the legate, the bishops of Winchester, Worcester, and Chichester; the earls of Pembroke, Chester and Ferrers, William de Briwere, Walter de Lacy, John of Monmouth, Savaric de Mauleon, Falkes de Breauté, and Aimeric de S. Maur, the Master of the Temple; Foed. i. 144.

Fatal influence of the pope in John's favour.

bishop whom all had learned to regard as the interpreter of the constitution, and he had to the last blessed and strengthened the tyrant. But for his influence John could not have repudiated his oath to the charter, or driven the barons to call in a foreign invader as their only possible deliverer. Innocent leaves a deep mark on our history, and, readily as we recognise the grandeur of his aims, it must be allowed to be a deep mark of aggression and injustice. The unhappy design of turning a free kingdom into a fief of the Roman see was the key to a policy that seems utterly inconsistent with that great zeal for righteousness with which he was no doubt inspired. We cannot guess what might have been his policy if he had survived John, but, so far as we can see, it would have been morally impossible for him to recede from the position that he had taken. He knew the worst of John and yet sustained him: he had nothing more to learn which would justify him in forsaking him. His successor reaped the fruit of his experience and adopted a wiser plan.

Coronation of Henry III, Oct. 28, 1216.

170. John was buried, as he had directed in his will, at Worcester, a few days after his death; and the coronation of Henry III was celebrated at Gloucester on the 28th of October, with such slight ceremony as was possible, and with a smaller attendance of bishops and barons than had appeared since the coronation of Stephen. The boy of nine years old was made to take the solemn constitutional oaths, dictated by the bishop of Bath, and to do homage also to the pope in the person of the legate Gualo [1]. A plain circlet of gold was the substitute for the crown, which was no doubt beyond the reach of the royal party; and the bishop of Winchester, in the absence of the two archbishops and the bishop of London, anointed and crowned the child [2]. That done, the homage and fealty of the magnates

[1] Rot. Claus. i. 335; Foed. i. 145; Ann. Waverley, p. 286; W. Cov. ii. 233. Matthew Paris, iii. 1, gives the form of the oath: 'Quod honorem, pacem ac reverentiam portabit Deo et sanctae ecclesiae et ejus ordinatis, omnibus diebus vitae suae; quod in populo sibi commisso rectam justitiam tenebit; quodque leges malas et iniquas consuetudines, si quae sint in regno, delebit et bonas observabit et ab omnibus faciet observari.'

[2] According to the Annals of Tewkesbury, Gualo placed the crown on Henry's head; p. 62: see also Ann. Winton. p. 83; Ann. Wigorn. p. 407; and the same might be inferred from the royal letter announcing the issue

present was taken, and a council summoned for the 11th of November at Bristol. Council summoned.

The news of John's death had already affected the balance of parties, and gone far to reverse their constitutional attitude. Hubert de Burgh, who had just made a truce with Lewis for the siege of Dover[1], hastened to join the legate; and, although Lewis took advantage of the respite to secure the castles of Hertford and Berkhampstead[2], as well as to receive the surrender of the Tower of London, the gain of time was not purchased too dearly. Berkhampstead was made the price of a general armistice which was to last until the 13th of January. The interval was well employed. At Bristol, on the 11th of November, eleven bishops presented themselves. Langton and the bishop of Lincoln, and probably the archbishop of York also, were still abroad; the bishops of Salisbury and London were ill; the sees of Durham, Norwich, and Hereford were vacant. The earls of Pembroke, Chester, and Derby represented their own branch of the council; William of Aumâle also had returned to his allegiance before John's death; Hubert de Burgh and the two Williams de Briwere, father and son, represented the administrative body; Savaric de Mauleon and Falkes de Breauté, the military strength which John had laboured so hard to maintain. Of the other barons present the most famous names are those of Beauchamp, Basset, Clifford, Mortimer, Lacy, and Cantilupe, most of them from the western shires and the march, where the personal influence of John had been longest and least oppressively felt. Of the twenty-five executors of the charter, William of Aumâle alone appeared, but William of Albini, the defender of Rochester, who had just been

Truce and armistice.

Council at Bristol. Nov. 11, of bishops, earls, ministers, and warriors.

The western barons attend.

of the charter; Foedera, i. 145; but the coronation, although performed under Gualo's authority, which was necessary to overrule the protests of the Westminster and Canterbury monks, was solemnised by the English bishops, Winchester, Bath, Worcester, and Exeter; Ann. Dunst. p. 48; M. Paris, iii. 2: and Wykes (p. 60) mentions that the legate did not even put his hand on the crown.

[1] Oct. 14; R. Coggesh. p. 182; W. Cov. ii. 232; cf. M. Paris, iii. 5.

[2] Hertford was besieged from Nov. 11 to Dec. 6, and Berkhampstead from Dec. 6 to Dec. 20; Lewis reached Lambeth Nov. 4, and the Tower was surrendered on the 6th; Liber de Ant. Legg. p. 202; M. Paris, iii. 5, 6, 8; Ann. Waverley, p. 286.

ransomed, had determined to support the young king, and several of the gallant company were now dead[1].

Question of guardianship and regency.

Since the days of Ethelred the crown of England had never fallen to a child, and the first business of the council was to determine in whose guardianship the king and the kingdom lay. We are not told by what arguments this was decided; but it may be presumed that there would be conflicting claims, and competing analogies. The pope might fairly claim the custody of a ward who had so recently recognised his feudal superiority. The queen was the natural guardian. Near kinsman the young king had none at hand; and, if the principle of the civil law were to be adopted, it might have been a critical point whether the count Palatine or the king of Castille or even Lewis himself might not demand the regency. In France no such emergency had as yet arisen; the miserable minority of Henry IV in Germany was a warning rather than a precedent, and that of Frederick II presented a parallel full of evil omen. Nor could the common feudal analogy apply, by which the care of the estate belonged to the heir, and that of the person of the minor to the next kinsman who could not inherit. Even if the persons were eligible, the circumstances of the case admitted no such solution; and the plan adopted was that which the vassals of the Frank kingdom of Palestine used in such cases[2]; the barons of the realm determined to appoint a regent, and they, by common consent, chose the earl of Pembroke to be 'rector regis et regni[3].' With him were associated, as chief councillors, the legate and Peter des Roches bishop of Winchester; the former to satisfy the claims and to secure the support of the Pope, the latter perhaps, however inadequately, to fill the place that belonged to the archbishop of Canterbury[4].

The Earl of Pembroke 'rector regis et regni.'

[1] The names are given in the reissue of the Charter; Select Charters, p. 340.

[2] See the Assises de Jerusalem, i. 261, and Count Beugnot's note.

[3] 'Commissa est ex communi consilio cura regis et regni legato, episcopo Wintoniensi, et Willelmo Marescallo;' W. Cov. ii. 233. 'Remansit in custodia Willelmi comitis Pembroc, magni videlicet Mareschalli;' M. Paris, iii. 2.

[4] There is a writ tested at Bristol on the 13th of November by William Marshall as justiciar of England (Rot. Claus. i. 293), which seems to show

The first act of the government proved its wisdom and defined its policy. The Great Charter was republished[1], not indeed in its completeness, but with an express statement that no permanent infraction was contemplated. All the material provisions for the remedy of administrative oppressions were retained; but the constitutional clauses, those touching taxation and the national council, were omitted. The articles that concerned the debts of the Jews, the right of entering and leaving the kingdom, the forests, warrens, and rivers, were likewise put in respite until fuller counsel could be had; then all things were to be fully deliberated and faithfully amended. The reasons for this course are obvious. The baronage was for the moment in the place of the king: to limit the taxing powers of the crown would be to tie their own hands; and the Jews, the forests, and other demesne rights, were at the moment too ready sources of revenue to be dispensed with. The country was at war, and the government must not be crippled. There are other indications that the hands which drew up the new charter were not those which drew up the old. There could be no question about the banishment of aliens, when aliens formed the mainstay of the government. Some idea too of removing the restrictions on feudal action may have prompted other changes, for the feudal instinct must have been stronger at Bristol than at Runnymede. It is, however, by no means the least curious feature of the history, that so few changes were needed to transform a treaty won at the point of the sword into a manifesto of peace and sound government; that the papal power, which a year before had anathematised the charter and its advocates, could now accept and publish it as its own; and that the barons who had to the last supported John in repudiating it, should, the moment he was taken out of the way, declare their adhesion to it. Nor is it less a proof that the

Reissue of the Great Charter, Nov. 12, 1216.

Modifications in it.

Reasons for these changes.

The Charter becomes the rallying point for union.

Inferences from this.

that it was intended that he should bear that title, but it may be a clerical error. Hubert de Burgh is called *justitiarius noster* in the charter issued the day before, and continues in office.

[1] Statutes of the Realm (Charters), p. 14; Select Charters, p. 340. Letters for the publication of the Charter were issued June 27, 1217; Rot. Claus. i. 336.

baronial body, whether for or against the king, was in the main actuated by patriotic feeling, and ready to take the same line of reform. The omission of the constitutional clauses does not disprove this, for it is by no means clear that their importance was fully realised; it is at least as strange that they were never forced on Henry III by the triumphant barons after the parliament of Oxford, as that they were omitted now. It is equally conceivable, as has been already observed, that they embodied and enunciated an accepted constitutional practice[1], as that they imposed a new restriction on arbitrary government. The struggle over taxation is unintermitted; yet, until the reign of Edward I, there is no formal attempt made to supply an omission which dates from the accession of his father. John's tyrannical designs are thus seen to have been the great hindrance to the pacification of the country; his vanity would not be bound by terms within whose as yet unwritten limits his father had been content to act. Now John was dead, and the charter at once might be made the basis of peace. At the same time we need not suppose that either legate or regent overlooked the importance of winning the people, or of dividing still more the ill-assorted elements that were sustaining the cause of the invader.

Omission of the constitutional clauses in the reissue of the Charter.

Disappointment of the barons at the behaviour of Lewis.

The unfortunate barons had already found out their mistake. John, shortly before his death, had at Newark received promises of adhesion from forty of the lords who wished to rejoin him; and although after his death and Henry's coronation the malcontents had bound themselves to Lewis more strictly than ever, and had renounced by oath the heirs of John, mutual confidence was not restored. Robert Fitz-Walter, 'the marshal of the army of God,' was made to feel that not even he was trusted. After the capture of Hertford he asked to have the charge of the castle, as he had held it in the early years of John. Lewis answered, by the advice of his French counsellors, that Englishmen having been traitors to their own lord were not fit to have the charge of castles[2]. He soothed the offended baron by the

[1] See below, p. 30, note 1, and Vol. I. p. 534.
[2] M. Paris, ii. 668; iii. 6; see too Ann. Dunst. p. 47.

assurance that when he was king all men should have their own; but the word had sunk deep, and later events strengthened the impression.

After Christmas each party held a council: Henry's friends met at Oxford[1], those of Lewis at Cambridge. At the expiration of the truce war was renewed; the regent strengthening his positions of defence; the legate trying to bring the influence of the church to bear on Lewis; Lewis securing as many as he could of the castles of the eastern shires, in order to gain a compact base of operations, and connect London with the camps of Lincoln, Rochester, and Dover. He took Hedingham, Orford, Norwich, and Colchester; conceding, for the surrender of the last, a new truce which was to last until April 23. This truce was as necessary to himself as to Henry, for his father had peremptorily summoned him to a council, called to avert the interdict which the pope threatened to issue on account of his behaviour in England. Early in March, under the strictest obligation to return speedily, Lewis departed, and from that moment his chances of success were over: perhaps they had never been so great as the desperation of John had augured. He had indeed secured a large proportion of the barons, but the military advantages were on the king's side. In the whole of the north, the fortresses were in the king's hands. The towns received Lewis, but the moment that his troops quitted a district, it was reduced by the royal garrisons that he had failed to dislodge. Of the castles, those only which had been in the hands of the barons when war broke out, the few that he had taken whilst pursuing John to Winchester, and those of the eastern counties which had been taken since John's death, were in his hands; these captures were the limit of his success.

Councils in Jan. 1217.

Lewis secures the Eastern Counties.

He visits France, in March.

Limits of his success.

As soon as he was gone the earl of Salisbury, who had long been wavering[2], forsook him, and, with many other lords anxious

[1] The court was at Oxford from the 13th to the 30th of January (Rot. Pat.). The council is mentioned in a writ in the Close Rolls, i. 319. The Close Rolls are full of writs ordering the restitution of the estates of the men who had come in and made peace, from December 1216 onwards.

[2] See Chr. Mailros, p. 194; R. Coggesh. p. 185; W. Cov. ii. 235. The earl of Salisbury and William Marshall the younger had letters of safe

Lewis, on his return, finds his cause declining.

to find a reasonable pretext for desertion, declared himself a crusader; Lewis returned but three days after the truce expired, to find that the younger William Marshall had joined his father, that the castles of Marlborough, Farnham, Winchester and Chichester were lost, that Mountsorel was besieged by the earl of Chester, and that Lincoln still presented an impregnable front[1]. He determined that Dover must be his first object, and dispatched Robert Fitz-Walter with a French reinforcement to raise the siege of Mountsorel and strengthen the besieging force at Lincoln. In the first Robert was successful. The earl of Chester left Mountsorel, but only to join the regent who was advancing in full force to Lincoln. The decisive day was the 20th of May: after a bloody struggle in the streets the royal host was completely victorious: Saer de Quincy, Robert Fitz-Walter, Richard of Montfichet, William Mowbray, Robert de Ros, leaders among the twenty-five, with Gilbert of Ghent, Lewis's new-made earl, were taken. So far as concerned the English, the battle of Lincoln practically ended the struggle[2]. London however was still obdurate, and Lewis had hope of succour from France. But even this was short-lived. On the 24th of August Hubert de Burgh completely defeated and destroyed the fleet on which the only remaining hope depended. Lewis had already left Dover for London. The march of the regent on London compelled him to come to terms: negotiations

Battle of Lincoln, May 20, 1217.

Naval victory, Aug. 24.

conduct on the 8th of December; Rot. Pat. 1 Hen. III (twenty-sixth report of the Deputy Keeper, p. 67): the earl, who had been at the council at Oxford in January (Rot. Claus. i. 319), had restitution of his estates on the 7th of March, Rot. Claus. i. 299; and the younger Marshall immediately afterwards appears in the king's service, and has custody of the estates of the men with whom he had just before been in alliance, such as Saer de Quincy; ibid. From this moment crowds of penitents come in; see Rot. Claus. i. 300 sq.: Gilbert of Clare has safe conduct, March 27; the earl of Warenne, who had made a truce April 16 (Foed. i. 146), comes in on the 5th of May.

[1] Rot. Claus. i. 297.

[2] W. Cov. ii. 237; R. Coggesh. p. 185. Negotiations for peace began before the 12th of June; Foed. i. 147; the earl of Arundel had come in on July 14; the constable of Chester, August 9; John Fitz-Robert, another of the twenty-five, July 25. After the peace, on the 17th of September, the countess of Gloucester, John's divorced wife, submitted, Sept. 17; Saer de Quincy, Sept. 29; William of Mandeville, Oct. 4; Rot. Claus. i. 315–348. Cf. Foed. i. 149.

began at Kingston, and were completed by a treaty at Lambeth on the 11th of September[1]: on the 20th Lewis received absolution from Gualo[2]; and on the 23rd the final arrangements were made at Merton for his departure[3].

Treaty of Lambeth, Sept. 11, 1217.

The treaty of Lambeth is, in practical importance, scarcely inferior to the charter itself, and bespeaks an amount of sound policy, honesty and forbearance on both sides, which could scarcely have been expected after so long and bitter a contest. Lewis stipulates for the safety of his confederates, and the royal party shows no desire of vengeance. All parties alike, individuals and communities, are restored to their lands, and are to enjoy the right customs and liberties of the realm. Prisoners are to be set free, and ransoms remitted under a careful arrangement to prevent fraud. All who had been on Lewis's side are to give assurance of fidelity to Henry by homage, oaths and charters. Hostages are to be restored. Cities, boroughs, towns, castles and lands that are in foreign hands, especially the Channel islands, are to be surrendered to the king. The Scots and Welsh, if they will, are to be included in the terms. Lewis releases all who have bound themselves to him, and swears to do his best to obtain papal confirmation of the treaty[4]. The clergy however who had defied the papal threats were left to the mercies of the legate. Payments due to Lewis were secured, and the regent bound himself to pay him ten thousand marks, under the title of expenses, really as the price of peace[5]. Lewis made terms with the legate in another document dated on the 27th of September[6], promising a tenth of his own revenues and a twentieth of those of his French companions for two years towards the expenses of

General pacification.

Hard lot of the clergy.

Lewis's terms with Gualo.

[1] Foedera, i. 148; it was proclaimed on the 19th, ibid., and the absolution was confirmed by the pope on the 13th of January; ibid. 149.

[2] W. Cov. ii. 239. The form is given in the Foedera, i. 143.

[3] Liber de Antt. Legg. p. 203.

[4] Foedera, i. 148; W. Cov. ii. 239; M. Paris, iii. 30–32.

[5] The earl engages to pay 10,000 marks 'pro bono pacis,' Royal Letters of Henry III (ed. Shirley), i. 7; 'nomine expensarum,' W. Cov. ii. 239. Cf. Ann. Wav. p. 288. Ann. Dunst. p. 51 and Ann. Mailros, p. 195, say £10,000. The king also mentions a debt incurred 'secundum formam pacis,' Rot. Cl. i. 360. That this sum was collected by a tallage appears from Rot. Cl. i. 457, 'tallagium quod assisum fuit in Dunewico ad opus nostrum post pacem factam inter nos et Lodovicum.' He speaks of it as 'magnum negotium nostrum;' Rot. Cl. i. 479.

[6] Foedera, i. 143.

Second reissue of the Charter, Nov. 6, 1217.

the crusade. The general pacification was crowned by a second reissue of Magna Carta, this time accompanied by a new charter, the Carta de Foresta, in which the forest articles of John's charter were renewed and expanded. This was done on the 6th of November[1].

Character of the work of William Marshall.

The work of William Marshall's administration, the restoration of peace and good government, may be compared with the similar task undertaken by Henry II at the beginning of his reign[2]. William Marshall adopted the same firm but conciliatory policy. He showed no vindictiveness; had he done so his own son must have been the first to suffer. He had not to create a new administrative system, but only to revive and adapt one that had been long at work, and that wanted but little adjustment to present needs. He could not dispense with the aid of the legate or of the foreign servants of John; he could but use and regulate them so as to do the most good and the least harm; and he thus tolerated the existence of elements foreign to the constitution, and in their results full of difficulties to his successors. Hubert de Burgh had to stem the tide of these evils, and he overcame them, although he fell under the reaction caused by his own measures. William Marshall could scarcely have carried into effect plans which were premature even under his successor. The glory of his administration then is the pacification, and the two editions of the charter by which the stages of the pacification are marked.

Distinctive points of the Charter of 1217.

The charter of 1217 differs from the two earlier editions in several points: it does not contain the respiting clause of 1216, although it provides a substitute in its 46th article, reserving to all persons lay and clerical the liberties and free customs they possessed before. Two new clauses form a germ of later legis-

[1] Select Charters, p. 344; Statutes of the Realm (Charters), pp. 17 sq. These charters were sent to the sheriffs to be published and sworn at the county courts, Feb. 22, 1218; Foed. i. 150; Rot. Claus. i. 377.

[2] By a general writ issued Sept. 29, the sheriffs were ordered to ascertain by jury the royal demesnes in their counties, and to take them into the royal hands; Rot. Claus. i. 336. On the 3rd of November the earl of Chester is called on to account for the counties of Lancaster, Stafford, and Salop; ibid. 340. These Rolls contain an enormous mass of evidence on the restoration of estates consequent on the peace.

lation; the 39th, which directs that no freeman shall henceforth alienate so much of his land that the residue shall be insufficient to furnish the legal services due to his lord, is said to be the first legal restraint on alienation on record in this country[1], and, in another aspect, contains the principle of the statute 'Quia Emptores;' the 43rd, forbidding the fraudulent transfer of lands to religious houses, stands in the same relation to the statute 'de religiosis.' The 47th clause, again, which orders the destruction of adulterine castles, and the 44th, which provides that scutages shall be taken as in king Henry's time[2], may show that in some points the current of recent history had been retrogressive. The 42nd article orders the county court to be held monthly, and the sheriff's tourn, which now first appears in the charters, twice a year[3]. The same clause also regulates the view of frankpledge and affords the first legal evidence of its general obligation. The annual sessions of the itinerant justices are reduced from four to one, and their functions are somewhat limited: this was possibly a concession to the feudal feeling which long continued hostile to the king's aggressive judicature. This reissue presents the Great Charter in its final form; although frequently republished and confirmed, the text is never again materially altered.

Prospective and retrospective interest of the changes.

Minor alterations.

Final form of the Charter.

Forest Charter.

The Charter of the Forest[4], put forth at the same time and in like form, was probably no less popular or less important; for the vast extension of the forests, with their uncertain boundaries and indefinite privileges, had brought their peculiar

[1] See Reeves, Hist. of English Law, i. 239; Report on the Dignity of a Peer, i. 397 sq.

[2] The exact force of the clause is however uncertain; if, as may be thought (Report on the Dignity of a Peer, i. 79), it was to restrict the amount of scutage, it was a concession on the part of the crown; if it means that scutages should be taken without asking the commune concilium, it was a retrograde act. The scutage taken nearly at this time was assessed by the commune concilium; see p. 30, note 1.

[3] This clause was explained and modified by Henry III in 1234, in an edict which directs the holding of hundred and wapentake courts every three weeks, instead of every fortnight as had been usual under Henry II; Ann. Dunst. p. 140; Royal Letters, i. 450.

[4] It is to be remembered that John issued no Forest Charter, as is commonly stated; that given by Matthew Paris in his name is Henry's Charter of 1225; see M. Paris, ii. 598.

Its importance.

jurisdictions and minute oppressions into every neighbourhood, and imposed on all the inhabitants of the counties in which they lay burdensome duties and liabilities, rivalling in number and cogency the strict legal and constitutional obligations under which they still groaned. The forest courts stood side by side with the county courts, the forest assizes with the sessions of the shire and hundred; the snares of legal chicanery, the risks of offence done in ignorance, lay in double weight on all. This charter was a great measure of relief: the inhabitants of the counties not living within the forests are released from the duty of attending the courts except on special summons[1]; the forests made in the last two reigns are disafforested; much of the vexatious legislation of Henry II is annulled, and the normal state of the rights of landowners adjusted to their condition at the time of that king's coronation. Both the charters are sealed with the seals of both legate and regent[2].

Remedial character of the Forest Charter.

The reissues of the Charter a representative act of a representative man.

The aged warrior, who had shared the rebellion of the younger Henry in 1173, and had stood by his deathbed; who had overthrown the administration of William Longchamp, and joined in the outlawing of John; who had been in 1215 the mainstay of the royal party, and had seen his son the leading spirit of the opposition; who had secured the crown for Henry III, by holding out the promises of good government which his father had broken; now puts forth, as a constitutional platform, the document whose growth and varying fortunes he had so carefully watched. Honorius III saw clearly how and where he must recede from the position of his predecessor; he too has his share of credit; and Gualo, who from first to last acted in close concert with the regent, may be pardoned if he tried to make his own profit out of the task. The later history of the twenty-five barons[3] may be briefly told: Geoffrey Mandeville and Eustace de Vescy

Action of Honorius III.

Later history of the twenty-five.

1 Cf. Royal Letters, i. 360.

2 Select Charters, pp. 347 sq.; Statutes (Charters), pp. 20, 21. The perambulation ordered for the purpose of ascertaining and settling the boundaries of the forests was made in the summer of 1218, under writs issued at Leicester, July 24; Foed. i. 151.

3 The later history of the twenty-five is worked out by Thompson, in his notes on Magna Carta; but the dates given in the text are drawn from the contemporary writers, and supplemented from Dugdale's Baronage.

died before John; William of Lamvalei in 1217, the earl of Hertford in 1218, Saer de Quincy in 1219 at Damietta; the earls of Hereford and Norfolk in 1220; Robert de Vere in 1221; William Mowbray in 1222. Robert Fitz-Walter, who from the moment of his release took up the position of a good subject, went on the crusade, and died, long after his return, in 1235; William of Albini in 1236. Gilbert of Clare, who became earl of Hertford in 1218 and of Gloucester in 1226, died in 1230, leaving a son who played a part, like that of his father and grandfather, under Simon de Montfort. Hugh Bigod became earl on his father's death, and died in 1225. John de Lacy became earl of Lincoln in 1232, and died in 1240; he and Richard de Percy both lived to act among the king's friends in his first constitutional difficulties. Of the whole number Richard of Montfichet alone, who was afterwards justiciar of the forests, lived to see the barons' war. The younger William Marshall and William of Aumâle are the only two who come again into the bright light of history. As so often happens in constitutional contests, the fruit of their labours fell to the men who had thwarted them: their only reward was the success of the cause which had been won with so great a risk of their own destruction.

Their comparative obscurity.

The reign of Henry III may be regarded as really beginning with the treaty of Lambeth. He was now ten years old: the leading men in the administration might reckon on ten years more of unimpeded usefulness. Langton's period of suspension was over [1], and he had in Walter Gray, now, and for nearly forty years after, archbishop of York, an experienced colleague in the government of the church, and a helper of great official knowledge, honesty, and ability. Hubert de Burgh, the justiciar, had already by his faithfulness, by his military prowess, and by his wise moderation in public policy, proved his fitness to rule. Gualo, in spite of the charges of avarice, and the general dislike of a legate who claimed so strong a feudal

Henry's advisers during his first years.

[1] Langton's sentence of suspension was removed in February 1216 (M. Paris, ii. 648), but he was not to return to England until peace was made. He returned in May 1218; Ann. Mailros, p. 196.

position as representing the pope, and who might call himself the king's guardian, was earnest in his support of the secular government, and faithful to his public duties. But the difficulties of the situation were such as might have proved fatal to far stronger men. The necessity of securing immediate peace had forced the regent to tolerate the retention, by John's personal favourites, of an amount of power which could not safely be trusted to any section of the baronage, much less to a class of adventurers who were viewed with distrust and jealousy by all. Some of these were still numbered in the inner circle of the king's advisers.

Rising difficulties.

The foreign adventurers.

Close of the administration of the earl of Pembroke.

The measures for securing the position of the young king, the execution of the remedial enactments of the charters, the exaction of the due homages from the barons who had not yet presented themselves in person, from the king of Scots and from the prince and lords of Wales, occupied the few remaining months of the earl Marshall's life. He seems, in the measures taken for raising money, to have acted strictly with the counsel and consent of the common council of the realm[1]. One of his last public acts was to induce that council to issue a provision, that no charter, letters patent of confirmation, alienation, sale or gift, or any other act that implied perpetuity, should be sealed with the great seal before the king reached full age. This must have been done soon after Michaelmas 1218[2], probably on

[1] The Rolls contain evidence of the ways in which money was raised in 1217 and 1218:—(1) June 7, 1217, the king mentions a hidage, carucage, and aid, 'quod de praecepto nostro assisum est,' Rot. Claus. i. 310. (2) The Pope, July 8, 1217, orders an aid to be granted by the prelates; Royal Letters, i. 532. (3) Jan. 9, 1218, Henry mentions a carucage and hidage, 'quod assisum fuit per consilium regni nostri;' Rot. Claus. i. 348. (4) Henry mentions a scutage of two marks on the fee, 'quod exegimus' (Jan. 17), and 'scutagium de omnibus feodis militum quae de nobis tenet in capite, quod ultimo assisum fuit per commune consilium regni nostri' (Jan. 24), ibid. 349; cf. ii. 87. As the orders for the collecting this scutage were issued Feb. 22, the same day on which the writs for proclaiming the charters are dated (Rot. Claus. i. 377), it would seem certain that it was granted by the assembly in which the charters were renewed, and that thus, although the constitutional articles were omitted, they were so far observed. Besides these, tallages are mentioned; ibid. 359, 364, 370, &c.

[2] Foedera, i. 152; between Oct. 7, 1218, and Feb. 24, 1219; Ann. Waverley, p. 291; Rot. Claus. i. 381. The Annals of Waverley, p. 290, mention a reissue of the charters at Michaelmas, sealed by both the arch-

November 5, on which day the king's seal was first used, and in an assembly in which it is said that the charters were again confirmed. Immediately after this Gualo returned to Rome, Pandulf, who was already too well known in England, being his successor. Early in the spring of 1219 the regent died, to the great regret of the whole nation [1].

Departure of Gualo.

Death of the regent, May 14, 1219.

171. We have no record of any arrangement made to supply his place. It had been proposed to the pope, in 1217, that the earl of Chester should be nominated as his colleague [2], but he was not chosen as his successor. Henry remained under the care of the bishop Peter of Winchester; but that ambitious prelate did not venture to call himself 'rector regis et regni,' nor did Pandulf assert any such right on behalf of his master. The personal pre-eminence which had been allowed to the earl Marshall seems to have been inherited by the justiciar, although the writs which had been hitherto attested by the regent as the king's representative were frequently from this time attested by Bishop Peter. The bishop's functions were probably those of the king's personal guardian and president of the royal council. His policy was to support the foreign influences, which it was the great aim of Langton and the justiciar to eliminate. The amicable relations which had subsisted under the earl Marshall were for a short time maintained; the crusade called away many of the leaders in the late quarrel, and the specific policy of the government could not be at once reversed. The second coronation of Henry, which was performed on the 17th May 1220 [3]

Peter des Roches acts as the king's guardian.

His peculiar policy.

Second coronation of Henry, May 17, 1220.

bishops and by Gualo. No original charter of this issue is known to be extant, and possibly the statement is a mistake.

[1] He died at Caversham, May 14 (Ann. Waverley, p. 291), and was buried on the morrow of the Ascension, May 17; R. Coggesh. p. 187. Gualo left on the 23rd of November, 1218; Pandulf arrived on Dec. 3; R. Coggesh. p. 186.

[2] July 8, 1217; Royal Letters, i. 532. In the statement of the charges against Hubert de Burgh, made in the twenty-third year of Henry III (M. Paris, ed. Luard, vi. 64), the king's agent says that, after the earl Marshall's death, the legate Gualo was, 'de communi consensu et provisione totius regni,' 'primus consiliarius et principalis totius regni Angliae.' This is impossible, and it shows how very soon the very order of events was forgotten. A council, to be held on June 16, had been called before the earl's death (Royal Letters, i. 27); possibly something was done in it.

[3] W. Cov. ii. 244: the coronation oath was renewed, 'scilicet quod

by the archbishop at Westminster, was regarded as typical of the full restoration of peace and good government. The young king renewed his coronation oaths and received the diadem of S. Edward. Shortly afterwards the primate went to Rome, and obtained a promise from the pope [1] that, after the expiration of Pandulf's legation, no successor should be appointed, at least during Langton's life; the legate resigned his commission at midsummer 1221 [2].

Pandulf's departure.

Character of the work of Hubert de Burgh.

As William Marshall's work was to restore the administrative system, that of Hubert was to replace the working of that system in English hands; his victory was no easy one. The formal homages paid at the coronation were to be followed by the resumption into the hands of the government of the royal castles which were still held by the lords to whom John had entrusted them. The barons swore to enforce the surrender, on the day after the coronation [3]. The measure was one of ordinary prudence; it had been frequently practised by Henry II, and by John himself, and was now enforced by a papal mandate [4]. The men who professed to be devoted to Henry III had no justification in resisting. They determined however to resist, and, at the instigation of the bishop of Winchester, to allege as their excuse their distrust of the justiciar, a cry which they so pertinaciously raised as ultimately to draw into their schemes men of experience and independent position, who had no other ground of sympathy with them. The chiefs of the party were, as might be expected, William of Aumâle, Falkes de Breauté, and Peter

Resumption of royal demesne, 1220.

Party formed against Hubert.

ecclesiam Dei tueretur, pacemque tam cleri quam populi, et bonas regni leges custodiret illaesas.'

1 Ann. Dunst. p. 74.

2 July 19; 'cessit legationi suae ex mandato domini papae;' M. Westm., Flores Hist. ed. Luard, ii. 172; cf. Ann. Dunst. p. 75; Ann. Waverley, p. 295: 'a legationis officio revocatur;' Cont. Flor. Wig. p. 173.

3 W. Cov. ii. 244; Ann. Dunst. p. 57.

4 The papal letter ordering the prelates to surrender the royal castles is dated May 26, 1220; Royal Letters, i. 535: on May 28, Honorius directed that no one should hold more than two castles; ibid. i. 121; Foed. i. 160: on the 9th of August, Henry ordered the sheriffs to inquire what demesnes were in John's hands at the beginning of the war; Rot. Claus. i. 437. In 1221, April 29, Honorius ordered the resumption of escheats that had been alienated; Foed. i. 167. A general inquiry into the rights which John had possessed at the beginning of the war was ordered by Henry, Jan. 30, 1223, Foed. i. 168; and April 9, Rot. Cl. i. 569.

de Mauley; with them was a number of minor leaders, such as Philip Mark, Engelard of Cigognies, and Gerard of Athies, who had been proscribed by the charter of Runnymede, but had contrived during the succeeding hostilities to maintain and strengthen their position[1]. Ralph de Gaugi as early as 1218 had refused to surrender Newark, until he was besieged by the regent[2]. William of Aumâle in 1219 had been declared to be in rebellion for attending a prohibited tournament, and was then fortifying Sauvey[3]. Now, following the example of his grandfather, who had refused to admit Henry II into Scarborough, he declined to surrender Sauvey and Rockingham; and the young king immediately after the coronation was brought up with an armed force to demand admittance. Assisted by the men of the county, who were called together as of old, he frightened the garrisons into flight, and took both castles[4]; but after Christmas the earl renewed the quarrel, collected forces at Biham and seized Fotheringay, a castle of the earl of Huntingdon, whence, with an assumption of feudal or royal style, worthy of the days of Stephen, he issued letters patent granting safe conduct to traders moving from one to another of his castles[5]. Vigorous action was taken against him; Pandulf excommunicated him, and the earl of Chester, who, having just returned from the crusade, was not yet implicated in the design against Hubert, threw himself zealously into the king's cause. The council of the kingdom granted a scutage of ten shillings[6] on the knight's fee, and before the end of February Biham was dismantled and the earl a fugitive suing for pardon. The alarm however was so great that the pope on the 29th of April wrote to urge the bishops to apply themselves to enforce peace[7].

Uneasy state of the country.

Contumacy of William of Aumâle.

His castles taken in June, 1220.

He revolts early in 1221.

The scutage of Biham.

1 M. Paris, iii. 33. 2 Ib. iii. 33; Ann. Dunst. p. 54; Rot. Cl. i. 379.

3 Royal Letters, i. 57; Rot. Claus. i. 434.

4 June 28, 1220; M. Paris, iii. 59. The force was composed of 'tam pauperes quam divites ex illo comitatu;' W. Cov. ii. 245. See Ann. Dunst. p. 60.

5 W. Cov. ii. 247; Royal Letters, i. 168. See Rot. Claus. i. 448, 450.

6 The 'Scutagium de Biham;' Rot. Claus. i. 458, 465, 475. Biham was taken Feb. 8; M. Paris, iii. 61. See Ann. Dunst. p. 64. The expenses of the siege are noted in Rot. Claus. i. 453.

7 'Cum, sicut audivimus, gravis guerra in regno Angliae incipiat pullulare;' Foed. i. 167; Royal Letters, i. 174.

Peter des Roches goes abroad.

The resignation of Pandulf[1], the return of Langton, and the defeat of his friend, had now weakened the position of Peter des Roches; he determined to join the crusade, but, finding that Damietta was already lost, contented himself with a pilgrimage to Compostella. His absence did not however insure peace.

Alarms in 1222.

The year 1222 opened with still more alarming auguries. At Whitsuntide Peter de Mauley and Engelard de Athies were arrested and compelled to surrender their castles[2]; and in June the earl of Derby was ordered to surrender Bolsover and the Peak[3].

The earl of Chester joins the opposition.

The disaffection which had begun with William of Aumâle showed itself in another direction, and now the earl of Chester deigned to be the spokesman of the malcontents. But the prompt intervention of the archbishop met the difficulty: a threat of excommunication seconded by argument and persuasion silenced the earl, who however from this time ranked himself among Hubert's enemies[4].

Hubert endeavours in 1223 to recover the royal castles.

The next outbreak was in 1223. In the April of that year Honorius III declared Henry, although not yet of age, competent to govern, and issued letters to the barons charging them to obey[5]. At the close of the year Hubert, having just completed a successful campaign in Wales[6], thought himself strong enough to act upon this mandate; and the earl of Chester, William of Aumâle and Falkes de Breauté, attempted to anticipate him. Disappointed in a design for seizing the Tower of London, they encamped at Waltham, and sent to the king demanding the dismissal of the justiciar. A discussion took place in the royal

1 The particular circumstances of Pandulf's resignation are detailed by Dr. Shirley in the preface to the Royal Letters, vol. i; and Pearson, Hist. Eng. ii. 126.

2 Ann. Dunst. p. 68; M. Paris, iii. 60, 83.

3 June 27; Rot. Claus. i. 502.

4 W. Cov. ii. 251.

5 April 13; see Royal Letters, i. 430; M. Paris, iii. 79; Ann. Dunst. p. 83. Curiously enough the bull of Gregory IX, to the same effect (Foed. i. 190), is dated April 13, 1227. By another letter, Nov. 20, 1223, the pope permits Henry to leave the castles in the hands of their present holders; Royal Letters, i. 539. Dr. Shirley has collected the notices of changes in the holders of castles and counties between Nov. 15, 1223, and March 21, 1224; in Royal Letters, i. 508 sq.

6 For this a scutage, the scutage of Montgomery, was taken, two marks on the fee, and a great tallage from the towns. See Rot. Claus. i. 553, 565, 570; ii. 34, &c.

presence, Hubert answering for himself and denouncing the bishop of Winchester as the secret prompter of the disturbance [1]. Langton again mediated, and a formal reconciliation took place at Christmas at Northampton. Six months after, Falkes de Breauté [2] drew down upon himself the final storm. This clever adventurer was a Norman refugee, who had devotedly attached himself to John. John had repaid his services with lavish munificence. Sheriffdoms, wardships, escheats, castles, were showered upon him; he was married to the countess of Wight and Devon, was executor of John's will, a chief counsellor in Henry's court, and, just before the outbreak, was sheriff of six counties [3]. He no doubt had the confidence of Peter des Roches, and held the strings of the confederation against Hubert. His fall, however, was caused, not by defeat in a deliberate conflict of parties, but by a subordinate incident in his career of aggression. He had entrusted the castle of Bedford to his brother William, who in the insolence of power arrested and imprisoned one of the royal judges itinerant whilst they were inquiring into his misdoings. Hubert, who probably had been watching for his opportunity, and who with the king was at Northampton at the time, besieged Bedford at Midsummer, and took it on the 14th

Resistance prompted by Peter des Roches.

Outbreak of Falkes de Breauté, in 1224.

Siege of Bedford.

[1] Ann. Dunst. p. 83; M. Paris, iii. 83; Royal Letters, i. 225. Matthew Paris mentions amongst the malcontents the earl of Chester, William of Aumâle, the constable of Chester, Falkes de Breauté, Philip Mark, and even William Cantilupe.

[2] There is a great mass of information on the history of Falkes de Breauté. He was, it would seem, secretly supported by Peter des Roches, and was used if not supported by the earl of Chester and others, as the leader of opposition to the justiciar. He had negotiated with the Welsh and also with France. But it is difficult to distinguish between the true statements and the mere suspicions about him, and in some instances mere political sympathy was probably construed as connivance. The annals of Tewkesbury describe him in 1219 as 'plusquam rex in Anglia'; p. 64. His position was no doubt complicated by private quarrels with the Marshalls, against whom he intrigued with the Welsh. But, when he left England, he declared with tears that he had acted throughout at the instigation of the great men of the realm; M. Paris, iii. 94. See Ann. Waverley, p. 300; W. Cov. ii. 253 sq.; Prynne's Records, &c.; Shirley, Royal Letters; and Luard, Relations between England and Rome under Henry III.

[3] He was ordered to surrender Bedfordshire, Bucks, Cambridgeshire, and Huntingdonshire, Jan. 18, 1224; Rot. Claus. i. 581. June 9, at Dunstable he was convicted of thirty-five acts of disseisin; Ann. Dunst. p. 90: Henry in a letter to the pope says sixteen, Royal Letters, i. 225. See too Rot. Claus. i. 619, 655.

Fall of Falkes.

of August[1]. The garrison was hanged; Falkes threw himself on the king's mercy and was allowed to leave the kingdom. He went to Rome and there prevailed on Honorius to write a somewhat touching letter of intercession to the king[2], but was not suffered to return. The importance of his position, and the great constitutional significance of his humiliation, is shown by the fact that the earls and barons, as well as prelates, of the whole province of Canterbury, joined to grant a carucage towards the expenses of the struggle[3], and that the pope regarded him as worthy of his protection. His fall crowned for the moment the power of Hubert; it extinguished the influence of the foreigners who had been imported by John, and reduced the bishop of Winchester to political insignificance[4]. The recurrence of like influences in the later years of Henry was due to other causes.

His importance.

The power of the aliens falls with Falkes de Breauté, 1224.

Threats of war with France.

The recent expenses were not sufficiently met by the carucage, and new ones were already incurred. Lewis VIII, who succeeded Philip II in 1223, had laid hold on Poictou, and great part of the year 1224 was devoted to planning an expedition to recover the last remnant of Eleanor's inheritance. Up to this time taxation had not been heavy; and, although the constitutional articles of the charter were unconfirmed, they had been practically acted upon[5]. Besides the scutage of 1218, a carucage of two shillings had been taken at the coronation of

Increase of taxation.

[1] M. Paris, iii. 89; Cont. Flor. Wig. p. 174.

[2] W. Cov. ii. 272 sq. He had already written strong letters in his favour before he knew of his surrender; Royal Letters, i. 543 sq.

[3] A carucage was made by the prelates for themselves, their tenants and their rustics; Foed. i. 175; W. Cov. ii. 254, 255; Ann. Dunst. p. 86. The grant was half a mark on the carucate of demesne, two shillings on the carucate from tenants, and two labourers from each hide, to work the engines: on the latter point, see Rot. Claus. i. 655. The payment by the lay barons is mentioned by Matthew Paris, iii. 88; Rot. Claus. i. 640; and there was a scutage coinciding with the scutage of Bedford, two marks on the fee, which the tenants-in-chief paid to the king, but which the king allowed them to exact from their tenants; M. Paris, iii. 88.

[4] The bishop was summoned, Sept. 28, to appear before the king at Westminster in three weeks, to account (quo waranto) for the essarts and purprestures made in the forests of Hampshire; Rot. Claus. i. 655. On the 18th of January, 1225, the pope wrote to remonstrate with Henry for hindering the bishop's proposed visit to Rome; Royal Letters, i. 218; and it is clear that he was regarded as prompting all the attacks on Hubert; ibid. p. 224.

[5] See above, p. 30, note 1.

1220[1], and a scutage of ten shillings after the capture of Biham[2]; one of two marks for the Welsh war in 1223, and one of a like amount for the siege of Bedford: in 1219 the clergy[3], and in 1223 the whole population had been called on to contribute to the crusade[4]. But now a much larger supply was needed, and when the justiciar, at the Christmas court of 1224, demanded a fifteenth of all moveables, he was met by a petition for the reconfirmation of the charters. They had been twice confirmed since the last edition, in 1218 and 1223[5]. They were now re-issued with no material alteration[6], but with a change in the enacting words. Instead of the 'counsel' of the barons, which had hitherto formed part of the moving clause, Henry III issues the charters 'spontanea et bona voluntate nostra,' and the magnates, whose names had been before recounted as counselling and consenting, now appear as witnesses. The change was probably intended to make the obligation more binding on Henry, who had been declared old enough to act for himself; but it must be acknowledged that Hubert, in trying to bind the royal conscience, forsook the normal and primitive form of legislative enactment, and opened the way for a claim on the king's part to legislate by sovereign authority without counsel or consent. The condition on which the grant is made is openly stated: for the concession of the two charters, the archbishops, bishops, abbots, priors, earls, barons, knights, freeholders, and all persons of the realm, give the fifteenth of all moveables. A careful

The charters confirmed and a fifteenth granted, Feb. 11, 1225.

Change in the words of the Charter.

[1] Ann. Winton, p. 83; Ann. Waverley, p. 293; Ann. Dunst. p. 60; Select Charters, p. 351.

[2] See above, p. 33.

[3] The general tax of a twentieth ordered by the Lateran council; Ann. Theokesb. p. 64; Ann. Osney, p. 80; R. de S. Germano, p. 47.

[4] 'Provisum est et concessum coram nobis et consilio nostro praesentibus Archiepiscopo Cantuariae, episcopis, comitibus, baronibus et magnatibus nostris de communi omnium voluntate;' Rot. Claus. i. 516, 567. 'Provisum est communi consilio regni;' an earl was to pay three marks, a baron one, a knight a shilling, and each householder a penny; W. Cov. ii. 252; Ann. Dunst. p. 67; Ann. Waverley, p. 296; where however it is stated that the tax was never paid. It was unpaid in Dec. 1223; Rot. Claus. i. 630.

[5] See p. 30, note 2. The confirmation in January 1223 is mentioned by Matthew Paris, iii. 76, who describes a dispute between Langton who was urging, and William Briwere who opposed, the act. It was closed by the king's declaration, 'omnes illas libertates juravimus et omnes astricti sumus ut quod juravimus observemus.'

[6] Select Charters, p. 353; Statutes of the Realm (Charters), pp. 22–25.

scheme was at the same time drawn out for the assessment of the grant, and its collection by local machinery[1]: a survey of the forests, by twelve legal men chosen by the counties, was a necessary supplement[2]: and finally the clergy were moved, by a papal and archiepiscopal mandate, to add a voluntary vote[3], 'making a virtue of necessity,' from the property which was not assessed to the fifteenth. The exact amount, raised by the fifteenth, was calculated to be 86,758 marks and twopence[4]. Great sums were also borrowed from the bishops, and extorted from the Jews. The money was collected by special justices assigned for the purpose, and placed in the castles of Winchester and Devizes. It did not pass through the hands of the sheriffs except for transmission, and does not appear in the usual form in the Pipe Rolls.

Grant by the clergy.

Amount of money raised.

The expedition to France, 1225.

The expedition equipped at this great cost was placed under the command of the king's brother Richard, and his uncle William of Salisbury. It was so far successful that Gascony was again secured, but it had the further result of reopening England to the influx of foreign adventurers. After the first victories the war languished; the death of the earl of Salisbury, the prosecution by Lewis VIII of his war against Toulouse, and his death in November 1226, led to a succession of truces which lasted for three years.

Demands made by the pope in 1226.

The year 1226 witnessed the first of those exorbitant demands on the part of the pope which, next to the influence of the aliens, were the great cause of Henry's later troubles. A special envoy, Otho, was sent to ask that in every cathedral and collegiate church one prebend should be assigned to papal uses, an equal revenue from the episcopal estate, and a proportionate sum from each of the monasteries. The demand was a general

[1] Select Charters, p. 355; Foed. i. 177; Rot. Claus. ii. 21.

[2] M. Paris, iii. 91, 92. Order for the proclamation of the Charters was given Feb. 16; Rot. Claus. ii. 70: May 1; ibid. 72. An inquest into the liberties and free customs confirmed by the Charter was directed July 8; Rot. Claus. ii. 48.

[3] Ann. Dunst. p. 39; W. Cov. ii. 257; 'ut sic necessitatem transferant in virtutem.' The clerical grant was made in 1226; see p. 39, note 2.

[4] Liber Ruber: see Hunter's Three Catalogues, p. 22; Rot. Claus. ii. 40, 45, 70, 71, 73.

one, based on the plea that the court of Rome might reduce the expenses of litigation[1]. In France it was successfully resisted by a council at Bourges; in England the king refused to admit it without the consent of the magnates, and forbade them to bind their lay fees in any liability to the pope. The proposal was discussed in councils held on January 13 and April 13, and a formal answer was returned, which saved the nation's credit at the expense of her dignity; whatever other kingdoms might do, England was freed from such an exaction by her tribute paid annually under the terms of John's submission[2].

The barons and bishops evade the demand.

Henry now considered himself of age to govern, as the pope had declared. He was not yet twenty, but he was tired of the tutelage of Peter des Roches, and was no doubt prompted by Hubert to throw off the yoke. Accordingly, in a council at Oxford in January 1227[3], he announced that from henceforth he should regulate the affairs of the realm by himself. Hubert continued to be justiciar, and was made earl of Kent; the bishop went on crusade, and stayed away until 1231. The new pope, Gregory IX, renewed in April the letters issued by Honorius in 1223, recognising the king's competency.

Henry determines to emancipate himself, Jan. 1227.

On the occasion of his majority, Henry first showed how lightly his constitutional obligations sat upon him. The ordinance made in 1218, by which until he came of age he was restrained from making grants in perpetuity, was now interpreted to imply the nullity of all charters sealed during the minority, and on the 21st of January[4], 1227, by the common counsel of the

He orders all charters of perpetuity, sealed in his minority, to be resealed.

[1] W. Cov. ii. 279. The demand was based on a papal bull (*Super muros Jerusalem*), dated Jan. 28, 1225; ibid. p. 274; Martene, Thesaurus, i. 929; Wilkins, Conc. i. 558; M. Paris, iii. 102, 103, 105 sq.

[2] Wilkins, i. 559; W. Cov. ii. 279. The annals of Dunstable say that the province of Canterbury refused to make the concession without the consent of the patrons, and the authority of a general council, p. 99; Ann. Osney, p. 66; M. Paris, iii. 109. This was in the council of April 13. This year the inferior clergy, after consultation in their dioceses, granted to the king a sixteenth of their ecclesiastical revenue in a council held Oct. 13; see Wilkins, Conc. i. 605; Royal Letters, i. 299; Ann. Wykes and Osney, pp. 67, 68; Rot. Claus. ii. 143.

[3] M. Paris, iii. 122: who places the event in February; but the king himself mentions the council at Oxford, in his writ of Jan. 21; Rot. Claus. ii. 207; and he was at Oxford only on Jan. 8–10.

[4] 'Scias quod per commune consilium Archiepiscopi Cantuariensis, episcoporum, abbatum, comitum, baronum et aliorum magnatum et fidelium

kingdom, he issued letters directing that all who had received such charters should apply for their renewal. The renewal was, according to Matthew Paris, to be purchased at a valuation fixed by the justiciar [1]. It was for the moment uncertain whether the charters of the forests, and even the great charter of liberties, might not be included in the same repudiation. The historian asserts that the former were annulled [2], and the Close Rolls contain letters of February 9, by which the disafforestments of Lincoln, Rutland, Leicester, Nottingham, Cambridge, and Huntingdon were set aside [3]. But the declaration seems merely to have been a contrivance for raising money; £100,000 was obtained by the repurchase of the grants imperilled [4]; a tallage was asked of the towns and demesne lands of the crown [5], and the charters remained in force, although the partial disafforestments were made a ground of complaint by the earls [6]. If the king intended his threat to be more than a sign of emancipation and self-confidence, the influence of the justiciar probably hindered him from acting further upon it.

The forest charters and perambulations endangered.

Money raised by this means.

Constitutional results of the minority of Henry III.

At the termination of the king's minority, the machinery of the government might be expected to rid itself of all the temporary expedients which the tutelage of the royal person had made necessary. In most respects it did so; but the period leaves its mark on the framework, and even on the theory, of the government. It is from this point that we first distinctly trace the action of an inner royal council, distinct from the curia regis as it existed under Henry II, and from the common council of the realm. The king's personal advisers begin to

nostrorum providimus nuper apud Oxoniam quod de cetero cartas et confirmationes sub sigillo nostro fieri faciamus;' Rot. Claus. ii. 207.

[1] M. Paris, iii. 122.

[2] Ibid. See the remarks of Dr. Pauli, Gesch. v. Engl. iii. 564, and Lingard, ii. 196.

[3] Rot. Claus. ii. 169. The reason given is that the knights employed had misunderstood their commission.

[4] Hardy, preface to the Rotuli Cartarum, pp. v, vi.

[5] The writs were issued Feb. 16, 1227; Rot. Claus. ii. 171; but the matter had been on foot as early as Nov. 3, 1226; ibid. ii. 204; the tallage is mentioned in the annals of Tewkesbury; but very large remissions in it were made; Rot. Claus. ii. 180 sq.; and each man was to be taxed 'per se secundum facultatem,' Jan. 30; ibid. ii. 208.

[6] See p. 42.

have a recognised position as a distinct and organised body, of which the administrative officers, the judges, and other ministers of state and household, form only a part. The growth and functions of this body must be discussed in another chapter; the political importance of what may be regarded either as a new element in the state or as a new embodiment of an old principle, becomes more and more marked as we proceed, and as the changes in the character of royalty and its relations to the three estates are gradually developed. Another point of like significance comes also into light: as soon as the constitutional disputes of the reign begin, the common council of the realm claims the right of nominating or confirming the nomination of the great officers of state, the justiciar, the chancellor, and the treasurer. In previous times, although new appointments would no doubt be announced in the meetings of the great council, there is no trace of such a claim. During the minority it is not unlikely that that assembly was formally consulted: Hubert de Burgh may have been continued in the justiciarship by the same body that conferred the regency on William Marshall; we are distinctly told that Ralph Neville received the chancellorship and the great seal in 1226 by the 'assent' and 'by the common counsel' of the kingdom [1], on the understanding that he should not be removed except by the same authority; and in 1236 he refused to resign his office without a requisition from the body that had appointed him. It is probable then that the events of Henry's minority had a considerable effect in creating the idea of limited monarchy, which almost immediately springs into existence. It is at all events not improbable that the constitutional doctrine that the king can do no wrong, and that his ministers are responsible to the nation, sprang up whilst the king was a child, and the choice of his ministers was actually determined by the national council.

Growth of the king's council.

Claim to elect great officers of state.

A new claim.

Possible change in the theory of the monarchy.

172. Hubert's administration lasted for five years longer, and he was able during this time to exercise a directing power in

Hubert's administration, 1227–1232.

[1] M. Paris, iii. 74, 364; M. Westm. Flores, ii. 176. The grant by which the appointment was made for life, Feb. 12, 1227, does not mention this; Madox, Hist. Exch. p. 43.

the state, although hampered by Henry's interference even more than he had been by the hostility of Peter des Roches. He had in fact to hold himself responsible not only for his own strong measures, but for the king's imprudences; nor is it easy, in the somewhat hostile narrative of the contemporary writers, to distinguish the one from the other[1]. The rising of the earls in July 1227, by which Henry was compelled to make a large provision for his brother Richard[2], and to restore the forest charters, may have been provoked by the economy of the justiciar; the failure in the Welsh war of 1228 can hardly be attributed to anything but the inexperience of the king. Hubert's foreign policy was one of peace, but it was probably his distrust of Henry's firmness of purpose that led him to oppose the design of a Gascon campaign in 1229. This distrust was justified by the events of 1230, when Henry, having landed in Brittany and overrun Poictou, returned to England to raise supplies. A scutage of three marks was granted, notwithstanding the opposition of the clergy[3]; but a truce for three years was concluded almost immediately, and the war was not resumed for ten years.

The earls rise in favour of earl Richard.

Hubert tries to keep the king at home.

His position is gradually shaken.

Many circumstances combined to make the position of the justiciar difficult. On the 9th of July, 1228, he lost his most able and honest coadjutor, Archbishop Langton, the man who more than any other had helped to give form and consistency to the constitutional growth, and had also staved off difficulties

[1] He was 'consiliarius, immo concilium et quasi cor regis,' Ann. Margan, p. 39; 'regis et regni rector et pro libito dispositor et dispensator,' Ann. Waverley, p. 311.

[2] M. Paris, iii. 123-125. The earls were those of Pembroke, Chester, Gloucester, Warwick, Warenne, Hereford, and Ferrers: the king made the required concessions August 2 at Northampton. Writs were issued August 21 at Abingdon; Rot. Claus. ii. 197. The quarrel originated in an attempt of Richard to dispossess Waleran le Tyes, a mercenary of John's, of a castle which the late king had given him.

[3] See Royal Letters, i. 394; M. Paris, iii. 200. 'Dixerunt quod non tenentur viri ecclesiastici judicio laicorum, cum absque illis concessum fuisset scutagium in finibus transmarinis.' They accepted however the king's promise that it should not be made a precedent. This appears in the Pipe Rolls in 1231, as 'Scutagium Pictaviae post primam transfretationem regis'; a similar tax had been raised in preparation for the expedition in 1230, 'Scutagium de primo passagio regis in Britanniam,' also at three marks; Rot. Pip. Ann. 14, 15. There was a scutage of two marks in 1229, 'Scutagium de Kery,' for the Welsh campaign in 1228.

with the papacy. Honorius III had died the year before, and Gregory IX took immediate advantage of the removal of Langton's influence. In 1229 he demanded a tenth of all property for the war against the emperor [1]. A great assembly of tenants-in-chief was held at Westminster on the 29th of April; the earls and barons, led by the earl of Chester, opposed the grant; the king assented in silence; he had pledged himself by his proctors at Rome to agree to the impost, in order to obtain the confirmation of his nominee to the primacy; and from the clergy the tax was rigidly collected [2]. Master Stephen, the pope's collector, provoked a popular rising; an anti-Roman league [3] was formed, with the connivance, it was thought, of the justiciar, and the papal agents were insulted and ill-treated. Henry, whose devotion to the papacy was the most permanent result of his education, if not also the strongest feeling of which he was capable [4], began from this time to look on Hubert with aversion. He was only saved by the interposition of his personal enemy, the earl of Chester, from being disgraced because of his opposition to the Gascon war. The king, himself suspicious, listened to every one who was jealous of Hubert's greatness, or who had suffered under his strong hand. He was, however, far too useful to be dismissed until a substitute was provided. In July 1232 he fell: with his fall Henry's own administration of government begins, and the history of the next six-and-twenty

The clergy are compelled to grant a tenth to the pope; 1229.

Hubert encourages the opposition to the pope.

Fall of Hubert de Burgh, 1232.

[1] M. Paris, iii. 169, 186, describes this as a general impost; but all the other authorities refer it to the clergy only; Ann. Theokesb. p. 73; Ann. Burton, p. 245; Ann. Winton, p. 85; Ann. Waverley, p. 305; Ann. Dunst. pp. 114, 125; Ann. Osney, p. 70.

[2] Ann. Theokesb. p. 77.

[3] Ann. Burton, p. 239; Ann. Dunst. p. 129: 'per conspirationem quorundam clericorum et laicorum machinatum est ut per quosdam satellites blada Romanorum violenter excussa venderentur; et cum per ballivos regis talia praesumentes arguebantur, ostenderunt litteras patentes ipsius justitiarii.' A papal inquiry was made into the matter by the bishop of Winchester and the abbot of St. Edmund's, and the names of the offenders sent to Rome; Ann. Dunst. p. 130. The letter directing this is in the Foed. i. 104; dated June 7, 1232. Cf. M. Paris, iii. 218.

[4] See the letter of Grosseteste to the Pope, Epistt. pp. 338, 339. Henry declares himself bound more closely to the Roman church than any other prince; 'cum enim essemus orbati patre, adhuc in minore aetate constituti, regno nostro non solum a nobis averso sed et nobis adversante, ipsa mater nostra Romana ecclesia. . . . idem regnum ad nostram pacem et subjectionem revocavit. . . .'

years is a continuous illustration of the king's insincerity and incapacity.

Estimate of the work of Hubert.

Hubert had done a great work. Following in the footsteps of William Marshall, he had taken a middle path between the feudal designs of the great nobles and the despotic theories of John which had still some support among the old officials of the court. In so doing he had found himself adopting for the most part the principles of the barons of Runnymede. He had attempted to govern England for English interests, husbanding her resources and keeping her at peace. The King of Scots he had bound by giving him a daughter of John to wife, and he had himself married a daughter of William the Lion; he had kept peace with France until his personal influence was on the wane, and the young king began to listen to rasher if not bolder counsels.

Hubert's policy of strengthening the crown, and humbling the aliens.

He had attempted to strengthen the royal connexion with the barons, especially with the great house of the Marshalls, which inherited not only the reputation of the regent, but the enormous claims of the lords of Striguil in Wales and Ireland; he had married the younger earl William to the king's sister[1], and Richard of Cornwall to a sister of the earl. His hardest task had been the humiliation of the foreigners, and in this he had succeeded, to the great benefit of the king and to the increase of public security. The policy which made this humiliation necessary was indisputably right, but those on whom the humiliation fell were men who had had no small share in placing Henry on the throne. Hubert taught the boy that personal gratitude must give way to state policy. Henry was an apt scholar in learning the lesson of ingratitude; policy he could not learn. He had thrown off the yoke of Peter des Roches when the justiciar bade him; now he threw off the justiciar at the bidding of the bishop, and reversed the policy that he had failed to

He was too good a minister for the time.

comprehend. Like Hubert Walter and Geoffrey Fitz-Peter, Hubert de Burgh had served the king too well to please the nation, and had spared the nation too much to please the king. His fall, however, was not the result of any general demand. He was first dismissed and then persecuted. His persecution,

[1] See Royal Letters, i. 245: an argument on the policy of this marriage.

like Wolsey's, was based upon untenable accusations, on charges which are for the most part so far from reasonable probability, that they prove the innocence of the man against whom nothing more plausible could be alleged.

Peter des Roches recovers his influence with Henry.

173. Peter des Roches had returned from the crusade in 1231. He entertained the king at Christmas at Winchester [1], recovered the royal confidence, reformed his party in the council, and resumed his designs. Henry was in want of money; in a council on the 7th of March, 1232, the barons, led by the earl of Chester, demurred to a grant of aid for the French war, on the plea that they had served in person; the clergy objected on account of insufficient representation [2]. The Welsh, too, were in arms; and the king complained to Peter that he was too poor to enforce order. The bishop at once urged the dismissal of the ministerial staff;—it was no wonder that the king was poor when his servants grew so rich. The hint was not wasted. Henry forthwith dismissed the treasurer, Ranulf le Bret, an old clerk of Hubert, and on the 4th of July appointed bishop Walter of Carlisle in his place: three weeks later Hubert, who but a month before had been made justiciar of Ireland for life, was summarily dismissed, July 29, and Stephen Segrave appointed to succeed him. Three sets of charges were brought against him immediately after [3]. In the first Henry followed the plan adopted by his grandfather for the ruin of Becket; he demanded an account of all sums received by the justiciar on the king's account during his tenure of office, and an answer to all the complaints for wrongs at which he was said to have connived, especially the late outrages on the servants of the pope. The second series of charges concerned foreign affairs: Hubert had defeated a proposal to marry Henry to a daughter of the duke of Austria; he had first corrupted and then married the sister of the king of Scots; he had stolen from Henry and given to the prince of Wales a talisman, which rendered its wearer invulnerable; he had contrived that William de Braiose should

Henry dismisses his ministers; and supersedes Hubert, July 29, 1232.

Henry's charges against Hubert similar to those against Becket, Wolsey, and Cromwell.

[1] M. Paris, iii. 204, 211; Ann. Dunst. p. 127. [2] M. Paris, iii. 211, 212.

[3] M. Paris, iii. 221–223. See the answers to the charges revived against Hubert in 1239, drawn up by Laurence of S. Alban's; M. Paris, vi. 63–74.

be hanged as a thief. A third series was founded on public report: he had poisoned the earl of Salisbury, the young earl Marshall, Falkes de Breauté, and archbishop Richard; he had kept the king under his influence by witchcraft, and in contempt of the rights of the city of London had hanged Constantine Fitz-Alulf. The first set of charges he endeavoured to rebut by producing accounts and quittances; but, when he heard the second series, he took sanctuary at Merton, and refused to present himself for trial. The interposition of the earl of Chester saved him from being dragged violently from the sanctuary; but having obtained a delay of his trial and roused the king's suspicions by a journey to S. Edmund's, he was torn from the chapel at Brentwood and lodged in the Tower. After bringing him before a tribunal of earls and judges[1], Henry allowed himself to be soothed by the surrender of his victim's treasures, accepted the security of four earls for his good behaviour, and placed him in honourable captivity at Devizes, restoring the estates that he had inherited or bought, and those which he held of other lords besides the king[2].

Hubert's reply and flight.

His imprisonment and forfeiture.

He is imprisoned at Devizes.

Questionable character of Henry's proceedings.

The question of the legality of Henry's proceedings against Hubert can scarcely be decided on constitutional grounds; he might, indeed, have pleaded the action taken by William Rufus against the bishop of Durham, by Stephen against Roger of Salisbury, or by Henry II against Becket; but in each of these cases the clerical character of the accused minister furnished an element of complication that was absent in the case of Hubert. That the whole transaction was extrajudicial may be inferred from the fact that the king thought it necessary to give his own account of it in the form of letters patent. In this curious document, which must be regarded as an admission that the nation had a right to know how and why the justiciar was dismissed[3], the only distinct charges made against him are the wrongs inflicted, contrary to the king's peace, on the pope's envoys and the Italian clerks.

His manifesto on the occasion.

The death of the earl of Chester, which occurred during these

[1] Foed. i. 208.

[2] See Royal Letters, i. 408 (October 12, 1232).

[3] Foed. i. 207.

Death of the earl of Chester. proceedings[1], removed the foremost of the nobles who had taken part in the quarrels of John, and who could remember the days of Henry II and Richard. **His career.** The son of earl Hugh, who had imperilled the throne in 1173, he had been loyal to Henry and Richard. As a crusader he had taken part in the capture of Damietta in 1219. He was the stepfather of Arthur of Brittany. In 1215 he had been faithful to John, and had been trusted by him more entirely than any other Englishman. The peculiar jurisdiction of his palatine earldom, and the great accumulation of power which he received as custos of the earldom of Leicester, made his position in the kingdom unique, and fitted him for the part of a leader of opposition to royal or ministerial tyranny. On more than one occasion he refused his consent to taxation which he deemed unjust: his jealousy of Hubert, although it led him to join the foreign party in 1223, did not prevent him from more than once interposing to avert his overthrow. **Disappearance of the Conquest families.** He was, moreover, almost the last relic of the great feudal aristocracy of the Conquest, the estates and dignities of which were soon to be centred in the royal family. Cornwall was already given to the king's brother; Leicester was soon to be the portion of his brother-in-law; on earl Ranulf's death without children the great Palatine inheritance, having passed to his nephew John, son of David of Huntingdon, was within a few years appropriated as a provision for a son of the king.

Peter des Roches provokes opposition. Peter des Roches did not long enjoy the fruits of his victory. He was strong enough however to persuade the king to dismiss his new treasurer, to substitute for him Peter de Rivaux, a creature of his own[2], and to make some important changes in the sheriffdoms. One of the first measures of the new administration was to obtain, September 14, a grant of a fortieth of moveables, amounting to 24,712 marks, 7*s.* 2*d*[3]. The removal of the English servants of the royal household to make way

[1] October 28, M. Paris, iii. 229; October 26, Ann. Theokesb. p. 87.

[2] M. Paris, iii. 220.

[3] M. Paris, iii. 223, 230. From this the spiritualities were exempted; see Ann. Waverl. p. 310; Ann. Dunst. p. 131; Ann. Osney, p. 74; Foed. i. 207; Royal Letters, i. 415. And there was a scutage the same year, the 'Scutagium de Elveyn,' for the Welsh war, at 20*s.* on the fee.

for Bretons and Poictevins soon followed at the Christmas court at Worcester[1]. These measures produced great and widespread apprehensions of further change, and raised at once a formidable opposition under the earl Marshall, Richard, the second son of the regent, the most accomplished and patriotic member of the baronage, who had succeeded his brother in 1231[2]. On receiving a summons to meet the king at Oxford on the 24th of June 1233, the earls and barons determined to absent themselves, and announced their resolution in plain terms to the king. Robert Bacon, a Dominican friar, told Henry that so long as the influence of the bishop of Winchester prevailed there could be no peace[3]. The king in alarm issued a new summons for the 11th of July, promising that if the barons would then meet him at Westminster he would make all rightful and necessary reforms. They replied that unless the alien counsellors were dismissed they would call together the common council of the realm and elect a new king. The bishop carried matters with a high hand: it ill became him, the chief adviser of the pope and emperor, to yield. Foreign forces were levied, hostages demanded of the barons; the king was ready for war. On the 1st of August at London the party of opposition met to face the king, but the earl Marshall, warned by his sister, the countess of Cornwall, that Henry intended him to share the fate of Hubert de Burgh, absented himself, and in his absence nothing was done. A general assembly of all the military tenants of the crown was next called for the 14th of August at Gloucester. In that meeting Richard was declared a traitor: the king invaded his estates and fixed a day for his trial[4]. On the 8th of October there was another stormy meeting at Westminster: the barons denied the legality of the proceedings against the earl Marshall,

Opposition of Richard Marshall.

The earls and barons refuse to meet Peter, June, 1233.

Henry promises compliance.

The barons insist on the dismissal of the bishop.

Councils in the summer of 1233.

The earl Marshall declared a traitor.

[1] M. Paris, iii. 240; Ann. Winton, p. 86.

[2] 'Vir omni morum honestate praeditus, nobilitate generis insignis, artibus liberalibus insigniter eruditus, in armorum exercitio strenuissimus, in omnibus operibus suis Deum habens prae oculis, regis et regni praevidens et verens excidium, ut pacem et concordiam reformaret, se ipsum exponens discrimini, se murum inter dominum regem et magnates opposuit;' Ann. Waverley, p. 313. See the loving terms in which Grosseteste addresses him, Epist. vi. pp. 38 sq.

[3] M. Paris, iii. 244, 245.

[4] Ibid. iii. 247, 248.

and insisted that he should be tried by his peers. The bishop replied contemptuously, and with a perverse misrepresentation of the English law, which justifies the suspicious hatred with which he was regarded: there were, he said, no peers in England as there were in France, and the king had a full right through his justices to proscribe and condemn his enemies [1]. This provoked an immediate outcry; the bishops declared that they would excommunicate Peter of Winchester and the rest of the counsellors, and went so far as to pronounce a general sentence against the men who had turned the king's heart away from his natural subjects. Civil war broke out immediately; Hubert escaped from Devizes and joined the earl; the king, having marched in person against the malcontents, suffered an entire defeat at Monmouth in November; and the beginning of the next year saw the earl Marshall in league with the Welsh, ravaging the estates of the royal partisans.

Peter des Roches declares that there are no peers in England.

The bishops threaten him with excommunication.

Civil war.

Bishop Peter, however, was cunning as well as violent. He had forced the earl Marshall into armed resistance, he now took measures for completely destroying him. He drew him into Ireland to defend his estates there. Geoffrey de Marisco, the old justiciar of Ireland, was trusted to allure him to open war, to desert him, and then overwhelm him. The plan was too successful. The earl was mortally wounded on the 1st of April, 1234, and died in prison on the 16th. He might, if he had lived, have anticipated some of the glories of Simon de Montfort; but the craft of the Poictevins had already separated him from the party which he would have led, and he had no advisers who could compete in policy with his foes. His death left the headship of the opposition vacant for many years [2].

Peter's plot against the earl Marshall.

Defeat and death of the earl Marshall, April, 1234.

But before he died his great foe had fallen. Henry, incapable of any lasting feeling, weary of his new friends, and cowed by the threats of the clergy, was ready to give way. In a council at Westminster on the 2nd of February, 1234, the bishop of Lichfield had indignantly denied that friendship with the earl

Proceedings against Peter des Roches.

[1] M. Paris, iii. 252.
[2] Ibid. iii. 249, 273, 279, 288; Ann. Dunst. p. 136.

Marshall implied enmity to the king, and obtained from his brethren a sentence of anathema against the accusers[1]. But the bishops soon found a more able leader in Edmund Rich, the new primate, whom the pope had appointed by an assumption of power as great as that by which Innocent III had compelled the election of Langton. His first act after his consecration was to visit the king and insist on the reform of abuses and the dismissal of the bad advisers. On the 9th of April at Westminster a long list of grievances was read, and Edmund declared himself ready to excommunicate the king in person[2]. Henry gave way: on the 10th he sent word to Peter des Roches that he must henceforth confine himself to his spiritual duties[3]. Peter de Rivaux was dismissed and compelled to resign all his offices. Stephen Segrave, too, fell with his patron, and both treasurer and justiciar were called to a strict account for their dealings, especially for their treatment of Hubert de Burgh and the earl Marshall[4]. Hubert was soon afterwards restored to his estates; but the bishops who were sent to treat with the earl brought back only the tidings of his death and a demand for the punishment of his enemies. Henry placed himself under the advice of the archbishop, and prepared to begin to be a good king. All the evil influences that had hung round him since his childhood were apparently extinct, all the aliens were displaced, and all who had suffered wrong at their hands restored to their rights[5].

Archbishop Edmund insists on his dismissal, April, 1234.

He is dismissed, and his dependents with him.

Hubert de Burgh restored to his estates.

174. Henry seems from this time forward to have conceived the idea of acting without a ministry, such as he had hitherto employed. The justiciarship was not again committed to a great baron; the treasurership he filled from time to time with clerks

Henry's attempt to govern alone.

[1] M. Paris, iii. 268.

[2] Ibid. iii. 269, 272. Edmund was consecrated April 2. The pope wrote on the 3rd of April to the Archbishop urging him to persuade the English to put away their prejudice against the aliens; Royal Letters, i. 556.

[3] M. Paris, iii. 272; Ann. Theokesb. p. 93; Ann. Dunst. p. 136; Ann. Osney, p. 78; Ann. Wigorn. p. 426.

[4] M. Paris, iii. 292–298; Ann. Waverl. p. 315; Royal Letters, i. 445, 446.

[5] The pardons of Gilbert Marshall and Hubert de Burgh are dated May 26, Royal Letters, i. 439, 440; and the outlawry against Hubert annulled June 8 (ib. 443), 'eo quod injuste et contra legem terrae in eos fuit promulgata.'

of his own selection, and, although he was unable to deprive Ralph Neville of the chancellorship, he got the great seal out of his hands, and after his death appointed no successor for many years [1]. There was no doubt some convenience in this plan; the nation would at least for a time bear more patiently the demands of the king than those of his officers: the great revenues, which had been administered by those officers to their own advantage, would help to defray the expenses of the court; and the personal grievances which had been made the pretext of discontent could less easily be alleged against a king who was his own minister. But such a scheme required for success a much more persevering and careful man than Henry: nor could any success be more than temporary: the king's personal administration might present a barrier against disorder and an answer to discontent, longer than that of a servant who could be sacrificed to appease complaints, but this could only last until the discontent became overwhelming, and then the flood of disorder would sweep away the royal power itself. In this case, however, Henry's tenure of power and misuse of it were prolonged by the fact that the baronial party had no competent leader. For many years after the death of Richard Marshall, the only powerful remonstrances addressed to the king proceeded from his own brother Richard and archbishop Edmund. Richard was as yet a hopeful English baron, the very reverse of Henry both in faults and virtues, of much more practical wisdom and more patriotic sympathies. Edmund was a bishop of the type of Anselm, with somewhat of the spirit and political instincts of Langton: but he lived in an unhappy period for the display of either class of qualities, under a pope whom he knew only as a taskmaster, and under a king whose incapacity and want of firmness made it as hard to support as to resist him. But the influence of earl Richard was soon to be diverted into other channels, and Edmund in a few years died worn out with labour and disappointment. It was not until Simon de Montfort arose

Suspension of the great offices of State.

The constitutional opposition was without a recognised leader, except the archbishop and earl Richard of Cornwall.

[1] Mr. Foss does not recognise any person as full chancellor until Walter de Merton was appointed in 1261. In the interval the seal was held by seven successive keepers for short periods. Foss, Tabulae Curiales, p. 10.

as the champion of the nation that Henry found himself obliged to face reform.

Henry incapable of acting for himself, or resisting the influence of his surroundings.

But although he had determined to take on himself all the responsibilities of governing, it was not in his nature to stand without a staff to lean upon. He could not exist without favourites, whose influence with him was unbounded, and England furnished no aspirants for so pernicious a distinction. The unpopularity of Hubert had to be set against the hatred felt for Peter: the too powerful minister was only one degree less odious than the foreign favourite. Henry had scarcely energy or purpose enough to seek out worthy advisers; his choice of confidants was determined largely by accident: he liked the more refined manners, the magnificent appearance, the absolutist politics of the French and Provençals: he fell directly under the rule of any stronger mind with which he was brought in contact.

Reasons for the general dislike of foreigners.

The detestation of the foreigners, which, with the maintenance of the charters, gave tone to the popular politics of the reign, was by no means an irrational outcry. The English believed and had good cause to believe that the men whom the king chiefly loved and trusted were either strangers or actual enemies to the constitutional rights that had already become so precious.

Misconduct of the foreigners.

They knew that they evaded English law, that they misused English influence and money abroad, and that at home they engrossed power and employed it by illegal means for illegal ends. So much the earlier and later foreign influxes had in common. In an age in which leaders were few and political knowledge small, it is no wonder that personal influences, sympathies, and antipathies are more prominent in the chronicles than the progress of political principles.

Events of 1235 and 1236.

The chief business of the year 1235 was the marriage of the king's sister Isabella with the emperor Frederick, which was discussed in the national council and made the occasion of a grant of two marks on the fee[1]. The next year Henry

[1] M. Paris, iii. 319, 327; Ann. Theokesb. p. 97, where it is stated that the bishops paid nothing; Ann. Dunst. p. 142: 'petitum et concessum fuit . . . non solum de feodis habitis in capite de rege sed etiam de aliis cultis.' It was granted by the 'commune concilium regni,' Madox, Hist.

himself was married. After a long series of negotiations for alliance with ladies of the chief houses of France and Germany[1], Eleanor, the second daughter of Raymond Berenger IV of Provence, and sister of the queen of France, accepted his offer. She was brought to England by her uncle William, bishop elect of Valence, who almost immediately acquired supreme influence over the king[2]. The marriage took place in January, 1236; on the 23rd of that month, in a great council called at Merton after the festivities were over, the statute of Merton was passed, in which the barons emphatically declared that they would not have the laws of England changed. Yet on the 29th of April the alarm was raised that the foreigners were too powerful; that the king had chosen a body of twelve sworn counsellors, William of Valence at the head, and had bound himself to do nothing without their advice; and here was an attempt to substitute the French court of twelve peers for the common council of the kingdom. The storm in the assembly of the barons rose so high that Henry had to take refuge in the Tower. Thoroughly cowed, he made promises of good government, and removed some of the sheriffs in consequence of complaints of misbehaviour; but he persevered in his new scheme of administration, attempted to compel the bishop of Chichester to surrender the great seal, recalled to court Stephen Segrave and Robert Passelew, the most unpopular of his late ministers[3], and allowed Peter des Roches, against whom he had but lately written the bitterest accusations

Henry's marriage, Jan. 1236.

Council of Merton.

Rumours of foreign influences in the government.

Henry recalls the late ministers.

Exch. p. 412, where an 'auxilium praelatorum' is mentioned as made separately. The form for collection is in the Select Charters, p. 364.

[1] Negotiations were on foot in 1224 for an Austrian princess, Foed. i. 176; in 1225 for a Breton, ibid. i. 180; Royal Letters, i. 295; for a Bohemian, Foed. i. 185; Royal Letters, i. 249; for a Scottish princess, in 1231, M. Paris, iii. 206; and for a lady of the house of Ponthieu as late as April, 1235, M. Paris, iii. 328.

[2] M. Paris, iii. 362, 387. 'Factus est consiliarius regis principalis, cum aliis undecim, qui super sacrosancta juraverunt, quod fidele consilium regi praestarent, et ipse similiter juravit quod eorum consiliis obediret;' Ann. Dunst. p. 146. This plan, if really adopted, may not unreasonably have led to the general impression that the foreigners were intent on a change in the constitution; but the authority is scarcely sufficient to prove the fact, in the silence of other writers.

[3] They had made their peace and been employed again as early as February 1235; M. Paris, iii. 306. They were in full favour again in June, 1236; ibid. iii. 368; Ann. Dunst. p. 144.

to the emperor[1], to return to his see, where he closed his long and turbulent career in 1238.

Statement of the king's necessities in 1237.

Henry was now in sore want of money. On the 13th of January, 1237[2], William of Raleigh, one of his confidential clerks, laid before an extraordinary assembly of barons and prelates the necessity to which the ki g, as he said, was reduced by the dishonesty or incapacity of his late advisers. He proposed that the council of the nation should determine the mode of collecting an aid, and that the money when collected should be placed in the hands of a commission elected by the assembly, to be laid out according to the needs of the realm. The barons, either mistrusting or not understanding the vast importance of this concession, declared in reply that there was no reason for such constant demands; the king was engaged in no great enterprise; if he was poor it was because he wasted his money on foreigners. Henry professed himself ready to make amends, to dismiss his present counsellors and accept as advisers three nobles named by the barons, and to authorise the excommunication of all who impugned the charters. In the end it was determined to add to the council the earls of Derby and Warenne and John Fitz-Geoffrey. On these conditions a grant of a thirtieth of moveables was made by the archbishops, bishops, abbots, priors, earls, barons, knights, and freeholders for themselves and their villeins, with a provision however that nothing should be taken of the poor who possessed less than forty pennyworth of goods. The careful scheme adopted for the assessment and collection, by sworn officers elected in each township, affords a valuable illustration of the growth of constitutional life[3]. The sum raised was 23,891 marks, two shillings and a penny[4]. But the hope of peace and reform was premature. William of

Proposal to give the council the control of expenditure.

Henry's promises of reform.

Grant of a thirtieth, Jan. 1237.

[1] Royal Letters, i. 467 (April 27, 1235). He is free to return, May 4, 1236; ibid. ii. 12.

[2] M. Paris, iii. 380–382; Ann. Theokesb. pp. 102–104.

[3] Select Charters, pp. 366–368; Foed. i. 232; M. Paris, iii. 383; Ann. Winton, p. 87; Ann. Waverley, p. 317; Ann. Dunst. p. 147; Ann. Wykes, p. 84. To the same council must be referred the discussion on the state of the forests and the statutes of limitations, dated Feb. 5, 1237; given in the Annals of Burton, pp. 252, 253.

[4] Hunter, Three Catalogues, p. 22.

Valence indeed left England for a short time, but no sooner had the king secured a revenue for the year than by his secret invitation the legate Otho, who had been repelled by the nation in 1226, arrived, on the plea of enforcing necessary reforms in church and state. He held an important council in November[1], and showed a wise moderation; but the archbishop, not trusting appearances, went to Rome immediately afterwards to procure his recall.

Departure of William of Valence; and arrival of the legate Otho.

It is at this point that Simon de Montfort first comes prominently forward. He was the youngest son of the great leader of the crusade against the Albigenses[2], the elder Simon, who was nephew and one of the co-heirs of the last earl of Leicester. The father had borne the title of earl of Leicester, but had never been able to obtain possession of his inheritance. Although the English barons, in their struggle with John, had thought, it is said, of electing him king[3], he had been too busy in his attempt to secure the county of Toulouse to care for his interests here, and after his death the Leicester estates had remained in the hands of the earl of Chester. A family arrangement was made in contemplation of the earl of Chester's death; Amalric, the eldest son of Simon, claimed the inheritance, and after some negotiation resigned his rights in favour of his youngest brother[4]. The younger Simon inherited his father's piety, his accomplishments, his love of adventure, and his great ambition. Sprung from a family which had more than once signalised itself by unscrupulous aggression, and trained by a youth of peril, Simon had had little in his early career that seemed to fit him to be a national deliverer. He was, in the eyes of the English lords, a foreigner, an adventurer, and an upstart, combining all that they had found

Rise of Simon de Montfort.

Simon's inherited and personal qualifications.

[1] M. Paris, iii. 395, 403, 416 sq.; Ann. Theokesb. p. 105; Ann. Burton, p. 253; Ann. Waverley, p. 318. Henry had written for a legate in 1230, but the justiciar had prevailed on him to recall the messenger; Royal Letters, i. 379.

[2] See, for Simon de Montfort generally, Dr. Pauli's Simon von Montfort, and the Life of Simon de Montfort by G. W. Prothero, 1876.

[3] Ann. Dunst. p. 33.

[4] Simon, on April 8, 1230, has a pension of 400 marks until he receives the earldom; Royal Letters, i. 362, 401; Foed. i. 203, 205.

Simon de Montfort.

objectionable in Hubert de Burgh, Peter des Roches, and William of Valence. That he was able to overcome this repugnance, and to throw himself heart and soul into the position of an English baron, statesman, and patriot, is no small proof of the greatness and versatility of his powers. The respect with which the chroniclers almost invariably mention him is justified by the friendships which he formed with the best men of his time; his great reputation for honour and probity, as well as for warlike skill and statesmanship, is indisputable. Such qualifications he had for undertaking the part of the champion and deliverer of an oppressed people; a part which when honestly played is the grandest that ever falls into the hands of man, but one which has its special temptations; for it must not endure the least suspicion of vindictiveness or self-seeking; it demands peremptorily that the hero must understand and not go beyond the exact terms of his high commission, and the risks of it are so great that the undertaking can only be completely justified by success.

His secret marriage with the king's sister, Jan. 1238.

Richard of Cornwall declares against him.

To the English of 1238 Simon was a foreigner and a royal favourite[1]. The news that the king had secretly married him to his sister Eleanor, the widow of William Marshall, a lady too who had taken a vow of chastity, provoked an immediate outcry. Richard of Cornwall, indignant at Henry's folly and his sister's disparagement, headed the malcontents. He was joined by the earl Marshall Gilbert, the majority of the barons, and even by the citizens of London: only Hubert de Burgh stood by the king. Earl Richard peremptorily rejected the mediation of the legate; why, he asked, should the king of England sacrifice the welfare of the realm to strangers: such was not the way of the emperor and the king of France; England had become like a vineyard with a broken hedge; all that went by plucked off her grapes[2]. The dispute threatened to become a civil war: on the 3rd of February[3], the marriage having taken place on the 7th

[1] 'Consiliarios quoque habuit infames et suspectos . . . et hi erant J. comes Lincolniae, S. comes Legrecestriae, frater G. Templarius;' M. Paris, iii. 412.

[2] M. Paris, iii. 470, 475–478; Ann. Theokesb. p. 106.

[3] Royal Letters, ii. 15.

of January, Richard was in arms, and the king was summoning forces to crush him. Henry begged for a respite. On the 22nd a plan of reform was produced, the first of the many schemes of the sort that leave such important marks on the reign, and which show the instinctive tendency of the national wishes towards a limited monarchy acting through responsible advisers. Henry undertook to abide by the decisions of a chosen body of counsellors for the reform of the state. Articles were written out and sealed, when Richard drew back. He was, after all, the heir to the crown; the royal hands must not be too tightly bound: he admitted Simon to the kiss of peace; and the great design came to naught, except as a precedent for other days in which the two leaders should have changed places. Simon soon after, having raised large sums from his vassals on the Leicester estates, went to Rome to purchase the papal recognition of his marriage[1]. This he succeeded in obtaining. He returned to England in October, and in February 1239 received from Henry the full investiture of his earldom[2]. Before the end of the year he was again in disgrace, but the preparations for the Crusade gave him an opportunity of making his peace. The earl of Cornwall and the heir of Salisbury had taken the cross; again, as in 1218, the troubles of the East drew away the more active spirits from domestic politics. Simon left with the rest in the early summer of 1240 and did not return before 1242.

The first plan of constitutional reform.

Richard hangs back.

Simon admitted to favour, Feb. 1239.

During these years England looked in vain for peace. The presence of the legate, the vast assumptions of the court of Rome, which rested not only on spiritual claims but on the new relation created by John's submission; the demands not only of direct subsidies, but of the patronage of churches to the detriment of clerical and lay patrons, the constant intrusion of foreigners into the richest livings, the ceaseless disputes between the crown and the chapters on the election to bishoprics, the steady flow of appeals to Rome and the equally steady rise in the judicial pretensions of the Curia, produced a feeling of irritation in all classes, which can scarcely be overstated. It is to this period,

Difficulties with Rome

[1] M. Paris, iii. 479.

[2] Ibid. iii. 524.

Ecclesiastical disaffection.

too, at which the king, strengthened by the presence of the legate, began to regard himself as supreme over all classes of his subjects, that we must refer the beginning of the ecclesiastical disaffection which appears in constant councils and in the long bills of gravamina so common in the annals of the time. The constant interference of the lay courts in spiritual matters, the compelling of the clergy to answer before secular judges for personal matters, not concerning land or otherwise pertaining to secular jurisdiction [1], the forcing of clerks into benefices for which they were unqualified, to the contempt of the bishops' right of institution, are the burden of these complaints: they begin with the legatine council of 1237; Grosseteste is their first exponent; and they speedily fall in with the general tide of remonstrance against misgovernment, of which Grosseteste was the guiding mind, and which served to build up the party and arm the hands of earl Simon as champion of both church and nation. Archbishop Edmund saw only the beginning of the strife; and he was fitted to be a victim rather than a champion. After vainly imploring both pope and king to hold their hand before the destruction of the church was completed, he left England, to die quietly in France. He started, late in the autumn, on his way to Rome, rested at Pontigny, and died at Soissi, November 16, 1240. The legate, who had collected, as it was said, half the money of the realm, departed, leaving the church without a constitutional head, in January 1241. Then the queen's kinsmen poured in, bringing their foreign manners and the hateful suspicion that they wanted to change the laws. Thomas of Savoy, the titular count of Flanders, obtained from Henry a grant of a groat on every sack of English wool carried through his territories; and the king took away the great seal from the officer who had refused to seal the writ [2]. William of Valence he tried to force into the see of Winchester, and thus

Grosseteste leader of the clerical opposition.

The archbishop dies, 1240.

Departure of Otho, Jan. 1241.

Influx of Savoyards.

[1] An instance of this is the summoning of Grosseteste before the curia regis for neglecting to observe a writ of inquiry into the legitimacy of a presentee. Taken in connexion with Grosseteste's strong opposition to the statute of Merton on the subject, this very case may have led to the complaint; Grosset. Ep. xxvi. p. 104; but all these points are illustrated by Grosseteste's letters, especially Ep. lxxii. See also Bracton's Note Book, ed. Maitland, vol. i. pp. 104–108, 117.

[2] M. Paris, iii. 629.

provoked the monks into electing Ralph Neville, whom he had failed to remove from the Chancery[1]. Peter of Savoy appeared early in 1241 to claim the earldom of Richmond[2] as the king's gift: and Boniface, another brother, the bishop elect of Belley, was chosen the same year to succeed the saintly Edmund. The vacancy of the popedom, which lasted from 1241 to 1243, might have given the king breathing time, if he had had the good sense to take it: but he had fallen into utter contempt. To complete the degradation of the Plantagenets, Lewis IX chose the moment to bestow Poictou, which was titularly claimed by Richard of Cornwall, on his brother Alfonso. One glimpse of successful administration is seen in the submission of the Welsh to the king, who appeared on the border with an armed force in August 1241. The same year he was delivered from one foe by the accidental death of Gilbert Marshall, who had stayed from the crusade in order to settle his differences with the king, the ever-recurring differences arising from Henry's determination not to do justice to the children of his great benefactor[3].

The queen's uncles.

Loss of Poictou.

Success in Wales.

175. It was in expectation of a war in France to which he was summoned by his stepfather Hugh of La Marche, that Henry called his bishops and barons to London on the 28th of January, 1242. Earl Richard arrived in time to join in the proceedings, which were formally recorded and are the subject of the first authorised account of a parliamentary debate[4]. They are of singular importance both in form and in matter. Earl Richard, archbishop Walter Gray, and the provost of Beverley, came before the assembled body, which contained all the prelates in person or by proxy, all the earls, and nearly all the barons, and delivered the king's message, requesting aid for the recovery of his foreign possessions. The assembly seems to have laboured under none of the reticent cautious modesty that prompted the parliaments of Edward III; they replied that before the king went to war he would do

Parliament of 1242.

First report of a debate.

The king's demand of an aid.

Reply of the parliament.

[1] M. Paris, iii. 495; Ann. Theokesb. p. 110. [2] Ann. Theokesb. p. 118.
[3] June 27, 1241; Ann. Waverley, p. 328; Ann. Theokesb. p. 119.
[4] M. Paris, iv. 185–188; Select Charters, pp. 368–370.

Advice of the parliament.

well to await the termination of the truce by which he was bound to France, and try to prevail on Lewis to do the same. If the king of France refused, then the question of aid might be entertained. They had, they said, been very liberal in former years: very early in the reign they had given a thirteenth, in 1225 a fifteenth, in 1232 a fortieth, a very great aid for the marriage of Isabella in 1235, and a thirtieth in 1237; besides carucages, scutages, and tallages[1]. The grant of 1237 had been made under special conditions as to custody and expenditure; no account of it had been rendered; it was believed to be still in the king's hands. Besides these extraordinary sources of revenue the king had enormous resources in the escheats, the profits of vacant churches and the like; and for five years the itinerant justices had been inflicting fines which impoverished the innocent as well as the guilty. If, however, the king would wait for the expiration of the truce, they promised to do their best. Henry, professing himself satisfied with the reply, asked next what, if he should wait, their grant would be; they answered that it would be time to consider when the case arose: as for the promises of reform with which he tried to stimulate their liberality, they said that they were not disposed to try the question with the king, they knew too well how he had kept the engagements made in 1237.

They distrust the king.

Conditional promises.

Henry negotiates separately with the magnates.

Unable to draw out a distinct answer, and hopeless of obtaining a general grant, Henry then called the prelates and barons singly, and tried to make a separate bargain with each. So, although the council broke up without coming to a vote, he contrived by force, fraud or persuasion, to raise a large sum with which he equipped an expedition. He then declared the truce broken, sailed from Portsmouth on the 9th of May, and after an ignominious campaign, in which he escaped capture only through the moderation of Lewis and the counsel of

[1] Of the first of these imposts we can only conjecture that it was raised in 1217, previous to the scutage and tallage (above, p. 30); the others will be found noted under their respective years: the scutages under 1218, 1220, 1223, 1224, 1225, 1229, 1230, 1231, 1233. The tallages were probably supplementary to the scutages, but more varied in their incidence. The list forms a complete account of the taxes raised constitutionally during the first half of the reign.

Richard, sent home his forces. He remained in Gascony until September 25, 1243, leaving England under the archbishop of York[1], as guardian, lieutenant or regent, with the bishop of Carlisle and Walter Cantilupe as chief counsellors. The archbishop, Walter de Gray, who had been John's chancellor nearly forty years before, contrived to ameliorate the condition of the realm, whilst he could, and to prevent any undue exactions in the king's name. For Henry wished to raise, as his father had done, a scutage by way of fine from the barons who had left him alone in Gascony, besides that which he received, twenty shillings on the fee, from those who had stayed at home[2]. **His expedition to Gascony, May 1242 to Sept. 1243.**

Two important results followed incidentally from this expedition: the influx of a new body of Poictevin kinsmen into England, and the marriage of earl Richard, who had lost his first wife before the Crusade, with the queen's sister, Sanchia of Provence. The first marriage of Richard with the countess of Gloucester had made him brother-in-law of the Marshalls and the earls of Norfolk and Derby, and stepfather to the earl of Gloucester. His new alliance on the other hand drew him away from the baronage. Once or twice afterwards he appears in opposition, but it is no longer as heading his party against the aliens: his prudence and his wealth saved Henry in more than one threatening crisis, but on the whole he disappointed the hopes of the nation, and lost the place which Simon de Montfort was not unwilling to take. His desertion of the good cause was in after years alleged against him more bitterly perhaps than justice demanded. A resistance to the royal power, headed by the king's nearest kinsman, was an experiment **Influx of Poictevin.** **Earl Richard changes his policy.** **Excuse to be made for him.**

[1] He is called, in the Liber de Antiquis Legibus, *capitalis justitiarius domini regis*; p. 9; Foed. i. 244. On the 8th of June the king wrote for men and money, and directed five hundred good Welshmen to be sent him in a way that seems to correspond with the later commissions of array; Foed. i. 246.

[2] M. Paris, iv. 227, 232; where the reading 'viginti solidos' seems to be that of the author; 'iii marcas' is the reading of one MS. In the Historia Anglorum, ii. 466, M. Paris has the smaller sum. A scutage of 40*s.* in 1242 is mentioned in the Annals of Dunstable, p. 160; Ann. Wykes, p. 91; Cont. Fl. Wig. p. 178. The Pipe Rolls contain 'fines militum ne transfretarent cum rege in Wasconiam praeter scutagia sua quae regi sponte concesserunt.' Cf. Pearson, ii. 188.

from which a wise man might well shrink. Richard's change of attitude may be justified by the history of the royal house during the next two centuries.

Parliament of 1244.

The political history of 1244[1] shows a steady advance made by the barons from their position in 1238 and 1242. A parliament met, the date of which is uncertain, but which must have been held in autumn after Henry's return from the north; it contained the usual elements, and sat in the Refectory at Westminster. Henry, who had been reduced to the necessity of collecting money from the Jews with his own hands, and had even applied for aid to the general chapter of Cîteaux[2], had to act as his own spokesman in order to avoid a flat contradiction. He had, he said, gone to Gascony by the advice of his barons, and had there incurred debts from which without a liberal and general grant he could not free himself[3]. The magnates replied that they would take counsel; the prelates, the earls, and the barons, all three deliberated apart. After some discussion the bishops proposed to the lay nobles that they should act conjointly; they knew one another's minds, the prelates would draw up the answer if the barons would assent. The barons answered that they would do nothing without the assent of the whole body of the national council. Thereupon a

Personal application for money by the king.

Deliberations of the lords.

[1] M. Paris, iv. 364 sq., 372.

[2] Ibid. iv. 234, 235, 257.

[3] Matthew Paris describes this parliament as adjourned until three weeks after the Purification, February 2, and so would lead us to suppose that it was the usual Hilarytide session of 1244. Brady and Carte have both noticed that this is incompatible with the history of the year. Boniface, the archbishop-elect, only reached England on the 22nd of April (Ann. Waverley, p. 333); and the bishop of Winchester only obtained admission to the king's favour on the 9th of September (Ann. Dunst. p. 164; Ann. Waverley, p. 332). Henry moreover laid before the bishops a papal bull dated July 29, 1244, which could not have arrived in England before the end of August (Carte, ii. 80), and Henry himself only returned from Scotland at the end of August. On the other hand, the bishop of Lincoln went to Lyons on the 18th of November (M. Paris, iv. 390). The parliament must then be placed between these limits. There was a parliament at Windsor on the morrow of the Nativity of the blessed Virgin (Ann. Dunst. p. 164). If Matthew Paris gives the order of events correctly, the Westminster Parliament was probably held at Michaelmas or soon after. The refusal of the barons to grant further aid he places on the 3rd of November (iv. 395). The aid for the marriage was granted (Ann. Dunst. p. 167) three weeks after the Purification in 1245; hence perhaps the confusion.

joint committee was chosen to draw up the reply. This committee consisted of twelve members, four chosen by each of the three bodies, the prelates, earls and barons. The bishops were represented by Boniface, the primate elect; William Raleigh, bishop of Winchester, who had once been the king's minister, but had since then been the object of his vindictive persecution; the bishop of Lincoln, Robert Grosseteste; and the bishop of Worcester, Walter Cantilupe, who throughout the long contest that followed never deserted the cause of freedom. The earls of Cornwall, Leicester, Norfolk and Pembroke, represented their brethren. The barons chose Richard of Montfichet, one of the few survivors of the twenty-five executors of the great Charter, and John of Balliol, with the abbots of S. Edmund's and Ramsey. Their reply to the king stated that the charters, although often confirmed, were never observed; that the money so freely given had never been spent to the good of the king or of the realm; and that owing to the want of a chancellor the great seal was often set to writs that were contrary to justice. They demanded therefore the appointment of a justiciar, a treasurer and a chancellor, by whom the state of the kingdom might be strengthened. Henry refused to do anything on compulsion, and adjourned the discussion. It was however agreed that, if the king would in the meantime appoint such counsellors, and take such measures of reform, as the magnates could approve, a grant should be made, to be expended under the supervision of the joint committee. Henry was very much disinclined to accept these terms, and, in order to detach the bishops from the league, produced a papal letter, ordering them to vote a liberal subsidy. They postponed their answer however until the general question was settled; and when, after the departure of the lay barons, the king renewed his application, both by messengers and in person, Grosseteste closed the discussion by reference to the agreement made with the barons: 'We may not be divided from the common counsel, for it is written, if we be divided we shall all die forthwith [1].'

The bishops, earls, and barons form a joint committee.

Their remonstrance.

Demand of a ministry.

Reply of Grosseteste.

[1] M. Paris, iv. 366. Cf. Grosseteste, Ep. 79, which may possibly refer to this demand.

Record of a second scheme of constitutional reform, 1244.

Matthew Paris has preserved a scheme of reform under the same year[1], which purports to be the result of the deliberations, and to contain provisions made by the magnates with the king's consent to be inviolably observed for the future. Amongst these provisions are some propositions of a far more fundamental character than any that have yet been broached, and to a curious degree typical of later forms of government. According to this plan a new charter was to be drawn up, embodying and strengthening the salutary provisions of the old one, and to be proclaimed under the same sanctions: the execution of it was not to be left to the royal officers, but to be committed to four counsellors chosen by common assent, sworn to do justice, and not to be removed without common consent. Of these four, two at least were to be in constant attendance on the king, to hear all complaints and find speedy remedies, to secure the safe custody of the royal treasure, and the proper expenditure of money granted by the nation, and to be conservators of all liberties; two of them might be the justiciar and chancellor, chosen by the whole body of the realm, and not to be changed without the consent of a regular assembly, 'a solemn convocation.' Two justices of the bench and two barons of the exchequer were also to be appointed, in the first instance by general election, afterwards by the four conservators. 'As these officers are to treat of the concerns of all, so in the selection of them the assent of all should concur.' This form, whether or no it were more than a paper constitution, anticipates several of the points of the later programme of Simon de Montfort, and some at least of those which for centuries afterwards were the chief subject of contention between king and people. For the time however the attention of the magnates was distracted by the appeals and other interference of Master Martin, the envoy of Innocent IV, whose demands exceeded all that had been claimed by former popes. Nothing was really settled.

The discussion closed.

On the 3rd of November the barons refused to grant money; but, after an adjournment, a scutage of twenty shillings was,

[1] 'Haec providebant magnates rege consentiente inviolabiliter deinceps observari;' M. Paris, iv. 366–368.

in February 1245, granted for the marriage of the king's eldest daughter[1].

Action of England in the council of Lyons in 1245.

The council of Lyons, in which Innocent IV deposed Frederick II, and in which Roger Bigod and others, representing the 'communitas' of the realm of England, made a bold but vain demand for the relaxation of papal tyranny[2], and even attempted to repudiate the submission of John, concentrated the gaze of the world in 1245. Henry seems to have rested on the little victory he had won, eking out his revenue by vexatious tallages imposed on the Londoners. The wrongs of the church form for a time the chief matter of debate in the national gatherings.

Gravamina drawn up in 1246.

A parliament held at Westminster, March 18, 1246, drew up a list of grievances, which were sent to the pope with special letters from each of the great bodies present, the king, the bishops, the abbots, and the earls, with the whole baronage, clergy, and people[3]. Another parliament met at Winchester on the 7th of July to receive the answer. Innocent threatened Henry with the fate of the emperor[4]. He at once succumbed, and the barons lost heart.

Payment to the pope.

Six thousand marks were wrung from the clergy to support the Anti-Cæsar[5].

Monotonous discontent.

The parliamentary history of the following years is of the same complexion: the councils meet and arrange fresh lists of grievances; year after year resistance becomes more hopeless. Now and then the king and his people seem to be drawn more closely together, as from time to time new elements appear in the councils, and each throws in its lot with the rest. The pope, however, found means to detach Henry finally from his alliance with the nation.

Silence of earl Simon.

No great signs are apparent of the action of any one leader: Simon de Montfort may have taken part in the

[1] 'Auxilium regi concessum ad primogenitam filiam suam maritandam, de quolibet feodo xx*s*.;' Pipe Roll, 29 Hen. III.

[2] Roger Bigod, John Fitz Geoffrey, Ralph Fitz Nicolas, Philip Basset, William Cantilupe, and Master William of Powick; Cole's Records, p. 350; Trivet, p. 234; M. Paris, iv. 420, 441, 478; Ann. Dunst. p. 168.

[3] M. Paris, iv. 511, 518–536; Ann. Burton, pp. 277–285; Foed. i. 265; Ann. Winton, p. 90. See Grosseteste, Ep. 119.

[4] M. Paris, iv. 560. The letters of Innocent dated June 12 (Foed. i. 266) do not bear out the statement of the historian.

[5] M. Paris, iv. 577. A scutage for the Welsh war, 'Scutagium de Gannoc,' three marks on the fee, appears in the Pipe Roll of 1246.

counsels of Grosseteste, who both in his writings and in parliament consistently opposed the tyranny of king and pope alike, but he must have led a quiet life on his own estates until 1248, when Henry sent him to govern Gascony. Archbishop Boniface lived generally in Savoy, regarding his English see only as a source of revenue: on his occasional visits he offended the English by his arrogance and violence, and, if now and then he saw that his real interest was to resist Roman extortion, he, like the king, was easily recalled by a share of the spoil. This period of our history is dismal indeed; but the sum of grievances was mounting so high that they must compel their own remedy, and men were growing up with a sense of injury that must sooner or later provide its vindication. For a third time within the century the business of the Crusade, now preparing under Lewis IX, postponed the violent determination of the crisis.

Archbishop Boniface.

Ecclesiastical questions of 1247.

The events of these years may be briefly summed up: in 1247 in a Candlemas parliament new protests were made against papal exactions, to which the prelates were, in the second session held at Oxford, at Easter, obliged to yield; and 11,000 marks were granted[1]. The same year Henry tried to restrict by law the ecclesiastical jurisdiction in temporal matters, such as breaches of faith, tithe suits and bastardy, and to confine it to matrimonial and testamentary causes. The proceedings of Grosseteste, who had encouraged the disciplinary assumptions of the spiritual courts, had called for a similar prohibition in 1246[2]. In 1248 the constitutional struggle began again, partly provoked by the arrival of a new brood of foreigners, half-brothers of the king. At a very great parliament held on the 9th of February, money was asked and grievances registered as usual[3]: the demand for a justiciar, chancellor, and treasurer, appointed by the common council of the realm, was again made, and declared to be based on the precedents of former reigns. Henry replied with general promises, and the barons rejoined with general professions made

Parliaments of 1248; in February, when money is asked;

[1] M. Paris, iv. 590, 594, 622, 623; Ann. Winton, p. 90; Ann. Wykes, p. 96.

[2] M. Paris, iv. 580, 614.

[3] Ibid. v. 5.

contingent on his fulfilment of his promises. After a delay of five months[1] he returned an arrogant refusal :—the servant was not above his master, he would not comply with the presumptuous demand; yet money must be provided. The answer of the barons was equally decided; and Henry in his disappointment turned his anger against his foolish advisers. They proposed that he should sell his jewels to the citizens of London. The king however, thinking that if the Londoners were rich enough to buy the jewels they might afford to help him freely, kept his Christmas at London, taking large sums as New Year's gifts[2].

and July, when it is refused.

Henry's tyrannies.

At Easter, 1249, the annual debate was repeated. Again the appointment of the three great officers was demanded, but in consequence of the absence of earl Richard, who had taken the side of the barons, nothing was done[3]. The next year, under the pressure of debt and poverty, Henry took the cross, begged forgiveness of the Londoners, whom he never ceased to molest by interference with their privileges, as well as by extortion of money, and issued a stringent order for the reduction of his household expenses in order that his debts might be paid, consoling himself with a heavy exaction from the Jews[4].

Parliament of 1249.

Henry's repentance in 1250.

The king's economical resolutions lasted over the following Christmas; but his savings were chiefly devoted to the enrichment of his half-brothers, for one of whom, Ethelmar, he had obtained by personal advocacy the election to the see of Winchester. The year 1251 however passed without a quarrel, and the next year the complications of royal and papal policy took a new form. Henry had probably as little intention of visiting Palestine as his father and grandfather had had; if he had ever intended it, the resolution was no stronger than the rest of his purposes. The pope now tried to rouse him to his duty, and by way of inducement authorised him to exact, for his expenses on Crusade, a tenth of the revenues of the clergy of England and his other dominions, for three years, to be taken after a new and stringent assessment[5]. This demand, which was announced in a papal

Lull of 1251.

Crusade proposed in 1252, and made an occasion for asking money, which is resisted.

[1] In 1248 'mense Julii magnum parliamentum apud Lundoniam;' Ann. Winton, p. 91; M. Paris, v. 8, 20.

[2] M. Paris, v. 20–22, 47, 49.

[3] Ibid. v. 73.

[4] Ibid. v. 101, 114–116, 136.

[5] Foed. i. 272, 274.

Debate on the papal demand, Oct. 1252.

letter dated April 11, 1250, was laid before the clergy on the 13th of October, 1252, and was indignantly opposed by Grosseteste, who declared it to be an unprecedented and intolerable usurpation. Ethelmar, on his brother's part, argued that the French clergy had submitted, and that the English had no means of successful resistance. Grosseteste replied that the submission of the French was itself a reason for the resistance of the English; two such submissions would create a custom. After a long discussion, in which they attempted to prevail on Henry to make an independent remonstrance, the clergy resolved that in the absence of the archbishops they were not competent to decide; the clergy of the province of York, when in the preceding September the matter was laid before them, had declined to act without consulting their brethren of the southern province[1]. The barons, whom the king next consulted on making an expedition to Gascony, replied that their answer would depend on that of the clergy[2]. Disgusted at finding that Ethelmar was inclined to side with the bishops, Henry now resorted to the meaner expedients of extortion, especially from the Londoners, a policy which afterwards cost him dear.

Continuance of the discussion, at Easter, 1253.

After a preliminary discussion at Winchester at Christmas, the debate was continued the next Easter, 1253, and then in a very large assembly of barons and clergy the king obtained his wish; the three years' tenth was to be paid when the Crusade should start; a scutage of three marks was granted by the tenants-in-chief for the knighting of the king's eldest son[3]; and in return Henry confirmed the charters.

The Parliament yields, and Henry confirms the charters.

On this occasion the act was performed with peculiar solemnity: a solemn sentence of excommunication was passed on all impugners; the king himself was made to say 'So help me God, all these will I faithfully

[1] M. Paris, v. 324–328. They replied, 'Quod cum dictum negotium totam tangat ecclesiam Anglicanam ac in talibus communis inter clerum utriusque provinciae, Eboracensis videlicet et Cantuariensis, consueverit tractatus haberi, antequam certum daretur responsum, a modo illo recedere non credunt esse congruum vel honestum;' Royal Letters, ii. 95.

[2] M. Paris, v. 335.

[3] Cont. F. Wig. p. 184; M. Paris, v. 373–378; Ann. Burton, pp. 305, 318; Ann. Dunst. p. 186; Ann. Waverl. p. 345; Foed. i. 289, 290; Liber de Antt. Legg. p. 18.

keep inviolate as I am a man, a Christian, a knight, a crowned and anointed king.' Thus provided with funds, after some discussion with the barons at Oxford, London, Winchester, and Portsmouth, as to their obligation to foreign service[1], he went to Gascony in August. **He goes to Gascony, Aug. 1253.**

The kingdom was left in the care of the queen and earl Richard, whose administration is marked by the first distinct case, since the reign of John, of the summons of knights of the shire to parliament[2]. On January 28 and the following days the prelates and magnates in parliament promised an aid for themselves, but said that they did not believe that the clergy would follow the example unless the tenth granted for the Crusade were given up or postponed[3]. The barons would go to Gascony but not the rest of the laity, unless the charters were confirmed. The regents therefore summoned a great council to Westminster on the 26th of April, at which two chosen knights from each county, and representatives of the clergy of each diocese, were directed to report the amount of aid which their constituents were prepared to grant. The only result of the meeting was the renewal of complaints; and earl Simon took the opportunity of warning the assembled estates against the policy of the king[4]. **Parliament of 1254.** **Knights of the shire in parliament, Apr. 26, 1254.**

After wasting the money which the queen in spite of the reluctance of the barons succeeded in collecting, the king returned at the end of 1254 only to begin the contest where it had left off; the demand for an elective ministry was made and refused as usual at the Hoketide parliament of 1255[5]. But matters had now reached a point at which a stoppage of all governmental machinery was imminent; and several other causes served to bring about the long deferred crisis. These must be definitely distinguished. **Hoketide parliament of 1255, April 6.**

[1] Ann. Theokesb. p. 155; Ann. Dunst. p. 186; Ann. Winton, p. 93; Foed. i. 291: 'convenit Oxoniis omnis generaliter Anglorum universitas,' July 20; J. Oxen. p. 179.

[2] Royal Letters, ii. 101; Select Charters, p. 375; Lords' Report, i. 95, and App. i. 13; Prynne, Register, i. 3.

[3] M. Paris, v. 423; vi. 282–284.

[4] M. Paris, v. 440; Ann. Dunst. p. 190.

[5] M. Paris, v. 493; Ann. Dunst. p. 195; Ann. Winton, p. 95; Ann. Burton, p. 336.

Variations of papal manipulation exercised on Henry III.

176. The popes, who had practised successively on the pliant will of Henry, had by no means employed the same methods of dealing with him. Honorius III, who exercised a sort of paternal care over him, and felt a certain responsibility for his well-being, contented himself with a demand of patronage, which was to enable him to provide for the officers of the curia, without overtaxing those who brought appeals to Rome. The demand was not restricted to England, and both in England and in France it was refused. Gregory IX took a long step in advance of this when in 1229 he demanded a tenth of the moveable property of the whole realm to defray the cost of his war against Frederick II. This exaction, to which the king was bound by his proctors at Rome, and which was enforced with spiritual penalties, was intended to furnish the pope with money to execute his own schemes, not to be the means of drawing England into a European war. The legation of Cardinal Otho, which lasted from 1237 to 1241, and was issued at the king's request, proved very lucrative to the Holy See; with Henry's connivance every conceivable expedient for raising money was adopted: procurations, licences for neglecting the vow of Crusade, multiplication of appeals, usurpation of patronage, and

Direct exactions.

direct imposts on beneficed foreigners. Not content with this, the legate in 1240 demanded a direct grant of a fifth of all ecclesiastical goods within the realm, which was actually wrung from the bishops, whilst Peter de Rubeis was obtaining by separate negotiation promises of money from the monasteries and from individuals [1]. A twentieth of clerical income for the Crusade for three years was demanded by the Council of Lyons in 1245 [2]. In 1246 Innocent demanded a half, a twentieth, and a third from different classes of the clergy. But the personal connexion between Henry and Frederick was so close, that, although English money was freely spent in war against the emperor, the pope did not venture to give the king a stake in the great game. Innocent IV, having in his earlier years exhausted all the older methods of extortion, took, upon

[1] M. Paris, iv. 10, 15; Ann. Dunst. p. 154; Ann. Burton, p. 265.
[2] M. Paris, iv. 458.

Frederick's death, a measure which led directly to the ruin of the king. As early as 1250 it was reported in England that the pope had proposed the election of Richard of Cornwall to the empire; some said that he was to be emperor at Constantinople; the next year it was said that he had declined to be nominated as successor of Frederick II [1]; the earl himself stated that he had refused the offer of the Sicilian crown. But the papal offers and promises were regarded merely as expedients for obtaining money. In 1252, however, the proposal took a tangible form: Master Albert, the pope's notary, presented himself with full powers to treat on the pope's behalf with Richard for the kingdom of Sicily, which he regarded as a papal fief [2]. Richard, who was bound by friendship to Conrad, Frederick's heir, and was unwilling to supplant his own nephew Henry, the titular king of Jerusalem, refused either to accept the crown or to lend his money. The offer was next made to the king for one of his sons; he held back as long as his nephew Henry of Hohenstaufen lived. That prince died early in 1254 [3], and then, the pope having offered to lend him money and commuted his vow of pilgrimage, Henry accepted Sicily for his second son Edmund. The formal cession was made by Albert to Edmund at Vendôme on the 6th of March, 1254 [4], and the arrangement was confirmed by the pope at Assisi on the 14th of May [5]. Innocent IV died on the 7th of the following December, and one of the first acts of Alexander IV was to repeat the confirmation [6]. Henry, after exemplifying his characteristic indecision by pleading his vow of Crusade, on the 18th of October, 1255, directed John Mansel to set the seal to the act of acceptance [7].

Proposal to grant the crown of Sicily to earl Richard; and to Edmund the king's son.

Negotiations about the Sicilian crown.

Such a negotiation was of course unpopular in England. The

[1] M. Paris, v. 112, 118, 201, 347, 457.

[2] Foed. i. 284. Henry undertook that the clergy should grant an aid to Richard, 28th January, 1253; ibid. 288. Both the sons of Frederick died in 1254.

[3] Foed. i. 302; M. Paris, vi. 302. Innocent offered to lend the king £50,000 of Tours; ibid. p. 303; prolonged the grant of tithe for two years more, May 23, 1254, and commuted his vow of pilgrimage for the attempt on Sicily, May 31; ibid. 304. See also Royal Letters, ii. 114

[4] Foed. i. 297.

[5] Ibid. i. 301.

[6] April 9, 1255; Foed. i. 316–318.

[7] Foed. i. 331.

Unpopularity of this policy.

design combined the objectionable characteristics of being originated by papal avarice, of being directed to the acquisition of foreign dominion, whence would flow a new tide of aliens, and of leading Henry into a war, for the direction of which he had neither skill nor experience. But the nation was unprepared to find him prompt and thorough in carrying the plan into execution. The pope began the war with Manfred, who now represented the house of Hohenstaufen, on his own account, but in Henry's name and on Henry's credit. Peter of Aigueblanche, the Provençal bishop of Hereford, who was the king's agent at Rome[1], allowed himself to be guided by Alexander, and bound the king to repay the money which the pope spent. The war was prolonged, and the pope became pressing for payment[2]. In November, 1256, the archbishop of Messina was despatched as papal ambassador, and he, in the chapter-house at Westminster on the Sunday after Midlent, 1257, laid the statement of the royal debt before the assembled magnates[3]. It amounted to 135,000 marks. Henry, who was accompanied by his brother, recently elected king of the Romans, led forth the boy Edmund in an Apulian dress and confessed his position. It was, he declared, with the consent of the English church that he had accepted the throne of Sicily, and he had bound himself, under the penalty of forfeiting his kingdom, to pay the pope 140,000 marks. He asked therefore a tenth of ecclesiastical revenue and, besides other contributions, the income of all vacant benefices for five years[4]. The prelates denied that they had consented or had been consulted on the matter. They had not even heard of the king's under-

The king's debt to the pope laid before parliament, Mar. 25, 1257.

Exaction from the prelates, in 1257.

[1] It was by his advice that the king had asked and obtained from many of the prelates blank sheets sealed with their seals, which were filled up with promises to pay money at the king's discretion. See Ann. Osney, p. 110; M. Paris, v. 510.

[2] On the 5th of February, 1256, he wrote to the king to pay him, or he would cancel the grant; Foed. i. 336. Soon after Henry confesses that he owes 135,501 marks at Rome, ibid. 337; and Alexander allows him to put off payment until Michaelmas, ibid. 342: and on the 6th of October, 1256, allows him to defer it until the 1st of May, 1257, sending the Archbishop of Messina to England; ibid. 350.

[3] M. Paris, v. 621–624; Foed. i. 354; Ann. Osney, p. 114; Ann. Burton, p. 384. Richard was elected king of the Romans, Jan. 13, 1257. He accepted the offer April 10, at London; and was crowned May 17.

[4] Ann. Burton, p. 390.

taking until it was completed. In their helplessness they offered 52,000 marks, which were ungraciously accepted[1]. The grant was accompanied by a series of fifty articles of grievances[2].

Retrospect of 1255 and 1256.

The political feeling had been rising high ever since Henry's return from Gascony. The history of the year 1255 is a continuous record of quarrels in parliament and council. The charters were confirmed and republished in vain. In vain Rustand, the pope's envoy, attempted to carry out his instructions to raise money. Political memory awoke, and, for the first time on record, the magnates on the 13th of October, to which day the Hoketide parliament had been adjourned[3], refused to give an aid on the distinct ground that they had not been summoned in the form prescribed by the great charter[4]. The year 1256 was full of the same contests; the Londoners, the Jews, the sheriffs, were mulcted in turn; the system of fines for distraint of knighthood was enforced; the renewal of the charters was proposed; the clergy were canvassed singly and in every form of council. The mission of Rustand, of the archbishop of Messina, and of Herlottus with like instructions, only brought discontent to a head. The king was helplessly in debt; when he returned from Gascony he had spent 350,000 marks, now 140,000 more were gone, and it was calculated that since his wasteful days began he had thrown away 950,000 marks[5].

Amount of the king's debt.

Simon de Montfort and his wrongs.

Another train of circumstances had prepared a leader for the afflicted church and nation. Simon de Montfort had returned home with his sense of public injustice sharpened by the feeling of his private wrongs. Appointed in 1248 to govern Gascony, he had encountered extraordinary difficulties. He had to contend with a body of nobles whom Henry II and Richard I had failed

[1] M. Paris, v. 624, 627. The answer was returned on the 22nd of April; Ann. Burton, pp. 392, 401. Another convocation was held on the 22nd of August, in which both reforms and gravamina were discussed; ibid. pp. 401–407.

[2] M. Paris, vi. 353 sq.: 'Articuli pro quibus episcopi Angliae fuerant pugnaturi.'

[3] See above, p. 69; Ann. Burton, p. 336. At this parliament proxies for the clergy (procuratores clericorum beneficiatorum archidiaconatus) were present; Ann. Burton, pp. 360, 362.

[4] M. Paris, v. 520; Ann. Burton, p. 360.

[5] M. Paris, v. 627.

to reduce, and whose only object in acknowledging Henry III was to evade submitting to the stronger hand of Lewis IX. In this contest Henry supplied him with neither men nor money; Simon had to raise funds either from his own estates or by taxing the Gascons; the king acted as if he had sent him abroad simply to ruin his fortunes and wreck his reputation, for, far from strengthening his hands, he lent a willing ear to all complaints against him. We have not to decide whether Simon ruled Gascony with judgment; he maintained Henry's hold on it in the greatest straits and under the most unfair treatment[1]. Against the latter both earl Richard his personal enemy, and Edward the king's son, who was now growing into the grievous knowledge of his father's folly and ingratitude, had found themselves obliged to protest. His term of office expired when Henry visited Gascony in 1253, but he had stayed some time longer abroad, and after his return had stood aloof from politics, not however avoiding the court or acting against the king, although he was engaged in a tedious litigation with him about his wife's jointure.

Simon's attitude in politics.

Henry's party among the earls.

Henry was not without friends. He had spared no pains to attach to himself some of the most powerful earls. Those of Gloucester, Warenne, Lincoln, and Devon, had been on his side in 1255[2]. The king of the Romans supported him, although he would not lend him money. Boniface, although more independent than might be expected, was bound too closely to the king to venture to maintain the freedom of the church. Walter Gray, the inheritor of the traditions of good government, and Robert Grosseteste, the prophet and harbinger of better days coming, were dead. The aliens were in possession not only of royal favour but of substantial power, holding castles and revenues, and trampling on law and justice far more unrestrainedly than even William of Aumâle or Falkes de Breauté[3]. The programme of

The king's strength.

[1] See Adam de Marisco, Ep. 30.

[2] M. Paris, v. 514.

[3] The Annals of Waverley, p. 350, describe the miserable state of the kingdom: 'Quatuor etiam fratres domini regis . . . prae ceteris alienigenis dignitatibus et divitiis supra modum elevati, intolerabili fastu superbiae in Anglos saevientes, multis ac variis injuriis et contumeliis crudeliter eos afficiebant, nec ausus fuit aliquis praesumptiosis eorum actibus propter regis timorem obviare. Non solum autem isti, sed, quod magis dolendum est, Anglici in Anglos, majores scilicet in minores

reform had been so often mooted and put by, that faith in it was nearly lost. Never before had the cause of liberty sunk so completely out of sight, if its chances of success were to be judged by the prominence of its defenders or the loudness of its advocates. It was out of the desperate humiliation of the kingdom that the remedy must be made to spring.

The first parliament of 1258.

The parliament of 1258 met at London in the second week after Easter, and sat until the 5th of May[1]. The king had only complaints and petitions to offer, the truce with the Welsh was at an end, and the Scottish barons had formed an alliance offensive and defensive with them[2]. The clergy had drawn up a long list of gravamina embodying the complaints which had been first reduced to form by Grosseteste[3]. Three papal envoys in rapid succession had arrived, each with more stringent orders than the last, and the sentence of excommunication was hanging over the king in consequence of his delay in invading Apulia. The court was full of foreigners whose wealth and extravagance were in strong contrast with the state of beggary to which Henry declared himself reduced. The meeting was a stormy one. On the 28th of April the king's petition for money was rejected, a petition which was said to involve a tallage of one third of all the goods of the realm[4]. It was openly declared that the king's exceptional delinquency must be met by exceptional measures[5]; Roger Bigod, who acted as spokesman of the baronage, insisted on the acceptance of distinct terms, the banishment of the Poictevins, and the appointment

Demand of money, and profession of penitence.

insurgentes, cupiditatis igne succensi, placitis et merciamentis, tallagiis et exactionibus variisque aliis incommodis unicuique quod suum erat conabantur auferre. Leges etiam et consuetudines antiquae aut nimis corruptae aut penitus cassatae et ad nihilum erant redactae, et quasi pro lege erat cuique sua tyrannica voluntas.'

[1] M. Paris, v. 676, 689. The date of the opening is given by M. Paris, 'post diem Martis, quae vulgariter Hokedai appellatur;' i.e. April 2. The king describes it as called together, 'in quindena Paschae;' Foed. i. 370. Easter fell on March 24. There is some evidence showing that representative knights for certain shires were present during a part of the proceedings; Lords' Report, i. 460. An earlier meeting had been summoned, for the third Sunday in Lent; see the writ to the Abbot of S. Alban's, dated January 24; but the day was changed; M. Paris, vi. 392.

[2] Foed. i. 370.

[3] Ann. Burton, pp. 412 sq.

[4] Ann. Theokesb. p. 163.

[5] 'Excessus regis tractatus exigit speciales;' M. Paris, v. 689.

Henry submits to the plan of reform.

of a commission of reform. Having found himself only partly successful in collecting offerings from the greater monasteries, Henry professed penitence, and in the end placed himself, on the 30th of April, in the hands of the barons[1]. A committee of twenty-four, chosen half from the royal council and half by the barons, were to enforce all necessary reforms before the following Christmas; on this understanding the question of a money grant might be considered. The king's consent to this scheme was published on the second of May[2], and the parliament was the next week adjourned to the 11th of June, at Oxford. By that time the barons were to have prepared the list of grievances and the scheme of provisional government by which they were to be remedied. The archbishop held a council at Merton on the 6th of June[3]; the acts of this assembly seem to show a complete sympathy with the desire of reform and indignation at the king's conduct shown in parliament.

Parliament of Oxford, June 11, 1258.

On the 11th of June, at Oxford[4], the Mad Parliament, as it was called by Henry's partisans, assembled. It seems to have been a full assembly of the baronage and higher clergy[5]. Fearful of treachery from the foreigners, the barons had availed themselves of the summons to the Welsh war[6], and appeared in full military array. The list of grievances, the petition of the barons now presented, contained a long series of articles touching the points in which the king's officers had transgressed either the letter or the spirit of the charters. The committal of royal castles to native Englishmen, the bestowal of heiresses on native husbands, the honest fulfilment of the charter of the forests, the freedom of ecclesiastical elections, the right of the lords to the wardship of their tenants, are claimed as a matter

Articles of complaint, brought forward by the barons.

[1] Ann. Theokesb. p. 164; cf. Ann. Wykes, p. 119.

[2] Foed. i. 370, 371; Select Charters, pp. 380–382; M. Paris, v. 689.

[3] Ann. Burton, p. 412 sq.; Ann. Dunst. p. 163.

[4] Ann. Dunst. p. 208; M. Paris, v. 695. 'Insane parliamentum;' Liber de Antt. Legg. p. 37.

[5] The presence of the clergy at Oxford is expressly stated; Ann. Burton, p. 438; Ann. Dunst. p. 208.

[6] This was issued March 14, for a meeting at Chester on the Monday before midsummer; Lords' Report, App. pp. 16–19. The king was to start from Oxford after the parliament, ibid. p. 19. A truce however was concluded for a year on the 17th of June, Foed. i. 372. See the Lords' Report, i. 126.

of justice. The complaints touch especially the illegal exaction of feudal services, the illegal bestowal of estates as royal escheats and the denial of justice to their lawful owners, the vexatious fines for non-attendance exacted by the itinerant justices and by the sheriffs who had multiplied the number of local courts beyond endurance, the erection of castles on the coast without national consent, the abuse of purveyance, the dealings with the Jews and other usurers who impoverished the kingdom and played dishonestly into the hands of the great, the delays of justice owing to the licences issued by the king to the knights exempting them from service on juries, assizes and recognitions, and other like points which require a minute collation with the articles of the Great Charter to illustrate their full meaning [1]. The justice of the petitions was beyond question, but the immediate conclusion to be drawn from them was the necessity of having a fully qualified justiciar; and this at once opened the question of the new provisional government, the creation of the committee of twenty-four, by whose action the articles of complaint were to be redressed and by whom the ministry, the justiciar, chancellor, treasurer, and council were to be named. Preparations had probably been made for this in the earlier parliament; these were now completed. The idea of a commission of twenty-four may have been derived from the executive body appointed at Runnymede; the mode of appointment bore more distinct marks of the character of arbitration. The two parties were definitely arrayed against each other, for Henry was not in the forlorn state to which his father had been reduced. The king nominated his nephew Henry of Cornwall, his brother-in-law John of Warenne, his three half-brothers Ethelmar, Guy, and William of Lusignan, the earl of Warwick, John Mansel, John Darlington, a friar who was afterwards archbishop of Dublin, the abbot of Westminster, Henry Wengham keeper of the Seal, the bishop of London, and probably archbishop Boniface [2]. The community of the barons elected

Complaints.

Petitions for redress.

Demand of a commission of reform.

Method of nomination.

[1] Ann. Burton, pp. 439–443; Select Charters, pp. 382–388.
[2] Ann. Burton, p. 447. Only eleven names are given; the one omitted seems to be that of the archbishop.

Election of the Twenty-four.

the earls of Gloucester, Leicester, Hereford and Norfolk; Roger Mortimer, John Fitz-Geoffrey, Hugh Bigod, Richard de Gray, William Bardulf, Peter de Montfort, Hugh le Despenser, and the bishop of Worcester, Walter Cantilupe. The king's party was very poor in the historic names of England, and the baronial selection included most of those which come into prominence both before and after this crisis. This body, after having received promises of faithful co-operation and obedience from the king and his son[1], proceeded to draw up a provisional constitution.

Project of government under the Provisions of Oxford, 1258.

The king was to be assisted by a standing council of fifteen members; these were to have power to counsel the king in good faith concerning the government of the realm, and all other things that appertained to the king and the kingdom, to amend and redress all things which they saw needed amendment and redress, and to exercise supervision over the great justiciar and all others. They were in fact not only to act as the king's private council, but to have a constraining power over all his public acts, just as, in the scheme propounded in 1244[2], the four chosen counsellors were to have done, and as was actually done by the council of nine chosen after the battle of Lewes. To these fifteen, as the king's perpetual council, was assigned the function of meeting, in three annual parliaments at Michaelmas, at Candlemas, and on the 1st of June, with another body of twelve chosen by the barons to discuss common business on behalf of the whole community[3]. In the selection of the fifteen great precaution was to be taken. The twenty-four divided into their two original halves. The king's half selected two out of the opposite twelve, and the twelve appointed by the barons chose two out of the king's half; these four were to choose the fifteen[4]. The

Council of Fifteen.

Three annual parliaments.

Election of the Fifteen.

[1] Ann. Burton, p. 457; M. Paris, vi. 401; Foed. i. 373; Ann. Theokesb. pp. 164, 171; Ann. Wykes, p. 119; Chron. Rishanger (Camd. Soc.), p. 3.

[2] Above, p. 64.

[3] 'Les duze ke sunt eslu per les baruns a treter a treis parlemenz per an oveke le cunseil le rei pur tut le commun de la tere de commun besoine;' Ann. Burton, p. 449.

[4] This elaborate plan seems to have been not uncommon in cases of arbitration. In the treaty of Lambeth (Foed. i. 148), it is arranged that, for the decision of questions touching prisoners taken before Lewis's landing, Henry's council is to choose three members of Lewis's council to make

twelve appointed to meet at the annual parliaments were chosen by the general body of the barons; another committee of twenty-four, chosen by the whole parliament on behalf of the community[1], was to treat of the aid which the king demanded for the war; and the reform of the church was committed to the original twenty-four to be enforced as they should find time and place[2].

Committees of parliament, and aid.

The somewhat confused details of the annalists seem to warrant the following conclusions. The machinery now devised was partly provisional, partly permanent; the provisional arrangement comprised first the redress of grievances in church and state, and secondly the providing of an aid. These two sets of functions were committed to two bodies of twenty-four, the former chosen in equal parts by the king and the barons, the latter chosen by the assembled body. The most influential of the barons served on both of these committees.

Analysis of the new scheme.

Provisional machinery.

The permanent machinery included the formation of a regular council and the reconstitution of the ministerial body, the nomination of the officers of state and sheriffs. The council of fifteen was selected in the complex manner described already, which was borrowed no doubt from the method of proceeding used in treaties, arbitrations, and ecclesiastical councils, where two well-defined parties were in opposition. We are not told how the great officers were chosen[3], but the claim of the parliament to appoint

Permanent machinery.

Appointment of ministers.

inquiry; while for the decision of questions of ransom, Lewis's council is to choose three of Henry's councillors. Bartholomew Cotton (p. 175) gives a case of an arbitration between Yarmouth and the Cinque Ports: 'provisum fuit per ipsos quod barones quinque portuum eligerent sex homines bonos et legales de villa Gernemutae, et burgenses Gernemutae sex homines bonos et legales de quinque portubus.' In point of intricacy the arrangements now adopted may be compared with the Venetian rule for choosing the Doge, Woolsey, Pol. Science, ii. 49; and with the Florentine constitutions, ib. pp. 68, 69 sq. But the best parallel is with the cross elections of Lords of Articles in Scotland; see especially, for 1367, 1524, 1633, and 1663, Acts of Parl. of Scotl. i. 143; ii. 289; v. 9, 10; vii. 449.

[1] 'Ces sunt les vint et quatre ke sunt mis per le commun a treter de aide del rei;' Ann. Burton, p. 450; Select Charters, p. 390.

[2] 'Ke le estat le seint Eglise seit amende par les vint et quatre esluz a refurmer le estat del reaume de Engletere;' Ann. Burton, p. 450.

[3] 'In parliamento Oxoniae factus fuit justitiarius Angliae dominus Hugo le Bigot;' Ann. Burton, p. 443. 'Illi duodecim, de consensu et voluntate domini regis, elegerunt unum justitiarium principalem;' Ann. Dunst. p. 209, where the twelve appear to be put for the twenty-four. 'Communi

them had been so often and so distinctly asserted and denied, that it may now have been compromised in such a way as to save all existing rights. This would easily be done by vesting the appointment in the hands of the king, advised by the twenty-four. The result was certainly a compromise; Hugh Bigod [1], a younger brother of the earl Marshall, a man of the strictest integrity and a member of the baronial party, was named justiciar at once; the great seal remained in the hands of Henry of Wengham, and Philip Lovell the king's treasurer continued in office until the following October, when he was removed by the barons, and John of Crakehall, who had been steward to Grosseteste, was appointed in his place [2]. The necessary security was supposed to be obtained by stringent oaths imposed on these officers, and drawn up in the parliament [3]. All the offices of state and the sheriffdoms [4] were to be held subject to an annual audit and for a year only, but there seems to be no distinct prohibition of reappointment [5].

The ministry of 1258.

Oaths and audits.

Oligarchic character of the scheme.

The new form of government bears evidence of its origin; it is intended rather to fetter the king than to extend or develop the action of the community at large. The baronial council clearly regards itself as competent to act on behalf of all the estates of the realm, and the expedient of reducing the national deliberations to three sessions of select committees, betrays a desire to abridge the frequent and somewhat irksome duty of attendance in parliament rather than to share the central legislative and deliberative power with the whole body of the people. It must however be remembered that the scheme makes a very indistinct claim to the character of a final arrangement.

consilio constituerunt Hugonem Bigod justitiarium Angliae;' Ann. Osney, p. 119, referring to the twenty-four. 'Per electionem baronum;' Lib. de Antt. Legg. p. 38; 'in praedicto parlamento;' Cont. Gerv. ii. 207.

[1] Hugh Bigod was the younger brother of Roger Bigod, earl of Norfolk (1225–1270), and was father of earl Roger (1270–1307), who took part in the proceedings of 1297.

[2] M. Paris, v. 719; Ann. Dunst. p. 210. Lovell died in December.

[3] Ann. Burton, pp. 447–449; Select Charters, pp. 388, 389.

[4] Ann. Dunst. p. 210.

[5] Ann. Burton, p. 457; Ann. Dunst. p. 210. The sheriff was not to hold office 'fors un an ensemble.' The justiciar 'ne seit fors un an.' It is possible that it was intended to forbid reappointments, but as regards the sheriffs it was not observed. See the 31st Report of the Deputy Keeper of the Records.

But before the new system was fully constituted a great victory was won. One of the first resolutions of the twenty-four was, that the king should at once resume all the royal castles and estates which had been alienated from the crown; and a list was made of nineteen barons, all of them Englishmen, to whom the castles should be entrusted; amongst these the justiciar appears as warden of the Tower of London[1]. When however it was proposed that the resolution should be enforced, the king's half-brothers and their friends refused compliance. In vain Simon de Montfort, as Hubert de Burgh had done before him, formally gave up Odiham and Kenilworth[2]; the alien party left the court in haste on the 22nd of June, and threw themselves into the bishop's castle at Winchester[3]. There they were besieged, and after some ignominious negotiations capitulated on the 5th of July[4]. Immediately after the surrender the Lusignans with their followers left the kingdom, carrying off only 6000 marks out of the enormous treasures which they had accumulated. This struggle however did not interrupt the progress of reform; on the 26th of June, Henry[5] directed the four elected lords to proceed to nominate the council. Edward, as soon as the aliens had departed, swore to observe the provisions[6]; on the 23rd of July they were accepted by the Londoners[7]; on the 28th directions were issued for inquiry into abuses[8]; on the 4th of August Henry published his consent to abide by the decisions of his new council[9]; and on the 18th of October, in the assembly which appointed the new treasurer, and in which four knights of each shire presented the complaints against the sheriffs, he solemnly reiterated his adhesion in a document drawn up in English, French, and Latin[10].

The foreigners refuse to surrender the royal castles. June 22, 1258.

Their flight,

and banishment.

Execution of the reforms.

[1] Ann. Burton, pp. 444, 453.
[2] M. Paris, v. 697. [3] Ann. Burton, p. 444; Ann. Dunst. p. 209.
[4] Foed. i. 375. They appear to have carried off more money than the government allowed them; ibid. 377. They sailed on the 14th of July; Ann. Burton, p. 445; Liber de Antt. Legg. p. 38.
[5] Royal Letters, ii. 127. The names of the council are given below, p. 85. Cf. Liber de Antt. Legg. p. 37.
[6] Ann. Burton, p. 445. [7] Liber de Antt. Legg. p. 39.
[8] Foed. i. 375; Ann. Burton, p. 456. [9] Royal Letters, ii. 129.
[10] Foed. i. 378; Select Charters, p. 396; Ann. Dunst. p. 210; Royal Letters, ii. 130; Brady, Introd. p. 141.

Conduct of the government.

The provisional government lasted from June 1258 to the end of 1259 without any break, and from that date, with several interruptions, until the spring of 1263, when war began. During this time the three annual parliaments were held, the council of fifteen meeting the twelve representatives of the community, and with them publishing ordinances and taking other measures for the good of the state. Peace was made with Wales, Scotland, and France. The negotiations with Lewis IX employed the energies of earl Simon for the best part of two years, and were completed by the king in a visit to France which lasted from November 1259 to April 1260, and in which, acting as it was believed under the advice of the earl of Gloucester[1], he finally renounced his claims on Normandy.

Division in the government.

The remedial measures were executed but slowly[2]. One section of the baronage was no doubt satisfied by the expulsion of the aliens, and little inclined to hasten reforms which would limit their own action and terminate the commission of their nominees. Their reluctance to proceed was probably the cause of the great quarrel which took place in the February parliament of 1259 between the earls of Gloucester and Leicester[3], and may have given occasion for the ordinance published by the king on the 28th of March, by which the barons of the council and the twelve representatives of the parliament undertook for themselves and their heirs to observe towards their dependents all the engagements which the king had undertaken to observe towards his vassals[4]. This undertaking, which stands in direct relation to the corresponding articles of the charters of Henry I, John, and Henry III, might be suspected to be the result of pressure on the king's part applied to force the two parties into a quarrel, but it was more probably the result of a

Proclamation of March, 1259.

[1] Chron. Dover, MS.; Cont. Gerv. ii. 209.

[2] 'Postea (sc. Jul. 23, 1258) praedicti barones habuerunt de die in diem colloquium, quandoque apud Novum Templum quandoque alibi, super usibus et consuetudinibus regni in melius conformandis;' Liber de Antt. Legg. p. 39.

[3] M. Paris, v. 737, 744; M. Westm. p. 366. There were two parliaments in the spring, February 9 and April 28; Ann. Winton, p. 98.

[4] Foed. i. 381. See on this the Lords' Report, i. 130.

victory gained by Simon over Gloucester in the council itself. If we may trust the popular belief of the time[1], Gloucester headed a strong party that would have been content with the acquisition of power for themselves, whilst Simon was regarded as a deliverer who was to make tyranny for the future impossible, whether from the side of the king or from that of the barons. Between these parties Henry himself may be supposed to have wavered; he had no reason to love the one more than the other, although he feared earl Simon the most of all.

Parties of Leicester and Gloucester.

The position of affairs is still more distinctly shown by the events of the October parliament of 1259, in which we find Edward, probably now in concert with Simon, acting with decision against the dilatory conduct of the council. On S. Edward's day, October 13, we are told, the 'community of the bachelors of England[2],' that is, no doubt, the body of knights—the tenants in chivalry, the landowners below the rank of the baronage—signified to the lord Edward, the earl of Gloucester, and others sworn of the council, that, whereas the king had done all that was required of him, the barons had fulfilled none of their promises. In fact they had contented themselves with providing for their own interest and damaging that of the king; if amends were not made, the complainants urged that another scheme of reform should be devised. Edward replied that, although he had unwillingly taken the oath, he would keep it honourably and was willing to risk death for the 'community;' he then urged the barons to produce their remedial provisions; and the result was the issuing of a series of ordinances known as the Provisions of Westminster, and enrolled in the Close Rolls with the date October, 1259. Of this document there are two

Edward and the knights come forward to compel the barons to proceed with the reforms: Oct. 1259.

The Provisions of Westminster are published in consequence.

[1] The Latin poem preserved by Rishanger (Wright's Political Songs, p. 121) seems to belong to this period rather than to 1264:—

'O comes Gloverniae comple quod coepisti,
Nisi claudas congrue, multos decepisti;
Age nunc viriliter sicut promisisti,
Causam fove fortiter cujus fons fuisti. . . .
O tu comes le Bigot, pactum serva sanum,
Cum sis miles strenuus nunc exerce manum,' &c.

[2] 'Communitas bacheleriae Angliae;' Ann. Burton, p. 471. Bachelarii is used by M. Paris, v. 83, for the knights: 'Multi de militibus universitatis regni qui se volunt bachelarios appellari.'

Certain articles found in French but not enrolled.

versions, one in Latin and one in French. The French version [1] contains some articles which are not in the Latin, and are not enrolled. We may therefore suspect that the council took advantage of their position to omit from the final form of statute some of the points which were at the moment yielded to the pressure of the knights. The Provisions, as they are enrolled [2], remedy most of the complaints urged in the Oxford Petition, but they do not contain the stringent articles found in the French version, by which the county organisation was empowered to watch and limit the action of the council and the courts. By one of these, which agrees exactly with one of the Provisions of Oxford [3], four knights were appointed in each shire to watch the sheriffs; by another the appointment of sheriffs was arranged; in the current year they were to be named by the justiciar, treasurer, and barons of the Exchequer; after that four good men were to be chosen in the county court, one of whom was to be selected by the barons of the Exchequer [4]: other articles provide for the redress of forest abuses and for the legal observance of the courts [5].

Provisions of Westminster.

The barons all-powerful in the council.

With the issue of these articles the commission of the twenty-four must have ended, but their action had already become indistinguishable from that of the council of fifteen. The two bodies were composed largely of the same persons; nine out of the baronial half of the commission of reform had seats in the permanent council, and another was the justiciar; of the king's half, two only besides the archbishop, the earl of Warwick and John Mansel, were in the council, but of the rest of his nominees nearly all had taken part with his half-brothers and practically surrendered their places on the commission; only three of the councillors, the earl of Aumâle, Peter of Savoy, James of Aldithley, possibly also the archbishop, were not of the twenty-four [6].

Composition of the Council.

[1] Ann. Burton, pp. 471–479. Cf. Liber de Antt. Legg. p. 42.
[2] Royal Letters, ii. 394; Statutes of the Realm, i. 8–12; Select Charters, pp. 400–405; Ann. Burton, pp. 480–484.
[3] Ann. Burton, pp. 446, 477.
[4] Ibid. p. 478.
[5] Ibid. pp. 478, 479.
[6] The *personnel* of the administration is so important that the following

As soon as the parliament broke up Henry went to France, where he finally resigned his claims on Normandy. But from that moment the prospect began to darken. Before Christmas the Welsh were in arms: the pope was interceding for the return of Ethelmar. Early in 1260 the king heard that his half-brothers were preparing to invade England[1], that Simon de Montfort was importing arms and horses[2], that the king of the Romans was insisting on the payment of the money which he had lent to his brother. The earl of Gloucester was in attendance on the king and took advantage of his position to alarm him and incite him to hostility[3]. He had an old grudge against Edward, to whom the king had given his castle at Bristol; Edward was embittered against him for advising the renunciation or sale of the Norman heritage, a feeling in which he probably had the sympathy of earl Simon. The alarming

Henry goes to France, Nov. 13, 1259.

table is necessary to show the comparative influence of individual members. See Royal Letters, ii. 153.

	The Twenty-four chosen to reform the State.	*The Council of Fifteen.*	*The Twelve Commissioners of Parliament.*	*The Twenty-four Commissioners of the Aid.*
The King's party.	Abp. of Canterbury (?)	Abp. of Canterbury.		
	Bp. of London.		Bp. of London.	Bp. of London.
	Bp. of Winton elect.		Earl of Winton.	Earl of Winton.
	Henry of Almain.	Ct. of Aumâle.		Ct. of Aumâle.
	John, E. of Warenne.	Peter of Savoy.		Peter of Savoy.
	Guy of Lusignan.	James of Aldithley.	John de Verdun.	Giles of Erdinton.
	William of Valence.			Bp. of Sarum.
	John, E. of Warwick.	John, E. of Warwick.		Earl of Oxford.
	John Mansel.	John Mansel.		John Kyriel.
	John Darlington.		Roger de Monthaut.	Roger de Monthaut.
	Abbot of Westminster.		Thomas Gresley.	Thomas Gresley.
	Henry Wengham.		Giles d'Argentine.	Giles d'Argentine.
The Baronial party.	Bp. of Worcester.	Bp. of Worcester.		Bp. of Worcester.
	Simon, E. of Leicester.	Simon, E. of Leicester.		Simon, E. of Leicester.
	Rich. E. of Gloucester.	Rich. E. of Gloucester.		Rich. E. of Gloucester.
	Humf. E. of Hereford.	Humf. E. of Hereford.	Humf. E. of Hereford.	Humf. E. of Hereford.
	Roger, E. of Norfolk.	Roger, E. of Norfolk.		Roger, E. of Norfolk.
	Roger Mortimer.	Roger Mortimer.		Roger Mortimer.
	John Fitz-Geoffrey.	John Fitz-Geoffrey.		John Fitz-Geoffrey.
	Hugh le Bigod.		Roger de Sumery.	Roger de Sumery.
	Rich. de Gray.	Rich. de Gray.	John de Gray.	John de Gray.
	Will. Bardulf.		Philip Basset.	Philip Basset.
	Peter de Montfort.	Peter de Montfort.		Peter de Montfort.
	Hugh le Despenser.		Hugh le Despenser.	Fulk de Kerdiston.
			John Balliol.	John Balliol.

[1] Foed. i. 396. [2] Ibid.

[3] A great gathering of the magnates at London, April 19, is mentioned, Ann. Winton, p. 98. Richard king of the Romans came to London in Easter week and called a Parliament for April 25; Liber de Antt. Legg. p. 44. This is possibly the assembly called to assure the king of a good reception; Ann. Wykes, p. 124.

He is recalled by news from home, April 23, 1260. news that Edward, his son and heir, was conspiring with Simon to depose him caused the king to return in haste on the 23rd of April[1]. In fear, or pretended fear, for the issue of the struggle, he would not trust himself at Westminster[2], and, having reached London on the 30th, assembled the barons at S. Paul's. **Quarrels and reconciliations.** There Edward was reconciled with his father: but the king and Gloucester fiercely attacked earl Simon, and after a long discussion the points in dispute between them were referred to arbitration. The king further laid before the parliament certain conclusions at which he had arrived as to his obligation to observe the Provisions. The storm blew over for the time; but the unity of the provisional government was already broken up, and Edward, if not his father also, was learning the policy of employing the one party to destroy the other.

Parliament in July, 1260. The Welsh war furnished employment for the Midsummer parliament[3]; but, although it was in that quarter that the cloud at last broke, the time was not come for an open schism. **Hugh le Despenser becomes justiciar, Oct. 1260.** The October session[4], in which Hugh le Despenser succeeded Hugh Bigod as justiciar[5], was merely an occasion for solemn ceremonial. Henry however, in opposition to the advice of his son, who held himself bound by his solemn engagement, was treating meanwhile for a dispensation from his oath and for the resumption of the design upon Sicily[6]. **Proceedings during 1261.** Rumour was already active, and, on the 14th of March, 1261, the king, who in alarm had thrown himself into the Tower, had to forbid malignant reports about the collection of tallage[7]. Having been compelled by the remonstrances of Edward and the earls to dismiss his counsellor John Mansel, and believing himself no longer safe

[1] Ann. Dunst. pp. 214, 215; Ann. Wykes, p. 123; Ann. Winton, p. 99; Liber de Antt. Legg. p. 44; M. Westm. Flores, ii. 446; Chron. Dover, MS. Cont. Gerv. ii. 210.

[2] M. Westm. p. 373.

[3] This was called for July 8; Liber de Antt. Legg. p. 45; Foed. i. 398.

[4] October 13; M. Westm. Flores, ii. 457. October 25; Liber de Antt. Legg. p. 45.

[5] The relations of the three rival justiciars were curious; Philip Basset was the father of Alina, who married first Hugh le Despenser, and after his death Roger the son of Hugh Bigod. Foss, Biographia Juridica, p. 59.

[6] M. Westm. Flores, ii. 466, 467.

[7] Foed. i. 405.

in London, he went down to Winchester; there, on the 24th of April, he removed the new justiciar and appointed Philip Basset in his place [1]. He also removed Nicolas of Ely the chancellor, and substituted Walter de Merton [2]. In May he had gained courage to threaten the expulsion of the foreign followers of earl Simon; and on the 12th of June he produced the bull of absolution [3] which Alexander IV just before his death had granted, with letters of excommunication against all who should contravene it. The arbitration between him and Simon, which was referred in July 1261 to queen Margaret of France, helped to prolong the suspense.

The two parties seem to have now prepared for overt war. Henry on the 16th of August [4] published a manifesto declaring his purpose of observing the rights and liberties of his subjects and appealing to the history of the last five and forty years as a proof of his sincerity: he complained too of the slanders of his enemies and justified his precautions in removing the sheriffs and wardens of the castles appointed by the council. Leicester, Gloucester, and the bishop of Worcester, who notwithstanding the recent quarrel were acting together as the chiefs of the provisional government, summoned to S. Alban's an assembly to which three knights of each shire were invited by writs addressed to the sheriff. This was a most timely and important recognition of the position of the county organisation and of the attitude taken up by the knights in 1259, as well as of the expanding policy of Simon and his advisers. Hearing of this, and fearful of throwing the knights into determined opposition, Henry ordered the sheriffs to send the knights not to S. Alban's but to Windsor [5], where he proposed to treat for

Henry appeals to his subjects, Aug. 1261.

Counter-councils at S. Alban's and Windsor,

to which knights representative are summoned, Sept. 18, 1261.

[1] Liber de Antt. Legg. p. 49; M. Westm. Flores, ii. 470; Rishanger, p. 10. Cf. Ann. Wykes, pp. 125, 129.

[2] Ann. Wykes, p. 129.

[3] Ann. Wykes, p. 128. The bulls are dated April 13 and May 7. Alexander died May 25; Foed. i. 405, 406. The archbishop ordered the execution of the bulls August 8; ibid. 408.

[4] Foed. i. 408.

[5] Royal Letters, ii. 179; Select Charters, p. 405. The writ is directed only to the sheriffs 'citra Trentam.' According to the statement of a strong royal partisan given in the Flores, iii. 255, only the bishop of Worcester, the earls of Gloucester and Leicester, Hugh le Despenser and

peace on the 18th of September. Little result however followed either the military preparations or the negotiation for peace. Before the day fixed for the meeting the earl of Leicester went to France, leaving the management of affairs in the hands of his uncongenial colleagues [1]. He was fettered by the still pending arbitration, and probably by the co-operation of Gloucester: the king by the fact that the pope had died immediately after granting the absolution, and it had not yet been confirmed by his successor. In a meeting at London in October, terms were drawn up, but the pacification failed; the council removed the king's sheriffs and appointed keepers (custodes [2]) of the counties: on the 18th the king ordered by proclamation that his own sheriffs should remain in office [3]. Ten days later negotiations were resumed at Kingston. An arbitration was determined upon, on the 21st of November, and on the 7th of December Henry announced the conclusion of a treaty and the pardon of all who should seal the agreement before the 6th of January: all points in dispute were to be adjusted by the following Whitsuntide [4]. Whether Simon and his friends accepted this agreement is uncertain; on the 16th of December they had not sealed the act, and were formally invited by the king to do it [5]. It mattered little however except so far as the storm passed over again without bloodshed.

Negotiations about the sheriffs.

Peace made, Dec. 7.

Events of 1262.

One of the most important questions in dispute was the right to nominate the sheriffs, and this was referred to the king of the Romans, who early in 1262 decided in favour of the king [6]. On the 25th of February [7] Urban IV renewed the absolution

Peter de Montfort out of the twenty-four were still faithful to the provisions.

[1] Foed. i. 409; Cont. Gerv. ii. 213. The king, writing to Lewis IX on Sept. 2, mentions the earl's departure.

[2] Liber de Antt. Legg. p. 49; M. Westm. Flores, ii. 473.

[3] Ann. Dunst. p. 217; Royal Letters, ii. 192.

[4] Foed. i. 411, 412; Ann. Osney, p. 218 (December 5); Ann. Wykes, p. 129.

[5] Royal Letters, ii. 196. The Osney Annals, p. 129, state that Simon refused to accept this, and left England in consequence. Cf. Ann. Dunst. p. 217.

[6] See Royal Letters, ii. 197; Foed. i. 415; Ann. Wykes, p. 130.

[7] Henry had begun to intrigue for Urban's absolution in September, 1261; his proctor at Rome found himself opposed by another agent, acting

of the king from his oath; the bull was laid before the parliament on the 23rd of April[1], and on the 2nd of May the sheriffs were informed of it[2]. Leicester prolonged his stay abroad. The king was in France from July to Christmas[3]. During his absence the earl of Gloucester died, and his son, a young man of nineteen, threw himself into the arms of Leicester. In October earl Simon paid a short visit to England, bringing with him it was said papal letters in favour of the Provisions of Oxford, revoking the absolution of the king. These were read in the October parliament in spite of the opposition of the justiciar, and Simon went back to France[4]. Henry accordingly, finding himself on his return without support in the council, soon after Christmas again confirmed the Provisions[5].

The king absolved.

He goes to France. Gloucester dies.

Henry returns at Christmas, 1262.

As usual Henry's promises were only made to be broken; his very renewal of them provoked the suspicion that he was trying to annul the hateful measures which had so limited his authority. He brought back with him a host of foreigners: the arbitration with Simon failed[6], and war was raging between the Marchers and the Welsh. The king's demand made on the 22nd of March, 1263[7], that the oath of allegiance should be taken to Edward, provoked a new struggle. The earl of Gloucester refused to take it[8], and at Whitsuntide Simon, who had come home early in the spring, raised the standard of revolt. Having demanded of the king a re-confirmation of the Provisions, which was refused[9], he began to collect armed

He demands the oath of allegiance to Edward, Mar. 1263.

He refuses to confirm the Provisions.

in the king's name for the council, and urging the confirmation of the new system; Royal Letters, ii. 188. The letter of absolution was obtained early in February, and dated February 25; Foed. i. 416. It was published in London in Lent; Liber de Antt. Legg. p. 49. See Royal Letters, ii. 206, 208, 209. Another bull of release, dated at Orvieto, Aug. 23, 1263, is in the Bodleian MS. 91.

[1] Ann. Wykes, p. 130.

[2] May 2, 1262; Foed. i. 419.

[3] Ann. Dunst. pp. 218, 219; Ann. Osney, p. 130. He returned Dec. 20; Cont. Gerv. ii. 218.

[4] Chron. Dover, MS.; Cont. Gerv. ii. 217.

[5] About Jan. 25, 1263; Ann. Osney, p. 131; Liber de Antt. Legg. p. 52.

[6] Simon was negotiating a truce with Edward to last until Midlent, March 4, 1263; Royal Letters, ii. 244.

[7] Foed. i. 425. Sent to the Cinque Ports June 15, ibid. 427; taken in London, March 11, Liber de Antt. Legg. p. 53.

[8] Ann. Dunst. p. 220.

[9] Before Whitsuntide; Liber de Antt. Legg. pp. 53, 54.

Simon begins war, 1263.

adherents, and proceeded to attack the king's friends. The bishop of Hereford was the first victim; he was taken prisoner on the 11th of June. Gloucester and the town of Bristol were next taken. Simon then betook himself to Kent to secure the Cinque Ports. Edward on the other hand made Windsor the head-quarters of an armed force and seized the treasure in the New Temple. The king and queen fled to the Tower of London, and the king had to confirm the Provisions [1]. Here the king of the Romans intervened, and, although Edward still refused to submit to force, the intervention secured the conclusion of a temporary peace on the 15th of July [2], by which the aliens were banished and Hugh le Despenser restored to the justiciarship. Edward held out until the 18th of August [3]. On the 8th of September [4] the Provisions were again proclaimed at S. Paul's, and Henry and Simon made another attempt to obtain a satisfactory arbitration in a short visit to France, which lasted from September 19th to October 7th [5]. The attempt as usual failed: the parliament which met on the 14th of October witnessed a stormy debate on the redress to be given by the baronial party to those who had suffered wrong at their hands; the king left London, Edward re-occupied Windsor. After some brisk manœuvres mediation again prevailed, and on the 16th of December [6] it was determined to refer to Lewis IX the whole question of the validity of the Provisions, and the final decision whether or no they were to continue in force.

Mediation of king Richard.

Attempt at arbitration.

The quarrel is referred to Louis IX, December 16, 1263.

The act of compromise, which was executed by Henry at Windsor and by Simon and his party at London, rehearses [7]

[1] This is probably the confirmation recorded in the Patent Rolls of 47 Hen. III (Statutes, i. 8, note *a*; p. 11, note 11), and published June 12, 1263.

[2] July 15, Liber de Antt. Legg. p. 55; Foed. i. 427, June 29; peace proclaimed July 20, ibid. 56; July 26, Windsor surrendered, ibid. 57.

[3] Foed. i. 430. See Royal Letters, ii. 247, 248, 249.

[4] See Ann. Theokesb. p. 176, where an assembly of clergy is mentioned as meeting on September 8, and sitting for a fortnight with no result; Ann. Dunst. p. 224.

[5] See Royal Letters, ii. 249; Ann. Dunst. p. 225. September 22–October 7, Liber de Antt. Legg. p. 57.

[6] Royal Letters, ii. 252; Ann. Dunst. 227; Liber de Antt. Legg. p. 58.

[7] The two acts of consent are printed in the notes to the Chronicle of Rishanger (Camd. Soc.), pp. 121, 122, from the original documents. Select

on the part of each a consent to the arbitration and a distinct promise to observe it. The names of the barons who joined in the act, being given in the two documents, furnish some data as to the composition of the two parties at the moment. With the earl are found the bishops of London and Worcester, Hugh le Despenser the barons' justiciar, and Humfrey de Bohun the heir of Hereford and Essex. With the king, besides his son and his nephew Henry, his brother William of Valence, and his brother-in-law John of Warenne, are Humfrey de Bohun the father, Hugh le Bigod the late justiciar, Roger le Bigod earl of Norfolk, Philip Basset and Roger Mortimer. Few of the twenty-four or of the fifteen appear in either list, more however on the king's side than on that of the earl. Nor is it easy to draw a geographical line between the parties; Bruce and Balliol, Clifford, Percy, Vaux and Marmion are with the king, Ros, Vipont, Vescy and Lacy are with the earl. Gloucester, on whose attitude it is probable much of the later course of events depended, stood aloof altogether.

The act of compromise.

Division of parties to the compromise of 1263.

Gloucester stands aloof.

Henry went in person to Amiens to attend the arbitration; Simon was prevented by an accident from doing the same: it is not however probable that the decision of Lewis was affected by his absence. The king of France had his own idea of the dignity of royalty, and was too humble and charitable not to credit other men with the same desire of doing their duty which was predominant in himself. He decided, on the 23rd of January, 1264, all points in favour of Henry, annulled the Provisions of Oxford and all engagements founded upon them; in particular he left the king free to appoint his own ministers, council and sheriffs, to employ aliens, and to enjoy his royal power as fully as he had done before the enactment of the Provisions. Two provisoes are added to console the barons; this award is not intended to derogate from the liberties of the realm as they were established by royal charter, privilege, franchise, statute, or praiseworthy custom; and all feuds arising from the recent proceedings are peremptorily suppressed. Thus

Decision of Lewis IX: the *Mise of Amiens*, Jan. 23, 1264.

He annuls the Provisions of Oxford.

Charters, pp. 406–409; Foed. i. 433, 434; Ann. Theokesb. p. 177; Liber de Antt. Legg. p. 58.

the charter of liberties is saved; the king may take no revenge on the barons, or the barons on the king. The Mise of Amiens, as the arbitration was called, received the papal confirmation on the 16th of March[1].

War in Wales, Feb. 1264.

The arbitration disregarded by the barons.

Attitude of London.

177. It was scarcely to be expected that the baronial party would patiently acquiesce in this decision[2]. They were already, under the pretext of the Welsh war, fighting and seizing the royal castles in the West, Llewelyn and earl Simon against Edward and Mortimer; and when the king on the 15th of February returned from France, bringing a considerable force and fresh papal letters, he found his way open to full revenge. Technically the fault must lie with Simon, who never thought of observing the award which he had so recently bound himself to accept, and whose conduct on the occasion is, except on the plea of absolute necessity, as unjustifiable as that of the king. It is however certain that a great part of the baronage, nearly the whole of the lower population[3], and especially the city of London and the Cinque Ports, had not joined in the compromise, and were not bound by the award. It was on the aid of these that Simon threw himself and by it he prevailed. The king summoned a parliament, or rather a conference[4], to Oxford in March; but the earl of Leicester and his companions attended it merely to declare their adhesion to the Provisions and to disclaim the compromise. This was a declaration of war. Henry accordingly seized Northampton and Nottingham, and Simon with the Londoners besieged Rochester. Hearing that Tutbury and Kenilworth had fallen into his hands, the king then marched south to relieve Rochester, and, learning that the siege was abandoned, encamped in great force before Lewes. Simon and the Londoners, still making a show of negotiation, followed him: an offer of £30,000 was made for the confirmation of the

War begins.

[1] Foed. i. 436.

[2] Ann. Theokesb. p. 179; Liber de Antt. Legg. p. 61.

[3] 'Fere omnis communa mediocris populi regni Angliae;' Liber de Antt. Legg. p. 61.

[4] A conference was proposed at Brackley March 18; the king summoned his forces to Oxford on the 20th; Foed. i. 437; cf. Liber de Antt. Legg. p. 61; marched from Oxford towards Northampton, April 3; Ann. Osney, p. 143.

Provisions. The debate ended in a formal defiance addressed by Henry, his brother, and his son, to the earls of Leicester and Gloucester, on the 12th of May[1]. On the 14th[2] the battle of Lewes, won through a singular conjunction of skill and craft on the one side, rashness and panic on the other, placed the king with his kinsmen and chief supporters as prisoners at the mercy of the earl.

Henry defeated and taken at Lewes, May 14.

The 'Mise of Lewes,' the capitulation which secured the safety of the king, contained seven articles[3]. By the first and second, after a re-confirmation of the Provisions, a new body of arbitrators was named: the archbishop of Rouen, the bishop of London, Peter the chamberlain of France, and the new legate the cardinal bishop of Sabina, with the duke of Burgundy or count of Anjou as umpire in case of need; the third directs that the arbitrators shall swear to choose only English counsellors; by the fourth the king is bound to act on the advice of his counsellors in administering justice and choosing ministers, to observe the charters and to live at moderate expense; by the fifth Edward and his cousin Henry are given as hostages; a sixth provides for the indemnity of the earls of Leicester and Gloucester; and the seventh fixes the next Easter as the time for the completion of the compromise. Peace was declared on the 25th of May[4] and published at London on the 11th of June[5].

The *Mise of Lewes*.

Peace proclaimed.

This treaty furnished the basis of the new constitution which Simon proposed to create, and forms the link between it and the earlier one devised in 1258. As soon as the royal castles had been placed in fit hands, on the 4th of June[6], writs were issued appointing guardians of the peace in each shire and ordering the election of four knights of each shire to meet the king in parliament on the 22nd of the same month. The parliament met and drew up the new scheme of government, which was to be observed as long as Henry lived, and under Edward also for a term to

Measures of security.

New scheme of government, June 1264.

[1] Foed. i. 440; Liber de Antt. Legg. p. 64.
[2] Ann. Winton, p. 101; Ann. Waverley, p. 537; Ann. Dunst. p. 232.
[3] See Chronicle of Rishanger (Camd. Soc.), p. 37; Select Charters, p. 334; cf. Liber de Antt. Legg. p. 63.
[4] Foed. i. 441.
[5] Foed. i. 443. May 27, Liber de Antt. Legg. p. 63.
[6] Foed. i. 442; Select Charters, p. 411.

be afterwards settled[1]. The king is to act by a council of nine members, nominated by three electors; the electors are to be chosen by the barons and to receive full powers from the king for the purpose. Of the nine counsellors three are to be in constant attendance: by their advice the ministers and the wardens of the castles are to be appointed. Electors and counsellors are bound by special oaths; in case of dissension, two-thirds of each body are competent to act; the appointment of successors or substitutes for the electors rests with the king and the barons and prelates; vacancies among the counsellors are to be filled up by the electors. All these must be native Englishmen, but aliens shall be free to come and go and stay. The charters and the provisions of 1263[2], which were a republication of those of 1259, were confirmed, and the two parties enjoined to forgiveness and forbearance[3]. It is observable that the knights of the shire are not recognised as having a voice in the choice of either electors or counsellors: yet the fact of their summons to this and the following parliament seems to show that Simon regarded them as an integral part of the national council or parliament. And in this we trace a marked difference between his earlier and later policy. The provisions of 1258 restricted, the constitution of 1264 extended, the limits of parliament; the committee of twelve that was to sit with the council of fifteen, the cumbersome and entangled duties of the several commissions, disappear; and some confidence is shown in the community of knights which had been assembled by representation in 1254, which had come forward to urge reform in 1259, and whose importance had been recognised by both parties in the summons of 1261. But the provision for freedom of election showed more than a confidence in the knights; it extended that confidence to the freeholders by whom they were to be chosen, a confidence which was in a few months extended to the inhabitants of the boroughs. Either Simon's views of a constitution had rapidly developed, or the influences which had checked them in 1258 were removed.

Standing council.

Confirmation of charters.

Relation of this constitution to that of 1258.

Rapid expansion of the reforms.

[1] Select Charters, p. 412; Foed. i. 443: where also is the scheme of church reform; cf. Liber de Antt. Legg. p. 66.

[2] See p. 89, note 7.

[3] Foed. i. 443.

Anyhow he had had genius to interpret the mind of the nation and to anticipate the line which was taken by later progress.

The new ministers. The three electors chosen were the earls of Leicester and Gloucester and the bishop of Chichester, Stephen Berksted[1]. Hugh le Despenser continued to be justiciar[2], and Thomas of Cantilupe, nephew of the bishop of Worcester, was made Chancellor. The names of the council do not appear; but it no doubt contained Peter de Montfort, Roger St. John, and Giles of Argentine.

Threats of invasion by the queen and archbishop. The new government was called on for immediate action. John of Warenne and the other fugitives from Lewes had joined the queen in France, and were preparing an invasion[3]. **Threats of the legate.** Boniface and the whole foreign party had combined to aid them, and the legate, who was not disarmed by his nomination as an arbitrator, was threatening excommunication. In a great meeting of the clergy held in July at S. Paul's, bishop Walter of Cantilupe solemnly appealed against the action of the legate[4]. On the 6th of the same month the whole armed force of the country was summoned to meet at London on the 3rd of August[5], to resist the attack, but adverse weather prevented the sailing of the queen's fleet, and early in September Henry of Cornwall was sent to France to open the arbitration determined at Lewes. **Appeals to the pope.** The legate was ready to anathematise[6] the new government, and the ambassadors were ill-treated on landing; the business of the arbitration was stopped, and the English church had to appeal to the Pope on the 19th of October[7] against the sentence of anathema. Urban IV, however, was already dead, and his successor, who was not elected

[1] Foed. i. 444. Stephen Berksted had been a chaplain of S. Richard, 'vir summae simplicitatis et innocentiae;' Wykes, p. 312.

[2] It is sometimes stated that Simon made himself justiciar; this is a mistake caused by running together in particular documents the attestation of the earl and that of Hugh le Despenser.

[3] See Royal Letters, ii. 257, 262 sq.

[4] Cont. Gervas. ii. 239–242.

[5] Foed. i. 444; Royal Letters, ii. 259, 269. The forces of the shires also are called out: the feudal tenants are summoned 'in fide et homagio;' and the sheriffs are bidden to send from each township eight, six, or four armed foot-men, whose expenses are to be paid 'de commune.' See Royal Letters, ii. 271.

[6] October 20; Foed. i. 448.

[7] October 19; Ann. Dunst. p. 234.

until the following February, was none other than the legate himself.

The great parliament of 1265.

The famous parliament of Simon de Montfort was summoned to meet at Westminster on the 20th of January, 1265. A previous meeting had been called at Oxford on the 30th of November, and a great military levy had been summoned at Northampton on November 25, for the purpose of taking active measures against the recalcitrant marchers, with whom it was suspected that Gloucester was already intriguing[1]. From Oxford the king and Simon went on to Worcester, where an agreement was made that several of the discontented lords should absent themselves from England for a year and a day, and the other marchers came to terms[2]. There, on the 13th of December, the king confirmed the Provisions of 1259[3], and on the following day was issued a first series of writs for the great parliament of 1265. A second series followed, ten days later[4].

Composition of earl Simon's parliament.

Important as this assembly is in the history of the constitution, it was not primarily and essentially a constitutional assembly. It was not a general convention of the tenants-in-chief, or of the three estates, but a parliamentary assembly of the supporters of the existing government. This was a matter of necessity. It would have been a mere mockery to summon the men who were on the other side of the channel uttering anathemas or waiting for an opportunity of invasion. Archbishop Boniface therefore was not cited, nor the other bishops who were avowedly hostile. The archbishop of York, the bishops of Durham and Carlisle, ten abbots and nine priors of the northern province, ten bishops and four deans of the southern were summoned, and by a later writ, issued December 24 at Woodstock, fifty-five abbots, twenty-six priors, and the heads of the military orders: a sufficient proof that the clergy as a body were on the side of the earl. With the baronial body this was not the case; only five earls (Leicester, Gloucester,

[1] Ann. Dunst. p. 235; Ann. Osney, pp. 154, 159; Ann. Wykes, p. 159.
[2] Liber de Antt. Legg. p. 70; Ann. Osney, p. 159; Foed. i. 449.
[3] Statutes of the Realm, p. 11.
[4] Foed. i. 449; Select Charters, p. 415; Ann. Dunst. p. 235; Lords' Report, iii. 32-36.

Norfolk, Oxford, and Derby) were summoned, and with them only eighteen barons [1], of whom ten had acted with Simon in the arbitration of Amiens. But the great feature of the parliament was the representation of the shires, cities, and boroughs: each sheriff had a writ ordering him to return two discreet knights from each shire; a like summons addressed to the cities and boroughs ordered two representatives to be sent from each, and the barons of the Cinque Ports had a similar mandate. The writs to the cities and boroughs are not addressed to them through the sheriff of the county, as was the rule when their representatives became an integral part of the parliament, and so far the proceedings of Simon do not connect themselves directly with the machinery of the county courts; nor is there any order for the election of the representatives, but the custom of election was so well established that it could not have been neglected on this occasion [2].

Representation of shires and boroughs.

Peculiarities of summons.

The parliament thus organised continued its session until late in March [3]; its chief business was the conclusion of the arrangements entered into in the Mise of Lewes. On the 14th of February [4] the king swore to maintain the new form of government, the charters and provisions; the negotiations for the release of Edward began on the 16th [5] and were completed on the 8th of March [6]; on the 14th Henry published a statement of the circumstances and terms of the pacification [7]; on the 17th oaths of fealty were taken by all who had been defied by the king before the battle of Lewes [8]; on the 20th, in pursuance of the treaty with Edward, the county of Chester, with valuable

Parliament of 1265, Jan. to March.

[1] The barons are Camoys, S. John, le Despenser (justiciar), Fitz John, Montchensi, Segrave, Vescy, Basset of Drayton, Hastings, Lucy, Ros, Eyville, Neuf Marché, Colevill, Marmyun, Bertram, Basset of Sapcote, and Gant; Lords' Report, iii. 34.

[2] The Liber de Antt. Legg. is the only printed Chronicle which notices the composition of Simon's parliament, p. 71, adding to the usual formula 'et de quinque Portubus, de qualibet civitate et burgo quatuor homines.'

[3] The knights of the shires however had their writs of expenses on February 15; Prynne, Reg. iv. p. 3; Lords' Report, App. p. 35. On the 23rd of February the sheriff of Shropshire and Stafford, who had not returned knights on the former summons, was directed to send them on March 8; ibid. 39.

[4] Liber de Antt. Legg. p. 71.

[5] Foed. i. 450.

[6] Foed. i. 452.

[7] Foed. i. 453; Select Charters, p. 416.

[8] Liber de Antt. Legg. p. 73.

appurtenances, was transferred to Simon, to be compensated by an exchange of lands[1].

Quarrel of Gloucester and Leicester.

But the new government was already breaking up. Gilbert of Gloucester was not more likely than his father had been to submit to Simon's supremacy; and, if he were, he stood at the head of a body of jealous kinsmen and vassals. A tournament fixed for Shrove Tuesday[2] at Dunstable, to be held by the followers of the two earls, was peremptorily forbidden by Simon. The surrender of the castle of Bristol to him, although the rights of Gloucester to the great stronghold of his ancestral power were provided for in the agreement, may have increased the misunderstanding. Notwithstanding the pacification at Worcester in 1264 the war on the Marches had never ceased, and Gloucester was known to be supporting the Mortimers. Soon after Easter the earls had a personal quarrel; Gloucester insisted that the Mise of Lewes and the Provisions of Oxford had not been executed, hinting unmistakeably that Simon was one of the aliens who were forbidden to take charge of castles or a share in the government. Matters had gone so far that on the 20th of May[3] Henry, who had gone with earl Simon to Hereford to enforce peace, was obliged to contradict the rumour that the two earls had gone to war. On the 28th Edward escaped from his half-captivity at Hereford and joined the Mortimers. With the earl of Gloucester he mustered his adherents in Cheshire and Shropshire, whilst Simon was engaged in Wales. When fully prepared he marched southward, and on the 29th of June took

Escape of Edward, May 28, 1265.

[1] Foed. i. 454.

[2] February 17; Ann. Dunst. p. 238; adjourned to Hokeday at Northampton, ibid. 239. The Waverley Annals place the quarrel and pacification in the January parliament, p. 358: and say that the imprisonment of earl Ferrers alarmed Gloucester into flight. 'Inter Pascha et Pentecosten;' Liber de Antt. Legg. p. 73.

[3] Foed. i. 455. See Ann. Theokesb. p. 180; where the two weak points in Simon's position, his foreign birth and his reputed greed of acquisition, are noted clearly by a partisan of Gloucester; and also Ann. Waverley, p. 358; Rishanger, p. 32; Ann. Wykes, p. 153. The two earls consented to an arbitration, May 12; Ann. Waverley, p. 361: the umpires were to be the bishop of Worcester, Hugh le Despenser, John Fitz John, and William of Montchensy; Liber de Antt. Legg. p. 73. It is probable that for this business the king's writ, dated May 15 at Gloucester, was issued for an assembly of prelates and magnates at Winchester, on the 1st of June; Lords' Report, iii. 36.

Gloucester[1]. Simon had summoned his eldest son from Pevensey to Kenilworth, and prepared to surround Edward's forces in the vale of Evesham. Edward's promptness forestalled the plan; marching rapidly on Kenilworth[2], he routed the force of the younger Simon and then advanced to crush the father. At Evesham, on the 4th of August, the verdict of Lewes was reversed, and the great earl was slain. With him fell Hugh le Despenser the justiciar, and, for the time, the great cause for which he had contended.

Battle of Evesham, Aug. 4.

On the 7th of August Henry proclaimed himself free, and on the 16th of September the war was reputed to be at an end, and peace might have followed at once if the victors had been content to be moderate. But the proceedings of the council called by the king at Winchester on the 8th of September[3] drove the remnant of the baronial party into desperate rebellion. The widows of the slain lords laid their complaints before the king, and in October a general sentence of forfeiture or 'exheredation' was issued against those who had fought at Kenilworth and Evesham on the side of Simon. The citizens of London made their submission on the 6th of October[4], and afterwards purchased peace: the Cinque Ports received Edward in the following March[5], and a new legate, Cardinal Ottobon, was sent to punish the bishops who had acted against the king. The disinherited lords were, however, organising resistance. Kenilworth castle was their head-quarters at first, and thither, after the capture of the earl Ferrers at Chesterfield[6] on the 15th of May, the king led the host which he had collected for the extinction of the rebels. The siege lasted from Midsummer to December[7]; and Henry took advantage of the long-continued

Forfeiture of the rebel lords.

They prepare for resistance.

Siege of Kenilworth, 1266.

[1] Ann. Waverley, p. 362.
[2] August 2; Liber de Antt. Legg. p. 74. August 1; Ann. Osney, p. 166.
[3] Liber de Antt. Legg. p. 76; Cont. Fl. Wig. p. 194; Ann. Osney, p. 173; Ann. Wykes, p. 176; Foed. i. 462.
[4] Royal Letters, ii. 293. Cf. Ann. Winton, p. 105; Foed. i. 464; see Liber de Antt. Legg. pp. 78–80. The citizens were admitted to favour January 10; ibid. 82.
[5] March 25; Ann. Waverley, p. 369; Liber de Antt. Legg. p. 82.
[6] Ann. Waverley, p. 369; Ann. Dunst. p. 241; Liber de Antt. Legg. p. 86; Cont. Fl. Wig. p. 197; Ann. Wykes, p. 188.
[7] June 25 to December 13; Ann. Winton, p. 104; Ann. Waverley,

attendance of the tenants-in-chief to draw up, under the walls of Kenilworth, a form of agreement by which the Disinherited might upon submission be allowed to recover their estates. It was arranged by a committee of arbitrators chosen in the same way as the council of 1258; three bishops and three earls were chosen by the assembled parliament[1], and these nominated six colleagues. Their ordinance, called the 'Dictum de Kenilworth,' was published on the 31st of October[2], 1266. It contains 41 articles, some declaring the plenary power of the king, the nullity of the acts of Simon, the royal obligation to keep the charters, the freedom of the church, and the remedy of some of the minor grievances touched by the Provisions. But the majority of the articles concern the rebels: Simon de Montfort is not to be reputed a saint, the fate of his children is to be determined by the king of France; the general sentence of forfeiture is to be commuted for a fine of five years' value of the forfeited estates; earl Ferrers is to pay seven years' revenue and give up his castles. All who will submit within forty days are to be forgiven and spared. The terms were very hard, and some of the defenders of Kenilworth, unwilling to accept them, assembled again after the surrender, and held out in the Isle of Ely until July 1267. But the most formidable hindrance to peace arose from the conduct of the earl of Gloucester. Distrusting the king's gratitude, and provoked by the greed and vindictiveness of Roger Mortimer, who was attempting to disturb the arrangements made in the Dictum of Kenilworth, he declared himself the champion of the Disinherited. On the pretext of conferring with the legate, he marched on London, and, with the co-operation of the

The *Dictum de Kenilworth*, 1266.

The earl of Gloucester seizes London, April 1267.

p. 373; Ann. Dunst. p. 242; Liber de Antt. Legg. pp. 87, 89; Cont. Fl. Wig. p. 198.

[1] The Dictum was drawn up in the Parliament begun at Kenilworth, Aug. 24th; the mode of election is thus given (Ann. Wav. p. 372):—

Bp. of Bath,		E. of Gloucester.
Bp. of Worcester,		E. of Hereford.
Bp. of Exeter,	nominate	Bp. of S. David's.
Rog. Sumery,		John Balliol.
Robert Walleran,		Phil. Basset.
Alan de la Zouche,		Warin Bassingbourn.

[2] Statutes, i. 17. Oct. 25, Ann. Winton, p. 104: Oct. 26, Ann. Waverley, p. 372; confirmed Nov. 1, Ann. Osney, p. 191. The charter of 1225 was re-proclaimed, Sept. 30; Liber de Antt. Legg. p. 87.

inhabitants, occupied the city[1] and admitted the refugees from Ely, the leaders of whom, John d'Eyville, Nicolas Segrave, and William Marmion, were three of the barons who had supported earl Simon in the famous parliament of 1265. But earl Gilbert's act was probably meant only to secure better terms for the Disinherited. Under the joint pressure of the king and legate he could not hold out long. On the 16th[2] of June he made his peace, and the three barons were admitted to grace. The defenders of Ely[3] also were allowed the terms of the Dictum of Kenilworth. The struggle ended here, and Henry was able with a good grace and under sound advice to adopt a healing policy. The parliament of Marlborough, Nov. 18, 1267, re-enacted the provisions of 1259 as a statute[4]. Except the demand for the appointment of the ministers and the election of sheriffs, the statute of Marlborough concedes almost all that had been asked for in the Mad Parliament; and from its preamble it seems not improbable that the shires were represented by their chosen knights in the assembly that passed it.

He submits, in June.

The parliament of Marlborough, Nov. 1267.

178. In 1268 Edward took the cross[5], and two years after left England for Palestine[6]. The remaining years of Henry were uneventful: he had survived all his enemies and very many of his difficulties; and some of his proceedings show that he reverted to the constitutional system of his earlier years. On the occasion of the translation of S. Edward, October 13, 1269[7], he brought together in a great assembly at Westminster not only

Parliament of 1269;

[1] April 8, 1267; Ann. Winton, p. 105; Ann. Dunst. p. 245. April 9–12; Liber de Antt. Legg. p. 90; Cont. Fl. Wig. p. 200; Ann. Wykes, p. 299.

[2] June 16; Foed. i. 472; Liber de Antt. Legg. p. 95. The arbitration was referred to the pope, who decided that the earl should give either his daughter or his castle of Tunbridge in pledge for three years; Henry released him from the obligation July 16, 1268; Foed. i. 476; Liber de Antt. Legg. p. 93.

[3] Ely surrendered July 11; Cont. Fl. Wig. p. 201.

[4] B. Cotton, p. 143; Hemingb. i. 329; Statutes of the Realm, i. pp. 19–25.

[5] At a parliament at Northampton; Ann. Winton, p. 107. June 24; Liber de Antt. Legg. p. 107; Ann. Wykes, p. 217.

[6] 1270; Ann. Winton, p. 109; cf. Foed. i. 484; Liber de Antt. Legg. p. 125; Cont. Fl. Wig. p. 205.

[7] Henry proposed to wear his crown at this festival, Ann. Winton, p. 108; but did not, Liber de Antt. Legg. p. 117.

the magnates lay and clerical, but the more powerful men of all the cities and boroughs[1]. After the ceremony the magnates held a parliament, and debated on a grant of a twentieth of moveables to the king[2]. We are not told that the citizens and burghers were consulted. Two or three parliaments were held in 1270[3] to complete the taxation of 1269 and to relieve the king from his vow of crusade by a formal prohibition. In July the Londoners were received into favour and recovered their forfeited charters. In a parliament held on the 13th of January, 1271, the lands of all the Disinherited[4] were restored, and, though some uneasiness was created by attempts at papal taxation, the kingdom was at peace. The king of the Romans died on the 12th of December the same year; and Henry closed his long and troubled career on the 16th of November, 1272.

Parliaments of 1270

and of 1271.

Henry dies, 1272.

Importance of Henry's character.

The character of Henry III may be best read in the history of his reign, for he is always among the foremost actors and has a very distinct idiosyncrasy. Accomplished, refined, liberal, magnificent; rash rather than brave, impulsive and ambitious, pious, and, in an ordinary sense, virtuous, he was utterly devoid of all elements of greatness. The events of his reign brought out in fatal relief all his faults and weaknesses, making even such good points as he possessed contribute to establish the general conviction of his folly and falseness. Unlike his father, who was incapable of receiving any impression, Henry was so susceptible of impressions that none of them could last long; John's heart was of millstone, Henry's of wax; yet they had in common a

Contrast of Henry and John.

[1] Ann. Wykes, p. 226.

[2] Liber de Antt. Legg. p. 122. The twentieth was debated in October, granted in the following year; B. Cotton, p. 144; cf. Lords' Report, i. 162.

[3] April 27; Ann. Winton, p. 108; adjourned to July 2. The first was a long session. On the 12th of May, 1270, Henry wrote to the clergy that it was impossible to collect a parliament, but that he hoped that they would give him a twentieth as the prelates had done; Royal Letters, ii. 336. May 13, the bishops proclaim the charter, Liber de Antt. Legg. p. 122. May 20, he writes to the bishops to come to him, Foed. i. 483. In the July parliament Edward takes leave, Liber de Antt. Legg. p. 125, at Winchester, p. 129; and in a parliament at Westminster on the 13th of October an ordinance was made about wool; Liber de Antt. Legg. p. 127.

[4] Ann. Winton, p. 110; Ann. Wigorn. p. 460: a tax of a twentieth had been raised from the clergy for their relief in 1268; Wykes, p. 220; Lords' Report, i. 160.

certain feminine quality of irresolute pertinacity which it would be a mockery to call elasticity. Both contrived to make inveterate enemies, both had a gift of rash, humorous, unpardonable sarcasm; both were utterly deficient in a sense of truth or justice. Henry had, no doubt, to pay for some of the sins of John; he inherited personal enmities, and utterly baseless ideas as to the character of English royalty. He outlived the enmities, and in the hour of his triumph found that his ideas could not be realised. Coming between the worst and the best of our kings, he shares the punishment that his father deserved, and the discipline that trained the genius of his son, without himself either unlearning the evil or learning the good. His character is hardly worth analysis except as a contrast to that of his brilliant rival.

Simon de Montfort.

Simon had all the virtues, the strength, the grace that Henry wanted; and what advantages he lacked the faults of the king supplied. If he be credited with too great ambition, too violent a temper, too strong an instinct of aggression, his faults will not outweigh his virtues. His errors were the result of what seemed to him necessity or of temptations that opened for him a position from which he could not recede. Had he lived longer the prospect of the throne might have opened before him, and he might have become a destroyer instead of a saviour. If he had succeeded in such a design, he could not have made a better king than Edward; if he had failed, England would have lain at the feet of Edward, a ruler whose virtues would have made him more dangerous as a despot than his father's vices had made him in his attempt at despotism. Simon cannot be called happy in the opportunity of his death, yet it may have been best for England that he lived no longer. He was greater as an opponent of tyranny than as a deviser of liberties; the fetters imposed on royal autocracy, cumbrous and entangled as they were, seem to have been an integral part of his policy; the means he took for admitting the nation to self-government wear very much the form of an occasional or party expedient, which a longer tenure of undivided power might have led him either to develope or to discard. The idea of representative government had, however, ripened under his hand; and although the germ of the growth

The position of Simon de Montfort in English history.

lay in the primitive institutions of the land, Simon has the merit of having been one of the first to see the uses and the glories to which it would ultimately grow.

Change in the character of the struggle.

The history of the latter years of Henry III shows that the character of the constitutional contest was undergoing a change. The humiliation of the baronial party, as led by Simon, was complete. The continuity of the struggle seemed to depend rather on the persistency of royal assumption than on the obstinacy of resistance. Henry had, as has been said already, out-lived most of his dangerous friends and all his dangerous enemies. The genius of Edward already made itself felt in his father's councils. The comparative moderation of the Dictum of Kenilworth shows that personal enmities were dying out, and that both sides were withdrawing extreme claims; it indicates that for the future the power of the crown was to be increased by legal and politic management, not by unwarranted claims or despotic aggression. Still clearer is the change when Edward becomes king. He had learned a great lesson from his father's faults and misfortunes: he had reaped the fruits of an education which had been a long struggle on the one hand to remedy his father's errors, and on the other to humble his father's enemies. He had inherited to the full the Plantagenet love of power, and he possessed in the highest degree the great qualities and manifold accomplishments of his race. He had been brought up in a household of which purity and piety were the redeeming characteristics, and had been impressed with these virtues rather than with the vices of insincerity and dishonesty which they had not served to conceal. Truthful, honourable, temperate and chaste; frugal, cautious, resolute; great in counsel, ingenious in contrivance, rapid in execution, he had all the powers of Henry II without his vices, and he had too that sympathy with the people he ruled, the want of which alone would have robbed the character of Henry II of the title of greatness. He was a law-abiding king, one who kept his word. If sometimes he kept the law in the letter rather than in the spirit, and used his promises as the maximum rather than the minimum of his good intentions;—if

Increasing influence of Edward.

Edward had learned wisdom in his father's reign.

His character.

Compared with Henry II.

we trace in his conduct a captiousness, an over-readiness to make the most of his legal advantages, and to strain legal rights beyond the line of equity, we have but to compare him with the kings that went before and that come after, and we shall see cause not so much to justify his conduct as to wonder at the greatness of his moderation, at the wise and temperate use of the position which he had made for himself. It is in his foreign transactions that this spirit of over-legality chiefly appears: upon one great occasion it is manifested in his home-politics, and then it determines against him the formal issue of the long struggle for the maintenance of the charters.

His weakness in one point.

Henry's irresolution and impolicy had one good result; they incapacitated him from becoming a successful tyrant. He had thrown away the chances that came to him in the exhaustion of political parties, the length of his reign, and the great advantages of his personal position. He had failed to gather, out of the many schemes of reform that were presented to him, a single element of strength for his own cause, or to attach to himself one of the many interests among which the nation was divided. Among the magnates only those who were foreigners by birth or who shared his foreign predilections adhered to him, and in the lower ranks of clergy and laity alike he made no friends. Had it been otherwise, had he been able to divide the national opposition, or to guide, as perhaps he attempted to do, the several components of that opposition to mutual destruction, he might have created a lasting despotism. He reigned so long that the chance of such a consummation passed away, and his son, who possessed the qualities which were wanting to his father for success, lacked the opportunity which the father had failed to grasp. Edward loved power. He would not have been so great a king as he was, if he had not estimated at its full value the kingly power that he inherited. It is only by clearly understanding this that we can appreciate the good faith and self-restraint implied in his keeping the engagements by which he was forced to limit the exercise of that power. He did not, like his father, obstinately reject conditions of reform, or, like Edward III,

Incapacity of Henry III.

His inability to use his opportunities.

Importance of the length of his reign.

Strength of Edward's position and character.

accept with levity terms which he did not intend to keep. Believing in his own right, in his own power of governing, and in his own intention to govern well, he held fast to the last moment every point of his sovereign authority; but when he was compelled to accept a limit, he observed the limit. The good faith of a strong king is a safer guarantee of popular right than the helplessness of a weak one. Edward had, besides force and honesty, a clear perception of true policy, and such an intuitive knowledge of the needs of his people as could proceed only from a deep sympathy with them. The improvement of the laws, the definite organisation of government, the definite arrangement of rights and jurisdictions, the definite elaboration of all departments, which mark the reign and make it the fit conclusion of a period of growth in all these matters, were unquestionably promoted, if not originated, by the personal action of the king. What under Henry I was the effect of despotic routine, and under Henry II the result of law imposed from without, becomes under Edward I a definite organisation worked by an indwelling energy. The incorporation of the spirit with the mechanism is the result of the discipline of the century, but the careful determination of the proper sphere and limit of action in each department, the self-regulating action of the body politic, was very much the work of Edward.

His place in the development of the constitution.

Edward succeeds without question, Nov. 20, 1272.

179. The beginning of the reign illustrates these positions. Edward at the time of his father's death was far away in the East, but no one questioned his right to succeed, or proposed conditions, or raised a finger to disturb the peace which had prevailed since 1267. The great seal was delivered to the archbishop of York, November 17; it was broken on the 20th; on the 21st a meeting of the council was held at the New Temple, and a new seal made, Walter de Merton being Chancellor[1]. The new king's reign began on the day of his father's funeral, when, without waiting for his return or coronation, the earl of Gloucester, followed by the barons and prelates, swore to observe the peace of the realm and their fealty to their new lord[2].

Oaths of fealty taken, Nov. 20.

[1] Foed. i. 497; Liber de Antt. Legg. p. 153; M. Westm. Flores, ii. 28.

[2] November 20; Foed. i. 497; Ann. Winton, p. 112. The earl had

For the first time the reign of the new king began, both in law and in fact, from the death of his predecessor; and, although in the coronation service the forms of election and acceptance were still observed, the king was king before coronation; the preliminary discussion, which must have taken place on every vacancy since the Norman Conquest, was dispensed with, and the right of the heir was at once recognised[1]. The doctrine of the abeyance of the king's peace during the vacancy of the throne was thus deprived of its most dangerous consequences, although it was not until the reign of Edward IV that the still newer theory was accepted, that the king never dies, that the demise of the crown at once transfers it from the last wearer to the heir, and that no vacancy, no interruption of the peace, occurs at all.

Proclamation of the king's peace.

Three days after the funeral, on the 23rd of November, 1272, the royal council put forth a proclamation in the name of the new king, announcing that the kingdom had, by hereditary succession and by the will and fealty of the 'proceres,' devolved on him, and enjoining the observance of the peace[2]. The question of regency was already settled. No claim seems to have been made either on behalf of the queen mother or on behalf of the judicial body[3]; the rights of Isabella of Angoulême had been set aside in 1216, and there was now no officer in the position held then by Hubert de Burgh. The king of the Romans was dead; Edmund of Lancaster was absent from the kingdom: Gilbert of Gloucester, who as the greatest of the barons might have asserted a claim, had been the last to lay down arms in the late war, and, although he gladly contributed to strengthen the government, could not be expected to guide it. The see of Canterbury was vacant. But no question arose; the delivery of the great seal of Henry III to the archbishop

No question about regency.

sworn to Henry on the day of his death to do this; Liber de Antt. Legg. p. 155.

[1] 'Magnates regni nominarunt Edwardum filium suum in regem;' Ann. Dunst. p. 254. 'Recognoverunt paternique successorem honoris ordinaverunt;' Rishanger, p. 75; Trivet, p. 283.

[2] Liber de Antt. Legg. p. 155; Foed. i. 497.

[3] Neither the queen nor the chief justice is mentioned in the records, but 'de assensu reginae matris statuerunt custodes;' Rishanger, p. 75. Edmund of Cornwall was present at the council; Foed. i. 497.

of York had placed supreme power in his hands as first lord of the council, and in his hands, assisted by Roger Mortimer a baron and Robert Burnell a royal clerk, the government remained until the king came home[1]. This arrangement, which had been made for the guardianship of the realm during Edward's absence as early as 1271, was confirmed in a great assembly of the magnates held at Hilarytide 1273[2], at which the oath of allegiance was taken not only by the prelates and barons, but by a body of representatives, four knights from each county and four citizens from each city. Walter de Merton the chancellor was directed, until the king's return, to stay at Westminster, where 'in banco' all cases were to be heard that required the action of the king's judges. This provision, which prevented the jealousies excited by the proceedings of the itinerant justices, spared the money of the country at a slight additional cost to litigants, and concentrated the judicature under the eye of the government.

It is administered by the council.

Convention of 1273.

Quiet during Edward's absence.

The regency worked economically and well. The political lethargy was unbroken. There was no man able or willing to revive the recent quarrels, and the ordinary revenue sufficed for the expenses of the government. The absence of the court gave opportunity for saving; and, although in 1273[3] under legatine pressure a tenth of ecclesiastical revenue was granted towards Edward's expenses on the Crusade, and the church was called on for a similar exaction for six years by the council of Lyons in 1274, the general resources of the country were not taxed until 1275, nor was the peace broken during the same period by more than mere local tumults.

Taxation only ecclesiastical.

Edward arrives in England, Aug. 2, 1274.

Edward returned to the West in the middle of 1273, but he was detained in France and Gascony, and did not reach

[1] See the 7th Report of the Deputy Keeper, App. ii. 259; cf. Madox, Exch. p. 678; Royal Letters, ii. 346. They are described as 'tenentes locum incliti viri domini Edwardi' in a letter dated April 28, 1272.

[2] Ann. Winton, p. 113; Ann. Wigorn. p. 462.

[3] February 15, 1273; Liber de Antt. Legg. p. 157. The grant made was one year's tenth to Edward, one to his brother Edmund; Ann. Winton, p. 113; Ann. Osney, p. 256; Cont. Fl. Wig. p. 211. The grant at the Council of Lyons was for six years; Ann. Dunst. pp. 260–264; Ann. Osney, p. 260; Ann. Wykes, p. 258.

home until August 2, 1274, when he landed at Dover. A fortnight after, on the 19th of August[1], he was crowned by[2] Robert Kilwardby, a Dominican friar, nominated by the pope in preference to Edward's minister Burnell, and the first of a series of primates who attempted to impress a new mark on the relations of church and state in England. On the 21st of September Burnell was made Chancellor. From that date, and with the able assistance of that minister, began the series of legal reforms which have gained for Edward the title of the English Justinian; a title which, if it be meant to denote the importance and permanence of his legislation and the dignity of his position in legal history, no Englishman will dispute.

And is crowned Aug. 19.

Burnell chancellor.

A comparison of the legislation of Edward I with that of Henry II brings out conclusively the fact that the permanent principles of the two were the same; that the benefits of

Edward's legislation.

[1] Ann. Winton, p. 118; Ann. Dunst. p. 263; Foed. i. 514.

[2] The oath taken on this occasion is not recorded. This is unfortunate, as that taken by Edward II was very differently worded from that of Henry III, and it would be an important point to ascertain when the change was introduced. We know from Edward's own statement at the parliament of Lincoln in 1301 that he had sworn not to alienate the rights of the crown; and there is a form of coronation oath preserved in Machlinia's edition of the Statutes, which contains this promise, although it does not occur in any of the Pontificals or other ritual books. It is as follows: 'Ceo est le serement que le roy jurra a son coronement, que il gardera et meinteynera les droites et les fraunchises de seynt esglise grauntes auncienment dez droitz roys Christiens d'Englitere et que il gardera toutz ses terres, honours et dignitees droitturelx et franks del coron du roialme d'Englitere, en tout maner d'entierte sans nul maner d'amenusement; et les droites disperges dilapides ou perdus de la corone a son pouoir reappeller en launcien estate, et que il gardera la peas de seynt esglise, et al clergie et al people be bon acorde, et que il face faire en toutz ses jugements owel et droit justice ove discrecion et misericorde et que il grauntera a tenure les leyes et custumes du royalme, et a son pouoir les face garder et affirmer, que les gentes de people averont faitz et eslies et les malvoys leyes et customez de tout oustera, et ferme peas et establie al people de son royalme en ceo garde esgardera a son pouoir; come Dieu luy ayde;' Statutes of the Realm, i. 168; Taylor, Glory of Regality, pp. 411, 412. This oath certainly has a transitional character, and may possibly be that of Edward I. The writer of the Opus Chronicorum (ed. Riley), p. 37, says of him, 'Nihil erat quod rex Edwardus IIItius pro necessitate temporis non polliceretur,' possibly referring to some novelty in the oath. The following extract from a MS. Chronicle perhaps may illustrate the point: 'Qui statim coronam deposuit, dicens quod nunquam capiti suo resideret donec terras in unum congregaret ad coronam pertinentes quas pater suus alienavit, dando comitibus et baronibus et militibus Angliæ et alienigenis.' MS. Rawlinson, B. 414; and Ann. Hagnebie.

a sound administration of the law conferred by the first were adapted by his great-grandson to the changed circumstances and amplified to suit the increasing demands of a better educated people.

Relation of Edward's legislation to that of Henry II, as to clergy;

The principle of restricting the assumptions of the clergy, which, although enunciated by the Conqueror, had in the Norman polity been neutralised by the practical independence of the church-courts and by the arbitrary action of the kings, had been made intelligible in the Constitutions of Clarendon.

feudal armies,

The institution of scutage had disarmed the feudal lords whilst it had compelled them to a full performance of their duties either in arms or in money; the assize of arms had entrusted the defence of the country to the people at large and placed arms in the hands of all.

and feudal courts.

The extension of the itinerant judicature in like manner had broken down the tyranny of the feudal franchises and brought the king's justice within the reach of all. The intervening century had seen these three points contested, now extended, now restricted, sometimes enforced and sometimes obstructed; but the course of events had amply justified the principles on which they rested.

Statutes *de religiosis*,

Edward's statute 'de religiosis' and the statute of Carlisle prove his confidence in Henry's theory, that the church of England as a national church should join in bearing the national burdens and should not risk national liberty or law by too great dependence on Rome.

and *quia emptores*.

What the statute 'de religiosis' was to the church the statute 'quia emptores' was to feudalism; but it was only one of a series of measures by which Edward attempted to eliminate the doctrine of tenure from political life.

Grand principle of Edward's policy.

Henry had humbled the feudatories, Edward did his best to bring up the whole body of landowners to the same level, and to place them in the same direct relation to the crown, partly no doubt that he might, as William the Conqueror had done at Salisbury, gather the whole force and counsel of the realm under his direct control, but chiefly that he might give to all alike their direct share and interest in the common weal.

Continuity of his policy.

Hence the policy of treating the national and the feudal force alike; the extension of compulsory knighthood from the tenants-in-chief to all landowners of sufficient means; hence the expansion of the assize of arms by the statute of Winchester. The legal reforms of the statutes of Westminster and Gloucester bear the same relation to the assizes of Clarendon and Northampton, the inquest of 1274[1] and the 'quo warranto' of 1279 to the inquest of sheriffs in 1170. Edward's legislation was no revolution, nor in its main principles even an innovation; the very links which connect it with that of Henry II are traceable through the reign of Henry III; the great mark of his reign, the completion of the parliamentary constitution by which an assembly of estates, a concentration of all national energies, was substituted for a court and council of feudal tenants, was the result of growth rather than of sudden resolution of change. But he contributed an element that marks every part of his policy, the definition of duties and spheres of duty, and the minute adaptation of means to ends.

His peculiar contribution to the result.

Edward was by instinct a lawgiver, and he lived in a legal age, the age that had seen Frederick II legislating for Sicily, Lewis IX for France, and Alfonso the Wise for Castille; the age that witnessed the greatest inroad of written law upon custom and tradition that had occurred since the date of the Capitularies; that saw the growth of great legal schools in the universities, and found in the revived Roman jurisprudence a treasury of principles, rules, and definitions applicable to systems of law which had grown up independently of the Imperial codes. Bracton had read English jurisprudence by the light of the Code and the Digest, and the results of his labour were adapted to practical use by Fleta and Britton. Edward had by his side Francesco Accursi, the son of the great Accursi of Bologna, the writer of the glosses on the Civil Law, a professional legist and diplomatist[2]; but he found

The thirteenth century an age of law-givers.

Edward's legal advisers.

[1] The articles for inquiry into the liberties and the 'status communitatis comitatuum' are in the Foedera, i. 517, dated October 11, 1274. The sheriffs were changed about the same time; Ann. Dunst. p. 263.

[2] Francesco was in attendance on Edward at Limoges, in May, 1274, Foed. i. 511, 512; and sent as a proctor to the French court, September 2, ibid. 516, 524. On December 7, 1276, the sheriff of Oxford was directed to provide him with lodgings in the king's manor-house there; Selden, on Fleta, p. 526, from Rot. Pat. 4 Edw. I. He was at the parliament of 1276,

probably in his chancellor Burnell and in judges like Hengham and Britton practical advisers to whose propositions, based on their knowledge of national custom and experience of national wants, the scientific civilian could add only technical consistency.

The first half of Edward's reign given to legislation.

The first half of Edward's reign is mainly occupied with this work. The other events that diversify the history of this period are only indirectly connected with our subject; the transactions with France only so far as they cause demands for money and stimulate political life. The conquest of Wales has a more important bearing; it marks the extension of direct royal authority over the whole of Southern Britain, and consequently the extinction of exceptional methods of administration, which had hitherto tended to diminish or to intercept the exercise of royal authority. The existence of the Welsh principalities had involved the maintenance of exceptional jurisdictions to keep them in order. Both the Welsh princes and the lords marchers, who with a sort of palatine authority held the border against them, were in name vassals of the crown, but in fact were able to oust all direct influences of the king in their respective territories. The extinction of the one involved for the other either extinction or insignificance; and left the field open for the introduction of the English system of administration. Politically the result was the same. The Welsh princes had meddled in every English struggle, had fanned the flame of every expiring quarrel, had played false to all parties, and had maintained a flickering light of liberty by helping to embarrass any government that might otherwise have been too strong for them. In the long quarrels of the Norman reigns they had had their share: now the day of account was come, and the account was exacted. The annexation of Wales contributed on the whole to increase the royal power, the personal influence of the sovereign, and the peace of the kingdom. Yet Edward, although he introduced the English shire system

Constitutional importance of the Welsh wars.

The annexation of Wales.

Statutes, i. 42; was sent to Rome in 1278, Foed. i. 562; he swore fealty to Edward at Lyndhurst, October 1, 1281, Foed. i. 598; he has his arrears of pay in 1290, Foed. i. 741. He is the Francesco mentioned by Dante in the Inferno, canto xv.

into Wales, did not completely incorporate the principality with England. It remained for more than two centuries isolated from the operation of general reforms, specially legislated for, separately administered, and unrepresented in parliament.

Parliament of Westminster, 1275. Edward's first parliament met at Westminster on the 22nd of April, 1275. It was a remarkable assembly, a great and general parliament, and is described as containing not only the prelates and barons, but 'the community of the land thereto summoned[1]:' the king legislates 'par sun conseil,' and with the common consent of the persons summoned. It is possible that knights of the shires were present, as they certainly were in the later parliament of the year. The statute of Westminster the First was the work of the session. This act is almost a code by itself; it contains fifty-one clauses, and covers the whole ground of legislation. Its language now recalls that of Canute or Alfred, now anticipates that of our own day: on the one hand common right is to be done to all, as well poor as rich, without respect of persons; on the other, elections are to be free, and no man is by force, malice, or menace, to disturb them. The spirit of the Great Charter is not less discernible: excessive amercements, abuses of wardship, irregular demands for feudal aids, are forbidden in the same words or by amending enactments. The Inquest System of Henry II, the law of wreck and the institution of coroners, measures of Richard and his ministers, come under review, as well as the Provisions of Oxford and the Statute of Marlborough[2]. This great measure was however not granted without its price. In the same parliament was made a grant of custom on wool, woolfells and leather, which marks a definite and most important step in the history of the revenue[3]. A second parliament was held on the 13th of October for the purpose of raising money.

Marginal notes: Its composition. — Statute of Westminster the First. — Its comprehensive character. — Taxation of 1275.

[1] 'Magnum parliamentum,' Ann. Winton, p. 119; 'famosum et solemne,' Ann. Wykes, p. 263; 'la communaute de la tere ileokes somons,' Stat. Westm. i. preamble.

[2] Statutes of the Realm, pp. 26–39.

[3] Parl. Writs, i. 2; Select Charters, p. 451. On the exact importance of this grant see below, § 276; and especially Hall's Custom Revenue of England, i. 3, 66; ii. 177 sq., where the whole subject is treated carefully and minutely.

Second parliament of 1275.

To this assembly knights of the shire were summoned, and the session is one of the landmarks in the history of representation [1]. In it a fifteenth of temporal moveables was bestowed for the relief of the royal necessities [2]. Measures for enforcing and regulating the collection of this tax were taken in an Easter parliament in 1276, on the occasion of a general pardon extended to all the disinherited of the late reign [3], and a recognition of the validity of the Charters [4].

Legislation of 1276.

Statute of Rageman.

The work thus begun was actively carried on: the October parliament of 1276 passed two minor acts [5], the statute 'de bigamis,' supplementary to that of Westminster, and the statute of Rageman, which ordered a visitation by the justices to determine all suits for trespass committed within the last twenty-five years. This session is marked by the attendance of Francesco Accursi, the Bolognese lawyer whom Edward had retained whilst in France, and who remained for several years in his service. The year 1277 was occupied with the Welsh war [6], on account of which a scutage of forty shillings was taken in 1279 [7]. The statute of Gloucester was the work of 1278 [8]; its object was to improve the process of provincial judicature by regulating the territorial franchises. It was based on the returns of a great commission of inquiry appointed by the king immediately after his arrival in 1274 [9], the results of which

Statute of Gloucester, 1278.

[1] See below under § 214; p. 234, note 5.

[2] 'Magnum parliamentum,' Ann. Winton, p. 119. The clergy made a promise of an aid from the spiritualities, Wykes, p. 266; see too, Ann. Waverley, p. 385; Dunst. p. 266; Cont. Fl. Wig. pp. 214, 217; Cont. Gerv. ii. 281; B. Cotton, p. 154; Ann. Osney, p. 265; Rot. Parl. i. 224.

[3] Ibid. M. Westm. Flores, iii. 47. In 1284 Martin IV issued letters of absolution for all crimes committed in the barons' war; Foed. i. 641.

[4] Ann. Waverl. p. 386; Ann. Winton, p. 120.

[5] Statutes of the Realm, i. pp. 42, 44.

[6] Llewelyn had avoided doing homage to Edward, although several times summoned. On November 12, 1276, 'Concordatum est de communi consilio praelatorum baronum et aliorum,' that the king should march against him, and the force of the kingdom was summoned to Worcester at Midsummer, 1277; Foed. i. 536 sq. July 21, Edward marched from Chester; Llewelyn submitted November 11, at Rhuddlan, and kept Christmas with the king at London; Foed. i. 545, 546. In 1278 he married Eleanor de Montfort.

[7] Ann. Wykes, p. 274; Madox, Exch. p. 449.

[8] August; Statutes, i. 45. There was another parliament at Westminster in October, at which the king of Scots did homage; Foed. i. 563; Ann. Waverley, p. 390.

[9] Above, p. 111, note 1.

were recorded in the 'Rotuli Hundredorum,' or Hundred-Rolls[1]. In pursuance of the main purpose of the act, proceedings were directed under which the itinerant justices were to inquire by what warrant the franchises reported by these commissioners were held; and a writ of 'quo warranto' was issued in each case. This proceeding was viewed with great jealousy by those barons who retained the old feudal spirit, and who were as suspicious as their forefathers had been of an attempt to limit the exercise of their local rights. The earl of Warenne in particular resented the inquiry[2]. When he was called before the justices he produced an old rusty sword and cried, 'See, my lords, here is my warrant. My ancestors came with William the bastard and conquered their lands with the sword; with the sword I will defend them against any one who wishes to usurp them. For the king did not conquer and subdue the land by himself, but our forefathers were with him as partners and helpers.' The speech was mere bravado on the part of the earl, who, although in the female line he represented the house of Warenne, was descended from an illegitimate half-brother of Henry II, but it expressed no doubt the view of the great feudatories of the preceding century; and it may have helped to call Edward's attention more closely to the abuses of the system against which the statute of 1290 was aimed. But the rigour with which the Quo Warranto writ was enforced shows that the king was already obliged to make extraordinary efforts to obtain money. In the summer of the same year, 1278, he issued a writ compelling all freeholders possessed of an estate of £20 a year[3], of whatsoever lord they held, to receive knighthood or to give such

Quo warranto inquest.

The earl of Surrey resists the *quo warranto.*

The king's expedients for raising money.

Distraint of knighthood.

[1] Ann. Waverley, p. 395 (A. D. 1280). See the introduction to the Rotuli Hundredorum published by the Record Commission, where the conclusion is thus stated: the Hundred-Rolls were the results of the inquiry of 1274; the Statute of Gloucester was based on the Hundred-Rolls, and the quo warranto visitations of the following years were carried out in accordance with the directions of the Statute of Gloucester.

[2] Hemingb. ii. 6.

[3] Parl. Writs, i. 214; Select Charters, p. 457. The writ is dated June 26, 1278, and directions for the execution were issued March 12, 1279, Foed. i. 567, when another inquiry into demesne rights was also instituted.

security as was equivalent to the price of a licence for evasion. No heavy taxation had yet been imposed, the impoverishment of the country was still unremedied, and the crown, notwithstanding its economy, was also poor. This was not a new measure, but Edward sought by it not merely to obtain money but to increase the knightly body, and to diminish the influence of the mesne tenures. Probably the great lords saw this; and John of Warenne marked by his speech an awakening of the baronage to the sense that their privileges were endangered by the new legislation. The alarm extended the next year to the clergy [1].

Alarm of the lords.

State of the Church.

Archbishop Kilwardby, whose energy had not answered the expectations of the papal court, had been summoned to Rome and made a cardinal in 1278. Nicolas III, rejecting Edward's application for Burnell, nominated in his place an Englishman of great reputation, John Peckham, a Franciscan friar and a pupil of Adam de Marisco, the friend of Grosseteste and earl Simon. Peckham signalised the first year of his primacy by a bold attempt at political independence. He held a council at Reading in August 1279 [2], in which, not satisfied with formally accepting the legatine constitutions of Ottobon, and passing some strictly spiritual articles, he directed the clergy of his province to explain to their parishioners, among other things, the sentences of excommunication issued against the impugners of Magna Carta, against those who obtained royal writs to obstruct ecclesiastical suits, and against all, whether the king's officers or not, who neglected to carry out the sentences of the ecclesiastical courts. Edward, not unnaturally, regarded this as an act of aggression. In the Michaelmas parliament he compelled the archbishop to renounce the objectionable articles [3], and to order that the copies of the Charter which had been

Archbishop Peckham.

Council at Reading, Aug. 1279.

Edward offended.

Peckham gives up the obnoxious articles.

[1] Edward went to France at the beginning of May 1279, and did homage for Ponthieu, renouncing Normandy; Cont. Fl. Wig. p. 222: he returned on the 19th of June; Foed. i. 575. The regents were the bishops of Hereford and Worcester, and the earls of Cornwall and Lincoln; Foed. i. 568.

[2] The council was summoned for the 29th of July; Wilkins, Conc. ii. 33; Ann. Wykes, p. 281; Cole's Records, pp. 362–370; Peckham's Register, ed. Martin, i. 9.

[3] Wilkins, Conc. ii. 40; Rot. Parl. i. 224.

fixed on the doors of the churches should be taken down. Not content with this, he took the opportunity of bringing forward a statute which, although it seems to have been an integral part of his policy, he had kept back until then, waiting probably for the assistance that Burnell, as archbishop, might have lent him.

Statute de Religiosis passed.

This was the famous Statute de Religiosis, which forbids the acquisition of land by the religious or others, in such wise that the land should come into mortmain[1]. The king and other lords were daily losing the services due to them, by the granting of estates to persons or institutions incapable of fulfilling the legal obligations. In future all lands so bestowed were to be forfeited to the immediate lord of the fee, or, in case of his neglect, to the next superior; the crown standing in the position of ultimate sequestrator. The principle of this statute was not new. The impoverishment of the nation by endowments, which deprived the state of its due services, had been a matter of complaint as early as the time of Bede; and in recent days it had formed one of the articles brought forward at the parliament of Oxford in 1258, and remedied by the provisions of Westminster in 1259. But the enactment of 1259, that no religious persons should be allowed to acquire land without the licence of the next lord of whom the donor held it, had not been enrolled with the rest of the provisions or re-enacted in the statute of Marlborough; it lacked, moreover, the penal clause and the inducement to the immediate lord to exact the forfeiture. The statute now enacted does not imply any hostility to the clergy, and the policy which dictated it is clearly the same as that which prompted the statute 'quia emptores' in 1290; but the archbishop's attitude had given the opportunity, and Edward was not likely to overlook it. Nor did he stop here. The spiritualities of the clergy had escaped the general taxation of 1275, partly as being burdened by papal grants, and partly in consideration of a promise to make a voluntary grant. Edward now applied for a fifteenth, the same proportion that had been

Importance of the measure.

Compared with the statute *quia emptores.*

Taxation of the clergy, in 1279 and 1280.

[1] Ann. Waverley, p. 392; Ann. Dunst. p. 282; B. Cotton, p. 158; Wykes, p. 282; M. Westm. Flores, iii. 53; Select Charters, p. 458; Statutes of the Realm, i. 51; Fleta, lib. iii. c. 5.

obtained from the lay property. After much discussion in the provincial convocations, the clergy of York granted a tenth for two years, those of Canterbury a fifteenth for three[1]: this arrangement was completed in the spring of 1280.

Peckham renews the struggle for ecclesiastical privilege.

The intrepid archbishop was not turned away from his purpose; and the king, having failed in an attempt to translate Burnell from Bath to Winchester, was even less inclined than before to bow to ecclesiastical dictation. The struggle was renewed in 1281, when in a council at Lambeth the prelates proposed to exclude the royal courts from the determination of suits on patronage, and from intervention in causes touching the chattels of the spiritualty[2]. The king interfered[3] with a peremptory prohibition, and Peckham gave way; but his conduct had no doubt suggested the definite limitation of spiritual jurisdiction which was afterwards enunciated in the writ 'circumspecte agatis.' On both sides are seen signs of an approaching contest on questions identical with those which had from time to time divided church and state since the Norman Conquest.

He has again to submit.

General uneasiness.

The Welsh war obliges Edward to raise money.

The renewal of the Welsh war in 1282[4], and the business which arose out of it, interrupted the progress of legislation for some time; and Edward's financial necessities were the most important part of the domestic business of the country. Whilst he was subduing Wales, his ministers were trying all possible plans for raising supplies. The nation might have been expected to be generous. Edward had been king for eight years,

[1] Edward applied for a grant November 15, 1279; Wilkins, Conc. ii. 41. Peckham summoned the convocation November 6, to meet January 20, 1280; ibid. p. 37; cf. Ann. Osney, p. 286; Cont. Fl. Wig. p. 224; B. Cotton, p. 160. The diocesan synod of York was summoned December 27, to meet at Pomfret on February 9. The clergy of the diocese, excepting those of the archdeaconry of Richmond, granted a tenth on that day; Wilkins, Conc. ii. 41, 42. The diocese of Carlisle did the same on the 24th of October; Ann. Lanercost, p. 105.

[2] Ann. Wykes, p. 285; M. Westm. Flores, iii. 54. The constitutions actually passed are in Wilkins, Conc. ii. 51–61, dated October 10.

[3] September 28, 1281; Foed. i. 598; Wilkins, ii. 50; Reg. Peckham, ed. Martin, i. 235 sq.

[4] The barons are summoned to meet at Worcester at Whitsuntide, April 6; Foed. i. 603. The prelates are summoned for August 2, to Rhuddlan, ibid. 607: and the knights also, p. 608; Parl. Writs, i. 222–225.

but only one general grant had been asked for, and a scutage of forty shillings taken for the war of 1277. Yet either the king or his chief adviser was reluctant to ask the parliament for money; and recourse was had to the old expedient of negotiating separately with individuals and communities instead of obtaining a national vote. In June, 1282, John Kirkby was sent by the king to obtain a subsidy from the shires and boroughs[1]. The autumn was spent in the transaction, and in October Edward wrote to thank the several communities for their courteous promises, and to ask for immediate payment[2]. But notwithstanding the compliance of the people, it had become clear that a general tax must be imposed. The king was at Rhuddlan, attended by most of the barons; he could not bring the clergy and commons to parliament in the midst of a hostile country and during the operations of war. A new expedient was therefore tried[3]: two provincial councils were called for the 20th of January, 1283, one at York for the province of York, the other at Northampton for the province of Canterbury; clergy and laity were summoned to each; the sheriffs were ordered to send all persons who possessed more than twenty librates of land, four knights to represent the community of each shire, and two representatives of each city, borough, and market town: the bishops were to bring their archdeacons, the heads of the religious orders, and the proctors of the cathedral clergy. But although called in ecclesiastical form, the two estates formed separate bodies; at Northampton the commons granted a thirtieth[4] on the condition that the barons should do the same, and that all who held more than twenty librates should also be charged; the clergy refused to make any grant[5], alleging that the parochial clergy were unrepresented: they might also plead poverty, and were already bound by the vote made in 1280,

Separate negotiations by John Kirkby, June, 1282.

Curious assemblage of estates.

Two provincial parliaments of representatives of laity and clergy.

Grant of the laity at Northampton,

[1] Parl. Writs, i. 384; Select Charters, p. 464; cf. Cont. Fl. Wig. pp. 225, 226; B. Cotton, p. 162. In October similar loans are asked from the Irish barons, Foed. i. 617; Parl. Writs, i. 386.

[2] Parl. Writs, i. 387; Select Charters, p. 464.

[3] Parl. Writs, i. 10; Select Charters, p. 465; Foed. i. 625.

[4] See Ann. Waverley, p. 399; Cont. Fl. Wig. p. 228. The writ for collection is dated Feb. 28, 1283; Select Charters, p. 469; Parl. Writs, i. 13.

[5] Ann. Dunst. p. 295; Wilkins, Conc. ii. 93.

and at York. Their reluctance delayed proceedings for nearly a year[1]. At York the commons declared themselves ready to contribute, and the king took a thirtieth; the clergy satisfied the royal commissioner with promises, which were still unfulfilled in 1286[2].

Collection of a thirtieth. The thirtieth was collected early in the year without any oppressive strictness, allowance being made for the sums collected by John Kirkby, for loans made to the king before the granting of the tax, for the services of the knights who were taking part in the war, and for those communities which, like the Cistercians, were accustomed to contribute in other ways[3].

Edward seizes the treasure of the Crusade. Possibly the relaxation was due to the fact that Llewelyn had perished in December, 1282[4], between the summoning and the meeting of the councils, or to the readier supply which Edward found in seizing the treasure accumulated at the Temple for the Crusade.

Another anomalous assembly, to witness the trial of David of Wales. The capture of David, the brother of Llewelyn, which occurred on the 22nd of June, was the occasion of another anomalous assembly, which Edward used as a parliament[5]. This unhappy man, whose conduct had been one of the causes of the war and of the destruction of the Welsh power, was a sworn liegeman of Edward, from whom he had received knighthood, and against whom, in spite of kindness and patience, he had conspired. He had been delivered up by the Welsh themselves, and the king determined that he should be tried in the presence of a full representation of the laity.

Representatives of shires and towns. The writs for this assembly were issued on the 28th of June; the sheriff of each county was to return two elected knights, and the governing bodies of

[1] Peckham, on January 21, called the full convocation at the Temple for May 9; Reg. Peck. ii. 508, 536. The king seized the money for the Crusade on March 28; and the archbishop about May 13 summoned a new convocation for October 20, to give time for the diocesan synods to declare their mind. A twentieth was granted for three years, in the convocation held in November; Ann. Dunst. p. 299. On the discussion by the clergy, and gravamina, see Ann. Dunst. p. 205; B. Cotton, p. 165; Rishanger, p. 103; Ann. Wigorn. p. 486; M. Westm. Flores, iii. 57; Cont. Fl. Wig. p. 231; Wilkins, Conc. ii. 93–95.

[2] See Foed. i. 673; Wilkins, Conc. ii. 127.

[3] Parl. Writs, i. pp. 12, 13.

[4] Cont. Fl. Wig. p. 229; B. Cotton, p. 164; Foed. i. 631.

[5] Foed. i. 630; Parl. Writs, i. 16; Select Charters, p. 467.

twenty cities and boroughs were to return two representatives for each. Eleven earls, ninety-nine barons, and nineteen other men of note, judges, councillors, and constables of castles, were summoned by special writ. The day of meeting was fixed, September 30, and the place was Shrewsbury. The clergy, as the business was a trial for a capital offence, were not summoned. At Shrewsbury accordingly David was tried, condemned and executed; his judges were a body chosen from the justices of the Curia Regis under John de Vaux [1]; the assembled baronage watched the trial as his peers, and the commons must be supposed to have given a moral weight to the proceedings. A few days later the king at Acton Burnell issued an ordinance or establishment called the Statute of Merchants, or the Statute of Acton Burnell [2], an enactment which, although it was put forth by the king and council, in an assembly which was not properly a national parliament, was accepted as a law, and has won the name of parliament for the body which accepted it. Edward doubtless availed himself of the presence of the deputies from the towns to promulgate an act which so closely concerned their interests; but, although the occasion is important as marking an epoch in the growth of the idea of representation, and as analogous to the parliament of 1265, it was not one of the precedents which were followed when the national council took its final form.

At Shrewsbury, Sept. 30, 1283.

Statute of Acton Burnell.

Not a true parliament.

The affairs of Wales furnished Edward with constant occupation during 1284. The Statutes of Wales, which he published at Rhuddlan at Midlent, were drawn up, as he states, by the advice of the nobles of the realm [3], but were not the result of parliamentary deliberation. They were intended to assimilate the administration of Wales to that of England, a principle which Edward had in vain attempted to enforce in his Welsh

Edward's employment in Wales in 1284.

[1] Cf. Ann. Waverley, p. 400, 'in curia regis tractatum est a regni potentioribus qua poena mortis plecti debuit;' Ann. Dunst. p. 294, 'per totum barnagium Angliae quatuor judicia suscepit;' Cont. Fl. Wig. p. 229, 'in ipsa domini regis curia, praesidente in judicio auctoritate regia Johanne de Wallibus;' see also B. Cotton, p. 164; 'per deputatos ad hoc justitiarios,' Rishanger, p. 104; Trivet, p. 307; Cont. Gerv. ii. 292.

[2] Statutes of the Realm, i. 53; Trivet, p. 309.

[3] Statutes of the Realm, i. 55–68.

territories before he became king [1]. They throw much light on the existing institutions of the shire in England itself, but do not further illustrate the king's policy. Another legislative act issued at the same time, the Statute of Rhuddlan, was merely a royal ordinance, like that of John, for the regulation of the exchequer of receipt, and would not require parliamentary authorisation. Its most important clause is one which forbids pleas to be holden or pleaded in the Exchequer unless they specially concern the king and his official servants [2]. This marks a stage in the division of legal business between the three courts now actively at work under distinct bodies of judges.

Statute of Rhuddlan.

Legislation of 1285.

At Christmas Edward was able to leave Wales and hold his court at Bristol [3]. Immediately on his return to London, he returned to the work of legislation. Two statutes of the first importance were passed in 1285: the statute of Westminster the second, drawn up at the midsummer parliament [4], June 28; and the statute of Winchester, dated on the 8th of October [5]. These two acts have, by the very fact of their juxtaposition, a special interest in the illustration of Edward's place in legal history. The statute of Westminster has great prospective importance: its first article, 'de donis conditionalibus,' forms one of the fundamental institutes of the medieval land law of England; the law of dower, of advowson, of appeal for felonies, is largely amended; the institution of justices of assize is remodelled, and the abuses of manorial jurisdiction repressed; the statute 'de religiosis,' the statutes of Merton and Gloucester, are amended and re-enacted. Every clause has a bearing on the growth of the later law. The whole, like the first statute

Statute of Westminster the Second.

Prospective importance of it.

[1] The attempt had been made by Henry III, in 1251 and 1252; M. Paris, v. 227, 288. Edward had tried to introduce the system of shires and hundreds in 1256; Ann. Dunst. pp. 200, 201; Ann. Theokesb. p. 138; Pearson, ii. 216.

[2] Statutes of the Realm, i. 69.

[3] He held there 'singulare non generale parliamentum,' Ann. Osney, p. 300; 'non universali seu generali, sed tanquam particulari et speciali,' Ann. Wykes, p. 300.

[4] Statutes of the Realm, i. 71–95; Ann. Waverley, 402. A scutage of 40*s*. for Wales was taken this year, for the Welsh war of 1282; Ann. Dunst. p. 317; Cont. Fl. Wig. p. 235; Madox, Exch. p. 457.

[5] Statutes, i. 96–98; B. Cotton, p. 166.

of Westminster, is a code in itself, and justifies the praises of the annalist who describes it thus: 'Certain statutes the king published, very necessary for the whole realm, by which he stirred up the ancient laws that had slumbered through the disturbance of the realm; some which had been corrupted by abuse he recalled to their due form; some which were less evident and clear of interpretation he declared; some new ones useful and honourable he added [1].'

Statute of Winchester. The statute of Winchester, on the other hand, carries us back to the earliest institutions of the race; it revives and refines the action of the hundred, hue and cry, watch and ward, the fyrd and the assize of arms. If the statute of Westminster represents the growth and defined stature of the royal jurisdiction, the statute of Winchester shows the permanence and adaptability of the ancient popular law. Both illustrate the character of the wise lawgiver, the householder bringing out of his treasure things new and old. **The crowning period of Edward's legislation.** Together they form the culminating point of Edward's legislative activity, for, although several important acts were passed in his later years, there are none which show so great constructive power or have so great political significance, unless indeed we except the statute of 1290. It is possible to trace in them also the highest point of influence obtained by the territorial magnates in Edward's legal policy.

Settlement of the ecclesiastical courts. To the year 1285 [2] must also be referred the decision of the contest which had been so long proceeding, on the jurisdiction of the ecclesiastical courts. These tribunals had been for many years attempting both by canon and in practice to extend their powers, and to base new claims on the foundation of the success which they had won by the efforts of the clergy against papal and regal tyranny in the late reign. Peckham had not been intimidated by his failure in 1281. In 1285 articles of complaint were presented to the king by the clergy of the southern province, with petitions for the regulation of the practice of prohibitions, which were issued from the king's court whenever a suit was entered in the ecclesiastical courts against one rich

[1] Ann. Osney, p. 304.
[2] Cf. Ann. Dunst. p. 318; B. Cotton, pp. 166, 197; Flores, iii. 63, 64.

enough to obtain such a prohibition[1]. After a detailed reply by the chancellor, and a rejoinder by the clergy, Edward seems to have published an ordinance restricting the spiritual jurisdiction to matrimonial and testamentary cases; shortly, however, followed by a writ, 'circumspecte agatis,' which, as defining the sphere of these courts, has received the title of a statute. This recognises their right to hold pleas on matters merely spiritual, such as offences for which penance was due, tithes, mortuaries, churches and churchyards, injuries done to clerks, perjury and defamation.

Circumspecte agatis.

The king's long visit to France, 1286–1289.

In May 1286[2] Edward went to Gascony, leaving the kingdom under the care of his cousin, Edmund of Cornwall, and taking with him the chancellor and the great seal. He returned in August 1289. For three years the annalists are content to follow his movements and to leave the domestic history blank. The administration proceeded smoothly and steadily, but the difficulties, which in both church and state had already shown themselves, gained strength; the country was gradually drained of money to be spent in foreign undertakings, and the king's servants were left without adequate supervision. In 1288, by taking a new vow of crusade, Edward obtained a grant of an ecclesiastical tenth for six years[3] from Nicolas IV. In the same year the regent had to prohibit very peremptorily the warlike preparations of the earls of Surrey, Warwick, Norfolk, and Gloucester, and in 1289 the earls of Gloucester and Hereford were at open war on their Welsh estates. Taxation, however, was not heavy; no great demand had been made since 1283[4], the harvest of 1288 had been most abundant, and, when early in 1289 the king sent a pressing appeal to the treasurer for money, he might have expected a favourable reply.

Grant of ecclesiastical tenth.

Private war.

Taxation moderate.

[1] Wilkins, Conc. ii. 115–119. The so-called Statute 'Circumspecte agatis' is not dated, and is referred by Prynne to the reign of Edward II; Statutes i. 101; Prynne, Records, iii. 336 sq. Cf. Barrington, Obs. on the Statutes, ed. 3, p. 139.

[2] Foed. i. 665.

[3] Foed. i. 714, 725, 732, 750. The grant was based on one of Honorius IV; it was the occasion of the new and stringent valuation known as the Taxation of Pope Nicolas, and was renewed in 1291; ibid. 747; see below, p. 130.

[4] There was a scutage in 1285; see above, p. 122, note 4.

The parliament met at Candlemas[1]. John Kirkby, now bishop of Ely and treasurer, laid the king's needs before the magnates: three years he had been in Gascony, he wanted a general aid. The earl of Gloucester, the same Gilbert of Clare who had fought for Edward at Evesham, and had been the first to swear fealty at his accession, who was now betrothed to the king's daughter, was the spokesman of the barons; nothing, he affirmed, should be granted until they should see the king's face in his own land. The discomfited treasurer, pressed on the one side by his master, and hampered on the other by the established understanding that taxation was the province of the parliament, determined to take a tallage from the towns and demesne lands of the crown. Before this was done, however, Edward, alarmed by the attitude of the barons, and not less perhaps by the imprudence of the minister, returned home, landing at Dover on the 12th of August[2]. **Parliament of 1289.** **The lords refuse a grant.** **Edward returns.**

The absence of the chancellor had been even more mischievous than that of his master. Edward found himself besieged with complaints against the judges. On the 13th of October he appointed a commission under Burnell[3] to hear the complaints at Westminster on the 12th of November, and to report to him at the next parliament. The result of the inquiry was the removal of the two chief justices Hengham and Weyland, Henry Bray the escheator, Adam Stratton clerk to the exchequer, and many others[4]. In the parliament at Hilarytide, 1290, Edward completed the consequent arrangements and received petitions[5]. In April he married his daughter Johanna to the earl of Gloucester[6], receiving from the bridegroom the surrender of his **Proceedings against the judges.** **Proceedings of 1290.**

[1] Ann. Wykes, p. 316.

[2] Foed. i. 711.

[3] Foed. i. 715. The Commissioners were Burnell, the earl of Lincoln, the bishop of Winchester, John S. John, William Latimer, William de Louth, and William de March.

[4] The removal of the judges is placed by the Annals of Waverley in the Michaelmas parliament, p. 408; by the Worcester annalist in the January one, p. 494; cf. Ann. Dunst. p. 356; B. Cotton, p. 171; Cont. Fl. Wig. p. 241. Stratton was tried on the 15th of January; Ann. Lond. i. 98.

[5] It was summoned for January 13, Ann. Wykes, p. 319, and sat until February 14, Cont. Fl. Wig. p. 241.

[6] The marriage was first proposed in 1283, Foed. i. 628, when the earl was divorced from his first wife; it was sanctioned by the pope in 1289; ibid. 721.

Parliaments in 1290.

estates, and restoring them with a settlement of the English estates on the earl and his heirs by Johanna. He likewise bound the earl by oath to maintain the succession of his son Edward and any other son he might have, and of his elder daughter Eleanor, before the crown could descend to Johanna[1]. Although Johanna was not the king's eldest daughter, the marriage seems to have suggested the plan of raising money on the old customary plea, and Edward determined to have parliamentary authority for the exaction, either as a justification for taking an increased rate, or as an opportunity for pleading his greater necessities.

Grant of an aid *pur fille marier*.

The January parliament had left business on hand to be completed in a second session three weeks after Easter; but the marriage festivities must have occasioned further delay, for it is not until the 29th of May that the full parliament is found sitting. On that day a grant of aid *pur fille marier* is made at forty shillings on the fee. The assembly, which is called a full parliament, contained only the bishops and barons, who are said to make the grant on their own behalf, and so far as lies in them for the community of the whole kingdom[2]. The impost fell on the tenants in chief only, and these might be fairly regarded as represented by the barons. The terms of the great charter were not infringed by the act. Nor, nearly as we are approaching the time at which the consent of the representatives of the commons became necessary for legislation, does either king or baronage show any desire for their co-operation in that department. The parliament continued to sit, employed no doubt in hearing the pleas and petitions which are found in the Rolls of Parliament[3], and on the 14th of June Edward issued writs, directing the sheriffs to return two or three elected knights for each shire, who were to appear at Westminster on or before the 15th of July[4]. We can only guess at the object of this summons; it was probably to get an additional grant of money. It

Knights of the shire summoned.

[1] Dugdale's Baronage, i. 214, 215; Foed. i. 742; Lords' Report, i. 205.
[2] Select Charters, p. 477; Rot. Parl. i. 25; Parl. Writs, i. 20; Lords' Report, i. 200.
[3] Rot. Parl. i. 15. Ralph Hengham was again in employment, ibid. p. 17.
[4] Parl. Writs, i. 21.

can hardly have been for the purpose of obtaining the assent of the commons to the statute of Westminster the Third, 'Quia emptores,' which was enacted by the king at the instance of the magnates on the 8th of July, a week before the day for which the knights were summoned[1]. The importance of this act, like the aid which preceded it, would at the moment be chiefly apparent to the baronage; although Edward must have seen that whatever influence it gave to the lords over their tenants, it gave in tenfold force to the king over the lords[2]. It directed that in all future transfers of land, the purchaser, instead of becoming the feudal dependent of the alienor, should enter into the same relations in which the alienor had stood to the next lord. In this way the king and the chief lords would not lose the services and profits of feudal incidents, a danger with which the constant repetition of the process of subinfeudation threatened them. But the operation of the statute had far wider consequences. As a part of Edward's policy it bears, as has been already noted, a close analogy to the statute *de religiosis*, which is partly rehearsed in it.

Statute *quia emptores*.

Of the business transacted in the assembly called for the 15th of July, we have no formal record; but it is shown by what follows to have been of a financial character, and comprised the grant of a fifteenth of all moveables, made by clergy and laity alike. It would appear that the king proposed this to the parliament, and also demanded a tenth of the spiritual revenue[3]. At the same time, by an act done by himself in his private council[4], he banished the Jews from England: the safe conduct granted them on their departure is dated on the 27th of July[5]. The writs for the collection of the fifteenth are dated at Clipstone on the 22nd of September[6]: the clergy met at Ely on the 2nd of October, and there granted the tenth[7]. The delay was probably caused by the business of valuation, the assessment of

July parliament.

Grant of a fifteenth of lay property.

Grant of a tenth of spiritual revenue.

[1] Select Charters, p. 478; Statutes of the Realm, i. 106.
[2] Lords' Report, i. 169.
[3] B. Cotton, p. 178; Ann. Osney, p. 326: Ann. Wigorn, p. 503.
[4] 'Per regem et secretum concilium,' Hemingb. ii. 20; M. Westm. Flores, iii. 70; P. Langtoft, ii. 126.
[5] Foed. i. 736.
[6] Parl. Writs, i. 24.
[7] Ann. Dunst. p. 362; Cont. Fl. Wig. p. 243; B. Cotton, p. 179.

the fifteenth being made on the quantity of goods in hand between August 1st and September 29th. The collection of the aid *pur fille marier* was deferred for many years. The boon in consideration of which the new grant was made is stated by the annalists to have been the banishment of the Jews, a measure which was popular owing to the abuses of usury, and which Edward favoured on economical as well as religious grounds[1]. The autumn parliament at Clipstone was merely a legal session of the king and council for the hearing of petitions. The proceedings of the year are especially interesting, as illustrating the transitional character of the period and the industry of the king.

Banishment of the Jews.

Business of 1291.

The next three years, although in some respects they are among the most interesting in our annals, afford little that bears directly on the growth of the constitution. The death of the young queen of Scots on the 2nd of October, 1290, threw the settlement of the succession into the hands of Edward. On the 3rd of June, 1291, he obtained an acknowledgment of his right as overlord of Scotland, and in this character he ordered a recognition of the claims of the two nearest in blood, Robert Bruce and John Balliol. The recognitors having reported in favour of Balliol, Edward on the 17th of November, 1292, gave sentence accordingly, and on the 26th of December received the homage of Balliol for the whole kingdom of Scotland. During this time, too, the great quarrel between the earls of Gloucester and Hereford was receiving legal examination, which ended in the mulcting and temporary imprisonment of both, in a parliament held at London in January, 1292[2]. Shortly after difficulties arose with France; a quarrel between the Cinque Ports and the Normans was followed by a war between the Gascons and the French; and the same year which saw Edward summon John Balliol to Westminster to answer the complaints of his malcontent subjects, saw Edward himself summoned to Paris as a vassal of Philip the Fair to answer for the misconduct of his own dependents. In February, 1294, he was declared

Scottish questions.

Great suit between Clare and Bohun.

Trouble of 1292.

[1] See the arguments of Grosseteste, in his letters, ed. Luard, p. 33. The whole of this subject is illustrated by the careful work of Mr. Joseph Jacobs, 'The Jews of Angevin England,' 1893.

[2] Rot. Parl. i. 70–77; Ann. Dunst. p. 370.

contumacious, his fiefs were forfeited to the French crown, and he was compelled to prepare for war, and in consequence to ask for money.

The critical period approaches.

During this busy time, only the routine work of England could receive attention. The schemes of legal reform gave way to those of territorial ambition or defence, and in the personal character of the king the weaker but more violent instincts of his family come into greater prominence than before. The death of his wife in November, 1290, may have contributed to sour him, and must have robbed him of a faithful and gentle counsellor: in 1292 he lost bishop Burnell, his most able and experienced minister; John Kirkby the financier had died in 1290. The domestic work of 1291 and 1292 seems to have been confined to the formal parliaments. In the former year petitions and pleas were heard at Ashridge in January[1], and in 1292 in the same month at London. There the great quarrel of the earls of Gloucester and Hereford was decided, and four or five short statutes were enacted 'de communi consilio,' supplementary to the earlier legislation[2]. No writs, however, have been preserved to show the constitution of the assemblies. The year 1293 had two parliaments, one after Easter, the other after Michaelmas, in the first of which a statute was passed to define the circuits of the judges[3], and in the second an edict providing for the regulation of juries[4]. Some indications may be traced in the records of increasing financial pressure, aggravated as usual by papal intervention. In March, 1291, the pope directed the king to take a tenth of ecclesiastical revenue for six years for his promised crusade[5]. In February, 1292, all freeholders possessing £40 a year in land were ordered to receive knighthood[6], and in the following January the estates of the defaulters were seized by the king's command. In 1292 the barons who held estates in Wales were persuaded to give a fifteenth, and the same was taken of the 'probi homines' and 'communitas' of

Edward loses his old ministers.

Parliaments of 1293.

Exactions.

Exigencies increasing.

[1] Rot. Parl. i. 66.
[2] Ibid. i. 70; Statutes, i. 108.
[3] Statutes, i. 112; Rot. Parl. i. 91.
[4] Statutes, i. 113.
[5] Foed. i. 747; M. Westm. Flores, iii. 83; Ann. Dunst. p. 367; Cont. Fl. Wig. p. 264; B. Cotton, p. 183; Ann. Osney, p. 331; Ann. Wigorn, p. 506.
[6] Cont. Fl. Wig. p. 266; Parl. Writs, i. 257.

Chester [1]. But, notwithstanding some symptoms of irritation, the country seems to have rested content, and to have been in no degree prepared for the threatening state of affairs which arose in 1294, and which brought on with unprecedented rapidity both the political crisis and the constitutional consummation of the period.

War with France.

180. The behaviour of Philip the Fair had made war inevitable; and although the English baronage had given, more than once, indisputable proofs that they cared little about preserving the king's Gascon inheritance, they were not disinclined to war on a reasonable pretext. In a great court or parliament held at Westminster on the 6th of June [2], war was unanimously agreed on, and money almost enthusiastically promised; John Balliol undertook to devote the whole revenue of his English estates for three years to the good cause, and, other barons being liberal in proportion, measures were taken for obtaining the aid of the Spaniards and Germans. The defence of the coast was organised on a plan which marks an important step in the growth of the English navy [3]. No time was wasted. On the 14th of June the king summoned the whole body of the knightly tenants to meet at Portsmouth on the 1st of September [4]. It is impossible to ascertain exactly the cause that led to confusion and delay; possibly it was the king's impetuosity, possibly the resistance of the clergy who were groaning under the taxation of pope Nicolas, and who, in the absence of their natural leader, acted with impolitic slowness. For the see of Canterbury had been vacant since the death of Peckham in 1292, and the pope had not yet confirmed the election of his successor. Unable to wait, Edward summoned the clergy of both provinces to meet at Westminster on the 21st of September, providing for the representation of the parochial and cathedral clergy by elected

Parliament of June, 1294.

Assembly of forces.

Assembly of the clergy, Sept. 21, 1294.

[1] Parl. Writs, i. 390, 391.

[2] B. Cotton, p. 233; M. Westm. Flores, iii. 274. Rishanger however (p. 151) states that the king seized the Balliol fiefs because John quitted the parliament without leave.

[3] B. Cotton, pp. 234, 236; Trivet, pp. 331, 332; and see the next chapter.

[4] Foed. i. 801, 803; Parl. Writs, i. 259–261.

proctors [1]. But his measures had already alarmed them. Even before the June parliament he had seized all the wool, wool-fells and leather of the merchants, releasing it only on the payment of five marks on the sack of approved wool, three on inferior wool, and five on the last of hides [2]: this impost, by some undescribed process, received the legal consent of the owners of wool, and was prolonged to the end of the war [3]. On the 4th of July he had seized and enrolled all the coined money and treasure in the sacristies of the monasteries and cathedrals [4]. The assembled clergy were no doubt prepared for a heavy demand, when the king appeared in person, and, after apologising for his recent violence on the plea of necessity, asked for aid. A day's adjournment was granted. On the third day they offered two tenths for one year. Edward's patience was already exhausted; indignant at their shortsightedness, he let them know that they must pay half their entire revenue or be outlawed [5]. The clergy were dismayed and terrified; the dean of S. Paul's died of fright in the king's presence. In great alarm they proposed conditions;—if the statute *de religiosis* were repealed they would make the sacrifice [6]. The king replied that the statute was made by the advice of the magnates and could not be repealed without it. Other small demands he readily granted, and they were obliged to submit to the exorbitant requisition [7]. The expedition had already been delayed until the 30th of September [8]: the condition of

Seizure of wool and treasure.

Edward demands half the ecclesiastical revenue.

Further delay.

[1] August 19; Parl. Writs, i. 25, 26; Ann. Lanercost, p. 157; Flores, iii. 275; B. Cotton, p. 247.

[2] Hemingb. ii. 55; Ann. Wigorn, p. 516. The order for release was given July 26; B. Cotton, p. 247.

[3] Edward distinctly asserts that the impost on the wool was regularly granted; see Carte, Hist. Engl. ii. p. 236, where the record, Rot. Fin. 22 Edw. I. m. 1, is quoted. Cf. B. Cotton, p. 246, and § 276 below. Probably it was done in an assembly of the merchants, such as we shall find later on becoming more and more common.

[4] Cont. Fl. Wig. p. 271; Hemingb. ii. 53; Flores, iii. 274.

[5] 'Medietatem omnium bonorum suorum tam temporalium quam spiritualium;' B. Cotton, p. 248; Cont. Fl. Wig. p. 273; Hemingb. ii. 57; Ann. Wigorn. p. 517.

[6] Hemingb. ii. 57.

[7] The writ for collection is dated September 30; B. Cotton, p. 249.

[8] Foed. i. 808.

Wales now stopped it for the year. Edward improved the time by calling a parliament and asking for supplies.

Great parliament of 1294.

To this parliament were summoned not only the magnates but the knights of the shires. The writs were issued on the 8th of October, the meeting was to be at Westminster on the 12th of November[1]; each sheriff was to return two knights, and by a second writ issued on the 9th of October, two more. From the cities and boroughs no representatives were called. The laity showed themselves more tractable than the clergy, and fared better; they had had their warning. They granted the king a tenth of all moveables, but in the exaction allowance is made for the goods of the clergy who had promised a half[2]. At the same time a sixth was collected from the cities and boroughs by separate negotiation conducted by the king's officers: the Londoners made a separate offering through Walter Langton, the keeper of the wardrobe; other towns may have done the same. The events of the year, although they show unconstitutional violence on the king's part, and somewhat of panic on the part of the nation, mark the acquisition by the clergy and the counties of the right of representation in their proper assemblies, and an acknowledgment of the need of their consent to taxation, two steps which were never revoked.

Knights of the shire.

Grant of a tenth,

and sixth.

Period of county representation.

Increasing difficulties with Wales, Scotland, and France.

The Welsh rebellion was followed by other difficulties. John Balliol found himself obliged to choose between leading the national revolt and sinking into a powerless dependent of England; the Scots were looking to France for help. War began with Scotland before the Welsh were subdued. Instead of invading France, Edward saw his own shores devastated by a French fleet, and his hopes of revenge indefinitely postponed. His difficulties, however, whilst they tried his patience to the utmost, called out his great qualities as a general and a ruler.

The third Welsh war occupied the king until May, 1295.

[1] Foed. i. 811; Parl. Writs, i. 26.

[2] Parl. Writs, i. 391. The laity of the baronage and of the shires granted a tenth, the towns paid a sixth, and the merchants a seventh; cf. M. Westm. iii. 275; P. Langtoft, ii. 213; B. Cotton, p. 254; Cont. Fl. Wig. p. 275; Rishanger, p. 143; Hemingb. ii. 57. The writ for the collection of the sixth is given by Brady, Boroughs, pp. 31, 32.

Great council of 1295, Aug. 15.

After the capture of Madoc he returned to London, where two papal legates had arrived in hopes of negotiating peace with France. On the 24th of June [1] he summoned a great council to be held at Westminster on the 1st of August, and to comprise the archbishops, bishops, abbots, priors, heads of orders, earls, barons, judges, deans sworn of the council, and other clerks of the council, but no representatives of the commons or inferior clergy. This assembly met and dispatched the judicial business on the 15th of August; the question of peace was likewise discussed, and the legates departed with powers to conclude a truce [2]. The magnates probably considered also the question of supplies, and determined to make a great effort before winter.

Summons for a great and model parliament.

For this purpose Edward took the last formal step which established the representation of the commons. On the 30th of September and on the 1st of October he issued writs [3] for a parliament to meet on the 13th of November at Westminster. The form of summons addressed to the prelates is very remarkable, and may almost be regarded as a prophetic inauguration of the representative system. It begins with that quotation from the Code of Justinian which has been already mentioned, and which was transmuted by Edward from a mere legal maxim into a great political and constitutional principle [4]: 'As the most righteous law, established by the provident circumspection of the sacred princes, exhorts and ordains that that which touches all shall be approved by all, it is very evident that common dangers must be met by measures concerted in com-

Form of the writs.

[1] Foed. i. 822; Parl. Writs, i. 28; B. Cotton, p. 294.

[2] The Rolls of Parliament give the petitions, vol. i. 132–142. The king's authorisation of the action of the legates is dated August 14; Foed. i. 825.

[3] Parl. Writs, i. 30, 31; Select Charters, p. 485; B. Cotton, p. 297; Foed. i. 828.

[4] The maxim occurs in the fifth book of the Code, title 56, law 5: 'ut quod omnes similiter tangit ab omnibus approbetur.' It is found also in the Canon Law, but in a portion unpublished at this time, the Sexta Pars Decretalis, containing the Extravagants of Boniface VIII, *de Regulis juris*, c. 30. That it was, however, familiarly known in England, is shown by the reference made to it by Matthew Paris, v. 225, in the year 1251: 'quod enim omnes angit et tangit ab omnibus habet trutinari.' See also the constitution scheme of 1244, above, p. 64; and the life of Edward II by the monk of Malmesbury (Chronicles of Edw. I and II; ii. 170), ed. Hearne, p. 111.

mon:' the whole nation, not merely Gascony, is threatened: the realm has already been invaded; the English tongue, if Philip's power is equal to his malice, will be destroyed from the earth: your interests, like those of your fellow citizens, are at stake. The writs to the barons and sheriffs are shorter but in the same key. The assembly constituted by them is to be a perfect council of estates; the archbishops and bishops are to bring the heads of their chapters, their archdeacons, one proctor for the clergy of each cathedral, and two for the clergy of each diocese. Every sheriff is to cause two knights of each shire, two citizens of each city, and two burghers of each borough, to be elected and returned. Seven earls and forty-one barons have special summons. The purpose of the gathering and the time of notice are definitely expressed, as the great charter prescribed. The share of each estate in the forthcoming deliberation is marked out; the clergy and the baronage are summoned to treat, ordain, and execute measures of defence; and the representatives of the commons are to bring full power from their several constituencies to execute, 'ad faciendum,' what shall be ordained by common counsel. This was to be a model assembly, bearing in its constitution evidence of the principle by which the summons was dictated, and serving as a pattern for all future assemblies of the nation.

Representation of clergy,

and commons.

Meeting of the parliament, Nov. 27, 1295.

It met, after a postponement, on the 27th of November[1]; and the estates, having heard the king's request for an aid, discussed the amount separately. The barons and knights of the shires offered an eleventh, the borough members a seventh. The archbishop of Canterbury offered a tenth of ecclesiastical goods for two years. The last offer did not satisfy the king; he demanded a third, or at least a fourth. The clergy held out, and the king on the 9th of December eventually accepted the tenth.

Different contributions of the estates.

Further delay.

But now the renewal of the Scottish war prevented the king's departure, and wasted the funds thus collected. Edmund of

[1] The writ of postponement is dated November 2; Parl. Writs, i. 32, 33; Foed. i. 831; B. Cotton, p. 298. The account of the business done is given in the Flores, iii. 282, sq.; B. Cotton, p. 299; Cont. Fl. Wig. p. 278; Ann. Wigorn. p. 524; Parl. Writs, i. 45.

Lancaster, instead of his brother, took the command in Gascony, and Edward spent the spring and summer of 1296 in the conquest of Scotland. During these events a new element was introduced into the already complicated relations of the king and kingdom. Boniface VIII published on the 24th of February, 1296, the famous bull 'Clericis laicos[1],' by which he forbade the clergy to pay, and the secular powers to exact, under penalty of excommunication, contributions or taxes, tenths, twentieths, hundredths, or the like, from the revenues or the goods of the churches or their ministers. The pope was at this very time busily negotiating for peace, and it is not to be supposed that he intended wittingly to add to the embarrassments of Edward in particular. It was a general enactment, intended to stay the oppression of the clergy, and to check the wars which were largely waged at their cost. Although the bull was clothed in the imperious language which had special charms for the enthusiastic temper of Boniface, it did not at first arouse the king's suspicions. At any rate he availed himself of the international diplomacy of the pope to gain time and to draw together the strings of the alliance, by which, as soon as Scotland was quiet, he hoped to overwhelm Philip.

The bull *clericis laicos.*

The parliament of 1296 was summoned by writs, dated at Berwick on the 26th of August: it was to meet at Bury S. Edmund's on the 3rd of November[2]. Its constitution was exactly the same as that of the preceding year, and its proceedings took the same form. The barons and knights who in 1295 granted an eleventh now granted a twelfth; the burghers who had then given a seventh now gave an eighth. The clergy had been reminded by the king in the writ of summons that his acceptance of a tenth in 1295 was accompanied by a promise on their part that further aid should be given on the next demand, until peace should be made. Archbishop Winchelsey, however, instead of announcing the willingness of the clergy to con-

Parliament of Bury S. Edmund's, Nov. 3, 1296.

[1] Foed. i. 836. It was published formally by Winchelsey, January 5, 1297; Wilkins, Conc. ii. 222.

[2] Parl. Writs, i. 47–51; B. Cotton, p. 312; Hemingb. ii. 116; Ann. Wigorn. p. 528; Trivet, p. 352; Flores, iii. 288; P. Langtoft, ii. 269.

The clergy are unable to grant money.

tribute, alleged to the king that it was impossible for them, in defiance of the papal prohibition, to make any grant at all[1]. Edward now awoke to the importance of the crisis. Without waiting for the clerical grant, he issued hasty orders for the collection of the lay contribution[2], and directed the archbishop to return his final answer on the 13th of January, 1297.

Convocation, Jan. 13, 1297.

Winchelsey immediately called together an ecclesiastical assembly or convocation of his province for Hilarytide[3]; but the papal prohibition was too distinct to be evaded; the council after deliberating returned the same answer as before, and the king replied by putting the clergy out of the royal protection. The threat produced an immediate effect. Although the collective convocation could not yield, individual members prepared to make separate terms for themselves, and the king accepted offers of a fifth. After seven days' discussion the bishops of Hereford and Norwich were sent to treat with the king[4], but without result. On the 30th of January the king outlawed the clergy[5]; on the 10th of February the archbishop replied by excommunicating the enemies of that body[6]. The clergy of the northern province who had yielded obtained letters of protection on the 6th of February[7]; but on the 12th the lay fees of the clergy of the province of Canterbury were taken into the king's hands, the archbishop protesting and ordering the excommunication of aggressors[8].

Futile negotiations.

Seizure of Church property.

Assembly of the baronage at Salisbury, Feb. 24, 1297.

On the 24th of February[9] the king met the barons, whom he had called together at Salisbury, without the clergy or commons. He was in no patient frame, and the ecclesiastical opposition

[1] Ann. Dunst. p. 405; B. Cotton, p. 315; P. Langtoft, ii. 271.

[2] December 16; Parl. Writs, i. 51.

[3] Wilkins, Conc. ii. 219; Wake, State of the Church, App. p. 23; B. Cotton, p. 317; Hemingb. ii. 116; Ann. Wigorn. p. 528; Flores, iii. 99, 100 sq.; P. Langtoft, ii. 273.

[4] On the 20th of January; Wilkins, Conc. ii. 220.

[5] B. Cotton, p. 318.

[6] Ibid. p. 321.

[7] Lords' Report, i. 219. Commissions for taking recognisances of the clergy who were willing to submit were issued March 1; Parl. Writs, i. 393. The archbishop was deprived of his property for twenty-one weeks and five days; Chron. Cant. Ang. Sac. i. 51.

[8] Ann. Wigorn. p. 530.

[9] B. Cotton, p. 320; Hemingb. ii. 121; Flores, iii. 100. The writs were issued on the 26th of January; Parl. Writs, i. 51.

which chafed him had encouraged the instinct of insubordination in the great vassals. They saw that they had been brought together apart from their fellow counsellors, and determined to make no dangerous concessions. Six earls and eighty-nine barons and knights had been invited, and most of them attended. Among the earls the marshall Roger Bigod of Norfolk and the constable Humfrey Bohun of Hereford now occupied the first place. Gilbert of Gloucester had died in 1295; Edmund of Lancaster in 1296. The earldoms of Leicester and Lancaster, with the lands of the earls of Derby, were held by the king's nephew, a minor; Chester was in the king's own hand, Cornwall in that of his cousin Edmund; Richmond in that of his brother-in-law; Pembroke was held by Aymer of Valence, another cousin. The earldoms of the Norman reigns were almost entirely concentrated in the royal family. Bohun and Bigod represented the second rank of the Conquest baronage, and each now held with his earldom a great office of state. Bigod inherited the traditions of the baronial party; his father Hugh had been justiciar under the Provisions of Oxford, and in the female line he represented the Marshalls. Bohun's father had taken part in the same great constitutional struggle, and had fought on the side of earl Simon at Evesham. Neither of the two was a man of much ability or policy, nor, except in pride and high spirit, distinguished above the rest of the baronage. But both had heard of the old quarrel about foreign service, both shared the hatred of the alien, and were averse to spending English blood and treasure in the recovery of Gascony. It is one of the curious coincidences of this important period that Edward himself, when staying at Acre in May, 1271, had been consulted by king Hugh of Cyprus on the parallel question, what feudal service the knights of Cyprus owed within the kingdom of Jerusalem. He heard the evidence, but his decision was not recorded[1].

Heads of the baronage.

Bohun and Bigod.

[1] John of Ibelin has laid down the rule: 'Three things are they bound to do outside the realm for their lord; 1. For the marriage of him or any of his children; 2. To guard and defend his faith and honour; 3. "Por le bosoing de sa seignorie ou le commun profit de sa terre";' Assises de Jerusalem, i. 347, ii. 427.

Refusal of the earls to go abroad.

When Edward proposed to the barons singly that they should go to Gascony whilst he took the command in Flanders, he was met by a series of excuses, and to these he replied with threats. The Marshall and the Constable alleged no general principle of law or policy: they might have complained that the king had strained his rights in every possible way, in assembling the national force for service to which they were not bound, and raising money by expedients which were unprecedented and unparalleled. Instead of doing this they pleaded that their tenure obliged them to go with the king; if he went to Gascony they would go with him; to Flanders they were under no obligation to go at all. From threats Edward turned to prayers: he felt that the battle of English freedom must be fought in France; surely the earl Marshall would go; Bohun might feel a grudge for his late imprisonment and fine. 'With you, O king,' Bigod answered, 'I will gladly go: as belongs to me by hereditary right, I will go in the front of the host before your face.' 'But, without me,' Edward urged, 'you will go with the rest.' 'Without you, O king,' was the answer, 'I am not bound to go, and go I will not.' Edward lost his temper: 'By God, earl, you shall either go or hang.' 'By God,' said Roger, 'O king, I will neither go nor hang[1].' The council broke up in dismay.

Personal altercation.

Preparations for civil war.

More than thirty of the great vassals joined the two earls, and they immediately assembled a force of fifteen hundred well-armed cavalry. They did not, however, take an aggressive attitude, but contented themselves with preventing the king's officers from collecting money or seizing the wool and other commodities on their lands.

Edward's provocations.

Some allowance must be made for Edward's irritation. He must have felt that the self-restraint and moderation which he had hitherto practised had been sadly unappreciated. He must have been provoked at the conduct of men who thus from sheer wilfulness imperilled the peace of the nation which he had so diligently cultivated, and at the same time were frustrating the great design which was to repay him for the pains he had taken to increase the national strength. The people had not

[1] Hemingb. ii. 121.

been heavily taxed, and the clergy had passed, compared with their fate in the late reign, scot-free. The improved administration of justice, the amendments of law, the consolidation of governmental machinery, had increased security, and with security had increased the resources of all. And yet when he wished to reap the fruit of his labour, to strike a blow at the ancient foe, to recover the last fragment of the ancient inheritance, he was met by a refusal, justified by an antiquated quibble. Although he was himself inclined to even captious legality, he was scarcely likely to allow the validity of such a plea as that of Bigod. The provocation and the exigency of the occasion were too much for him. His engagements with his allies, costly engagements as they were, were not to be broken because of the obstinacy of his vassals. He had recourse to a proceeding which, except on the plea of necessity, was unjustifiable, and which fortunately, whilst it was an exception to all his other dealings with his people, led to a determination of the crisis which deprived the crown for ever of the power of repeating it.

Edward tries to assume a dictatorship.

The first measure was an edict that all the wool and wool-fells of the country should be carried to the seaports under penalty of forfeiture and imprisonment. The staple commodity was then weighed and valued, all merchants who had more than five sacks received tallies as security for payment, those who had less paid a maletote of forty shillings on the sack and were allowed to retain it. No legislative authorisation was pleaded, as had been done in 1294, for this exaction, which served to give a standing ground and a gravamen to a body of men whom Edward had been most anxious to propitiate. At the same time each county was ordered to furnish 2000 quarters of wheat, as many of oats, and a supply of beef and pork [1]. This was done on S. George's day, April 23.

Seizure of wool, and demands of other supplies.

The clergy were still undecided. The king was persuaded by

[1] Hemingb. ii. 119; Flores, iii. 101; Rishanger, p. 169; Trivet, p. 354. The demand for supplies of corn had been made in November, probably with full authority; it was to be paid for at market price. See Madox, Hist. Exch. p. 260, and Hall, Customs Revenue, ii. 170, where some important illustrations of the subject, from the Exchequer Records, will be found, pp. 175 sq.

Continuation of the ecclesiastical difficulty.

the archbishop on the 7th of March to suspend the execution of the edicts against them; but the new council summoned for the 26th of March[1] was warned by a royal writ not to attempt anything dangerous to the king's authority, and broke up without coming to a formal vote. Winchelsey felt that he had no right to involve in the penalties which he had himself incurred men who, without doing violence to their consciences, saw their way to evade the papal mandate. He recommended the clergy to act each on his own responsibility, or in other words to make a separate bargain with the commissioners whom the king had appointed for the purpose. The difficulty was not solved, but the momentary emergency was provided for.

A military levy of the whole force of the kingdom called for July 7.

But although funds were thus furnished, Edward did not intend either to carry on the war with mercenaries, or to leave the contumacious lords to trouble the kingdom in his absence, much less to defy him with impunity. On the 15th of May he issued writs for a military levy of the whole kingdom, to meet at London on the 7th of July[2]; this levy was to include all who held lands of the annual value of £20, of whomsoever they held. Bishops, barons and sheriffs were directed to bring up their forces prepared with arms and horses to cross the sea under the king's command. Wales was to furnish infantry raised by the new plan of commissions of array. The king stationed himself at Portsmouth to complete the preparations. Such a design of employing the whole force of the country, irrespective of tenure, in anything but a defensive war in England itself, although it might be justified perhaps by early precedent in the Norman reigns, seems scarcely more constitutional than the seizure of wool, or the levying of taxes without a grant[3].

Great gathering at S. Paul's.

On the 7th of July the barons who had brought up their forces met at S. Paul's. The Marshall and the Constable were called on to discharge their official functions and draw up the lists of

[1] Wilkins, Conc. ii. 224; B. Cotton, p. 323; Flores, iii. 100, 101; Ann. Wigorn, p. 531.

[2] Parl. Writs, i. 281; Foed. i. 865.

[3] Lords' Report, i. 220. Edward allowed finally that the vassals were not bound to serve in Flanders except for wages; B. Cotton, p. 327; p. 150 below, note 1.

the men intended for the war. They had been concerting their measures in a little parliament of their own in Wyre forest, and refused to obey: they attended, they said, not by virtue of summons, but at the king's special prayer; they begged him to employ some other officer for the purpose. Whether this plea was suggested by any informality in the writ, or by their conviction of the illegality of the demand of service, is not clear. Edward had, by the use of the words 'affectuose requirimus et rogamus'[1] to the barons, based his claim on moral rather than on legal grounds, and on this they took their stand. He indignantly superseded them in their offices and determined to appeal to the people at large against them. They meanwhile prepared their list of grievances.

The lords plead the wording of the writ, in objection.

Edward's first measure was to reconcile himself with the archbishop. This he did with great ceremony on the 14th of July[2]. On a stage erected before Westminster Hall, he presented himself with his son Edward and the earl of Warwick, and addressed the people in an affecting speech. He had not, he allowed, governed them so well or so peaceably as became a king, but they must remember that such portions of their property as they had given him, or his servants without his knowledge had extorted from them, had been spent in securing the nation from enemies thirsting for their destruction. 'And now,' he added, 'I am going to put myself in jeopardy for you; I pray you, if I return, receive me as you have me now, and I will restore all that I have taken. If I return not, crown my son as your king.' Winchelsey with tears replied that he would be faithful: the people lifted up their hands and promised fealty. Unfortunately the demonstration did not affect the baronage in the same way. From prayers and tears Edward turned in a most business-like way to ask for money. Winchelsey undertook to call the clergy again together; the barons, although

The king makes peace with the archbishop, July 14.

New demands for money.

[1] Foed. i. 865. The words used to the sheriffs are 'praecipimus in fide qua nobis tenemini;' to the prelates 'mandamus . . . sicut nostri et vestri et totius regni nostri honorem et salvationem diligitis;' to the earls and barons, 'affectuose requirimus et rogamus.'

[2] M. Westminster, Flores, iii. 295; Birchington, Ang. Sac. i. 16. Winchelsey had restitution of his property on the 19th of July; Chron. Cant. Ang. Sac. i. 51.

their leaders had gone, urged that it was not for the good of the country that the king should go to Flanders, especially when the Scots and Welsh were planning rebellion; the country was moreover sadly impoverished, the custom of taking tallages ought to be abandoned, and the charters, which Edward had, perhaps, never yet expressly confirmed, should be reissued, confirmed, and observed. After some consideration Edward proposed to confirm the charters if an aid of an eighth were granted by the barons and knights, and a fifth by the towns[1]: under the circumstances the clergy would no doubt see their way to make a grant. The archbishop agreed to consult the clergy about obtaining papal permission to pay, and summoned his convocation for the 10th of August[2]. In the meanwhile he was to negotiate with the two earls and, if possible, to bring them to submission.

Proposal to renew the Charters.

Edward persuades the chief men at the court to grant money.

But the rest were amenable to more speedy treatment. Edward brought together in his own chamber the most important men who had attended the military levy, and although they had not been summoned to a parliament, nor possessed the credentials of representatives, he chose to regard them as qualified to make a grant on the instant. They agreed, for the leading men had left the court[3]; and an aid of an eighth from the barons and knights, a fifth from the towns, was declared to be granted. The king, still unwilling to act without the co-operation of the earls, spent several days in fruitless negotiation. On the 19th of July the archbishop proposed to meet the earls at Waltham, Barking, or Stratford; they chose the first, and on the 23rd Winchelsey fixed the 27th as the day of meeting. On that day Robert Fitz Roger and John Segrave appeared for their masters and with the archbishop visited the king at S. Alban's on the 28th. The earls, however, although furnished with safe-conducts, neither presented themselves nor sent excuses[4]. Unable to wait longer,

Obstinacy of the earls.

[1] M. Westm. Flores, iii. 295, 296.

[2] B. Cotton, p. 327; Parl. Writs, i. 53; Wilkins, Conc. ii. 226. The archbishop's writ was issued on the 16th of July, clearly in consequence of his reconciliation.

[3] Ann. Dunst. p. 407; M. Westm. Flores, iii. 102, 296.

[4] Foed. i. 872, 873; Wilkins, Conc. ii. 227.

Edward on the 30th of July issued letters for the collection of the eighth and fifth, and for the seizure of 8000 sacks of wool to be paid for by tallies[1]. On the 31st[2] he received the clergy into his protection, and then went down to Winchelsea to prepare for embarkation. On the 7th of August[3] he wrote to the archbishop desiring prayers for the success of the expedition, and on the 12th he published in letters patent an appeal to the people against the earls.

Edward prepares to embark.

This document, which we have in a French version only, is a curious proof of the importance which Edward attached to the support of the people, and furnishes a fine illustration of the influence which was thus formally recognised by so high-spirited a king. After recapitulating the circumstances of the quarrel and the attempts at reconciliation, he says that he has heard that a formal list of grievances has been drawn up by the earls, and that there is a report that he had refused to receive it when it was presented to him. This is not true, no such list has been offered him. If, as he supposes, such list contains references to the many pecuniary aids that he has been obliged to ask for, he has felt the grievance as much as any; but the people must remember that he spent the money not in buying territory but in defending himself and them[4]. If he return, he will gladly amend all; if not, his heirs shall do so. But in the interest of all the war must be fought out; he must keep his engagements; the lords have on condition of a confirmation of the charters granted an aid; he prays that nothing will hinder the nation from doing their best to help him, that they will not believe that he has refused redress, and that they will keep the peace, as indeed they must under pain of excommunication.

His manifesto of excuse, addressed to the nation at large.

The result of this appeal seems to have been that the list of grievances was at last formally presented, but whether the document which the chroniclers have preserved was really, as it purports to be, a list regularly drawn up by the whole of the estates, must ever remain uncertain. It is hard to see how any

The bill of grievances, drawn up by the magnates, is presented to the king.

[1] B. Cotton, p. 338; Parl. Writs, i. 53–55, 395, 396; Rot. Parl. i. 239.
[2] Rot. Cl. 25 Edw. I; Brady, Hist. iii. App. p. 20.
[3] Foed. i. 872.
[4] B. Cotton, p. 330; Foed. i. 872, 873.

Articles of grievance.

assembly could have been held at which such a list could be framed, or that the clergy and commons could have joined in it without conspiring to deceive the king. It is more probable that the heading of the list, which declares their co-operation, was a mere form, analogous to the preamble of a modern bill which contains the enacting words before it becomes a statute[1]. 'These are the grievances which the archbishops, bishops, abbots, priors, earls, barons, and the whole community of the land, show to our lord the king, and humbly pray him to correct and amend, to his own honour and the saving of his people.' The first grievance is the insufficiency of the summons for the 7th of July; it did not state the place to which the king proposed to go, or enable the persons summoned to adapt their preparations to the length of the journey; if, as was reported, the king wished to go to Flanders, the remonstrants were of opinion that they were not bound to serve in that country, there being no precedent for such service; but, supposing that they were so bound, they had been so much oppressed with tallages, aids, and prises, that they had no means of equipment. In the second place they state that the same oppressions had left them too poor to grant an aid. Thirdly, the Great Charter is not kept; and fourthly, the assize and charter of the Forest are a dead letter. Fifthly, the late exaction on the wool is out of all proportion. Lastly, the nation does not think it expedient that the king should go to Flanders. Edward replied that he could not at the moment return a precise answer; of his council part was in London, part had already sailed[2]. He was himself prepared to follow, but seems to have waited for the report from the clergy.

Grievance about the summons.

Plea of poverty.

Demand of charters.

Exaction on wool.

Opposition to the king's expedition.

Report from convocation.

The convocation on the 10th of August reported that they had good hopes of obtaining the pope's leave to grant an aid[3].

[1] In French in Hemingb. ii. 124, and B. Cotton, p. 325; in Latin in Trivet, p. 360; Rishanger, p. 175. It might be inferred from B. Cotton that this list was drawn up on the 30th of June, the Sunday before the meeting at London; but if this were so, it is impossible to account for Edward's ignorance of the fact; and it is more likely that the annalist has mistaken the date of the council.

[2] Rishanger, p. 175.

[3] The details of this somewhat important negotiation may be made out. On the 10th of August the archbishop put four questions to the clergy:

Boniface had in fact on the 28th of February issued an explanatory bull, at the instance of Philip the Fair[1], exempting from the prohibition all voluntary gifts of money and all taxes necessary for national defence. Edward and the bishops may not have known this, and the king was certainly unwilling to allow further delay. Provoked by their firmness or suspecting them of collusion with the earls, he issued on the 20th of August letters for the collection of a third of the temporalities of the clergy; their lay fees were to be taxed with those of the laity; their spiritualities, tithes and oblations, were not to be taxed, but any clergyman might compound for the whole by the payment of a fifth of his income[2]. The day before he had written to the archbishop to forbid the excommunication of the officers who were seizing corn and other supplies[3], and perhaps the peremptory character of the writ of collection may have been caused by the report that such excommunication was impending. His last act before his departure was to summon a number of barons and knights who were staying at home, to meet his son Edward at Rochester on the 8th of September[4]. Two days afterwards, on the 22nd of August, he embarked for Flanders, and on the 23rd he set sail[5].

Modification of the bull.

Edward taxes the clergy, Aug. 20.

He embarks, Aug 22.

'Utrum liceat nobis regi contribuere, secundo de contributionis quantitate, tertio quid petendum de libertate, quarto de regis magna necessitate.' They answer that they cannot contribute without the pope's leave, however great the king's need may be; Ann. Wigorn. p. 533. This is signified to the king, with an expressed hope that the pope's leave may be asked for and obtained (Wilkins, Conc. ii. 226), in three articles: 1. The clergy could not give because of the papal prohibition; 2. They would, if the king pleased, apply to the pope for leave; 3. The king must not be offended if they excommunicate the usurpers of ecclesiastical property in obedience to the bull. Edward replied to each article: 1. If they could not give he must take, but would do it with moderation; 2. He refused his consent to the application proposed; 3. He prohibited the excommunications; B. Cotton, pp. 327, 335.

[1] See Ann. Wigorn. pp. 531, 535; Raynald. Annals, iv. 235. The explanatory letter to the clergy is dated February 28, 1297. A letter to Philip to the same effect is printed in the Proofs of the Liberties of the French Church, with the date July 22 (ed. 1639, pp. 1089, 1090); Prynne, Records, iii. 725, 726.

[2] Parl. Writs, i. 396.

[3] August 19; Foed. i. 875. Notwithstanding this the sentences were published on the 1st of September; B. Cotton, p. 335.

[4] Parl. Writs, i. 296–298.

[5] The king was on board on Aug. 22, on which day the chancellor gave

Bohun and Bigod forbid the collection of the aid.

The Marshall and Constable, once assured of the king's departure, lost no time. On the very day of embarkation, Thursday the 22nd of August[1], they appeared in the Exchequer, protested against the prise of wool, and forbade the barons to proceed with the collection of the aid until the charters had been formally confirmed. The citizens of London joined them, and they were able to bring up a military force which gave to the whole proceeding the appearance of a civil war. This was instantly reported to the king who, before he set sail from Winchelsea, found time to write to the ministers of the Exchequer: the collection of the eighth was to be proceeded with, but a proclamation was to be made that the levy of the tax was not to be turned into a precedent; the wool was still to be taken, but only by way of purchase. The following day, by letters dated at sea, off Dover, he instructed the young prince, who was left as regent, and the council to the same effect. The proclamation was accordingly issued on the 28th[2]. But it was now evident that nothing but the confirmation and amplification of the charters would insure peace. Before the 8th of September, the day fixed for the meeting at Rochester, the necessity of calling a full council was apparent. On the 5th the bishop of London and most of the lords of the royal party were summoned for the 30th; on the 9th the archbishop and the two earls; and on the 15th writs were issued to the sheriffs for the election of knights of the shire[3]. The latter were to attend on the 6th of October to receive their copies of the charter; the representatives of the inferior clergy and of the towns were not summoned; and these two points take from the assembly the character of a full and perfect parliament like that of 1295.

Summons to council.

Summons of knights.

up to him the great seal; Foed. i. 876. Rishanger (p. 177) makes him embark on the 21st. The Annals of Worcester (p. 133) make him sail on the 23rd, as also does M. Westminster, p. 430.

[1] M. Westminster, Flores, iii. 103, 296; Parl. Writs, i. 32, note; Carte, ii. 271; quoting Maynard, Year Book, Mem. in Scacc. 25 Edw. I, p. 39. This notice from the Memoranda Roll is printed at length in the Transactions of the Royal Historical Society for 1886, pp. 282–291.

[2] Foed. i. 877.

[3] Parl. Writs, i. 55, 56, 298; B. Cotton, 336; Foed. i. 878.

The proceedings of the assembly, too, were tumultuary[1]; the earls attended with an armed force and insisted that the regent should accept and enact certain supplementary articles based on the list of grievances. The prince by the advice of his counsellors granted all that was asked, and immediately sent the new articles and the confirmed charters to his father for his corroboration. The same day, October 10, the fifth day of the session, the question of the aid again arose. The earls took advantage of their strength to force on the government the principle, which both before and long after was a subject of contention among English statesmen, that grievances must be redressed before supplies are granted. They insisted that the grant of the eighth and fifth should be regarded as null, and, as redress was now really obtained, they consented to an aid of a ninth from the laity there assembled; and this was shortly after extended to the towns[2]. The charters were confirmed by *inspeximus* on the 12th[3]; the king on the 5th of November at Ghent confirmed both the charters and the new articles[4]. On the 15th of October the archbishop summoned a new convocation for the 20th of November[5]. In this assembly, Winchelsey, either knowing of the explanatory bull or anticipating the solution of the difficulty, adopted a plan for avoiding both royal and papal censures. The Scots had invaded the north, the occasion demanded a national effort, the clergy might take the initiative and tax themselves for defence before the king applied for an aid. The bull which forbade compliance with such a request did not forbid them to forestall it. Accordingly the southern province granted a tenth and the northern a fifth[6]. The archbishop's writ for collection is dated on the 4th of December[7].

The charters confirmed and enlarged, Oct. 10.

The grant of aid is annulled.

The clerical difficulty overcome.

The new articles are extant in two forms, so different that they can scarcely be regarded as representing the same original.

The new articles.

[1] Hemingb. ii. 147.
[2] Parl. Writs, i. 63, 64.
[3] Statutes of the Realm, i. 114–119; Foed. i. 879.
[4] Foed. i. 810.
[5] Wilkins, Conc. ii. 228.
[6] B. Cotton, p. 339; Rishanger, p. 182; M. Westm. Flores, iii. 296; P. Langtoft, ii. 303; Hemingb. ii. 155.
[7] Wilkins, Conc. ii. 230; Ann. Wigorn. p. 534.

The two forms.

One is in French[1], containing seven articles, attested by the regent and sealed with the great seal. The other is in Latin[2], preserved by the annalist Walter of Hemingburgh, containing six articles, and purporting to be sealed not only by the king but by the barons and bishops. This last is generally known as the statute *de Tallagio non concedendo;* as a statute it is referred to in the preamble to the Petition of Right, and it is recognised as such by a decision of the judges in 1637. The contents of the two documents are different. The French version (1) declares the confirmation of the charters, (2) recognises the nullity of all proceedings taken in contravention of them, (3) authorises the publication of them at the cathedrals and the reading of them once a year to the people, (4) directs the excommunication of offenders against them, (5) grants that the recent exactions, aids and prises, shall not be made precedents, (6) grants that from henceforth no such exactions shall be taken without the common consent of the realm and to the common profit thereof, and (7) lastly gives up the maletote of forty shillings on wool, promising that no such tax shall be taken in future without the common consent and goodwill, the king's right to the ancient aids, prises, and custom on wool being saved by a distinct proviso in each case.

The French version.

The act *de tallagio non concedendo.*

The Latin articles are; (1) no tallage or aid shall be taken without the will and consent of all the archbishops, bishops, and other prelates, earls, barons, knights, burghers, and other freemen in the realm; (2) no prises of corn, wool, leather, or other goods, shall be taken without the goodwill of their owners; (3) the maletote is forbidden; (4) the charters are confirmed together with the liberties and free customs of clergy and laity, and all proceedings in contravention of them are annulled; (5) the king renounces all rancour against the earls and their partisans, and (6) the securities for the observance of the charter by publication and excommunication are rehearsed.

The French version does not contain the word *tallage;* the

[1] Hemingb. ii. 149; Statutes of the Realm, i. 124, 125.
[2] Hemingb. ii. 152; B. Cotton, p. 337; Rishanger, p. 181; Trivet, p. 366; Statutes, i. 125.

Latin does not reserve the rights of the king. The former omits the amnesty. It renounces 'such manner of aids,' whilst the Latin contains no such qualifying words, but distinctly declares that no tallage or aid shall be imposed. Yet the differences are scarcely such as to indicate any want of good faith on either side. They do not suggest that the one was the form understood by the earls, the other the form granted by the king. It is true that now and at a later period the legal advisers of the crown, when they drew up a statute in its final shape, exercised a discretion in modifying the terms of the petition which was the initial stage of legislation: but there was no chance for such an expedient on this occasion. The earls were too vigilant, and the aid would have been withheld if the document sent to the king had not been quite satisfactory. It may be questioned whether the Latin form may stand to the French enactment in the same relation as the articles of the barons stand to the charter of John, or whether it is a mere imperfect and unauthoritative abstract of the formal document, in which the terms of pacification have been confused with the details of permanent legislation. Certainly the French form is that in which the enactment became a permanent part of our law, by the exact terms of which Edward held himself bound, and beyond the letter of which he did not think himself in conscience obliged to act, in reference to either prise or tallage.

Variations of the two forms.

The French version is the original.

These articles are the summary of the advantages gained at the termination of the struggle of eighty-two years, and in words they amount to very little more than a re-insertion of the clauses omitted from the great Charter of John. But in reality they stand to those clauses in the relation of substance to shadow, of performance to promise. For the common consent of the nation of 1297 means not, as in 1215, the assent of a body which is conscious of its existence and common interest but unable to enforce its demands, without proper machinery, continuity of precedent, or defined arrangement of parts and functions, but the deliberate assent and consent of a parliament formed on strict principles of organisation, summoned by dis-

Importance of these articles.

tinct writs, for distinct purposes,—a well-defined and, for the time, completely organised expositor of the national will.

Peculiarities of the occasion on which the charters were confirmed.

The 'Confirmatio Cartarum' is one of the most curious phenomena of our national history, whether it be regarded as the result of an occasional crisis, or as the decision, no longer to be delayed, of a struggle of principles. At first sight it seems strange that such a concession should be extorted from a king like Edward, when neither arms nor oaths had been sufficient to compel Henry III to yield it. The coincidence of the clerical with the baronial action at this juncture has so much of the character of accident as to seem conclusive against the supposition that the result was a triumph of principle. Boniface VIII, when he issued the bull of 1296, had no thought that he was acting in practical concert with Bohun and Bigod; yet without the quarrel with the clergy Edward would have easily silenced the earls. Neither do the earls on the other hand seem to have conceived the idea of a constitutional revolution until the ecclesiastical question arose. Their ancient grudge about foreign service had no direct connexion with the confirmation of the charters, or with the greater part of the list of grievances on which the new articles were founded: it is not so much as named in the act to which the royal seal was affixed. Although it probably was made the subject of a separate convention, in which the king allowed that, except for wages, those who owed him services and the owners of twenty librates of land were not bound to go with him to Flanders, this important concession was no formal part of the national pacification [1]. The leaders of the rising were almost as much below the confederates of 1215 in political foresight, deliberate constitutional policy and true national spirit, as John was below Edward in his idea of honour and true royalty.

Coincidence of distinct lay and clerical difficulties.

Edward had not overtaxed the nation;

Nor again is it easy to see what occasion Edward had given for so violent an attack. His ordinary exactions were small in proportion to those of his father, and even his recent ex-

[1] 'Eodem anno post multas et varias altercationes concessit dominus rex omnibus qui debebant sibi servitia et omnibus viginti libratas terrae habentibus, non teneri ire secum in Flandriam nisi ad vadia et pro stipendiis dicti regis;' B. Cotton, p. 327.

traordinary measures were regulated by orderly management, and were acknowledged by him as exceptional expedients, not to be drawn into custom, and to be excused only on the ground of necessity. The charges of infringing the charters generally were mere vague declamation, for although he may never have formally reissued them, and had even forbidden archbishop Peckham to use them for political ends, Edward's reign had been devoted to legislation in the very spirit and on the very lines of the charters. So far as he is personally concerned, it may be said that by his legislation he had largely helped to train the spirit of law which was to bind, and did in him bind, the royal authority.

or habitually disregarded the charters.

As to the greater question, we may grant that the opportunity given by the French war, the bull *Clericis laicos*, and the discontent of the earls, was humanly speaking accidental; but it is not the less true that the forces which seized that opportunity were ready, and were the result of a long series of causes, and the working of principles which must sooner or later have made an opportunity for themselves. Such a crisis, if they had separately attempted to bring it about, might have changed the dynasty, or subverted the relations of church and state, crown and parliament, but, accepted as it came, it brought about a result singularly in harmony with what seems from history and experience to be the natural direction of English progress.

Character of the crisis.

The bull of Boniface VIII sums up a series of measures which date from the submission of John: it was not intended for England alone, but it struck a chord which had been in tension from that hour to this. The weapon that John had placed in the hands of Innocent had been used unsparingly, and the English Church had been the greatest sufferer. The king had connived at papal exaction; the pope had placed the clergy under the heel of the royal taskmaster. The church was indeed rich, too rich in proportion to the resources of the country, or for the moral welfare of the clergy; but the wealth which tempted the king and pope had been honestly acquired and was liberally expended. The demands of the popes drew a large

The ecclesiastical difficulty, traced to the act of John.

portion of the revenues of the church into foreign channels; the aids furnished to the king by the clergy under papal pressure enabled him to rule without that restraint which the national council, armed with the national grievances, had a right to place upon him. Men like S. Edmund, Grosseteste and the Cantilupes, had seen themselves obliged by papal threats to furnish material support to an administration against the tyranny of which they were at the very time contending; and thus to defeat the principle for which they were striving. Under Edward I the same policy had been adopted; but the wise and frugal government of his early years had given little occasion for complaint, and little opening for aggression. Boniface VIII must have forgotten that in destroying the concordat with the king he was not merely embarrassing the secular power but casting away the material chain by which he curbed it. The bull *Clericis laicos* at once gave occasion for a decisive struggle, and began a new phase of ecclesiastical and civil relations. The tacit renunciation of papal homage, the vindication of ecclesiastical liberties, the legislation marked by the statutes of provisors and præmunire, were the direct consequences of an act which was intended to place the secular power under the feet of the spiritual.

The constitutional opposition led by churchmen.

The new starting-point.

Bohun and Bigod were not great men.

The action of Bohun and Bigod was not dictated, as that of Simon de Montfort had been, and still more that of the barons of Runnymede, by a constitutional desire to limit the royal power. It arose chiefly from personal ambitions and personal grievances. Bohun had been fined and imprisoned in 1292; Bigod had been in arms in 1289, and was then very peremptorily ordered to keep the peace. Gloucester, who had shared their offence, and was by character and position qualified to lead them, had not lived long enough to resume his ancient part, but the spirit that had inspired him lived in the two earls, who by his death were left almost the sole relics of the great nobility of feudalism, and the last inheritors of the political animosities of the late reign. A victory won by these alone might, in spite of Edward's reforms, have revived the feudal spirit, to be sooner or later extinguished in a more bloody conflict.

Conduct of archbishop Winchelsey.

Winchelsey[1] was a great man, although he did not reach the stature of Langton. An eminent scholar and divine, he had been placed at the head of the church by a unanimous voice, which the pope had not cared to resist. To him the coincidence of the baronial and ecclesiastical quarrels seems at once to have suggested the cry of the restoration of the Charters. As the laws of King Edward had been in the days of the Conqueror, and the laws of Henry I in the days of John, so now the great Charter was the watchword of the party of liberty, the popular panacea. This fact showed at least a comprehension and a common feeling on the part of all classes as to the real state of the case; and the result of the struggle amply justifies the decision brought about by these complicated and accidental causes, in other respects not so closely connected with the constitutional development. Edward's designs were really premature. The conquest of Scotland and the retention of Gascony were beyond the present strength of the nation: the very conception of the former was premature, and the latter was a scheme incompatible with the now existing relations of king and people, although it required a century and a half more to convince them of the fact. No doubt Edward believed himself morally as well as legally justified in these aims: his weakness for legal exactness led him to overrate the importance of his claims and of the recognition of them: his experience of both Welsh and Scottish neighbours convinced him of the political expediency of annexation, and the fact that the chief competitors for the Scottish crown were his own vassals stimulated his pride and provoked his appetite for vengeance when his decision had been set aside and the faith pledged to him had been broken. The history of three centuries proves that, whether or no the two countries could have been benefited by union, the time of union was not come: England was not strong enough to hold Scotland, and there was no such sympathy between the nations as could supply the place of force. It would have been well if the case had been made clear as early with regard to Gascony.

Premature designs of Edward.

181. The remaining years of Edward's reign owe such con-

[1] See his character drawn by an admirer, in Birchington, Ang. Sac. i. 11 sq.

Supplementary confirmations.

stitutional interest as they have to the fact that they witnessed the supplementary acts by which the Confirmation of the Charters was affirmed and recognised as the end of the present disputes, and especially as the close of the long dispute about the limits and jurisdictions of the Forests. The king returned in March, 1298[1], after making with France a truce which in the following November became a permanent peace, cemented by a royal marriage. In the summer he invaded Scotland, but not before the earls had demanded as a condition of their attendance a re-confirmation of the act done at Ghent. The claim was made in an assembly of the lay estates held at York on the 25th of May, 1298[2], and was answered by a promise made on the king's part by the bishop of Durham and the earls of Surrey, Warwick, and Gloucester, that if he were victorious, he would on his return do all that was required. The promise was fulfilled in the spring of 1299, but again not without a contest. The earl of Hereford was now dead, but the steady determination of the nation had already superseded the action of the class; and the victory which had been won for the charter of liberties was now repeated in the demand and concession of the forest reforms. In a council of magnates called for the 8th of March[3] Edward confirmed the charters[4], but, in the case of the forests, with a reservation which provoked new suspicions.

Edward returns, March, 1298.

His promise to re-confirm the charters, May, 1298.

Contest in 1299.

Parliament, March 8.

[1] March 14; Foed. i. 889.

[2] Parl. Writs, i. 65; Foed. i. 890, 891, 892; Rishanger, p. 186; Hemingb. ii. 173; Trivet, p. 371; Flores, iii. 104; P. Langtoft, ii. 309.

[3] Parl. Writs, i. 78; Rishanger, p. 190; Hemingb. ii. 183; Trivet, p. 375; M. Westminster, p. 431.

[4] In what is called the statute *de finibus levatis*, Statutes, i. 126 sq., dated April 2. The words are very important in their relation to Edward's later action: 'Quos autem articulos supradictos firmiter et inviolabiliter observari volumus et teneri, volentes nihilominus quod perambulatio fiat, *salvis semper juramento nostro, jure coronae nostrae et rationibus nostris atque calumpniis ac omnium aliorum*; ita quod perambulatio illa nobis reportetur antequam aliqua executio vel aliquid aliud inde fiat; quam quidem perambulationem volumus quod fiat sicut praedicitur ad citius quod fieri potest post negotia quae habemus expedienda cum nunciis qui de Romana curia sunt venturi, quae vero ita sunt ardua quod non solum nos et regnum nostrum sed totam Christianitatem contingunt, et ad ea sanius pertractanda totum consilium nostrum habere plenarie indigemus.' The negotiations at Rome probably concerned the crusade, but the king may have known of the pope's views on Scotland and also have been negotiating for a recall of the bull *Clericis laicos*.

The words 'salvo jure coronae nostrae' turned the blessings of the people into curses; a second confirmation was demanded, and, on the 3rd of May[1], granted without the salvo. The perambulations necessary for enforcing the forest reforms were ordered, and the people for the moment were satisfied. But the struggle was not yet over. The delay of the forest reforms had revived the mutual distrust. The next year the debate was renewed, in the most completely constituted parliament that had been called since 1296, on the 6th of March, 1300[2]. On this occasion an important series of twenty articles, in addition to the charters, was passed, but those of 1297 were not re-enacted. By the first of these 'articuli super cartas' commissioners were appointed to investigate all cases in which the charters had been infringed; by others the abuses of purveyance and of the jurisdiction of the steward, the marshall, and the constable of Dover Castle, were restrained; the Statute of Winchester was enforced; the jury system received some slight reforms; the assaying and marking of gold and silver were ordered; and other enactments of purely legal interest were adopted. Two or three of these illustrate the character of this supplementary legislation[3]. The 4th orders that no common pleas shall be henceforth held in the Exchequer contrary to the form of the Great Charter, a rule which legal artifice easily overcame; the 5th directs that the Chancery and the Bench shall still follow the king, a trace of the old system of the Curia Regis which was soon to be lost; the 6th forbids the issue of common law writs under the Privy Seal. The 8th is a curious relic of the ideas of 1258;—the sheriffs, in those

Edward hesitates to alienate his forest rights, but yields, May 3.

Parliament at London, March 6, 1300.

The *articuli super cartas*, 1300.

[1] The writs for the council on the 3rd of May were issued April 10; Parl. Writs, i. 80. The king consented that the perambulation should be made under the view of three bishops, three earls, and three barons; Hemingb. ii. 182, 183. Neither of these assemblies contained the commons or inferior clergy. The statute *de falsa moneta* (Statutes, i. 131) was made in the May meeting.

[2] Parl. Writs, i. 82–84. The parliament was called for the 6th of March, and contained both commons and clergy. The confirmation is dated on the 28th; Statutes (Charters), i. 41; on which day was issued the order for the Great Charter to be read four times a year; Foed. i. 919. The additional articles were promulgated April 15; ibid. p. 920. See, too, the Chron. Ang. et Scot., ed. Riley, pp. 404–406; Hemingb. ii. 186; Ann. Wigorn. p. 544; Trivet, p. 377.

[3] Statutes of the Realm, i. 136–141.

counties in which the office is not of fee or heritable, may be elected by the people if they please. This enactment was of no long duration, and is limited by the 13th article, which forbids bribery and oppression on the sheriffs' part, as well as by the 14th, which defines the terms at which the profits of the hundreds are to be fermed. The most significant part of the legislation, however, concerns the point on which Edward seems to have determined to make his last stand against the demands of the nation, the administration of the forests: for the reform of these, very stringent measures were taken in obedience to the first article, and it was not without significance that, in the last, a proviso was inserted saving the right and prerogative of the crown in all things. The perambulation, however, was at last made; and to receive the report of the commissioners the king, on the 20th of January, 1301, met his parliament at Lincoln[1].

The forest reforms.

Report on the perambulations.

Parliament of Lincoln, Jan. 20, 1301.

This assembly is of considerable historical importance. Its composition was peculiar, for the king directed the sheriffs to return the same representatives, if they were alive, as had attended on the last occasion, no doubt that they might hear the report of the commission issued at their request[2]: all persons who had claims or complaints against the perambulations were to attend to show their grievances; the universities of Oxford and Cambridge were also ordered to send a number of lawyers to advise on the subject of debate. The proceedings indicate a feeling of continued mistrust on both sides. Edward, who negotiated through his clerk Roger Brabazon, attempted to guard his future action with regard to the forests by refusing to ratify the disafforestments until he had obtained a distinct assurance from the prelates and baronage that it could be done without a breach of his royal obligations and without detriment to the crown[3]. He sent down a bill to the magnates, in which

Edward's reluctance to yield unconditionally.

[1] Parl. Writs, i. 88–91; Foed. i. 923, 924; Flores, iii. 109, 303; P. Langtoft, ii. 329. The placing the parliament at Stamford instead of Lincoln is no doubt a mistake of the annalists.

[2] The writ, which was issued Sept. 26, 1300, rehearses the provisions and reservations made in the statute *de finibus*, above, p. 154, note 4. The proctors of the clergy were not summoned to this parliament, although the representatives of the commons were.

[3] Parl. Writs, i. 104. The oath referred to is probably the coronation oath, which may have contained a promise not to alienate the crown pro-

he declared that, if they would, after due examination, declare on their homage and fealty that the measures in question were well and loyally completed, and that he could confirm them without breaking his oath or injuring the crown, he would sanction them: or, if they would take some other convenient way of redressing the abuses, they should be redressed by their advice. The barons in reply declined to undertake the responsibility which the king wished to throw upon them, and, under the advice of archbishop Winchelsey, presented, through Henry of Keighley, knight of the shire for Lancashire, a bill of twelve articles [1], to each of which the king returned a formal answer. They demanded, in the name of the whole community, the complete confirmation of the charters in all points, the cancelling of all acts opposed to them, the definition, in parliament, of the functions of the justices assigned, the immediate execution of the disafforestments, the immediate abolition of the abuse of purveyance, a new commission to hear complaints, the redress of grievances by officers who should be free from suspicion, and the enforcement of general reforms before money was granted. This done, they proposed to grant a fifteenth in lieu of the twentieth already granted; it was to be assessed, collected and paid to the king by knights chosen by the common consent of the county after the next Michaelmas, the date at which the reforms were to be completed. Finally the prelates, with the consent of the barons, declared that they could not assent to any contribution to be made from the goods of the church in defiance of the pope's prohibition. At the same time, it would seem, although the subject is not mentioned in the Bill, they petitioned for the removal of Walter Langton, bishop of Coventry, the treasurer, and made bitter complaints against the king's other servants [2]. Edward keenly felt the ungenerous suspicions to which he was subjected, and ordered the knight who had pre-

Bill of twelve articles.

Claims made by the barons in the name of the community.

Grant of money.

Imprisonment of Henry Keighley.

perty, such as was taken by the king of the Romans: 'Vis jura regni et imperii conservare, bonaque ejusdem injuste dispersa recuperare et fideliter in usus regni et imperii dispensare?' Taylor, Glory of Regality, p. 412, and p. 109, note 2, above.

[1] 'Billa Praelatorum et procerum regni liberata domino regi ex parte totius communitatis in parliamento Lincolniensi;' Parl. Writs, i. 104.

[2] Pet. Langtoft, ii. 329; M. Westm. Flores, iii. 303.

sented the bill to be imprisoned[1]. The disafforestation in particular was repulsive to him, for he was called on to ratify arrangements which were not yet made. He yielded however to compulsion which he did not hesitate to call outrageous, and consented, either expressly or with some modification, to all these claims, except that which recognised the necessity of the pope's consent to the clerical payment; on the 30th of January the knights of the shire were allowed their expenses and suffered to go home; and on the 14th of February Edward confirmed the charters.

The king yields.

Confirmation of Charters, Feb. 14, 1301.

Resistance of the parliament to the demands of Boniface VIII.

But although the baronage were disposed to press their advantage to the utmost, and perhaps even to purchase too dearly the aid of the ecclesiastical party which was headed by Winchelsey, they showed themselves ready to support the king to the utmost in his resistance to the further assumptions of Boniface. The pope had now claimed Scotland as a fief of Rome and forbidden Edward to molest the Scots. This extraordinary assumption, made in a bull dated at Anagni, June 27, 1299[2], Edward determined to resist with the united voice of the nation. He had received the bull from Winchelsey at

[1] The following letter seems to give so true and clear an impression of the king's feelings on this occasion, and to be so full of character, that it is given entire. We see in it his determination to uphold his right, or what he deemed his right, and his desire that the victim of the moment should not suffer, but that his kindly treatment should be attributed to the unpopular minister:

'*Thesaurario pro rege.*—Eduard par la grace de Dieu &c. al honorable piere en Dieu Wautier par meisme la grace Evesqe de Cestre notre tresorier salutz. Nous envoions a vous par les porturs de ces lettres monsieur Henri de Kighele, qui ad este devant nous, et avoms bien trove par sa reconnisaunce demeine quil est celi qui nous porta la bille de par l'ercevesqe de Cantebiris et de par les autres qui nous presserent outraiousement au parlement de Nichole, et le quel nous avoms taunt fait serchier, et vous mandoms qe le dit Henri facez mettre en sauve garde en la tour de Loundres a demorer y, tant que nous puissons saver qil soit repentaunt de ce quil en ad fait, et que nous eons sur ceo autrement ordene. Et sachez que nous volons que le dit Henri soit curteisement et sauvement gardez en la dite Tour, hors des fers, mes qe cele curtesie et cele garde soit ensi ordenee quil puisse entendre qe ce viegne de votre cortesie e ne mye de nous. Done souz notre prive seal a Thindene, le V jour de Juyn;' Memoranda of the Exchequer, a° 33. 34 Edw. I. Memb. 40; Madox, Hist. Exch. p. 615. It is satisfactory to know that Keighley soon reappears in parliament and in public employment; Parl. Writs, i. 686.

[2] Hemingb. ii. 196; M. Westminster (ed. 1601), p. 436; Wilkins, Conc. ii. 259; Foed. i. 907.

Sweetheart Abbey in Galloway on the 27th of August, 1300[1], and, in acknowledging the receipt, had re-asserted the principle already laid down in the writ of 1295, 'it is the custom of the realm of England that in all things touching the state of the same realm there should be asked the counsel of all whom the matter concerns[2].' He laid the bull therefore before the parliament at Lincoln, explaining that the pope had ordered him to send agents to Rome to prove his title to the lordship of Scotland; and thereon he requested the barons to take the matter into their own hands. The barons complied, and a letter was written, briefly stating the grounds of the English claim and affirming that the kings of England never have answered or ought to have answered touching this or any of their temporal rights before any judge ecclesiastical or secular, by the free preeminence of the state of their royal dignity and by custom irrefragably preserved at all times; therefore, after discussion and diligent deliberation, the common, concordant and unanimous consent of all and singular has been and is and shall be, by favour of God, unalterably fixed for the future, that the king shall not answer before the pope or undergo judgment touching the rights of the kingdom of Scotland or any other temporal rights: he shall not allow his rights to be brought into question, or send agents; the barons are bound by oath to maintain the rights of the crown, and they will not suffer him to comply with the mandate even were he to wish it. This answer is given by seven earls and ninety-seven barons for themselves and for the whole community of the land, and is dated on the 12th of February[3]. The king soon after forwarded a detailed historical statement of his claim[4]. We miss on this occasion the co-operation of the clergy; and

Letter from the barons to the pope, Feb. 12, 1301.

Numbers of barons signataries.

[1] M. Westminster, p. 438. The archbishop reported to the pope his proceedings in a letter dated Otford, October 8, 1300; ibid. 439.

[2] M. Westminster, p. 439: 'consuetudo est regni Angliae quod in negotiis tangentibus statum ejusdem regni requiratur consilium omnium quos res tangit.'

[3] Foed. i. 926, 927; Parl. Writs, i. 102, 103; Rishanger, pp. 208–210; Hemingb. ii. 209–213; Ann. Lanerc. pp. 199, 200; Trivet, pp. 392–394; M. Westminster, pp. 443, 444.

[4] Rishanger, pp. 200–208; Hemingb. ii. 196–209; Trivet, pp. 381–392; M. Westminster, pp. 439–443; Foed. i. 932, 933.

there can be little doubt that Winchelsey, by his action in this parliament, provoked Edward to the somewhat vindictive proceedings which he took against him after the death of Boniface. Not only had he, as it would seem, adhered to the pope in this matter, or at least been silent when he ought to have spoken, but he had joined the barons in an attempt to embarrass the king in executing the internal reforms. He had, we may suspect, asked a recompense for the assistance he had given to the earls in 1297, and, whilst joining in the bill of twelve articles presented to Edward at Lincoln, had obtained the consent of the barons to add one which the king declined to accept—the exception of ecclesiastical property from grants made contrary to the papal prohibition. The answer to this proposal recorded on the bill is this, 'Non placuit regi sed communitas procerum approbavit[1].' That this co-operation went any further, or concealed, as Edward suspected, deeper designs against him, is improbable: the king however never forgave it. He regarded it at the least as an attempt to repeat the crisis of 1297. Probably the hearty confidence with which he threw himself on their sympathy prevented the barons from further concessions either to Winchelsey or to Boniface, and served to unite them in other respects more closely with the king than they had been united since 1290. His hands were thus strengthened for the completion of the design on Scotland.

The provoking policy of Winchelsey.

Edward's suspicions.

Measures for keeping the great earls quiet.

No more quarrels with the barons occur during the rest of the reign. In 1302 Roger Bigod[2] surrendered his earldoms and estates and received them back for life only: the earl of Hereford had, on his marriage with the king's daughter Elizabeth, in the same year, to make a resettlement like that made by Gloucester in 1290[3]: the earldom of Gloucester was now

[1] Parl. Writs, i. 105. Birchington acknowledges the archbishop's share in this: 'Unde quia ipse praelatis et proceribus regni, perambulationem de foresta et quaedam alia jura regali potentia usurpata petentibus, pro se et utilitate publica, se conjunxit, regis aemulus et suorum aemulorum fautor et temerarius censebatur;' Ang. Sac. i. 16.

[2] Hemingb. ii. 223; M. Westminster, p. 452; Foed. i. 940. They were surrendered April 12, 1302, and restored July 12; to revert in default of heirs of the body, to the king as heir; ibid. The earldom was promised to the king's son Thomas in 1306; Foed. i. 998.

[3] October 8, 1302; Foed. i. 944.

in the hands of Ralph de Monthermer the second husband of Johanna of Acre; and thus the great fiefs were already, as if in anticipation of the policy of Edward III, centring in the royal house. Edward's relations with Winchelsey were of course less friendly. He had imprisoned Henry of Keighley as a matter of form; but the archbishop was the real offender. He could not wholly forgive the man who had brought on him the greatest humiliation of his life. Walter Langton, too, his chief adviser, had engaged in a life-long quarrel with the archbishop[1]. In 1301, after the attempt made in the parliament of Lincoln to remove him, he was suspended by the pope from his bishopric, in consequence of a charge of adultery, concubinage, simony, and intercourse with the devil, made against him by John Lovetot. Edward ascribed the accusation to the odium which he had incurred by his faithful service. The charges against him collapsed, and, after an investigation held before the archbishop himself, he was acquitted and restored by the pope. Whether Winchelsey had any share in this attack there is nothing to show positively, but, from this moment until the archbishop's death, the two prelates were in constant hostility. In 1306 the king laid before Clement V a series of charges against Winchelsey[2], including an accusation of treasonable designs which he believed the archbishop to have carried on in the parliament of Lincoln. The pope in consequence called him to his court and suspended him. He had had a hard part to play, urged on the one hand by the imperious Boniface and on the other by the no less

Prosecution of Winchelsey at Rome, 1306.

Langton's quarrel with Winchelsey.

Charges against Winchelsey.

His suspension.

[1] Foed. i. 956, 957. Walter Langton became treasurer in 1295, and was made bishop of Lichfield in 1296. I have attempted to give a more detailed account of these struggles in the Introduction to the Chronicles of Edw. I and Edw. II, pp. ciii. sq.

[2] The king's charges against Winchelsey are given in the Foedera, i. 983, in a letter to Clement V, dated April 6, 1306. The pope promised to send a nuncio, May 6, and subsequently suspended the archbishop and appointed an administrator. Edward objected to this, but surrendered the profits of the archbishop's temporalities to the pope, and although at the parliament of Carlisle he had issued a prohibition to the pope's agents, he allowed them to execute their functions by letter of April 4, 1307; Foed. i. 1014. Immediately after his death Winchelsey was recalled and Langton imprisoned. When Winchelsey took the side of the Ordainers, Langton reconciled himself with Edward II and became minister again.

uncompromising king; he had yielded and persevered at the wrong times, and lost the confidence of both his masters.

Edward obtains absolution from his oaths.

It would have been well for Edward's reputation if this somewhat vindictive proceeding had satisfied him. Unfortunately, for once in his long career, he deigned to follow the example of his father and grandfather, and applied for a bull of absolution from the oaths so lately taken[1]. This was granted by Clement V in 1305, and although, like the award of S. Lewis in 1264, it contained a salvo of the rights of the nation, it amounted to a full cancelling of the royal obligations incurred in November, 1297. But it can scarcely be doubted that Edward's purpose in applying for it was to evade the execution of the forest articles which he had conceded under strong protests in 1299 and 1301. It is only in reference to these concessions that the absolution was used. He was probably ashamed of an expedient so much opposed to his own maxim 'pactum serva'; he mentions it but once in any public act: in the ordinance of the Forests issued in 1306 he states that he has revoked the disafforestations made at the Lincoln parliament, but only to pardon trespasses committed in consequence[2]. Although in the permanently important parts of constitutional law he refrained from acting on this licence, it is not the less convincing proof that, great and noble as his character was, it did not in this particular point rise above the morality of his age.

Probable purpose of this,

his dislike to the Forest reforms.

Winchelsey did not return to England during Edward's life.

[1] 1305, November 7, the king sends the pope a certified copy of the bull of Clement IV, annulling the Provisions of Oxford; and October 27, sends Henry de Lacy and Hugh le Despenser to tell his troubles to the pope; Foed. i. 975. At the same time he petitions for the canonisation of Thomas Cantilupe; p. 976. The bull of absolution is dated at Lyons, December 29, 1305; it contains a saving clause of the rights of the people existing before the concessions of November, 1297; Foed. i. 978.

[2] Ordinatio Forestae, Statutes, i. 147–149: 'Quia deafforestationem eandem, et ut sententia excommunicationis in contravenientes fulminaretur, quanquam de nostra bona voluntate minime processisset, concessimus, quam quidem sententiam dominus summus pontifex postmodum revocavit; et quas concessionem et deafforestationem ex certis causis revocamus et etiam adnullamus,' May 27, 1306. 'Super absolutione juramenti domini regis Angliae de foresta, quae vulgariter et Anglice dicebatur *porale*.' Ann. London, i. 146.

The king took advantage of his absence to begin the famous course of anti-Roman legislation which distinguishes our church history down to the Reformation. In the February parliament of 1305 the consent of the barons had been given to a statute forbidding the payment of tallages on monastic property and other imposts by which money was raised to be sent out of the country [1]. Not being fortified by the assent of the clergy, this act was not published until 1307, when, in the parliament of Carlisle held in January, it was formally passed, and at the same time a long petition from the whole of the laity was presented, praying for legislation against the abuses of papal patronage exercised in the form of provisions, the promotion of aliens, the diversion of the monastic revenues to foreign purposes, the reservation of first-fruits, Peter's pence and other exactions [2]. The parliament drew up a strong remonstrance, but further legislation, if it were contemplated, was not then proceeded with. Edward did not wish to quarrel with Clement, and in fact after the session was over, at the request of the Cardinal Peter of Spain who was present, he stopped the enforcement of the prohibitions issued against the papal agents, and superseded to some extent the recent legislation [3]. Before the matter was settled he died.

Anti-Roman legislation.

Restriction of papal claims.

Statute of Carlisle, 1307.

Edward hesitates about executing it.

The other constitutional incidents of this period may be briefly enumerated. The parliaments are regularly called and held, although, as we shall see, not invariably guided by the same rules. In 1302 Edward collected the aid *pur fille marier* granted in 1290 [4]. In 1304 he took a tallage of a sixth from the demesne lands, cities and boroughs. In 1306, on the occasion of the knighting of the prince of Wales, an aid

Parliaments and taxes of the latter years.

[1] Statutes, i. 150, 151; Rot. Parl. i. 217.

[2] Hemingb. ii. 254, 259; M. Westminster, p. 457; Rot. Parl. i. 207, 217–223. It is not clear why the delay occurred. In the statute of Carlisle, the ordinance of 1305 is described as made 'de consilio comitum, baronum, magnatum, procerum et aliorum nobilium et regni sui communitatum' (Statutes of the Realm, i. 151; Rot. Parl. i. 217), no mention being made of the clergy. The consent of the clergy is not mentioned in the statute of Carlisle itself. Perhaps the vacancy in the popedom is as probable a reason for the suspense. See Maitland, Memoranda de Parliamento 1305, p. li.

[3] Rot. Parl. i. 222.

[4] Rot. Parl. i. 266; Foed. i. 945.

was granted in parliament, the barons and knights voting a thirtieth, the cities and boroughs a twentieth[1]. In 1303 Edward largely extended the system of customs-duties; on the 1st of February he granted a charter to the foreign merchants in which, in return for an undertaking to pay additional duties according to a fixed tariff, which was substituted for the older and less definite customary imposts, he bestowed on them freedom of trade and immunity from arbitrary exactions. He was less successful when, on the 25th of June, he attempted to obtain from a representative assembly of citizens and burghers their consent on similar terms to a similar increase of the custom on wine, wool, and other commodities; this was unhesitatingly refused[2]. The increase, the *nova custuma*, was however collected from the foreign merchants without parliamentary sanction, in the terms of the *Carta Mercatoria*. Two of these measures, the tallage of 1304 and the *nova custuma* of 1303, were contrary to the spirit of the articles of 1297; but in the latter of the two the exaction was taken by consent of the payers, and as the price of important privileges; and for the tallage the king obtained the connivance of the magnates by allowing them to tax, in the same way, their tenants of ancient demesne of the crown[3]; and this must have constituted his justification.

Customs-duties.

The *Carta Mercatoria.*

Questionable character of these acts.

Although every year of the reign continued to be marked by legislation, there can be no doubt that the constructive part of Edward's work was completed before his political difficulties arose; and the constant employment of both king and baronage in Scotland gives to the statutes of this period a supplementary and fragmentary character. None of them affects the machinery or the balance of the constitution; and, where they illustrate its technical working, they may be noticed in another chapter.

[1] Foed. i. 982; Parl. Writs, i. 164.

[2] Parl. Writs, i. 134, 135; Select Charters, p. 500. The charter of the foreign merchants was declared illegal in 1311; Foed. ii. 749; Statutes, i. 159; see §§ 195, 250 below. The great importance of this incident, with especial reference to the prisage of wine, is carefully drawn out by Mr. Hall in the History of the Customs Revenue, i. 70; ii. 120: and the *Carta Mercatoria* is printed in the same work, i. 202 sq.

[3] Rot. Parl. i. 266; Select Charters, p. 501; Hemingb. ii. 233. On this see Dr. Schanz's remarks, Englische Handelspolitik, i. 392; Maitland, Memoranda, &c., 1305, p. liv; and Vinogradoff, Villainage, pp. 92, 93.

182. Edward died on the 7th of July, 1307. How far the events of his reign justify us in regarding him as an original worker, as founder, reviver or reformer of the Constitution,—with what moral intention he worked, for the increase of his power, for the retention of it, or for the benefit of his people,—it is scarcely within the province of the historian to determine. Personally he was a great king, although not above being tempted to ambition, vindictiveness, and impatient violence. He was great in organising: every department of administration felt his guiding and defining hand. The constitution of parliament which was developed under his hands remains, with necessary modifications and extensions, the model of representative institutions at this day. His legislation is the basis of all subsequent legislation, anticipating and almost superseding constructive legislation for two centuries. His chief political design, the design of uniting Britain under one crown, premature as it was at the moment, the events of later ages have fully justified. A more particular estimate of his work may be made by summing up the general results of this long and varied period[1].

Edward dies, July 7, 1307.

[1] The later parliaments of Edward I were these:—

1302. July 1, at Westminster; summoned by writ of June 2. The clergy and commons were not summoned; Parl. Writs, i. 112.

1302. Sept. 29, at Westminster, summoned by writ of July 20 and 24 and prorogued to Oct. 14. The commons were summoned, but not the clergy; Parl. Writs, i. 114.

1305. Feb. 16, at Westminster, summoned by writ of Nov. 12. Both the clergy and commons were present; Parl. Writs, i. 136: prorogued to Feb. 28; ibid. p. 138. This parliament sat until March 21.

1305. Aug. 15, at Westminster, summoned by writ of May 24 and July 13, prorogued to Sept. 15. This assembly did not comprise either clergy or commons, but was attended by the representatives of the community of Scotland; Parl. Writs, i. 159 sq.

1306. May 30, at Westminster; summoned by writ of April 5; the parochial clergy were not summoned, and the commons in an irregular form. The subject of deliberation was the grant for the prince's knighthood; Parl. Writs, i. 164 sq.

1307. Jan. 30, at Carlisle, summoned Nov. 3. Both clergy and commons were fully represented; Parl. Writs, i. 181 sq. The parliament was opened by the treasurer Langton and the earl of Lincoln. The deliberations lasted until the 20th of March.

CHAPTER XV.

THE SYSTEM OF ESTATES, AND THE CONSTITUTION UNDER EDWARD I.

183. Idea of Constitutional Government.—184. Double character of the English Constitution.—185. System of Estates.—186. The Spiritual estate.—187. The estate of Baronage.—188. Nobility of blood.—189. Connexion of barony with tenure.—190. Barony by summons.—191. The Commons.—192. The Shire Communities.—193. Growth of union among the Commons.—194. Sub-estate of Lawyers.—195. Sub-estate of Merchants.—196. Cross-divisions.—197. The National Councils.—198. The Spiritual estate in Synods and Parliaments.—199. Growth of representation among the Clergy.—200. Parliamentary representation of the Clergy.—201. The Baronage in Parliament.—202. The Commons in Parliament.—203. The Shiremoot.—204. The Sheriff.—205. The work of the Shire, judicial.—206. The work of the Shire in Police.—207. The Military work of the Shire.—208. Share in public measures.—209. Fiscal work of the Shire.—210. Access of the Shire to the King's Council.—211. Communities of towns.—212. Diversities of constitution in Towns.—213. Powers of the Town communities.—214. Summons of the Commons to Parliament.—215. Complete idea of Parliament.—216. Election of Knights of the Shire by the County Court.—217. Practice not necessarily in accordance with Theory.—218. Election in boroughs.—219. Numbers of Parliament.—220. Powers of Parliament.—221. These powers limited by Royal Prerogative;—222. and by individual action.—223. Transition from special to general Taxation.—224. Rights of the three estates in Legislation.—225. Difference in the share or nature of right in Legislation.—226. Judicial power of Parliament.—227. Deliberative power of Parliament.—228. Form of Summons.—229. Ideal of 1295.—230. The King's Council.—231. Petitions in Council.—232. Legislation in Council.—233. The judicial system: division of Courts.—234. Chancery.—235. Justices of Assize.—236. Conservation of the peace.—237. Exchequer.—238. Military system: feudal force.—239. Distraint of Knighthood.—240. The Militia of the period.—241. Commissions of Array.—242. Coast-Guard.—243. Foundation of Navy and Admiralty.—244. Review of the period.

Ideal of constitutional growth.

183. THE idea of a constitution in which each class of society should, as soon as it was fitted for the trust, be admitted to

a share of power and control, and in which national action should be determined by the balance maintained between the forces thus combined, never perhaps presented itself to the mind of any medieval politician. The shortness of life, and the jealousy inherent in and attendant on power, may account for this in the case of the practical statesman, although a long reign like that of Henry III might have given room for the experiment; and, whilst a strong feeling of jealousy subsisted throughout the middle ages between the king and the barons, there was no such strong feeling between the barons and the commons. But even the scholastic writers, amid their calculations of all possible combinations of principles in theology and morals, well aware of the difference between the 'rex politicus' who rules according to law and the tyrant who rules without it, and of the characteristics of monarchy, aristocracy and democracy, with their respective corruptions, contented themselves for the most part with balancing the spiritual and secular powers, and never broached the idea of a growth into political enfranchisement. Yet, in the long run, this has been the ideal towards which the healthy development of national life in Europe has constantly tended, only the steps towards it have not been taken to suit a preconceived theory. The immediate object in each case has been to draw forth the energy of the united people in some great emergency, to suit the convenience of party or the necessities of kings, to induce the newly admitted classes to give their money, to produce political contentment, or to involve all alike in the consciousness of common responsibility.

Ideal of constitutional growth.

The history of the thirteenth century fully illustrates this. Notwithstanding the difference of circumstances and the variety of results, it is to this period that we must refer, in each country of Europe, the introduction, or the consolidation, for the first time since feudal principles had forced their way into the machinery of government, of national assemblies composed of properly arranged and organised Estates. The accepted dates in some instances fall outside the century. The first recorded appearance of town representatives in the Cortes of Aragon is

Assemblies of Estates summoned in Spain.

Representation in Germany and France.

placed in 1162[1]; the first in Castille in 1169[2]. The general courts of Frederick II in Sicily were framed in 1232[3]: in Germany the cities appear by deputies in the diet of 1255, but they only begin to form a distinct part under Henry VII and Lewis of Bavaria[4]; in France the States General are called together first in 1302. Although in each case the special occasions differ, the fact, that a similar expedient was tried in all, shows that the class to which recourse was for the first time had was in each country rising in the same or in a proportional degree, or that the classes which had hitherto monopolised power were in each country feeling the need of a reinforcement. The growth of the towns in wealth and strength, and the decline

[1] In that year queen Petronilla summoned to the Cortes at Huesca 'prelados, ricos hombres, caballeros y procuradores;' and the names of the towns which sent procuradores to the Cortes at Saragossa in 1163 are known. See Zurita, lib. ii. cc. 20, 24; Schäfer, Spanien, iii. 207, 208; Hallam, M. A. ii. 56. The earlier instances, given by Hallam and Robertson (Charles V, vol. i. note 31), are scarcely cases of Cortes.

[2] 'Se sabe que habiendo don Alonso VIII tenido cortes generales en Burgos en el año de 1169, concurrieron a ellas no solamente les condes, ricos hombres, prelados y caballeros sino tambien los ciudadanos y todos los concejos del reino de Castilla;' quoted by Marina, Teoria de las Cortes, c. 14, vol. i. p. 138, from the Cronica General, pt. iv. cap. viii. fo. 387. In 1188 the Cortes of Carrion, attesting the treaty of marriage between Berenguela and Conrad, contained representatives of the towns; 'estos son les nombres de las ciudades y villas cuyos mayores juraron;' ibid. p. 139.

[3] 'Mense Septembris imperator a Melfia venit Forgiam et generales per totum regnum litteras dirigit, ut de qualibet civitate vel castro duo de melioribus accedant ad ipsum pro utilitate regni et commodo generali;' Ric. de S. Germano, A.D. 1232. Frederick's general courts instituted in 1234 are very like the English county courts; 'Statuit etiam ipse imperator apud Messanam, bis in anno in certis regni provinciis generales curias celebrandas . . . et ibi erit pro parte imperatoris nuntius specialis . . . Hiis curiis, bis in anno, ut dictum est, celebrandis, intererunt quatuor de qualibet magna civitate de melioribus terrae, bonae fidei et bonae opinionis, et qui non sint de parte; de aliis vero non magnis et de castellis duo intererunt curiis ipsis;' ibid. A.D. 1234.

[4] In the negotiations for the great confederation of Rhenish cities: see Hermann. Altah. A.D. 1255; Pertz, Scr. xvii. 397; Annales Stadenses, A.D. 1255; Pertz, Scriptt. xvi. 373; Datt, de pace publica, c. 4. 20; Zoepfl, Deutsche Rechtsgeschichte, vol. ii. p. 262; and the Essay on the subject by Arnold Busson, Innsbruck, 1874. In 1277 we find the 'communitates civitatum et civium' swearing fealty to Rudolf of Hapsburg; Eberhard. Altah. ap. Canis. Lectt. Antt. iv. 218; Pertz, Scr. xvii. 593: in 1309 Henry VII discusses the Italian expedition in a diet at Speyer, 'cum principibus electoribus et aliis principibus et civitatum nunciis,' Alb. Argentin. (ed. Urstisius), p. 116.

of properly feudal ideas in kings, clergy and barons, tended to the momentary parallelism. The way in which the crisis was met decided in each country the current of its history. In England the parliamentary system of the middle ages emerged from the policy of Henry II, Simon de Montfort and Edward I; in France the States General were so managed as to place the whole realm under royal absolutism; in Spain the long struggle ended in the sixteenth century in making the king despotic, but the failure of the constitution arose directly from the fault of its original structure. The Sicilian policy of Frederick passed away with his house. In Germany the disruption of all central government was reflected in the Diet; the national paralysis showed itself in a series of abortive attempts, few and far between, at united action, and the real life was diverted into provincial channels and dynastic designs.

Variety of results.

Double character of the English parliament.

184. The parliamentary constitution of England comprises, as has been remarked already, not only a concentration of local machinery but an assembly of estates[1]. The parliament of the present day, and still more clearly the parliament of Edward I, is a combination of these two theoretically distinct principles. The House of Commons now most distinctly represents the former idea, which is also conspicuous in the constitution of Convocation, and in that system of parliamentary representation of the clergy which was an integral part of Edward's scheme: it is to some extent seen in the present constitution of the House of Lords, in the case of the representative peers of Ireland and Scotland, who may also appeal for precedent to the same reign[2]. It may be distinguished by the term local representation as distinct from class representation; for the two are not necessarily united, as our own history as well as that of foreign countries abundantly testifies. In some systems the

Local representation and class representation.

[1] Vol. i. pp. 45, 564.

[2] Edward's design of having Scotland represented by a Parliament to be held in London on the 15th of July 1305 (see above, p. 165, note), to consist of ten persons, two bishops, two abbots, two earls, two barons, and two for the commune, one from each side of the Forth, chosen by the 'Commune' of Scotland at their assembly, may be seen in Parl. Writs, i. 155, 156, 161–163. These representatives were summoned to the parliament, but rather as envoys than as proper members.

Varieties of usage.

local interest predominates over the class interest; in one the character of delegate eclipses the character of senator; in another all local character may disappear as soon as the threshold of the assembly is passed; in one there may be a direct connexion between the local representation and the rest of the local machinery; in another the central assembly may be constituted by means altogether different from those used for administrative purposes, and the representative system may be used as an expedient to supersede unmanageable local institutions; while, lastly, the members of the representative body may in one case draw their powers solely from their delegate or procuratorial character, and in another from that senatorial character which belongs to them as members of a council which possesses sovereignty or a share of it. The States General of the Netherlands under Philip II were a mere congress of ambassadors from the provincial estates; the States General of France under Philip the Fair were a general assembly of clergy, barons, and town communities[1], in no way connected with any system of provincial estates, which indeed can hardly be said to have existed at the time[2]. In Germany the representative

[1] 'Statim idem dominus rex de baronum ipsorum consilio barones ceteros tunc absentes et nos, videlicet archiepiscopos, episcopos, abbates, priores conventuales, decanos, praepositos, capitula, conventus, atque collegia ecclesiarum tam cathedralium quam regularium ac secularium, necnon universitates et communitates villarum regni, ad suam mandavit praesentiam evocari; ut praelati, barones, decani, praepositi et duo de peritioribus uniuscujusque cathedralis vel collegiatae ecclesiae personaliter, ceteri vero per oeconomos syndicos et procuratores idoneos cum plenis et sufficientibus mandatis, comparere statuto loco et termino curaremus. Porro nobis ceterisque personis ecclesiasticis supradictis, necnon baronibus, oeconomis, syndicis, et procuratoribus communitatum et villarum et aliis sic vocatis juxta praemissae vocationis formam ad mandatum regium hac die Martis 10ma praesentis mensis Aprilis, in ecclesia beatae Mariae Parisius in praefati regis praesentia constitutis,' &c.—Letter of the French Clergy to Boniface VIII; Dupuy, Proofs of the Liberties, &c., p. 125; Prynne, Records, iii. 953; Savaron, États Généraux, p. 88.

[2] The very important illustrations of the existence of assemblies of estates in Languedoc given by Palgrave, Commonwealth, ccccxxxv. sq., from Vaissette's Preuves de l'Histoire de Languedoc, show that that territory possessed these institutions, but at a time when it could scarcely be called a part of France. S. Lewis writes to the men of Beaucaire, 'congreget senescallus consilium non suspectum, in quo sint aliqui de praelatis, baronibus, militibus et hominibus bonarum villarum,' p. ccccxxxviii. In 1271 there was at Beziers 'consilium praelatorum et baronum et aliorum

elements of the Diet,—the prelates, counts and cities,—had a local arrangement and system of collective as distinct from independent voting[1]; and in the general cortes of Aragon the provincial estates of Aragon, Catalonia and Valencia, were arranged in three distinct bodies in the same chamber[2]. Nor are these differences confined to the systems which they specially characterise. The functions of a local delegate, a class representative, and a national counsellor, appear more or less conspicuously at the different stages of parliamentary growth, and according as the representative members share more or less completely the full powers of the general body. A detailed examination of these differences however lies outside our subject[3], and in the constitutional history of foreign nations the materials at our command are insufficient to supply a clear answer to many of the questions they suggest.

Different combinations in different constitutions.

185. An assembly of Estates is an organised collection, made by representation or otherwise, of the several orders, states or conditions of men, who are recognised as possessing political power. A national council of clergy and barons is not an assembly of estates, because it does not include the body of the people, 'the plebs,' the simple freemen or commons, who on all constitutional theories have a right to be consulted as to their own taxation, if on nothing else. So long as the prelates and barons, the tenants-in-chief of the crown, met to grant an aid, whilst the towns and shires were consulted by special

An assembly of estates;

it should contain a representation of all the political factors.

bonorum virorum,' p. ccccxli, and in it the representatives brought procuratorial powers as in England. These instances are the more interesting as coming from the land which had been ruled by the elder Simon de Montfort. Cf. Boutaric, Premiers États Gen. p. 5.

[1] The fully developed diet contained three colleges—I. The Electors; II. The Princes; comprising (1) those voting *sigillatim,* (α) ecclesiastical, (β) temporal; (2) those voting *curiatim,* (α) ecclesiastical; the Prelates on two benches, the Rhine and Swabia; (β) the Counts, on four benches, Swabia, Wetterau, Franconia, and Westphalia; III. The Imperial Cities voting *curiatim* in two benches, the Rhine and Swabia.

[2] Schäfer, Spanien, iii. 215.

[3] The changes in the form of the States General of France are especially interesting, but are not parallel with anything that went on in England. The introduction of representation into the first and second State, and the election of the representatives of the three orders by the same constituent body, in 1483, are in very strong contrast with English institutions; see Picot, 'Les Elections aux États generaux,' Paris, 1874.

commissions, there was no meeting of estates. A county court, on the other hand, although it never bore in England the title of provincial estates, nor possessed the powers held by the provincial estates on the continent, was a really exhaustive assembly of this character.

Arrangement of the political factors in three estates. The arrangement of the political factors in three estates is common, with some minor variations, to all the European constitutions, and depends on a principle of almost universal acceptance. This classification differs from the system of caste, and from all divisions based on differences of blood or religion, historical or prehistorical [1]. It is represented by the

[1] 'Thæt bith thonne cyninges andweorc and his tol mid to ricsianne, thæt he hæbbe his land full mannod, he sceal hæbban *gebedmen* and *fyrdmen* and *weorcmen*;' Alfred's Boetius (ed. Cardale, p. 90). 'Aelc riht cynestol stent on thrim stapelum the fullice ariht stænt; an is *oratores*, and other is *laboratores* and thridde is *bellatores*;' a writer of the tenth century quoted by Wright, Political Songs, p. 365. 'Ther ben in the Chirche thre states that God hathe ordeyned, state of prestis and state of knyghtis and state of comunys;' Wycliffe, English Works (ed. Arnold), iii. 184. Compare 'Piers the Plowman,' Prol. v. 112 sq., ed. Skeat, p. 4. 'Constituitur autem sub te regnum illud in subjectione debita triplicis status principalis: status unus est militantium, alius clericorum, tertius burgensium;' Gerson, 'De considerationibus quas debet habere princeps.' The same writer interprets the three leaves of the fleur de lys (among other explanations) as the three estates, 'statum dico militantium, statum consulentium, statum laborantium;' Gerson, Sermon on S. Lewis, Opp. pt. ii. p. 758. The following passage from Nicolas of Clemangis (De lapsu et reparatione Justorum, c. 16) forms almost a comment on the constitution of Edward I: 'Nulli dubium est omne regnum omnemque politiam recte institutam ex tribus hominum constare generibus, quos usitatiori appellatione tres ordines vel status solemus dicere; ex sacerdotali scilicet ordine, militari et plebeio . . . Perutile immo necessarium mihi videtur ad universalem regni hujus in cunctis suis membris et abusibus reformationem concilium universale trium statuum convocari . . . Congruum nempe esse videtur ut in ruina vel periculo universali universale etiam quaeratur auxilium, et *quod omnes tangit ab omnibus probetur*.' The address of the Commons to Henry IV, in 1401, rehearses 'coment les estates du roialme purroient bien estre resemblez a une Trinite, cest assavoir la persone du Roy, les Seigneurs Espirituelx et Temporelx et les communes;' but, as Hallam remarks, the reference here is to the necessary components of the parliament; see his very valuable note, Middle Ages, iii. 105, 106, where other authorities are given. 'This land standeth,' says the Chancellor Stillington, in the 7th of Edward IV, 'by three states, and above that one principal, that is to wit lords spiritual, lords temporal, and commons, and over that state-royal, as our sovereign lord the king;' Rot. Parl. v. 622. Thus too it is declared that the treaty of Étaples, in 1492, was to be confirmed 'per tres status regni Angliae rite et debite convocatos, videlicet per praelatos et clerum, nobiles, et communitates ejusdem regni;' Rymer, xii. 508.

philosophic division of guardians, auxiliaries and producers, of Plato's Republic. It appears, mixed with the idea of caste, in the *edhilingi*, *frilingi*, and *lazzi* of the ancient Saxons. In Christendom it has always taken the form of a distinction between clergy and laity, the latter being subdivided according to national custom into noble and non-noble, patrician and plebeian, warriors and traders, landowners and craftsmen. The English form, clergy, lords and commons, has a history of its own which is not quite so simple, and which will be noticed by and by. The variations in this classification when it is applied to politics are numerous. The Aragonese cortes contained four brazos, or arms, the clergy, the great barons or ricos hombres, the minor barons, knights or infanzones, and the towns[1]. The Germanic diet comprised three colleges, the electors, the princes, and the cities, the two former being arranged in distinct benches, lay and clerical[2]. The Neapolitan parliament, unless our authorities were misled by supposed analogies with England, counted the prelates as one estate with the barons[3], and the minor clergy with the towns. The Castilian cortes arranged the clergy, the *ricos hombres*, and the *communidades*, in three estates[4]. The Swedish diet was composed of clergy, barons, burghers and peasants[5]. The

Arrangement in three estates,

with minor variations, in Spain, Germany, and Sweden.

[1] In Aragon proper (1) brazo de ecclesiasticos; (2) brazo de nobles, later, ricos hombres; (3) brazo de caballeros y hijosdalgo, called later infanzones; (4) brazo de universidades. In Catalonia and Valencia there were three, the ecclesiastico, militar, and real, for only royal towns, 'pueblos de realengo,' were represented; Schäfer, iii. 218.

[2] Above, p. 171, note 1.

[3] Giannone, History of Naples, Book 20. chap. 4. sect. 1. So too it is said that in Aragon the prelates first appear as a separate brazo in 1301; having before attended simply as barons, henceforth they represent the ecclesiastical estate or interest; Schäfer, Spanien, iii. 217.

[4] The following are the words of the 'Lei fundamental' of the Cortes of 1328–9: 'Porque en los hechos arduos de nuestros reinos es necessario el consejo de nuestros subditos y naturales especialmente de los procuradores de las nuestras cibdades y villas y lugares de nuestros reinos, por ende ordenamos y mandamos que sobre los tales hechos grandes y arduos se hayan de ayuntar cortes y se faga consejo de los tres estados de nuestros reinos, segun lo hicieron los reyes nuestros progenitores;' Recopilacion, L. ii. tit. vii. lib. vi; quoted by Marina, i. 31.

[5] Universal History, xii. 213. The estates comprised (1) the nobles, represented by one from each family, with whom sat the four chief officers of each regiment of the army; (2) the clergy, represented by the bishops, superintendents, and one deputy from every ten parishes; (3) representa-

In Scotland, and France.

Scottish parliament contained three estates, prelates, tenants-in-chief great and small, and townsmen, until James I, in 1428, in imitation of the English system, instituted commissioners of shires, to supersede the personal appearance of the minor tenants-in-chief; then the three estates became the lords, lay and clerical, the commissioners of shires, and the burgesses[1]; these throughout their history continued to sit in one house. In France, both in the States General and in the provincial estates, the division is into 'gentz de l'eglise,' 'nobles,' and 'gentz des bonnes villes[2].' In England, after a transitional stage, in which the clergy, the greater and smaller barons, and the cities and boroughs, seemed likely to adopt the system used in Aragon and Scotland, and another in which the county and borough communities continued to assert an essential difference, the three estates of clergy, lords, and commons, finally emerge as the political constituents of the nation, or, in their parliamentary form, as the lords spiritual and temporal and the commons[3]. This familiar formula in either shape bears the impress of history. The term 'commons' is not in itself an appropriate expression for the third estate; it does not signify primarily the simple freemen, the plebs, but the plebs organised and combined in corporate communities, in a particular way for particular purposes[4]. The commons are the 'communitates' or 'universitates,' the organised bodies of freemen of the shires

Stages in England.

The estate of the Commons.

tives of the towns, four from Stockholm, two or one from smaller towns; and (4) 250 peasant representatives, chosen one from each district.

[1] The first occasion on which the boroughs are known to have been represented in the Scottish parliament was in the parliament of Cambuskenneth, July 15, 1326; Acts of Parl. of Scotl. i. 115. The act for electing commissaries of shires, passed at Perth, Mar. 1, 1428, remained a dead letter for more than a century. The project was renewed in 1567, but the regular attendance dates from 1587. See Lords' Report on the Dignity of a Peer, i. 111 sq.; Acts of Parliament of Scotland, vol. i, Preface.

[2] Savaron, États Généraux, p. 74.

[3] The writer of the *Modus tenendi parliamentum* divides the English parliament into six grades, (1) the king, (2) the prelates, i.e. archbishops, bishops, abbots and priors holding by barony, (3) the proctors of the clergy, (4) the earls, barons and other magnates, (5) the knights of the shire, (6) the citizens and burghers; but this is not a legal or historical arrangement. See Select Charters, p. 508.

[4] On the use of Commons as a mere equivalent for plebs, see New English Dictionary, s.v. Commons.

and towns; and the estate of the commons is the 'communitas communitatum,' the general body into which for the purposes of parliament those communities are combined. The term then, as descriptive of the class of men which is neither noble nor clerical, is drawn from the political vocabulary, and does not represent any primary distinction of class. The communities of shires and boroughs are further the collective organisations which pay their taxes in common through the sheriffs or other magistrates, and are represented in common by chosen knights or burgesses; they are thus the represented freemen as contrasted with the magnates, who live among them but who are specially summoned to parliament, and make special terms with the Exchequer; and so far forth they are the residue of the body politic, the common people, so called in a sense altogether differing from the former. It is not to be forgotten, however, that the word 'communitas,' 'communauté,' 'la commune,' has different meanings, all of which are used at one time or another in constitutional phraseology. In the coronation oath[1] 'la communauté,' 'vulgus,' or folk, that chooses the laws, can be nothing but the community of the nation, the whole three estates: in the Provisions of Oxford 'le commun de la terre' can only be the collective nation as represented by the barons[2], in other words the governing body of the nation, which was not yet represented by chosen deputies; whilst in the Acts of Parliament[3], in which 'la commune' appears with 'Prelatz et

Meaning of the 'Commons.'

Uses of the words *Commons* and *Community*.

[1] 'Les queux la communaulte de votre realm aura esluz,' 'quas vulgus elegerit;' Statutes of the Realm, i. 168. It is needless to state at length that the idea of the lex Hortensia, 'ut eo jure quod plebes statuisset omnes Quirites tenerentur,' was never accepted in England except in the days of the Great Rebellion.

[2] 'Ces sunt les vint et quatre ke sunt mis per le commun a treter de aide le rei;' 'Ces sunt les duze ke sunt eslu per les baruns a treter a treis parlemenz per an oveke le cunseil le rei pur tut le commun de la tere de commun bosoine;' Select Charters, p. 390. In the later passage 'le commun de la tere' seems to mean the nation, in the former the baronage which for the moment represented it.

[3] The words 'le commun' and 'la commune' seem to be used without any apparent difference of meaning in the Revocation of the Ordinances (Statutes, i. 189) and elsewhere; and at the period at which the commons were growing into recognition as a third estate of parliament, it is extremely difficult to distinguish the passages in which 'le commun' is used discretively for the commons from those in which it is used comprehen-

Seigneurs' as a third constituent of the legislative body, it can mean only the body of representatives. The inconsistency of usage is the same in the case of the boroughs, where 'communitas' means sometimes the whole body of burghers, sometimes the governing body or corporation, sometimes the rest of the freemen, as in the form 'the mayor, aldermen, and commonalty.' As ordinarily employed then the title of 'commons' may claim more than one derivation, besides that which history supplies [1].

Order of the Three Estates.

The commons are the third estate: between the clergy and baronage the question of precedency would scarcely arise, but it is clear from the arrangement of the estates in the common constitutional formulae, both in England and in other countries, that a pious courtesy gave the first place to the clergy. For the term first or second estate there does not seem to be any sufficient early authority [2]. It is scarcely necessary to add that on no medieval theory of government could the king be regarded as an estate of the realm. He was supreme in idea if not in practice; the head, not a limb, of the body politic; the impersonation of the majesty of the kingdom, not one of several co-ordinate constituents.

The system of Estates a product of the thirteenth century.

186. In the earlier chapters of this work we have traced the history of the national council through the several stages of Anglo-Saxon and Norman growth: we have seen in the witenagemot a council composed of the wise men of the nation; in the court of the Conqueror and his sons a similar assembly

sively for the whole body. In the petitions also the word sometimes seems to mean the whole parliament and sometimes only the third estate. But many volumes might be written on this, and indeed every case in which the word occurs from the reign of Henry III to that of Edward III might be commented on at some length. Here I can only refer to the discussions on the word in the Lords' Report on the Dignity of a Peer; Brady's Introduction, pp. 71–84.

[1] The fact however of its use on the continent for the *communitates* or *universitates* of the towns is conclusive as to its historical derivation.

[2] 'In England where the clergy have been esteemed one estate, the peers of the realm the second estate, and the commons of the realm, represented in parliament by persons chosen by certain electors, a third estate;' Lords' Report, i. 118. So in Scotland the barons were the second estate in parliament; ibid. p. 116. 'Les Etats, soit generaux soit particuliers, sont composez des deputez des trois ordres du royaume, qui sont le clergé, la noblesse et les deputez des communautez;' Ordonn. des Rois, iii. p. xx.

with a different qualification; and in that of Henry II a complete feudal council of the king's tenants. The thirteenth century turns the feudal council into an assembly of estates, and draws the constitution of the third estate from the ancient local machinery which it concentrates. But the process of change is not quite simple; it is a case of growth quite as much as of political treatment; and, before examining the steps by which the representative system was completed, we must ask how the other two estates disentangled themselves from one another, and were prepared for the symmetrical arrangement in which they appear permanently; what were the causes of their mutual repulsion or internal cohesion.

The estate of the clergy.

The first or spiritual estate comprises the whole body of the clergy, whether endowed with land or tithe, whether dignified or undignified, whether sharing or not sharing the privileges of baronage. It possesses in its spiritual character an internal principle of cohesion, and the chief historical question is to determine the way in which the material ties which united it with the temporal estates were so far loosened as to allow to that principle of cohesion its full liberty. This of course affects mainly the prelates or ecclesiastical lords. Although during both the Anglo-Saxon and the Norman periods the ecclesiastical and temporal magnates possessed a distinct character and special functions, in the character of counsellors it is difficult to distinguish the action of the two. The ealdorman and sheriff would never usurp the function of the bishop, nor would the bishop, as a spiritual person, lead an army into the field; if he did so, or acted as a secular judge over his dependents, he did it as a landlord, not as a bishop. In the shiremoot the ealdorman declared the secular law, and the bishop the spiritual; but in the witenagemot no such definite line is drawn between lay and clerical counsellors. Under the Norman kings again the supreme council was not divided into bishops and barons, although, where ecclesiastical questions were raised, the prelates might and would avail themselves of their spiritual organisation, which they possessed over and above their baronial status, to sit and deliberate apart. Even after the system of

The prelates in the Anglo-Saxon system;

under the Norman kings;

taxation had been formally arranged, as it was under Henry I and Henry II, the bishops and abbots, as alike tenants-in-chief, sat with the barons to grant aids, took part 'sicut barones ceteri[1]' in the judicial proceedings of the supreme court, and counselled and consented to the king's edicts. They had certainly added the title of 'barones' to that title of 'sapientes,' by which they had originally held, and had never ceased to hold, their seats. This latter title during all the later changes is not forfeited; the guardian of the spiritualities of a vacant see, who of course could not pretend to a baronial qualification, received the formal summons[2]; and even now, when they no longer hold baronies, the bishops are summoned to the house of lords. The prelates were not the whole clergy; but so long as taxation fell solely on the land, the inferior clergy, who subsisted on tithes and offerings, scarcely came within view of the Exchequer. Thus, although of course the radical distinction between layman and clerk was never obliterated, still in all constitutional action the spiritual character was inseparable from the baronial, and the prelates and barons held their places by a common tenure, and as one body.

as barons of the king.

Union of prelacy and barony.

Ever since the Conquest, however, there had been causes at work which could not but in the end force upon the clergy the realisation of their constitutional place, and on the prelates a sense of their real union with the clergy[3]. Foremost among these was the growth of conciliar action in the church under Lanfranc and Anselm. The foreign ecclesiastics who sat on English thrones were made by the spirit of the time to take their place in the growing polity of the Western Church, and, whatever may have been the later practice of the Anglo-Saxon kings with regard to synods, there is no obscurity about their history under the Normans, or as to their distinctly spiritual character. In these synods the clergy had a common field into which the barons could not enter, and a principle of union second only to that which was inherent in their common

Causes of the growth of unity in the estate of clergy:—

(1) Conciliar action.

[1] Constitutions of Clarendon, Art. 11.

[2] See Hallam, Middle Ages, iii. 5. Abundant proof will be found in the summonses given in the Lords' Report.

[3] Cf. Lords' Report, i. 73.

spiritual character. In the various synods of the nation, the province, and the diocese, the clergy had a complete constitution; the assemblies contained not only the prelates but the chapters, the archdeacons, and, in the lowest form, the parochial clergy also. Here was an organisation in most respects the counterpart of the national system of court and council.

(2) Growth of Canon law.

Canon law distinguishing the clerical from the lay estates.

A second impulse in the same direction may be found in the introduction and growth of the canon law, the opening for which was made by the Conqueror's act forbidding the ecclesiastical judges to hold their pleas, that is to hear ecclesiastical causes, in the popular courts. The ecclesiastical law, which had hitherto been administered either by spiritual men in the popular courts, or, where it touched spiritual matters, by the bishop himself in his diocesan council, now received a recognition as the system by which all ecclesiastical persons were to be tried in courts of their own[1]. The clergy were thus removed from the view of the common law, and a double system of judicature sprang up; bishops, archdeacons, and rural deans had their tribunals as well as their councils. Burchard of Worms, Ivo of Chartres, and after them Gratian, supplied manuals of the new jurisprudence. The persecution of Anselm, the weakness of Stephen, and the Becket controversy, spurred men on in the study of it: the legislative abilities of the archbishops were tasked to the utmost in following the footsteps of Alexander III and Innocent III.

(3) Struggles for clerical immunities.

In the third place, the questions of church liberties and immunities, as fought out under Henry I and Henry II, had brought before all men's eyes the increasing differences of status. Appeals to Rome, the action of legates, the increased number of questions which arose between the temporal and spiritual powers in Christendom generally, were impressing a distinct mark on the clergy.

(4) Taxation of clerical property.

But it is in a fourth and further point that this distinctive character, so far as concerns our subject, chiefly asserts itself. This is the point of taxation. The taxable property of the

[1] 'Non secundum hundret sed secundum canones et episcopales leges rectum Deo et episcopo suo faciat;' Will. I, Select Charters, p. 85.

clergy was either in land, which, whether held by the usual temporal services or in free alms, shared the liability of the rest of the land, under the name of temporalities, or in tithes and offerings, technically termed 'spiritualia,' spiritualities. So long as the land only was taxed, the bishops might constitutionally act with the baronage, paying scutages for their military fiefs and carucages for their lands held by other tenure. When taxation began to affect the spiritual revenue, it touched the clergy generally in a point in which the laity had nothing in common with them. It provoked a professional jealousy which later history abundantly justified. Just as the taxation of moveables led to the constitutional action of the commons [1], so the taxation of spirituals served to develope the constitutional action of the clergy [2].

Growth of the custom of clerical taxation.

The stages of the process may be traced thus. Up to the reign of Stephen it is scarcely apparent. The king seized the castles and estates of the bishops just as he did those of the barons. Under Henry II we first find archbishop Theobald objecting to the payment of scutage by the bishops [3]; and, although his objections were overruled by general acquiescence, they seem to point to the idea that previously all ecclesiastical payments to the crown were regarded as free gifts, and that even the lands were held rather on the theory of free alms than on that of feudal service. But such an idea must have been swept away by Henry II, who called on the bishops as well as the barons to give account of the knights' fees held of them and to pay accordingly [4]. In the ordinance of the Saladin tithe, the first occasion probably on which revenue and moveables were regularly taxed, as the books, vestments, and sacred

[1] See vol. i. p. 581 sq.

[2] The French parochial clergy were not summoned either in person or by proctors to the States General, as not possessing 'temporel et justice;' Hervieu, Rev. de Legislation, 1873, p. 381.

[3] Vol. i. pp. 454, 578. Some tradition of this theory must have remained even under Edward I, who in 1276 issued letters patent declaring that the contribution of the archbishop and bishops to the grant of a fifteenth proceeded from the free grace of the bishops, 'et non nomine quintae decimae;' and was not to be construed as a precedent; Parl. Writs, i. p. 5. Cf. p. 14.

[4] Vol. i. p. 472.

apparatus of the clergy required special exemption [1], it can scarcely be expected that spiritual revenue, tithes and offerings, escaped. But this tax was raised for an ecclesiastical purpose, and was imposed by a council far larger than was usually consulted. In the case, again, of Richard's ransom, there is no mention of spiritual revenue as excepted; indeed, seeing that the sacred vessels of the churches were taken, it may be assumed that all branches of such revenue were laid under contribution: this however, again, was a very exceptional case, and one for which the authority of the saints might be pleaded. In the carucage of 1198 the freehold estates of the parish churches are untaxed [2], and during the rest of Hubert Walter's administration it is not probable that any extraordinary demand was made of the clergy, who, under bishops like Hugh of Lincoln, were prepared to resist any such aggression. The question however arose in its barest form under John, who in his demand of a share of the spiritual revenue showed an idea of legal consistency which only the want of money could have suggested to him. He approached the matter gradually. He began by applying to the Cistercians in 1202 [3]. Their wool then, as before and after, afforded a tempting bait to his avarice, a source of profit easily assessed and easily seized. He then demanded a subsidy from the whole clergy of the province of Canterbury for the support of his nephew Otto IV, whose cause was at the moment a holy one under the patronage of Innocent III [4]. The petition was renewed in 1204 [5]. Of the result, however, of these demands we have no account, nor does the demand itself contain distinct reference to the spiritual revenue, or prove more than the wish to obtain a grant from the clergy apart from the laity. After the death of Archbishop Hubert this obscurity ceases. On the 8th of January, 1207,

Increase of taxation under John.

[1] Select Charters, p. 160.

[2] 'Libera feoda ecclesiarum parochialium de hoc tallagio excipiebantur,' Hoveden, iv. 46; Select Charters, p. 257.

[3] Rot. Claus. i. 14; Foed. i. 86.

[4] Foed. i. 87; Rot. Pat. i. 18. The letter is directed 'universo clero;' of course the vast majority of the clergy could only contribute from moveables or spiritual revenue.

[5] M. Paris, ed. Luard, ii. 484.

Taxation of spirituals still a novelty.

the king called together the bishops, and asked them severally to allow the beneficed clergy to pay him a certain proportion of their revenues for the recovery of Normandy[1]. After an adjournment the request was repeated at Oxford on the 9th of February, and was unanimously refused; both provinces replied that such an exaction was unheard of in all preceding ages, and was not to be endured now[2]; and the king had to content himself with a thirteenth of moveables and such voluntary gifts as individual clergy might vouchsafe. The same idea must have occurred about the same time to Innocent III; he demanded a pecuniary aid, and an assembly of bishops, archdeacons and clergy, was convoked on the 26th of May at S. Alban's[3] to grant it, when John, at the instance of the barons, interfered to forbid it. The royal attempt in 1207 was lost sight of in the general oppressions that followed the interdict, and it is probable that until the end of the reign the spiritual revenues escaped direct taxation, simply because they ceased regularly to accrue. As soon, however, as the pope and king were at peace, the long struggle began between the clergy and their united taskmasters, both of whom saw the wisdom of humouring them in their desire to separate their interests from those of the laity. In 1219, in accordance with the decree of the Lateran council of 1215, a twentieth of church revenue was assigned for three years to the crusade[4]; in 1224 the prelates

Taxation of spirituals by the Lateran Council,

[1] Ann. Waverl. p. 258.

[2] 'Anglicanam ecclesiam nullo modo sustinere posse quod ab omnibus saeculis fuit prius inauditum;' Ann. Waverl. p. 258. See above, vol. i. p. 579; Select Charters, p. 273.

[3] 'Conquerente universitate comitum baronum et militum et aliorum fidelium nostrorum audivimus quod, non solum in laicorum gravem perniciem sed etiam in totius regni nostri intolerabile dispendium, super Romscoto praeter consuetudinem solvendo et aliis pluribus inconsuetis exactionibus, auctoritate summi pontificis consilium inire et consilium celebrare decrevistis;' Rot. Pat. i. 72.

[4] 'Vicesima ecclesiarum,' Ann. Theokesb. p. 64. The tax was paid the same year also in Sicily and France;' 'vicesima a personis ecclesiasticis, a laicis vero decima;' Ric. S. Germ. p. 47. The decree of the Lateran council was: 'ex communi approbatione statuimus ut omnes omnino clerici, tam subditi quam praelati, vigesimam partem ecclesiasticorum proventuum usque ad triennium conferant in subsidium Terrae Sanctae;' Labbe and Cossart, xi. 228. See above, p. 37.

granted a carucage separately from the barons[1]; in 1225, when the nation generally paid a fifteenth, the clergy contributed an additional sum from the property which did not contribute to that tax[2]. In 1226 the beneficed clergy at the pope's request gave the king a sixteenth for his own necessities[3]; in 1229 Gregory IX claimed a tenth for himself[4]. It was from such applications for grants from the spiritualty that the custom arose of assembling the clergy in distinct assemblies for secular business, which so largely influenced the history of both Parliament and Convocation. In 1231 the bishops demurred to a scutage which had been imposed without their consent[5]; in 1240 they refused to consider a demand of the legate because the lower clergy were not represented[6]. Successive valuations of ecclesiastical property, spiritual as well as temporal, were made[7]. The discussion of public questions in ecclesiastical

And by pope and king.

Custom of assembling the clergy for secular business.

[1] Above, p. 36. [2] W. Cov. ii. 256, 257; above, p. 38.

[3] Probably this was the same contribution as the last-mentioned, see above, p. 39; but it is important as showing the way in which the precedent of 1219 was applied; 'ad petitionem domini papae, ad urgentissimam necessitatem domini regis . . . spontanea voluntate concessa fuit eidem regi Henrico sexta decima pars aestimationis ecclesiarum, secundum taxationem qua taxatae erant ecclesiae in diebus illis quando vicesima pars ecclesiarum collata fuit ad instantiam domini papae in subsidium Terrae Sanctae; Ann. Osney, p. 68. 'Archiepiscopi, episcopi, abbates, priores et domorum religiosarum magistri per Angliam constituti decimam quintam partem omnium mobilium suorum et feodorum suorum, et clerus inferior aestimato annuo valore singularum ecclesiarum sextam decimam partem inde nobis concesserint;' Royal Letters, i. 299. 'Auxilium de beneficiis suis de quibus quindenam non recepimus impendant;' Wilkins, Conc. i. 620. Probably the grant was made in diocesan synods.

[4] See above, p. 43. 'Decimam reddituum et proventuum clericorum et virorum religiosarum;' Ann. Osney, p. 70.

[5] M. Paris, iii. 200; above, p. 42.

[6] M. Paris, iv. 37; 'omnes tangit hoc negotium, omnes igitur sunt conveniendi.' Cf. pp. 38–43.

[7] From the year 1252 onwards a tenth of ecclesiastical revenue was generally taken by the pope's authority; in 1252, 'decimam ecclesiasticorum proventuum in subsidium Terrae Sanctae,' for three years, Foed. i. 280; in 1254 for five years, Ann. Osney, p. 112; Royal Letters, ii. 101; in 1266 for three years, Foed. i. 473; in 1273 for three years; in 1274 a tenth of spirituals for six years; in 1280 and onwards the grants of spirituals to the king in convocation have been noted above. A taxation for the twentieth in 1219 was mentioned in note 4, p. 182. In 1256 Alexander IV ordered a new taxation of benefices to be made 'secundum debitam et justam taxationem,' Foed. i. 345; in consequence of this a taxation was made by Walter Suffield, bishop of Norwich, called the Norwich Taxation; this lasted until the new taxation of 1291, called that

Petitions and gravamina.

assemblies became more frequent as the constitution of those assemblies took form and consistency under oppression. Innumerable petitions for the redress of grievances illustrate the increased spirit of independence in the clergy, as well as the persistency of the king and pope in crushing it; and, interpreted by the life of Grosseteste, show a more distinct comprehension by the leaders of the church of their peculiar position as the 'clerus,' the Lord's inheritance. These points will come before us again in reference to the history of Convocation. It is enough to say here that it was by action on these occasions that the clerical estate worked out its distinct organisation as an estate of the realm, asserting and possessing deliberative, legislative, and taxing powers, and in so doing provided some not unimportant precedents for parliamentary action under like circumstances.

Growth of the clerical estate.

Growth of the estate of baronage.

187. It is less easy to determine, either by date or by political cause, the circumstances that ultimately defined the estate of the baronage, drawing the line between lords and commons. The result indeed is clear: the great landowners, tenants-in-chief, or titled lords, who appeared in person at the parliament, are separated by a broad line from the freeholders, who were represented by the knights of the shire; and legal authority fixes the reigns of Henry III and Edward I as the period of limitation, and recognises the change in the character of qualification, from barony by tenure to barony by writ, as the immediate and formal cause of it. This authority, however, whether based on legal theory or on the historical evidence of custom, rather determines the question of personal and family right than the

of pope Nicolas (see above, pp. 129 sq.), which was in force until the Reformation, and comprised both temporals and spirituals. Curiously enough during Simon de Montfort's administration the spirituals were taxed by the prelates and magnates;' 'cum per praelatos et magnates regni nostri provisum sit et unanimiter concessum quod decimae proventuum omnium beneficiorum ecclesiasticorum in regno nostro conferantur ad communem utilitatem ejusdem regni et ecclesiae Anglicanae,' Foed. i. 445; but perhaps this merely means that the tithe collected under the papal authority should be applied to the good of the country instead of the Crusade. The assessment of the lands acquired after the taxation of pope Nicolas was, as we shall see, a subject of difficulty throughout the fourteenth century.

intrinsic character of the baronage, at all events during its present stage of development.

188. An hereditary baronage may be expected to find its essential characteristic in distinction of blood, or in the extent and tenure of its territory, or in the definitions of law and custom, or in the possession of peculiar privilege bestowed by the sovereign, or in the coincidence of some or all of these.

Characteristics of barony.

The great peculiarity of the baronial estate in England as compared with the continent, is the absence of the idea of caste: the English lords do not answer to the nobles of France, or to the princes and counts of Germany, because in our system the theory of nobility of blood as conveying political privilege has no legal recognition. English nobility is merely the nobility of the hereditary counsellors of the crown, the right to give counsel being involved at one time in the tenure of land, at another in the fact of summons, at another in the terms of a patent; it is the result rather than the cause of peerage. The nobleman is the person who for his life holds the hereditary office denoted or implied in his title. The law gives to his children and kinsmen no privilege which it does not give to the ordinary freeman, unless we regard certain acts of courtesy, which the law has recognised, as implying privilege. Such legal nobility does not of course preclude the existence of real nobility, socially privileged and defined by ancient purity of descent or even by connexion with the legal nobility of the peerage; but the English law does not regard the man of most ancient and purest descent as entitled thereby to any right or privilege which is not shared by every freeman.

English nobility as contrasted with foreign.

English nobility of peerage.

The cause of this difference is a question of no small interest. Nobility of blood, that is, nobility which was shared by the whole kin alike, was a very ancient principle among the Germans, and was clearly recognised by the Anglo-Saxons in the common institution of wergild. The Normans of the Conquest formed a new nobility, which can scarcely be suspected of feeling too little jealousy of the privileges of blood; nor has the line which socially divided the man of ancient race from the 'novus homo,' who rises by wealth or favour, ever been entirely

Nobility of blood.

obliterated[1]. The question is not solved by reference to the custom of inheritance by primogeniture, or to the indivisibility of fiefs, so far as it prevailed, because, although these causes may have helped to produce the result, they were at work in countries where the result was different. It is possible that the circumstances of the great houses in the twelfth century, when the noble lines were very much attenuated, when many of them were rich enough to provide several sons with independent fiefs, and those who could not sent their younger sons into holy orders, may have affected the constitutional theory. The truth is, however, that English law recognises simply the right of peerage, not the privilege of nobility as properly understood; it recognises office, dignity, estate, and class, but not caste; for the case of villenage, in which the question of caste does to some extent arise, is far too obscure to be made to illustrate that of nobility, and the disabilities of Jews and aliens rest on another principle. Social opinion and the rules of heraldry, which had perhaps their chief use in determining an international standard of blood, alone recognise the distinction.

Distinction of blood.

Question of land-tenure as touching barony.

189. The nobility of blood then does not furnish the principle of cohesion, or separate the baronage from the other estates. The question whether the distinctions of land tenure created such a separation, has its own difficulties. Upon feudal theory all the king's tenants-in-chief were members of his court and council; and, as their estates were hereditary, their office of counsellor was hereditary too; but in practice the title and rights of baronage were gradually restricted to the greater tenants who received special summons, when the minor tenants

[1] A story told in the Opus Chronicorum about Johanna of Acre, the daughter of Edward I, who married a simple knight, Ralph of Monthermer, of whose extraction nothing is known, shows how slight was the influence of blood nobility at this time: 'Aderat unus e magnatibus terrae qui in auribus domini regis patris sui intonuit, quod ejus honori adversum foret hujusmodi matrimonium, cum nonnulli nobiles, reges, comites et barones eam adoptabant toro legitimo. Cui illa respondit "non est ignominiosum neque probrosum magno comiti et potenti pauperculam mulierem et tenuem sibi legitimo matrimonio copulare; sic vice versa nec comitissae non est reprehensibile nec difficile juvenem strenuum promovere;"' Trokelow, ed. Riley, p. 27. The idea of disparagement in marriage must have been on the wane.

received a general summons, to the council and the host; and the baronage of the thirteenth century was the body of tenants-in-chief holding a fief or a number of fiefs consolidated into a baronial honour or qualification. This qualification was not created by the possession of a certain extent of territory; for although the law defined the obligations of a barony in proportion to those of earldoms and knights' fees, in the ratio of the mark to the pound and the shilling[1], the mere acquisition of thirteen knights' fees and a third[2] did not make the purchaser a baron. Neither was it created by the simple fact of tenancy-in-chief of the crown, which the barons shared with knights and freeholders. The peculiar tenure of barony is recognised in the Constitutions of Clarendon: the relief due for a barony is prescribed by Magna Carta. Whether the baronial honour or qualification was created by the terms of the original grant of the fief, or by subsequent recognition, it is perhaps impossible to determine. As we do not possess anything like an early enfeoffment of a barony, it is safer to confine ourselves to the assertion that, in whatever form the lands were acquired or bestowed, the special summons recognised the baronial character of the tenure, or in other words, that estate was a barony which entitled its owner to such special summons.

Barony not created by extent of tenure;

nor by nature of tenure.

But although the extent and nature of tenure of estate in land may not explain the origin of the distinction, they do, more clearly than the theory of nobility, furnish a clue to the causes of the social distinction of the baronage. The twelfth century saw the struggle made by a body of feudatories, thoroughly imbued with the principles of feudalism, for the possession of political power and jurisdiction. Their attempts were defeated by Henry I and Henry II; but the policy of those kings did not require the limitation of the other parts of the feudal theory; on the contrary, it is to their reigns that many of the innovations are ordinarily referred, which, by developing the land-laws, gave considerable impulse to the

Tenure of land illustrates the social idea of barony.

[1] Bracton, lib. ii. c. 36; Magna Carta (Edw. I. A.D. 1297), art. 2. Cf. Pollock and Maitland, History of English Law, i. 238 sq.

[2] Modus tenendi Parliamentum, Select Charters, p. 503.

Rule of primogeniture.

growth of the baronage as a separate class. It was the feudal custom or rule that encouraged the introduction of succession by primogeniture, and discouraged the division and alienation of fiefs. In the absence of anything like exact evidence, the general acceptance of these principles is placed at this point. The law by which Geoffrey of Brittany introduced the right of primogeniture into his estates[1] was the work of his father Henry II, who would not have forced on that province a rule which he had not incorporated with his own legal practice. The whole process of the assize of Mort d'ancestor would seem to prove that in estates held by knight-service this was already the rule. In Glanvill's time estates held in socage were equally divided among the sons, the eldest however receiving the capital messuage; the exclusive rights of the eldest-born date from the thirteenth century[2]. During the same period of unrecorded change the rule that the tenant must not alienate his land without his lord's consent, a rule which had been formally promulgated in the empire by Lothar II[3], and which was in general use on the continent, must have been at least partially admitted. The power of alienation, a power which no one would value unless he was debarred from it, had under the Anglo-Saxon law been restricted by the rights of the family, only when such rights were specially mentioned in the title-deeds of the estate; and, when Glanvill wrote, this power was subject only to some undefined claims of the heir. First in the Great Charter of 1217 it was limited by the provision that the tenant must not give or sell to any one so much of his estate as to make it incapable of furnishing the due service to his lord[4]. The hold of the lord on the land of his tenant, which a century

Restraint on alienation.

[1] See it in Palgrave, Commonwealth, ii. p. ccccxxxv.

[2] Glanvill, vii. c. 3; Digby, Real Property, p. 72.

[3] Hallam, M. A. i. 174, 175. 'Per multas enim interpellationes ad nos factas comperimus milites sua beneficia passim distrahere, ac ita omnibus exhaustis suorum servitia subterfugere; per quod vires imperii maxime attenuatas cognovimus, dum proceres nostri milites suos omnibus beneficiis suis exutos, ad felicissimi nostri numinis expeditionem nullo modo transducere valeamus; . . . decernimus, nemini licere beneficia quae a suis senioribus habent sine ipsorum permissione distrahere;' A.D. 1136; Lib. Feudorum, ii. tit. 52. l. 1. Cf. the law of Frederick in tit. 55.

[4] Magna Carta (1217), art. 39.

before had been construed as implying so great rights of jurisdiction, was rapidly being limited to rights of service and escheat: but these rights the tenant-in-chief laboured hard to retain[1]: before the end of the century great obstacles had been put in the way of any such alienation, and were tasking the ingenuity of the lawyers to overcome them. These were devised no doubt to preserve the equitable rights of the lords or the reversionary rights of donors: the latter was the object of the statute *de Donis*, the former was thought to be secured by the statute *Quia emptores*. The principle that a tenant-in-chief of the crown could not alienate without licence had been long admitted[2] before it was exemplified in the document called *de Praerogativa*, the very title of which seems to show that the privileges it contains were not yet shared by the other 'capitales domini[3],' against whom Bracton argues in favour of liberty. But although these measures were justified by legal theory, there are indications that there was, in a section at least of the lords, an inclination to grasp at the ultimate possession of all land not in the royal hands, just as a century before they had grasped at exclusive jurisdiction. The statute of Merton[4], which gives to the lord of the manor the right of inclosing all common land that is not absolutely required by the freeholders, is an early illustration of this. Complaint was made too in the Oxford parliament of 1258, that certain great men bought up mortgages from the Jews and so entered on the lands of the mortgagors[5]. The charge was perhaps directed against the

Growth of English law on this point.

Aggressive instincts of the baronage.

[1] Bracton, ii. c. 19: 'sed posset aliquis dicere quod ex hoc quod donatorius ulterius dat et transfert rem donatam ad alios, quod hoc facere non potest, quia per hoc amittit dominus servitium suum, quod quidem non est verum, salva pace et reverentia capitalium dominorum.'

[2] In 1225, Thomas of Hoton sold the bailiwick of Plumpton, a serjeanty of the king's forest of Inglewood, with two carucates and four bovates of land to Alan de Capella, 'quam bailliam in manum domini regis cepit (Hugo de Nevilla) eo quod idem Thomas eam dicto Alano vendidit sine licentia domini regis;' Rot. Claus. ii. 38.

[3] Statutes of the Realm, i. 227. The date of the *de Praerogativa* is uncertain; it was formerly attributed to 17 Edw. II, but is probably earlier. See on it the Lords' Report, i. p. 400; Cutbill, Petition of Right, p. 12; Pollock and Maitland, i. 318.

[4] Statutes of the Realm, i. 2.

[5] 'Judaei aliquando debita sua, et terras eis invadiatas, tradunt magnatibus et potentioribus regni, qui terras minorum ingrediuntur ea occasione,

foreign favourites of Henry III, but it was not met adequately by legislation, and possibly it points to an increasing divergency of interest between the barons and the body of knights. But the policy of Edward I and the craft of the lawyers prevented the reduction of the English land system to the feudal model, if it ever were contemplated. The hold which the statutes of 1285 and 1290 gave to the chief lords over their vassals made the king supreme over the chief lords. On the whole, however, restraints on alienation, whether general or affecting the tenants-in-chief only, must have tended to the concentration and settlement of great estates and so must have increased the distinction between greater and smaller landowners.

Double effect of Edward's land-laws.

The definitions of the law as touching barony.

190. The definitions of the law recognise rather than create the character of barony; but the observance of the rule of proportion in the payment of relief, the special provision that the baron must be amerced by his equals or before the royal council, and the rule that by his equals only he should be tried, must have served to mark out who those equals were, and to give additional consistency to a body already limited and beginning to recognise its definite common interest[1].

Barony finally created by royal action.

Having, however, all these rights, privileges and interests in common, the baronage was ultimately and essentially defined as an estate of the realm by the royal action in summons, writ, and patent. It was by special summons 'propriis nominibus[2]' that Henry I, Henry II[3], and the barons of Runnymede, separated the greater from the smaller vassals of the crown; and the constitutional change which at last determined the character of peerage was the making of the status of the peers depend on the hereditary reception of the writ, rather than

et licet ipsi qui debitum debent parati sint ad solvendum praedictum debitum cum usuris, praefati magnates negotium prorogant, ut praedictae terrae et tenementa aliquo modo sibi remanere possint;' Select Charters, p. 385.

[1] Roger of Muntbegon, as 'magnus homo et baro regis,' has the right of swearing by his steward in a court of justice, and of not being personally detained by the county court, in 1220; Royal Letters, i. 102, 104.

[2] See vol. i. 567.

[3] 'Barones secundae dignitatis;' W. Fitz-Stephen, S. T. C. i. 235. Hallam (Middle Ages, iii. 8) rightly understands this to refer to the knightly tenants-in-chief; Lyttelton and Hume refer it to the mesne tenants.

on the tenure which had been the original qualification for summons. We may not suspect the great men who secured the liberties of England of struggling merely for their own privilege: their successes certainly did not result in the vindication of the rights of blood or of those of tenure. The determination of the persons who should be summoned as barons rested finally with the crown[1], limited only on one side by the rule of hereditary right.

The 'majores barones.'

We have already recognised the distinctive character, traceable as early as the reign of Henry I, of a class of vassals who, besides receiving special summons to council[2], had special summons to the host, led their own dependents in battle, and made separate composition with the Exchequer for their pecuniary obligations. Henry III and Edward I either continued or introduced the custom of summoning by special writ to the council a much smaller number of these than were summoned by special writ to perform military service. The diminution was no doubt gratefully admitted both by those who were glad to escape from an irksome duty, and by those who saw their own political strength increased by the disappearance of many who might have been their competitors. There can be little doubt that the idea of a peerage, a small body of counsellors by whom the exercise of the royal functions could be limited and directed, a royal court of peers like those of France, was familiar to the English politicians of the reign of Henry III; and the influence of such an idea may be traced to the oligarchical policy of the barons of 1258 and 1264. But it never gained general favour: the saying of Peter des Roches, that there were no 'pares' in England, ignorant blunder as it was[3], is sufficient to prove this; and the apprehensions felt that William of Valence would change the English constitution[4], as well as the contemptuous way in which the historians

Diminution in the number summoned to parliament.

Growth of the idea of peerage.

[1] In France the dukes, counts, barons, bannerets, and 'hautes-justiciers' were always summoned; the seigneurs of secondary rank never. Hervieu, Rev. de Legisl. 1873, p. 384.

[2] The form 'majores barones,' for the lords specially summoned, subsisted as late as the reign of Edward II; see Parl. Writs, II. i. 181.

[3] Above, p. 49.

[4] Above, p. 53.

describe the Scottish attempt to create a body of twelve peers[1], show that the scheme, however near realisation, was disliked and ridiculed. The plan of thus limiting the royal power, so frequently brought forward under Henry III, Edward II, and his successors, is never once broached in the reign of Edward I.

Edward's plan a middle course.

The hereditary summoning of a large proportion of great vassals was a middle course between the very limited peerage which in France co-existed with an enormous mass of privileged nobility, and the unmanageable, ever-varying assembly of the whole mass of feudal tenants as prescribed in Magna Carta. It is to this body of select hereditary barons, joined with the prelates, that the term 'peers of the land' properly belongs; an expression which occurs first, it is said, in the act by which the Despensers were exiled[2], but which before the middle of the fourteenth century had obtained general recognition as descriptive of members of the house of lords.

Edward's reign a date of limitation.

It may be doubted whether either Edward I or his ministers contemplated the perpetuity of the restrictions which mark this important change: and it may be not unreasonably held that the practice of the reign owes its legal importance to the fact that it was used by the later lawyers as a period of limitation,

In the present period barony implies tenure and summons.

and not to any conscious finality in Edward's policy. It is convenient to adopt the year 1295 as the era from which the baron, whose ancestor has been once summoned and has once sat in parliament, can claim an hereditary right to be so summoned[3]. It is unnecessary here to anticipate the further questions of the degrees, the privileges, and the rights of peerage. For the period before us membership of the parliamentary

[1] 'Ad modum Franciae;' Hemingburgh, ii. 78; Rishanger, p. 151. 'More Francorum;' M. Westm. p. 425.

[2] Statutes of the Realm, i. 181, 184; Lords' Report, i. 281. The word is used so clumsily as to show that it was in this sense a novelty; first 'lui mustrent prelatz, countes, barounes, et les autres piers de la terre, et commune du roiaulme;' then 'nous piers de la terre, countes et barouns.'

[3] Courthope, Hist. Peerage, p. xli; but cf. Hallam, M. A. iii. 124, 125. The question of life peerage need not be considered at the present stage. The importance of 1264 and 1295 arises from the fact that there are no earlier or intermediate writs of summons to a completely constituted parliament extant; if, as is by no means impossible, earlier writs addressed to the ancestors of existing families should be discovered, it might become a critical question how far the rule could be regarded as binding.

baronage implies both tenure and summons. The political status of the body so constituted is thus defined by their successors: 'the hereditary peers of the realm claim, (i.) in conjunction with the lords spiritual, certain powers as the king's permanent council when not assembled in parliament, (ii.) other powers as lords of parliament when assembled in parliament and acting in a judicial capacity, and (iii.) certain other powers when assembled in parliament together with the commons of the realm appearing by their representatives in parliament, the whole now forming under the king the legislature of the country[1].' The estate of the peerage is identical with the house of lords.

Definition of peerage.

191. Had it depended upon the barons to draw the line between themselves and the smaller landowners, the latter might in the end have been swamped altogether, or have had to win political power by a separate struggle. The distinction was drawn, on the one hand by the royal power of summons, and on the other by the institution and general acceptance of the principle of shire-representation. For several reasons the minor freeholders might have been expected to throw in their lot with the barons, with whom they shared the character of landowners and the common bonds of chivalry and consanguinity. For a long time they voted their taxes in the same proportion with them, and it was not by any means clear, at the end of the reign of Edward I, that they might not furnish a fourth estate of Parliament. And ultimately perhaps it was rather the force of the representative system than any strong fellow-feeling with the town populations that made them merge their separate character in the estate of the commons. We have then to account first for their separation from the baronage, and secondly for their incorporation in the third estate: their separation from the baronage was caused not only by the circumstances which drew the baronage away from them, but by other circumstances which gave them a separate interest apart from the baronage; and their union with the town populations was the result of mutual approximation, and not

The line drawn between the barons and smaller landowners.

Effect of representation.

[1] Lords' Report, i. 151; cf. p. 14.

of simple attraction of the smaller to the greater, the weaker to the stronger body.

The freeholders;

192. That portion of the third estate which was represented by the knights of the shire contained not only the residue of the tenants-in-chief but all the freeholders of the county. The chosen knights represented the constituency that met in the county courts. This point admits of much illustration [1], but it is enough now to remark that practically the selection of representatives would depend on the more important landowners whether they held in chief of the crown or of mesne lords. Formally their bond of union was the common membership of the particular shire-moot; but as a political estate they had class interests and affinities [2], and the growth of these in contrast with the interests of the baronial class might form for the investigator of social history an interesting if somewhat perplexing subject. Almost all presumptions based on the principles of nobility and property are common to both bodies; and their political sympathies might be expected to correspond. Yet from the day when the Conqueror exacted the oath of fealty from all the landowners, 'whosesoever men they were,' the kings seem to have depended on the provincial knights and freeholders for aid against the great feudatories. The social tyranny of the great barons would fall first on their own vassals; the knights who held single fees in chief of the crown would stand in a position to be coveted by their vassal neighbours, and the two classes would be drawn together by common dangers. These political sympathies would be turned into a sense of real unity by the measures taken by the kings, and especially by Edward I, to eliminate the political importance of mesne tenure. The obligation to receive knighthood, imposed not only on the tenants-in-chief, not only on all tenants by knight-service, but on all who possessed land enough to furnish knightly equipment [3], whether that obligation were enforced or redeemed by fine, consolidated a knightly body irrespective of tenure. The common service in war, which

combined in the county courts.

Separation from the great feudatories.

Growth of political sympathy.

[1] See below, § 203.

[2] See Gneist, Verwaltungsrecht, i. 312.

[3] See below, § 239.

likewise Edward demanded of all freeholders, was another example of the same principle; and, although foreign service of the sort was strange to the institutions of England, the very attempt to compel it helped to draw men together. The abolition of subinfeudation in 1290[1] must have increased the number of minor tenants-in-chief whenever the great estates were broken up; and must have diminished the difference, if indeed any such difference still subsisted, between the two classes.

Increase of corporate feeling between minor tenants-in-chief and mesne free holders.

Drawn together by common dangers, and assimilated to one another by royal policy, both classes of freeholders had, in the work of the county court, an employment which the technical differences of their tenure did not disturb. Without any regard to tenure, 'discreet and legal' members of these classes acted together in the management of the judicial and financial business, the military work and the police of the shire. The body which, under the name of the 'communitas bacheleriae Angliae[2],' urged on Edward in 1259 the necessity of reforming the laws, was not, however new in its designation, a newly-formed association; it was a consolidated body of men trained by a century and a half of common interests and common work. The summons to elect two men to parliament, to grant an aid or to accept a law, was not the first occasion on which the forms of election or the principle of representation came before them. It is quite probable that the idea of a possible antagonism, or a possible equilibrium, between the county court and the baronage, may have suggested to Henry III, as it did to Simon de Montfort, the summoning of such representatives to council. The machinery of the county gave body

The county court a common field of work.

Cohesion of the freeholders in the county court.

[1] 'In the reign of Edward, provisions were made with respect to tenures, which had the effect of greatly increasing the number of Freeholders, and particularly the statute, "quia emptores terrarum," which prevented all future subinfeudation, making every alienee tenant to the immediate superior of the alienor, which tended gradually to increase very considerably the number of the tenants-in-chief of the crown, as the necessities of the greater tenants-in-chief and even the necessity of providing for the younger branches of their families, which was generally done by grants of land, compelled them to alienate parcels of land holden by them immediately of the crown;' Lords' Report, i. 129. See also Hallam, Middle Ages, iii. 16.

[2] Above, p. 83.

and form; the common political interest, sympathy and antipathy, gave spirit, to the newly-formed 'communitas terrae.'

The knights draw off from the magnates.

When once made a part of the national council, the knights of the shire would have in their character of delegates or proctors another cause of separation from the barons, which would further react on their constituencies. Men who knew themselves to be delegates, called together primarily to give on behalf of their counties an assent to action already prescribed for them by the magnates, not only would be made to feel themselves a separate class from the magnates, but would be inclined to assume an attitude of opposition. As delegates too, local influences would affect them in a way which must have increased the divergency between them and the barons, who were less identified with local interests and more imbued with the interest of class. The constant changes in the representative members, none of whom would feel that he had a certain tenure of power, would incline the whole body to seek their strength in harmonious action and mutual confidence, not to indulge the personal ambition of particular leaders. And this delegate character, shared with the town representatives, drew the knights to them, and away from the barons. But too much importance must not be attached to these influences: we shall see in the history of the fourteenth century that local and personal interests were strong in all the three estates, and that there was far more to draw them together, or to divide them, so to speak, vertically, than to separate them according to class interests.

Their representative character draws them to the town representatives.

These points, it is true, illustrate the position of the knights of the shire rather than those of their constituents, but it is to be remembered that it is in the character of 'communitates,' represented by these elected knights, that the landowners of the shires become an estate of the realm.

Approximation of shire and town communities.

193. The causes that drew together the knights of the shire and the burghers in parliament may be similarly stated. The attraction which was not created by like habits of life and thought was supplied by their joint procuratorial character, their common action in the county court, and the common

need of social independence in relation to the lords. As time went on, and the two branches of the landed interest became in social matters more entirely separated, no doubt the townsmen were drawn nearer to their country neighbours. The younger sons of the country knight sought wife, occupation, and estate, in the towns. The leading men in the towns, such as the De la Poles, formed an urban aristocracy, that had not to wait more than one generation for ample recognition. The practice of knighthood, the custom of bearing coat-armour as a sign of original or achieved gentility, as well as real relationship and affinity, united the superior classes; the small freeholder and the small tradesman met on analogous terms, and the uniform tendency of local and political sympathy more than counteracted the disruptive tendency of class jealousies. Such agencies must be regarded as largely affecting the growth of the third estate into a consciousness of its corporate identity. Probably the proof of their effects will be found more plentifully in the fourteenth century than in the thirteenth. The policy however of raising the trading classes, which is ascribed to Edward III, may be traced in the action of his grandfather, and is far more in harmony with his statesmanship than with that of the founder of the order of the Garter. But notwithstanding the operation of these causes, both under Edward I and during the three succeeding reigns, the glare of a factitious chivalry must, in England as abroad, have rendered the relations of town and country gentry somewhat uneasy.

Country and town affinities.

Peculiarity of the Third Estate in England.

The third estate in England differs from the same estate in the continental constitutions, by including the landowners below baronial rank. In most of those systems it contains the representatives of the towns or chartered communities[1] only. And it was this that constituted the original strength of our representative system: as a concentration of the powers of the county courts, that system contained a phalanx of commoner members, seventy-four knights of the shires[2], who not

[1] The Spanish 'poblaciones,' although they contained landowners, were in reality chartered communities, not differing in origin from the town municipalities.

[2] This is a point to be kept carefully in mind when comparisons are

The shire system is the strength of the Third Estate.

only helped to link the baronage with the burghers, but formed a compact body which neither the crown nor the sheriff could diminish, as they could diminish the number of barons summoned, or of the representatives of the towns. These knights too were men likely and able to show themselves independent: certainly they could not be treated in the way in which Charles V and Philip II extinguished the action of the Spanish cortes or quelled the spirit of the Netherlands. Their rights were rooted not in royal privilege, which he who gave could take away, but in the most primitive institutions and in those local associations which are to all intents and purposes indelible.

Sub-estate of the lawyers.

194. In the uncertainty which for some half century attended the ultimate form in which the estates would rank themselves, two other classes or subdivisions of estates might have seemed likely to take a more consolidated form and to bid for more direct power than they finally achieved. The lawyers[1] and the merchants occasionally seem as likely to form an estate of the realm as the clergy or the knights. Under a king with the strong legal instincts of Edward I, surrounded by a council of lawyers, the patron of great jurists and the near kinsman of three great legislators, the practice and study of law bid fair for a great constitutional position. Edward would not, like his uncle Frederick II, have closed the high offices of the law to all but the legal families[2], and so turned the class, as Frederick did the knightly class, into a caste; or, like his

Foreign classes of lawyers.

drawn between the history of the third estate in Spain and that in England. The shires furnished the only absolutely indestructible part of the parliament.

[1] 'Qu'est il plus farouche que de veoir une nation ou, par legitime coustume, la charge de juger se vende, et les jugements soyent payez a purs deniers comptants, et ou legitimement la justice soit refusee a qui n'a de quoy la payer; et ayt cette marchandise si grand credit, qu'il se face en une police un quatriesme estat de gents maniants les proces, pour le joindre aux trois anciens, de l'eglise, de la noblesse, et du peuple;' Montaigne, Essais, liv. i. c. 22. See p. 200, note 1 below.

[2] See the Constitution of Roger, confirmed by Frederick II; Const. Reg. Sic. iii. 39. 1; cf. Giannone, Hist. Naples, i. 535. Gervase of Tilbury, Otia Imperialia, Leibnitz, Scr. Rer. Brunsv. i. 943, speaking of the emperor Henry VI, says, 'Hic legem instituit apud Teutones, ut militiae *more Gallorum et Anglorum*, successionis jure devolverentur ad proximiores cognationis gradus, cum antea magis penderent ex principis gratia.' He seems however by 'militiae' to mean knightly fiefs.

brother-in-law Alfonso the Wise, have attempted to supersede the national law by the civil law of Rome; or, like Philip the Fair, have suffered the legal members of his council to form themselves into a close corporation almost independent of the rest of the body politic; but where the contemporary influences were so strong we can hardly look to the king alone as supplying the counteracting weight. It is perhaps rather to be ascribed to the fact that the majority of the lawyers were still in profession clerks[1]; that the Chancery, which was increasing in strength and wholesome influence, was administered almost entirely by churchmen, and that the English universities did not furnish for the common law of England any such great school of instruction as Paris and Bologna provided for the canonist or the civilian. Had the scientific lawyers ever obtained full sway in English courts, notwithstanding the strong antipathy felt for the Roman law, the Roman law must ultimately have prevailed, and if it had prevailed it might have changed the course of English history. To substitute the theoretical perfection of a system, which was regarded as less than inspired only because it was not of universal applicability, for one, the very faults of which produced elasticity and stimulated progress and reform whilst it trained the reformers for legislation, would have been to place the development of the constitution under the heel of the king, whose power the scientific lawyer never would curtail but when it comes into collision with his own rules and precedents[2]. The action of

Peculiar growth of the profession of law in England.

[1] On the growth of the professional lawyer class, see Foss's Judges of England, ii. 200; iii. 46 sq., 370–390; iv. 195 sq., 251 sq.; and Gneist, Verwaltungsrecht, i. 341, 350. The frequent legislation of the ecclesiastical councils and the remonstrances of the better prelates of the thirteenth century withdrew the clergy in some measure from legal practice. Edward I in 1292 ordered the judges to provide and ordain seven score attorneys and apprentices to practise in the courts; a certain number to be chosen from the best in each county, and all others excluded; Rot. Parl. i. 84. Fleta mentions several degrees of practising lawyers, servientes, narratores, attornati, and apprentitii.

[2] It is a curious point, which should have been noted in the last chapter, that Bracton, although himself clearly a constitutional thinker, gives the preference in almost all cases to the decisions of Stephen Segrave, the justiciar of Henry III, who supplanted Hubert de Burgh, and was practically a tool of the foreign party. It is clear that Segrave, although a bad minister, was a first-rate lawyer.

An Estate of Lawyers not acceptable in England.

the Privy Council, which to some extent played the part of a private parliament, was always repulsive to the English mind; had it been a mere council of lawyers the result might have been still more calamitous than it was. The summons of the justices and other legal counsellors to parliament [1], by a writ scarcely distinguishable from that of the barons themselves, shows how nearly this result was reached.

Sub-estate of the Merchants.

195. The merchant class, again, possessed in the peculiar nature of their taxable property, and in the cosmopolitan character of their profession, grounds on which, like the clergy, they might have founded a claim for class representation. What the tithe was to the one class, the wool and leather were to the other; both had strong foreign connexions, and the Gilbertine and Cistercian orders, whose chief wealth was in wool, formed a real link between the two. Nor was the wool less coveted than the tithe by kings like Richard and John; the mercantile influence of Flanders and Lombardy might be paralleled with the ecclesiastical influence of Rome.

Their taxable value.

It was perhaps the seizure of the wool of the Cistercians for Richard's ransom that led John to bestow special favours on that order, and then to make the special applications for help in return for those special favours, applications which could scarcely be refused when the taxable fund lay so completely at the king's mercy. So long as the contribution to royal wants was made to bear the character of a free gift severally asked for and severally bestowed, the merchants shared with the clergy the privilege of being specially consulted. In 1218 the merchants whose wool was arrested at Bristol granted to Henry III six marks on the sack [2], making perhaps a virtue

[1] 'During the sitting of parliament the council . . . sat as a house, branch, or estate of Parliament;' Palgrave, King's Council, p. 21. This seems to be a mere rhetorical exaggeration. Yet in 1381 the commons petitioned that 'les prelatz par eux mesmes, les grantz seigneurs temporels par eux mesmes, les chivalers par eux, les justices par eux, et touz autres estatz singulerement,' might debate severally; Rot. Parl. iii. 100. In France in the reign of Henry II (1557, 1558) the 'Parliaments' seem to nave sat by their deputies as a separate estate of the states general. And in the Rolls of Parliament the judges are sometimes loosely mentioned as one of several 'status' in the general body. The dislike of having practising lawyers in parliament appears as early as the reign of Edward III.

[2] Rot. Claus. i. 351, 353.

of necessity, and preferring the form of a grant to that of a fine. Edward I very early in his reign obtained, from the lords and 'communitates' of the kingdom, a grant on the sack at the instance and request of the merchants[1]; possibly the parliament recognised the impost which the merchants by petition or otherwise had declared themselves willing to grant, in order to escape arbitrary seizures or 'prises.' This was in 1275; in 1294 when the king seized the wool, and took the consent of the merchants afterwards to an increased custom during the war, the consent was probably extorted from an assembly of merchants or by distinct commissions[2]. A similar exaction in 1297 was one of the causes of the tumultuous action of earls Bohun and Bigod, and the right of taking the maletote without the common consent and goodwill of the community of the realm was expressly renounced when the charters were confirmed. Still no legal enactment could hinder the merchants from giving or the king from asking. In 1303 Edward summoned an assembly of merchants to the Exchequer at York; ordering two or three burghers from each of forty-two towns to meet them and consider the matter of a grant. The foreign merchants had agreed to increase the custom, but the representatives of towns and cities refused[3]. In this assembly,

Use made by Edward I of merchant assemblies;

for taxing the wool and other merchandise.

Merchant assemblies.

[1] 'Cum archiepiscopi, episcopi, et alii praelati regni Angliae, ac comites, barones, et nos et communitates ejusdem regni ad instantiam et rogatum mercatorum . . . concesserimus;' Parl. Writs, i. p. 2; Select Charters, p. 451; below, § 223.

[2] Above, p. 131.

[3] See above, p. 164. Select Charters, p. 500; Parl. Writs, i. 134, 135. In this case the king, who on the 1st of February had granted a charter to a large body of foreign merchants, in return for the 'Nova Custuma' (above, p. 164), on the 16th of April ordered the Mayor and Sheriffs of London to send to York two or three merchants from each of the Italian trading companies on the 5th of May. Having secured their assent, he issued on the 8th of May writs to the Sheriffs of the several counties to cause two or three citizens and burghers from each city and borough to meet at York on June 25; on that day the meeting was held and the answer given: 'Dixerunt unanimi consensu et voluntate tam pro se ipsis quam pro communitatibus civitatum et burgorum . . . quod ad incrementum maltolliae nec ad custumas, in praedicto brevi contentas, per alienigenas et extraneos mercatores domino regi concessas, nullo modo consentient, nisi ad custumas antiquitus debitas et consuetas.' The king appointed collectors for the new customs granted by the foreign merchants, April 1st, 1304; Parl. Writs, i. 406.

which was not a parliament, it is clear that the elected burghers acted as representatives of the mercantile interest rather than of the third estate; and their prompt action no doubt checked in time Edward's scheme of providing himself with additional revenue from denizens, although he succeeded in obtaining a new custom from the foreigners. The gatherings of merchants by Edward III, which are sometimes regarded as a marked feature of his policy, are in analogy as well as in contrast with this, and may have been suggested by it. But although in that king's reign the wool was made a sort of circulating medium in which supplies were granted, and the merchants were constantly summoned in large numbers to attend in council and parliament, they wisely chose to throw in their lot with the commons, and sought in union with them an escape from the oppressions to which their stock and staple made them especially liable.

Inexactness of this division.

196. The three estates of the realm were thus divided, but not without subordinate distinctions, cross divisions, and a large residue that lay outside the political body. In the estate of baronage were included most of the prelates, who also had their place in the estate of clergy. The earls more than once took up a position which showed that they would willingly have claimed a higher political rank than their brother barons: for example, in 1242, the committee of parliament was chosen so as to include four bishops, four earls, and four barons. Many of the lines of distinction which separated the baron from the knight, such as relief and other matters of taxation, might have been made to separate the earls from the barons; but these points become more prominent as the ranks of the lords are marked out by new titles, duke, marquess, viscount. The townsmen, again, who were not included in the local organisations, and the classes of peasants who neither appeared nor were represented in the county courts, formed an outlying division of the estate of the commons. The classification is not either an exact or an exhaustive division of all sorts and conditions of men; such as it is, however, it presents a rough summary of the political constituents of the kingdom, and it

was the arrangement on which the theory of the medieval constitution was based. We have now to trace the process by which the English parliament grew into a symmetrical concentration of the three estates, and to examine the formal steps by which the several powers of the national council were asserted and vindicated, and by which the distinct share of each estate in those several powers was defined and secured, during the period at present before us.

Comparison of the condition of the national council at the close of the twelfth century.

197. The national council, as we have traced it through the reigns of Henry II, Richard I, and John, was an assembly of archbishops, bishops, abbots, priors, earls, barons, knights, and freeholders, holding in chief of the crown. Of the knights and freeholders few could attend the meetings, and they were already separated from the more dignified members by the fact that the latter were summoned by special writ, the former only by a general summons addressed to the sheriffs. In one or two instances before the end of the reign of John the summons to the sheriff had prescribed a form of representation, by which the attendance of elected knights from each shire was substituted for a general summons of the minor tenants-in-chief, which might or might not be obeyed.

with its condition at the close of the thirteenth.

The national council as it existed at the end of the reign of Edward I was a parliamentary assembly consisting of three bodies, the clergy represented by the bishops, deans, archdeacons, and proctors; the baronage spiritual and temporal; the commons of the realm represented by the knights of the shire and the elected citizens and burgesses, and in addition to all these, as attendant on the king and summoned to give counsel, the justices and other members of the continual council.

The various relations of the clergy to the state involve a threefold organisation.

198. The relations of the clergy to the body politic were threefold, and the result of these relations was a threefold organisation for council. The higher clergy, holding their lands as baronies, attended the king's court 'sicut barones ceteri;' the general body of the clergy, as a spiritual organisation, exercised the right of meeting in diocesan, provincial, and national councils, the monastic orders having likewise their

provincial and general chapters or councils[1]; and the whole body of beneficed clergy, as an estate of the realm possessing taxable property and class interests, was organised by Edward I as a portion of his parliament, by the clause of premunition inserted in the writ of summons addressed to the bishops. This clause, 'the *praemunientes* clause[2],' directs the attendance of proctors for the chapters and parochial clergy with the bishops, heads of cathedral chapters and archdeacons personally, in parliament.

Analogies with the secular assemblies.

It is in the second and third relations that the organisation of the clergy chiefly illustrates our subject. And in each aspect analogies may be traced which illustrate the development of the lay estates. The diocesan synod answers to the county court, the provincial convocation to the occasional divided parliaments, and the national church council to the general parliament. The practice of representation appears nearly at the same time in the church councils and in the parliaments: the same questions may be raised as to the character of the representative members of each, whether they were delegates or independent counsellors; the transition from particular consent to general consent in matters of taxation is marked in both cases; and in both cases the varying share of legislative and consultative authority may be traced according to circumstances, later history furnishing abundant illustration of the process which led to such different results.

Persistence of the clergy in granting money in convocation.

If the clergy had been content to vote their taxes in parliament instead of convocation, they might have been involved in a perpetual struggle for equality with the commons, which would have left both at the mercy of the crown

[1] In 1282 Edward commissioned John Kirkby to negotiate with these bodies severally; distinct writs being issued to the Cistercians, who were to meet at Oxford, the Austin Canons at Northampton, the Benedictines at Reading, the Premonstratensians, all abbots and other religious men in the province of Canterbury; Parl. Writs, i. 385.

[2] 'Praemunientes decanum (vel priorem) et capitulum ecclesiae vestrae, archidiaconos, totumque clerum vestrae diocesis, facientes quod iidem decanus et archidiaconi in propriis personis suis, et dictum capitulum per unum, idemque clerus per duos procuratores idoneos, plenam et sufficientem potestatem ab ipsis capitulo et clero habentes, una vobiscum intersint, modis omnibus tunc ibidem ad tractandum, ordinandum et faciendum nobiscum et cum ceteris praelatis et proceribus et aliis incolis regni nostri;' Parl. Writs, i. 30.

and baronage. By taking their stand on their spiritual vantage-ground they lost much of their direct influence in the parliament itself, but, so long as their chiefs sat with the baronage and enjoyed a monopoly of the highest offices of state, they retained more than an equitable share of political power. On the other hand, their resolution, to grant money in convocation only, secured for them a certain right of meeting whenever parliament was called for the same purpose, and that right of meeting involved the right of petitioning and, within certain limits, of legislating for themselves.

199. At an earlier period of our inquiries we have seen the clergy united in their special assemblies and in the national council. The developments of the thirteenth century may be briefly stated. The purely ecclesiastical convocations gain strength and consistency under the pressure of royal and papal aggression, especially after the introduction of the taxation of spiritualities. The diocesan synods, being an exhaustive assembly of the clergy, admitted of little modification. Like the cathedral chapters they were separately consulted on taxation, so long as separate consent was required: in 1254 the bishops were directed to summon their chapters, archdeacons, and clergy to consider a grant, and to report to the council at Easter; as late as the year 1280 the diocesan synods of the province of York gave their several consent to the grant of a tenth[1]. In them the representatives sent to the greater assemblies were chosen, and the gravamina drawn up. In some cases even subdivisions of the dioceses acted independently of one another; in 1240 the rectors of Berkshire refused to contribute to the expenses of the papal war against the emperor[2]; and in 1280 each archdeaconry of the diocese of York was separately consulted before the archdeacons and proctors reported to the diocesan synod, and the archdeacon of Richmond did not join in the general grant[3].

The ecclesiastical convocations, councils, and synods.

Diocesan synods. Consulted on taxation.

The growth of the provincial synod or convocation is chiefly

The provincial synod.

[1] Prynne, Register, i. p. 3; Hody, Hist. Conv. p. 340; Wilkins, Conc. ii. p. 42; Ann. Lanercost, p. 105; above, p. 118, note 1.

[2] M. Paris, iv. 38–43.

[3] Wilkins, Conc. ii. p. 42.

Growth of representation in the provincial synod.

marked by the institution or development of representation, of which there are few if any traces before the pontificate of Stephen Langton. In 1225 that archbishop directed the attendance of proctors of the cathedral, collegiate and conventual clergy in addition to the bishops, abbots, priors, deans, and archdeacons[1]. In 1254 the prelates refused to include the secular clergy in a money grant without their consent, and a great council was summoned in consequence[2]. In 1255 the proctors of the parochial clergy of several archdeaconries presented their gravamina in parliament. But it is not clear that the representative principle was regarded as an integral part of the system of convocation[3]. In 1256 to the meeting of the prelates who assembled to give an answer to the demands of Rustand, were summoned for January 18, the abbots, priors, deans of cathedrals with proctors for their canons, and the archdeacons accompanied by three or four more discreet clergy of their archdeaconries with procuratorial mandate of their fellows[4]. In 1258 archbishop Boniface directed that the archdeacons should be furnished with letters of proxy from the parochial clergy[5], and so empowered they attended the council at Merton which was held preparatory to the Mad Parliament of Oxford. In 1269 in a council at the New Temple, the proctors of the several dioceses declared their gravamina. In 1273 archbishop Kilwardby summoned the bishops, with an order to bring with them three or four of their principal clergy[6]. In 1277 the same prelate included in the summons the greater personae of the chapters, the archdeacons, and the proctors of the whole clergy of each diocese, but without prescribing the number or mode of nomination[7]. This deficiency was supplied by archbishop Peckham in 1283[8].

[1] Wilkins, Conc. i. 602; Select Charters, p. 453.
[2] Royal Letters, ii. 101; above, p. 69.
[3] Ann. Burton, p. 360; Select Charters, p. 332.
[4] M. Paris, vi. 314.
[5] Select Charters, p. 454; Ann. Burton, p. 411; see above, p. 76, note 3.
[6] Wilkins, Conc. ii. 20, 26; Select Charters, p. 455; Wake, State of the Church, App. p. 7.
[7] Wilkins, Conc. ii. 30; Select Charters, p. 455.
[8] Wilkins, Conc. ii. 93, 95; Select Charters, p. 466; Parl. Writs, i. 11.

At the council of Northampton held under the king's writ in the January of that year, it was determined to call a convocation at the New Temple three weeks after Easter: and the rule devised on the occasion was expressed in the writ: 'each of the bishops, as was provided in the said congregation, shall about the aforesaid day cause the clergy of his diocese to be assembled in a certain place, and shall there have carefully expounded to them the propositions made on behalf of the king, so that at the said time and place at London, from each diocese two proctors in the name of the clergy, and from each cathedral and collegiate chapter one proctor, shall be sent with sufficient instructions, who shall have full and express power of treating with us and our brethren upon the premisses, and of consenting to such measures as for the honour of the church, the comfort of the king, and the peace of the realm, the community of the clergy shall provide.' This rule was then or soon after accepted as authoritative, and has been treated as having the force of a canon [1]; and the body so constituted, including bishops, abbots, priors, and heads of religious houses, deans of cathedrals and collegiate churches, archdeacons and proctors, was the convocation of the province of Canterbury. That of the province of York is somewhat differently constituted, containing two proctors from each archdeaconry, an arrangement which dates at least as early as 1279 [2]. It is impossible to fix with any greater certainty the origin of the procuratorial system, but it was probably introduced at a much earlier period, and had long been used in foreign churches [3].

Rule for representation in convocation.

Representation in convocation.

Uses of York and Canterbury.

[1] The canon (so called) is given among the 'Statuta Johannis Peckham' in Wilkins, ii. 49; see also Johnson's Canons, ed. Baron, ii. 268. It is not really a canon; by its reference to the convocation at the Temple, three weeks after Michaelmas, it is shown to belong to the same year 1283. But the exact origin of the special form as inserted in the 'Statuta' is somewhat obscured by the words 'tempore parliamenti proximi post festum sancti Michaelis ad tres hebdomadas per Dei gratiam futura.' However, the convocation was summoned for that date in 1283, the parliament meeting at Shrewsbury on Sept. 30; and it would be difficult to find any other date, between 1278 and 1292, that would suit. See Peckham's Letters, ed. Martin, pp. 486-501, 508, 523, 536.

[2] Wilkins, Conc. ii. 41.

[3] Compare the account of the legatine council of Bourges held in 1225; W. Covent. ii. 277.

National church councils rarely called.

Owing to the unfortunate jealousy which subsisted between the two primates, the assembling of national church councils became, after the independence of York had been vindicated by Thurstan, almost a matter of impossibility. The disputes, amounting often to undignified personal altercation between the archbishops themselves, disturbed the harmony of even the royal courts and national parliaments. Only when the authority of a legate superseded for the moment the ordinary authority of both, were any national councils of the church summoned. The most important of these were the councils of 1237, in which the constitutions of Otho were published, and of 1268, in which those of Ottobon were accepted. The comparative rarity of these assemblies, and the fact that the prelates were the only permanent element in them, rob them of any importance they might otherwise have had in the history of our ecclesiastical organisation.

Proposals for conference between the two provincial synods.

This division between the two provinces was, in secular questions, remedied by the custom of bringing the leading men of both to the national parliaments[1]; but this was felt to be inadequate in cases in which the special rights of the clergy were concerned. Accordingly in 1252[2] we find the archbishop of York and the bishops of Carlisle and Durham declining to answer a request of the king on the ground that it was a matter which touched the whole English church, and that they did not think it consistent or honourable to depart from the customary procedure in such cases, in which a common debate was usually had between the clergy of the two provinces. But although such communication might in general terms be called customary, the extant evidence points rather to a discussion or arrangement by letter between the archbishops than to any common deliberation of the churches.

Parliamentary representation of the clergy.

200. When Edward I in 1295 determined to summon to parliament the whole clergy of the two provinces by their representatives, he probably desired not only to define the

[1] In 1207 John collected the clergy of both provinces to grant an aid; Ann. Waverley, p. 258.

[2] Royal Letters, ii. 94, 95; see above, p. 68.

relations between the several estates, but to obtain the joint action of the two provinces, and to get rid of the anomalous modes of summons and attendance which had been from time to time adopted in the innumerable councils of the century. There were precedents for summoning to councils, in which no specially ecclesiastical business was discussed, not only the prelates but the archdeacons and deans, as representing the parochial and cathedral clergy. One remarkable assembly of the kind, in 1177[1], on the occasion of the arbitration between Castille and Navarre, seems to show that Henry II regarded the presence of these 'minor prelates' as necessary to make his court sufficiently impressive to his foreign visitors. The council of 1255[2], in which the proctors of the beneficed clergy exhibited their gravamina, was a parliament, although it may not be certain that the proctors appeared as members rather than as petitioners. Simon de Montfort's parliament of 1265 contained cathedral deans and priors as well as prelates[3]. Later in the same year, Henry III, still in the hands of earl Simon, summoned proctors for the cathedral chapters to a parliament at Winchester[4]. In 1282 the proctors of the chapters were summoned to the two provincial parliaments of York and Northampton[5]. In 1294 Edward called what may be regarded as a clerical parliament at Westminster, apart from the other two estates and at a different time; summoning the clergy of the two provinces by their prelates, chapters, archdeacons, and proctors for the 21st of September[6], and the lay estates for the 12th of November. The following year he incorporated the three in one assembly and adopted for the representation of the clergy the method instituted twelve years before for the provincial convocations[7].

Early examples.

Council or convocation of 1294.

Parliament of 1295.

[1] Ben. Pet. i. 145; see above, vol. i. p. 486.
[2] Above, p. 206.
[3] Above, p. 96.
[4] Select Charters, p. 418; above, p. 98.
[5] Parl. Writs, i. 10; Select Charters, p. 466.
[6] Parl. Writs, i. 25, 26; Select Charters, p. 480.
[7] Ibid. p. 484. The 'modus tenendi parliamentum' describes the clerical proctors in parliament, as two from each archdeaconry, not, as was really the case, two from each diocese; ibid. p. 503. This is but one of the many misstatements of that document, but it may show that, even when it was written, the question of clerical representation was becoming obscure.

But, although so closely united in idea, the two representative bodies, convocation[1] and the parliamentary representation of the clergy, are kept clearly distinct. The convocations are two provincial councils meeting in their respective provinces, generally at London and York; the parliamentary representatives are one element of the general parliament and meet in the same place. The convocations are called by the writ of the archbishops addressed through their senior suffragans to each bishop of their provinces; the parliamentary proctors are summoned by the king's writ addressed directly to the bishops individually, and directing by the clause 'praemunientes'[2] the attendance of the proctors. The convocations contain the abbots and priors; these are not included in the 'praemunientes' clause. The convocations are two spiritual assemblies; the parliamentary assembly of the clergy is one temporal representation of the spiritual estate; and it is, as we shall see, only owing to the absolute defeasance of the latter institution that the convocations have any connexion with parliamentary history. Every step of the development of the two has however a bearing on the growth of the idea of representation, both in the nation at large and in the mind of the great organiser and definer of parliamentary action, Edward I[3].

Difference between the convocation and the parliamentary session of the clergy.

Later relation of convocation to parliament.

[1] The word *convocation* had not yet acquired its later technical meaning. The prior and convent of Bath, 1295, elect their proctor under the praemunientes clause, to appear in the 'generalis convocatio;' Parl. Writs, i. 34; in 1297 the writ of the archbishop for the spiritual assembly is entitled 'Citatio pro convocatione;' ibid. p. 53.

[2] See above, p. 204, note 2. Philip the Fair seems to have had an intention in 1297 of summoning the whole of the French clergy to Paris to make a grant; but, warned perhaps by the events of 1296 in England, he did not venture to do it, and wrung the money he wanted from provincial councils; Boutaric, Premiers États Gen. p. 6. The parochial clergy, the rectors or curés of parishes, were systematically excluded from the states general (Hervieu, Rev. de Legislation, 1873, p. 380), inasmuch as they did not possess temporalities or jurisdiction. Nor were the clergy assembled according to their ecclesiastical divisions; not in dioceses and provinces, but in bailliages and senechaussées, like the laity; ibid. 396.

[3] I need hardly remark here that, although the procuratorial system as used in clerical assemblies has a certain bearing on the representative system in England, it is much less important here than in those countries in which there were no vestiges of representative lay institutions left, and where the representation of communities in the states general must have been borrowed from the ecclesiastical system. In England the two forms

201. The baronial estate underwent during this period the great change in respect to its conciliar form, from qualification by tenure to qualification by writ, from which the hereditary peerage emerges. This change affected however only the simple barons[1]. As a rule all the earls and all the bishops were constantly summoned, the only exceptions being made when the individual omitted was in personal disgrace. The list of abbots and priors however varies largely from time to time; more than a hundred were summoned by Simon de Montfort in 1264[2]; nearly seventy by Edward I to the great parliament of 1295[3]; in the reign of Edward III the regular number fell to twenty-seven[4]; the majority being glad to escape the burden of attendance, and, by the plea that their lands were held in free alms and not by barony, to avoid the expenses by which their richer brethren maintained their high dignity[5]. The modification in the character of the lay baronage is a matter of great significance. This question has been made the subject of what may be called a large body of historical literature, out of which, observing the due proportion of general treatment, we can state here only a few conclusions.

Development of the baronage.

All bishops and earls summoned.

Diminished numbers of abbots and priors.

Diminished number of barons.

grow side by side, the lay representation is not formed on the model of the clerical.

[1] Occasionally bishops, abbots, and barons were allowed to appear by proxy; thus in the parliament of Carlisle (Parl. Writs, i. 185, 186) a great number of proxies or attorneys were present; and some even of the elected proctors of the clergy substituted others as their proxies. Abbesses and peeresses who had suits to prosecute or services to perform also sent proctors, but not as members of the parliament, simply as suitors of the high court.

[2] Ten abbots, nine priors, and one dean of the province of York, fifty-five abbots, twenty-six priors, and four deans of the province of Canterbury; and the heads of the military orders.

[3] Sixty-seven abbots and three heads of orders; Parl. Writs, i. 30.

[4] See the tables given by Gneist, Verwalt. i. 382–387.

[5] See Prynne, Register, i. pp. 141 sq. The position of the abbots and priors as distinguished from the bishops is historically important, in relation to council and also to tenure. Before the Conquest all the bishops attended the witenagemot, and only a few of the abbots. When the practice of homage was introduced, the bishops, we are told by Glanvill and Bracton, did no homage after consecration, but only fealty: whilst according to the latter writer, abbots 'ad homagium non teneantur de jure, faciunt tamen tota die de consuetudine;' lib. ii. c. 35. The reduction in the number of parliamentary abbots was probably owing to their dislike of attendance at secular courts, which suggested the excuse alleging their peculiar tenure.

Qualification for summons as a baron.

The 'majores barones' of the reigns of Henry II, Richard and John, were, as has been several times stated, distinguished from their fellows, by the reception of special summons to council, special summons to the army, the right of making special arrangements with the exchequer for reliefs and taxes, of leading their own vassals in battle, and of being amerced by their equals. The coincidence of these points enables us to describe if not to define what tenure by barony must have been; it may, as some legal writers have maintained, have comprehended the duties of grand serjeanty, it may have been connected originally with the possession of a certain quantity of land; but it certainly possessed the characteristics just enumerated. The number of these barons was very considerable: in 1263, a hundred and eighteen were specially summoned to the Welsh war[1]; a hundred and sixty-five in 1276[2]; a hundred and twenty-two in 1297[3]; and correspondingly large numbers on other occasions. That the occurrence of a particular name in the list proves the bearer to have held his estates *per baroniam* may be disputed, but it can scarcely be doubted that all who were summoned would rank among the *majores barones* of the charter. The extant writs of summons to parliament are much more rare, and these contain far fewer names than the writs of military service. Only eighteen barons were summoned by Simon de Montfort; ninety-nine were summoned by Edward I to Shrewsbury in 1283; only forty-one to the parliament of 1295[4]; thirty-seven in 1296[5]. Occasionally the number increases; especially when a number of counsellors is also summoned. To the parliament of March 6, 1300, ninety-eight lords and thirty-eight counsellors were called[6]; and the letter addressed by the parliament of Lincoln to the pope was sealed by ninety-six lay lords, eighty of whom had been summoned by special writ[7]. It is clear from these facts, nearly all

Great number of barons summoned for military service.

Smaller numbers summoned to parliament.

[1] Lords' Report, iii. 30.

[2] Parl. Writs, i. 193–195.

[3] Parl. Writs, i. 282. Not less than 174 were summoned for the defence against Scotland in the autumn of the same year, but many of these were addressed as knights; ibid. pp. 302–304.

[4] Parl. Writs, i. 31.

[5] Ibid. i. 48.

[6] Ibid. i. 82, 83; seventy-two abbots, &c. were also summoned.

[7] Ibid. i. 90. The whole list summoned to Lincoln contained two

of which belong to the parliaments properly so called in which the three estates were assembled, that very large discretionary power remained in the royal hands; and that, unless he was warranted by earlier custom, the existence of which we can only conjecture [1], Edward I must, in the selection of a smaller number to be constant recipients of special summons, have introduced a constitutional change scarcely inferior to that by which he incorporated the representatives of the commons in the national council: in other words, that he created the house of lords as much as he created the house of commons. The alteration or variation in the number of the barons summoned implied also an alteration in the qualification for summons; if the king were at liberty to select even a permanent number of lords of parliament from the body of tenants-in-chief or barons, the qualification of tenure ceased to be the sole qualification for summons. But it is probable that the change went still further, and that of the diminished number some at least did not possess the qualification by baronial tenure, but became barons simply by virtue of the special writ, and conveyed to their heirs a dignity attested by the hereditary reception of the summons. If this be true, and it is supported by considerable evidence [2], the tenure *per*

Importance of the principle established by Edward I.

Institution of hereditary writs.

archbishops, eighteen bishops, eighty abbots, three masters of orders, ten earls, and eighty specially summoned barons and knights; the letter (ibid. pp. 102–104) is sealed by seven earls and ninety-six other lords. See the Fourth Report of the Lords' Committee, pp. 325–341; where it is maintained that the occurrence of a name among these ninety-six signataries does not by itself imply a peerage.

[1] The famous quotation of Camden, Britannia (ed. 1600), p. 137, has never been, I believe, verified; it runs as follows: 'Ille enim' (sc. Henricus III) 'ex satis antiquo scriptore loquor, post magnas perturbationes et enormes vexationes inter ipsum regem, Simonem de Monteforti et alios barones, motas et sopitas, statuit et ordinavit quod omnes illi comites et barones regni Angliae quibus ipse rex dignatus est brevia summonitionis dirigere, venirent ad parlamentum suum et non alii, nisi forte dominus rex alia consimilia brevia eis dirigere voluisset.' Cf. Brady, Intr. p. 145; Hallam, M. A. iii. 7.

[2] See Courthope's edition of Nicolas's Historic Peerage, pp. xxv sq.; Third Lords' Report, p. 235 sq. An example is Thomas de Furnival, of whom it was found in the 19th Edw. II that he did not hold his estates per baroniam, who yet was summoned from 1295 to 1332; nine other persons summoned in 1295 are 'not anywhere stated to have been previously barons of the realm.' The last statement is I think somewhat arbitrary; all the nine had had special military summons repeatedly.

baroniam must have ceased to have any political importance, and we have in the act, or in the policy suggesting it, a crowning proof of Edward's political design of eliminating the doctrine of tenure from the region of government. The later variations, in number and qualification, of the house of lords, may be noted when we reach the time at which those variations become important.

Continuation of baronial assemblies, in the *magnum concilium*.

The baronage spiritual and temporal did not, however modified, merge its independent existence in the newly constituted parliament of Edward I. It had been in possession of the functions of a common council of the realm far too long not to have acquired powers with which it could not part. Under the title of 'magnum concilium regis et regni' it retained, like the convocation of the clergy, distinct methods of assembly, and certain powers which ultimately fell to the house of lords. But these must be considered in another part of our work.

Representation of the commons.

202. The great mark which the century and the reign of Edward I leave on our constitutional history is the representation of the commons: the collecting in parliament of the representatives of the communities of both shires and boroughs, the concentration of the powers which had been previously exercised in local assemblies or altogether superseded by the action of the barons, and the admission of such representatives to a share in the supreme work of government.

Arrangement of the following pages.

In order to avoid needless repetition it will be desirable to examine this part of our subject under the several heads of (1) the constitution of the local courts and communities, (2) their powers and functions, and (3) the periods and causes of the introduction of their representatives into the national parliament. So much however has been already said on the first and second points in the earlier chapters of this work, that it will be enough briefly to recapitulate our chief conclusions about them and to account for the modifications which affected them in the century before us.

1. Constitution of the county court.

203. (1) The county court in its full session, that is, as it attended the itinerant justices on their visitation, contained the archbishops, bishops, abbots, priors, earls, barons, knights, and freeholders, and from each township four men and the

reeve, and from each borough twelve burghers[1]. It was still the folkmoot, the general assembly of the people, and, in case of any class or person being regarded as outside the above enumeration, the sheriff was directed to summon to the meeting all others who by right or custom appeared before the justices. It contained thus all the elements of a local parliament—all the members of the body politic in as full representation as the three estates afterwards enjoyed in the general parliament.

Its times of meeting.

The county court, according to the 42nd article of the charter of 1217[2], sat once a month; but it is not to be supposed that on each occasion it was attended by all the qualified members; the prelates and barons were generally freed from the obligation of attendance by the charters under which they held their estates; every freeman might by the statute of Merton appear by attorney[3], and by the statute of Marlborough all above the rank of knight were exempted from attendance on the sheriff's tourn[4], unless specially summoned: the charters of the boroughs implied and sometimes expressed a condition that it was only

Persons excused attendance.

[1] The writ of 1217 for the promulgation of the charter orders the sheriff to publish it, 'in pleno comitatu tuo convocatis baronibus, militibus et omnibus libere tenentibus ejusdem comitatus;' Brady, App. 166. The writs containing the list of names given in the text begin in 1217; Rot. Claus. i. 380: 'Rex Vicecomiti Ebor. salutem. Summone per bonos summonitores omnes archiepiscopos, episcopos, abbates, comites et barones, milites et libere tenentes de tota baillia tua, et de qualibet villa quatuor legales homines et praepositum, et de quolibet burgo xii legales burgenses per totam bailliam tuam, et omnes alios de baillia tua qui coram justitiis itinerantibus venire solent et debent, quod sint apud Eboracum coram justitiis nostris a die Sancti Martini in xv dies, audituri et facturi praeceptum nostrum.' Cf. Rot. Claus. i. 463, 473, 476. There is one of 1231 in the Select Charters, p. 358. See too Bracton, lib. iii. tr. i. c. 11.

[2] Select Charters, p. 346.

[3] Statutes of the Realm, i. 4: 'provisum insuper quod quilibet liber homo qui sectam debet ad Comitatum, Trithingam, Hundredum et Wapentachium, vel ad curiam domini sui, libere possit facere attornatum suum ad sectas illas pro eo faciendum.' Such an appointment of a proxy, by Thomas de Burgh, to appear in the shiremoot of Staffordshire in 1223, is given in the Close Rolls, i. 537. See further below, vol. iii. c. xx. § 420.

[4] Statutes of the Realm, i. 22: 'de turnis vicecomitum provisum est quod necesse non habeant ibi venire archiepiscopi, episcopi, abbates, priores, comites, barones nec aliqui viri religiosi seu mulieres nisi eorum praesentia specialiter exigatur.' Cf. on the whole question, Pollock and Maitland, i. 524 sq.

when the court was called to meet the justices that their representatives need attend[1]; in some cases the barons and knights compounded for attendance by a payment to the sheriff[2]; and the custom of relieving the simple knights, by special licence issued by the king, prevailed to such an extent that the deficiency of lawful knights to hold the assizes in the county court was a constant subject of complaint[3]. The monthly sessions then were only attended by persons who had special business, or owed special suit, and by the officers of the townships with their lawful men qualified to serve on the juries. For the holding of a full county court, for extraordinary business, a special summons was in all cases issued; our knowledge of its composition is derived from such special writs.

Ordinary monthly sessions.

Special sessions.

History of the sheriffs.

204. The sheriff is still the president and constituting officer of the county court; to him is directed the writ ordering the general summons, and through him is made the answer of the county to the question or demand contained in the writ. Successive limitations on his judicial power have been imposed from the reign of Henry II to the date of Magna Carta, but have scarcely diminished his social importance[4]; and although the general contributions of the country, the fifteenths, thirtieths and the like, no longer pass necessarily through his hands, he retains the collection of scutages and other prescriptive imposts, and considerable power of amercement for non-attendance on his summons. The king retains the power of nominating the sheriffs, but not without a struggle; the right of nomination being at one time claimed for the baronage in parliament, and at another for the county court itself. By the Provisions of Oxford in 1258 it was ordered that the sheriff should be a vavasour of the county in which he was to reside and should

Struggles to change the mode of appointing the sheriffs.

[1] Charter of Dunwich, Rot. Cart. p. 51: 'et quod nullam sectam faciant comitatus vel hundredorum nisi coram justitiis nostris; et, cum summoniti fuerint esse coram justitiis, mittant pro se xii legales homines de burgo suo qui sint pro eis omnibus.'

[2] As in the honour of Aquila in Sussex; see vol. i. p. 102.

[3] See the 28th article of the petition of the barons in 1258; Select Charters, p. 386. An instance will be found as early as 1224; Rot. Claus. i. 627.

[4] Vol. i. pp. 606, 607; see Gneist, Verwalt. i. 320.

retain office for a year only[1]. In 1259, it was provided that for the current year appointment should be made by the chief justice, treasurer, and barons of the Exchequer, absolutely; and in future from a list of four good men chosen in the county court[2]. The efforts made by Henry III to get rid of the provisionary council involved in each case an attempt to remove their sheriffs and to nominate his own. In 1261, at the Mise of Merton concluded in December, a committee of arbitration was named to determine the question of right; the six arbitrators referred it to Richard of Cornwall as umpire, and he decided in favour of the king, though he attempted to introduce the principle of election[3]: and the decision was confirmed by the award of S. Lewis. After this no attempt was made by the barons to renew the quarrel; but under Edward I the question of a free election by the shires was mooted. Such free election had long been the right of the citizens of London; the freeholders of Cornwall and Devon had purchased the like privilege from John and Henry III[4]; and the lawyers of Edward I seem to have held, and foisted into the copies of the laws of the Confessor an article declaring, that such election was an ancient popular right[5]. It was possibly in concession to this opinion that in 1300, by one of the *Articuli super Cartas*, Edward granted the election of the sheriffs to the people of the shire where they desired to have it, and where the office was not 'of fee' or hereditary[6]. But the privilege was sparingly exercised if it were exercised at all, and was

Election of sheriffs.

[1] Select Charters, p. 391.

[2] Ann. Burton, p. 478; above, p. 84. The securing a sheriff from among the inhabitants of the county was probably as material a point as the obtaining the right of election; see Ann. Dunst. p. 279: 'eodem anno, 1278, amovit rex omnes vicecomites Angliae clericos scilicet et extraneos, et substituit loco eorum milites de propriis comitatibus.'

[3] Above, pp. 87, 88.

[4] Madox, Hist. Exch. pp. 283, 288; Rot. Claus. i. 457; ii. 25, 169, 184.

[5] 'Per singulos comitatus in pleno folcmote, sicut et vicecomites provinciarum et comitatuum eligi debent;' Thorpe, Ancient Laws, p. 197.

[6] Statutes of the Realm, i. 139: 'le roi ad grante a soen poeple qil eient esleccion de leur viscontes en chescun conte, ou visconte ne est mie de fee, sil voelent.' An examination of the lists of sheriffs shows that the privilege could only have been slightly valued; the changes in 1300 and 1301 are few.

Final settlement of the question.

withdrawn by the Ordinances of 1311[1]. In 1338 Edward III ordered the sheriffs to be elected by the counties, but in 1340 it was finally provided that no sheriff should continue in office for more than a year, the appointment remaining, as prescribed by the Ordinances, in the hands of the officers of the Exchequer[2]. It would seem that during this period it was more important to the king and to the barons to secure the right of appointment, than to limit the powers of the sheriff; and consequently his position and influence underwent less change than they had done under the legislation of Henry II. The real loss of his ancient importance resulted from the limitation of his period of office.

II. Business of the county transacted in the county court.

205. (II) In the county courts and under the guidance of the sheriffs was transacted all the business of the shire: and the act of the county court was the act of the shire in matters judicial, military, and fiscal, in the details of police management, and in questions, where such questions occurred, connected with the general administration of the country. It is unnecessary to repeat what has been said on these points in a former chapter; but some illustration may be given of the completeness of the county administration for each purpose; of the use, in each department, of representation; and of the practice of electing representatives who thus act on behalf of the whole community of the shire. The ideas of representation and election are not inseparable; at certain stages the sheriff in the county, or the reeve in the township, might nominate, from a fixed list, by choice, or in rotation; but the tendency of the two ideas is to unite, and the historic evidence shows their joint use generally at this time. The custom of electing representatives in the county court was in full operation before such representatives were summoned to parliament.

(1) The judicial work of the county court.

The judicial work of the county was done in the county court: except in the county court even the itinerant justices

[1] Statutes of the Realm, i. 160.

[2] Foed. ii. 1049, 1090; the Act passed in 1340 ordered that the appointment should be made in the Exchequer by the Chancellor, Treasurer, and Chief Baron, with the justices, if present; Statutes, i. 283. In 1376 the commons again petitioned for elective sheriffs; Rot. Parl. ii. 355.

could not discharge their functions; and the county was the sphere of jurisdiction of the justices of assize and justices of the peace. The county was the *patria* whose report was presented by the juries; and a process by assize was 'per judicium et consilium totius comitatus[1].' The uses of representation and election have already been illustrated sufficiently in our discussion of the origin of juries.

(2) The conservation of the peace.

206. The conservation of the peace, or police, a department that links the judicial with the military administration of the shire, was fully organised on the same principles. For each necessary measure the county was an organic whole; the action was taken in the county court; and in the execution of the law the sheriff was assisted or superseded by elected representatives. The writs for the conservation of the peace, directing the taking of the oath, the pursuit of malefactors, and the observance of watch and ward, were proclaimed in full county court; attachments were made in obedience to them in the county court before the coroners; and, when the institution was modified, as in 1253, the sheriffs were ordered to summon all the knights and freeholders of their counties, four men with the reeve from each township, and twelve burghers from each borough, to receive and execute the royal mandate[2]. The coroners, whose duty was to watch the interests of the crown in this region of work as well as in the fiscal and judicial business, were always elected by the full county court[3]. In the fifth year of Edward I, an officer called 'custos pacis,' whose functions form a stage in the growth of the office of justice of the peace, was elected by the sheriff and community of each

[1] 'Nihil fecimus in facto memorato nisi per consilium et judicium totius comitatus . . . ex recordo dictae assisae quod de communi consensu et testimonio totius comitatus fideliter conscriptum vobis transmittimus;' Royal Letters, i. 21. On the general subject, see Gneist, Verwaltungsrecht, i. 317 sq.

[2] 'Summone per bonos summonitores omnes milites et omnes libere tenentes de comitatibus praedictis, et de qualibet villa quatuor homines et praepositum, et de quolibet burgo duodecim legales burgenses, quod sint coram dilecto et fideli nostro Henrico de Colevilla ad dies et loca quos tibi scire faciet, ad audiendum et faciendum praeceptum nostrum;' Foed. i. 291; Select Charters, p. 374.

[3] See below, p. 239.

Election of conservators.

county in the full county court; and the conservators who carried out the provisions of the statute of Winchester, although no mention of the mode of appointment occurs in the act itself, were after the first vacancy elected in the same way[1]. In this instance the principle was extended to the election of constables for the hundreds.

(3) The military business of the shire.

207. The military administration of the county, except so far as it was connected with the conservation of the peace, was less capable of being conducted on a symmetrical plan of representation. It furnishes, however, illustrations of the completeness of the local agencies, and of the concentration of those agencies for national purposes, which are of the first importance: for both the feudal military system and the system of the national defence have their exact analogies in the system of the national council; and, if the parliament is not the host in council as it was in primitive times, the national force is the presentment in arms of those elements which in the parliament meet for council.

Character of the national force.

The national force, as a whole, falls into three divisions; the armed vassals of the tenants-in-chief who served under their own lords, each of those lords receiving a special summons to arms; the minor tenants-in-chief who served under the sheriff; and the body of freemen sworn under the assize of arms. Of the second and third divisions the sheriff was the proper leader; they were the men who served on assizes and juries, and who in other matters acted constitutionally with him. In every change of military organisation, and there were several such changes in the course of the thirteenth century[2], the sheriff retains his place. In 1205 John warned the sheriffs that by assent of the national council every nine knights throughout all England were to furnish a tenth, and ordered the whole effective force of the country to be incorporated and sworn under an organisation of constables for the national defence[3]. In 1223 Henry III directed the sheriffs to impose the oath on those who had been 'jurati ad arma' in

The minor tenants in chief and the *jurati ad arma* commanded by the sheriff.

[1] See below, p. 237, and § 236; Gneist, Verwalt. i. 320 sq.; Stat. i. 98.
[2] See below, § 238; Gneist, Verwalt. i. 313–317.
[3] Above, vol. i. pp. 590, 592.

the time of John[1]. In 1231 Henry III ordered them to furnish a fixed contingent of men-at-arms to be provided by the men of the county sworn under the assize of arms[2]. On the great occasions during the troubled period of the reign of Henry III, or in the wars of Edward I, when writs of military summons are directed to the barons, the sheriffs are ordered to bring up the force of the freeholders, and, when the system of commissions of array is adopted, the letters investing the commissioners with their powers are addressed to the sheriffs[3]. But over and above the authority they possessed over the minor freeholders, they exercised a sort of vigilant superintendence over the forces of the barons, under the king's writ. Thus in 1217 Henry III directed them to bring to Oxford the whole military force of the shire, whether due from prelates, barons, and tenants-in-chief, or others; in 1221, they were to summon to Cockermouth barons, knights, freeholders, all who owe the king service and all the 'jurati ad arma[4].' In 1223 he ordered them to summon all the tenants-in-chief by knight-service, whether archbishops, bishops, abbots, priors, earls, barons, knights, or others[5]; and this plan was followed in later years as if the agency of the sheriff were more to be trusted than that of the special messengers. The writs for distraint of knighthood were also directed to the sheriffs. The writs of Edward I, being more peremptory, are also more full, and exhibit his design of consolidating the national force without distinction of tenure; they reach the climax when in 1297 he orders the sheriffs to give notice to all who possess twenty librates of land or more, whether holding in chief or not, whether within or without franchises, to prepare at once with horses and arms to follow the king whenever he shall demand their service[6]. The military progress of the period must however be traced in a separate section.

Military work of the sheriff; summoning the entire force; compelling knighthood.

[1] Rot. Claus. i. 628.
[2] Select Charters, p. 359.
[3] See below, § 241.
[4] Rot. Claus. i. 336; Lords' Report, App. pp. 2, 3.
[5] Lords' Report, App. p. 3.
[6] 'Firmiter injungentes quod, statim visis litteris istis, scire facias omnibus illis de bailliva tua infra libertates et extra qui habent viginti libratas

His orders published in the county court.

The military orders of the sheriff were published in the county court; of this practice the year 1295 furnishes a good instance; Edward, having appointed the bishop of Durham and the earl of Warenne to provide for the defence of the northern shires, ordered the sheriffs to assemble before them all the knights of their shires and two good men of each township, to hear and execute the orders of the newly appointed officers[1]. For all questions touching the character of tenure, and the extent of obligation, the juries employed in other matters would be necessarily employed by the sheriff in this department likewise.

(4) The remedial measures executed by the county court.

208. In the execution of the remedial measures which form so large a part of the political history of the century, the agency of the counties is employed, generally by means of elected representatives. In 1215, immediately after the charter of Runnymede, John directed twelve lawful knights to be chosen in each shire, at the first county court held after the receipt of the writ, to inquire into the evil customs which were to be abolished[2].

Remedial work of the county.

The same plan was followed at each renewal of the charters. In 1222 two knights were sent up from Wiltshire to lay the forest liberties before the king[3]. In 1226 and 1227, on occasion of a dispute as to the administration of the counties, Henry III ordered the sheriffs in the next county court to bid the knights and good men of the counties to choose from among themselves four lawful and discreet knights to appear

terrae et redditus per annum, et illis similiter qui plus habent, videlicet, tam illis qui non tenent de nobis in capite quam illis qui tenent, ut de equis et armis sibi provideant et se praeparent indilate, ita quod sic sint prompti et parati ad veniendum ad nos et eundum cum propria persona nostra pro defensione ipsorum et totius regni nostri praedicti quandocunque pro ipsis duxerimus demandandum;' Parl. Writs, i. 281; Lords' Report, App. p. 79; below, § 239.

[1] 'Et mandatum est vicecomiti Ebor. quod venire faciat coram praefatis episcopo et comiti vel eorum altero apud Eboracum, in crastino festi Omnium Sanctorum proximo futuri, omnes milites de comitatu praedicto et de qualibet villa ejusdem comitatus duos probos homines ad audiendum et faciendum,' &c.; Parl. Writs, i. 270.

[2] Rot. Pat. i. 180: 'Quod xii milites de comitatu tuo, qui eligentur de ipso comitatu in primo comitatu qui tenebitur post susceptionem litterarum istarum in partibus tuis, jurent de inquirendis,' &c. Select Charters, p. 307.

[3] Rot. Claus. i. 498.

at Lincoln and at Westminster to allege the grounds of complaint [1]. In 1258 four knights brought up the complaints of the shires to the October parliament [2]. By the articles of 1259 four such officers were appointed to watch the action of the sheriffs in each shire [3]. The close connexion of this occasional work with the general government is shown by the fact that in 1297 the knights of the shire were summoned to the national council expressly to receive copies of the confirmation of the charters [4], and that in 1301 the great object for which the parliament of Lincoln was summoned was to receive the report of the perambulations made under the new forest articles [5].

(5) The fiscal business of the county.

209. But the fiscal business is that in which the shire system most closely approached, before it actually touched, the national council; and in it therefore the special action of the shire has the greatest constitutional interest. The practice of assessing and collecting taxes by chosen juries, and the practice of obtaining money grants by special and several negotiation, ultimately brought the crown and the tax-payer into very close communication. Many instances of this tendency have been already given [6], and they may be multiplied. In 1219 two knights are appointed in each county to collect the amercements [7]. In 1220 the sheriffs are ordered to cause two lawful knights to be chosen in full county court, by the will and counsel of all men of the county, to take part in the assessment and collection of the carucage [8]. In 1225, when the management of the fifteenth was taken out of the hands of the sheriff, committed to special justices, and audited by special

Assessment of juries.

Special negotiations for grants of money.

Election of assessors and collectors.

[1] 'Et in proximo comitatu tuo dicas militibus et probis hominibus bailliae tuae quod quatuor de legalioribus et discretioribus militibus ex se ipsis eligant, qui ad diem illum sint apud Lincolniam pro toto comitatu, ad ostendendum ibi querelam quam habent,' &c.; Select Charters, p. 357; Rot. Claus. ii. 153, 212.

[2] Foed. i. 375; Brady, Intr. p. 141. See above, p. 81.

[3] Ann. Burton, p. 477.

[4] Parl. Writs, i. 56. See above, p. 146.

[5] Parl. Writs, i. 88–90; above, p. 156.

[6] Vol. i. pp. 577–587.

[7] Royal Letters, i. 28; Rot. Claus. i. 398.

[8] 'Convocato comitatu tuo pleno, de voluntate et consilio eorum de comitatu, facias eligi duos de legalioribus militibus totius comitatus qui melius sciant velint et possint huic negotio ad commodum nostrum intendere;' Rot. Cl. i. 437; Select Charters, p. 352.

commission, the collection and assessment were entrusted to four elected knights of each hundred, who inquired by jury into all disputed cases[1]. In 1232 the fortieth was assessed in each township by the reeve and four chosen men of the township, in the presence of knights assigned[2]; a similar mode was adopted in 1237[3]. The precise regulation of the method of assessment becomes less important when the grants are made in duly constituted assemblies; but the practice of choosing four knights to assess, tax, levy, and collect a money grant in each shire was continued under Edward I[4], and the directions for the purpose were promulgated in the county court[5]. The Customs were under like management: in 1275 the sheriffs of London and Gloucestershire were ordered to cause two lawful men to be chosen in London, Bristol, and other ports, as sub-collectors of the custom on wool[6].

Assessment in the townships.

Election of collectors of customs.

Important illustration of the position of the county court in taxation.

But the reign of Henry III supplies at least one clear proof that not merely the assessment but the concession of a grant was regarded as falling within the lawful power of a local assembly. We have seen how Henry I, when directing the customary assembling of the shiremoots, declared his intention of laying before them his sovereign necessities whenever he required an aid; and although we do not find a grant made during the twelfth century in the county courts, we have abundant evidence of the transactions of the justices of the Exchequer in the matter of taxation, which took place in those sessions. The business of setting the tallage, when it was dispatched between the justices or barons of the Exchequer and the

[1] Foed. i. 177; Select Charters, p. 355; and see Rot. Claus. ii. 40, 45, 71, 95, and p. 38, above.

[2] 'Quod videlicet de qualibet villa integra eligantur quatuor de melioribus et legalioribus hominibus una cum praepositis singularum villarum, per quorum sacramentum quadragesima pars omnium mobilium praedictorum taxetur et assideatur;' M. Paris, iii. 231; Select Charters, p. 361.

[3] Foedera, i. 232; Select Charters, p. 366.

[4] Parl. Writs, i. 106; the fifteenth granted in 1301 was thus collected. The king even furnished a speech which was to be delivered by the royal commissioners to the knights and good people of the county assembled, to prevail on them to furnish supplies in kind, to be paid for by the fifteenth; ibid. p. 401; cf. pp. 404 sq.

[5] Parl. Writs, i. 403.

[6] Parl. Writs, i. 2.

payers, and when the payers ascertained their liability and apportioned their quota by jury, approached, within one step, a formal consent to taxation. So when the fourteenth article of the charter mentions, as a part of the process of holding the 'commune consilium,' that the minor tenants-in-chief should be summoned by the general writ addressed to the sheriff, it is at least possible that the business announced in that general writ would be discussed in the assembly which was the proper audience of the sheriff. In the year 1220 we have an important illustration which must be compared with the cases of grants, before adduced, by ecclesiastical assemblies of diocese and archdeaconry.

Case of the shiremoot of Yorkshire in 1220.

Geoffrey Neville, the king's chamberlain, was sheriff of Yorkshire, and had to collect the carucage, already mentioned as the occasion on which two knights of the shire were elected to make the assessment. The writ declaring the grant to have been made by the 'magnates et fideles' in the 'commune consilium' was dated on the 9th of August [1]. In the month of September, the chamberlain writes to the justiciar [2]: he had received the writ on the 2nd, and had summoned the earls, barons, and freeholders, to hear it on the 14th. On that day the earls and barons had sent their stewards, as was usual, and did not attend in person. The writ was read: to the disgust of the sheriff the stewards replied with one accord, that their lords had never been asked for the aid and knew nothing of it; without consulting them, they dared not assent to the tax; they insisted that the lords of Yorkshire, like those of the southern shires, ought to have been asked for the grant by the king either by word of mouth or by letter. The sheriff attempted to answer them, but was obliged to grant a postponement until the next county court, that in the meantime they might lay the king's command before their lords. He learned, however, that if Henry, in a visit which he was shortly to make to York, should call together the magnates, and make the proposal in form, it would be accepted; if the justiciar recommended compulsion he was ready to employ it.

The stewards of the lords refuse to pay a tax.

The matter referred to the next county court.

[1] Rot. Claus. i. 437; Select Charters, p. 353. [2] Royal Letters, i. 151.

The case is perhaps exceptional: the Yorkshire barons would ordinarily have been consulted before the question of collection could arise; but the event clearly proves that the county court claimed a right to examine the authority under which the tax was demanded, and to withhold payment until the question was answered. The county court of Worcester thus declined to pay the illegal exaction of the eighth in 1297[1]. The knights who were summoned in 1254 to the parliament could scarcely have done more. It is however certain that in 1220 the sovereign authority had been given to the collection before the writ was issued. The county court therefore, in its greatest force, was far from the independent position of an assembly of provincial estates.

Worcestershire refuses in 1297.

(6) Access of the counties to the king.

210. It might be inferred, as a corollary from these facts, that the several county courts had the power of directly approaching the king as communities from a very early period. As the crown recognised their corporate character by consulting them through inquests, and taxing them as consolidated bodies, they must have had, through their sheriffs or through chosen representatives, the right of approaching the crown by petition or of negotiating for privileges by way of fine. There is sufficient proof that they did so from time to time, just as the several town communities and the ecclesiastical bodies did. When the men of Cornwall agreed by fine with John, that their county should be disafforested and they should elect their own sheriff[2]; when the men of Devon, Dorset, and Somerset treated for the same or the like privileges with John and Henry III, the negotiation may or may not have been carried on through

[1] See above, p. 142. The passage is curious and important: 'Sexto kalendas Octobris, cum ministri regis exigerent sextam partem infra burgum bonorum omnium et octavam extra burgum, responsum fuit eis per comitatum, "rex Henricus aliquando promisit communitati regni quod libertates magnae cartae et forestae concederet et confirmaret si daretur ei quinta decima quam tunc petebat, sed pecunia accepta libertates tradidit oblivioni. Ideo quando habuerimus libertatum saisinam gratis dabimus pecuniam nominatam;"' Ann. Wigorn. p. 534. In 1302 the sheriff of Lincoln is ordered to assemble the taxors and collectors of the fifteenth, and the knights and others of his county, 'quos praemuniendos esse videris,' to the next county court, to meet the king's officers; Parl. Writs, i. 403.

[2] Above, p. 217.

the sheriff; it must have been initiated and authorised by the county court. So likewise with petitions: in the parliament of 1278 the county of Chester petitions, as 'la commune de Cestresire,' for the usages which it enjoyed before it fell into the king's hands [1]. After the consolidation of the parliamentary system such memorials became more frequent, and were no doubt presented by the knights of the shire.

Analogy of the town communities with the shires.

211. The communities of cities and boroughs, the organisations which in foreign constitutions composed the whole estate of the commons, present points of analogy and contrast with the county communities, under both of the heads just noticed. Being in their origin sections of the shire, and lying locally within the area of the shire, they retain for the most part the same constituent elements and the same administrative functions which were common to them and the shire before their separation. Trained throughout their subsequent history on a plan of privilege and exemption, exposed far more than the shires to the intrusion of foreign elements and foreign sympathies, and open to the influx of the political ideas which came in along with the trade of the foreign merchants, they were subject to internal jealousies and class divisions, of which there are fewer traces in the counties, where the local interests of the great lords were the chief dividing causes. Any complete generalisation upon the constitutional history of the towns is impossible for this reason, that this history does not start from one point or proceed by the same stages. At the time at which they began to take a share in the national counsels through their representatives, the class of towns contained communities in every stage of development, and in each stage of development constituted on different principles. Hence, by the way, arose the anomalies and obscurities as to the nature of the constituencies, which furnished matter of deliberation to the House of Commons for many centuries, and only ended with the

Difficulty of generalisation on this head.

[1] Rot. Parl. i. 6. In 1300 Edward summoned seven knights from each of the ridings of Yorkshire to meet the barons of the Exchequer at York, 'super quibusdam negotiis nos et communitatem comitatus praedicti specialiter tangentibus tractaturi;' Parl. Writs, i. 86.

Reform Act of 1832. The varieties of later usage were based on the condition in which the borough found itself when it began to be represented, according as the local constitution was for the moment guided by the court leet, the burgage holders, the general body of householders, the local magistrates or landlords, the merchant guild, or the like. Of these points something may be said when we reach the subject of the suffrage; it is noticed here in order to show that the obscurity of the subject is not a mere result of our ignorance or of the deficiency of record, but of a confusion of usages which was felt at the time to be capable of no general treatment; a confusion which, like that arising from the connexion between tenure and representation, prevailed from the very first, and occasioned actual disputes ages before it began to puzzle the constitutional lawyers.

Actual obscurity of the question.

I. Constitution of the towns and their courts.

212. I. We look in vain then for any uniform type of city or borough court which answers to the county court[1]: in one town the town-meeting included all householders, in another all who paid scot and lot—analogous to the modern ratepayers —in another the owners of burgages, in another the members of the merchant guild or trade guilds: every local history supplies evidence of the existence of a variety of such courts, with conflicting and co-ordinate jurisdictions. Roughly, however, we may divide them into two classes, those in which the local administration was carried on by a ruling body of magistrates or magnates, and those in which it remained in the hands of the townspeople in general; the former being the type of the larger and more ancient municipalities, the latter that of the smaller towns and of those whose corporate character was simpler and newer[2]. In London and the other great towns

(a) One class under close corporations; (b) another with simpler and freer organisation.

[1] This was the case in France also, where similar questions arise as to the elections to the States General; Boutaric, pp. 20, 21.

[2] Thus in 1245, the magnates of London elected one person as sheriff, 'quidam de vulgo' chose another; Lib. de Antt. Legg. p. 11; in 1249, when the justices wished to negotiate with the mayor and aldermen, 'universus populus contradixit non permittens illos sine tota communa inde aliquid tractare,' ibid. p. 16; in 1254 the whole communa passed several by-laws, p. 20; in 1255 the citizens refused to pay queen-gold, p. 23; in 1257 the alderman and four men of each ward met the council in

which in the reign of Edward I much more nearly rivalled London than they do now, there was a doubt whether the jurisdiction of the magistrates were not, so far as it touched questions of finance and general politics, a usurped jurisdiction. And this division of opinion caused the tumults which arose in the capital, on the right of the magistrates to determine the incidence of taxation, and to elect the mayor, to the exclusion of the general body of the citizens. Of these disputes the reign of Henry III furnishes a continuous record, the divisions being complicated by the political affinities of their leaders as royalists or as members of the baronial party [1]. And this feeling could not be confined to London; something of the kind was felt everywhere except in those small towns where the more ancient type of moot and court still retained its efficiency.

Political struggles of the governing bodies with the general body of inhabitants.

213. II. As there were many types of town constitution existing at the same time, so too there were many degrees of completeness of functions. Some were almost independent republics, some mere country townships that had reached the stage at which they compounded severally for their ferm, but were in all other respects under the influence of the sheriff and the county court. There were, however, some points in which—London with sheriffs and a shire constitution of its own being perhaps the only exception—the sheriff and the county court still reviewed or incorporated the town constitution.

II. Variety of powers and functions in towns.

Functions of the sheriffs in the towns.

In matters of jurisdiction, the towns, however completely organised, could not exclude the itinerant justices, whose court being the shiremoot involved the recognition of the sheriff.

the Exchequer, and discussed the question whether the assessment of tallage ought to be made by the mayor and other officers, or 'per viros ad hoc per totam communam electos et juratos,' p. 33. In 1263 a popular mayor 'ita nutrierat populum civitatis, quod vocantes se communam civitatis habuerant primam vocem in civitate;' on all matters of business he said to them 'vultis vos ita fiat,' they replied 'Ya, ya,' and it was done, the aldermen and magnates not being consulted; p. 55. In 1272 there was a struggle between the magnates and 'ille populus vocans se communem civitatis,' about the election of mayor; p. 152.

[1] So it is remarked by the French writers referred to above, Boutaric and Picot, that the universal suffrage prevailed more in the *villes prévotales* than in the *communes*; the former being the towns administered by a royal bailiff or praepositus, the latter being independent corporations, where the suffrage was exercised by the magistrates.

(1) Attendance before the justices in eyre.

Hence in the general summons of the county court before those officers the boroughs were ordered to send twelve burghers to represent the general body[1].

(2) View of the arms under the Assize, watch and ward.

In the measures for the conservation of the peace, the sheriff had orders to enforce the observance of watch and ward, to forbid tournaments and other occasions of riot, and to examine into the observance of the Assize of Arms, not only in the geldable or open townships of the shire, but in the cities and boroughs as well[2]. The details of the system were carried out by the local officers; the great towns elected their own coroners, mayors, bailiffs and constables, but they were under view of the sheriff.

(3) The armed force of the towns was under the sheriff.

The military contingents of the towns, composed of the men sworn under the Assize of Arms, were also led by the sheriffs; these contributions to the national force being, except in the case of a few large towns, too small to form a separate organised body.

(4, 5, 6) Direct negotiation of the towns with the crown.

In point of direct dealing with the crown, whether in the executive measures resulting from reform, in fiscal negotiations, or in transactions which took the form of fine or petition, every town, as indeed every individual, had a distinct and recognised right to act; and these points, which serve in regard to the counties to show the corporate unity of the community, and therefore require illustration in relation to that point, need no further treatment here.

Were the towns to be treated as parts of the shire?

Under these circumstances, we can well imagine that Simon de Montfort and Edward I, when they determined to call the town communities to their parliaments, may have hesitated whether to treat them as part of the shire communities or as independent bodies. Earl Simon adopted the latter course, which was perhaps necessary under the local divisions of the moment: as he summoned out of the body of the baronage only those on whom he could rely, so he selected the towns which were to be represented, and addressed his summons directly to

[1] Select Charters, p. 358; above, p. 219.

[2] Select Charters, pp. 362, 371. 'Vicecomites . . . circumeant comitatus suos de hundredo in hundredum, et civitates et burgos;' p. 371.

the magistrates of those towns[1]. And this plan was adopted by Edward I on one of the first occasions on which he called the borough representatives together[2]. But when the constitution took its final form, a form which was in thorough accordance with the growth of the national spirit and system, it was found more convenient to treat them as portions of the counties; the writ for the election was directed to the sheriff, and the formal election of the borough members, as well as that of knights of the shire, was in many cases, if not generally[3], completed in the county court. Thus the inclusion of the boroughs in the national system was finally completed in and through the same process by which the general representation of the three estates was insured.

Writs for borough elections directed to the sheriffs.

The towns of England, neither by themselves nor in conjunction with the shires, ever attempted before the seventeenth century to act alone in convention like the Scottish boroughs, or in confederation like the German leagues. The commons had no separate assembly, answering to the convocation of the clergy or the great council of the baronage. In 1296, however, Edward summoned representative burghers from the chief towns to meet first at Bury and afterwards at Berwick to advise on the new constitution of the latter town; and this plan may have been occasionally adopted for other purposes[4].

The English boroughs had no collective organisation.

214. III. We have now to link together very succinctly the several cases in which, before the year 1295, the representative principle entered into the composition of the parliaments; the political causes and other phenomena of which have been treated in the last chapter. From the year 1215 onwards, in the total deficiency of historical evidence, we can only conjecture that the national council, when it contained members over and above those who were summoned by special writ as barons, comprised such minor members of the body of tenants-in-chief as found it convenient or necessary to obey the general summons which was

III. Early cases of representation.

Obscurity during the years 1215 to 1254.

[1] Foedera, i. 449; Select Charters, p. 415.
[2] In 1283; above, p. 121; Select Charters, p. 476.
[3] Prynne, Writs, iii. 175–188, 251 sq. Cf. Privy Council Acts, 1558, vol. vii. p. 41, for an illustration of the continuity of the custom.
[4] Parl. Writs, i. 49, 51. Cf. p. 164, above.

prescribed, for the purpose of granting special aids, by the fourteenth article of the charter. These would be more or less numerous on occasion, but would have no right or title to represent the commons; they attended simply by virtue of their tenure. When Matthew Paris describes a parliament of 1246 as containing the 'generalis universitas' of the clergy and knighthood of the kingdom, his words, suggestive as they are, cannot be safely understood as implying representation[1].

Summons of knights of the shire in 1254.

The year 1254 then is the first date at which the royal writs direct the election and attendance in parliament of two knights from each shire: the occasion being the granting of an aid in money to be sent to the king in Gascony, and the parliament being called by the queen and the earl of Cornwall in the belief that, as the bishops had refused to grant money without consulting the beneficed clergy, the surest way to obtain it from the laity was to call an assembly on which the promise of a renewal of the charters would be likely to produce the effect desired[2].

No representation in 1258 or 1259.

There is no reason to suppose that the counties were represented either in the first parliament of 1258[3] or in the Oxford parliament of the same year, or that the knights who brought up the complaints of the shires to the October parliament were elected as representatives to take part in that parliament, or that the 'bacheleria,' which in 1259 took Edward for its spokesman, was the collective representation of the shires. The provisionary

[1] M. Paris, iv. 557: 'In parlamento regis ubi congregata fuerat totius regni tam cleri quam militiae generalis universitas.' It is however observable that this is 'parlamentum generalissimum;' ib. p. 518.

[2] Above, p. 69. That the knights of the shire assembled on this occasion represented the minor tenants-in-chief seems to be too lightly admitted by Hallam, Middle Ages, iii. 19; apparently on the argument of the Lords' Committee, i. 95. There is nothing in the writ that so limits their character; Select Charters, p. 376.

[3] There were knights at the first parliament, but apparently summoned for local business only. The question turns on the meaning of a writ of expenses, dated Nov. 4, 1258, for four knights of Northumberland who had attended at Westminster a month after Easter: similar writs were issued for Yorkshire, Lincolnshire, Huntingdonshire, and Northamptonshire; Lords' Report, i. 463; ii. 5, 7. It is however certain from the form of the writ 'pro quibusdam negotiis communitatem totius comitatus praedicti tangentibus' that the summons was not a parliamentary one; in that case the form is 'super diversis negotiis nos et populum regni nostri specialiter tangentibus,' or some similar expression; Parl. Writs, i. 85.

government which lasted from 1258 to 1264 restricted rather than extended the limits of the taxing and deliberative council. In the intervening struggle however both parties had recourse to the system of representation: in 1261 the baronial leaders summoned three knights of each shire to a conference at S. Alban's, and the king retaliated by directing the same knights to attend his parliament at Windsor[1]. In 1264, immediately after the battle of Lewes, Simon summoned four knights of each shire to a parliament at London[2], and in the December of the same year he called together the more famous assembly, to which not only knights of the shire were summoned by writs addressed to the sheriffs, but two discreet and lawful representatives from the cities and boroughs were summoned by writs addressed to the magistrates of the several communities[3]. It is not impossible that Henry III, or earl Simon, may have summoned representatives of the commons, when he summoned proctors for the cathedral chapters[4], to the parliament at Winchester which was to have been held in June 1265. The preamble to the statute of Marlborough in 1267 states that the king had called to parliament the more discreet men of the realm, 'tam de majoribus quam de minoribus[5],'—the discretion, which was the peculiar qualification of the knights of the shire, affording a presumption

Kings and barons adopt it in 1261.

Two parliaments of Simon de Montfort.

Possible cases of representation in 1265 and 1267.

[1] Above, p. 87. [2] Above, p. 93.

[3] Above, p. 96. The fact that the peculiar constitution of this parliament did not attract the notice of the historians has led to the conclusion that borough representation was not such a novelty as to call for much remark at the time; see Edin. Rev. vol. xxxv. p. 38. As however there is no real evidence of any summons of the boroughs before this time, there seems little reason to question that this was the first occasion. The case of S. Alban's, in which in the reign of Edward II the burghers claimed a right of sending two members to parliament in discharge of all service due to the crown, as customary in the days of Edward I and his progenitors (see Brady, Introduction, p. 38; Hallam, Middle Ages, iii. 29), and that of Barnstaple (see Hallam, iii. 32), where, in the 18th of Edward III, the burghers alleged a lost charter of Athelstan to support their claim to representation, need not be discussed. They were both cases of imposture, got up with the intention of escaping from the services due to the lords of the towns, the abbot of S. Alban's and the lord Audley; and the S. Alban's claim was part of a great effort, which lasted for more than half a century, to throw off the authority of the abbey; see Vitae Abb. S. Alb. (ed. Riley), ii. 156 sq.

[4] Select Charters, p. 418. The assembly, called on May 15 for June 1, was of course prevented by the outbreak of the war. See above, p. 98, note 3.

[5] Statutes, p. 19.

Attendance of representatives in 1269, not in parliament.

that they were present. In 1269, at the great court held for the translation of S. Edward the Confessor, attended by all the magnates, were present also the more powerful men of the cities and boroughs; but, when the ceremony was over, the king proceeded to hold a parliament with the barons [1], and the citizens and burghers can only be supposed to have been invited guests, such as attended, by nomination of the sheriffs, at the coronations and other great occasions [2]. In 1273 we find a more important illustration of the growth of the custom: at Hilary-tide a great convocation of the whole realm was held to take the oath of fealty to Edward I, and to maintain the peace of the realm: 'thither came archbishops and bishops, earls and barons, abbots and priors, and from each shire four knights and from each city four citizens [3].' This assembly was, in its essence if not in its form, a parliament, and acted as the common council of the kingdom. The preamble of the statute of Westminster passed in the first parliament of 1275 declares the assent of archbishops, bishops, abbots, priors, earls, barons, and the community of the land thereunto summoned [4]; an assertion which distinctly implies, besides the magnates, the attendance of a body which can hardly have been other than the knights, though not necessarily elected representatives. In the second parliament of that year we have direct record of the presence of elected knights of the shire; it was summoned for the purpose of raising money, an occasion on which it was expedient that the counties should be represented, and the recent discovery of the writ by which the election was ordered may tend to show the probability that the usage was being regularly adopted. At any rate the first parliament at which Edward asked for a general contribution was a representative parliament [5]. After

Great convention in 1273.

First Parliament of 1275.

Second Parliament of 1275.

[1] Ann. Wykes, pp. 226, 227.

[2] Thus for the coronation of Edward II, the sheriffs were ordered, 'et milites, cives, burgenses ac alios de comitatu praedicto, quos fore videris invitandos, ut dictis die et loco solempnizationi praedictae personaliter intersint, ex parte nostra facias invitari;' Foed. ii. 28.

[3] Ann. Winton, p. 113.

[4] Statutes, i. 26.

[5] The writ for this election was discovered a few years ago in the search made preparatory to the Return of Members' names ordered by the House of Commons and published in August, 1879. It is so very interesting and important that it is here given entire:—

1275 the earlier obscurity and uncertainty recur. In 1278 the statute of Gloucester was enacted with the assent of the most discreet, 'ausi bien les greindres cum les meindres[1].' In 1282 the two provincial councils of Northampton and York contained four knights of each shire and two representatives of each city and borough[2]. In 1283 the parliament of Shrewsbury comprised representatives of twenty-one selected towns separately summoned as in 1265, and two knights of each shire[3]. In 1290 two knights of each shire attended the Westminster parliament[4]; in 1294 four[5]; and in 1295 two knights from each shire, two citizens from each city, and two burghers from each borough[6].

Parliament of Gloucester.

Councils of 1282 and 1283.

Parliaments of 1290, 1294, and 1295.

The last date, 1295, may be accepted as fixing finally the right of shire and town representation, although for a few years the system admits of some modifications. The great councils of the baronage are sometimes, until the writs of summons are examined, almost indistinguishable from the parliaments; they are in fact a permanent survival from the earlier system. But even in the parliaments proper there were, as we shall see, a variety of minute irregularities, such for instance as the summoning to the parliament of Lincoln of the representatives who had sat in the preceding parliament, and in 1306 of one representative from the smaller boroughs; but such anomalies only illustrate the still tender growth of the new system.

Later variations of parliamentary constitution.

'Edwardus Dei Gratia Rex Angliae dominus Hiberniae et dux Aquitanniae vicecomiti Kanciae salutem. Cum praelatis et magnatibus regni nostri mandaverimus ut ipsi parliamento nostro, quod apud Westmonasterium in quindena Sancti Michaelis proxime futura tenebimus, Domino concedente, intersint ad tractandum nobiscum tam super statum regni nostri quam super quibusdam negotiis nostris quae eis exponemus ibidem, et expediens sit quod duo milites de comitatu praedicto de discretioribus et legalioribus militibus ejusdem comitatus intersint eidem parliamento, ex causis praedictis tibi praecipimus quod in pleno comitatu tuo de assensu ejusdem comitatus eligi facias dictos duos milites et eos ad nos usque Westmonasterium pro communitate dicti comitatus venire facias ad dictum diem ad tractandum nobiscum et cum praedictis praelatis et magnatibus super negotiis praedictis. Et hoc non omittas. Teste me ipso apud Cestr. primo die Septembris anno regni nostri tertio.

'DORS. Nomina militum qui eliguntur eundum ad parlementum Domini regis in quindena Sancti Michaelis apud Westm.

¶ Fulco Peyforer.
¶ Henricus de Apuldrefeud.'

[1] Statutes, i. 45.
[2] Above, p. 119.
[3] Above, p. 121.
[4] Above, p. 126.
[5] Above, p. 132.
[6] Above, p. 134.

The parliament of 1295 a model parliament.

The parliament of 1295 differed, so far as we know, from all that had preceded it, and was a precedent for all time to come, worthy of the principle which the king had enunciated in the writ of summons. The writs for assembling the representatives are addressed to the sheriffs; they direct the election not only of the knights but of citizens and burghers; the return to the writ is not merely as in 1265 and 1283 the reply of the separate towns but of the county courts, in which the final stage of the elective process is transacted; and the parliament that results contains a concentration of the persons and powers of the shiremoot. In that assembly, on great occasions, the towns had appeared by their twelve burghers, now they appear, by their bailiffs or otherwise, to make their return to the sheriff, who thereupon makes his report to the government.

The name of parliament not restricted to representative assemblies.

215. In thus tracing the several links which connect the parliament of 1295 with those of 1265 and 1254, we must be content to understand by the name of parliament all meetings of the national council called together in the form that was usual at the particular time. We must not take our definition from the later legal practice and refuse the name to those assemblies which do not in all points answer to that definition. After 1295 it is otherwise; that year established the precedent, and although, in the early years that follow, exceptional practices may be found, it may be fairly questioned whether any assembly afterwards held is entitled to the name and authority of parliament which does not in the minutest particulars of summons, constitution, and formal dispatch of business, answer to the model then established. This rule, however, was not at once recognised, and for many years both the terminal sessions of the king's ordinary council, and the occasional assemblies of the magnum concilium of prelates, barons and councillors, which we have noticed as a great survival of the older system, share with the constitutional assembly of estates the name of parliament[1].

[1] For example, the summons to the council called for Sept. 30, 1297, is entitled 'de parliamento tenendo:' in 1299 a writ 'de parliamento tenendo,' dated Sept. 21, is addressed only to the archbishop of Canterbury, five bishops, four earls, and five others, barons of the council; Lords' Report, App. pp. 87, 111. On the other hand the great council of the

216. Before proceeding to inquire into the powers of the body thus composed, we have to meet the natural question, who were the electors of the representative members? On any equitable theory of representation, the elected representatives represent those members of the body politic who have not the right of appearing personally in the assembly, and they are elected by the persons whom they represent. The knights of the shire represented the community of the shire which was intermediately represented by the county court; the representatives of the towns represented the community of the several towns intermediately represented by their agents in the county court. The two cases must be considered separately.

By whom were the representatives elected?

It is most probable, on the evidence of records, on the analogies of representative usage, and on the testimony of later facts, that the knights of the shire were elected by the full county court. The institution of electing representative knights for local purposes was in active operation for nearly eighty years before such representatives were summoned to parliament; those earlier elections were made by the full county court; and in the writs ordering the parliamentary elections no words are contained which restrict the liberty heretofore exercised. The four knights elected under the eighteenth article of Magna Carta, to assist the itinerant justices in taking recognitions, are elected *per comitatum* [1]: the county court which attended the itinerant justices was, as we have seen, of the fullest possible character [2]. The twelve knights chosen to inquire into the forest abuses, under the forty-eighth article [3], are chosen 'per probos homines comitatus,' and in the first county court after the issue of the writ [4]. The two knights, collectors of the

Election of knights of the shire.

Knights elected by the shire for local purposes.

barons called at Salisbury, Feb. 5, 1297, is entitled 'de parliamento tenendo apud Sarisburiam;' Ibid. p. 77.

[1] Select Charters, p. 299.

[2] Above, p. 215. On the whole subject see Riess, Geschichte des Wahlrechts zum Englischen Parlament; Leipzig, 1885, a book which contains much illustrative material.

[3] Select Charters, p. 302: 'qui debent eligi per probos homines ejusdem comitatus.'

[4] 'Qui eligentur de ipso comitatu, in primo comitatu qui tenebitur post susceptionem litterarum istarum;' Select Charters, p. 307.

carucage of 1220, are elected 'de voluntate et consilio omnium de comitatu in pleno comitatu[1].' The four knights of the shire summoned to meet the sheriffs in 1226 are to be chosen in the county court by the knights and good men of the county[2]. In 1254 the knights summoned to grant an aid are described as 'four lawful and discreet knights of the aforesaid counties, that is to say, two of the one county and two of the other, whom the same counties shall choose for the purpose to represent all and singular of the same counties[3].' The knights summoned to the first parliament of Simon de Montfort are chosen 'per assensum ejusdem comitatus[4].' In 1275 the sheriff is instructed to cause the election of two knights in full county court and by assent of the same county[5]. In 1282 he is ordered to send four knights from each county 'having full power to act for the communities of the same counties[6].' In 1283 he is directed to cause two knights to be chosen in each county, to attend the king on behalf of the community of the same county[7]. In 1290 the knights are described as elected from the more discreet and able, and as having full power for themselves and the whole community of the counties[8]. In 1294 and 1295 the qualification and authorisation are stated in the same words[9].

Cases of election in the shire-moot for local purposes.

These are elections by the full county.

No restriction implied in the writs of summons to parliament,

There is then no restriction on the common and prescriptive usage of the county court. Nor does any such restriction appear in the extant returns of the sheriffs in 1290 and 1295[10].

[1] Select Charters, p. 352.

[2] 'In proximo comitatu dicas militibus et probis hominibus bailliae tuae, quod quatuor de legalioribus et discretioribus militibus ex se ipsis eligant;' Select Charters, p. 357.

[3] 'Tibi districte praecipimus, quod praeter omnes praedictos venire facias coram consilio nostro apud Westmonasterium in quindena Paschae proximo futuri, quatuor legales et discretos milites de comitatibus praedictis quos iidem comitatus ad hoc elegerint, vice omnium et singulorum eorundem comitatuum, videlicet duos de uno comitatu et duos de alio, ad providendum, una cum militibus aliorum comitatuum quos ad eundem diem vocari fecimus, quale auxilium nobis in tanta necessitate impendere voluerint;' Select Charters, p. 376; Lords' Report, App. p. 13.

[4] Foed. i. 442; Select Charters, p. 412.

[5] See above, p. 234, note 5.

[6] Select Charters, p. 465; Parl. Writs, i. 10.

[7] Select Charters, p. 468; Parl. Writs, i. 16.

[8] Select Charters, p. 477; Lords' Report, App. p. 54.

[9] Select Charters, pp. 481, 486. Compare the writs of the 28th and 34th years; Parl. Writs, i. 84, 167.

[10] Parl. Writs, i. 21–24, 38, 40, 41.

nor in the wording of the returns.

In 1290 the knights are described as elected 'per assensum totius comitatus,' or 'per totam communitatem,' or 'in pleno comitatu;' in 1295 the knights for Lancashire are elected 'per consensum totius comitatus;' those for Oxfordshire and Berkshire 'per assensum communitatis;' those for Dorset and Somerset, 'per communitatem' and 'in plenis comitatibus.' In 1298 the knights for Cornwall are elected 'per totam communitatem;' those for Dorset, Somerset, and Hertford 'in pleno comitatu per totam communitatem [1];' the diversity of form in the several returns serving to prove the uniformity of the usage.

Analogy of the election of coroners, verderers, and conservators.

Analogous examples may be taken from the election of coroner and conservator, and from the practice of the ecclesiastical assemblies, in which the representative theory is introduced shortly before it finds its way into parliament; and these instances are the more convincing because the continuity and uniformity of practice has never been questioned. The writ for the election of coroners orders it to be done 'in pleno comitatu per assensum totius comitatus [2];' the election of verderers is made 'convocato toto comitatu,' 'per eundem comitatum [3];' the election of conservator is made 'in pleno comitatu de assensu ejusdem comitatus [4].' The election of proctors for the clergy is made, as it is hardly necessary to say, by the whole of the beneficed clergy of each archdeaconry.

Royal decisions in favour of the full county court.

The later modifications of the right of election belong to a further stage of our inquiries; but we may adduce now the answer made by Edward III in 1376 to a petition that the knights should be elected by common choice from [5] the best men

[1] Parl. Writs, i. 70, 74.

[2] 'Praecipimus tibi quod in pleno comitatu Wigorniae per assensum totius comitatus eligi facias de fidelioribus et discretioribus militibus de comitatu . . . duos coronatores;' Rot. Claus. i. 414; cf. pp. 419, 463, 506, 522.

[3] 'Praecipimus tibi quod sine dilatione convocato comitatu tuo statim per eundem comitatum eligi facias unum de legalioribus et discretioribus militibus . . . qui melius esse possit viridarius;' Rot. Claus. i. 409; cf. pp. 410, 493, 497.

[4] 'Tunc in pleno comitatu tuo de assensu ejusdem comitatus et de consilio Simonis de Wintonia . . . eligi facias unum alium de fidelibus regis;' 8th March, 1287; Parl. Writs, i. 390.

[5] 'Par commun election de les meillours gentz des ditz counteez;' Rot. Parl. ii. 355. It is clear that the 'de les' means the body from which the

of the county, and not certified by the sheriff alone without due election. The king replied that they should be elected by the common assent of the whole county[1]; in 1372, when a proposition was made to prevent the choice of lawyers, he ordered that the election should be made in full county court[2]. These replies, made within a century of the introduction of the usage, seem to be conclusive as to the theory of election.

We must not, however, suppose that this theory was universally understood, or generally accepted, or that it was not in practice limited by some very strong restrictions.

Theory that the knights of the shire represented the minor tenants-in-chief of the crown.

It seems almost unquestioned that the national assemblies between 1215 and 1295 were composed on the principle stated in the fourteenth article of the charter, and thus contained a considerable number of minor tenants-in-chief attending in obedience to the general summons; it might then not unreasonably be contended that the new element of the representative knights was a substitute for those minor tenants, and so that the knights of the shire represented not the body of the county but simply the tenants-in-chief below the rank of baron. If this were the case, the assembly by which the election was made would not be the full county court; the electors would be the tenants-in-chief, not the whole body of suitors; and the new system, instead of being an expedient by which the co-operation of all elements of the people might be secured for common objects, would simply place the power of legislation and taxation in the hands of a body constituted on the principle of tenure[3]. It has been accordingly supposed that the court summoned for the election was not the court leet of the county, at which all residents were obliged to

choice was made; see Riess, Geschichte des Wahlrechts zum Englischen Parlament, p. 38, where the danger of a mistake is carefully pointed out.

[1] Rot. Parl. ii. 355: 'le roi voet q'ils soient esluz par commune assent de tout le Contee.'

[2] Rot. Parl. ii. 310.

[3] This appears to be the theory of the Lords' Report on the dignity of a Peer, to which only a general reference need here be given. The Lords however confess that it is involved in very great obscurity. It was the theory of Blackstone, Brady, and Carte; Prynne on the other hand maintained that the knights were elected in full county by and for the whole county; Regist. ii. p. 50; and this view is followed by Hallam, Middle Ages, iii. 19, 216–219.

attend, but the court baron, composed of persons owing suit and service to the king, and excluding the tenants of mesne lords[1]. To this must be objected that there is no authority for drawing at this period any such distinction between the two theoretical characters of the county court[2], and that it is impossible that an election known to be made by a mere fraction could be said to be the act of the whole community, or to be transacted 'in pleno comitatu.' If such, moreover, were the case, the whole body of mesne tenants who were not included in the town population would be represented in parliament by their feudal lords, or, if their lords were below the degree of barony, would be unrepresented altogether. But it was certainly opposed to the policy of the crown, from the very date of the Conquest, that the feudal lords should stand in such a relation to their vassals, although from time to time they had assumed it, and the assumption had been tacitly admitted. And it is impossible to suppose that Edward I, who in so many other ways showed his determination to place the whole body of freeholders on a basis of equality, exclusive of the question of tenure, should have instituted a system which would draw the line more hardly and sharply than ever between the two classes. These considerations would seem to be conclusive as to the original principle on which the institution was founded. But the facts that questions did arise very early on the point, that the doctrines of tenure more and more influenced the opinions of constitutional lawyers, and that there was always a class among the barons who would gladly have seen the commons reduced to entire dependence on the lords, have led to much discussion, and perhaps the question may never be quite satisfactorily decided.

This theory is wanting in authority;

is opposed to the policy of the crown;

and irreconcileable with the other measures of Edward I.

Yet questions arose very early upon this.

As the knights of the shire received wages during their attendance in parliament, it was fair that those persons who

[1] Lords' Report, i. 149, 150. This view, which need not be here re-argued, was by anticipation refuted by Mr. Allen in the Edinburgh Review, vol. xxvi. pp. 341–347; on the ground that the vavassores of the barons, the mesne tenants, are spoken of as attending the courts, both in the charters of Henry I (above, vol. i. p. 393), and in the 'Extenta Manerii' of the reign of Edward I; Statutes, i. 242.

[2] Hallam, Middle Ages, iii. 217.

How far does the question of wages paid to the knights of the shire illustrate the question?

were excluded from the election should be exempt from contribution to the wages. To many of the smaller freeholders the exemption from payment would be far more valuable than the privilege of voting; and the theory that the knights represented only the tenants-in-chief would be recommended by a strong argument of self-interest. The claim of exemption was urged on behalf of the mesne tenants in general, on behalf of the tenants in socage in the county of Kent, as against the tenants by knight service, and on behalf of the tenants of land in ancient demesne of the crown[1]. In the last of these three cases the exemption was occasionally admitted, for, as the crown retained the power of tallaging such tenants without consulting parliament, they were without share in the representation[2]. As to the two former cases, opinions were divided at a very early period, and petitions for a legal decision were presented in many parliaments from the reign of Edward III to that of Henry VIII. The petitions of the commons generally express their desire that the expenses should be levied from the whole of the commons of the county, a desire which is in itself sufficient to show that no exemption could be urged on the ground of non-representation[3]. The reiteration of the petition shows that it met with some opposition, which must have proceeded from those lords who retained the idea that they represented their tenants, and were anxious to maintain the hold upon them which that idea implied. The crown as constantly avoids a judicial decision, and orders that the usage customary in the particular case shall be maintained. This hesitation on the part of the government in several successive reigns may have arisen from a desire to avoid a quarrel with either estate, but more probably proceeded from the recognised obscurity of the question, the theory having been from the first subject to the doubts which we have noted. In consequence of the authority

Exemption claimed for tenants in socage, for mesne tenants, and for tenants in ancient demesne.

Petitions of the commons opposed to such exemptions.

The crown decides in favour of custom.

[1] See Hallam, Middle Ages, iii. 114–116.

[2] Lords' Report, i. 58, 232; Prynne, Reg. iv. 431.

[3] Lords' Report, i. 330, 331, 366, 369. Cases might be pleaded that would lead to almost any conclusion: e.g. in 1307 the sheriff of Cambridgeshire is forbidden to tax the villein tenants of John de la Mare for the wages of the knights, because he had attended personally in parliament; Parl. Writs, i. 191.

of custom thus recognised, the Kentish socagers secured their exemption[1], but between the general body of freeholders and the tenants-in-chief the dispute was never judicially settled; as the awakening political sense showed men the importance of electoral power, the exemption ceased to be courted, and the laws which defined the suffrage must have practically settled the question of contribution[2]. The discussion of the matter, in which the belief of the commons was uniformly on one side, and in which no adverse decision by the crown was ever attempted, tends to confirm the impression that, although there was real obscurity and conflict of opinion, both the right of election and the burden of contribution belonged to the whole of the suitors of the county court. Had the counter pleas been successful, had the tenants in ancient demesne, the mesne tenants, and the tenants in socage, been exempted, the county constituencies would have been reduced to a handful of knights, who might as easily have attended parliament in person, as their compeers did for many ages in Aragon and Scotland.

The dispute never decided on its merits.

General conclusion.

217. Yet it is almost equally improbable that, in an age in which political intelligence was very scanty, the whole county court on each summons for an election was fully attended, carefully identified the qualified members, and, free from all suspicion of undue influence, formally endeavoured to discover the most discreet, or most apt, or most able, among the knights of the shire. Unquestionably the tenants-in-chief of the crown, men who still received their summons to the host, or held their lands by barony, the knightly body too, who had interests of their own more akin to those of the baron than to those of the socager, would possess an influence in the assembly, and a will to exercise it. The chief lord of a great manor would have

Theory and practice may not have coincided.

Influence of the greater men in the shire-moot.

[1] Lords' Report, i. 364.

[2] 'We are of opinion that no conclusion whatever can be drawn from the disputes concerning the payment of wages.' 'Villeins contributed.' Allen, Edinb. Rev. xxxv. 27. Brady (Introd. p. 141) points out that the payment of wages to knights appointed for county business was not a novelty. In 1258 the knights appointed, four in each shire to present before the council at Michaelmas the complaints against the sheriffs, had writs for their expenses 'de communitate;' Rot. Claus. 42 Hen. III. m. 1 dors.

Early traces of undue influence in elections.

authority with his tenants, freeholders as they might be, which would make their theoretical equality a mere shadow, and would moreover be exercised all the more easily because the right which it usurped was one which the tenant neither understood nor cared for. Early in the fourteenth century undue influence in elections becomes a matter of complaint. But it is long before we have sufficient data to determine how far the suitors of the county court really exerted the power which we cannot but believe the theory of the constitution to have given them: when we do reach that point, the power often seems to be engrossed by the great men of the shire. The office of representative was not coveted, and we can imagine cases in which the sheriff would have to nominate and compel the service of an unwilling member. But by whomsoever the right was actually used, the theory of the election was that it was the act of the shire-moot, that is, of all the suitors of the county court assembled in the county court, irrespective of the question of whom or by what tenure their lands were held.

No competition for the office of knight of the shire.

General conclusion.

Elections in boroughs.

218. With regard to the boroughs analogous questions arise. It may be asked whether the towns which were directed to return representatives were the demesne boroughs of the crown only[1], or all the town communities which the sheriff regarded as qualified under the terms of the writ. The former theory has been maintained, on the same principle of the all-importance of tenure which suggested the limitation of the county constituencies to the tenants-in-chief[2]; and there may have been

[1] In favour of the restriction is Brady, who however regards the term 'demesne cities and boroughs' as including all towns that had charters and paid fee farm rent; p. 35. In favour of the more liberal view, are Prynne, Hallam, Allen. The Lords' Report seems to halt between the two. The question is however practically decided by the cases mentioned in the text and in the note on the next page. There is a good deal of thoughtful argument on this in Riess's Geschichte des Wahlrechts, pp. 24 sq.

[2] On this point we may look for illustration from the elections of representatives of the third estate in the States General. M. Boutaric gives the data for the States General of Tours in 1308: he concludes that the municipal magistrates were not representatives except when specially elected and commissioned, but that the representatives were generally chosen from among the magistrates; that sometimes a town entrusted the commission to a clergyman, and the clergy to a layman; that in the com-

periods at which it was acted upon, for the number of borough representatives long and greatly fluctuated. But the evidence of fact seems decisive in favour of the more liberal interpretation, so far at least as concerns the reign of Edward I, to which we must naturally look as the fairest and first source of precedent. In the great parliament of 1295 many towns which were held in demesne by other lords than the crown, were represented: such were Downton, a borough of the bishop of Winchester, Ripon and Beverley, two towns which until recent times were dependent on the archbishop of York, and in 1298 North-Allerton a borough of the bishop of Durham; no doubt the instances might be multiplied [1]. Yet the matter is not so clear, but that in the writs for collecting money granted in these assemblies, whether from confusion of idea, or owing to the observance of routine forms, expressions are found that might lead to a different conclusion. The writ in 1295 asserts that the citizens and burghers and good men of the demesne cities and boroughs had courteously granted a subsidy [2]. If this expression be understood as a statement of fact, then the term 'dominicae civitates et burgi' must be made to include all

The towns returning members were not merely the demesne towns of the crown.

Yet there were early doubts on this.

Writs of 1295.

munes the deputies were chosen in the regular general assembly; and in the districts which had no communal organisation, in similar general gatherings, where all inhabitants had an equal voice; Premiers États Généraux, p. 21. M. Hervieu, Rev. de Législation, 1873, pp. 410 sq., limits this conclusion very materially: 'Tantôt, en effet, c'est le suffrage à deux degrés qui est la base de ces elections, et tantôt le suffrage universel.' An immense variety of usages prevailed, many of them exactly analogous to the later usages in England, when the various classes of burghers, the corporations, the householders, the freemen, the scot and lot payers, claimed the right. The subject has been still further illustrated by M. Picot in his paper on 'Les Élections aux États Généraux,' Paris, 1874.

[1] The following boroughs represented in the parliaments of Edward I were of the same class; Lynn belonged to the see of Norwich, Salisbury to the bishop, S. Alban's to the abbot; Evesham to the abbot; Tunbridge and Bletchingley to the earl of Gloucester; Arundel and Midhurst to the earl of Arundel; Farnham to the see of Winchester; Edinb. Rev. xxxv. pp. 36, 37. Compare the returns given in the Parliamentary Writs, i. 34 sq.

[2] Parl. Writs, i. 45: 'cum . . . cives, burgenses et alii probi homines de dominicis nostris civitatibus et burgis ejusdem regni septimam de omnibus bonis suis mobilibus . . . nobis curialiter concesserint et gratanter:' here 'curialiter' simply means courteously, not as the Lords' Committee understood it, as a formal act of a court.

boroughs whether held in chief or through mesne lords: if it be understood to state a theory, then the mesne boroughs which had sent members had gone beyond their duty in doing as they had done. It is perhaps more likely to be an old form applied without much definiteness on a new occasion, and the form used in 1296[1] must be taken to express both theory and fact. In this the grant is distinctly said to be made by the citizens, burghers, and other good men of all and singular the cities and boroughs of the kingdom of whosesoever tenures or liberties they were, and of all the royal demesnes. But again, the fact that neither of the counties palatine, Chester or Durham, furnished either knights of the shire, citizens, or burghers, until the reigns of Henry VIII and Charles II respectively, shows that the doctrine of demesne, qualified by the possession of peculiar privileges, created early anomalies and with them obscurities which nothing will explain but the convenient, almost superstitious, respect shown to ancient usage. The third of the great palatinates, Lancaster, is constantly represented, although for many years, from the reign of Edward III onward, the towns of the county were too much impoverished to send members to parliament.

The form in 1296 is distinct enough.

Inconsistency in practice.

Of the elections of city and borough members we have, except in the case of London, no details proper to the present period. In the capital, in 1296, all the aldermen and four men of each ward met on the 26th of September, and chose Stephen Aschewy and William Herford to go to the parliament of S. Edmunds; and on the 8th of October the 'communitas' was called together, namely six of the best and most discreet men of each ward, by whom the election was repeated and probably confirmed[2]. Whether these two gatherings in the

Example of city elections only in London.

[1] Parl. Writs, i. 51: 'cives, burgenses et alii probi homines de omnibus et singulis civitatibus et burgis regni nostri de quorumcunque tenuris aut libertatibus fuerint et de omnibus dominicis nostris . . . curialiter concesserint et gratanter.' So too in France in 1308, not merely the demesne towns but all the 'insignes communitates' were represented in the states general; Boutaric, pp. 16, 20, 28–35.

[2] Parl. Writs, i. 49. A similar plan was used for the election of the sheriffs of London, who were chosen 'per assensum duodecim proborum hominum singularum wardarum,' in the 29th and 31st parliaments of Edward I; Brady, Boroughs, p. 22.

case of London correspond with the two processes which must have taken place in the election of borough members, it would be rash to determine. In the latter case it must be supposed that the members were nominated in the borough assembly, or that delegates were appointed in that assembly to elect them, and a return thereon made to the sheriff before the election was made in the county court [1]. The proceedings before the sheriff seem to be the election, or report of nomination, by the citizens and burghers, the manucaption or production of two sureties for each of the elected persons, and the deliverance, by act or letter, of the full powers to act on behalf of the community which elected them. The difficulty of determining who the real electors were need not be re-stated.

Proceedings before the sheriff relating to borough elections.

All the representatives of the commons received wages to defray their necessary expenses: these were fixed in the 16th of Edward II at four shillings a day for a knight and two shillings for a citizen or burgher; and they were due for the whole time of his service, his journey to and fro, and his stay in parliament [2]. The notices of these payments are as early as the attendance of representative members; on the 10th of February, 1265, Henry III orders the sheriffs to assess by a jury of four lawful knights the expenses of the journey, so that the county be not aggrieved [3], the community of the county being clearly both electors and payers. The writ reads so much as a matter of course as to suggest that the practice was not new [4].

Wages of the representative members.

219. The number of cities and boroughs represented in the reign of Edward I was 166; the number of counties 37: as

Number of representative members.

[1] The return for the town of Oxford in 1295 is thus recorded: 'Nulla civitas neque burgus est in comitatu Oxoniensi nisi villa Oxoniensis; et breve quod michi venit returnatum fuit ballivis libertatis villae praedictae, qui habent returnum omnimodorum brevium, et ipsi mihi responderunt quod ex assensu communitatis villae Oxoniensis electi sunt secundum formam brevis duo burgenses subscripti.' But in Somersetshire the return is general: 'In plenis comitatibus Somerset et Dorset per communitatem eorundem eligere feci quatuor milites et de qualibet civitate duos cives et de quolibet burgo duos burgenses;' Parl. Writs, i. 41. See however Riess, Wahlrecht, p. 59.

[2] Hallam, Middle Ages, iii. 114; Prynne, Register, iv. p. 53.

[3] Lords' Report, i. 489 and App. p. 35.

[4] See above, p. 243, note 2.

each returned two members[1], the whole body at its maximum would number 406; but the towns almost always varied, and no doubt this number is very far ahead of the truth. To the parliament or great council of 1306 the sheriffs were directed to send two members for the larger, one for the smaller boroughs; several of the latter availed themselves of the relief. But this assembly was in other respects anomalous.

Further questions as to the powers of the parliament.

Such in its constituent parts was the ideal parliament of 1295. The growth and extent of its powers is a further question of equal interest. We have in former chapters examined the powers of the national council under the Norman and Plantagenet kings, and in the last chapter have watched the constant attempts made by personal and political parties to extend them. We have seen too how those attempts coincide in time with an irregular but continuous enlargement of the constitution of the national council. The next question is to determine how far and by what degrees the new elements of parliament were admitted to an equal share with the older elements in the powers which were already obtained or asserted; how far and by what steps were the commons placed on a constitutional level with the other two estates during the period of definition.

Powers of parliament under John.

(1) In taxation.

220. The great council of the nation[2], before the end of the reign of John, had obtained the acknowledgment and enjoyed the exercise of the following rights. In respect of taxation, the theoretical assent, which under the Norman kings had been taken for granted, had been exchanged for a real consultation; the *commune concilium* had first discussed the finance of the year under Henry II, had next demurred to the nature of the exaction under Richard, and under John had obtained in the Great Charter the concession that without their consent given in a duly convoked assembly no tax should be levied beyond the three prescriptive feudal aids. They had further, by the practice of the king's ministers in the exchequer, been consulted as to the mode of assessment, and had given counsel

[1] See Parl. Writs, i. 72, note; and above, p. 165. Cf. Hallam, iii. 117.

[2] On the exact relations of the several powers of the parliament, whilst it consisted of prelates and barons only, see Gneist, Verwalt. i. 366 sq.

and consent to the form in which the taxes were collected. In respect of legislation they had received similar formal recognition of their right to advise and consent, and had, as it would appear from the preamble of some of the assizes, exercised a power of initiating amendments of the law by means of petition. As a high court of justice they had heard the complaints of the king against individuals, and had accepted and ratified his judgments against high offenders. And lastly as a supreme deliberative council they had been consulted on questions of foreign policy, of internal police and national defence; in the absence of the king from England they had practically exercised the right of regulating the regency, at all events in the case of the deposition of Longchamp; and by a series of acts of election, acknowledgment, and acceptance of the kings at their accession, had obtained a recognition of their right to regulate the succession also.

(2) In legislation.

(3) In judicature.

(4) In general business.

During the minority and in the troubled years of Henry III they had fully vindicated and practically enlarged these rights. In matters of taxation they had frequently refused aid to the king, and when they granted it they had carefully prescribed the mode of collection and assessment; in legislation they had not only taken the initiative by petitions, such as those which led to the Provisions of Oxford, and by articles of complaint presented by the whole or a portion of their body, but they had, as in the famous act of the council of Merton touching the legitimising of bastards by the subsequent marriage of their parents, refused their consent to a change in the law, by words which were accepted by the jurists as the statement of a constitutional fact[1]. Their judicial power was abridged, in practice by the strengthened organisation of the royal courts, but it

Progress during the minority of Henry III.

(1) In taxation.

(2) In legislation.

(3) As to judicature.

[1] 'Nolumus leges Angliae mutari;' Bracton states the principle: 'leges Anglicanae . . . quae quidem cum fuerint approbatae consensu utentium, et sacramento regum confirmatae, mutari non possunt nec destrui sine communi consilio et consensu eorum omnium quorum consilio et consensu fuerunt promulgatae. In melius tamen converti possunt etiam sine illorum consensu;' lib. i. c. 2. Thus we have seen Edward I refusing to annul the statute de Religiosis: 'illud statutum de consilio magnatum suorum fuerat editum et ordinatum et ideo absque eorum consilio non erat revocandum;' Hemingb. ii. 57; above, p. 131.

remained in full force in reference to high offenders, and causes between great men; the growth of the privileges of baronage gave to the national council, as an assembly of barons, the character of a court of peers for the trial and amercement of their fellows; and, even where a cause was brought against the king himself, although it must begin with a petition of right and not as in causes between subjects with a writ, the lawyers recognised the *universitas regni* as the source of remedy, and the king's court as one of the three powers which are above the king himself[1]. Their general political power was greatly increased; they had determined the policy of the crown in foreign affairs; they had not only displaced the king's ministers but had placed the royal power itself in commission; they had drawn up a new constitution for the country and imposed new oaths on the king and his heir. It is true that the most important of these were party measures, carried out in exceptional times and by unconstitutional means, but it was as

(4) As to general deliberation.

[1] In 1223 the pope declared Henry III of age, 'quantum ad liberam dispositionem de castris et terris et gwardiis suis, non autem quoad hoc ut in placito posset ab aliquo communiri;' Ann. Dunst. p. 83. If the last word be read *conveniri* or *summoneri*, it is conclusive as to the fact that the king might be sued at law; and we thus have a passage proving the method in which he could be compelled to give redress before the form of petition of right was instituted. The statement of Chief Justice Wilby (Year Book, 24 Edw. III. fo. 55), that he had seen a writ 'Praecipe Henrico regi Angliae,' &c., would thus become more probable than it has been generally regarded. Bracton, however, writes so that we must suppose the practice to have been changed before his time; 'contra ipsum [regem] non habebitur remedium per assisam, immo tantum locus erit supplicationi ut factum suum corrigat et emendet, quod si non fecerit, sufficiat ei pro poena quod Dominum expectet ultorem . . . nisi sit qui dicat quod universitas regni et baronagium suum hoc facere debeat et possit in curia ipsius regis;' lib. iii. tract. i. c. 10. Mr. Horwood, in his preface to the Year Book of 33–35 Edw. I, gives some valuable references in support of Wilby's statement; especially one at p. 471 of that volume: 'en auncien temps chescun bref e de dreit e de possessioun girreit ben ver le roi, de quei nest ore rens raunge mes qe tant qil voet qe home siwe ver luy par bille ou home siwist avant par bref;' he also cites Year Book 22 Edw. III. fo. 3 b, and 43 Edw. III. 22 a. Matthew Paris under the year 1244 speaks of 'brevia impetrata contra regem;' ed. Luard, iv. 367; but only with a view to their revocation with those impetrated 'contra consuetudinem regni.' The passages quoted by Prynne, Plea for the Lords, p. 97, stating that the king might be *sued*, are scarcely relevant, for they belong to the year 1259, and are apparently misconstrued. See however Mr. Cutbill's pamphlet on Petition of Right (London, 1874), and Allen on the Prerogative, pp. 94 sq., 190, 191.

representing the supreme council of the kingdom that the baronial party acted, and the rights they enforced were enforced in the name of the nation.

Further claims made by the parliament.

But the claims of the same body had gone further, and had in some respects run far in advance of the success which was actually achieved at the time or for ages later; nay, in one or two points they had claimed powers which have never yet been formally conceded. The principles that the grant of money should depend on the redress of grievances, and that the parliament should determine the destination of a grant by making conditions as to expenditure [1], were admitted by the royal advisers, although the king contrived to evade the concession. The right of electing the ministers, a premature and imperfect realisation of the doctrine of a limited monarchy, was likewise demanded as authorised by ancient practice [2]. The right of controlling the king's action by a resident elective council also was asserted; but, though Henry was constrained to accept these terms, he steadily refused to admit them as a matter of right, and they were ultimately rejected with the acquiescence of the nation [3].

Grants should depend on redress and supplies should be appropriated to special purposes.

Right of electing ministers and council.

Rights exercised in the early years of Edward I.

The early years of Edward I saw all the privileges which had been really used or acquired under Henry III fully exercised. The parliament of prelates and barons had been asked for and had granted aids [4], had given counsel and consent to legislation, had acted as a supreme court of justice [5], and had discussed questions of foreign policy and internal administration [6]. The further steps gained by the constitutional assembly in this reign were gained by it in its new and complete organisation.

Two drawbacks:—

(1) The king's prerogative.

(2) The right of the individual.

Two drawbacks materially affected the value of these rights: the recognition of certain power on the king's part to do by his own authority acts of the same class as those for which he asked counsel and consent; and the recognition of certain undefined rights of individual members to concede or refuse consent to the determinations of the whole body; the latter drawback was

[1] Above, pp. 54, 55.
[2] Above, pp. 41, 63, 64.
[3] Above, pp. 54, 64, 78.
[4] Above, pp. 113, 126.
[5] Above, pp. 128, 129.
[6] Above, pp. 128–130.

seriously increased by the incompleteness of the national representation before the 23rd of Edward I.

(1) The parliament did not yet exclude the power of the crown to tax and legislate.

221. Although the national council had made out its right to be heard on all four points of administrative policy, it had not obtained an exclusive right to determine that policy. The taxes might be granted in parliament, but the king could still take the customary aids without reference to parliament; he could tallage his demesnes and could interpret the title of demesne so as to bring the chartered towns, or a large portion of them, under contribution; he could increase the customs by separate negotiations with the merchants, and at any time raise money by gifts negotiated with individual payers, and assessed by the officers of the exchequer.

Legislation by ordinance.

The laws again were issued with counsel and consent of the parliament, but legal enactments might, as before, in the shape of assizes or ordinances, be issued without any such assistance; and the theory of the enacting power of the king, as supreme legislator, grew rather than diminished during the period, probably in consequence of the legislative activity of Frederick II, Lewis IX, and Alfonso the Wise.

Jurisdiction of the king's court.

The king's court, the curia regis, might be influenced and used to defeat the right of the barons to be judged by their peers, and there was not in the article of the charter anything that so fixed the method of such judgment as to make it necessary to transact it in full council. And the political action of the crown, in matters both foreign and domestic, could, as it always can, be determined without reference to anything but the royal will. Nor, as we shall see, was the failure of the national council to secure exclusive enjoyment of these rights owing to their own weakness:

The king's council.

both Henry III and Edward I possessed, in their personal inner council, a body of advisers organised so as to maintain the royal authority on these points, a council by whose advice they acted, judged, legislated, and taxed when they could, and the abuse of which was not yet prevented by any constitutional check. The opposition between the royal and the national councils, between the privy council and the parliament, is an important element in later national history.

222. The second, however, of these points, the uncertainty of the line dividing corporate and individual consent, and the consequent difficulty of adjusting national action with incomplete representation, bears more directly on the subject before us. The first question has already arisen[1]: did the consent of a baron in council to grant a tax bind him individually only, or did it form part of such a general consent as would be held to bind those who refused consent? When Geoffrey of York, or Ranulf of Chester, refused to agree to a grant, was the refusal final or was it overborne by the consent of the majority? Did the baron who promised aid make a private promise or authorise a general tax? Was taxation the fulfilment of individual voluntary engagements or the legal result of a sovereign act? Secondly, how far could the consent, even if it were unanimous, of a national council composed of barons and superior clergy, bind the unrepresented classes, the commons, and the parochial clergy? The latter question is practically answered by the contrivances used to reconcile compulsion with equity. The writ of Edward I for the collection of the aid *pur fille marier* rehearses that it was granted in full parliament by certain bishops and barons, for themselves and for the community of the whole realm, 'so far as in them lay[2].' As a parliamentary assembly, legally summoned, they authorised a tax which would bind all tenants of the crown, but they did it with an express limitation, a conscious hesitation, and the king did not at the time venture to collect the tax. This was on the very eve of the contest for the confirmation of the charters. The documentary history of the reign of Henry III illustrates the difficulty at an earlier stage. In 1224 the prelates granted a carucage of half a mark on their demesne lands and those of their immediate tenants[3], and two shillings on the lands of the under tenants of those tenants: the feudal lord thus represented all who held directly or mediately under him. In 1232 the writ for collecting

(2) Difficulty arising from individual right to consent or dissent.

The unrepresented classes.

Difficulty of reconciling theory with practice.

[1] Vol. i. pp. 578, 579.

[2] 'Magnates et proceres tunc in parliamento existentes, pro se et communitate totius regni quantum in ipsis est, concesserunt;' Rot. Parl. i. 25; above, p. 126; Select Charters, p. 477.

[3] Above, p. 36, note 3.

the fortieth states that it was granted by the archbishops, bishops, abbots, priors, clergy, earls, barons, knights, freeholders, and villeins [1], implying that not only the national council but the county courts had been dealt with: but in 1237 a similar writ rehearses the consent of the prelates, barons, knights and freeholders for themselves and their villeins [2]. Yet it is certain that in neither of the parliaments in which these taxes were granted were the villeins represented, and almost as certain that the commons were unrepresented also. The consent thus rehearsed must have been a simple fabrication, a legal fiction, on a theoretical view of parliament; or else the exacting process of the central assembly must have been supplemented by the consent of the county courts, in which alone, at the time, the liberi homines and villani assembled, that consent being either taken by the itinerant judges or presumed to follow on a proclamation by the sheriff. The expressions, however used, show a misgiving, and warrant the conclusion that the line between corporate and individual, general and local, consent was lightly drawn: the theory that the lord represented his vassal was too dangerous to be unreservedly admitted when all men were the king's vassals; the need of representation was felt. But the line continued uncertain until 1295; and even after that the variety of proportion in which the several estates taxed themselves shows that the distinction between a voluntary gift and an enacted tax was imperfectly realised.

Possible action of the county courts.

Refusal of individuals;

The idea that the refusal of an individual baron to grant the tax absolved him from the necessity of paying it, although now and then broached by a too powerful subject, could be easily overborne by force: ordinarily the king would seize the lands of

[1] 'Sciatis quod archiepiscopi, episcopi, abbates, priores, et clerici terras habentes quae ad ecclesias suas non pertinent, comites, barones, milites, liberi homines et villani de regno nostro concesserunt nobis,' &c.; M. Paris, iii. 230; Select Charters, p. 360.

[2] 'Scias quod cum in octavis sancti Hilarii . . . ad mandatum nostrum convenirent apud Westmonasterium archiepiscopi, episcopi, abbates, priores, comites et barones totius regni nostri et tractatum haberent nobiscum de statu nostro et regni nostri, iidem archiepiscopi, episcopi, abbates, priores et clerici terras habentes quae ad ecclesias suas non pertinent, comites, barones, milites et liberi homines pro se et suis villanis, nobis concesserunt,' &c.; Foedera, i. 232; Select Charters, p. 366.

the contumacious, and take by way of fine or ransom what could not be extracted by way of gift. The claim of a particular community to refuse a tax which had not been assented to by its own representatives, such as was claimed in the sixteenth century by Ghent, was based on the same idea, and would be overcome in the same way. Such a hypothesis, however, could only arise in a community which had not realised the nature of sovereign rights or of national identity. The refusal of an estate of the realm to submit to taxation imposed in an assembly at which it had not been represented, or to which its representatives had not been summoned, rested on a different basis. Such was the plea of the clergy in 1254[1], and it was recognised by the spirit of the constitution.

of communities; of an estate of the realm.

The practice had long been to take the consent of the communities by special commission. The year 1295 marks the date at which the special commissions, as a rule, cease, and the communities appear by their representatives to join in the act of the sovereign body. The process of transition belongs to the years 1282 and 1295, and the transition implies the admission of the commons to a share of taxing power, together with the clergy and the baronage.

Cessation of special commissions to raise money.

223. The dates may be more precisely marked. In 1282 the king's treasurer negotiated with the several shires and boroughs for a subsidy, just as might have been done under Henry II: the money so collected being insufficient, the king at Rhuddlan summoned the clergy and commons to two provincial councils, in one of which the commons granted a thirtieth on condition that the barons should do the same[2]. In 1289 a special negotiation was proposed, but not carried into effect[3]. In 1290 the barons granted an aid *pur fille marier*; the knights of the shire were subsequently summoned to join in a grant of a fifteenth; and the clergy in a separate assembly voted a tenth of spirituals; the boroughs probably, and the city of London certainly, paid the fifteenth without having been represented in the assembly that voted it, except as parts of the shires represented

Chronological summary.

[1] Above, pp. 69, 205.
[2] Above, pp. 119, 120; Parl. Writs, i. 12.
[3] Above, p. 125.

by the knights[1]. In 1294 the clergy in September granted a moiety of their entire revenue in a parliamentary assembly of the two provinces held at Westminster[2]; the earls, barons, and knights granted a tenth in November[3], and commissioners were sent out in the same month to request a sixth from the cities and boroughs[4]; the three estates, roughly divided, thus granted their money at different dates, in different proportions, and in different ways. In 1295 the special negotiation disappears: the three estates, although making their grants in different measure and by separate vote, are fully represented, and act in this, as in other respects, in the character of a consolidated parliament.

The right to grant customs claimed by the parliament,

Nor was the recognition of this right of taxation confined to direct money grants. The impost on wool, woolfells and leather, has a similar history, although the steps of reform are different and the immediate burden fell not on an estate but on individual merchants. In 1275 we are told that the prelates, magnates, and communities, at the request of the merchants granted a custom on these commodities[5]: in 1294 a large increase of custom was imposed by the king's decree, rehearsing however the consent of the merchants[6], not that of the parliament.

[1] Above pp. 126, 127: 'Assessores et collectores quintae decimae in civitate London. et infra totum praecinctum ejusdem civitatis regi concessae, anno regni sui decimo octavo, reddunt compotum de £2860 13*s*. 8*d*. de eadem quintadecima;' cf. Brady, Boroughs, p. 27.

[2] Above, p. 131.

[3] Above, p. 132.

[4] Above, p. 131: 'Rex dilectis et fidelibus suis custodi, vicecomitibus, Aldermannis et toti communitati civitatis suae London. salutem. Cum vos, in forma qua nuper nobis quintamdecimam concesseratis, sextam partem bonorum et mobilium vestrorum in subsidium guerrae nostrae nobis concesseritis liberaliter et libenter,' &c. 'Per consimiles litteras assignantur infrascripti ad petendam sextam partem in singulis dominicis civitatibus et aliis villis regiis in comitatibus subscriptis,' &c.; Brady, Boroughs, pp. 31, 32. These writs are not in Sir F. Palgrave's Collection.

[5] Above, pp. 114, 201; Select Charters, p. 451; Parl. Writs, i. 2. Yet the language of the several writs on this subject is scarcely consistent; the earl of Pembroke describes the custom as granted by the archbishops, bishops, and other prelates, the earls, barons, and communities of the realm, at the instance and request of the merchants; the king describes it as 'de communi assensu magnatum et voluntate mercatorum;' and as 'grante par touz les granz del realme e par la priere des communes de marchanz de tot Engleterre.'

[6] Above, p. 131, note 3; Hale, Concerning the Customs, p. 155; and ch. xvii, below.

In the articles of 1297 the royal right of taxing wool was placed under the same restrictions as the right of direct taxation [1]; but the idea was still maintained that an increase of the impost might be legalised by the consent of the payers, and an attempt [2] to substitute the action of a 'colloquium' of merchants for that of the national parliament was defeated by the representatives of the boroughs in 1303.

The confirmation of charters in 1297 recognised on the king's part the exclusive right of the parliament to authorise taxation: 'for no occasion from henceforth will we take such manner of aids, tasks, or prises, but by the common assent of the realm and for the common profit thereof, saving the ancient aids and prises due and accustomed [3].' Already the right of the commons to a share in the taxing power of parliament was admitted.

and recognised in 1297.

224. The right of the three estates to share in legislation was established by a different process and on a different theory; it was a result rather than a cause of the recognition of their character as a supreme council. The consent of individuals was much less important in the enacting or improving of the law than in the levying of a tax; the power of counsel in the one case might fairly be supposed to belong to one of the three estates in larger proportion than to the others; and the enacting, if not also the initiative, power belonged to the king. The nation granted the tax, the king enacted the law: the nation might consent to the tax in various ways, severally by estates, communities, or individuals, or corporately in parliament; but the law was enacted once for all by the king with the advice and consent of parliament; it was no longer in the power of the individual, the community, or the estate to withhold its obedience with impunity. In very early times it is possible that the local assemblies were required to give assent to the legal changes made by the central authority, that a publication of the new law in the shiremoot was regarded as

Share of the estates in legislation.

Different conditions of legislation and taxation.

Early cases of acceptance of legislation in local assemblies.

[1] Above, p. 148; Select Charters, p. 495.
[2] Above, pp. 163, 164, 201.
[3] Select Charters, pp. 495, 496. On this a good résumé will be found in Gneist, Verw. i. 393–396.

denoting the acceptance of it by the people in general, and that it would be contrary to natural equity to enforce a law which had not been so published[1]. But from the existing remains of legislation, we are forced to conclude that, whilst customary law was recorded in the memories of the people, legislative action belonged only to the wise, that is to the royal or national council. That council in the twelfth century contained only the magnates; at the end of the thirteenth it contained also the inferior clergy and the commons: the latter, fully competent as they were to discuss a tax, were not equally competent to frame a law; and such right of initiation as the right of petition involved could be set in motion outside as easily as inside parliament. Yet the right of the nation to determine by what laws it would be governed was fully admitted. Canute and the Conqueror had heard the people accept and swear to the laws of Edgar and Edward. The Great Charter and the Provisions of Oxford were promulgated in the county courts, and all men were bound by oath to obey them, as if without such acceptance they lacked somewhat of legal force. Bracton, in the words of Justinian, enumerates the 'consensus utentium'[2] as well as the king's oath among the bases of law. It is to the conservation of the laws which the folk, vulgus, communauté, shall have chosen, that the later coronation oath binds the king. The enactment of Edward II in 1322, that matters to be established touching the estate of the king and his heirs, the realm and the people, shall be treated, accorded, and established in parliaments by the king and by the assent of the prelates, earls, and barons and the commonalty of the realm,

Legislation proper to the king's council;

but the right of the people admitted.

In the coronation oath,

and by the statute of 1322.

[1] See the passage quoted from Bracton, above, p. 249. In France the royal ordinances had no force in the territories of the barons until approved by them; Ordonnances des Rois, i. 54, 93; Boutaric, Premiers États généraux, p. 4. Coke, 4 Inst. p. 26, records a decision of 39 Edw. III: 'although proclamation be not made in the county, every one is bound to take notice of that which is done in parliament; for as soon as the parliament hath concluded anything, the law intends that every person hath notice thereof; for the parliament represents the body of the whole realm; and therefore it is not requisite that any proclamation be made, seeing the statute took effect before.'

[2] See above, p. 249, note. The *consensus utentium* is from the Institutes, lib. i. tit. 2.

is but an amplification of the principle laid down by his father in 1295.

Legislation by baronial parliaments.

The legislation, however, of the reign of Henry III, and most of that of Edward I, was the work of assemblies to which the commons were not summoned. It has been well remarked that, whereas for his political work Edward found himself obliged to obtain the co-operation of the three estates[1], his legislative work was done without the co-operation of the commons, until in the question of taxation they had enforced their right to be heard. By whatever process the consent of the 'communaulté' to the statute of Westminster the first was signified, and whatever were the force of the summons by virtue of which the 'communaulté' was supposed to be present, it is certain that in 1290 the statute 'quia emptores' was passed in a council at which no representatives of the commons attended, and as certain that the statute of Carlisle was published after deliberation not only with the magnates but with the 'communitates' of the realm[2]. The statute 'quia emptores' was not improbably the last case in which the assent of the commons was taken for granted in legislation: for in the later enactments by ordinance it is not the commons only but the parliament itself that is set aside; and, although some few statutes made after 1290 do not declare expressly the participation of the three estates, it is possible, by comparing the dates of those acts with the extant writs of summons, to show that all such acts as were really laws were enacted in full parliaments to which the words of the statute of Carlisle are equally applicable[3]. The commons had now a share of the 'commune consilium regni' which was indispensable to the abrogation or amendment of a law. It is true that some of

The statute *Quia Emptores.*

The statute of Carlisle.

[1] Shirley, Royal Letters, ii. pref. xxii.

[2] Above, p. 163. 'Dominus rex post deliberationem plenariam et tractatum cum comitibus, baronibus, proceribus et aliis nobilibus ac communitatibus regni sui, habitum in praemissis, de consensu eorum unanimi et concordi ordinavit et statuit;' Statutes, i. 152.

[3] 'Si quae statuta fuerint contraria dictis cartis vel alicui articulo in eisdem cartis contento, ea de communi consilio regni nostri modo debito emendentur vel etiam adnullentur;' Edward I. Feb. 14, 1301; Statutes (Charters), i. 44. See on these points Gneist, Verwalt. i. 399 sq.

The share of the commons in legislation recognised.

the most important acts of parliament are dated several days after the writs were issued for the payment of the wages of the knights and burghers, e.g. in 1300 the Articuli Super Cartas are published April 15, the writs for wages are issued March 20; in 1301 the letters to the pope are dated February 12; the writs, January 30. Not much however can be argued from this, for the final form which the law took would be settled at the end of the parliament; the representatives might leave as soon as the important business of petition and consultation was over. There could be no reason why they should stay until the charters were actually sealed or the copies of the statutes written out for circulation [1].

The share of the several estates in legislation not necessarily an equal share.

225. But neither this conclusion nor even the principle stated by Edward II in 1322, implies the absolute equality of the share of each estate. Counsel and consent are ascribed to the magnates, but it is a long time before more is allowed generally to the commons than petition, instance, or request: and the right of petition the commons possessed even when not called together to parliament; the community of a county might declare a grievance, just as the grand jury presented a criminal. Further, so long as the enacting power was exercised by the king, with the counsel and consent of the magnates only, a statute might be founded on a petition of the clergy; and it may be questioned whether, according to the legal idea of Edward I, an act so initiated and authorised would not be a law without consent of the commons, just as an act framed on the petition of the commons would, if agreed to by the magnates, become law without consent of the clergy either in convocation or in parliament. The determination of this point belongs to the history of the following century. We conclude that, for the period before us, it would be true to say, that, although in theory legislation was the work of the king in full parliament, he exercised the power of legislating without a full parliament, and that in the full parliament itself the functions of the three estates were in this respect imperfectly defined. It is certain however, from the action of the king in reference

Right of petition.

Imperfect definition of powers.

[1] Foedera, i. 920, 926, 927; Parl. Writs, i. 85, 102–104.

to mortmain, that a statute passed with the counsel and consent of parliament, however constituted, could not be abrogated without the same counsel and consent[1].

The commons did not share the judicial power of parliament. Trial of David of Wales.

226. The third attribute of the old national council, that of a supreme tribunal of justice, for the trial of great offenders, and the determination of great causes, was never shared by the commons. The nearest approach to such a participation was made when in 1283 they were summoned to Shrewsbury, on the trial of David of Wales: but they attended merely as witnesses of the trial; he was tried by the king's judges and only in the presence, not by a tribunal, of his peers. It is true that the abundant facilities which the system of jury gave for the trial of commoners by their peers superseded any necessity for criminal jurisdiction to be exercised by the assembly of the commons; but it is not quite so clear why the right of advising the crown in the determination of civil cases was restricted to the lords, or why they should continue to form a council for the hearing of petitions to the king, when the commons did not join in their deliberations. This resulted however from the fact that the system of petition to the king in council had been perfected before the commons were called to parliament; and thus the whole subject of judicature belongs to the history of the royal council rather than to that of parliament strictly so called. But it is noteworthy in connexion with the fact that the estate which retained the judicial power of the national council retained also the special right of counsel and consent in legislation, these rights being a survival of the time when the magnates were the whole parliament; and on the other hand the smaller council which, as the king's special advisers, exercised judicial authority in Chancery, or in Privy Council and Star-chamber, claimed also the right of legislating by ordinance.

Petitions on civil matters.

Powers of the national council in judicature engrossed by the baronage.

Obscurity of deliberation on points of general policy.

227. The general deliberative functions of parliament, and the right of the representatives of the commons to share with the magnates in discussing foreign affairs or internal administration, scarcely come before us during this period with sufficient distinctness to enable us to mark any steps of progress. On

[1] Above, p. 131.

the other hand the right of deliberation had been exercised by the great men long before the time of the Great Charter, and abundant evidence shows that they retained the right. The stories of the debate on the 'Quo Warranto' and the action of the earls in 1297 fully illustrate this. The action of the commons is distinctly traceable in the presentation of the Bill of twelve articles at the parliament of Lincoln in 1301. That bill was a bill of the prelates and proceres delivered on behalf of the whole community, but presented by a knight of the shire for Lancashire. The representatives of the commons had left before the barons drew up their letter to the pope[1]. Here again it is probable that the theory of the constitution was somewhat in advance of its actual progress. The principle declared by Edward I in 1295 would seem to touch this function of the national council more directly even than taxation or legislation; but in practice, as had been done long ago, silence was construed as assent and counsel taken for granted from the absent as well as the present.

Illustration, from the forms of writ, of the share of the several estates in deliberation.

Form of writ, for magnates.

228. The forms of the writs of summons furnish illustrations if not conclusive evidence on the general question. The special writs addressed to the magnates usually define their function in council by the word *tractare*. In 1205 the bishop of Salisbury is summoned to treat on the common interest of the realm[2]; in 1241 the bishops and barons are summoned *ad tractandum*[3]; in 1253 to hear the king's pleasure and to treat with his council[4]; in Simon de Montfort's writ for 1265 the words are *tractaturi et consilium vestrum impensuri*[5]; to the

[1] See above, pp. 157–159. The proceedings of Edward in the parliament of Lincoln, as touching the papacy, may be compared with those taken by Philip the Fair in 1302 and 1303. The latter king, having in 1302 called together the states general, in which each estate remonstrated by letter with the pope, in 1303 called a council of barons, in which he appealed against the pope, obtaining a separate consent to the appeal from the provincial estates of Languedoc and from the several communities singly throughout the rest of France. See Boutaric, Premiers États Généraux, pp. 12–15.

[2] Lords' Report, App. p. 1; Select Charters, p. 283; see Hallam, Middle Ages, iii. 36, 37.

[3] Lords' Report, App. p. 7.

[4] Lords' Report, App. p. 12.

[5] Lords' Report, App. p. 33; Select Charters, p. 415.

first parliament of Edward I the archbishop of Canterbury is invited *ad tractandum et ordinandum*[1]; to the parliament of Shrewsbury in 1283 the barons are summoned *nobiscum locuturi*[2]; in 1294 the king declares his wish to hold *colloquium et tractatum*[3]; in 1295 earls, barons, and prelates are summoned *ad tractandum, ordinandum et faciendum nobiscum et cum praelatis et ceteris proceribus et aliis incolis regni nostri*[4]; in 1297 the barons only, *colloquium et tractatum specialiter habituri vestrumque consilium impensuri*[5]; in 1298 the form is *tractatum et colloquium habituri*[6]; and from 1299 generally *tractaturi vestrumque consilium impensuri*[7]. In this last formula we have the fullest statement of the powers which, on Edward's theory of government, were exercised by those constituents of the national council that had for the longest time been summoned: and these functions must be understood as being shared by the judges and other councillors who are summoned in almost exactly the same terms[8].

Writs for knights of the shire.

The writs ordering the return of representative knights run as follows; in 1213 John summons them *ad loquendum nobiscum de negotiis regni nostri*[9]; in 1254 the special purpose is expressed *ad providendum . . . quale auxilium . . . impendere velint*[10]; in 1261 the words are *colloquium habituros*[11]; in 1264 *nobiscum tractaturi*[12]; under Simon de Montfort in 1265 all the representatives are summoned in the same form

[1] Parl. Writs, i. p. 1; Lords' Report, App. p. 36.
[2] Parl. Writs, i. p. 15; Lords' Report, App. p. 49.
[3] Parl. Writs, i. p. 25; Lords' Report, App. p. 56.
[4] Parl. Writs, i. p. 31; Lords' Report, App. p. 67.
[5] Parl. Writs, i. p. 51; Lords' Report, App. p. 77.
[6] Parl. Writs, i. p. 65.
[7] Parl. Writs, i. p. 82; Lords' Report, App. p. 102.
[8] The differences are slight; the barons are summoned *in fide et homagio*, the prelates *in fide et dilectione*, the judges and councillors without any such adjuration. The barons and prelates are summoned 'quod . . . personaliter intersitis nobiscum ac cum ceteris praelatis, magnatibus et proceribus,' or 'magnatibus' simply; the judges and councillors 'ac cum ceteris de consilio nostro,' all alike 'tractaturi vestrumque in praemissis consilium impensuri.'
[9] Lords' Report, App. p. 2; Select Charters, p. 287.
[10] Lords' Report, App. p. 13; Select Charters, p. 376.
[11] Lords' Report, App. p. 23; Select Charters, p. 405.
[12] Foedera, i. 442; Select Charters, p. 412.

Form of *full powers.*

as the magnates[1]; in 1275 the form is *ad tractandum*[2]; in 1282 the character of the full power which they receive from their constituencies is expressed, *ad audiendum et faciendum ea quae sibi ex parte nostra faciemus ostendi*[3]: in 1283 the words are *super hiis et aliis locuturi*[4]: in 1290 the full powers are described, *ad consulendum et consentiendum pro se et communitate illa hiis quae comites, barones et proceres praedicti tunc duxerint concordanda*[5]; in 1294 *ad consulendum et consentiendum*[6]; in 1295 both knights of the shire and representatives of the towns are to be chosen *ad faciendum quod tunc de communi consilio ordinabitur*[7]; and this form is retained until under Edward II the words *ad consentiendum* are added[8].

Form in the case of representatives generally.

General inference from these forms.

The variations of expression may safely be interpreted as showing some uncertainty as to the functions of the representatives, although, as in the case of the barons, it may often merely show the difference of the occasion for which they were summoned. But it would be wrong to infer from the words in which their full representative powers were described that their functions were ever limited to mere consent to the resolutions of the magnates. Certainly this was not the case in questions of taxation, in which the several bodies deliberated and determined apart. The fact that the representative or delegate powers are so carefully described in the later writs shows the care taken, at the time of transition from taxation by local consent to taxation by general enactment, that no community should escape contribution by alleging the incompleteness of the powers with which it had invested its delegates; *ita quod pro defectu hujus*

1 Lords' Report, App. p. 33; Select Charters, p. 415.
2 See above, p. 234, note 5.
3 Parl. Writs, i. 10; Select Charters, p. 465.
4 Parl. Writs, i. 16; Select Charters, p. 468.
5 Parl. Writs, i. 21; Select Charters, p. 477.
6 Parl. Writs, i. 26; Select Charters, p. 481.
7 Parl. Writs, i. 29; Select Charters, p. 486. The summons to the parliament of Lincoln orders the representatives to be sent 'cum plena potestate audiendi et faciendi ea quae ibidem in praemissis ordinari contigerint pro communi commodo dicti regni;' Parl. Writs, i. 90.
8 The form in which the third estate was called to the States General at Tours in 1308 is thus given by M. Boutaric, p. 18: 'Pour entendre, recevoir, approuver et faire tout ce qu'il serait commandé par le roi, sans exciper du recours a leurs commettants.'

potestatis negotium praedictum infectum non remaneat quoquo modo[1]. The delegates had full procuratorial power both to advise and to execute. The fact however remains that, although the assembly was called for advice and co-operation, it was co-operation rather than advice that was expected from the commons: counsel is distinctly mentioned in the invitation to the magnates, action and consent in the invitation to representatives[2]. Similar variations are to be found in the writs directing the parliamentary representation of the clergy; in 1295 the proctors as well as the prelates are summoned *ad tractandum, ordinandum et faciendum*[3]; in 1299 the form is *ad faciendum et consentiendum*[4]. Under Edward III *faciendum* is frequently omitted, and in the reign of Richard II their function is reduced to simple consent.

Relation of the commons to the lords.

History has thrown no light, as yet, on the way in which the powers of the representatives, whether procuratorial or senatorial, were exercised; and when, in the long political discussions of the fourteenth century, some vestiges of personal independent action can be traced amongst the commons, it is difficult to see that the constitutional position of the representatives in their house differed at all from that of the peers in theirs. It is of course possible that some change for the better followed the definite arrangement of parliament in two houses. In fact, until that arrangement was perfected, the discussion would be monopolised by those members who, by skill in business, greatness of personal position, or fluency in French or Latin, were accustomed to make themselves heard; and few of these would be found amongst the knights, citizens, and burghers. The obscurity of details does not stop here. No authentic record has yet been found of the way in which the general assent of the assembly was taken, or the result of a division ascertained. We might infer from the procuratorial character of the powers of the representatives, that on some questions, taxation in par-

No light as yet on the method of voting.

[1] See the Writs of 1294 and 1295.

[2] This point is strongly urged by Mr. Gairdner in his interesting article on the functions of the House of Lords; Antiquary, ix. 149 sq.

[3] Parl. Writs, i. 30.

[4] Parl. Writs, i. 83.

ticular, the two members for each community would have only a joint vote. The so-called 'Modus tenendi parliamentum' might be thought likely to illustrate this[1]. But that curious sketch of the parliamentary constitution cannot have been drawn up until a period much later than that on which we are now employed, and seems to describe an ideal of the writer rather than any condition of things that ever really existed.

The 'modus tenendi parliamentum' not to be trusted.

Relation of the events of 1295 to those of 1297;

229. To this point then had the parliamentary constitution grown under the hand of this great king. The assembly definitely constituted in 1295,—at once a representation of the three estates and a concentration of the local institutions,—the clergy, the barons and the communities, associated for financial, legislative, and political action—obtained in 1297 the fullest recognition of its rights as representing the whole nation. It had come into existence by a growth peculiar to itself, although coinciding in time with the corresponding developments in other nations, and was destined to have a different history. Of this representative body the king was at once the hand and the head, and for foreign affairs the complete impersonation. He called together the assembly when and where he chose; the result of the deliberations was realised as his act; the laws became valid by his expressed consent, and were enforced under his commission and by his writ; his refusal stayed all proceedings whether legislative or executive. It was no part of the policy of Edward to diminish royal power and dignity; probably for every concession which patriotism or statesmanship led him to make, he retained a check by which the substance of power would be kept in the hand of a sovereign wise enough to use it rightly. The parliamentary constitution was by no means the whole of the English system: there still remained, in varying but not exhausted strength, by no means obsolete, the several institutions royal and popular, central and local, administrative and executive, out of which the parliamentary constitution itself sprang, whose powers it

and of the king to the new parliament.

Checks on the system.

[1] Select Charters, p. 512. There all the laity appear to vote together, and with equal votes; two knights, we are told, could outweigh one earl; and in the house of clergy two proctors could outvote a bishop. But this seems purely imaginary.

concentrated and regulated but did not extinguish, and whose functions it exercised without superseding them. The general reforms in law, army and finance, which were completed by Edward I, bear the same mark of definiteness and completeness which he so clearly impressed on parliament; a mark which those departments continued to bear for at least two centuries and a half, and which in some respects they bear to the present day. The permanent and definite character thus impressed gave strength to the system, although it perhaps diminished its elasticity and in some points made the occasion for future difficulties.

Edward's character as a definer.

The high court of parliament had for one of its historical antecedents the ancient court and council of the king, which was as certainly the parent of the house of lords, as the shire system was of the house of commons. The king's court had in its judicial capacity been the germ of the whole higher judicial system of the country, as well as of the parliamentary and financial machinery. But so far from having lost strength by dividing and subdividing its functions, the magical circle that surrounded the king remained as much as ever a nucleus of strength and light. Such strength and light Edward was well able to appreciate; and in it he found his royal as contrasted with his constitutional position; in other words he organised the powers of his prerogative, the residuum of that royal omnipotence, which, since the days of the Conquest, had been on all sides limited by the national growth and by the restrictions imposed by routine, law, policy, and patriotic statesmanship. The primitive constitution, local, popular, self-regulating, had received a new element from the organising power of the Normans. The royal central justice had come to remedy the evils of the popular law; the curia regis was a court of equity in relation to the common law of the county court. Now, the curia regis had incorporated itself with the common law system of the country, just as parliament had become a permanent institution. The royal chancery was now regarded as a resource for equitable remedy against the hardships of the courts of Westminster, as the courts of Westminster had been a remedy against the inequalities of the shiremoot. The vital

Continuity of the king's personal influence.

and prolific power remained unimpaired, and side by side with the growth of the power of parliament, grew also the power of the crown exercised in and through the council[1].

Origin of the king's council.

230. The special circle of *sapientes*, councillors, and judges, to which Henry II reserved the decision of knotty cases of finance and law[2], was perhaps the first germ of the later council, as the little circle of household officers may have formed the nucleus of the Exchequer and the Curia Regis. But, beyond the short mention of it in the Gesta Henrici and the Dialogus de Scaccario, we have no traces of its action. Richard I had his staff of personal counsellors, his clerks and secretaries such as Philip of Poictiers, but they were rather a personal than a royal retinue, and, as he was constantly absent from England, his personal council had no constitutional status as apart from that of his justiciar. John however had a large body of advisers, many of them foreigners, who, except as his servants, could have had no legal position in the country, and for whom he obtained such a position by appointing them to definite offices, sheriffdoms and the like. But although it may fairly be granted that the king's private advisers had thus early gained definite recognition, and together with the officers of the household, court, and exchequer, may have been known as the royal council, it is to the minority of Henry III that the real importance of this body must be traced. Notwithstanding the indefiniteness of the word *concilium*, it is clear that there was then a staff of officers at work, not identical with the *commune consilium regni*. The *supernum* or *supremum concilium*[3], to which jointly with the king[4] letters and petitions are addressed, clearly comprised the great men of the regency, William Marshall the *rector regis et regni*, Gualo the legate and Pandulf after him, Peter des Roches, the justiciar,

The early council of Henry III.

[1] On the History of the Council, see Sir P. Palgrave's Essay on the King's Council, Dicey's Essay on the Privy Council, and Gneist, Verwalt. i. 352 sq. In the last of these the history of the council is given with too little regard to historical sequence or development, but the subject is one of exceedingly great difficulty.

[2] Vol. i. 603.

[3] 'Quoniam in praesentia domini legati et superni concilii domini regis estis;' F. de Breauté to Hubert de Burgh, Royal Letters, i. 5.

[4] Royal Letters, i. 37, 43.

chancellor, vice-chancellor, and treasurer[1]. It is addressed as *nobile consilium*[2], *nobile et prudens consilium*[3]; its members are *majores* or *magnates de consilio*[4], *consiliarii* and *consiliatores*[5]. Its action during the minority is traceable in every department of work, and it worked in the king's name. It may be indeed inferred from the mention made in the treaty of Lambeth of the *consilium* of Lewis, that such a body was generally regarded as a part of the royal establishment, and the institution may have been borrowed from France, where in consequence of the dismemberment of the monarchy there was nothing answering to the *commune consilium regni*. But however this may have been, from the accession of Henry III a council comes into prominence which seems to contain the officers of state and of the household, the whole judicial staff, a number of bishops[6] and barons, and other members who in default of any other official qualification are simply counsellors; these formed a permanent, continual[7] or resident council, which might transact business from day to day, ready to hold special sessions for special business, to attend the king in parliament and act for him[8], but the distinguishing feature of which

The titles of the council.

Its composition under Henry III.

[1] Royal Letters, i. 44; addressed to Henry, Pandulf, Peter des Roches, 'ceterisque consiliatoribus domini regis.' The archbishop of Dublin writes to Ralph Neville asking him to excuse him 'apud concilium domini regis;' ibid. 89.

[2] Royal Letters, i. 94.

[3] Royal Letters, i. 123.

[4] Royal Letters, i. 60, 70; Foedera, i. 400.

[5] Royal Letters, i. 13, 32, 44, 129, &c.

[6] Letters of the pope allowing the bishops to be members of the council are in the Royal Letters, i. 549.

[7] 'Son continuel conseil;' Rot. Parl. iii. 16, 349; Nicolas, Proceedings of the Privy Council, i. p. 3. 'Familiare consilium,' M. Paris, v. 549; 'secretum concilium,' Hemingb. ii. 20.

[8] The several sorts of business transacted before the council in the early years of Henry III are given by Sir T. Hardy from the Close Rolls, in his preface to the first volume; 'it had a direct jurisdiction over all the proceedings of the courts below, with the power of reversing any judgment of those courts founded in error;' 'whenever the council thought it expedient to have the advice and assistance of any particular persons, whether barons, bishops, or others, the chancellor by order of the council issued writs of summons to such persons, according to circumstances; and if any information was required, writs and commissions emanating from the council were dispatched out of Chancery, and the inquisitions made by virtue of such writs being presented to the council, instructions upon the matter at issue were thereupon delivered as the case required. Conventions,

was its permanent employment in the business of the court. The historians now and then inform us of the addition and removal of members[1]. The foreign favourites of Henry acted as members of this council, and provoked the hatred of the nation by their opposition to the king's constitutional advisers, whose functions they usurped and whose influence in the council they were sufficiently numerous to overpower.

Council under Henry III.

Plans for having an elective council.

Among the many schemes of reform which we have seen brought forward between 1237, 1244[2], and 1258, were plans for imposing a constitutional oath on the councillors, and for introducing special nominees of the baronage into the body; thus making the permanent council a sort of committee of the commune concilium; and, when in the provisionary schemes of 1258[3] and 1264 the royal power was in the hands of the barons, a regularly constituted council, of limited number and definite qualifications, was appointed to attend and act for the king.

The obscurity which hangs over the council during Henry's

recognisances, bails, and agreements were also made before the Council. Oaths, vouchers, and protestations were also made before it. Orders for payments of money were issued from it. Judgment was given in matters tried before it upon petition. Persons were ordered to appear before the Council to show why they opposed the execution of the king's precepts; and so also persons aggrieved, to state their complaints; and the aggressors were commanded to appear and answer the charges preferred against them.' 'It was declared by the king that earls and barons should only be amerced before the Council,' &c.

[1] Thus friar Agnellus was a counsellor of Henry III in 1233; M. Paris, iii. 257; the king called Friar John of S. Giles to his council in 1239; ibid. 627; Simon the Norman and Geoffrey the Templar were expelled from the council; ibid. 629; Paulin Piper and John Mansell in 1244 were appointed by the king to be his principal counsellors; and Lawrence of S. Martin 'consiliorum regalium moderatorem;' ibid. iv. 294. William Perepound, an astrologer, was in the council in 1226; ibid. iii. 111. In 1237 William, bishop elect of Valence, 'factus est consiliarius regis principalis, cum aliis undecim, qui super sacrosancta juraverunt quod fidele consilium regi praestarent; et ipse similiter juravit quod eorum consilio obediret;' Ann. Dunst. p. 146. In 1255 Sir John de Gray retired from the Council, M. Paris, v. 523; in 1256 John Darlington was called to it, ibid. 549; in 1257 Hurtaldus, a royal counsellor, special clerk, and treasurer of the king's chamber, died; ibid. 655. In 1253, the king wished the bishop of Salisbury to attend the council, 'et praebuit se difficilem propter quod ad praesens nolumus habere alios consiliarios quam ordinavimus;' Prynne, Reg. i. 390.

[2] Above, pp. 54, 64.

[3] Above, p. 78.

reign is not altogether dispelled in that of his son. Henry had retained a special council as long as he lived, and Edward's absence from England at his accession left the power in the hands of his father's advisers[1]. He seems thus to have accepted the institution of a council as a part of the general system of government, and, whatever had been the stages of its growth, to have given it definiteness and consistency. It is still uncertain whether the baronage generally were not, if they chose to attend, members ex officio, but it is quite clear that, where no such qualification existed, members were qualified by oath and summons. In the oath taken by the king's councillors in 1257[2], they bind themselves to give faithful counsel, to keep secrecy, to prevent alienation of ancient demesne, to procure justice for rich and poor, and to allow justice to be done on themselves and their friends, to abstain from gifts and misuse of patronage and influence, and to be faithful to the queen and to the heir. The oath taken under Edward I contains twelve articles, the last of which is to be sworn by the judges also: these are to give, expedite, and execute faithful counsel; to maintain, recover, increase, and prevent the diminution of, royal rights; to do justice, honestly and unsparingly, and to join in no engagements which may prevent the counsellor from fulfilling his promise; and lastly, to take no gifts in the administration of justice, save meat and drink for the day[3].

Council under Edward I.

Oaths of the councillors.

We find among the writs of summons many addressed to these sworn councillors, the deans and clerks sworn of the council[4], and others; and we may fairly conclude that it now contained all the judges and officers of the household, although the former at least would not be able to keep continual residence. At any rate it was as members of the royal council

Qualification of councillors by oath.

[1] Thus on the day after Henry's death the great seal was delivered to the archbishop of York and R. Aguillun 'et ceteris consiliariis domini regis in praesentia eorundem consiliariorum;' Foed. i. 497.

[2] See Ann. Burton, p. 395.

[3] Foed. i. 1009; also Parl. Writs, II. ii. 3.

[4] Select Charters, p. 484. See the oath taken by the bishop of London, 'quem rex vult esse de consilio regis,' in 1307; Foed. i. 1009.

that the judges were from the year 1295 summoned to the parliaments and great councils of the kingdom.

Place of the council and its members in parliament.

Although a large proportion of its members would, as earls, barons, and bishops, be members of the *commune concilium*, the judges and special counsellors, who owed their place there simply to the royal summons, or to royal nomination independent of feudal or prescriptive right, were not necessarily parts of that constitutional body; and the *commune concilium*, after it had taken its ultimate form and incorporated representative members, contained a very large number who were not members of the permanent council. Nor were the relations of the two bodies to the king of the same sort; he acted with the counsel and consent of the commune concilium, but in and through the permanent council; the functions of the latter were primarily executive, and it derived such legislative, political, taxative and judicial authority as it had, from the person of the king, although many of its members would have a constitutional share of those powers as bishops and barons. Thus the permanent council might claim a share in those branches of administration which emanated directly from the king rather than in those which emanated from the subject; in legislation and judicature rather than in constitutional taxation. In the latter department each member of the council would either as a baron tax himself personally, or as a commoner tax himself through his representative. Hence the mere counsellor would not as such have a voice in taxation; and hence probably arose the custom of regarding the judges and other summoned counsellors as rather assistants than members of the parliament or great council; and thus perhaps the judges and the lawyers with them lost their chance of becoming a fourth estate[1].

Conciliar and parliamentary functions.

[1] 'For ages past the members of the concilium ordinarium who are not also members of Parliament have been reduced to the humble station of assistants to the House of Lords;' Edinb. Rev. xxxv. 15. On this subject see Prynne's Register, i. pp. 341 sq., 361 sq. He argues that as they are not uniformly summoned, as they are not mentioned in the writs to the magnates, but apparently summoned at the will of the king, and simply as counsellors, cum ceteris de consilio nostro, and as they could not appear

It would be dangerous to decide by conjecture on a point which has been discussed with so much learning and with such discordant views by many generations of lawyers, when the terms used are in themselves ambiguous and at different periods mean very different things. The fact that the word council implies both an organised body of advisers, and the assembly in which that organised body meets; that it means several differently organised bodies, and the several occasions of their meeting; that those several bodies have themselves different organisations in different reigns although retaining a corporate identity; and that they have frequently been discussed by writers who have been unable to agree on a common vocabulary or proper definitions, has loaded the subject with difficulty. We may however generalise thus: (1) there was a permanent council attendant on the king, and advising him in all his sovereign acts, composed of bishops, barons, judges and others, all sworn as counsellors; and this council sitting in terminal courts assisted the king in hearing suits and receiving petitions. (2) In the parliaments of the three estates, from the year 1295 onwards, the judges and other legal members of this permanent body, who did not possess the rights of baronage, were summoned to advise the king. (3) In conjunction with the rest of the prelates and baronage, and excluding the commons and the minor clergy, the permanent council acted sometimes under the title of *magnum concilium;* and this name was, occasionally, given to assemblies in which the council and the Estates met, which are only distinguishable in small technical points from proper parliaments. Many of the assemblies of the reign of Henry III, the constitutions of which we have regarded as steps towards the realisation of the idea of parliament, may be regarded, in the light reflected from the fourteenth century, as examples of the *magnum concilium;* but in point of fact the *magnum concilium* under Edward II and Edward III was only a form of the general national assembly which had survived for certain purposes, when for other prac-

Variety of opinions on the council.

General conclusions as to the character of the king's council.

The *Magnum Concilium*.

by proxy, they are assistants only, not essential members of the parliament. See Gneist, Verwalt. i. 389.

tical uses of administration it had been superseded by the parliament of the three estates as framed by Edward I. The privy council, from the reign of Richard II onwards, although it inherited and amplified the functions of the permanent council of Edward I, differed widely in its organisation, and the steps by which the difference grew must be discussed later on.

The Privy Council.

General and special parliaments.

The name of parliament, the king's parliament, belonged to the sessions of each of the three bodies thus distinguished, the terminal session of the select council, the session of the great council, and the session of the commune concilium of the three estates [1]. The historians distinguish between general and special parliaments, the former [2] being the full assembly of the *commune concilium* in the completeness recognised at the moment; the latter the royal session for the dispatch of business [3]. In the Rolls of Parliament the confusion of name and distinction of functions are still more conspicuous, for most of the early documents preserved under that name belong to the sessions of the council for judicial business, held, as the Provisions of Oxford had ordered, at fixed times of the year, and resembling in idea, if not in fact, the crown-wearing days of the Norman kings.

Confusion of name.

The king acts both in Council and in Parliament.

Whilst the constitutional reforms of Edward I were gradually taking their final shape, it is not surprising that some confusion should arise between the functions of the king's council and those of the national council. In both we find the king legislating, judging, deliberating, and taxing, or attempting to tax. If in the one he enacted laws and in the other issued ordinances, if in the one he asked for an aid and in the other imposed a tallage or negotiated the concession of a custom, the ordinance and the statute differed little in application, the voluntary contribution and the arbitrary tallage were demanded

[1] See above, p. 236, note; Prynne, Reg. i. 397.

[2] 'Magnum parliamentum;' Ann. Winton, p. 119; Ann. Waverl. p. 390. 'Parliament general;' Stat. Westm. I; Select Charters, p. 450. The writs for the first parliament of 1275 call it a 'generale parliamentum;' Parl. Writs, i. 1.

[3] 'Singulare non generale tenuit parliamentum;' Ann. Osney, p. 299.

with equal cogency from the taxpayer. Some few facts, if not rules or principles may, notwithstanding the rapid changes of the times, be determined, but in general it may be affirmed that for all business, whether it were such as could be done by the king alone or such as required the co-operation of the nation, the action of the smaller circle of advisers was continually employed. The most important points, however, are those connected with judicature and legislation.

231. The petitions, addressed to the king, or to the king and his council, which are preserved in the early rolls of parliament, furnished abundant work to the permanent council, and the special parliaments were probably the solemn occasions on which they were presented and discussed. These stated sessions[1] were held by Edward I at Hilarytide, Easter, and Michaelmas, or at other times by adjournment. And then were heard also the great placita, or suits which, arising between great men or in unprecedented cases, required the judgment of the king himself; and the general parliaments, which were of course much less frequent, were for the sake of convenience or economy usually called at times when the council was in session; a fact which has increased the difficulty of distinguishing the acts of the two bodies. The placita on these occasions were either relegated to small bodies of auditors who reported their opinion to the council, or were heard in the full council itself. Of the former sort were the suits between the abbot of S. Augustine and the barons of Sandwich in 1280, and between the men of Yarmouth and the Cinque Ports in 1290, in which a small number of councillors were assigned as auditors[2]; of the latter was the claim of Gilbert of Clare to the castle and town of Bristol[3], and the king's demand of

I. Petitions in council.

Placita in council.

Committees of council.

[1] The provisions of Oxford ordered three parliaments in the year, October 7, February 2, and June 1; Select Charters, pp. 390, 392. Edward I is said to have held four, at Christmas, Hilarytide, Easter and Michaelmas; Lords' Report, i. 169; but these were not by any means regular. They frequently were held on the octaves of the festivals, and thus the Christmas Court would run on into the Hilarytide Council.

[2] Parl. Writs, i. 8, 19, 20; B. Cotton, p. 175.

[3] Parl. Writs, i. 6; two foreigners, Francesco Accursi and the bishop of Verdun were present, besides the magnates 'plurimorum magnatum terrae

T 2

a sentence against Llewelyn, at Michaelmas, 1276[1], both of which were heard and decided in full council, composed of magnates, justices, and others, whose names are recorded. The hearing of petitions was much more laborious work, and required more minute regulation. In the eighth year of Edward I it was ordered that all petitions should be examined by the judges of the court to which the matter in question properly belonged, so that only important questions should be brought before the king and council, especially such as were matters of grace and favour which could not be answered without reference to the king[2]. A further order of the twenty-first year provided that these petitions should be divided, by the persons assigned to receive them, into five bundles, containing severally the documents to be referred to the Chancery, the Exchequer, the judges, the king and council, and those which had been already answered, so that matters referred to the king himself might be laid before him before he proceeded to transact business[3]. For the hearing as well as the reception

Hearing of petitions.

Arrangement and answering of petitions in parliament.

in pleno consilio regis.' The list comprises the archbishop of Canterbury, four bishops, three earls, eleven barons, seventeen judges and clerks, Francesco Accursi, and G. de Haspal.

[1] Parl. Writs, i. 5.

[2] 'Pur ceo ke la gent ke venent al parlement le Roy sunt sovent deslaez et desturbez a grant grevance de eus e de la curt par la multitudine des peticions ke sunt botez devant le Rey, de queus le plus porroient estre espleytez par Chanceler e par justices, purveu est ke tutes les peticions ke tuchent le sel veynent primes al chanceler, e ceus ke tuchent le Escheker veynent al Escheker, e ceus ke tuchent justices u ley de terre veinent a justices, e ceus ke tuchent Juerie veynent a justices de la Juerie. Et si les bosoigns seent si grantz u si de grace ke le chanceler e ces autres ne le pussent fere sanz le rey, dunk il les porterunt par lur meins demeine devant le rey pur saver ent sa volente; ensi qe nule peticion ne veigne devaunt le roy e son conseil fors par les mains des avauntditz chaunceller e les autres chef ministres; ensi ke le rey e sun consail pussent sanz charge de autre busoignes entendre a grosses busoignes de sun reaume e de ses foreines terres;' Rot. Claus. 8 Edward I, m. 6, dorso; Ryley, Pleadings, &c. p. 442.

[3] 'Le roy voet et ordeine qe totes les petycions qe de si en avant serrunt liveres as parlemens a ceaus qil assignera a recevoir les, qe totes les peticions seient tot a primer, apres ce qe eles serrunt receves, bien examinees; et qe celes qe touchent la Chancelerie seient mises en un lyaz severaument, e les autres qe touchent le Escheker en autre liaz; et ausi seit fet de celes qe touchent les justices; et puis celes qe serront devant le rey e son consail severaument en autre liaz; et ausi celes qe aver ont este respondues devant en several liaz; et ensi seient les choses reportees devant le rey devant ceo qe il les comence a deliverer;' Rot. Claus. 21 Edward I, m. 7; Ryley, Pleadings, p. 459.

of these petitions provision was made in the parliament, or by the king before the parliament opened; and from the records of 1305 we find that they were now presented in the full parliament of the estates[1], for in that year Edward named special commissions of judges and barons to receive the petitions touching Scotland, Gascony, Ireland, and the Channel Islands. Those which could not be answered without reference to the king formed a special branch of business[2], and it was from the share taken by the Chancellor in examining and reporting on the bills of grace and favour that his equitable jurisdiction in the fourteenth century grew up. The nomination of receivers and triers became a part of the opening business of every parliament, and the ultimate division of the work, in the reign of Richard II, was into three portions, one for the king, one for the council, and one for the parliament itself.

Receivers and triers of petitions.

II. Share of the king's council in legislation.

232. Edward I, in the preamble of several of his statutes, some of which were distinctly the result of deliberation of the general parliament, mentions the participation of the council as well as that of the assembled estates. The first statute of Westminster was enacted by the king *par son conseil*, and by the assent of the magnates and community[3]: the statute *de religiosis* is made *de consilio praelatorum comitum et aliorum fidelium regni nostri de consilio nostro existentium*[4]; the statute, so called, of Acton Burnell is an enactment by the king, *par luy e par sun conseil a sun parlement*[5]. In such cases it seems impossible to understand by the *conseil* merely the advice of the persons who are afterwards said to have consented. In other cases, however, the king enacts, or ordains by his council, when the action of parliament is altogether unnoticed. The statute of Rageman is 'accorded by the king and by his council[6];' the statute 'de Bigamis' rehearses the names of a sort of committee of councillors, in whose presence the draught of it was read before it was confirmed by the king and the entire council[7].

[1] Parl. Writs, i. 155; Ryley, p. 508.
[2] See Hardy's Preface to the Close Rolls, i. p. xxviii.
[3] Statutes, i. 26. [4] Ibid. i. 51. [5] Ibid. i. 53, 54. [6] Ibid. i. 44.
[7] Statutes, i. 42. This statute gives the names of the councillors, of whom Francesco Accursi was one; it was approved by 'omnes de consilio,

It would seem certain from this that the king in his council made ordinances[1], as by the advice of his council he enacted laws with consent of parliament. All Edward's legislation may be received as of full and equal authority, but we have to look forward to days in which the distinction between statute and ordinance will be closely scrutinised.

Comparison with the institutions of France under Philip the Fair.

For this part of Edward's system a parallel may be sought in the practice of the French court under Philip the Fair. The parliament of Paris may be generally compared with the special judicial session or parliament of the council[2]. The somewhat later bed of justice, in which the king, with his court of peers and prelates, officers and judges, solemnly attested the decisions or the legislation put in form by parliament, loosely resembles the magnum concilium; and the States General answer to the parliament of the three estates. How far Edward I adopted from French usage the form of legal council which he seems to have definitely established, and the practice of giving to its legal members a place in parliament, and how far Philip the Fair borrowed from England the idea of the States General, need not be discussed, for it cannot be determined on existing evidence[3]. But the parallel, superficial as it may be, marks out the end of the reign of Edward in England and the period of Philip the Fair in France, as the point at which the two constitutions approximated more nearly than at any other in the middle ages. The divergences which followed arose not merely from the absolutist innovations in France, but from the working of more ancient causes, which had for the moment drawn together to develop stronger differences hereafter. In

justitiarii et alii;' the councillors named are two bishops, one dean, three archdeacons, five magistri, and nine others, who were employed at various times as itinerant justices and in like offices. The constitution is said to be made in parliament after Michaelmas, 1276; the assemby that gave sentence against Llewelyn, and decided the cause of the earl of Gloucester, mentioned above, pp. 275, 276.

[1] The statute 'de falsa moneta,' Statutes, i. 131, is quoted in the Wardrobe accounts as 'ordinatio facta per ipsum regem et consilium suum in parliamento tento apud Stebenhethe;' p. 5.

[2] One of the best illustrations of this analogy is the Statute de Bigamis; see above, p. 277, note 7.

[3] Compare Boutaric, les Premiers États Généraux, p. 30. Cf. Langlois, Origines du Parlement de Paris, Paris, 1890.

England the several bodies maintained more or less a right of co-operating in each branch of administration; in France the States General, although in the first instance called for the purpose of political deliberation, were soon limited to the subject of taxation and declaration of grievances, and lost their political weight with their deliberative power; whilst the judicial work, and the duty of registering rather than of joining in legislation, fell to the parliament of Paris. In England the jurisdiction of the House of Lords was co-ordinate with that of the council; the legislative power of the parliament did not exclude the ordaining power of the council; the council acted executively in all political matters on which the parliament deliberated, and, if in taxation the sole authorising body was the assembly of the three estates in parliament, the exclusion of the king's right of tallaging, and of the action of his ministers in obtaining loans and benevolences, was not completely secured until a comparatively late period.

Edward's changes in the judicial system.

233. The judicial machinery of the kingdom received during the period before us, and finally under Edward I, the form which with a few changes it has retained to recent times; the measures by which this was done may be briefly enumerated here, although from henceforth they cease to have any special bearing on our main subject[1]. The evolution of the several courts of supreme judicature from the personal jurisdiction of the king, first in the Curia Regis and Exchequer, we have already examined. We have traced to the arrangements made by Henry II in 1178 for the constant session of a limited number of judges in the Curia, the probable origin of the King's Bench as a distinct tribunal; and we have seen, in the 17th article of Magna Carta, the Common Pleas separated from the other suits that came before this court.

Division of the courts:

At the beginning of the reign of Henry III the three courts are distinguished; first, as to the class of causes entertained: the Exchequer hearing cases touching the king's revenue; the Court of Common Pleas the private suits of subjects; and the King's Bench, under the

[1] On this see Gneist, Verwalt. i. 317–320 sq., 337–352; Pollock and Maitland, i. 153–183.

head of *placita coram rege*, all other suits, whether heard before the king, or before the justiciar, or the limited staff of judges. They are distinguished, further, as to the place of session, the Common Pleas being fixed at Westminster, the other two following the king, although the Exchequer, in its proper character, was as a rule held at Westminster. The justiciar, however, was still the head of the whole system, and the body of judges was not yet divided into three distinct benches or colleges, each exclusively devoted to one branch. This final step is understood to have been taken shortly before the end of the reign of Henry III, but no legislative act has been found on which it was based, and it may have been originally a mere voluntary regulation adopted for convenience. The multiplication of suits, the increasing spirit of litigation, and the great development of legal ingenuity at this period, will account for the growth of distinct systems of rules, forms of pleading, and the like, in the three courts. The increasing difficulty of administering justice under three forms, by the same judges, would cause the gradual apportioning of particular individuals to particular courts; and as the office of great justiciar, after the fall of Hubert de Burgh, lost its importance, and may be said to have become practically extinct, the tendency to division was strengthened by the acephalous condition of the courts. This was remedied by the appointment of a head or capital member to each body. From the beginning of the reign of Edward I we find a series of Chief Justices of Common Pleas[1], as well as of the King's Bench, and from the middle of the next reign a regular succession of Chief Barons of the Exchequer. The tendency to specialisation was, however, somewhat neutralised by the exertions of the professional lawyers to attract business into the courts in which they practised. In 1282 the king had to prohibit the treasurer and barons of the Exchequer from hearing

Side notes: under Henry III. — Further separation. — Extinction of the justiciarship. — Three chief judges. — Co-ordinate jurisdictions.

[1] See Foss's Tabulae Curiales. In 1278, at Gloucester, the king in council re-nominated a chief justice and two others, 'Justitiae de Banco ad placita regis;' a chief and four others, 'justitiae de Banco Westmonasterii;' six justices in eyre for the north, and six for the south; with fixed sums, 'nomine feodi ad sustentationem,' varying from sixty to forty marks; Parl. Writs, i. 382.

common pleas, as contrary to the custom of the kingdom, except in cases which touched the king or the ministers of the Exchequer[1]. This custom was embodied in a statute in 1300; and, although the pertinacity of the lawyers contrived to evade it by the means of fictitious pleadings, it served to show the king's intention of completely defining the business of the tribunals. The same process is traceable in the division of the petitions presented to the king and council in 1280 and 1293, those referred to the justices being separated from those referred to the Exchequer[2]. The common law jurisdiction of the Chancellor was perhaps comprehended in the same scheme of specialisation: in 1280, after Epiphany, the king went to hunt in the New Forest, but the Chancellor returned to London as to a certain place where all who sought writs, and were prosecuting their rights, might find a ready remedy[3]. But if this were so, the plan was found impracticable for the present; Edward could not do without his Chancellor, who accompanied him in his long visit to France; and, in the Articuli super Cartas, the clause which forbade the hearing of Common Pleas in the Exchequer directed that the King's Bench and the Chancery should still follow the king's person; implying further that the Exchequer, which in 1277 had been taken to Shrewsbury, and in 1299 to York[4], should remain at Westminster.

The Chancellor as judge.

234. The origin of the equitable jurisdiction of the Chancellor is connected directly with the history of the king's council. The Chancellor had long been, as a baron of the Exchequer and as a leading member of the Curia, entrusted with judicial functions. To him, as well as to the justices of the land and the Exchequer, the ordinance of 1280 referred a distinct class of petitions. But as yet the king was the chief judge in equity, or

Equitable jurisdiction of the Chancellor.

[1] Foedera, i. 618.

[2] Above, p. 276.

[3] Ann. Waverl. p. 393. But see Pollock and Maitland, i. 172.

[4] In 1210 the Exchequer was taken to Northampton; Madox, p. 131: in 1266 the Exchequer and King's Bench were at S. Paul's; Lib. de Antt. Legg. p. 84: in 1277 the Exchequer, and in 1282 the Bench, went to Shrewsbury; in 1290 the Exchequer was held at the Hustings in London; in 1299, both Exchequer and Bench went to York. See Madox, Hist. Exch. pp. 552, 553; Ryley's Pleadings, p. 225; Parl. Writs, i. 86; Ann. Winton, p. 124; Ann. Dunst. p. 278.

'matters of grace and favour.' And 'matters which were so great, or of grace, that the Chancellor and others could not dispatch them without the king,' were ordered to be brought before the king, and, except by the hands of the Chancellor and other chief ministers, no petition was to come before the king and his council. At this period, then, the Chancellor, although employed in equity, discharged ministerial functions only[1]. When, early in the reign of Edward III, the Chancellor ceased to be a part of the king's personal retinue and to follow the court, his tribunal acquired a more distinct and substantive character, as those of the other courts had done under the like circumstances; petitions for grace and favour began to be addressed primarily to him, instead of being simply referred to him by the king, or passed on through his hands. In the 22nd year of that king such transactions are recognised as the proper province of the Chancellor[2], and from that time his separate and independent equitable jurisdiction began to grow into the possession of that powerful and complicated machinery which belongs to later history. Since the fall of the great justiciar, the Chancellor was in dignity, as well as in power and influence, second to the king. Robert Burnell was the first great chancellor, as Hubert de Burgh was the last great justiciar.

The Chancellor ceases to follow the king.

Court of chancery.

Edward's reform in itinerant judicature.

235. The provincial jurisdiction exercised by itinerant justices has a conspicuous place among the institutions reformed

[1] Neither Glanvill, the Mirror, Bracton, Briton, Fleta, nor the 'Diversité des Courtes,' ever alludes to the Chancery as a court of Equity; Hardy, Close Rolls, i. pref. p. xxiii. Yet the distinction was recognised between law and equity as early as the time of Glanvill, and was inherent in the double character of the judicature; and Fleta (ii. 13) mentions the hearing of petitions as one of the principal duties of the chancellor and his clerks, 'quorum officium sit supplicationes et querelas conquerentium audire et examinare, et eis super qualitatibus injuriarum ostensarum debitum remedium exhibere per brevia regis.'

[2] 'Quia circa diversa negotia nos et statum regni nostri Angliae concernentia sumus indies multipliciter occupati, volumus quod quilibet negotia tam communem legem regni nostri Angliae quam gratiam nostram specialem concernentia penes nosmet ipsos habens ex nunc prosequenda, eadem negotia, videlicet negotia ad communem legem penes venerabilem virum electum Cantuariensem confirmatum cancellarium nostrum per ipsum expedienda, et alia negotia de gratia nostra concedenda penes eundem cancellarium seu dilectum clericum nostrum custodem sigilli nostri privati, prosequantur;' Rot. Claus. 38 Edw. III; Hardy, Close Rolls, i. pref. xxviii.

by Edward I, and contributes an important element to the social and political history of his father's reign also. The 18th article of the Charter of John directed that for the purpose of taking assizes of mort d'ancestor, novel disseisin, and darrein presentment, two justices should visit each county four times a year [1]. This regulation was confirmed in the Charter of 1216, but materially altered by that of 1217 [2], which placed the assize of darrein presentment under the view of the justices of the bench and directed the other two to be taken only once a year. These itinerant justices were however properly justices for these assizes merely; and their sessions do not appear to have taken the place or to have superseded the necessity of the more important visitations for the purpose of gaol delivery and amercements which had been continued since 1166. These visitations seem to have been held at irregular intervals and under special articles of instruction; some of the justices being, as Bracton tells us, commissioned to hear all sorts of pleas [3], and some restricted to particular classes of causes. Throughout the reign of Henry III these courts are found everywhere in great activity, their judicial work being still combined with financial work, the amercement of shires and hundreds, of contumacious and negligent suitors, and the raising of money from the communities not represented in the *commune concilium*. Their exertions in one form or another brought a large revenue to the crown, and, whilst they enabled Henry to resist the reasonable demands for reform, they turned a measure which had been both welcome and beneficial into a means of oppression. Hence both the barons and the people generally looked on them with great jealousy. The petition that led to the Provisions of Oxford contains complaints of mal-administration and extortion [4]: the monastic annalists register long details of expensive litigation, and under the protection of their great neighbours the stronger towns refused to receive the itinerant judges unconditionally. In 1261 Worcester declined to admit them on the ground that seven years had not elapsed since the last visit [5], and Hereford

Earlier itinerant justices.

Eyres under Henry III.

Unpopularity of these courts.

[1] Select Charters, p. 299.
[2] Ibid. p. 345.
[3] Bracton, lib. iii. tr. i. c. 11.
[4] See articles 13, 14.
[5] Ann. Wigorn. p. 446.

did the same, pleading that their proceedings were contrary to the Provisions of Oxford[1]. That constitution however contained no regulation as to a septennial eyre, and the annals of Dunstable, Worcester, Winchester, and Waverley, furnish abundant evidence that the visitations were much more frequent. No fixed rule can be inferred from these notices, and it is most probable that the irregular system of earlier times was continued. If this be so, Edward I has the credit of reducing to definite rules the characteristic procedure of his great-grandfather, when he substituted regular visitations of judges of assize for the irregular circuits of the justices itinerant. The first measure of the reign, taken by his ministers before his arrival, was to stop the work of the itinerant justices[2]. In his fourth year, by the statute of Rageman[3], he ordered a general visitation for hearing complaints of trespass and offences against statutes committed during the last twenty-five years; but this seems to have been no more than a proceeding under special commission. The newer system is referred by the legal historians to the 30th article of the second statute of Westminster, A. D. 1285[4]; by which two sworn justices are to be assigned, before whom, in conjunction with one or two knights of the shire, all assizes of mort d'ancestor, novel disseisin and attaints, are to be taken, thrice a year, in July, September, and January. From the form of writ ordering the trial of questions of fact before the justices at Westminster, unless the sworn justices hold their visitation before a fixed day, these latter received the name of justices of Nisi Prius. The statute 21 Edward I divided the kingdom into four circuits, each of which had two justices assigned to it[5]: these were to take the assizes as before, but without a restriction of terms, and were to be on duty throughout the year. By a further act of the 27th year, the justices of assize were ordered to act as justices of gaol delivery[6]; and thus obtained all the judicial authority which

Frequency of their sessions.

Statute of Rageman.

Institution of justices of *nisi prius*,

and circuits of assizes;

of gaol delivery.

[1] Cont. M. Paris, ed. Wats, p. 990.
[2] Ann. Winton, p. 113.
[3] Statutes of the Realm, i. 44; in 1278 two bodies of six itinerant judges were appointed by the king and council; Parl. Writs, i. 382.
[4] Statutes, i. 86.
[5] Statutes, i. 112.
[6] Statutes, i. 129.

had belonged to their predecessors, although special commissions for criminal cases, such as that of the justices of Trailbaston appointed in 1305[1], were now and then issued. The system of division of business, now established in the courts of Westminster, so far affected the provincial jurisdiction, that it was necessary to provide that assizes and inquests might be taken before any one judge of the court in which the plea was brought and one knight of the shire[2]; and it was not until the 14th of Edward III that inquests of Nisi Prius were allowed to be heard by the justices of Nisi Prius, altogether irrespective of the court to which the justices belonged[3]. The commission of oyer and terminer dates from the 2nd of Edward III[4], and the commission of the peace completed the five several authorities possessed by the judges on circuit.

Modifications.

Various commissions of judges.

Conservation of the peace.

236. Intermediate between the provincial administration of the supreme courts and the ancient local administration of shire and hundred, come the offices connected with the maintenance of peace and police, derived from the higher source, and coordinate with the justiciary, as distinct from the popular, jurisdiction of the sheriff. Knights assigned, to enforce the oath of peace and the hue and cry, appear as early as the year 1195[5]. Their designation as *assigned* seems to prove that they were royal nominees and not elected officers; but their early history is obscure. To this class may be referred also the appointment by Henry III in 1230, of three[6], and in 1252 of two, knights assigned in each county to enforce the Assize of Arms[7], and the nomination of constables of hundreds and townships, to secure the conservation of the peace. In 1264 a single 'custos pacis' was assigned to each shire to conserve the peace, and possibly to watch, possibly to supersede, the sheriff, but with instructions not to interfere with his functions so as to diminish the revenue[8]. In the 5th of Edward I, it appears that this *custos*

Knights assigned.

Custodes pacis.

[1] Parl. Writs, i. 408.
[2] Statutes, i. 130.
[3] Statutes, i. 286.
[4] Statutes, i. 258.
[5] Select Charters, p. 264; see vol. i. p. 507.
[6] Royal Letters, i. 371 sq.
[7] Select Charters, pp. 371, 374.
[8] Select Charters, p. 411. 'Nolumus autem quod praetextu hujus mandati nostri de aliquibus quae ad officium vicecomitis pertinent, vos intro-

pacis had become an elective officer, chosen by the sheriff and the community of the county, in the county court and under the instructions of the king conveyed by the sheriff[1]. We are not however able to discover whether the office was a permanent or an occasional one. In 1282 the earl of Cornwall was assigned by the king to conserve the peace in Middlesex and several other counties, with power to appoint deputies[2]. After the passing of the statute of Winchester, the office of conservator of the peace, whose work was to carry out the provisions of that enactment, was filled by election in the shiremoot[3]. The act of the 1st Edward III, c. 16[4], which orders the appointment, in each county, of good men and loyal to guard the peace, connects itself more naturally with the statute of Winchester, and through it with the *milites assignati* of Henry III and Richard I, than with the chosen *custodes* of Edward I. These nominated conservators, two or three in number, were commissioned by the 18th Edward III, stat. 2, c. 2[5], to hear and determine felonies, and by 34 Edward III, c. 1[6], were regularly empowered to do so. The office thus became a permanent part of the county machinery in the hands of the Justices of the Peace.

Conservators of the peace.

Justices of the peace.

Courts of the shire and hundred.

The changes and improvements in the general judicial system inevitably tended to diminish the consequence of the ancient popular courts, withdrawing from them the more important suits and allowing the absence of the more important members. The changes which affected the position of the sheriff have been already noted. It is to the thirteenth century that the ancient machinery of the county court and hundred court owes its final form. The second charter of Henry III determines the times of

Times of meeting.

mittatis, quominus vicecomes de exitibus ejusdem comitatus nobis plene respondere valeat;' Lambarde, Eirenarcha, p. 19.

[1] 'Cum vicecomes noster Norfolk, et communitas ejusdem comitatus, elegerit vos in custodem pacis nostrae ibidem,' &c.; Rot. Pat. 5 Edw. I; Lambarde, Eirenarcha, p. 17.

[2] Parl. Writs, i. 384.

[3] See above, p. 239. Probably the conservators were in the first instance appointed by the crown, the vacancies being filled by election; see Parl. Writs, i. 389–391. An enumeration of the duties of these officers may be found in the Commissions issued by Edward II; Parl. Writs, II. ii. 8, 11, 12.

[4] Statutes, i. 257.

[5] Statutes, i. 301.

[6] Statutes, i. 364.

meeting: the shiremoot is henceforth to be held from month to month; the sheriff's tourn twice a year, after Easter and after Michaelmas; and view of frankpledge is to be taken at the Michaelmas tourn[1]. By a supplementary edict in 1234 Henry allowed the courts of the hundred, the wapentake, and the franchises of the magnates, to be held every three weeks, and excused the attendance of all but those who were bound by special service, or who were concerned in suits[2]. These courts, the continuance of which is based, according to this edict, on the fact that under Henry II they were held every fortnight, are thus shown to be still substantially the same as in Anglo-Saxon times, when the shiremoot was held twice a year and the hundred moot once a month. The Statute of Merton allowed all freemen to appear by attorney in the local courts; the attendance of the magnates of the county at the sheriff's tourn was dispensed with by the provisions of Westminster in 1259 and by the Statute of Marlborough in 1267[3].

Continuity of the popular courts.

The smaller manorial courts gradually adopted the improvements of the larger and popular courts, but great diversities of custom still prevailed, and the distinction between court leet and court baron, the jurisdiction derived from royal grant and that inherent in the lordship, whether derived from the original grant or from the absorption of the township jurisdiction, becomes more prominent. How much of the organisation which characterised these courts, and of which we have abundant illustration in the court rolls of every manor, was devised by the ingenuity of lawyers, and how much is of primitive origin, it would be hard to say. The whole jurisprudence of these courts rests on custom and is rarely touched by statute: custom is capable of much elaboration and modification; its antiquity can only be shown by record or by generalising from a large number of particulars. On the whole, however, the structure of these courts bears, as we have seen[4], so many marks

The manorial courts.

[1] Select Charters, p. 346; Pollock and Maitland, i. 518–547.

[2] Ann. Dunst. pp. 140, 141; Royal Letters, i. 450; Brady, Hist. vol. i. App. p. 254.

[3] Above, p. 215.

[4] Vol. i. pp. 88, 89, 399, 606; Pollock and Maitland, i. 547–622.

of antiquity, that we may fairly suppose the later lawyers to have merely systematised rules which they found prevailing. The increased importance of the minuter local franchises, as sources of revenue to the lords, after the passing of the statute Quia Emptores, will account for the large increase of local records. The Court Rolls of manors generally begin in the reign of Edward I; the necessity of keeping a formal record would have the effect of giving regularity and fixed formality to the proceedings.

Court Rolls.

Regulation of juries.

The regulations for juries occupy a prominent place among the minuter acts of Edward's legislation. The determination of the qualification of a juror, which had no doubt some bearing on the later question of the electoral suffrage, belongs to this reign. In 1285, for the relief of the poorer suitors who felt the burden of attendance at the courts very heavily, it was ordained that a reasonable number of jurors only should be summoned, and that none should be put on assizes within their own shire who could not spend twenty shillings a year, or out of their shire who could not spend forty[1]. In 1293 the qualification for the former was raised to forty shillings, and for the latter to a hundred; saving however the customs observed in boroughs and before the itinerant justices[2].

Qualification of jurors.

Every branch of judicature thus received consistency, consolidation and definition under the hands of Edward and his ministers.

Changes in the Exchequer.

237. The disappearance of the great justiciar, which left the chancellor at the head of the royal council and broke into three the general body of judges, had its results in the Exchequer also. There the Treasurer stepped into the place of the justiciar, and became, from the middle of the reign of Henry III, one of the chief officers of the crown[3]. In the same reign was created the office of Chancellor of the Exchequer, to whom the

Treasurer and Chancellor of the Exchequer.

[1] Statutes, i. 86, 89. There is an order to remove ignorant jurors in a particular case, and substitute nearer neighbours and better-informed men, in the Close Rolls of Henry III, vol. ii. p. 124.

[2] Statutes, i. 113.

[3] Madox, Hist. Exch. p. 564; the title of the Treasurer is sometimes Treasurer of the Exchequer, sometimes the King's Treasurer; in 1307 Walter Langton is called Treasurer of England; ibid. p. 579.

Exchequer seal was entrusted, and who with the Treasurer[1] took part in the equitable jurisdiction of the Exchequer, although not in the common law jurisdiction of the barons which extended itself as the legal fictions of pleading brought common pleas into this court[2]. But the financial business of the Exchequer underwent other great modifications. The official work of that great department was broken up into sections. Large branches of expenditure were reckoned among the private accounts of the king kept in the Wardrobe[3]. The grants of money in parliament, the fifteenths, thirtieths and the like, were collected by special justices and no longer accounted for by the sheriffs or recorded in the Great Rolls of the Pipe[4]. The constant complaints which were made, in the reigns of Edward III and Richard II, of the difficulty of auditing the national accounts show that the real value of the old system of administration was much impaired. In fact the king's household accounts were no longer the national accounts, and yet the machinery for managing the two was not definitely separated. Edward II paid his father's debts to the amount of £118,000. The debts of Edward II were not paid late in the reign of his son[5]. The banishment of the Jews, the employment of foreign merchants to farm the revenues, the alterations in the methods of taxation,

Jurisdiction in common pleas and equity.

Changes in the financial work of the Exchequer.

Decline in the fiscal system.

[1] Thomas, Hist. Exch. pp. 94, 95; Blackstone, Comm. iii. 44.

[2] John Mansell is regarded by Madox as filling this office in the 18th of Henry III; but the first person who is known to have borne the title is Ralph of Leicester, in the 32nd year; Madox, Hist. Exch. pp. 580, 581.

[3] The receipts at the Wardrobe begin as early as 1223; Rot. Claus. i. 628; Madox, p. 184. A Wardrobe Account of 1282–1285 is printed as an Appendix to Ellis's John of Oxenedes; it contains the expenses of the Welsh war, amounting to £102,621 0s. 4*d.*; pp. 308, 311. The whole wardrobe account of 1299–1300, accounting for expenses to the amount of £64,105, was published by the Society of Antiquaries in 1787; other accounts of the same kind are printed in the Archæologia, vols. 15, 16, 17, 28, 31.

[4] Thus the fifteenth raised in 1225 was assessed and collected under the superintendence of justices assigned, and called 'justitiarii quintae decimae;' and audited by the bishop of Carlisle, Michael Belet and William de Castellis; Rot. Claus. ii. 40, 45, 71, 95; Foedera, i. 177.

[5] Archbishop Islip (1349–1366) writes to Edward III: 'utinam . . . scires debita tua et debita patris tui, et intelligeres, id est, pericula animae tuae et periculum animae patris tui propter debita multimoda creditoribus non soluta . . . sed Deus propitietur animae ejus . . . forte filius tuus pro te non solvet;' MS. Bodl. 624.

and the varying use of gold, bills of exchange, and raw material, as a circulating medium for international transactions, furnished an amount of work to which the old machinery was unequal, and which accounts for some of the embarrassments which the following century, ignorant of the principles of political economy, failed to overcome. Of the details of taxation as a part of the financial work enough has been already said.

Military system in the thirteenth century.

238. In the development of military organisation the thirteenth century is not less fertile than it is in other respects[1], nor is the defining and distinctive policy of Edward I less conspicuous. Henry III, it is true, engaged in no such great war as

Mercenaries abandoned.

demanded any concentration of the national strength. The attempt made by John to hold the kingdom by a mercenary force was not repeated under his son, although during the struggle with the barons it was opportunity rather than will that was lacking, and England was in danger of being invaded by a foreign army, under the queen and the refugees, after the battle of Lewes. The impossibility of maintaining a force of mercenaries precluded the existence of a standing army; the loss of the foreign dominions of the crown took away the pretext which Henry II or Richard might have alleged; the small territory left to the king in the south of France was the only field for his warlike energies or military skill. Henry III, then, so far as he had need of an army, and Edward I after him, could only use and develop the materials already in existence, that is, the feudal service which was due from the tenants-in-chief, and the national militia organised by Henry II under the Assize of

Divisions of the national force.

Arms[2]. The military measures of these two reigns have, however, considerable interest, both in analogy with other branches of the royal policy and in their permanent effects on our military history. The armed force of the nation was divided by the same lines of separation which were drawn in matters of land tenure, judicature, council, and finance. It was the fixed and persistent policy of the kings, fully developed under Edward I, to unite the whole people for administrative purposes, whether

[1] On this see Gneist, Verwalt. i. 313–317.
[2] Vol. i. pp. 587–592.

by eliminating the feudal distinctions or by utilising them for the general objects of government; that, as the parliament should be the whole nation in council, and the revenue the joint contributions of the several estates, the national defence and its power for aggressive warfare should be concentrated, simplified, and defined; and thus the host should be again the whole nation in arms. Such a consummation would be perfect only when the king could demand immediately, and on the same plea, the services of all classes of his subjects; but the doctrine of feudal obligation was nowhere so strong as in the matter of military service, and Edward's design, so far as it failed to eliminate the importance of tenure from this branch of the national system, remained imperfect. It may be questioned, however, whether, with existing materials, he could have entirely dispensed with the feudal machinery, and whether the wars of the next century and a half were not needed to prove its weakness and to supply a substitute in the form of a regular military system [1].

Edward I tries to get rid of the feudal influence in military affairs.

His policy somewhat premature.

The military levy of the feudal tenants-in-chief presents a close analogy with the assembly of the *commune concilium* as described in Magna Carta. The great barons were summoned by special writ to appear on a certain day, prepared with their due number of knights, with horses and arms, to go on the king's service for a certain time, according to the king's orders [2]. At the same time the sheriff of each county had a writ directing him to warn all the tenants-in-chief of his bailiwick to obey the general summons to the same effect;

(1) Military levy of the feudal body.

Action of the sheriff.

[1] An important passage in M. Paris, vi. 374, 375, shows us how the military service of the abbot of S. Alban's was performed: 'consuetudo autem est et fuit ab antiquo, quod post summonitionem regiam debent convocari ad unum locum omnes tenentes de feodo militari, et de quolibet scuto provideri unus miles capitalis ad faciendum corporale servitium exercitui regis. Procurari autem debent expensae suae et levari a compartionariis suis, et ille capitaliter electus sumptibus suis ire debet ad exercitum. Senescallus autem abbatis, aut alius nomine suo missus, debet praesentare capitales electos ad faciendum servitium regale coram marescallo ad recipiendum servitium domini regis ei concessum per eundem regem constituto.'

[2] Countless examples of these summonses will be found, for the reign of Henry III and onwards, in the Appendix to the Lords' Report on the Dignity of a Peer; and for the reigns of Edward I and Edward II, in Palgrave's Parliamentary Writs.

under the general term tenants-in-chief were included not only the minor tenants, but the archbishops, bishops, abbots, earls, barons, and knights who had also received the special summons, the double warning being intended no doubt to secure the complete representation of the outlying estates of the baronage. But the chief business of the sheriff in this department would be to collect and see to the proper equipment of the minor tenants in chivalry.

Nature of the summons.

When the summons was issued for a purpose which fell within the exact terms of feudal obligation, as understood at the time, the vassals were enjoined 'in fide qua nobis tenemini,' or 'sub debito fidelitatis,' or 'sicut ipsum regem et honorem suum diligunt necnon et terras et tenementa quae de rege tenent,' or finally, 'in fide et homagio et dilectione.'

Term of service.

If the service demanded were likely to be prolonged beyond the customary period of forty days, or were in any other way exceptional, the summons took a less imperative

Service of courtesy.

form; thus in 1277 Edward I uses the words 'affectuose rogamus' in requesting the barons to continue their service against the Welsh, and engages that no prejudice should accrue to them by reason of their courtesy in complying[1]: and we have already seen how in 1297 the use of this form was made by the constable and marshal an excuse for disobeying the royal order[2].

Letters of thanks.

In such cases letters of thanks were issued at the close of the campaign[3], with a promise that such compliance should not be construed as a precedent.

Service by a quota.

For expeditions on which it was unnecessary to bring up the whole force of the tenants-in-chief, the king sometimes orders a definite quota

[1] Parl. Writs, i. 213.

[2] Above, p. 141. Still more urgent language is used in 1302; Parl. Writs, i. 366: 'mandamus in fide et homagio . . . quod sitis ad nos . . . cum toto servitio quod nobis debetis . . . et, ut fidelitatis vestrae constantia sibi famae laudem adaugeat, vos requirimus quatinus praeter servitium vestrum sic armatorum suffulti potentia pro communi praefati regni utilitate . . . veniatis.'

[3] Parl. Writs, i. 196: 'cum milites et alii de communitate comitatus Sallopiae curialitatem et subsidium de equis et armis et alio posse suo, non ratione alicujus servitii nobis ad praesens debiti, sed sponte et graciose . . . fecerint . . . concedimus . . . quod occasione hujusmodi curialitatis et subsidii hac vice nobis gratiose facti . . . nichil novi juris nobis vel heredibus nostris accrescere, nec eidem communitati aliquid decrescere possit,' &c.; cf. p. 252.

to be furnished by each, in proportion to his obligation; thus in 1234 Henry de Trubleville is ordered to attend 'te quinto militum[1],' that is, with four other knights, and Walter de Godarville 'te altero,' that is, with one. This plan was perhaps identical with the muster of a third or fourth part of the usual service, of which there are instances under Henry II and Richard[2]. We have already noticed the fact that the number of tenants who were specially summoned to the army was much larger than that of the barons so summoned to the council; and it is by no means improbable that the force so specially summoned constituted the largest part, if not the whole, of the available feudal army, many of the minor tenants being poor men, willing to serve under the greater lords, and certainly requiring the utmost pressure before they would undertake the expenses and other liabilities of knighthood.

Great number of tenants-in-chief.

From the statement contained in the writ of summons as to the purpose of the armament we gather a somewhat indistinct idea of the limits of feudal obligation. John, in 1205, summons his barons 'ad movendum inde cum corpore nostro et standum nobiscum ad minus per duas quadragesimas[3];' in 1213, 'ad eundum nobiscum[4];' and in 1215, 'ad transfretandum cum corpore nostro[5],' the destination being Gascony. Notwithstanding the refusal of the baronage to undertake service in Gascony as a duty of their tenure, Henry III continued his father's policy in this point, not only by summoning the tenants-in-chief to cross the seas with him, but in one instance, at least, by ordering them to join the Count of Brittany and to serve under his orders[6]. Edward I then, both in 1294 and 1297, had precedents for demanding foreign service from the barons, although the language in which he, at least in 1297, couched the request, showed that he had misgivings which were warranted by the result. This last case, however, opened a still wider question.

Extent of service required.

Foreign service demanded of the feudal force.

The second branch of the national force comprehended all those who were bound, not by homage but by allegiance, to

(2) Military service due as a matter of allegiance.

1 Lords' Report, App. pp. 6, 7.
2 Vol. i. pp. 589, 590.
3 Lords' Report, App. p. 1.
4 Lords' Report, App. p. 1.
5 Lords' Report, App. p. 2.
6 Lords' Report, App. pp. 5, 7.

attend the king in arms; in other words, the whole population capable of providing and wearing arms, who were embodied under the Assize of Arms, and in strict connexion with the shire administration. The measures taken for the efficiency of this force were very numerous. Henry III, in 1230 and 1252, issued stringent edicts for the purpose[1], and in 1285 Edward I still further improved the system by the statute of Winchester[2]. In these acts the maintenance of the 'jurati ad arma' is closely connected with the conservation of the peace, according to the idea that this force was primarily a weapon of defence, not of aggression. But as the Welsh and Scottish wars had in a great measure the character of defensive warfare, the service of the national militia, the qualified fighting men of the counties, was called into requisition; and in great emergencies Henry III and Edward I conceived themselves justified in using them as William Rufus had done, for foreign warfare. In 1255 Henry, in the general summons to the sheriffs for his expedition to Scotland, includes not only the tenants-in-chief, but other vavasours and knights who do not hold of the king in chief, and who are to attend 'as they love the king and their own honour, and as they wish to earn his grace and favour[3].' In this writ we have an early indication of the policy which tended, by the creation of a knightly class not necessarily composed of tenants-in-chief, to raise a counterpoise to the over-weight of feudal tenure in matters of military service. And we are thus enabled to explain the frequent orders for the distraint of knighthood as arising from something above and besides the mere desire of extorting money.

Assize of arms.

Foreign service demanded.

239. The distraint of knighthood was both in its origin and

[1] Royal Letters, i. 371; Select Charters, p. 371.

[2] Statutes, i. 96–98; Select Charters, p. 469.

[3] Foed. i. 326: 'Mandatum est singulis vicecomitibus Angliae, quod cum omni festinatione clamari faciant publice per totam balliam suam quod omnes illi qui de rege tenent in capite et servitium ei debent, quod, omni dilatione et occasione postpositis, veniant ad regem cum equis et toto posse suo, profecturi cum eo ad partes Scotiae, sicut ipsum regem et honorem suum necnon et terras et tenementa quae de rege tenent diligunt; et alios vavasores et milites qui de rege non tenent in capite, similiter veniant cum equis et armis, sicut ipsum regem et honorem suum diligunt, et gratiam et favorem regis perpetuum promereri voluerint.'

Distraint of knighthood.

in its effects a link between the two branches of the national force. The tenure of twenty librates of land by knight service properly involved the acceptance of knighthood; the Assize of Arms made the possession of arms obligatory on every one according to his wealth in land or chattels. Whoever possessed twenty librates of land, of whomsoever he held it or by whatsoever tenure, might on analogy be fairly required to undertake the responsibility of a knight. The measures for the enforcement of this duty began early in the reign of Henry III. In 1224 the king ordered the sheriffs to compel all laymen of full age who held a knight's fee or more, to get themselves knighted[1]: it may be doubted whether this applied to mesne tenants, for in 1234 the same order is given with reference to tenants-in-chief only[2]; but probably it was intended to be universal. The chroniclers under the year 1254 tell us that all who held land of ten or fifteen pounds annual value, were ordered to receive knighthood, but in this case there is possibly some confusion between the acceptance of knighthood and the provision of a full equipment[3]. In 1274 inquiry is made into the abuse, by the sheriffs and others, of the power of compelling knighthood[4]; in 1278 Edward imposes the obligation on all who possess the requisite estate, of whomsoever held, and whether in chivalry or not[5]; in 1285 owners of less than £100 per annum are excused[6]; in 1292 all holding £40 a year in fee are to be distrained[7]. In some

[1] Rot. Claus. ii. 69.

[2] Royal Letters, i. 456.

[3] 'Qui redditus (sc. uniuscujusque libere tenentis) si decem librarum constiterit, gladio cingatur militari et una cum magnatibus Angliae Londoniam citra clausum Paschae veniant prompti et parati cum dictis magnatibus transfretare;' Ann. Theokesb. p. 154. The summons however mentions only freeholders of £20 value, and does not specify knighthood; Select Charters, p. 376. In 1256, Matthew Paris and Bartholomew Cotton repeat the story 'ut quilibet qui haberet xv libratas terrae et supra cingulo militiae donaretur,' the latter adding 'vel per annum unam marcam auri regi numeraret;' M. Paris, v. 560, 589; B. Cotton, p. 136; Joh. Oxenedes, p. 187. The fines under Edward I varied in amount; Parl. Writs, i. 221.

[4] Foedera, i. 517.

[5] Select Charters, p. 456; Parl. Writs, i. 214, 219; Foed. i. 567; 'de quocunque teneant.'

[6] Foed. i. 653; Parl. Writs, i. 249.

[7] Foed. i. 758; Parl. Writs, i. 258.

cases the knighthood is waived and the military service alone demanded; thus in 1282 owners of £20 annual value are ordered to provide themselves with horses and arms, and to appear in the provincial councils at York and Northampton[1]: in 1297 the same class are called on for military service together with the barons[2]. There can be no doubt that this practice was one of the influences which blended the minor tenants-in-chief with the general body of the freeholders; possibly it led also to the development of the military spirit which in the following century sustained the extravagant designs of Edward III and was glorified under the name of chivalry.

Infantry force.

240. The barons, knights, and freeholders liable to knighthood, furnished the cavalry of Edward's armies, and were arranged for active service under bannerets, attended by a small number of knights and squires or *scutiferi*[3]. The less wealthy men of the shires and towns, sworn under the assize, furnished the infantry, the archers, the machinists, the carpenters, the miners, the coopers, the ditchers and other workmen[4]. Of these the men-at-arms, according to their substance, provided their own equipment, from the fully-armed owner of fifteen librates who appeared with his hauberk, helmet, sword, dagger, and horse, to the owner of less than forty shillingsworth of chattels, who could provide only a bow and arrows. These were under the regular inspection of the sheriffs and knights assigned to examine into their efficiency, and the force would, if assembled in arms, have included the whole adult male population. Such a levy was never even formally called for; it would have been quite unmanageable, would have robbed the land of its cultivators, and left the country undefended except at head-quarters. In 1205[5] and again in 1213[6], when John was in dread of invasion, he ordered that all men should on the rumour of the enemy's

Equipment of the ordinary men-at-arms.

Only a portion of this force ever actually employed.

[1] Parl. Writs, i. 10; Select Charters, p. 465.
[2] Parl. Writs, i. 285 sq.; Foedera, i. 864.
[3] The banneret received 3*s.*, the knight 2*s.*, and the squire 12*d.* a day, in 1300; Wardrobe Accounts, p. 195. This was in time of war; in peace the bannerets and knights received a fee of ten or five marks in lieu of wages; ib. p. 188.
[4] Copiatores, Parl. Writs, i. 252; fossatores, ibid.
[5] Rot. Pat. i. 55; Select Charters, p. 281.
[6] Foed. i. 110.

landing assemble to resist him, on pain of forfeiture and perpetual slavery. Henry III in 1220, in 1224, and again in 1267, called up the posse comitatus of the neighbouring counties only, for the sieges of Rockingham, Bedford, and Kenilworth[1]. In 1264, when Simon de Montfort found it necessary to make the utmost efforts to repel the invasion threatened by the queen, he called out a proportion only of this force; eight, six, or four men from each township armed at the discretion of the sheriff and provided with forty days' provision at the expense of the community that furnished them[2]. And this plan was followed in less pressing emergencies. Thus in 1231 the sheriff of Gloucestershire was ordered to send two hundred men with axes, furnished with forty days' provision at the expense of the men of the shire who were sworn to provide small arms, and at the same time to send to the king's camp all the carpenters of the county[3].

241. Under Edward I this arrangement was extended and developed by means of Commissions of Array. In 1282, on the 30th of July, he commissioned William le Butiller of Warrington to 'elect,' that is to press or pick a thousand men in Lancashire; on the 6th of December[4] writing from Rhuddlan, and at several other dates during the same winter, he informed the counties that he had commissioned certain of his servants to choose a fixed number of able-bodied men and to bring them to head-quarters to serve on foot: the commission for Nottingham and Derby fixes 300, that for Stafford and Salop 1000, that for Lancashire 200, that for Hereford and the Marches 2360. In 1294 the commissioners are not limited to fixed numbers[5]. In 1295 the counties of Hants, Dorset, and Wilts are ordered to provide 3000 archers and balistarii to man the fleet[6]; in 1297 large commissions are issued for the collection

Commissions of Array.

[1] Royal Letters, i. 56; Rot. Claus. i. 639; Foed. i. 467. In 1224 the posse comitatus of Devon was called up to watch or besiege Plympton castle; the knights of the county 'responderunt unanimiter se nec posse nec debere hujusmodi custodiam facere cum domini sui sint in exercitu vestro, quibus sua debent servitia.'

[2] Foed. i. 437.

[3] Foed. i. 200; Select Charters, p. 359.

[4] Parl. Writs, i. 228, 245 sq.

[5] Parl. Writs, i. 266.

[6] Parl. Writs, i. 270; at the same time Surrey and Sussex are ordered to

of Welshmen and men of the Marches to join in the expedition to Gascony[1]. Under Edward I the forces raised in this way were paid by the king; very large levies were thus made in 1297 and onwards to serve *ad vadia nostra*[2]. These and the county force generally were placed under the superintendence of a *capitaneus*[3] or *cheveteigne* in each shire, who must have been the prototype of the later lord-lieutenant. The abuse of the system, which threw the expense of additional arms and maintenance on the townships and counties, began under Edward II, although down to his last year his writs make arrangement for the payment of wages. The second statute of 1 Edward III, c. 5, was directed to the limitation of the power of compelling military service; and after a series of strong complaints by the commons, who were greatly aggrieved by the burden of maintaining the force so raised, it was enacted in 1349 that no man should be constrained to find men-at-arms, hobblers, or archers, other than those who held by such services, if it be not by the common assent and grant made in parliament. The maritime counties however even under Ed-

The king was pay-master of forces raised by these commissions.

Abuse of the system.

Restriction of commissions of array under Edward III.

find 4000, Essex and Herts 4000, Norfolk, Suffolk, Cambridge and Hants 8000, Kent 4000, Oxon and Berks 2000.

[1] Parl. Writs, i. 295, 296. Wales had furnished soldiers to Henry II, whose mercenaries are called by Ralph de Diceto, Marchiones, as well as Walenses; Opp. i. 387; ii. 55. In the commissions to raise a force in 1297 Edward instructs the commissioners to explain the business to the Welsh, 'en la plus amiable manere e la plus curteise que vous saverez;' a mild form certainly of impressment; ibid. 283.

[2] Parl. Writs, i. 224.

[3] See Parl. Writs, i. 193, 222, &c. These *capitanei* appear first in the Marches; in 1276 Roger Mortimer was made captain for Salop, Stafford, and Hereford, and William Beauchamp for Chester and Lancashire; and similar commissions were issued in 1282. In 1287 the earl of Gloucester was made 'capitaneus expeditionis regis in partibus de Brecknock;' Parl. Writs, i. 252; Edmund Mortimer and the earl of Hereford in Cardiganshire; ibid. p. 254. In 1296 Robert de la Ferete and William of Carlisle are named *capitanei et custodes pacis* for Cumberland, ibid. 278; in 1297, *capitanei munitionis* are appointed in Northumberland and Cumberland, ibid. 294; also 'capitanei custodiae partium Marchiae;' ibid. 301. At last in 1298 officers are generally appointed as 'Cheveteignes des gentz d'Armes;' William Latimer being named 'notre lieutenant e soverein cheveteine de vous e tutes les gentz de armes a cheval e a pie' for the northern counties, with a captain under him in each; ibid. p. 319. In 1315 Edward II allowed the Yorkshire and northern *lieges* to choose their own custodes et capitanei; ibid. II. i. 435.

ward I were liable for the charges of defending the coast, and found the wages of the coast guard.

Internal arrangement of the army.

242. The arrangement and classification of the last-mentioned force furnish a good illustration of the internal organisation of the army generally[1]. The coast guard of each county was under the command of a knight as 'major custos,' constable, or chief warden; under him was an 'eques supervisor' who managed the force of one, two, three, or more hundreds, with a 'vintenarius' and a 'decenarius' under him. The wages of the custos were two shillings a day, those of the supervisor sixpence, the two inferior officers each threepence, and each footman twopence. The general force of infantry and archers was arranged in bodies of a hundred, each under a mounted constable or *centenarius*, and sub-divided into twenties, each under a *vintenarius*: the constable had a shilling, the vintenarius fourpence, and the common soldier twopence a day[2]. The final arrangement of the men was the work of the king's constable, who claimed twopence in the pound on the wages of stipendiaries[3]. It would only be when assembled for local defence that the infantry could retain their local organisation.

Wages of infantry and archers.

Voluntary service.

The military action of the general population, who were not bound by tenure to serve in the field, sometimes wears the appearance of volunteer service, and as such is rewarded, like the extra service of the feudal tenantry, with the king's thanks. In 1277 Edward wrote to thank the county of Shropshire for their courtesy in furnishing aid to which they were not bound by tenure; and such cases were not uncommon on the border, where military zeal and skill were quickened by the instinct of self-preservation[4].

Employment of the whole force in 1297.

The great exigency of 1297 furnishes a complete illustration of the use of all these means of military defence and aggression: on the 5th of May[5] the king ordered all the freeholders of the kingdom possessing £20 a year in land, whether holding of the

[1] See Parl. Writs, i. 268, 272, 274 sq.; Foed. i. 826.
[2] Wardrobe Account, p. 241; Parl. Writs, II. i. 472. The payments varied; cf. p. 710.
[3] Foed. i. 615.
[4] Above, p. 292.
[5] Parl. Writs, i. 281.

king in chief or of other lords, to provide themselves with horse and arms to accompany him in defence of the kingdom whenever he should ask it. Ten days later[1] he called on the sheriffs to ask, require, and firmly enjoin upon the persons before described, to meet him at London prepared to cross the sea with him in person to the honour of God and themselves, for the salvation and common benefit of the realm: the same day he ordered all ecclesiastics and widows holding in chief to furnish their due service[2]; and further addressed to the earls and barons the letter of earnest request which furnished the marshal and constable with the ground of excuse when the crisis came. On the 24th of May he wrote to the sheriffs requiring a list of the freeholders and knights who were generally included in the summons of the 15th[3]. On the 16th of September Edward, the king's son, issued commissions for the selection in each county of knights and valetti, to be retained in his service during his father's absence, with a special view towards defence against the Scots[4]; on the 23rd of October commissions of array were issued for a force of 23,000 men, to be chosen in eleven northern and western counties, and 6400 more in Wales and Cheshire[5].

System of the navy.

243. The measures taken by Edward for the defence of the coast, which have been already mentioned, were a part of the system on which he laid the foundations of the later navy.

Growth of the fleet under John.

The attempt made successfully by John to create a fleet of mercenaries which, combined with the naval force furnished by the ports, would be a match for any other fleet in Europe, had not been renewed under Henry III. Probably the force of the ports was by itself sufficient to repel any fleet that Philip Augustus or Lewis could have mustered after the death of John.

Under Henry III.

Throughout the reign of Henry III, when ships were required, the necessary number were impressed by the sheriffs of the maritime counties or the barons of the Cinque Ports[6]. If they

[1] Parl. Writs, i. 282.
[2] Ibid. i. 281.
[3] Ibid. i. 285.
[4] Ibid. i. 299, 300.
[5] Ibid. i. 304.
[6] In 1207 the barons of the Cinque Ports were ordered to impress all ships; Foed. i. 96: and a like order is given by Edward in 1298; Parl.

were wanted for transport, the ports were summoned to furnish a proportion of proper size and strength. If it was desirable to take the offensive, the barons of the ports might be empowered to ravage the French coasts, and indemnify themselves with spoil; this was done by Henry III in 1242[1], and, if rumour is to be trusted, by Simon de Montfort in 1264[2]. The shores of England were never seriously threatened with invasion except in 1213, 1217, and 1264, and the invasion was prevented in the former years by the king's fleet, in the latter by the contrary winds assisting the efforts of Simon de Montfort. But in 1294 Edward saw the necessity of giving a more definite organisation to this the most natural means of defence. The piratic habits which the old system had produced in the seaport towns had led to a series of provincial quarrels which occasionally ended in a seafight; and they likewise imperilled the observance of treaties with foreign powers. The Cinque Ports went to war with the men of Yarmouth, or with the Flemings, with little regard to the king's peace or international obligations[3].

Edward organises the defence of the coast by the shipping.

It is uncertain whether the superintendence of naval affairs had been as yet in the hands of any permanent official; or whether the king, or the justiciar in his place, were not admiral as well as general in chief. In 1217 the victory which saved England from the last attempt of Lewis was won by the fleet nominally under the command of the justiciar, Hubert de Burgh, but Philip of Albini and John Marshall, to whom Henry's council had entrusted the guardianship of the coast, were the responsible commanders[4]. In 1264 Thomas de Multon and John de la Haye were appointed by Simon de Montfort 'custodes partium maritimarum,' with the charge of victualling and com-

Naval institutions.

Custodes partium maritimarum.

Writs, i. 308. In 1253, 300 great ships were pressed; M. Paris, v. 383. In less urgent circumstances a particular quota is asked for; ten ships are demanded of the ports of Norfolk and Suffolk, to convey the king's sister in 1236; Foed. i. 225: and eight ports provide ships carrying sixteen horses to convey the queen to France in 1254; ibid. 295. Philip the Fair got together a fleet by the same means; B. Cotton, p. 282.

[1] Foed. i. 246, 250; M. Paris, iv. 208, 209.

[2] Lib. de Antt. Legg. pp. 69, 73.

[3] See B. Cotton, 171, 174, 227; Royal Letters, ii. 244; Parl. Writs, i. 115.

[4] M. Paris, ii. 26.

manding the fleet[1]. In the earlier years of Edward I the officers of the Cinque Ports seem to have exercised the chief administrative power; and no attempt had yet been made to unite the defence of the coasts, the maintenance of a fleet of war or transport, and the general regulation of the shipping, under one department. In 1294 however, when the constitutional storm was rising, when the Welsh, the Scots, and the French were all threatening him, Edward instituted a permanent staff of officials. He appointed William Leyburne captain of all the portmen and mariners of the king's dominions, and under him John de Bottetourt warden of all from the Thames to Scotland[2]. For the manning of the fleet he issued orders to the sheriffs to collect the outlaws of their shires with the promise of wages and pardon[3]: besides these the chief captain was empowered to impress men, vessels, victuals, and arms, paying however reasonable prices[4]. It is not surprising that a force so raised signalised itself by a cruel devastation of Normandy in the following year: or that, whilst they were so employed, the French mariners, who had been brought together on the same plan, made a half-successful raid upon Dover, and shortly after threatened Winchelsea. It was in fear of such reprisals that the king instituted the system of coast guard already described, and agisted or rated the landowners of the maritime counties for its support[5]. In 1298 the orders for the superintendence of the fleet are given to Robert Burghersh as lieutenant-warden of the Cinque Ports, and John le Sauvage as lieutenant-captain of the mariners[6]. The negotiation of peace with France probably made further proceedings unnecessary for a time. In 1302 Robert Burghersh is still warden of the Cinque Ports and answerable for the service of fifty-seven ships

Admirals appointed.

Impressment.

Appointment of naval commanders;

[1] Foed. i. 447. See Selden, Mare Clausum; Opp. ii. 1327 sq.

[2] B. Cotton, p. 234. Walsingham (i. 47, and Rishanger, p. 143) gives these officers the title of Admiral, which was new in England, although common in Southern Europe, where it was derived from the Arabic Emir (Amyrail = Comes, Trokelowe, p. 30) and had been used for some centuries.

[3] B. Cotton, p. 235.

[4] B. Cotton, p. 237. Here again the Wardrobe Accounts afford abundant information.

[5] B. Cotton, p. 312.

[6] Parl. Writs, i. 308.

due from them[1]; in 1304 he with Robert le Sauvage and Peter of Dunwich has the charge of victualling the twenty ships furnished by the city of London[2]. In 1306 we find a further step taken; Gervas Alard appears as captain and admiral of the fleet of the ships of the Cinque Ports and all other ports from Dover to Cornwall[3]; and Edward Charles captain and admiral from the Thames to Berwick; a third officer of the same rank probably commanded on the coast of the Irish sea, and thus the maritime jurisdiction was arranged until the appointment of a single high admiral in 1360. The history of the jurisdiction of these officers is as yet obscure, both from the apocryphal character of all the early records of the Admiralty, and from the nature of their authority, which was the result of a tacit compromise between the king as sovereign and lord of the sea, entitled to demand for offence or defence the services of all his subjects, the privileged corporations of the sea-port towns with their peculiar customs and great local independence, and the private adventure of individuals, merchants, and mariners, whose proceedings seem to be scarcely one degree removed from piracy. Some organisation must have been created before Edward II could claim for himself and his predecessors the dominion of the sea, or his son collect and arm the navy with which he won the battle of Sluys. As a matter of administration however the navy was yet in its earliest stage.

Three admirals.

Obscurity of the history of the Admiralty.

Growth of the Navy.

In a general summary like the foregoing, it is impossible to do more than point out the chief departments in which Edward's energy and special sort of ability are prominent. Other points will arise as we pursue the history of his descendants. These, however, may help us to understand both the spirit and method which he displayed in definitely concentrating the national strength, and by which he turned to the advantage of the crown and realm, the interests of which he had made identical, the results of the victory that had been won through the struggles of the preceding century.

244. On a review of the circumstances of the great struggle which forms the history of England during the thirteenth century,

Attempt to adjust the

[1] Foedera, i. 936, 945. [2] Ib. i. 961, 962. [3] Ib. i. 990.

credit of constitutional progress.

and after realising as well as we can the constitution that emerges when the struggle is over, a question naturally arises as to the comparative desert of the actors, their responsibility for the issue, and the character of their motives. It is not easy to assign to the several combatants, or the several workers, their due share in the result. The king occupies the first place in the annals; the clergy appear best in the documentary evidence, for they could tell their own tale; the barons take the lead in action; the people are chiefly conspicuous in suffering. Yet we cannot suppose either that the well-proportioned and well-defined system which we find in existence at the death of Edward I grew up without a conscious and intelligent design on the part of its creators, or that the many plans which, under his father, had been tried and failed, failed merely because of the political weakness or accidental ill-success of their promoters. Comparing the history of the following ages with that of the past, we can scarcely doubt that Edward had a definite idea of government before his eyes, or that that idea was successful because it approved itself to the genius and grew out of the habits of the people. Edward saw, in fact, what the nation was capable of, and adapted his constitutional reforms to that capacity. But, although we may not refuse him the credit of design, it may still be questioned whether the design was altogether voluntary, whether it was not forced upon him by circumstances and developed by a series of successful experiments. And in the same way we may question whether the clerical and baronial policy was a class policy, the result of selfish personal designs, or a great, benevolent, statesmanlike plan, directed towards securing the greatness of the country and the happiness of the people.

Edward's action partly designed, partly the result of compulsion.

First, then, as to the king: and we may here state the conclusions before we recapitulate the premisses, which are in fact contained in the last two chapters. The result of the royal action upon the constitution during the thirteenth century was to some extent the work of design; to some extent an undesigned development of the material which the design attempted to mould and of the objects to which it was directed; to some extent the result of compulsion, such as forced the author of the design to carry out his own principles of design even when they told against his momentary policy and threatened to thwart his own object in the maintenance of his design. Each of these factors may be illustrated by a date; the design of a national parliament is perfected in 1295; the period of development is the period of the organic laws, from 1275 to 1290; the date of the compulsion is 1297. The complete result appears in the joint action of the parliaments of Lincoln in 1301 and of Carlisle in 1307.

The design. The design, as interpreted by the result, was the creation of a national parliament, composed of the three estates, organised on the principle of concentrating local agency and machinery in such a manner as to produce unity of national action, and thus to strengthen the hand of the king, who personified the nation.

Its character as the consummation of a growing policy. This design was perfected in 1295. It was not the result of compulsion, but the consummation of a growing policy. Edward did not call his parliament, as Philip the Fair called the States General, on the spur of a momentary necessity, or as a new machinery invented for the occasion and to be thrown aside when the occasion was over, but as a perfected organisation, the growth of which he had for twenty years been doing his best to guide. Granted that he had in view the strengthening of the royal power, it was the royal power in and through the united nation, not as against it, that he designed to strengthen. In the face of France, before the eyes of Christendom, for the prosecution of an occasional war with Philip, for the annexation of Wales and Scotland, or for the recovery of the Holy Sepulchre, a strong king must be the king of a united people. And a people, to be united, must possess a balanced constitution, in which no class possesses absolute and independent power, none is powerful enough to oppress without remedy. The necessary check on an aspiring priesthood and an aggressive baronage, the hope and support of a rising people, must be in a king too powerful to yield to any one class, not powerful enough to act in despite of all, and fully powerful only in

Edward's clear perception of the needs of the people.

the combined support of all. Up to the year 1295 Edward had these ends steadily in view; his laws were directed to the limitation of baronial pretensions, to the definition of ecclesiastical claims, to the remedy of popular wrongs and sufferings. The peculiar line of his reforms, the ever-perceptible intention of placing each member of the body politic in direct and immediate relation with the royal power, in justice, in war, and in taxation, seems to reach its fulfilment in the creation of the parliament of 1295, containing clergy and people by symmetrical representation, and a baronage limited and defined on a distinct system of summons.

Growth of his policy. But the design was not the ideal of a doctrinaire, or even of a philosopher. It was not imposed on an unwilling or unprepared people. It was the result of a growing policy exercised on a growing subject-matter. There is no reason to suppose that at the beginning of his reign Edward had conceived the design which he completed in 1295, or that in 1295 he contemplated the results that arose in 1297 and 1301. There was a development co-operating with the unfolding design. **National growth.** The nation, on whom and by whom he was working, had now become a consolidated people, aroused by the lessons of his father's reign to the intelligent appreciation of their own condition, and attached to their own laws and customs with a steady though not unreasoning affection, jealous of their privileges, their charters, their local customs, unwilling that the laws of England should be changed. The reign of Henry III, and the first twenty years of Edward, prove the increasing capacity for self-government, as well as the increased desire and understanding of the idea of self-government. The writs, the laws, the councils, the negotiations, of these years have been discussed in this and the preceding chapter: they prove that the nation was becoming capable and desirous of constitutional action; the capacity being proved by the success of the king's design in using it, the conscious desire by the constant aspiration for rights new or old.

Progressive plans. The adaptability of his people to the execution of his design may well have revealed to Edward the further steps towards the perfection of his ideal. The national strength was tried against Wales, before Scotland opened a scene of new triumphs, and the submission of Scotland encouraged the nation to resist Wales, Scotland, and France at once. In the same way the successful management of the councils of 1283 and 1294 led to the completion of the parliament in 1295. In each case the development of national action had led to the increase of the royal power. Edward could not but see that he had struck the very line that must henceforth guide the national life. The symmetrical constitution, and the authoritative promulgation of its principle, mark the point at which the national development and the fullest development of Edward's policy for his people met. He was successful because he built on the habits and wishes and strength of the nation, whose habits, wishes, and strength he had learned to interpret.

Power of resistance to royal power increased.

But the close union of 1295 was followed by the compulsion of 1297: out of the organic completeness of the constitution sprang the power of resistance, and out of the resistance the victory of the principles, which Edward might guide, but which he failed to coerce. With the former date then the period closes during which the royal design and the national development work in parallel lines or in combination; henceforth the progress, so far as it lies within the compass of the reign, is the resultant of two forces differing in direction, forces which under Edward's successors became stronger and more distinctly divergent in aim and character. It seems almost a profanation to compare the history of Edward I with that of John; yet the circumstances of 1297 bear a strong resemblance to those of 1215: if the proceedings of 1297 had been a fair example of Edward's general dealings with his people, our judgment of his whole life must have been reversed. They were, however, as we have seen, exceptional; the coincidence of war at home and abroad, the violent aggression of Boniface VIII, and the bold attempt at feudal independence, for which the earls found their opportunity in the king's difficulties, formed together an exigency, or a complication of exigencies, that suggested a practical dictatorship: that practical dictatorship Edward

Exceptional character of the crisis of 1297.

attempted to grasp; failing, he yielded gracefully, and kept the terms on which he yielded.

Edward inherited some sound institutions.

In an attempt to ascertain how far Edward really comprehended the constitutional material on which he was working, and formed his idea according to the capacity of that material, we can scarcely avoid crediting him with measures which he may have inherited, or which may have been the work of his ministers. Little as can be said for Henry III himself, there was much vitality and even administrative genius in the system of government during his reign. Local institutions flourished, although the central government languished under him. Some of his bad ministers were among the best lawyers of the age. Stephen Segrave, the successor of Hubert de Burgh, was regarded by Bracton as a judge of consummate authority; Robert Burnell and Walter de Merton, old servants of Henry, left names scarcely less remarkable in their own line of work than those of Grosseteste and Cantilupe. No doubt these men had much to do with Edward's early reforms. We can trace the removal of Burnell's influence in the more peremptory attitude which the king assumed after his death, and the statesmanship of the latter years of the reign is coloured by the faithful but less enlightened policy of Walter Langton. But, notwithstanding all this, the marks of Edward's constitutional policy are so distinct as to be accounted for only by his own continual intelligent supervision. If his policy had been only Burnell's, it must have changed when circumstances changed after Burnell's death, as that of Henry VIII changed when Cromwell succeeded Wolsey; but the removal of the minister only sharpens the edge of the king's zeal. His policy, whoever were his advisers, is uniform and progressive. That he was both well acquainted with the machinery of administration, and possessed of constructive ability, is shown by the constitutions which he drew up for Wales and Scotland: both bear the impress of his own hand. The statute of Wales not only shows a determination closely to assimilate that country to England in its institutions, to extend with no grudging hand the benefits of good government to the conquered province, but furnishes an admirable view of the

Edward's ministers.

Personal share of the king in administration.

local administration to which it was intended to adapt it. The constitution devised for Scotland is an original attempt at blending the Scottish national system as it then existed with the general administration of the empire, an attempt which in some points anticipates the scheme of the union which was completed four centuries later. A similar conclusion may be drawn from Edward's legislation: it is not the mere registration of unconnected amendments forced on by the improvement of legal knowledge, nor the innovating design of a man who imagines himself to have a genius for law, but an intelligent development of well-ascertained and accepted principles, timed and formed by a policy of general government. So far, certainly, Edward seems qualified to originate a policy of design.

Policy of genius or of expediency.

But was the design which he may be supposed to have originated the same as that which he finally carried out? Was the design which he actually carried out the result of an unimpeded constructive policy, or the resultant of forces which he could combine but could not thwart? Was it a policy of genius or of expediency? It may be fairly granted that the constitution, as it ultimately emerged, may not have been that which Edward would have chosen. Strong in will, self-reliant, confident of his own good-will towards his people, he would have no doubt preferred to retain in his own hands, and in those of his council, the work of legislation, and probably that of political deliberation, while his sense of justice would have left the ordinary voting of taxation to the parliament as he constructed it in 1295 out of the three estates. Such a constitution might have been more like that adopted by Philip the Fair in 1302 than like that embodied in the statement of parliament in 1322, or enunciated by Edward himself in his answer to the pope. The importance actually retained by the council in all the branches of administration proves that a simple parliamentary constitution would not have recommended itself to Edward's own mind. On the other hand, his policy was far more than one of expediency. It was diverted from its original line no doubt by unforeseen difficulties. Edward intended to be wholly and fully a king, and he struggled for power. For

How far Edward's policy was spontaneous.

twenty years he acted in the spirit of a supreme lawgiver, admitting only the council and the baronage to give their advice and consent. Then political troubles arose and financial troubles. The financial exigencies suggested rather than forced a new step, and the commons were called to parliament. In calling them he not only enunciated the great principle of national solidarity, but based the new measure on the most ancient local institutions. He did not choose the occasion, but he chose the best means of meeting the occasion consonant with the habits of the people. And when he had taken the step he did not retrace it. He regarded it as a part of a new compact that faith and honour forbad him to retract. And so on in the rest of his work. He kept his word and strengthened every part of the new fabric by his own adhesion to its plan, not only from the sense of honour, but because he felt that he had done the best thing. Thus his work was crowned with the success that patience, wisdom, and faith amply deserve, and his share in the result is that of the direction of national growth and adaptation of the means and design of government to the consolidation and conscious exercise of national strength. He saw what was best for his age and people; he led the way and kept faith.

Contrast with other kings of the time.

Thus he appears to great advantage even by the side of the great kings of his own century. Alfonso the Wise is a speculator and a dreamer by the side of his practical wisdom; Frederick II a powerful and enlightened self-seeker in contrast with Edward's laborious self-constraint for the good of his people. S. Lewis, who alone stands on his level as a patriot prince, falls below him in power and opportunity of greatness. Philip the Fair may be as great in constructive power, but he constructs only a fabric of absolutism. The legislation of

Alfonso.

Alfonso is the work of an innovator who, having laid hold on what seems absolute perfection of law, accepts it without examining how far it is fit for his people and finds it thrown

Frederick and Lewis.

back on his hands. Frederick legislates for the occasion; in Germany to balance opposing factions, in Italy to crush the liberty of his enemies or to raise the privileges of his friends: S. Lewis legislates for the love of his people and for the love of justice, but neither he nor his people see the way to reconcile freedom with authority. These contrasts are true if applied to the Mainzer-recht or the Constitutions of Peter de Vineis, the Establishments of S. Lewis or the Siete Partidas. Not one of these men both saw and did the best thing in the best way: and not one of them founded or consolidated a great power.

Distinctive policy of the baronial families.

In estimating the share of the baronage in the great work there is the difficulty, at the outset, of determining the amount of action which is to be ascribed to persons and parties. In Henry III's reign we compare, without being able to weigh, the distinct policies of the Marshalls, of the earls of Chester and Gloucester, Bohun and Bigod. Even the great earl of Leicester appears in different aspects at different parts of his career, and the great merit of his statesmanship is adaptative rather than originative: what he originates perishes, what he adapts survives. In the earlier period the younger Marshalls lead the opposition to the crown partly from personal fears and jealousies, but mainly on the principles of Runnymede; they perish however before the battle. The earl of Chester, the strongest bulwark of the royal power, is also its sharpest critic, and, when his own rights are infringed, its most independent opponent; his policy is not that of the nation but of the great feudal prince of past times. The earls of Gloucester, father and son, neither of them gifted with genius, try to play a part that genius only could make successful: like Chester, conscious of their feudal pretensions, like the Marshalls, ready to avail themselves of constitutional principles to thwart the king or to overthrow his favourites. In their eyes the constitutional struggle was a party contest: should the English baronage or the foreign courtiers direct the royal councils. There was no politic or patriotic zeal to create in the national parliament a properly-balanced counterpoise to royal power. Hence, when the favourites were banished, the Gloucesters took the king's side; when the foreigners returned, they were in opposition. They may have credit for an unenlightened but true idea that England was for the English, but on condition that the English should follow their lead. They have the credit

The earls of Gloucester.

of mediating between the English parties and taking care that neither entirely crushed the other. Further, it would seem absurd to ascribe to the Gloucesters any statesmanlike ability corresponding to their great position. The younger earl, the Gilbert of Edward I's reign, is bold and honest, but erratic and self-confident, interesting rather personally than politically.

Simon de Montfort.

To Leicester alone of the barons can any constructive genius be ascribed; and as we have seen, owing to the difficulty of determining where his uncontrolled action begins and ends, we cannot define his share in the successive schemes which he helped to sustain. That he possessed both constructive power and a true zeal for justice cannot be denied. That with all his popularity he understood the nation, or they him, is much more questionable: and hence his greatest work, the parliament of 1265, wants that direct relation to the national system which the constitution of 1295 possesses. In the aspect of a popular champion, the favourite of the people and the clergy, Simon loses sight of the balance of the constitution; an alien, he is the foe of aliens; owing his real importance to his English earldom, he all but banishes the baronage from his councils. He is the genius, the hero of romance, saved by his good faith and righteous zeal.

Bohun and Bigod.

Bohun and Bigod, the heroes of 1297, are but degenerate sons of mighty fathers; greater in their opportunity than in their patriotism; but their action testifies to a traditional alliance between barons and people, and recalls the resistance made with better reason and in better company by their forefathers to the tyranny of John. We cannot form a just and general judgment on the baronage without making these distinctions. On the whole, however, it must be granted that, while the mainspring of their opposition to Henry and Edward must often be sought in their own class interests, they betray no jealousy of popular liberty, they do not object to share with the commons the advantages that their resistance has gained, they aspire to lead rather than to drive the nation; they see, if they do not fully realise, the unity of the national interest whenever and wherever it is threatened by the crown.

Share of the clergy in the constitutional growth.

It is in the ranks of the clergy that we should naturally look, considering the great men of the time, for a moderate, constructive policy. The thirteenth century is the golden age of English churchmanship. The age that produced one Simon among the earls, produced among the bishops Stephen Langton, S. Edmund, Grosseteste, and the Cantilupes. The Charter of Runnymede was drawn under Langton's eye; Grosseteste was the friend and adviser of the constitutional opposition. Berksted, the episcopal member of the electoral triumvirate, was the pupil of S. Richard of Chichester: S. Edmund of Canterbury was the adviser who compelled the first banishment of the aliens; S. Thomas of Cantilupe, the last canonised Englishman, was the chancellor of the baronial regency.

How they are to be judged.

These men are not to be judged by a standard framed on the experience of ages that were then future. It is an easy and a false generalisation that tells us that their resistance to royal tyranny and the aid that they gave to constitutional growth were alike owing to their desire to erect a spiritual sovereignty and to depress all dominion that infringed upon their own liberty of tyrannising. The student of the history of the thirteenth century will not deny that the idea of a spiritual sovereignty was an accepted principle with both clerk and layman. The policy of the papal court had not yet reduced to an absurdity the claims put forth by Gregory VII and Innocent III. It was still regarded as an axiom that the priesthood which guided men to eternal life was a higher thing than the royalty which guided the helm of the temporal state: that the two swords were to help each other, and the greatest privilege of the state was to help the church. Religious liberty, as they understood it, consisted largely in clerical immunity. But granting that principle,—and until the following century, when the teaching of Ockham and the Minorites, the claims of Boniface VIII and their practical refutation, the quarrel of Lewis of Bavaria and John XXII, the schism in the papacy, and the teaching of Wycliffe, had opened the eyes of Christendom, that principle was accepted,—it is impossible not to see, and ungenerous to refuse to acknowledge, the debt due to

Grosseteste. men like Grosseteste. Grosseteste, the most learned, the most acute, the most holy man of his time, the most devoted to his spiritual work, the most trusted teacher and confidant of princes, was at the same time a most faithful servant of the Roman Church[1]. If he is to be judged by his letters, his leading principle was the defence of his flock. The forced intrusion of foreign priests, who had no sympathy with his people and knew neither their ways nor their language, leads him to resist king and pope alike; the depression of the priesthood, whether by the placing of clergymen in secular office, or by the impoverishment of ecclesiastical estates, or by the appointment of unqualified clerks to the cure of souls, is the destruction of religion among the laity. Taxes and tallages might be paid to Rome when the pope needed it, but the destruction of the flock by foreign pastors was not to be endured. It may seem strange that the eyes of Grosseteste were not opened by the proceedings of Innocent IV to the impossibility of reconciling the Roman claims with his own dearest principles: possibly the idea that Frederick II represented one of the heads of the Apocalyptic Beast, or the belief that he was an infidel plotting against Christendom, affected his mental perspicacity. Certainly as he grew older his attitude towards the pope became more hostile. But he had seen during a great part of his career the papal influence employed on the side of justice in the hands of Innocent III and Honorius III. Grosseteste's attitude towards the papacy however was not one of unintelligent submission. The words in which he expresses his idea of papal authority bear a singular resemblance to those in which Bracton maintains the idea of royal authority[2].

His characteristic views.

His attitude towards Rome.

His views of the papacy.

[1] Grosseteste's belief that the bishop receives his power from the pope and the pope receives his from Christ, a doctrine which in its consequences is fatal to the doctrine of episcopacy and the existence of national churches, is clear from his letter No. 127; ed. Luard, p. 369. But that he did not see to what it would lead, is clear from the whole tenour of his life.

[2] 'Praesidentes huic sedi sacratissimae principalissime inter mortales personam Christi induuntur, et ideo oportet quod in eis maxime sint et reluceant Christi opera, et nulla sint in eis Christi operibus contraria; et propter idem, sicut Domino Jesu Christo in omnibus est obediendum, sic et praesidentibus huic sedi sacratissimae, in quantum indutis Christum et

The pope could do no wrong, for if wrong were done by him he was not acting as pope. So the king as a minister of God can only do right; if he do wrong, he is acting not as a king but as a minister of the devil[1]. In each case the verbal quibble contains a virtual negation: and the writer admits without identifying a higher principle than authority. But it is not as a merely ecclesiastical politician that Grosseteste should be regarded. He was the confidential friend of Simon de Montfort, and the tutor of his children. He was more than once the spokesman of the constitutional party in parliament, and he was the patron of the friars who at the time represented learning and piety as well as the doctrines of civil independence in the Universities and country at large[2]. Bolder and more persevering than S. Edmund, he endured the same trials, but was a less conspicuous object of attack and gained greater success. Grosseteste represents a school of which S. Richard of Chichester and his disciple Berksted, with archbishops Kilwardby and Peckham, were representatives; a school, part of whose teaching descended through the Franciscans to Ockham and the Nominalists, and through them to Wycliffe. The baronial prelate was of another type. Walter of Cantilupe no doubt

His political position.

The baronial prelate.

in quantum vere praesidentibus, in omnibus est obtemperandum; sin autem quis eorum, quod absit, superinduat amictum cognationis et carnis aut mundi aut alicujus alterius praeterquam Christi, et ex hujusmodi amore quicquam Christi praeceptis et voluntati contrarium, obtemperans ei in hujusmodi manifeste se separat a Christo et a corpore ejus quod est ecclesia, et a praesidente huic sedi in quantum induto personam Christi et in tantum vere praesidente; et cum communiter in hujusmodi obtemperatur, vera et perfecta advenit discessio, et in januis est revelatio filii perditionis' (2 Thess. ii. 3); Grosseteste's sermon before the Council of Lyons; Brown's Fasciculus, ii. 256.

[1] 'Exercere igitur debet rex potestatem juris, sicut Dei vicarius et minister in terra, quia illa potestas solius Dei est, potestas autem injuriae diaboli et non Dei, et cujus horum opera fecerit rex, ejus minister est cujus opera fecerit. Igitur dum facit justitiam vicarius est Dei aeterni, minister autem diaboli dum declinet ad injuriam;' Bracton, Lib. iii. de Actionibus, c. 9.

[2] The sentiments not of the people but of the Universities, and incidentally of the Franciscans also, are exemplified in the long Latin poem printed in Wright's Political Songs, pp. 72–121. I have not quoted this curious document as an illustration of the belief of the people, who could not have read it or understood it; but it was clearly a manifesto, amongst themselves, of the men whose preaching guided the people.

had his sympathies with the English baronage as well as with the clergy and was as hostile to the alien favourites of the court as to the alien nominees of Rome. A man like Thomas of Cantilupe united in a strong degree the leading principles of both schools; he was a saint like Edmund, a politician like his uncle, and a bishop like Grosseteste. Another class, the ministerial prelate, such as was bishop Raleigh of Winchester, was forced into opposition to the crown rather by his personal ambitions or personal experiences than by high principle: the intrusion of the foreigner into the court and council was to him not merely the introduction of foreign or lawless procedure, but the exclusion from the rewards that faithful service had merited; and his feeling, as that of Becket had been, was composed, to a large extent, of a sense of injury amounting to vindictiveness. Yet even such men contributed to the cause of freedom, if it were only by the legal skill, the love of system, and ability for organisation, which they infused into the party to which they adhered. The opposition of the English clergy to the illegal aggressions of the crown in his father's reign taught Edward I a great lesson of policy. He at all events contrived to secure the services of the best of the prelates on the side of his government, and chose for his confidential servants men who were fit to be rewarded with high spiritual preferment. The career of Walter de Merton proves this: another of his great ministers, bishop William of March, was in popular esteem a candidate for canonisation and a faithful prime minister of the crown. Walter Langton, the minister of his later years, earned the gratitude of the nation by his faithful attempts to keep the prince of Wales in obedience to his father, and to prevent him taking the line which finally destroyed him. Of archbishop Winchelsey we have already seen reason to believe that he was an exceptional man, in a position the exceptional character of which must affect our judgments of both himself and the king. If the necessities of the case excuse the one, they excuse the other. He also was a man of learning, industry, and piety, and, if he did not play the part of a patriot as well as Stephen Langton had done, it

The secular prelate.

Opposition of the clergy to Edward I.

Winchelsey.

must be remembered that he had Edward and not John for his opponent, Boniface and not Innocent for his pope. But on the whole perhaps the feeling of the English clergy in the great struggle should be estimated rather by the behaviour of the mass of the body than by the character of their leaders. The remonstrances of the diocesan and provincial councils are more outspoken than the letters of the bishops, and the faithfulness of the body of the clergy to the principles of freedom is more distinctly conspicuous than that of the episcopal politicians: the growing life of the Universities, which towards the end of the century were casting off the rule of the mendicant orders and influencing every class of the clergy both regular and secular, tended to the same end; and, although, in tracing the history of the following century, we shall have in many respects to acknowledge decline and retrogression, we cannot but see that in the quarrels between the crown and the papacy, and between the nation and the crown, the clergy for the most part took the right side. Archbishops Stratford and Arundel scarcely ever claim entire sympathy, but they gained no small advantages to the nation, and few kings had better ministers or more honest advisers than William of Wykeham.

The body of the clergy.

They take the side of freedom.

If we ask, lastly, what was the share of the people, of the commons, of their leading members in town and shire, our review of the history furnishes a distinct if not very circumstantial answer. The action of the people is to some extent traceable in the acts of the popular leader. Simon de Montfort possessed the confidence of the commons: the knightly body threw itself into the arms of Edward in 1259 when it was necessary to counteract the oligarchic policy of the barons: the Londoners, the men of the Cinque Ports, the citizens of the great towns, the Universities under the guidance of the friars, were consistently on the side of liberty. But history has preserved no great names or programmes of great design proceeding from the third estate. Sir Robert Thwenge the leader of the anti-Roman league in 1232, and Thomas son of Thomas who led the plebeians of London against the magnates, scarcely

Sympathy of the people with the reforms.

No great names preserved.

rise beyond the reputation of local politicians. Brighter names, like that of Richard Sward, the follower of Richard Marshall, are eclipsed by the brilliance of their leaders. It was well that the barons and the bishops should furnish the schemes of reform, and most fortunate that barons and bishops were found to furnish such schemes as the people could safely accept. The jealousy of class privilege was avoided, and personal influences helped to promote a general sympathy. The real share of the commons in the reformed and remodelled constitution is proved by the success of its working, by the growth of the third estate into power and capacity for political action through the discipline of the parliamentary system; and the growth of the parliamentary system itself is due to the faithful adhesion and the growing intelligence of the third estate.

Concluding award.

Let then the honour be given where it is due. If the result is a compromise, it is one made between parties which by honesty and patriotism are entitled to make with one another terms which do not give to each all that he might ask; and justly so, for the subjects on which the compromise turns, the relations of Church and State, land and commerce, tenure and citizenship, homage and allegiance, social freedom and civil obligation, are matters on which different ages and different nations have differed in theory, and on which even statesmen and philosophers have failed to come to a general conclusion alike applicable to all ages and nations as the ideal of good government.

CHAPTER XVI.

EDWARD II, EDWARD III, AND RICHARD II.

245. BETWEEN the despotism of the Plantagenets and the despotism of the Tudors lies a period of three eventful centuries. The first of these we have now traversed; we have traced the course of the struggle between the crown and the nation, as represented by its leaders in parliament, which runs on through the thirteenth century, and the growth of the parliamentary constitution into theoretical completeness under Edward I. Another century lies before us, as full of incident and interest as the last, although the incident is of a different sort, and the men around whom the interest gathers are of very different stature and dissimilar aims. We pass from the age of heroism to the age of chivalry, from a century ennobled by devotion and self-sacrifice to one in which the gloss of superficial refinement fails to hide the reality of heartless selfishness and moral degradation—an age of luxury and cruelty. This age has its struggles, but they are contests of personal and family faction, not of great causes; it has its great constitutional results, but they seem to emerge from a confused mass of unconscious agencies

Relation of the thirteenth century to the fourteenth.

Change in the character of the struggle of the Constitution.

rather than from the direct action of great lawgivers or from the victory of acknowledged principles. It has however its place in the history of the Constitution; for the variety and the variations of the transient struggles serve to develop and exercise the strength of the permanent mechanism of the system; and the result is sufficiently distinct to show which way the balance of the political forces, working in and through that mechanism, will ultimately incline. It is a period of private and political faction, of foreign wars, of treason laws and judicial murders, of social rebellion, of religious division, and it ends with a revolution which seems to be only the determination of one bloody quarrel and the beginning of another.

Incidental effects.

But this revolution marks the growth of the permanent institutions. It is not in itself a victory of constitutional life, but it places on the throne a dynasty which reigns by a parliamentary title, and which ceases to reign when it has lost the confidence of the commons. The constitutional result of the three reigns that fill the fourteenth century is the growth of the House of Commons into its full share of political power; the recognition of its full right as the representative of the mass and body of the nation, and the vindication of its claim to exercise the powers which in the preceding century had been possessed by the baronage only. The barons of the thirteenth century had drawn the outline of the system by which parliament was to limit the autocracy of the king. Edward I had made his parliament the concentration of the three estates of his people; under Edward II, Edward III, and Richard II, the third estate claimed and won its place as the foremost of the three. The clergy had contented themselves with their great spiritual position, and had withdrawn from parliament; the barons were no longer feudal potentates with class interests and exclusive privileges that set them apart from king and commons alike. The legal reforms of Edward I and the family divisions which originated under Edward III changed the baronial attitude in more ways than one: in the constitutional struggle the great lords were content to act as leaders and allies of the commons or as followers of the court; in the dynastic struggles they ranged

Constitutional result.

Growth of the Commons.

Changed attitude of clergy and baronage.

Parties among the barons.

themselves on the side of the family to which they were attached by traditional or territorial ties; for the royal policy had placed the several branches of the divided house at the head of the great territorial parties which adopted and discarded constitutional principles as they chose.

Growth of the constitution through them and in spite of them.

In this aspect the fourteenth century anticipates some part of the history of the fifteenth; the party of change is only accidentally and occasionally the party of progress; constitutional truths are upheld now by one, now by another, of the dynastic factions; Edward II defines the right of parliament as against the aggressive Ordinances, and the party of the Red Rose asserts constitutional law as opposed to the indefeasible right of the legitimate heir, even when the cause of national growth seems to be involved in the success of the White Rose. Both sides look to the commons for help, and, while they employ the commons for their own ends, gradually place the decision of all great questions irrevocably in their hands. The dynastic factions may be able alternately to influence the elections, to make the house of commons now royalist now reforming, one year Yorkist and one year Lancastrian, but each change helps to register the stages of increasing power. The commons have now gained a consolidation, a permanence and a coherence which the baronage no longer possesses. The constitution of the house of commons, like that of the church, is independent of the divisions and contests that vary the surface of its history. A battle which destroys half the baronage takes away half the power of the house of lords: the house of commons is liable to no such collapse. But the battle that destroys half the baronage leaves the other half not so much victorious, as dependent on the support of the commons. The possession of power rests ultimately with that estate which by its constitution is least dependent on personal accident and change. It gains not so much because the party which asserts its right triumphs over that which denies it, as because it stands to some extent outside the circle of the factions whose contests it witnesses and between which it arbitrates. All that is won by the parliamentary opposition to the crown is won for the commons; what the

Permanent influence of the Commons.

Continuous victories of the Commons.

baronage loses by the victory of the crown over one or other of its parties is lost to the baronage alone. The whole period witnesses no great struggle between the lords and the commons, or the result might have been different. There was a point at which the humiliation of the baronage was to end in such an exaltation of the royal power as left the other two estates powerless; and with the baronage fell or seemed to fall the power of parliament. But the commons had a vitality which subsisted even when the church, deprived of the support of united Christendom, lay at the feet of Henry VIII, and a new baronage had to be created out of the ruins of the two elder estates. And when under the Stewarts the time came for the maturity of national organisation to stand face to face with the senility of medieval royalty, the contest was decided as all previous history pointed the way and subsequent history justified. But we do not aspire to lead on our narrative to so distant a consummation, and the discussion for the present lies within much narrower limits.

Vitality of the Commons.

The House of Commons gains definiteness and consolidation.

246. It was natural that a system thus gaining in power and capacity should gain in definiteness of organisation. The growth of the house of commons, as well as of the parliamentary machinery generally, during the fourteenth century, is marked by increased clearness of detail. With its proceedings more carefully watched, and more jealously recorded, more conscious of the importance of order, rule, and precedent, it begins to possess what may be called a literature of its own, and its history has no longer to be gleaned from the incidental notices of writers whose eyes were fixed on other matters of interest, or from documents that presume rather than furnish a knowledge of the processes from which they result. The vast body of Parliamentary Writs affords from henceforth a sufficient account of the personal and constitutional composition of each parliament: the Rolls of Parliament preserve a detailed journal of the proceedings, from which both the mode and the matter of business can be elucidated, and the increasing bulk of the statute-book gives the permanent result.

247. The transition from the reign of Edward I to that of

Edward II is somewhat abrupt; we find ourselves at one step in a new era, with new men, new manners, and new ideas. The greatness of the father's character gathers, so long as he lives, all interest around him personally, and we scarcely see that almost all that belongs to his own age has passed away before his death. When he is gone we feel that we are out of the atmosphere which had been breathed by Stephen Langton and Simon de Montfort. The men are of meaner moral stature. The very patriots work for lower objects: the baronial opposition is that of a faction rather than of an independent estate: the ecclesiastical champions aim at gaining class privilege and class isolation, not at securing their due share in the work of the nation: the grievances of the people are the result of dishonest administration, chicanery, and petty malversation, not of bold and open attempts at tyranny; the royal favourites are no more the great lords of Christendom, the would-be rivals of emperor and king, but the upstart darlings of an infatuated prince; and the hostility they excite arises rather from jealousy of their sudden acquisition of wealth and power than from such fears as their predecessors had inspired, that they would change the laws and constitution of the realm.

Change of men and principles on the accession of Edward II.

Some part of the change is owing to the influx of foreign manners. Very much of the peculiarities of national history is lost; and the growing influence of France by affinity or example becomes at once apparent in manners, morals, language and political thought. This influence is not new, but it comes into prominence as the older national spirit becomes weaker. S. Lewis had impressed his mark on Edward I himself, and the growth of education during the thirteenth century had taken a distinctly French form. Under Henry III French had become the language of our written laws; under Edward I it appears as the language of the courts of law. The analogies, already traced, between the constitutional machinery of Edward and that of Philip the Fair, testify to, at least, a momentary approximation between the two national systems. The idea of securing the power of the crown by vesting the great fiefs as appanages in the hands of the younger branches of the royal

Influx of foreign manners.

French language and customs.

Approximation of French and English history.

family, a plan which had been adopted in France by Lewis IX, must have been either borrowed from him by Henry III and Edward I, or in both countries suggested by the same circumstances,—the vanishing of feudal ideas and the determination that they should not revive; and in both countries the plan has the same result: it turns what had been local, territorial, traditional, jealousies into internecine struggles between near kinsmen; enmities that will not be appeased by humiliation, rivalries that cease only when the rivals themselves are extinct. French manners too, the elegancies with the corruptions of a more continuous old culture, luxury in dress and diet, vice no longer made repulsive by grossness, but toned down by superficial refinement and decked in the tinsel of false chivalry,—all these were probably working under Edward I, though he was free from the least imputation of them; they come into prominence and historical importance under his son and reach a climax in the next generation.

The system of Edward I was not likely to suit a bad king.

But there was a deeper source of danger. Edward I had systematised and defined the several functions of a form of constitution that worked well, although not without difficulties, under his own hand. His system was the system of a king who felt himself at one with the nation he governed, who was content to act as the head and hand of the national body. In sharing political power with his people, he gave to the parliament more than was consistent with a royal despotism, he retained in his own hands more than was consistent with the theory of limited monarchy. He was willing to have no interest apart from his people, but he would not be less than every inch a king. The share of power which he gave was given to be used in concert with him; the share that he retained was retained that he might control the aims and exertions of the national strength. There was what is called, in modern phrase, solidarity between him and his people. He had not calculated on the succession of a race that would maintain a separate interest, apart from or opposed to that of the nation. Until a few months before his death, he does not seem to have realised the danger of leaving the fortunes of the people he had loved at the mercy of a son, whose character he had reason to mistrust, and whose ability for government he had never found time to train.

Around Edward II, who was utterly incapable of recognising the idea of kingship, and Edward III, who realised that idea only so far as it could be made subservient to his personal ambition, there grew up a body of influences and interests centering in the king and his family, not always swayed by the same ideas, but consistently devoted to personal aims and employing personal agencies to the furtherance of political objects, which in turn were made to conduce to personal aggrandisement. This body of influences, the court or courtiers of the later Plantagenet kings, was by its very nature opposed to the baronage, which, however indebted to royal favour for its original character and constitutional recognition, took its stand on something far higher and nobler than royal favouritism. Scarcely less opposed was it to the administrative body of the king's constitutional advisers, who, although in theory the king's servants, had under Edward I become so thoroughly incorporated with the national system, and so thoroughly bound by the obligations of honour and conscience to the national interest, that they were already the ministers of the nation, rather than of the court or even of the king. It is to the action of the court that we must attribute the extravagance, the dishonesty, the immorality, private, social, and political, of the period; it is to the antagonism between the court and the administration, or in modern language the court and the cabinet, that many of the constitutional quarrels of the century are owing; it is to the unpopularity of the court that the social as distinct from the constitutional disturbances are chiefly due, and to the selfish isolation of the court that much of the national misery and no little of the national discontent are to be traced. A body of courtiers, greedy of wealth, greedy of land and titles, careless of the royal reputation and national credit, constantly working to obtain office for the heads of one or other of its factions, using office for the enrichment of its own members, contained in itself all the germs of future

Growth of a court party.

It is hostile to the baronage,

and to the administration.

It is the origin of the political irritation of the period.

It is in rivalry with all the more permanent elements.

trouble. In rivalry with the baronage which collectively looked upon the courtiers as deserters from its own body, although the barons individually or the several factions among them were ready enough to play the part in their turn; in rivalry with the clergy whose political power they begrudged and whose religious influence they uniformly thwarted; in rivalry with the ministry which, if it were composed of honest men, was in hostility to the court as a whole, or, if it were itself the creation of one half of the court, was in hostility to the other; the court furnished the king with his favourites and flatterers, the worst of his traitors, the most hateful, the most necessary, supporters and servants of his prerogative [1].

General existence of the evil.

Such surroundings of royalty are not, it is true, peculiar to any one age or country: the courtiers of the Conqueror and his sons, of Henry II, of John and Henry III; the *curiales* of whom the English chroniclers of the twelfth century complain so bitterly, and whose follies are so wittily exposed by the satirists of that and the next age, were a distinct social feature of each reign, varying very much as they reflected the character of the reigning king.

How it comes into the foreground.

It is not until the relations of king and nation have become settled and defined that the mischievous influences of the court begin to have substantive existence: when the king can no longer be a despot, when the nation can no longer be regarded as existing for the despot's pleasure, when the jealousy inherent in limited power leads the king to trust to personal friends rather than to constitutional advisers, to rely on his prerogative rather than on his constitutional right, to strain every colourable claim, to disclaim every questionable responsibility,—then it is that the ministers of his pleasures, the companions or candidates for companionship in

[1] The courtiers were the great promoters of the feud between Edward II and the earl of Lancaster :—'aulicis, quos idem comes meritis exigentibus exosos habuit, id jugiter procurantibus;' Cont. Trivet, p. 23. 'Videant amodo,' says the Monk of Malmesbury on the fall of Gaveston, 'curiales Anglici ne de regio favore confisi barones despiciant;' ed. Hearne, p. 124: 'tota iniquitas originaliter exiit a curia;' ibid. p. 171. (Chron. Edw. I. II., ii. 180, 223.) So too in 1340 and 1376; and throughout the reign of Richard II.

his follies, the flatterers of his omnipotence, become a baneful power in the state; and not less hateful than baneful, because their irresponsible position and the splendid obscurity in which they move prevent their being brought to a reckoning. It is only when the king's constitutional advisers have become an integral part of the national system, that his unconstitutional advisers, their rivals, detractors and supplanters, become a power in the state. A good and great king alone can rise superior to such influences. A king of weak will, one who has been cradled and nursed among them, a stay-at-home who has not seen the ways of other nations, a pleasure-loving king, even a strong king who is not at one with his people, must certainly in the end, even if it be with shame and remorse, acquiesce in the system in which he lives.

Its strength increases as the constitutional machinery strengthens.

248. The transitionary character of the period appears most distinctly when we look at the successor of the great Edward. Edward II is not so much out of accord with his age as might be inferred from a hasty glance at his history and fate. He is not without some share of the chivalrous qualities that are impersonated in his son. He has the instinctive courage of his house, although he is neither an accomplished knight nor a great commander[1]. But he has no high aims, no policy beyond

Transition from Edward I to Edward II.

[1] 'O si armorum usibus se exercitaret, regis Ricardi probitatem praecederet. Hoc enim deposcit materia habilis, cum statura longus sit et fortis viribus, formosus homo decora facie. Sed quid moror ipsum describere? Si tantum dedisset armis operam quantam impendidit circa rem rusticam, multum excellens fuisset Anglia, nomen ejus sonuisset in terra;' Mon. Malmesb. p. 136: Chron. Edw. I. II., ii. 192. Knighton calls him 'vir elegans corpore, viribus praestans, sed moribus, si vulgo creditur, plurimum inconstans. Nam, parvipenso procerum contubernio, adhaesit scurris, cantoribus, tragoedis, aurigis, fossoribus, remigibus, navigiis et ceteris artis mechanicae officiis; potibus indulgens; secreta facile prodens, astantes ex levi causa percutiens, magis alienum quam proprium consilium sequens; in dando prodigus, in convivando splendidus, ore promptus, opere varius;' c. 2532. His love of mechanical employments is also mentioned in the Chronicle of Lanercost, p. 236: 'Domino Edwardo seniori in nulla probitate similis videbatur. Dederat enim se in privato ab adolescentia sua arti remigandi et bigam ducendi, foveas faciendi et domos cooperiendi, ut communiter dicebatur; arti etiam fabrili de nocte cum suis sodalibus operando, et aliis artibus mechanicis, quibusdam etiam vanitatibus et levitatibus aliis in quibus filium regis non decuit occupari.' Edward's taste for theatrical entertainments is remarked on. Archbishop Reynolds, as a young man, 'in ludis theatralibus principatum tenuit et per hoc regis

Character of Edward II and his reign, 1307–1326.

the cunning of unscrupulous selfishness. He has no kingly pride or sense of duty, no industry or shame or piety. He is the first king since the Conquest who was not a man of business, well acquainted with the routine of government; he makes amusement the employment of his life; his tastes at the best are those of the athlete and the artisan; vulgar pomp, heartless extravagance, lavish improvidence, selfish indolence make him a fit centre of an intriguing court. He does no good to any one: he bestows his favours in such a way as to bring his favourites to destruction, and sows enmities broadcast by insult or imprudent neglect. His reign is a tragedy, but one that lacks in its true form the element of pity: for there is nothing in Edward, miserable as his fate is, that invites or deserves sympathy. He is often described as worthless. He does little harm intentionally except by acts of vengeance that wear the garb of justice. His faults are quite as much negative as positive: his character is not so much vicious as devoid of virtue. He stands in contrast with both Henry III and Richard II: he does not bend to the storm like the former, or attempt to control it like the latter; he has neither the pliancy of the one nor the enterprise of the other. History does not condemn him because he failed to sustain the part which his father had played, for the alternation of strong and weak, good and bad, kings is too common a phenomenon to carry with it so heavy a sentence: but he deliberately defied his father's counsels, and disregarded his example. If his faults had proceeded from deficient or bad training[1], his reign would have been the

favorem obtinuit;' M. Malmesb. p. 142; (Chron. Edw. ii. 197.) That he was a devoted hunter and breeder of horses and trainer of dogs, is clear from his letters; see the following note. And this is probably the 'res rustica' to which he devoted himself. He writes to the archbishop of Canterbury for stallions, to the abbot of Shrewsbury for a fiddler, and to Walter Reynolds, then keeper of his wardrobe, for trumpets for his little players; a curious illustration of the passage just quoted.

[1] In one instance, probably connected with the quarrel with Langton about Gaveston, we find the king severely punishing his son, and making him an example to the court: 'Quae quidem (viz. contemptus et inobedientia) tam ministris ipsius domini regis quam sibi ipsi aut curiae suae facta, ipsi regi valde sunt odiosa, et hoc expresse nuper apparuit;—idem dominus rex filium suum primogenitum et carissimum Edwardum principem

greatest slur on his father's statesmanship; but it is difficult to trace in his career any natural ability or goodness. It is certain that from the very beginning of his reign he was the victim of unrelenting hostility, and that during the whole of it he did nothing to prove that he was worthy of better treatment [1]. Nor is it true that he paid in any way the penalty of his father's sins, that he fell under the enmities that his father had provoked, or under the tide of influences that his father was strong enough to stem. He voluntarily threw away his advantages, and gave to his enemies the opportunities that they were ready to take. His position was of his own making; his fate, hard and undeserved as it was, was the direct result of his own faults and follies.

Edward was not the victim of his father's policy.

He was his own worst enemy.

249. Within a few days of his father's death Edward II was recognised as king. At Carlisle, on the 20th of July, he received the homage and fealty of the English magnates [2], and at Dumfries a few days later that of the Scots. The form in which his peace was proclaimed announced that by descent of heritage he was already king [3]; the years of his reign were computed from

He succeeds.

Proclaims his peace, July, 1307.

Walliae, eo quod quaedam verba grossa et acerba cuidam ministro suo dixerat, ab hospitio suo fere per dimidium anni amovit, nec ipsum filium suum in conspectu suo venire permisit, quousque dicto ministro de praedicta transgressione satisfecerat:' Abbreviatio Placitorum, annis 33, 34 Edw. I, p. 257. That Edward I attempted to train him for a life of business is clear from the great roll, still extant, which contains his letters during the thirty-third year of his father's reign. See the 9th report of the Deputy Keeper of the Records, App. ii. p. 246. In one of these he speaks of his father's severity, and begs to be allowed to have Gilbert of Clare and Perot de Gaveston to cheer him in his solitude (Aug. 4, 1305); p. 248.

[1] It has been thought that Edward showed much filial duty in paying his father's debts to the amount of £118,000, and that possibly the economy which he attempted to practise may have created some of the enmities under which he perished. I do not think that Edward's economies were at any period of his reign voluntary, or that the payment of his father's debts was more than the ordinary mechanism of the government would as a matter of course provide for. See Mr. Bond's article on Edward's financial operations in vol. 28 of the Archæologia. That he was a clever man with a profound design of making himself absolute, as some other writers have imagined, seems to be a mere paradox. I have endeavoured to look at the reign as it appears in contemporary records and in its results, rather than as an exemplification of royal character.

[2] Ann. Lanercost, p. 209.

[3] 'Come le tres noble prince, sire Edward, qui estoit n'adgueres roi d'Engleterre, soit a Dieu comande, e nostre seignur sire Edward, son fiuz et son heir, soit ja roi d'Engleterre par descente de heritage,' &c.; Parl.

the day following his father's death; and, as soon as he had received the great seal from his father's chancellor, he began to exercise without further ceremony all the rights of sovereignty. As king he summoned, on the 26th of August, the Three Estates to meet in full session at Northampton on the 13th of October, there to deliberate on the burial of his father and on his own marriage and coronation [1]. The assembly granted an aid for these purposes, the clergy giving a fifteenth of both spirituals and temporals according to the taxation of pope Nicolas, and the towns and the ancient demesne a fifteenth, the magnates and the counties a twentieth, of moveables [2]. From Northampton he went on to Westminster, where he buried his father on the 27th of October; and thence, after Christmas, to Dover on his way to France. At Dover, on January 18, he issued writs fixing the 18th of February for the coronation, and inviting the magnates to attend; at the same time he ordered the sheriffs to send up from the towns and cities such persons as might seem fit to be witnesses of the ceremony [3]. On the 25th of January, 1308, at Boulogne, he married Isabella, daughter of Philip the Fair, having the day before done homage to her father for the provinces of Aquitaine and Ponthieu. The coronation took place on the 25th of February, a week later than the day fixed; the bishop of Winchester performed the ceremonies of anointing and crowning, as deputy for Winchelsey, for whose restoration Edward had already applied to the Pope [4].

Parliament at Northampton, Oct. 13, 1307.

Grant of money, Oct. 1307.

His marriage, Jan. 1308,

and coronation, Feb. 1308.

Writs, II. ii. 3; Foed. ii. 1. 'Successit . . . non tam jure hereditario quam unanimi assensu procerum et magnatum;' Walsingham, i. 119. Archbishop Sudbury spoke of Richard II as succeeding, 'nemye par election ne par autre tielle collaterale voie, einz par droite succession de heritage:' Rot. Parl. iii. 3.

[1] Parl. Writs, II. i. 1. There were three subjects of discussion, the burial, the aid, and the question of the currency of the late king's coinage, which was enforced under penalties; Cont. Trivet, p. 2: Parl. Writs, II. ii. 8. The proclamation was repeated in 1309; Foed. ii. 84; and 1310, p. 114.

[2] Parl. Writs, II. i. 14, 15; Rot. Parl. i. 442; Wals. i. 120.

[3] Parl. Writs, II. i. p. 17. The invitation was accepted; 'burgenses singularum civitatum aderant;' Mon. Malmesb. (ed. Hearne), p. 98; Chron. Edw. ii. 157. See above, p. 234, note.

[4] The pope proposed that Edward should be crowned by a cardinal, but on the king's request commissioned the archbishop of York, and the bishops of Durham and London, to perform the ceremony. As soon however as Winchelsey was restored, he claimed the right, and, being too ill to attend

An elaborate record drawn up on the occasion contains the form of the coronation oath taken by the new king[1]. In this we may perhaps trace the hand of Edward I, or at any rate the result of the discipline of the previous century[2]. The ancient terms of the *Promissio Regis* had, it would seem, been long disused; for although Henry I had sworn to maintain peace, to forbid injustice, and to execute equity and mercy, as Ethelred had done before him, and although that ancient form was regarded by Bracton as the proper coronation oath[3], Richard, John, and Henry III had materially varied the expression. These kings had sworn to 'observe peace, honour and reverence to God, the church, and the clergy, to administer right justice to the people, to abolish the evil laws and customs and to keep the good.' The new promises, four in number, are more definite, and to some extent combine the terms of the more ancient forms. 'Sire,' says the primate or his substitute, 'will you grant and keep, and by your oath confirm, to the people of England, the laws and customs to them granted by the ancient kings of England your righteous and godly predecessors, and especially the laws, customs, and privileges granted to the clergy and people by the glorious king Saint Edward your predecessor?' The king replies, 'I grant them and promise.' 'Sire, will you keep towards God and holy Church, and to clergy and people, peace and accord in God, entirely, after your power?' 'I will keep them.' 'Sire, will you cause to be done in all your judgments equal and right justice and discretion, in mercy and truth, to your power?' 'I will so do.' 'Sire, do you grant to hold and to keep the laws and righteous customs which the community of your realm shall have chosen[4],

Changes in the form of the coronation oath, Feb. 25, 1308.

The king's four promises.

in person, commissioned the bishops of Winchester, Salisbury, and Chichester to represent him. Hence probably the delay of a week; Chron. Edw. i. 260. Edward had applied for the archbishop's restoration on the 16th of December; Foed. ii. 23.

[1] Foed. ii. 32–36; Parl. Writs, II. ii. 10; Statutes, i. 168.

[2] Carte in his MS. notes mentions the new form as the work of Stephen Langton, but he gives no authority for the statement, and, if it rests on his conjecture, it may safely be rejected.

[3] Bracton, lib. iii. de Actionibus, c. 9. The early forms are given in vol. i. pp. 147, 304, 524; and above, pp. 18, 108.

[4] 'Quas vulgus elegerit,' 'les quiels la communaute de vostre roiaume

Coronation Oath.

and will you defend and strengthen them to the honour of God, to the utmost of your power?' 'I grant and promise.' The increased stringency of the language may be due to the fact that since the accession of Henry II no formal charter, confirming the ancient laws and customs, had been granted at the coronation, and that the mention of Saint Edward, as well as the recognition of the right of the people to choose their own laws, was intended to supply the place of such a charter. It is however, at the least, an interesting coincidence that these particulars should first appear immediately after the consolidation of the constitution by Edward I, when for the first time it could be distinctly and truly affirmed that the community of the realm, the folk, or vulgus, that is the Three Estates, had won their way to a substantial exercise of their right. We read the oath in connexion with the maxim of the one king, that 'that which touches all shall be approved of all,' and with the constitutional law enunciated a few years later by the other, that 'matters to be established for the estate of our lord and king and of his heirs, and for the estate of the realm and of the people, shall be treated, accorded and established in Parliaments by our lord the king and by the assent of the prelates, earls, and barons, and the commonalty of the realm, according as hath been heretofore accustomed[1].' It is not unimportant to observe that Edward II took the oath, not in Latin but in the French form provided for the case, 'si rex non fuerit litteratus;' he was indeed the 'rex illitteratus,' whom his ancestor Fulk the Good had declared to be no better than a crowned ass[2].

Historical importance of the new form.

aura esleu;' Foed. ii. 36. On the dispute as to the meaning of elegerit, which Brady maintained to be equivalent to 'have already chosen,' whilst Prynne appealed to grammar, record, and history as proving it to mean 'shall choose,' see Prynne, Sovereign Power of Parliament, part ii. p. 67; and Brady, in his glossary, s. v. Elegerit; Taylor, Glory of Regality, pp. 337 sq.

[1] Above, p. 258.

[2] That Latin was becoming a rare accomplishment at court appears from the story of Lewis de Beaumont, bishop of Durham, who, when making profession of obedience on his consecration, stumbled over the word *metropoliticae;* after taking a long breath and having failed to pronounce it, he said 'seyt pur dite,' and went on. On another occasion, when conferring holy orders and failing to make out the words 'in aenigmate' (1 Cor. xiii. 12), he said aloud, 'Par seynt Lewis, il ne fu pas curtays qui cest parole icy

Whether new or not, the final words of the oath at once caught the attention of the baronage. A great council of the magnates had been called for the 3rd of March[1], to consult on the state of the church, the welfare of the crown, and the peace of the land, in other words, to consider whether the policy of the late king should be prosecuted. After the coronation, on the day appointed, or possibly in anticipation of it, Edward, through the Earl of Lancaster, his cousin, and Hugh le Despenser, intimated to the lords his willingness to proceed to business[2]. The message was hailed as a good omen. Henry de Lacy, Earl of Lincoln, the closest counsellor of Edward I, after blessing God for the happy beginning of the new reign, expressed a wish that the king should confirm by writ the promise to ratify whatever the nation should determine. Two only of the barons refused to join in the premature congratulation; and these, strange to say, were the king's envoys, the two men who perhaps knew him best. Thomas of Lancaster and Hugh le Despenser de-

Council called for March 3, 1308.

The king offers to proceed to business.

escrit;' Hist. Dunelm. Scr. p. 118. Yet the bailiff of every manor kept his accounts in Latin.

[1] Parl. Writs, II. i. 18. To this council were called, by writs issued on the 19th of January, the bishops, earls, forty-six barons, and thirty-seven judges and counsellors. The inferior clergy were not summoned; the praemunientes clause is omitted in the writs to the bishops. It has been supposed that the commons were summoned, as there is an imperfect writ on the Close Roll addressed to the sheriff of Kent, and two writs for the expenses of the knights of Wiltshire. As however the clergy were not summoned, as no returns for the commons are forthcoming, and as the solitary writ for expenses seems to have a very exceptional character, being applied for four years after the expenses were due, and then disputed by the county (Parl. Writs, II. i. 56, 116), it is more probable that the writ of summons was left imperfect because no such summons was really issued; and the writ of expenses may belong properly to the parliament of the year 1309, at which the knights mentioned in it represented Wiltshire. Neither clergy nor commons were called to the adjourned council in April, and the amount of expenses allowed in the writ, £23, is altogether out of proportion to the length of either session.

[2] Hemingb. ii. 270, 271. The Annales Paulini mention Feb. 27 as a parliament day, and the day of the quarrel; Chron. Edw., i. 262; the writs for the new assembly were issued Mar. 10. Stow, Chron. p. 213, mentions five articles or conditions laid by the barons before the king on this occasion; if he would undertake (1) to confirm the ancient laws, (2) to give up the right of purveyance, (3) to resume property alienated from the crown since his father's death, (4) to dismiss Gaveston and follow up the Scottish war, and (5) to do judgment and justice, and suffer others to do the same, —then they would grant a twentieth. But there must be a confusion of what had taken place at Northampton when the grant was made, and what had been done against the favourite at the coronation.

clared that until the king's mind was known it was too soon to rejoice. Their anticipation was justified. Edward knew that a storm was rising, and postponed the council for five weeks.

Delay of the council.

Rise of Piers Gaveston.

250. The occasion of the storm was the promotion of Piers Gaveston[1]. This man, the son of a Gascon knight who had earned the gratitude of Edward I, had been brought up as the foster-brother and play-fellow of Edward II, and exercised over the young king a most portentous and unwholesome influence. There is no authority for regarding Gaveston as an intentionally mischievous, or exceptionally vicious man; but he had gained over Edward the hold which a strong will can gain over a weak one, and that hold he had determinedly used to his own advancement, entirely disregarding the interest of his master.

Character of Gaveston.

He was brave and accomplished, but foolishly greedy, ambitious, and ostentatious, and devoid of prudence or foresight. The indignation with which his promotion was viewed was not caused, as might have been the case under Henry III, by any dread that he would endanger the constitution, but simply by his extraordinary rise and his offensive personal behaviour.

His banishment by Edward I, Feb. 1307.

In the late reign he had so far strained his influence with the prince as to induce him to demand for him the county of Ponthieu[2], the inheritance of queen Eleanor; and Edward I, indignant and apprehensive, had in the February before his death, with the unanimous assent of the lords, sent Gaveston out of the country, making both the prince and the favourite swear that without his command they would meet no more[3]. From this promise Edward II regarded himself as freed by his father's death; and, neither in this matter nor in the prosecution of the Scottish war, did he hold his father's wish as binding him, or his counsel as a command. His first act was to recall Gaveston; within a month of his accession he had given him the earldom

[1] On the rise of Gaveston, see M. Malmesb. pp. 109 sq.; Chron. Edw. ii. 167; Hemingb. ii. 271 sq.

[2] Hemingb. ii. 272.

[3] On the 26th of February, 1307, at Lanercost, the king ordered that Gaveston should leave England in three weeks from the 11th of April; and Gaveston and the prince swore obedience; Foed. i. 1010. The witnesses, the earls of Lincoln and Hereford, Ralph Monthermer, and Bishop Antony Bek, were also sworn to enforce it; Cont. Trivet, p. 2.

of Cornwall[1], with its appurtenant honours, as held by Earl Edmund son of the king of the Romans, and reserved by Edward I as a provision for one of his younger sons. At Gaveston's instigation he had removed his father's ministers, the chancellor, Ralph Baldock bishop of London, and the treasurer, Walter Langton bishop of Coventry[2], the latter of whom he imprisoned, probably as Gaveston's enemy; he had given him in marriage Margaret, the sister of the young earl of Gloucester and his own niece[3]; he had made him regent during his own visit to France[4], and had allowed him to carry the crown at the coronation. Report further declared that he had bestowed on him a large portion of the late king's treasure, especially £32,000 reserved for the crusade, and that Gaveston, expecting but a short career in England, had sent great sums to his kinsfolk in France[5]. The murmurs had long been growing louder: it was possibly owing to this cause that the coronation was deferred from the 18th to the 25th of February[6];

His recall and promotion, Aug. 1307.

Rumours of his avarice.

[1] On the 6th of August, four days after Edward had got possession of the great seal, Gaveston received the grant of the earldom of Cornwall; Foed. ii. 2: it is attested by the earl of Lincoln, who had given his opinion in favour of the king's power to grant it (M. Malmesb. ed. Hearne, p. 96; Chron. Edw. ii. 155), the earls of Lancaster, Warenne, Hereford, Arundel, and Richmond, and Aymer de Valence.

[2] Walter Langton was removed from office August 22, Walter Reynolds succeeding him; Dugd. Chr. Ser. p. 34; his lands were seized, Sept. 20; Foed. ii. 7. See Hemingb. ii. 273. Ralph Baldock, bishop of London, surrendered the great seal on the 2nd of August, and it appears soon after to have been given to John Langton, bishop of Chichester.

[3] The betrothal took place on Oct. 29; Cont. Trivet, p. 3; on the 2nd of December at the tournament at Wallingford Gaveston offended the earls of Hereford, Warenne, and Arundel; M. Malmesb. (ed. Hearne), p. 97; Chr. Edw. ii. 156.

[4] Dec. 26; Foed. ii. 24; Parl. Writs, II. ii. 9: his powers were enlarged Jan. 18; Foed. ii. 28.

[5] Hemingburgh mentions the seizure by Gaveston of £50,000 at the New Temple, belonging to Langton, and says that Edward gave him £100,000 of his father's; ii. 277; Walsingham, i. 115, 120. The table and trestles of gold taken from the Treasury were delivered to Amerigo Friscobaldi, to be carried to Gascony; Leland, Coll. ii. 473. It would appear that the jewels taken from Gaveston, and restored in 1312 to the king, were the royal treasure of jewels; some of them may be identified in the older list of the jewels of Henry III; Leland, Coll. iv. 171.

[6] See Walsingham, i. 121, where it is stated that on that day 'quo rex debebat coronari' the lords desired the banishment of Gaveston, and proposed to hinder the coronation. As late as Feb. 9 the day originally fixed was unaltered; but it is perhaps on the whole more probable that the

and it was, no doubt, in anticipation of an attack, that Edward postponed the council. When the assembly met on the 28th of April [1], Gaveston was the chief subject of discussion, and, as the result, his banishment was made known in letters patent of the 18th of May [2]: the prelates, earls, and barons had counselled it, the king had granted it, and promised that he would not frustrate the execution of the order. A month later, having consoled himself in the meantime by increased gifts to Gaveston [3], and having entreated the interposition of the pope and the king of France in his favour [4], he made him regent of Ireland. Before the end of the year he was scheming for a recall.

He is banished again, May 18, 1308.

Gaveston goes to Ireland, 1308.

Deprived of his friend, Edward showed himself singularly careless or incapable of governing. His father's counsellors had been discarded or had left him in disgust. His cousin, earl Thomas of Lancaster, the most powerful man in England, had been personally insulted by the favourite, and the insult had served to stimulate an ambition already too willing to grasp at an occasion of aggression. Earl Thomas was the son of Edmund, the second son of Henry III and titular king of

Character and position of Thomas earl of Lancaster.

postponement was the result of a difficulty as to who should crown the king.

[1] The writs were issued on March 10; the clergy and commons were not summoned; Parl. Writs, II. i. 20.

[2] The earls met at the New Temple, and drew up the ordinance of exile, on that day; Gaveston was to quit the kingdom on the 25th of June; Cont. Trivet, pp. 4, 5; Foed. ii. 44; Hemingb. ii. 274. The archbishop, who returned home in April, and the other bishops, undertook to excommunicate him and his abettors if he did not obey; Cont. Trivet, p. 5; Foed. ii. 59; M. Malmesb. p. 100; Chr. Edw. ii. 159. Only Hugh le Despenser favoured the offender; Gloucester was neutral; Lincoln, who had hitherto befriended him, was embittered against him, 'non ex vitio comitis sed ex ingratitudine ipsius Petri;' ibid. The Chronicle of Lanercost mentions among Gaveston's partisans besides Hugh le Despenser, Nicholas Segrave the marshal, William Berford and William Inge, the latter two being lawyers and afterwards chief justices.

[3] Foed. ii. 48; Parl. Writs, II. ii. 14.

[4] On the 16th of June Edward appointed him lieutenant of Ireland; Parl. Writs, II. ii. 15; and the same day asked the pope to annul the sentence of excommunication; Foed. ii. 50. Clement V, on the 11th of August, wrote him a letter of good advice, urging him to peace, but saying nothing about Gaveston; ibid. p. 54; on the 21st of May, 1309, the pope absolved the king from all sins committed during the past wars, but stated that he did not intend to do so again; Foed. ii. 74. On the 13th of April, 1309, Edward applied to one of the cardinals to intercede with the king of France in Gaveston's favour; Foed. ii. 71.

Sicily, by Blanche of Artois queen dowager of Navarre[1]. Cousin to the king, uncle to the queen, high steward of England, possessor of the earldoms of Lancaster, Leicester, and Derby, he stood at the head of a body of vassals who, under Montfort and the Ferrers, had long been in opposition to the crown. He was married to the heiress of Henry de Lacy, earl of Lincoln and Salisbury. A strong, unscrupulous, coarse, and violent man, he was devoid of political foresight, incapable of patriotic self-sacrifice, and unable to use power when it fell into his hands. His cruel death and the later development of the Lancastrian power, by a sort of reflex action, exalted him into a patriot, a martyr, and a saint. He was by birth, wealth, and inclination fitted to be a leader of opposition. Discontented, he made no secret of his feelings, and became the centre of general discontent. He was unappeased by the banishment of Gaveston; he regarded with contempt the new policy towards Scotland, by which Edward II was losing all that his father had won at so great a cost. The state of England under his frown was threatening. Already proposals were mooted for drawing up new ordinances for the government of the kingdom. Edward found it necessary to forbid tournaments, which served as a pretext for the meetings of the malcontents, and even to prohibit the lords from attending in arms[2] at the October meeting of the baronage which was called to complete the business left unfinished in the earlier sessions.

His earldoms.

Rising disturbances, May–Oct. 1308.

Such was the state of affairs at the close of the year 1308. No legislation had been begun; no supplies granted, no general assembly of the estates called since October 1307. Money was raised by negotiation with the Italian bankers, especially the Friscobaldi, who had been appointed to collect the new customs by which foreign merchants had obtained their charter of privileges from Edward I[3], but which were regarded by the nation

Want of money.

[1] They were married in 1275; Ann. Wykes, p. 267. Earl Thomas was about seven years older than the king.

[2] Foed. ii. 59; Parl. Writs, II. i. 23. The king (Aug. 16) called a 'parliament' of the magnates at Westminster for Oct. 20; Parl. Writs, II. i. 22.

[3] See above, p. 164. The Friscobaldi had been appointed by Edward I

Parliament of April, 1309.

as contrary to the Great Charter, and therefore illegal. On the 27th of April, 1309, Edward was compelled to face the full parliament of clergy, lords, and commons; the first of the three estates being again under the guidance of Archbishop Winchelsey [1].

Eleven articles presented to the king, April, 1309.

The session was held at Westminster, and it was the most important parliament since that of Lincoln in 1301. To the king's request for money the lay estates replied by a promise of a twenty-fifth, but the promise was accompanied by a schedule of eleven articles of redress [2], which the king was required to answer in the next parliament. These articles, like those of Lincoln in 1301, were presented in the name of the whole community, not of the commons separately, but they must have been dictated chiefly by regard to the interest of the third estate. They complain of (1) the abuses of purveyance, the prises of corn, malt, meat, poultry, and fish taken by the king's servants; (2) the imposts on wine, cloth, and merchandise, two shillings on the tun, two shillings on the piece of foreign cloth, and three pence in the pound sterling on other articles of avoirdupois, belonging to alien merchants [3]; (3) the uncertainty in the value of the coinage, which sellers depreciated one half, notwithstanding the ordinance which provided that it should pass at its nominal value [4]; (4 and 5) the usurped jurisdiction of the royal stewards and marshals; (6) the want of machinery for receiving and securing attention to petitions addressed to the king in parliament; (7) the exactions taken at fairs; (8) the delay of justice caused by the granting of writs of protection; (9) the sale of pardons to criminals; (10) the illegal

to receive both customs from April 1, 1304; Madox, Hist. Exch. p. 730; Bond, Archæol. xxviii. pp. 244, 293.

[1] A council of magnates was called Jan. 8, to meet Feb. 23; in consequence of the deliberations of this body, on the 4th of March, writs were issued for an assembly of the three estates on April 27. The parliament sat until May 13, on which day the knights had their writs of expenses; Parl. Writs, II. i. 25, 26, 35.

[2] The articles with the answers will be found in the Rolls of Parliament, vol. i. pp. 443-445: Hallam, M. A. iii. 40.

[3] These were among the new customs taken by Edward I by consent of the merchants; see above, p. 164; and declared by the Ordainers in 1311 to be illegal.

[4] Above, p. 330, n. 1.

jurisdiction of the constables of the royal castles in common pleas; and (11) the tyranny of the king's escheators, who, under pretence of inquest of office, ousted men from lands held by a good title. All these points were chiefly interesting to the commons; they betray not only an irritable state of public feeling, but an absence of proper control over the king's servants, and an inclination to ascribe the distresses of the people to the mismanagement of the court. The petition, taken in conjunction with the Bill of twelve articles presented at Lincoln, marks a step in the progress of the commons. On this occasion as on that, the third estate attempted the initiation of action in parliament: it does not amount to an initiation of legislation, for most of the grievances stated were contrary to the letter of the existing law. There is no reason to suppose that the schedule was presented in a humble or conciliatory spirit, for the king's proposal that he should be allowed to recall Gaveston was summarily rejected.

Importance of the occasion.

What negotiations for a clerical grant were set on foot there is nothing to show. The pope however, with or without the acquiescence of the clergy, granted a tenth for three years from the ecclesiastical estate; and no formal vote in parliament was required. It is not improbable that one of the reasons for this act of complaisance was the need of the king's help for the suppression of the Templars which was now proceeding. Possibly the papal interference on behalf of Gaveston was bought by a like concession [1].

Papal grant of money.

Notwithstanding the refusal to recall [2] the favourite, he

[1] In August, 1307, Clement V had granted a tenth for two years for the Crusade; Wilkins, Conc. ii. 288. The grant for three years was made early in 1309: it is referred to by the king, August 29, 1309, who agrees that the pope shall keep a quarter of it for himself; Foed. ii. 87. The liability of the clergy to pay this tenth is mentioned August 26 (Parl. Writs, I. i. 39), as a reason for exempting them from the twenty-fifth: and it was collected under writs from the king, Dec. 10, 1309, and June 18, 1310; Carte, MS.; Wake, State of the Church, p. 250. The most likely conclusion is that the subject was broached in parliament, and that the clergy made the promise conditional on the papal consent.

[2] Hemingb. ii. 275; Mon. Malmesb. p. 102; Chron. Edw. ii. 161. Edward writes to thank the pope for absolving Gaveston, and begs him further to release him from the promise he had made to satisfy the claims of the church, Sept. 4, 1309; Foed. ii. 88.

Gaveston returns, July, 1309.

The king accepts the articles in July, 1309.

returned to England in July, absolved by apostolic authority; the king met him at Chester. On the 27th of July the king, at Stamford, in an assembly of the barons, which was regarded as representing the April parliament, gave a favourable answer to the petition [1]; a statute on purveyance was issued; the illegal exactions were at once suspended, that the king might ascertain whether the relief affected the prices of goods; and the order for collecting the twenty-fifth was issued. The tide seemed suddenly to have turned, the earl of Gloucester had been drawn in to advocate the cause of his brother-in-law, and by his mediation a consent was obtained from a considerable part of the baronage to Gaveston's recall [2]. The earls of Lincoln and Warenne now took his part. Lancaster was neutral or silent; only the earl of Warwick remained implacable. But before October, Gaveston, by his imprudence and arrogance, had turned Lancaster against him. The great earl refused to attend a council called by the king on the 18th of October at York [3], and the earls of Lincoln, Warwick, Oxford, and Arundel joined in the refusal. In December the king had to forbid the publication of false rumours, and unauthorised gatherings of armed men [4]. The discussion of the great grievance was thus delayed until the following year, when Edward called the bishops and barons to meet on the 8th of February, at Westminster [5]. After some demur the opposing parties came

Lancaster takes offence, Oct. 1309.

Council summoned.

[1] See Foed. ii. 84; Parl. Writs, II. i. 37; the writs were issued June 11; the clergy and commons were not summoned. A formal remonstrance to the pope was drawn up on the 6th of August: Ann. Lond. p. 161. The writ for enforcing the law of 1300 on purveyance, called the Statute of Stamford, was issued Aug. 20; Statutes, i. 156. The exactions on wines, cloth, and merchandise belonging to aliens were suspended Aug. 20; Parl. Writs, II. ii. 22; and the writs for collecting the twenty-fifth were issued on Aug. 26; ibid. i. 38; but as the articles were not observed, the collection was stopped, Dec. 10; ibid. i. 41; and not renewed until after the election of the Ordainers, April 1, 1310; ibid. i. 42. On the 2nd of August, 1310, the collection of the new customs was resumed, on the ground that the abolition of them had not reduced prices; ibid. ii. 30. Cf. Rot. Parl. i. 444, 445.

[2] Edward had done all he could to purchase support, 'paterna et patriae fretus cautela; blandiuntur enim Anglici cum vires oneri sufficere non vident;' M. Malmesb. p. 101; Chr. Edw. ii. 160; cf. Hemingb. ii. 275.

[3] Hemingb. ii. 275.

[4] Foed. ii. 101, 102.

[5] The writs of summons 'de summonitione parliamenti,' for a parliament

together early in March: but the king had made his preparations as if he expected a tournament rather than a council. The earls of Lancaster, Hereford, Pembroke, and Warwick were forbidden to appear in arms; the earls of Gloucester, Lincoln, Warenne, and Richmond were appointed to enforce order[1]. Nevertheless, the barons presented themselves in full military array, and Edward found that he must surrender at discretion. His affairs were in much the same state as his grandfather's had been in the parliament of 1258, and the opposition took for their programme of reform the scheme adopted by the barons in that year.

Council in March, 1310.

251. The idea of intrusting the government to a commission of reform had been broached, if we may trust the annalists, as early as the council of 1308[2], when a joint committee of bishops and barons had been nominated to execute some articles of redress. This measure however, if ever it was attempted, had been frustrated or lost sight of. The council now assembled proceeded at once to renew the struggle for supremacy which in the previous century had for the time been decided by the battle of Evesham.

Propositions of Reform.

This assembly was strictly a council of the magnates; the bishops, the earls, and a large number of barons were summoned, but neither the commons nor the inferior clergy. The lords proceeded with a high hand. They presented a petition[3] in which they represented the dangers, impoverishment, losses and dishonour of the existing state of things; there was no money left for defence, although they had granted a twentieth for the war; and the king was maintaining his household and living by prises and purveyance contrary to the great charter, although by their gift of a twenty-fifth they had purchased

Composition of the council.

Petition of March, 1310.

to be held at York on Feb. 8, were issued Oct. 26; the clergy and commons were not summoned; Parl. Writs, II. i. 40; and the place of meeting was changed from York to Westminster, Dec. 12; ibid. i. 41. Eighty-four barons received the first summons, sixty-eight the second.

[1] Foed. ii. 103; Parl. Writs, II. ii. 26.

[2] Trokelowe (ed. Riley), pp. 66, 67; but the account is confused, and possibly should be referred to 1310. Cf. Walsingham, i. 123, and Stow in his Chronicle (ed. 1615), p. 213.

[3] 'Ceo est la Petition des Prelats, Contes et Barons;' Liber Custumarum, ed. Riley, pp. 198, 199; Chron. Edw. i. 168.

exemption from such extortion; of the crowns which his father had left him, that of Scotland was lost altogether, and both in England and in Ireland the crown was 'grossly dismembered' without the assent of the baronage and without occasion; they therefore prayed for his assent that these evils might be removed and redressed by ordinance of the baronage. Edward, willing to consent to anything that might save Gaveston, gave his formal assent, by letters patent of the 16th of March[1], to the election of a commission by which his own authority was to be superseded until Michaelmas 1311. On the 20th of March the barons made their election. Even on this point the proceedings of 1258 served as a precedent. The commons had no share in the matter: the bishops elected two earls, the earls two bishops; these four elected two barons; and the six electors added by cooptation fifteen others[2], the whole number being twenty-one. All were sworn to make such ordinances as should be 'to the honour and advantage of Holy Church, to the honour of the king, and to his advantage and that of his people, according to the oath which the king took at his coronation[3].' The action of the Ordainers was thus made to connect itself directly with the constitutional obligation enunciated in the new form of the coronation oath.

Election of the Ordainers, Mar. 20, 1310.

Persons chosen.

The Ordainers took their oath on the 20th of March in the Painted Chamber; foremost among them was archbishop Winchelsey, who saw himself supported by six of his brethren. Of these only one, John Langton the chancellor, who had filled the same office under Edward I[4], was of much personal im-

[1] The king's letter authorising the election is in Foed. ii. 105; Rot. Parl. i. 445; on the 17th the lords protested that the king and his heirs should not be prejudiced by the act; Parl. Writs, II. ii. 26; Rot. Parl. i. 443.

[2] The monk of Malmesbury mentions twelve as the number first fixed; p. 104; Chron. Edw. ii. 163; and so Hemingb. ii. 276; the king's consent is for the election of *certeines persones*; Foed. ii. 105. The details of the election show that Hallam (Middle Ages, iii. 42) was mistaken in supposing that the commons co-operated.

[3] Parl. Writs, II. ii. 27. The importance of the coronation oath is specially insisted on; M. Malmesb. p. 104; Chron. Edw. ii. 163.

[4] The others were Ralph Baldock, of London; Simon of Ghent, of Salisbury; John Salmon, of Norwich; David Martin, of St. David's; and John of Monmouth, of Llandaff. Baldock had been, and Salmon afterwards became, chancellor.

portance; none of the northern prelates were present, and no bishop appointed during the present reign was chosen. The two earls, elected by the bishops, were the heads of the two parties, Henry de Lacy the father-in-law of the earl of Lancaster, and Aymer de Valence earl of Pembroke the king's cousin and minister; the six added by cooptation were Lancaster, Hereford, Warwick and Arundel from the opposition, Gloucester and Richmond from the royal side: the six barons were Hugh de Vere, William le Mareschal[1], Robert Fitz Roger, Hugh de Courtenay, William Martin and John Gray of Wilton; none of whom were as yet prominent partisans. **The Ordainers of 1310.**

Gaveston, anticipating misfortune, had left the court in February. Edward, as soon as the council broke up, put himself at the head of his army, and marched against the Scots, leaving the earl of Lincoln as regent[2]; on whose death in February 1311 the earl of Gloucester was appointed in his place[3]. The chancellor, whom the king, without the consent of the Ordainers, appointed on the 6th of July, 1310, was bishop Reynolds, his old tutor[4], and he was succeeded as Treasurer by John Sandale afterwards bishop of Winchester. **Edward goes to the North.** Edward, having been rejoined by Gaveston at Berwick, remained on the border until the following July, trying every expedient to raise money[5]. **Gaveston joins him.** During this time England was quiet, and the strife was not renewed until it became necessary to receive the report of the Ordainers. On the 16th of June,

[1] William le Mareschal had served as marshal at the coronation, but was superseded in 1308 by Nicolas Segrave, with whom he went to war in 1311. It was probably his dismissal that offended Lancaster in 1308; see M. Malmesb. p. 103; Chr. Edw. ii. 162; and he may be considered as a strong adherent of the earl. William Martin was father to the second wife of Henry de Lacy; Cont. Trivet, p. 8; Courtenay was brother-in-law to Hugh le Despenser, and was one of the council appointed in 1318.

[2] Sept. 1, 1310; Foed. ii. 116; Parl. Writs, II. ii. 32.

[3] March 4, 1311; Foed. ii. 129; Parl. Writs, II. ii. 34.

[4] Reynolds received the great seal July 6, 1310, from Adam of Osgodby, the keeper. Langton had retired on the 11th of May; Foss, Tab. Cur. p. 17.

[5] April 14, the king wrote to the archbishop asking him to obtain from the convocation a grant of 12*d*. in the mark of spiritualities; Parl. Writs, II. ii. 34; at the same time he was borrowing largely both of the towns and individuals; ibid. II. ii. 35, 36. The York clergy refused to make the grant; Wake, State, &c., p. 262; Reg. Pal. i. 6; Foed. ii. 132.

Parliament of 1311.

1311, writs were issued for a parliament of the three estates, to be held on the 8th of August at London[1]. The king placed his friend in security at Bamborough, left Berwick at the end of July, and, after a pilgrimage to Canterbury, presented himself about the end of August to the assembly which had been some time waiting for him. The session, which was held at Blackfriars, lasted until the 9th of October[2].

The work of the Ordainers in August, 1310.

The Ordainers had not loitered over their work. Six Ordinances had been published and confirmed by the king as early as August 2, 1310[3]. By these provision was made for (i) the privileges of the Church, (ii) the maintenance of the peace, and (vi) the observance of the charters; (iii) no gifts were to be made by the king without the consent of the Ordainers; (iv) the customs were to be collected by native officers and to be paid into the Exchequer, that the king might live of his own without taking prises other than those anciently due and accustomed, and all others were to cease; and (v) the foreign merchants, who had been employed to receive the customs since the beginning of the reign, were to be arrested and compelled to give accounts of their receipts. The result of the deliberations of the parliament was the issue of thirty-five additional articles conceived in the same spirit, but of a more stringent character[4].

Additional Ordinances of 1311.

Final form of the Ordinances, Oct. 1311.

The ordinances, as finally accepted, afford not only a clue to the abuses and offences by which Edward had provoked the hostility of men already prejudiced against him, but a valuable illustration of the continuity of constitutional reform. It is clear from the first six that the royal demesnes had been diminished

[1] Parl. Writs, II. i. 37–39. Besides the clause *praemunientes* in the writs to the bishops, the king addressed a letter to each of the archbishops, ordering them to enforce attendance. This practice, which now occurs for the first time, continues until the 14th year of Edward III; Wake, State of the Church, p. 260.

[2] The writs for expenses were issued on the 11th of October; Parl. Writs, II. i. 55.

[3] Foed. ii. 113; Rot. Parl. i. 446, 447. Hemingb. ii. 278, mentions a solemn excommunication, at St. Paul's, by the archbishop, on Nov. 1, 1310, of all who should hinder the ordinances or reveal the secrets of the Ordainers.

[4] The ordinances are printed among the Statutes of the Realm, i. 157 sq.; Rot. Parl. i. pp. 281–286.

The Ordinances, Oct. 1311.

and the national revenue diverted from its proper objects; that the king had made most imprudent alienations, and allowed grievous acts of dishonesty, yet he was living on money raised by prises and by purveyance. The royal favourite was the recipient of the forbidden gifts, possibly the contriver of the malversation. By the seventh article the gifts made since the issue of the commission were revoked. Four articles (xx–xxiii) were devoted to the perpetual banishment and forfeiture of Gaveston, as having misguided the king, turned away his heart from his people, and committed every sort of fraud and oppression; to the expulsion of the Friscobaldi, the king's foreign agents, the dismissal of Henry de Beaumont [1], to whom Edward had given the Isle of Man, from the royal council, and the removal of his sister the lady de Vescy from court. If these clauses recall the expulsion of the Lusignans in 1258 and the resumption of royal demesne in 1155 and 1220, others as forcibly illustrate the permanent importance of the concessions made by John and Edward I. All the revenue (viii) is to be paid into the Exchequer. The abolition of (x) new prises, (xi) new customs [2], (xviii, xix) new forest usurpations, and (xxxiii) infractions of the statute of merchants; the (xxxi, xxxviii) confirmation of charters and statutes; (xxiv, xxv) the restriction of the court of Exchequer to its proper business; the prohibition (xxviii, xxxii, xxxiv, xxxvii) of writs by which justice was delayed and criminals protected, (xxxv) of outlawry declared in counties where the accused has no lands, and of (xii) interference with the church courts,—all these show that the legislation of the late reign had been

[1] Henry de Beaumont was the son of Lewis of Brienne viscount of Beaumont in Maine, and grandson of John Brienne king of Jerusalem and emperor of Constantinople. His brother Lewis was afterwards bishop of Durham. See Anselme, Histoire Généalogique, vi. 137.

[2] On October 9, 1311, it was ordered that all prises taken since the coronation of Edward I should cease, except half a mark on the sack and 300 woolfells, and a mark on the last of leather, which had been granted in 1275; Parl. Writs, II. i. 43. This was in consequence of the eleventh ordinance, which declares the *Carta Mercatoria* of Edward I (see above, p. 164) to have been issued without the consent of the baronage and contrary to Magna Carta.

Character of the Ordinances of Oct. 1311.

imperfectly enforced; and that even the gravamina of 1309 were not remedied by the king's perfunctory promises. But the ordinances were intended to cut deeper still. The old claim of the baronage to control ministerial appointments, first made in 1244, is now enforced. All the great offices of state (xiii–xviii) in England, Ireland and Gascony are to be filled up by the king with the counsel and consent of the baronage, and (xxxix) their holders are to be bound by proper oaths in parliament. The king (x) is 'to live of his own,' (ix) is not to go to war, to summon forces or to quit the realm without the consent of the baronage in parliament. Parliaments (xxix) are to be held once or twice every year, and in these pleas are to be heard and decided; and (xl) proper persons are to be named to hear complaints against the king's officers. The jurisdictions of the marshal, and the coroner within the verge of the court (xxvii, xxviii), are restricted; and the king is forbidden (xxx) to alter the coinage without consulting parliament. The act as a whole is a summary of old grievances and, in all respects but one, of new principles of government by restraint of the royal power. It is not, however, as regards the main feature of constitutional interest, in advance of the Provisions of Oxford; the privileges asserted for the nation are to be exercised by the baronage; the agency of the third estate is nowhere referred to, unless the very loose expression 'in parliament' be understood to allow to the commons the privilege of witnessing the acts of the magnates. And in this respect it would appear that the leaders of opposition were behind rather than before their time. No constitutional settlement could be permanent which did not provide for the action of the commons, and the neglect of that consideration actually furnished the plea for the reversal of the Ordinances by the hands of the Despensers.

The longest articles, and those perhaps to which the greatest importance was attached, were those directed against Gaveston and the other favourites.

The king, after a humble entreaty that his 'brother Piers' might be forgiven, was obliged by the urgent appeal of his council to yield[1]. On the 27th of September the completed ordinances were published in S. Paul's Churchyard; on the 30th the king's assent was declared at S. Paul's Cross by Hugh le Despenser, the earl of Gloucester, Sir Henry Percy and other lords of the council[2]. On the 5th of October the new statutes were reduced to the form of letters patent; they were sent to the sheriffs for publication on the 10th and 11th; the king on the latter day went away to Windsor and new officers were appointed in the chancery and treasury[3]. The parliament had been prorogued until the 12th of November and was again called for February 12, 1312; but nothing was done[4], although the three estates were duly summoned to both. Edward, no doubt, regarded himself as absolved from the obligation to observe the ordinances by the compulsion under which he acted[5]. In January, 1312, he returned to the north. No sooner had he reached York[6] than he set aside the ordinance touching Gaveston, recalled him to his side, and restored his forfeited estates. This was regarded by the hostile barons as a declaration of war. Archbishop Winchelsey excommunicated the favourite and his abettors[7]. Thomas of Lancaster, with his four confederate earls, took up arms, advanced northwards and, after very nearly capturing Gaveston at Newcastle, besieged

The king assents to the Ordinances, Oct. 1311.

Edward recalls Gaveston, Jan. 1312.

[1] See A. Murimuth (ed. Thompson), p. 15; M. Malmesb. p. 113; Chr. Edw. ii. 70.

[2] Liber de Antt. Legg. pp. 251, 252.

[3] Statutes, i. 163: they were sent to the sheriffs on the 10th; Foed. ii. 146. On the 23rd, Walter of Norwich was made lieutenant of the treasury, and Adam of Osgodby became keeper of the seal, Dec. 10.

[4] The commons were summoned for the 12th and the clergy for the 18th of November; Parl. Writs, II. i. 58; the same members were to attend. The clergy took offence at the shortness of the notice, and the king prolonged the time for them to Dec. 2. The knights were in attendance from Nov. 12 to Dec. 18; ibid. p. 67. For the February session all the estates were summoned on the 19th of December; but warned on January 10 not to attend.

[5] He complained that he was treated like an idiot, 'sicut providetur fatuo, totius domus suae ordinatio ex alieno dependeret arbitrio;' M. Malmesb. p. 117; Chr. Edw. ii. 174.

[6] Jan. 18, 1312, the king announces that Gaveston has returned to him and is ready to account for all his acts; Foed. ii. 153; on the 10th and 24th of February the king restores his estates; p. 157. Cf. Lib. de Antt. Legg. p. 252.

[7] M. Malmesb. p. 118; Chr. Edw. ii. 175, 180.

Capture and death of the favourite, June, 1312.

him in Scarborough castle. On the 19th of May he was obliged to capitulate, and under safe-conduct of the earl of Pembroke proceeded towards Wallingford, there to wait for the meeting of parliament in August. On his way he was carried off by the earl of Warwick, and after a pretence of trial was beheaded in the presence of earl Thomas of Lancaster, on Blacklow Hill on the 19th of June[1].

Important results of this crime.

The blood of Gaveston, thus illegally, if not unrighteously, shed, was the first drop of the deluge which within a century and a half carried away nearly all the ancient baronage and a great proportion of the royal race of England. Edward's revenge for his friend mingled the blood of Lancaster with the rising stream. The feuds of this reign were the source and the example of the internecine struggle under Richard II, and of all that followed until the battle of Bosworth field and the practical despotism of the Tudors exhausted the force of the impulse and left no more noble blood to shed.

Negotiations for peace; 1312, 1313.

The immediate results, however, of this violent act were not startling. Edward was too weak to bring the offenders to justice; the earls were perhaps shocked at their own boldness, and had not yet conceived the idea of deposing the king. He was left under the influence of the earl of Pembroke, who never forgave the injury done him by the earls in seizing the prisoner who was trusting to his honour, and of Hugh le Despenser, who had as yet no personal quarrel with the enemies of Gaveston. The pope and the king of France[2] sent envoys to mediate between the parties; the earl of Gloucester tried to make peace; the bishops also threw themselves between the threatening hosts, and civil war was averted. After a long negotiation carried on under a series of letters of safe-conduct, and a long discussion in parliament which sat from Septem-

Mediation in favour of peace.

[1] The Bridlington Chronicler (Chron. Edw. p. 43) says that the justices Inge and Spigurnell tried him under the Ordinances. Lancaster, Hereford, and Warwick were present, according to the Continuator of Trivet, p. 9. The monk of Malmesbury says that the earl of Warwick stayed in his own castle, the others followed afar off 'to see the end;' p. 123; Chr. Edw. ii. 180; cf. Lib. de Antt. Legg. p. 245.

[2] The papal envoys were the Cardinal of S. Prisca, Count Lewis of Evreux, and the bishop of Poictiers; Foed. ii. 180.

ber 30 to December 16, 1312[1], peace was proclaimed[2]; but another year passed before the earls were admitted to pardon. During this time the parliament, although duly summoned, granted no money; the king was obliged to borrow from every accessible quarter; the bishops, the merchants, even the pope, became his creditors. Walter Langton, the old enemy of Gaveston, had made his peace and resumed his office as treasurer[3] in March, 1312, in spite of the opposition of Winchelsey and the ordainers. It was probably under his advice that the royal council, in December, 1312, issued orders for a tallage[4], which the great towns, especially London and Bristol, resisted. The country was kept in alarm by constant proclamations and prohibitions of tournaments. The earls were forbidden to

Peace made in December, 1312.

Continued alarm, 1313.

[1] On the 3rd of June the king summoned the three estates to meet at Lincoln on the 23rd of July; Parl. Writs, II. i. 72; on the 8th of July the parliament was postponed to August 20, at Westminster; ibid. p. 74; the commons were dismissed on the 28th, to meet Sept. 30; ibid. ii. 53; the writs of expenses were issued Dec. 16; ibid. i. 79.

[2] The royal commissioners were the earl of Pembroke, Hugh le Despenser, and Nicolas Segrave; Foed. ii. 191; Chr. Edw. i. 221. The peace was proclaimed Dec. 22; ibid. p. 192. The king gave a receipt for Gaveston's jewels, which had been taken at Newcastle, on the 27th of February; ibid. p. 203.

[3] Langton had restitution of his temporalities, Oct. 3, 1308; Foed. ii. 58; but he did not get possession until Jan. 23, 1312; ibid. 154; and continued in prison. On July 1, 1311, he was removed from the king's prison at York to the archbishop's; ibid. 138. On the 24th of January, 1312, at York, the king wrote to the pope in his favour; ibid. p. 154; on the 14th March he was made treasurer; ibid. 159. On the 3rd of April the ordainers turned him out of the Exchequer and the archbishop excommunicated him for accepting office contrary to the ordinances; he appealed to Rome in June, 1312; A. Murimuth, p. 18. The king had urged him to defy the threat, April 13; Foed. ii. 164; and wrote to the pope to absolve him, May 1; ibid. p. 167. After his expulsion from the treasury, Walter of Norwich in May and John Sandale in October acted as lieutenants there. Sandale became treasurer before December.

[4] Parl. Writs, II. ii. 59; Rot. Parl. i. 449. The amount was a fifteenth of moveables, and a tenth of rents. The quarrels which arose in London and Bristol in consequence are described in the Parl. Writs, II. ii. 84; cf. Cont. Trivet, pp. 11, 18; M. Malmesb. p. 167; Chr. Edw. ii. 219; Foed. ii. 210. Lord Badlesmere, as warden of the castle of Bristol, earned great unpopularity in the struggle. Edward and Isabella went to France, May 23, 1313, to the coronation of the king of Navarre, leaving John Drokensford, bishop of Bath, as regent; Cont. Trivet, p. 10; M. Malmesb. p. 134; Chr. Edw. ii. 190, 191. The latter writer states that Gloucester was regent. Drokensford, Reynolds, Gloucester, and Richmond were commissioned to open parliament; Foed. ii. 220. The king returned on the 16th of July; ibid. p. 222.

move about the country in arms, and refused to attend the councils at which the king was present. Parliament met twice or three times in the spring and summer of 1313, but with no results. However, this phase of the struggle ended on the 16th of October, 1313[1], when the pardon[2], a general amnesty for all offences committed since the king's marriage, was publicly granted to the earls of Lancaster, Hereford, Warenne, and Warwick, with four hundred and sixty-nine[3] minor offenders, of whom the vast majority were men of the northern counties. The parliament that witnessed the pacification was prevailed upon to grant supplies, a fifteenth from cities and boroughs, and a twentieth from the lands of the barons and the counties[4]. The clergy, in their provincial councils the same year, granted four pence in the mark[5].

General pardon issued in Oct. 1313.

The year 1314.

In 1314[6] the war with Scotland was resumed, and the battle of Bannockburn, June 24, placed Edward before his people as a defeated and fugitive king. The year 1315 was spent in vain attempts to remedy the distress occasioned by dearth, murrain, and pestilence[7]. The parliaments were held

Famine in 1315.

[1] A parliament of the three estates was called Jan. 8, 1313, to meet on March 18: it sat from March 18 to April 7, and from May 6 to May 9; Parl. Writs, II. i. 80, 91. On the 23rd of May a second parliament was summoned for July 8; ibid. p. 94; on the 26th of July a third was called for Sept. 23; ibid. p. 102; and sat until Nov. 18; ibid. p. 115.

[2] Statutes, i. 169.

[3] M. Malmesb. p. 140; Chr. Edw. ii. 195; Foed. ii. 230, 231; Parl. Writs, II. ii. 66–70. Hugh le Despenser and the earl of Lancaster were not reconciled; M. Malmesb. p. 140.

[4] Foed. ii. 238; Trokelowe, p. 81; Parl. Writs, II. i. 116, 117; Rot. Parl. i. 448.

[5] Parl. Writs, II. ii. 63; May 27, 1313; Wake, p. 263; Wilkins, Conc. ii. 426; Reg. Palat. i. 416.

[6] A parliament called for April 21, 1314, was prevented from meeting by the outbreak of war. See below, p. 354, note 1. To raise more money Edward wrote to the archbishops, bidding them call together the clergy in convocation on May 17; this offended the clergy, and led to some important consequences. See Parl. Writs, II. i. 122, 123, 124; Wake, State of the Church, p. 265. The convocation of Canterbury met on the 18th of July; that of York, June 26, granted a shilling in the mark; Reg. Palat. i. 636, 641. For the second Parliament of 1314, see p. 354, note 3.

[7] See Cont. Trivet, pp. 17, 18; Trokelowe, pp. 90–95 sq.; Knighton, c. 2534. An attempt was made in 1315 to fix prices, but withdrawn the next year as pernicious; Rot. Parl. i. 295; Foed. ii. 266, 286; Trokelowe, pp. 89, 92; and a sumptuary edict, fixing the number of dishes at dinner for each rank, was issued, Aug. 6, 1315; Foed. ii. 275.

with regularity and completeness, but with few results in either legislation or general taxation. The importance of the earl of Lancaster increased as the king became more insignificant. He was now lord of five earldoms, Lincoln and Salisbury having come to him on the death of his father-in-law. The death of earl Gilbert of Gloucester, slain at Bannockburn, who in some degree inherited the noble character of his grandfather Edward I, and the death of the earl of Warwick in 1315, left earl Thomas without a rival among the lay barons; and he was relieved from the counsels as well as the independent spirit of archbishop Winchelsey, who died on the 11th of May, 1313.

Lancaster increases in power.

Wretched, however, as these years were, they were perhaps to Edward the happiest and safest period of his reign[1]: his children were gaining their due place in his affections, the queen was still faithful to him, the nation was entertaining better hopes. But Edward could not live without favourites or rule without ministers, and he was most unfortunate in the choice of both. Walter Reynolds, the new archbishop of Canterbury, who had been his tutor[2], and advanced from being clerk of the wardrobe to be treasurer, chancellor, and primate, was a mere creature of court favour, who could indeed contrive to obtain from the clergy money which enabled his master to dispense with the unwilling gifts of the parliament, but who neither by experience nor by influence strengthened his position. The old treasurer, Langton, had been too often matched

Time of peace for Edward, 1314–1317.

The king's friends—Reynolds, Langton, Pembroke.

[1] Trokelowe, p. 80.

[2] Edward describes him as one 'qui a nostro aetatis primordio, nostris insistens obsequiis, secreta prae caeteris nostra novit;' Foed. ii. 101. Thomas Cobham, who was chosen by the chapter, was a man of noble birth and a great scholar, who afterwards became bishop of Worcester. Walter Reynolds, the king's nominee, was a simple clerk, the son of a baker at Windsor, who had gained Edward's favour, it was said, by his skill in theatrical entertainments, but really had been his tutor. 'O quanta inter electum et praefectum erat differentia!' M. Malmesb. p. 141. The same writer is severe on the pope: 'octo annis et amplius papa Clemens quintus universalem rexit ecclesiam, sed quicquid profuit homini evasit memoriam;' p. 142: 'melius esset rectoribus papam non habere quam tot exactionibus indies subjacere;' 'Domine Jesu, vel papam tolle de medio vel potestatem minue;' p. 143; Chr. Edw. ii. 196, 197. See also the annals of Lanercost, p. 222.

with the barons to be conciliatory now. The earl of Pembroke was by no means an efficient leader of the royal party in or out of parliament. The division of the estates of the earl of Gloucester among his three brothers-in-law raised up three rival interests close to the throne. The ablest man who was faithful to the king was probably Hugh le Despenser the elder, whom the barons hated as a deserter, and who was gradually rising to supremacy among the king's personal advisers. Hugh le Despenser was the son of the great justiciar who had fallen with Simon de Montfort at Evesham, and step-son of Roger Bigod, who had compelled Edward I to confirm the charters. He had been in constant employment under Edward I; as his envoy he had obtained from Clement V the bull of absolution which relieved the king from his oath in 1305; and under Edward II he had, as we have seen, incurred the hatred of the magnates as supporting Gaveston. As early as 1308[1] or 1309 the king had been requested to remove him from the council, but notwithstanding the hostility of the lords his experience made him too valuable to be neglected. He rose in favour, he was god-father to the king's eldest son, and his rise was shared by his son, Hugh le Despenser the younger, whom, in 1313, Edward married to the eldest of the co-heiresses of Gloucester. Under such influence Edward made a vain attempt to govern.

Hugh le Despenser.

The Ordinances broached again, 1312.

But the question of the Ordinances never slumbered: Edward began, before the fall of Gaveston, to move for the revision, and, although he had just ordered the publication of them in the counties[2], issued a commission to a select body of his councillors to treat with the ordainers for the repeal of the articles which were prejudicial to the royal dignity. This was done on the 8th of March, 1312[3], but the troubles arising about Gaveston prevented the discussion at the time fixed. On

[1] In August, 1308, at Northampton, Edward was urged to dismiss Hugh le Despenser, Nicolas Segrave, William Bereford, and William Inge; Chron. Edw. i. 264; Ann. Lanercost, p. 212; and the attempt to remove him was made again in the negotiations on the ordinances. He was twenty-one years of age on March 1, 1283, and was thus sixty-four, not ninety, as the historians relate, at the time of his death; Dugdale, Baronage, p. 390.

[2] On the 26th of January, 1312; Foed. ii. 154; Parl. Writs, II. ii. 46.

[3] Foed. ii. 159; Parl. Writs, II. i. 71; Rot. Parl. i. 447.

The king's objections to the Ordinances, 1312, 1313.

the 4th of August, 1312 [1], in preparation for the parliament of that month, Edward summoned the earls of Lancaster, Hereford, and Warwick, to appear on the 27th to treat on the subject, and on that occasion laid before the ordainers his reasons for desiring a change [2]. The bill of exceptions, which was drawn up by two French lawyers, and brought up either on this occasion or at a later stage in the parliament of September, 1313, described the obnoxious regulations as invalid; the ordainers had not been properly elected; instead of being chosen by the prelates and barons they had been nominated by a small committee; the Ordinances were contrary to right and reason, derogated from the king's rights and dishonoured the crown: many points in them were doubtful, uncertain, inconsistent with one another; they were contrary to the charters and the coronation oath; the ordainers were ipso facto excommunicate as acting against the charters; the Ordinances themselves were but a reproduction of the provisions which S. Lewis had annulled in 1264, and his award had been confirmed by Urban IV and Clement V. To particular articles particular objections were raised: they were beyond the powers intrusted to the ordainers, or contrary to right, to natural equity, to the provisions of Magna Carta, to the royal coronation oath, to the constitutional doctrine respecting fiefs and benefices, and to the fundamental idea of the kingly character: if the king were forbidden to go abroad he would be more of a slave than the rustic who could go on pilgrimage; the whole matter and form of the Ordinances was accordingly opposed to the spirit of the constitution. The barons [3] in answer laid down as a principle that England is not governed by written law, but by ancient custom, and, if that were not enough, the king and his prelates, earls, and barons, 'ad queri-moniam vulgi' were bound to amend it and reduce it to a certainty. But the quarrel was not formally decided; Edward

General exceptions.

Particular objections.

[1] Foed. ii. 175; Parl. Writs, II. ii. 53; Rot. Parl. i. 447.

[2] See Annales Londonienses. Chron. Edw. i. 211 sq.

[3] By a misreading of the MS. I placed these words, in former editions, in the mouth of the king. The Chronicle is now printed; Chron. Edw. i. 215.

would not admit that Gaveston had been a traitor, the earls would not accept any concession that left them liable to legal vengeance. The pacification of 1313 was however accompanied by a distinct understanding that the Ordinances should hold good.

The struggle is renewed, 1314.

No sooner were the pardons issued than both parties renewed the contest. The Scottish war was imminent; the king contended that there was no time to call a parliament, and revoked the summons which had been issued for April 21, 1314; the earls declined, without consulting the nation, to join the expedition; Lancaster, Warenne, Arundel and Warwick refused to disobey the ninth Ordinance or to go without the order of parliament; they stayed at home, and the king was beaten at Bannockburn [1]. Having thus contributed by his absence, if not, as was suspected, by a secret understanding with the Scots, to the king's humiliation, earl Thomas took advantage of the crisis to proclaim [2] that the abeyance of the ordinances was the cause of the public misery, and in a full parliament, held at York in September, 1314 [3], Edward was obliged to confirm them again and to consent to the dismissal of his chancellor, treasurer, and sheriffs. Their places were immediately filled up by nominees of the earl [4]. The advantage was

The king yields, after the defeat at Bannockburn, 1314.

The Ordainers appoint the ministers.

[1] 'Responderunt comites melius fore ad parliamentum omnes convenire et ibidem unanimiter diffinire quid in hoc negotio oportet agere . . . nam et ordinationes hoc volunt. Dixit autem rex instans negotium magna acceleratione indigere, et ideo parliamentum exspectare non posse. Responderunt comites ad pugnam sine parliamento venire nolle, ne contingeret eos ordinationes offendere;' M. Malmesb. p. 146; Chr. Edw. ii. 200. Cf. Ann. Lanercost, p. 224; Trokelowe, p. 83. On the 26th of November a full parliament had been called to meet April 21, 1314, at Westminster; Parl. Writs, II. i. 119; but war being begun the king revoked the summons, March 24, calling the barons to meet at Newcastle on April 28; ibid. p. 121. Some elections had however been held, as in Cornwall; Return of Members (1879), p. 45.

[2] M. Malmesb. p. 154; Chr. Edw. ii. 208.

[3] This parliament was summoned July 29, to meet September 9: it sat until September 27; Parl. Writs, II. i. 126.

[4] Archbishop Reynolds had to surrender the great seal, and John Sandale was appointed chancellor, Sept. 26; Walter of Norwich, a baron of the Exchequer, was made treasurer the same day, and retained the office until May 1317; Dugdale, Origines, Chr. Ser. p. 36; Parl. Writs, II. ii. 81. Sandale was a protégé of archbishop Winchelsey, and had been lieutenant of the treasurer under the ordainers. The ordinances were confirmed at the same time; Ann. Lanercost, p. 229. Hugh le Despenser and Henry de

followed up the next year. In a general parliament, which lasted from January to March [1], 1315, regulations were drawn up for the royal household; Hugh le Despenser and Walter Langton were removed from the council, and the king was put on an allowance of ten pounds a day [2]. The estates made a grant of money contingent on certain terms; the clergy voted a tenth on condition that peace should be maintained between the king and the lords, that the rights of the church should be observed, that the ordinances should be kept, and all grants of land made in contravention of them should be annulled, that their contribution should be levied by ecclesiastics, and its expenditure determined by the earls and barons [3]. The lay estates granted a fifteenth and twentieth. Edward bent to the storm and yielded where he could not resist. In August the earl of Lancaster was made commander-in-chief against the Scots [4], thus superseding the earl of Pembroke, who had been commissioned a month before.

The king's expenses reduced, 1315.

Grants of money, 1315.

252. In January, 1316, the parliament met at Lincoln, and there earl Thomas took another step, which wrested the reins altogether from Edward's hands [5]. He was made president of the royal council on the express understanding that without

Lancaster made chief of the council in 1316.

Beaumont were also threatened, and the former went into hiding; M. Malmesb. p. 154; Chr. Edw. ii. 208.

[1] The parliament of 1315 was summoned Oct. 24, 1314; the clergy protested against the summons addressed to them through the archbishop; Parl. Writs, II. i. 137, 139. The session lasted from Jan. 20 to March 9; ibid. p. 149. The petitions are given in the Rolls of Parliament, i. 288 sq.

[2] M. Malmesb. p. 156; Chr. Edw. ii. 209. The expenditure accounted for in the Wardrobe Account for the 10th year of Edward II, July 1316 to July 1317, is £61,032 9s. 11¾d.; that of the eleventh year, July 1317 to July 1318, is £36,866 16s. 3½d.; in the fourteenth year, July 1320 to July 1321, only £15,343 11s. 11¾d. See Stapleton's article in the Archaeologia, xxvi. p. 319.

[3] Parl. Writs, II. ii. 92; Wilk. Conc. ii. 451–454.

[4] Parl. Writs, II. i. 457.

[5] The parliament was summoned Oct. 16, for Jan. 27, 1316; Parl. Writs, II. i. 152; it sat until Feb. 20; ibid. 157. Lancaster was not present until Feb. 12; on the 17th the bishop of Norwich, at the king's request, proposed that the earl should become 'de consilio Regis capitalis;' 'principalis consiliarius regis efficitur;' M. Malmesb. p. 166; 'ordinatum erat quod dominus rex sine consilio comitum et procerum nihil grave, nihil arduum inchoaret, et comitem Lancastriae de consilio suo principaliter retineret;' ibid. p. 172; Chron. Edw. ii. 218, 224; and after making some conditions he took the oath as a councillor; Rot. Parl. i. 350 sq.

the consent of the council no acts touching the kingdom should be done, and that any member of it who should do any act or give any advice dangerous to the kingdom should be removed at the next parliament. The king agreed to enforce the ordinances[1]; the complaints of the clergy, which show that they had begun to regard Lancaster as the champion of their privileges, were met by measures of redress[2]; and the parliament, hoping that a settlement of the quarrel was at last attained, made a liberal grant, the towns granting a fifteenth[3], the lords and knights promising the service of a foot soldier from every rural township, to be maintained by the township, and the clergy likewise declaring their willingness to grant money in their own assembly. The arrangements thus begun were completed in a July session of the knights, also held at Lincoln[4], where the counties compounded for their grant of men by paying a sixteenth of movables. The clergy of the southern province, in the following October, granted a tenth of spirituals: in consideration of this, as seems most probable, the king at York, on the 24th of November, published a series of 'Articuli Cleri,' or authoritative answers to questions touching the relation of Spiritual and Temporal courts, which had been laid before the parliament of Lincoln. This document was entered on the Statute Book, and, considered as a concordat between Church and State, is not the least important document of the reign[5].

The Ordinances renewed.

Grants of money in 1316.

But although summons after summons was issued for the Scottish war, the show of preparation was the sole result, and the pacification itself was futile. Earl Thomas, although he

[1] The order for enforcement was given March 6; Foed. ii. 287.

[2] See below, note 5.

[3] Foed. ii. 291; Parl. Writs. II. i. 157; Rot. Parl. i. 450, 451. The clergy promised a grant which they were called on to make in convocation on April 28; and again on October 10.

[4] The knights were summoned June 25, 1316, to meet July 29 before the king's council; Parl. Writs, II. i. 473; II. ii. 104, 105; the towns, having been taxed to the fifteenth, were not summoned. The session lasted till August 5; ibid. i. 167. The clerical tenth was granted Oct. 11 by the southern, and Nov. 23 by the northern convocation; Wilkins, Conc. ii. 458: the order for collection of the tenth was made Dec. 8; Parl. Writs, II. ii. 109; cf. Wake, p. 269.

[5] Statutes, i. 171–174; Wilkins, Conc. ii. 460–462.

had gained the object of his desire, control in both army and council, showed no capacity for either. His hatred for his cousin was a stronger motive than his ambition, or else he was a traitor to his country as well as to his king. He refused to follow the king to war; the Scots spared his estates when they ravaged the north; his own policy towards them was one of supineness if not of treacherous connivance[1]. He refused to attend the parliaments, and yet kept all internal administration as well as external business at a standstill. Edward could neither dispense with him nor defy him. Nor had he the excuse of being the chosen spokesman of a body of malcontents. The baronial opposition was no longer a compact body, although the largest section of it no doubt, as well as the ecclesiastical party, looked to Thomas as their leader. The earl of Warenne, who had been one of Gaveston's bitter enemies, had so far reconciled himself with Edward as to settle the succession to his estates on the king, in default of an heir of his body. The inheritance of the earl of Gloucester, which had fallen to his three sisters, raised up in their respective husbands three new claimants of political power, Hugh le Despenser the younger, Hugh of Audley, and Roger d'Amory, who were not likely to throw their weight into one scale. The earl of Pembroke since the death of Gaveston had been faithful to the king, but rather as the leader of a court party opposed to Lancaster than as a supporter of the royal policy. The unsettled condition of Wales, where the chief marcherships were in the hands of the great English earls, afforded, as it had done in the reign of Henry III, a battlefield for private war.

Strange conduct of earl Thomas.

Factions among the barons.

The middle party, 1314–1317.

[1] It was believed that he wished Robert Bruce to maintain the struggle, lest Edward should be strong enough to overwhelm him (Lancaster); M. Malmesb. p. 173; Chron. Edw. ii. 224, 225. But it is probable that both parties intrigued with Robert Bruce. Edward would have acknowledged him if he would have befriended Gaveston, or have helped him to avenge himself on Lancaster; and Lancaster was believed to have received a bribe of £40,000 to be neutral; M. Malmesb. pp. 194, 199; Chron. Edw. ii. 244, 245. It was said that Edward had offered carte blanche (alba carta) to Robert Bruce for Lancaster's death, and this report first attracted the people to the earl: 'hac de causa populus Anglicanus qui prius comitem fere spreverat . . . adhaesit comiti;' Cont. Trivet, p. 24; Wals. i. 152.

The earls, who were obliged to maintain a show of peace within the border, could wage war, train their men, and make their castles impregnable, on the other side. Meanwhile the condition of England was lamentable in the extreme; the dearth and pestilence in 1315, constant invasions by the Scots, the impossibility of raising money or of collecting it,—for several of the scutages of the last reign were yet unpaid,—the constant assemblies of riotous bands, the secret training of men in arms for suspected purposes, all of them evils which a wise administration would have been able to remedy, were fruitful causes of misery. Edward's thoughtless or wilful extravagance condemns him as heartless; his vain attempts to relieve himself from restraint condemn him as incapable. In 1317, on the proposition of a crusade, the Pope allowed him to take a tenth of spiritual revenue [1] for the payment of his debts, but refused to absolve him from his oath to the ordinances. An elaborate plan for borrowing of the merchants, 'the new increment' [2] as it was called, was devised the same year; enormous loans or 'finances' were taken from every possible lender [3], and for nearly two years no parliament was held.

Miserable state of the kingdom.

The king's extravagance.

War between Lancaster and Warenne in 1317.

A private war broke out in the spring of 1317 between the earls of Lancaster and Warenne. The countess of Lancaster had eloped from her unfaithful husband, with the assistance of Warenne, and, as was suspected, by the contrivance or with the connivance of the king [4]. But Edward was incapable of

[1] Mar. 27, 1317; Foed. ii. 320; Wilkins, Conc. ii. 464; M. Malmesb. pp. 175, 176; Chron. Edw. ii. 225, 226. The council of Vienne in 1312 had ordered a tenth for six years for the crusade. One year's tenth had been collected in England. This the pope makes over to the king, and suspends the payment of the rest for three years.

[2] Parl. Writs, II. ii. 115; by the advice of the merchants and in the character of a *mutuum*; on wool 6*s*. 8*d*. on the sack by denizens, 10*s*. by aliens; a similar impost was ordered on cloth, wine, avoirdupois and other merchandise, but was revoked soon after; Parl. Writs, II. ii. 118; see Hall, Customs Revenue, ii. 183.

[3] From merchants, bishops, the pope himself; see Foed. ii. 247, 258, 263.

[4] There was a suspicious council held by the king at Clarendon on Feb. 9, 1317; Parl. Writs, II. i. 170; Cont. Trivet, p. 20; Wals. i. 148: Lancaster refused to attend either at Clarendon or at a later council held at London on April 15; Cont. Trivet, p. 20; M. Malmesb. p. 176; Chron. Edw. ii. 228; Parl. Writs, II. i. 170. The countess was carried off on

taking advantage of the opportunity to overwhelm his rival Vain proclamations of peace, prohibitions against armed bands, futile summonses to parliaments which could not be brought together [1], display the unfortunate king as completely helpless. The earl of Pembroke, Roger d'Amory, and Bartholomew lord Badlesmere, went so far as to bind themselves by oath to an alliance for gaining supreme influence in the royal council [2]; Pembroke, as in position the rival of Lancaster, Badlesmere as a bitter enemy of the earl, and d'Amory as an aspirant to the Gloucester honours, seem to have conceived the idea of forming a middle party between Lancaster as the head of the old baronial faction, and the king sustained by the Despensers and the personal adherents of the royal house. Sieges and negotiations were in brisk operation when the country was brought to its senses by Robert Bruce.

The middle party is in power, 1317

Formal reconciliation of parties.

Berwick was taken on the 2nd of April, 1318, and its capture was the signal for a reconciliation. For this the earl treated as an independent power with the king, who had, by forbidding Lancaster to move, become a party in the private war. The mediation was undertaken by the earls of Pembroke and Arundel, Roger Mortimer, Badlesmere, and two other barons, with the archbishop of Dublin and the bishops of Norwich, Ely, and Chichester. The list of the king's sureties contains the names of his two brothers, the archbishop of Canterbury and nine other prelates, the earls of Pembroke,

Treaty of peace in August, 1318.

the 9th of May; Cont. Trivet, p. 20. This writer believed that the elopement was arranged at the Clarendon council; p. 22. In July Lancaster in a long letter to the king justifies his refusal to attend him and insists on a discussion in parliament; Chron. Bridl. (Chron. Edw. ii), p. 50. On the 24th of September Lancaster had letters of protection; Parl. Writs, II. i. 171: war must have already begun; Lancaster had taken the castles of the earl of Warenne in Yorkshire; Knaresborough castle had been seized by a rebel force in his interest, and he was forbidden to continue hostilities on Nov. 3; Foed. ii. 344.

[1] A parliament called for Jan. 13, 1318, was postponed by several writs to March, and then to June, when it was finally revoked.

[2] This was done by indenture, Nov. 24, 1317. Roger D'Amory bound himself in a penalty of £10,000 to give his diligence to induce the king to allow himself to be led and governed by the advice of Pembroke and Badlesmere; Parl. Writs, II. ii. 120. The monk of Malmesbury mentions as Lancaster's chief opponents at the time, Warenne, Audley, D'Amory, le Despenser, and William Montacute; p. 184; Chron. Edw. ii. 235.

Arundel, Richmond, Hereford, Ulster, and Angus, and twelve barons, of whom the greatest were Roger Mortimer, Hugh le Despenser the son, John and Richard Gray, John Hastings, and lord Badlesmere; the earl of Lancaster alone affixed his seal to the counterpart of the indenture of treaty. But although so strongly supported, Edward had to yield every point in dispute: a general pardon was granted to the earl and nearly 700 followers, the ordinances were confirmed, and a new council nominated [1]. This was to consist of eight bishops, Norwich, Ely, Chichester, Salisbury, S. David's, Hereford, Worcester, and Carlisle; four earls, Pembroke, Arundel, Richmond, and Hereford; four barons, Hugh Courtenay, Roger Mortimer, John Segrave, and John Gray, and a single banneret to be named by the earl of Lancaster [2]: of these, two bishops, one earl, one baron, and the banneret were to be in constant attendance, and with their concurrence everything that could be done without the assent of parliament was to be done [3]. At

Permanent council appointed.

[1] The arrangement was made at Leek, August 9, and confirmed by the parliament; Foed. ii. 370. The stages of the negotiation are given by Knighton, c. 2535, and in the Parliamentary Writs, I. i. 184, 185; II. ii. 123 sq.; Rot. Parl. i. 453, 454. Cf. Chr. Bridl. pp. 54, 55. The parliament was summoned August 25, to meet at York; Parl. Writs, II. i. 182; it sat until Dec. 9; ibid. i. 194. The Roll is printed in Cole's Records, pp. 1–54.

[2] To these were added in the parliament, Hugh le Despenser the son, Badlesmere, Roger Mortimer of Chirk, William Martin, John de Somery, John Giffard, and John Bottetourt; at the same time the earl of Hereford, Badlesmere, Mortimer of Wigmore, John de Somery, and Walter of Norwich were appointed to deal with the reform of the household, to whom the king added the archbishop of York and the bishops of Ely and Norwich; Cole, Records, p. 12.

[3] Cont. Trivet, p. 27; A. Murimuth, p. 29; M. Malmesb. p. 185; Chron. Edw. ii. 236. Under this arrangement Badlesmere was steward of the household, Gilbert of Wygeton controller of the household, Hugh le Despenser chamberlain; many other appointments were made, which are illegible in the Roll; Cole, Records, p. 3; and it was determined that the next parliament should be held at York or Lincoln; ibid. p. 4; the provision made by the king for Badlesmere, Despenser, Audley, D'Amory and others, was confirmed, and a good deal of other business done. Bishop Langton claimed £20,000 which he had lost in the king's service; but, on being asked whether he intended to burden the king with the payment, he avoided a direct answer, and received nothing. In June, 1318, Bishop Hotham of Ely, who had been treasurer since May, 1317, succeeded Sandale as chancellor, John Walwayn becoming treasurer; but Sandale in November resumed the treasurership, which he held until his death in November, 1319.

the next parliament a standing council was to be chosen. The treaty was arranged on the 9th of August and reported to a full parliament held at York on the 18th of October. This, which was the first parliament held since that of Lincoln in 1316, confirmed the treaty and the pardons, and passed a statute to improve the judicial procedure[1]. But the year was too far advanced for a campaign against the Scots. A parliament held, also at York, in the following May granted an eighteenth from the barons and the shires, and a twelfth from the towns[2].

Parliaments of 1318, and 1319.

Notwithstanding the pretences of reform in administration, and the imminent danger of the country, no united attempt was made to repel invasion. Lancaster would neither lead the army nor support the king. The year 1319 saw Edward obliged to retire from the siege of Berwick and to conclude a truce for two years with the enemy. Whilst the king was at the siege of Berwick, the unhappy Yorkshiremen made a luckless attempt to fight their own battle under archbishop Melton, and paid the forfeit in the White battle of Myton, where a great number of clerks were slain[3]. Lancaster offered to purge himself by ordeal from the charge of complicity with the Scots, but when summoned to the council of the baronage refused to attend what he called a parliament 'in cameris.' In 1320, under the shadow of the truce, Edward visited France[4] and did homage to Philip V; but the short period

Increasing perversity of Lancaster.

Defenceless state of the North.

[1] The Statute of York; Statutes, i. 177.

[2] A parliament was called March 20, 1319, to meet May 6; Parl. Writs, II. i. 197; it sat till the 25th; ibid. p. 210. The writs for collecting the grants were issued May 30; ibid. p. 211; Rot. Parl. ii. 454, 455. The clergy in the parliament of 1318 had declined to make a grant in convocation; the king requested the archbishops to summon one for Feb. 3, 1319; Parl. Writs, II. i. 196. The convocation was really held on April 20; Wake, State of the Church, p. 271. In the parliament held at York on the 6th of May following, the bishops reported that the clergy would make no grant without the pope's leave, and Adam of Murimuth was sent to Avignon to ask it; it was granted May 29; and on the 20th of July the king wrote to anticipate the payment of a tenth; Parl. Writs, II. ii. 140. See A. Murimuth, p. 30; Wilkins, Conc. ii. 492; Wake, pp. 271, 272.

[3] Ann. Lanerc. p. 239; Bridlington, p. 58; Trokelowe, p. 104; Wals. i. 156.

[4] He sailed on the 19th of June, leaving Pembroke regent, and returned on the 22nd of July; Foed. ii. 428; Parl. Writs, ii. 146.

Pembroke in power.

of calm ended in the following year. During this time the government was carried on apparently under the influence of Pembroke and Badlesmere, the earl of Lancaster acting through his agent in the council, and the king's personal adherents being led by the Despensers, one of whom, Hugh the younger, had been appointed chamberlain in the parliament at York in 1318. John Hotham, bishop of Ely, was chancellor from 1318 to 1320, when he was succeeded by John Salmon, bishop of Norwich.

The other ministers.

The character and position of the Despensers.

253. Edward had not learned wisdom from Gaveston's fate, although the men under whose influence he had now fallen were not liable to the same objections as those which had prejudiced the nation against the Gascon favourite. The younger Despenser had taken Gaveston's place in Edward's regard [1], and neither father nor son had shown any caution or moderation in using the advantages of the position. They had been willing or eager recipients of all that the king had to give. Though they were neither foreigners nor upstarts, they were obnoxious to charges and enmities as fatal as those which had overwhelmed Gaveston. Representing to some extent the views of the barons of 1264, they had attached themselves to the king, against whom Lancaster was trying to play the part of Simon de Montfort. As the husband of the eldest co-heiress of Gloucester, the younger Hugh came into collision with the other co-heirs and the rest of the rival lords of the marches, especially the Mortimers [2]. Lancaster, feeling that his conduct with regard to Scotland was diminishing his political influence, grasped the opportunity which was supplied by Edward's infatuation and the greediness of the Despensers. He revived the outcry against the favourites, and at once enlisted on his side all whom they had outraged and offended.

Greediness of the Despensers.

[1] See T. de la Moor, p. 595; Chron. Edw. ii. 301.

[2] The quarrel began however in Gower, where John Mowbray as heir had entered without the king's leave, which Hugh le Despenser asserted was necessary in Wales as well as in England; M. Malmesb. p. 205; Chron. Edw. ii. 254. The other marchers took occasion of the quarrel to attack Hugh. Lancaster had his 'antiquum odium' against the father, and involved him in it; M. Malm. p. 209; Chron. Edw. ii. 257; Trokelowe, p. 107.

He himself had an old grudge against the father, and had long insisted that all who had received gifts from the king contrary to the ordinances should be punished, a threat launched especially at the Despensers. Humfrey Bohun, earl of Hereford and lord of Brecon, the king's brother-in-law and the chief among the marchers, saw that his position was threatened by the son; the younger Hugh had received Glamorgan in the partition of the Gloucester inheritance; Hugh of Audley and Roger d'Amory in the same way had received castles and honours in the marches. Henry of Lancaster, the earl's brother, was lord of Kidwelly. Roger Mortimer of Chirk and his nephew Roger Mortimer of Wigmore ruled the northern marches almost as independent lords[1]. **Welsh quarrel of the Despensers, 1320.**

The troubles began in the autumn parliament of 1320[2], an assembly of the lords and commons only, to which the clergy were not summoned, the pope having by his grant of a tenth relieved the king from the need of asking a grant from spiritualities. A commission was issued soon after the dismissal of the assembly, and in consequence of a petition of the commons, for the trial of cases arising out of the unlawful assemblies which were held for political purposes. On the 30th of January 1321[3] the king issued writs to the earls of Hereford, Arundel, and Warenne, and twenty-six other lords, forbidding them to attend a certain unlawful assembly at which matters were to be treated concerning the crown, in contempt of the royal prerogative and to the disturbance of the peace of **Tumults and debates, 1320–1.**

[1] Roger Mortimer of Chirk was the second son, and Roger (III) Mortimer of Wigmore the grandson of Roger (II) Mortimer, the friend and ally of Edward I, who had also acted as his lieutenant at the beginning of his reign (see above, p. 107). Hugh Mortimer who resisted Henry II in 1155 was great-grandfather of Roger (II). Roger of Chirk was justiciar of Wales; he died in the Tower after his nephew's escape.

[2] This parliament was summoned Aug. 5, to meet Oct. 9; Parl. Writs, II. i. 219; it sat until the 25th; ibid. p. 229. The pope had granted, July 14, another tenth; the clergy therefore were not summoned. The Michaelmas parliament refused to allow the king to make gifts in perpetuity to the pope's brother and two nephews; Foed. ii. 438; and passed the Statute of Westminster the fourth, touching sheriffs and juries; Statutes, i. 180. The transactions are recorded in the Rolls of Parliament, i. 365 sq. The petition for inquiry is given, p. 371.

[3] Foed. ii. 442; Parl. Writs, II. ii. 155.

The king goes to the Marches, Mar. 1321.

the kingdom. Two months later, when at Gloucester[1], the king learned that there was war in the marches. Hugh of Audley was summoned for contumaciously refusing to obey the king's writ, and the earl of Hereford with others of the marchers was directed to appear at Gloucester to treat with the king[2]. The earl of Hereford and Roger Mortimer of Wigmore had before the 23rd of April refused to obey the writ or to attend any council at which the Despensers were present[3]. On the 1st of May Edward had formally to forbid Bohun and Mortimer to attack the Despensers; and on the 15th he called a full parliament[4] to meet at Westminster on the 15th of July. In the interim Lancaster assembled his adherents lay and clerical at Pomfret and Sherburn in Yorkshire, and drew up articles of complaint[5]. Before parliament met all parties had joined against the favourites; Pembroke alone ventured to mediate[6]; the earl of Warenne and lord Badlesmere joined with Lancaster in the attack, and a solemn proscription was the result.

Approach of war in 1321.

Attack on the Despensers in parliament, July, 1321.

The proceedings on this occasion were taken with much more circumspection than had been used against Gaveston. The three estates were summoned on the distinct plea that the absence of the clergy should not be alleged as invalidating the acts of the parliament[7]. The charges against the Despensers were formally stated[8]; they had attempted to accroach to themselves royal power, to estrange the heart of the king from his people and to engross the sole government of the realm. The younger Hugh had attempted to form a league by which the king's will should be constrained; he had taught that it is to the crown rather than to the person of the king that the subject is bound by homage and allegiance, and that thus, if the personal will of the king incline to wrong, it is the sworn

Charges against the Despensers.

[1] Foed. ii. 445; Parl. Writs, II. i. 231; Rot. Parl. i. 455.

[2] Parl. Writs, II. i. 231.

[3] Parl. Writs, II. i. 232.

[4] The clergy as well as the commons were summoned; Parl. Writs, II. i. 234.

[5] June 28. Chr. Bridlington, Chron. Edw. ii. 61 sq. gives interesting details.

[6] Adam Murimuth asserts that Pembroke was secretly in the plot against the Despensers; p. 33. So also T. de la Moor, p. 595; Chron. Edw. ii. 302; cf. Annales Paulini, Chron. Edw. i. 297.

[7] Parl. Writs II. i. 236.

[8] Statutes, i. 181 sq.

duty of the subject to guide or constrain him to do right[1]. The two had moreover prevented the magnates from having proper access to the king, had removed ministers appointed by the great men of the realm, had incited civil war, exercised usurped jurisdiction, and in every way perverted and hindered justice. The sentence is passed in the name of the peers, in the presence of the king: father and son are condemned to forfeiture and exile, not to be recalled but by the assent of prelates, earls, and barons, and that in parliament duly summoned. The award was accompanied by a formal grant of pardon to the prosecutors for all breaches of the law committed in bringing the accused to justice: the chief prosecutor had been the earl of Hereford; he with the two Mortimers, the Audleys and D'Amory, lord Badlesmere, the earl Warenne, John Mowbray, John Giffard, and Richard Gray, and a large number of their followers, received separate pardons on the 20th of August[2]. On the 22nd the parliament separated.

Sentence passed.

The prosecutors secured from vengeance, July, 1321.

254. Two months after this the king took courage. An insult offered to the queen by the lady Badlesmere, who had refused to admit her into Leeds castle, provoked Edward to take up arms[3]; six earls, Norfolk, Kent, Pembroke, Warenne, Arundel, and Richmond, obeyed his summons, and Lancaster, in his hatred of Badlesmere[4], allowed the king to gather strength. Finding himself stronger than he had hoped, the king proceeded to attack the castles of the earl of Hereford, Audley, and D'Amory; and empowered the Welsh to raise forces against them as rebels. This earl Thomas was not disposed to suffer: he called an assembly of the lords of his party to Doncaster on

Edward takes up arms, October, 1321.

His vigorous action.

[1] The statement of Hugh's teaching on this point, which is made one of the charges against him, curiously enough appears in the Bridlington Annals, and in the Annales Londonienses, as the justification of the proceedings against Gaveston; see Chron. Edw. i. 153; ii. 33.

[2] Parl. Writs, II. ii. 163–168. 302 pardons were issued on the 20th of August; and 146 more in the following six weeks.

[3] Trokelowe, p. 110. On the 16th of October the writ of summons was issued; the force was to be at Leeds on the 23rd; Foed. ii. 458; Parl. Writs, II. ii. 539. October 27, the archbishop and the earl of Pembroke came to mediate; A. Murimuth, p. 34.

[4] This is distinctly asserted by the monk of Malmesbury; p. 213; Chron. Edw. ii. 262.

the 29th of November[1], and prepared to succour the earl of Hereford in the marches, whither Edward was moving to attack him. But he had miscalculated the energy which the pressure of circumstances had developed in Edward's character. Early in December the king obtained an opinion from the convocation of the clergy, that the proceedings against the Despensers were illegal[2]. At Christmas he marched to Cirencester, and attempted to cross the Severn so as to reach Hereford. Having failed to effect a passage at Worcester, he proceeded to Bridgnorth, where he was resisted by the Mortimers. On the 22nd of January the Mortimers, despairing of help from Lancaster, yielded[3]; the king crossed at Shrewsbury, marched to Hereford and thence to Gloucester, where on the 11th of February[4] he felt himself strong enough to recall the favourites. The northern lords, now thoroughly awake, and joined by the fugitives from the marches, were besieging Tickhill, and Lancaster was preparing to march southwards. Edward called a general levy to Coventry on the 28th of February, with the purpose of intercepting the earl; but the latter, having reached Burton on Trent with an inferior force, turned and fled. On the news of his retreat the castles of Kenilworth and Tutbury surrendered, and the king ordered the earls of Kent and Warenne to arrest the pursuers of the Despensers[5]; one of them, Roger D'Amory, was captured at Tutbury and shortly afterwards died[6]. The battle of Boroughbridge, in which Sir Andrew Harclay defeated and took captive the earl of

The proceedings against the Despensers declared to be unlawful, Dec. 1321.

The Mortimers taken, Jan. 1322.

Flight of Lancaster.

Battle of Boroughbridge, Mar. 16, 1322.

[1] Foed. ii. 459. It was forbidden by the king Nov. 12: Parl. Writs, II. ii. 169.

[2] Dec. 10; A. Murimuth, p. 35; T. de la Moor, p. 595; Chr. Edw. ii. 303; cf. Foed. ii. 463, 470. On Nov. 30 the king wrote to the archbishop in reference to the approaching convocation; Parl. Writs, II. ii. 172; Wake, p. 172. On the 4th of January he applied to ten bishops who had been absent from the convocation to certify their assent or to dissent from the opinion there given; Parl. Writs, II. ii. 173; Wilkins, Conc. ii. 510.

[3] Jan. 17, Roger Mortimer of Wigmore had safe conduct; Foed. ii. 472; on the 22nd the king received the submission of both; Parl. Writs, II. ii. 176.

[4] Parl. Writs, II. ii. 177.

[5] March 11; Foed. ii. 477.

[6] M. Malmesb. p. 215; Chr. Edw. ii. 268. Roger d'Amory was tried and condemned to be hanged, but was spared 'inasmuch as the king had loved him much,' and he had married the king's niece; March 13; Parl. Writs, II. ii. 261.

Lancaster, was fought on the 16th of March. There the earl of Hereford and four other barons were slain. Six days after his capture the great earl, in his own castle of Pomfret, before a body of peers with Edward himself at their head, was tried, condemned, and beheaded as a rebel taken in arms against the king, and convicted of dealing with the Scots [1]. The haste and cruelty of the proceeding were too sadly justified by the earl's own conduct in the case of Gaveston. Yet cruel, unscrupulous, treacherous, and selfish as Thomas of Lancaster is shown by every recorded act of his life to have been, there was something in so sudden and so great a fall that touches men's hearts. The cause was better than the man or the principles on which he maintained it. A people, new as yet to political power, saw in the chief opponent of royal folly a champion of their own rights: rude, insolent, and unwarlike, an adulterer and a murderer, he was liberal of his gifts to the poor, and a bountiful patron of the clergy: his fame grew after his death. The fall of earl Thomas closes the second act of the great tragedy. The minor leaders fell one by one into the king's hands; Badlesmere was taken at Stow park [2] and hanged at Canterbury; John Mowbray and John Giffard, who were taken at Boroughbridge, shared the same fate: the Mortimers were already prisoners [3]: the two Audleys surrendered at Boroughbridge, and were spared owing to their connexion with the royal house. Fourteen bannerets and fourteen bachelors were put to death [4]. Eighty-six bachelors remained in prison. The

Lancaster beheaded, Mar. 22, 1322.

His position in history.

Fate of the other captives. April–June, 1322.

[1] The earls of Kent, Richmond, Pembroke, Warenne, Arundel, Athol, and Angus were present; Foed. ii. 479; Parl. Writs, II. ii. 196; Chr. Edw. ii. 77.

[2] Leland, Coll. ii. 463.

[3] On June 13 the commission was issued for the trial of Hugh of Audley and the Mortimers; Parl. Writs, II. ii. 193: on the 14th of July justices were appointed to pass sentence on the Mortimers; ibid. 213, 216: and on the 22nd the sentence of death was commuted for perpetual imprisonment; ibid.

[4] Henry le Tyeys at London, April 3; Henry Wylyngton and Henry de Montfort at Bristol, April 5; Bartholomew Ashburnham at Canterbury, the same day; Bartholomew lord Badlesmere, at Canterbury, April 14, were tried by the king's justices and condemned; Parl. Writs, II. ii. 284 sq. Roger Clifford and John Mowbray were drawn and hanged at York; Wals. i. 165: Giffard at Gloucester; Knighton, c. 2541. Eight barons, according to the Chronicler of Lanercost, were hanged, four immediately released, ten imprisoned; fifteen knights hanged, five liberated, sixty-two

earl of Warenne and Sir Richard Gray had already changed sides.

Political and constitutional result.

Thus far the king and his friends appeared to be inclined to make a moderate use of their victory; and, had it been possible to undo the work of the last fifteen years, Edward might still have reigned happily. The determination of the personal quarrel was not disadvantageous to the constitution. The king had never been a tyrant. The earl of Lancaster had never understood the crisis through which the nation was passing. His idea was to limit the royal power by a council of barons, to court the favour of the clergy, and to diminish the burdens of the people; not to admit the three estates to a just share in the national government. Hence during his tenure of power few parliaments were called, little or no legislation, except the Ordinances, had been effected; no great national act had been undertaken; he had not even attempted to arrest the decline of England in military strength and reputation, or to recover the ground lost by the incompetency of the king. Edward was now able to choose his own advisers; and, although they were chosen apparently at hap-hazard, they were men who entertained, or found it convenient to proclaim, a policy far more in accord with the real growth of the nation.

Lancaster's rule not constitutional.

Attitude of the Despensers.

The Despensers had not been blind supporters of royal power. The elder Hugh, as an old servant of Edward I, may have preserved some traditions of his constructive policy. The younger Hugh had professed a very distinct theory of the rights of the subject as limiting the despotic will of the sovereign. It is possible that both had an idea of re-establishing the league between the king and the nation at large which alone could keep the great nobles in their proper subordination, but which had been broken in the reign of John and had only partially been restored by Edward I. But, if this were so, the tide of public hatred had set in so strongly against the king and the favourites

imprisoned; p. 245. Cf. Trokelowe, p. 124; Eulogium, iii. 196, 197; Bridlington, p. 77. The list given in the Parliamentary Writs is not to be trusted as to details. On the 11th of July 138 persons submitted to a fine to save their lives and lands; the fines recorded amount to about £15,000; Parl. Writs, II. ii. 202 sq.

as to make it impossible. The acts however of the parliament which met at York on the 2nd of May, 1322 [1], intentionally or not, embody in a very remarkable way the spirit of the Constitution. Parliament of York, in May, 1322.

This parliament contained a full representation of the beneficed clergy and commons as well as the lords spiritual and temporal and the council. It included also for the first time, and, with one exception, the only time before the reign of Henry VIII, representatives of Wales, twenty-four discreet men empowered to act for the 'communitas' of each half of the principality. The three estates sat until the 19th of May, when the commons were dismissed: the magnates until the 7th of July. The great act of the session was the repeal of the Ordinances, which were revoked in their integrity as prejudicial to the estate of the crown; for the future all ordinances or provisions concerning the king or the kingdom, made by the subjects or by any power or authority whatever, are to be void; and 'the matters which are to be established for the estate of our lord the king and of his heirs, and for the estate of the realm and of the people, shall be treated, accorded and established in parliaments by our lord the king, and by the consent of the prelates, earls and barons, and the commonalty of the realm, according as hath been heretofore accustomed.' It did not matter, then, that the ordinances had received full legislative sanction in 1311; they had been forced upon the king, drawn up and published by men chosen only by the lords, and they had been approved and authorised, not treated and accorded, by the parliament. The importance of the wording lies in its prospective bearing. The great Charter had declared how the 'commune consilium regni' was to be had; Edward I had stated the principle that that which touches all shall be approved by all; Edward II, uttering words of which he could faintly realise the importance, enunciates a still more elaborate formula of constitutional law.

Representatives from Wales.

Revocation of the Ordinances, 1322.

Constitutional principle asserted.

Prospective importance of this principle.

[1] This parliament, which contained both clergy and commons, was summoned March 14; it sat from the second to the 19th of May, on which day the commons were dismissed: Parl. Writs, II. i. 245, 258; ii. 184. The magnates continued in council until July 7. The revocation of the ordinances is dated May 19; Statutes, i. 190.

But whilst the Despensers thus hastened to repeal the burdensome limitations placed on the action of the crown, they were careful to withdraw none of the concessions by which the ordainers had obtained the support of the nation. Another document[1] issued by Edward at the same time declares the state of the law on these points, and, by reference to his father's statutes, shows that no new legislation was required to secure the boons conferred in the Ordinances. He, by the assent of the archbishops, bishops, abbots, priors, earls, barons, and community here assembled, makes his own ordinances, confirms the rights of the church as contained in the Great Charter and other statutes, and the king's peace according to law and custom; the statute of 1300 touching purveyance and prises[2], that of 1316 touching sheriffs, the ordinance of 1306 on the Forests, that of 1300 on the courts of the steward and marshal; he relaxes the operation of the statute of Acton Burnell, and reforms the law touching appeals and outlawry in the very words of the ordinances of 1311. The articles by which the royal power of giving was restrained are the chief points which are not re-enacted. These measures were accompanied by a reversal of the acts against the Despensers and for the pardon of the pursuers; and a grant of money[3] and men[4] was made for the prosecution of the war.

Edward republishes some of the Ordinances as his own, May, 1322.

Renewed legislation, May, 1322.

As soon as the parliament was over the king marched towards Scotland. But it was now too late. The Scots had learned warfare whilst the English had been forgetting it. They avoided a pitched battle, wore out the enemy by hasty attacks

Edward's ill-success against the Scots, Oct. 1322.

[1] Rot. Parl. i. 456.

[2] An order for collecting the revived New Customs, given in consequence of the revocation of the Ordinances, was signed July 20; Parl. Writs, II. ii. 214: a subsidy, corresponding with the new increment of 1317, was granted by the merchants on the 16th of June 1322, and stopped July 4, 1323: ibid. ii. 193, 229.

[3] The clergy of the province of Canterbury granted 5*d.* in the mark on spirituals; but their authority being doubtful, the archbishop called a convocation for June 9; Parl. Writs, II. i. 259; Wake, p. 274. On the 20th of April the pope granted a tenth for two years; Wilkins, Conc. ii. 524.

[4] One man-at-arms was to be furnished by every township to serve for forty days; this was the contribution of the shires; but it was generally redeemed by a money payment; Parl. Writs, II. i. 573 sq.

and distressed the country with rapid inroads. Edward narrowly escaped capture at Byland on the 14th of October. The parliament, which had been summoned for November 14 to Ripon, had to be transferred to York [1], and even there many of the magnates found it impossible to attend [2]. Worse than all, treachery was discovered among the king's most trusted servants. Sir Andrew Harclay, now earl of Carlisle [3], and warden of the Scottish marches, was found intriguing with the Scots in January, 1323. On the 1st of February the order was given for his arrest; he was tried by a special commission of judges, and he died the death of a traitor on the 3rd of March [4]. The conclusion of a truce for thirteen years, in the following June, proved Edward's weakness or the general distrust, and left him to work out his own ruin without let or hindrance.

Parliament at York, Nov. 1322.

Harclay put to death, March, 1323.

Truce with the Scots, June, 1323.

255. The rest of the reign is one consistent story of desperate recklessness on the part of the Despensers, helpless self-abandonment on the part of the king, and treachery unjustifiable, unparalleled and all but universal, on the part of the magnates. The hatred of the favourites had risen to a pitch which seems irrational: Robert Baldock [5] the chancellor and bishop Stapledon the treasurer shared the odium of the

Hatred of the Despensers and other servants of the king.

[1] The parliament, to which the inferior clergy were not called, was summoned Sept. 18, to meet Nov. 14 at Ripon; Parl. Writs, II. i. 261: on the 30th of October, the place was altered to York; ibid. p. 263: it sat until Nov. 29; ibid. p. 277.

[2] Foed. ii. 499. This parliament granted a tenth from the barons and shires, and a sixth from the towns; ibid. p. 527; Parl. Writs, II. i. 280; Rot. Parl. i. 457; W. Dene, Ang. Sac. i. 362. As the clergy were not present the king asked the archbishops, Nov. 27, to summon their convocations at Lincoln and York; Parl. Writs, II. i. 280. The clergy of Canterbury were summoned Dec. 2, to meet on Jan. 14. They refused to make a grant, on the ground that the pope had granted the tenth for two years; ibid. 283. See W. Dene, Ang. Sac. i. 363; Wake, p. 275; Wilkins, Conc. ii. 517.

[3] Harclay was created earl March 25, 1322.

[4] Foed. ii. 504, 509; Parl. Writs, II. ii. 225, 262; A. Murimuth, p. 39; Ann. Lanercost, pp. 248, 251.

[5] Robert Baldock became chancellor on the 20th of August, 1323, in succession to bishop Salmon. On the death of bishop Sandale in November 1319, the treasury remained for a few months under Walter of Norwich the chief baron; Stapledon was treasurer from Feb. 18, 1320, to June 3, 1325, when he was succeeded by William de Melton, archbishop of York.

rest; the king had fallen into contempt; all public confidence had ceased; the military summonses were not obeyed, the taxes were not collected; the country was overrun by bands of lawless men; the law was unexecuted, and among the greatest offenders were Edward's most trusted friends. The most important of the great prisoners of state[1] was suffered to escape and go over to France. The elder Hugh le Despenser put no limit on his acquisitiveness and was unable to check the arrogance and violence of his son: the queen conceived a bitter hatred for him which scarcely needed opportunity and temptation to extend to her husband likewise. The people were told that Edward was a changeling, no true son of the great king. Miracles were wrought at the tombs of earl Thomas[2] and the other martyrs of the rebellion. No class was free from disaffection. Even Henry de Beaumont, who had been one of the obnoxious favourites in 1311, in May 1323 refused to advise the king and addressed him in words of insult for which he was put under arrest[3].

General disorder.

Escape of Mortimer, Aug. 1324.

Alienation of the queen.

False rumours.

Disaffection.

The relations of the king with the prelates were likewise critical. The archbishop of Canterbury was altogether unable to influence his brethren, and some of the most powerful among them had grievances or ambitions of their own. The weakness of Edward and the policy of the popes, who sometimes played into his hands, sometimes defied him with impunity, had promoted to the episcopate men of every shade of political opinion and of every grade of morality. Three of these, John Drokensford bishop of Bath, Henry Burghersh of Lincoln, and Adam Orlton of Hereford, had been implicated in the late rebellion. Burghersh, the nephew of lord Badlesmere, had under his uncle's influence been forced by the king, against the wish of the canons and when under canonical age, into the see of

Ingratitude and selfishness of the bishops, 1323–1326;

especially Burghersh and Orlton.

[1] Roger Mortimer escaped from the Tower on August 1, 1324; Blaneford, p. 145; Foed. ii. 530; Parl. Writs, II. ii. 232, 239. Robert Walkefare, the chief adviser of Humfrey Bohun, escaped from Corfe; Wals. i. 178.

[2] June 28, 1323; Foed. ii. 526. At Bristol also Henry de Montfort and Henry Wylyngton, who had been hanged there, were said to be working miracles; Foed. ii. 536, 547.

[3] Foed. ii. 520; Parl. Writs, II. i. 285.

Lincoln[1]; Orlton had been placed by the pope at Hereford in opposition to the king's nominee[2], and had with difficulty obtained admission to his see. The former had the wrongs of his uncle to avenge, the latter was attached to the queen and in league with his neighbours the Mortimers. John Stratford, a clerk of the council, was sent to Avignon by the king in 1322 to complain of their conduct[3]. Whilst Stratford was at Avignon the see of Winchester fell vacant, and Edward immediately wrote to the pope for the appointment of Robert Baldock, then keeper of the Privy Seal[4]. Instead of furthering his master's wishes Stratford obtained Winchester for himself, and, although after a year's resistance Edward admitted him to his temporalities, the new bishop let his resentment outweigh both gratitude and honesty. His example was an inviting one: William Ayermin by a similar process obtained the see of Norwich which the king had intended for Baldock, in 1325[5]. Official jealousies moreover created personal antipathies and partisanships among the bishops themselves; Drokensford had probably been offended at being outrun in the race for secular preferment; archbishop Reynolds took offence at the appointment of the archbishop of York to the treasurership[6], and the prelates who had risen under the influence of the ordainers were opposed as a matter of course to those who had been promoted by the king. Three or four good men amongst them stood aloof from politics; three or four were honestly grateful and faithful to Edward:

Bishop Stratford.

Bishop Ayermin.

Rivalry of the two archbishops, June, 1325.

[1] M. Malmesb. p. 201; Chr. Edw., ii. 251. The king wrote to the pope to give him the see of Winchester in 1319; Foed. ii. 404; and applied for Lincoln in 1320; ibid. 414. He was in his twenty-ninth year; ibid. 425.

[2] A. Murimuth, p. 31; Foed. ii. 328.

[3] Foed. ii. 504.

[4] Winchester became vacant on the 12th of April, 1323; Edward wrote in favour of Baldock, April 26; Stratford, who was bidden to urge the appointment, and who was agent to Baldock, presented the letter to the pope on the 9th of May: the pope nominated Stratford on the 20th of June; Foed. ii. 491, 518, 525, 531, 533. Adam Murimuth, p. 40, says, 'litterae ad curiam nimis tarde venerunt.' Stratford was admitted to his temporalities June 28, 1324; Foed. ii. 557.

[5] M. Malmesb. p. 239; Chr. Edw., ii. 284. Ayermin had been in 1324 elected to Carlisle, but the pope preferred John de Ross; Ann. Lanercost, p. 253.

[6] M. Malmesb. p. 237; Chr. Edw., ii. 283; W. Dene, p. 365; Parl. Writs, II. ii. 274.

the conduct of the rest proves that the average of episcopal morality had sadly sunk since the death of Winchelsey. Yet Edward in his infatuation or simplicity trusted all alike, except Orlton[1], against whom, when the prelates in the parliament of 1324 had refused to surrender him, he obtained a verdict from a jury of the country as guilty of high treason.

Edward's foolish confidence.

Threats from France.

The death of Philip V in 1322 caused the king of England to be summoned to do homage for Gascony and Ponthieu to his successor. A peremptory summons to Amiens for the 1st of July, 1324, was regarded as the prelude to a sentence of confiscation. The earl of Pembroke, who was sent over as envoy, died in France[2]; in him the king lost the last trustworthy friend who might have been able to save him. Edmund of Kent having failed to negotiate peace, in 1325 the queen was sent to use her influence with her brother. Edward, who might easily have complied with all that was demanded of him, was prevented by the Despensers from making the journey; they felt that they were safe neither in England nor in France without him. Isabella, freed from her husband's company, embittered against the Despensers by the measures of precaution which they had taken against her influence, and jealous of their ascendency over the king, found a lover and a counsellor in the fugitive Mortimer[3]. A deliberate plan for the overthrow of the Despensers was formed in France. The king's ambassadors, Stratford, Ayermin, Henry de Beaumont[4], whom he had rashly trusted, fell in with the design. The earl of Kent joined them. Edward the heir of the kingdom, the king's eldest son and earl of Chester, to whom, in the hope of avoiding the required

Death of the earl of Pembroke in 1324.

Isabella goes to France, 1325,

and forms a league against her husband.

[1] Blaneforde, p. 141; T. de la Moor, p. 597; Chr. Edw., ii. 305.

[2] June 23, 1324; Blaneforde, p. 150.

[3] On the relations of the queen and Mortimer the chroniclers of the time are very reticent; 'suspecta fuerat familiaritas . . . prout fama publica testabatur;' Ann. Lanercost, p. 266; Wals. i. 177; 'eam illicitis complexibus R. de Mortuomari devinctam;' Galfr. le Baker (ed. Thompson), p. 20; T. de la Moor, p. 305. According to the annals of Lanercost, Hugh le Despenser wished to obtain a divorce for Edward; p. 254. Froissart, liv. i. c. 23, is scarcely more positive. Avesbury says that Mortimer 'se cum dicta domina Isabella, ut facta secretius non dicenda taceam, alligavit;' p. 4.

[4] They were commissioned Nov. 15, 1324, and again May 5, 1325; Foed. ii. 579, 597. Stratford advised that the queen should be sent, and Edward reported this to the pope, March 8, 1325; Foed. ii. 595.

homage, the hapless king had made over his foreign estates[1], was sent to France to perform the ceremony: but no sooner had he reached his mother's side than he became her facile tool. By negotiating for him a marriage with a daughter of the count of Hainault, she obtained an escort and force for the invasion of England. Whether at that time she and her more intimate counsellors entertained any deeper design against the king can hardly be determined. The English bishops and earls were not likely to commit themselves to overt treason. And the later events seem to indicate that the spirit of hatred and revenge grew stronger in her and Mortimer as their scheme prospered.

The young Edward sent to France.

Edward meanwhile was holding session after session of parliament, council after council[2], in which no business was done, and summoning armies and fleets which he was unable to pay, and which were dispersed as soon as they were assembled. Henry of Lancaster, the brother of earl Thomas, now earl of

Edward's futile measures, 1323–1326.

[1] Ponthieu was transferred Sept. 2, 1325; Foed. ii. 607; and Aquitaine on the 10th; ibid. 608. The young Edward sailed on the 12th; ibid. 609; Parl. Writs, II. ii. 276. On the 1st of December the king had heard that the queen and her son refused to return to him; Foed. ii. 615.

[2] On the 20th of November, 1323, Edward summoned the barons and commons to meet at Westminster Jan. 20, 1324; and ordered the provincial convocations of the clergy to be held at London and York the same day. The bishops, except one, were summoned to the convocation, not to the parliament; Parl. Writs, II. i. 286–288. But on December 26 the writs were issued in the usual form for a parliament of the three estates on the 23rd of February; ibid. 289; and the convocations were consequently discharged; ibid. 291. It was in this session, which lasted until March 18, that the king made a vain attempt to obtain an aid for the ransom of the earl of Richmond, and to arraign bishop Orlton; Blaneforde, pp. 140, 141. On the 9th of May, 1324, the sheriffs were ordered to bring up all the knights of the kingdom to Westminster on May 30; Parl. Writs, II. i. 316. On the 13th of September the king summoned a large body of barons to meet on Oct. 20 at Salisbury, and on the 20th of September directed the sheriffs to send two elected knights from each shire to the same meeting; Parl. Writs, II. i. 317, 318; but on the 24th summoned the same bodies to London on the day before fixed; ibid. The assembly of barons and prelates held June 25, 1325, is called a parliament, but it contained neither the commons nor the beneficed clergy; Parl. Writs, II. i. 328. On the 10th of October, 1325, a parliament of the three estates was summoned to meet at Westminster, Nov. 18; Parl. Writs, II. i. 334. It sat until Dec. 5; ibid. i. 346. See Rot. Parl. i. 430 sq.: Wake, p. 277. And in 1326 the king summoned a council to Stamford for Oct. 13, for which day the archbishop had also called the convocation at London; Parl. Writs, II. i. 349.

The king's few supporters.

Leicester[1], notwithstanding the open hostility of the Despensers, and John of Warenne, sustained the government: the former was to be regent in case the king was prevailed on to go to France, the latter was to be commander-in-chief if the king stayed at home. Walter Stapledon, the bishop of Exeter, who had been sent in the retinue of the young Edward to France, returned home as a fugitive from the vindictive malice of the queen[2]. There was no longer any doubt of an approaching invasion. The king's measures did not reassure the nation; the stoppage of communication with the continent, the search of all the ships that came to Dover for letters, the threatened outlawry of the queen and her son, the vain summons addressed to the contumacious ambassadors, the issue of commissions of array under the view of the bishops[3], the order that they should equip themselves and their retainers, and preach sermons to animate the people for defence, seemed like the struggles of a drowning man. The Despensers, so mighty for aggression, were helpless for defence: their craft and selfish cunning was exemplified only in the retention of their hold on the king, without whom they could not hope to escape, and whom they would recklessly ruin rather than leave him free.

His alarm and precautions.

Helplessness of the favourites.

Isabella lands, Sept. 24, 1326.

At length, on the 24th of September, 1326, Isabella landed in Suffolk, proclaiming herself the avenger of earl Thomas and the enemy of the Despensers[4]. In a proclamation issued at Wallingford, Oct. 15, she charged the Despensers and Baldock with despoiling the church and crown, putting to death, disinheriting, imprisoning, and banishing the lords, oppressing widows and orphans, and grieving the people with tallages and exactions. Not even now was any ulterior design declared; her purpose might not be more dangerous or less salutary than that of the

[1] M. Malmesb. pp. 234–236; Chr. Edw., ii. 280–282. Leicester was somehow implicated in a charge of witchcraft practised against the king; but his name is not mentioned in the proceedings; Parl. Writs, II. ii. 269.

[2] The queen's estates were taken into the king's hands by order given to the bishop of Exeter the treasurer, Sept. 18, 1324; Foed. ii. 569.

[3] Parl. Writs, II. i. 665 sq., 741 sq., 748 sq.; Foed. ii. 564, 565. On the 12th of May, 1326, the bishops were ordered to equip themselves and their families for defence; ibid. p. 627; and on the 12th of August to preach sermons to the same effect; p. 637.

[4] Foed. ii. 645, 646.

ordainers; the king's brothers and his cousin of Leicester joined her; the bishops of Lincoln, Norwich, and Hereford obtained for her supplies of money from their brethren, and her march was a triumph. The king, on the news of her landing, after applying in vain to the Londoners for a force, hurried into the West of England; only two earls, Arundel and Warenne, held by him. Archbishop Reynolds, who with Stratford, Stapledon, and a few others remained in London, at first attempted to intimidate the invaders by publishing, on the 30th of September, the bulls of excommunication which the pope had launched against the king's enemies, that is, the Scots[1]. Stratford, clinging to the old idea that in such cases it was the office of the clergy to arbitrate, offered to mediate, but found no one willing to share the risk, and, when the proposal failed, obeyed the summons of the queen. Stapledon, on the 15th of October, fell a victim to the violence of the citizens. The archbishop fled into Kent to await the issue; although he was indebted for everything to Edward, he was already committed to the queen.

She is joined by the earls and bishops.

Affairs in London.

Unable to defend himself, the king fled first to Gloucester. Pursued thither, he passed into Wales, and thence tried to escape to Ireland. Failing in this, he took refuge at Neath Abbey, and there offered to treat with his wife. She had marched by Oxford, where Orlton preached rebellion before the University on the text 'My head, my head[2];' by Gloucester, where the lords of the north and of the marches joined her; by Berkeley, where she restored the castle to the rightful heir whom the Despensers had dispossessed; to Bristol, where she arrived on the 26th of October. There she avenged earl Thomas by hanging the elder Hugh le Despenser, and there the ultimate purpose of the invasion was made known. Young Edward was the same day proclaimed guardian of the realm, which the king had deserted, and was accepted by the assent of the assembled magnates in the name of the community[3]. On the 16th of

Flight of Edward.

The queen's march to Bristol.

Proclamation of Regency, Oct. 26, 1326.

[1] Ann. Paulini, Chr. Edw., i. 315.

[2] 'Caput meum doleo,' 2 Kings iv. 19; Galfr. le Baker, p. 23; Chr. Edw., ii. 310.

[3] Foed. ii. 646. The archbishop of Dublin, the bishops of Winchester, Ely, Lincoln, Hereford, and Norwich, the earls of Norfolk, Kent, and

November the king, with Hugh le Despenser the younger and the chancellor Baldock, was captured. Hugh, on the 24th, suffered the death of a traitor at Hereford. At the same place, on the 17th, the earl of Arundel had been beheaded by order of Mortimer. Baldock remained in the custody of Orlton until his death in the following spring. The king himself was reserved for more elaborate and protracted torture. The finishing stroke of the revolution was to be given by the parliament, which was to be held on the 7th of January, 1327.

Executions.

Parliament, Jan. 7, 1327.

This parliament was summoned in strict conformity with the precedent set in the parliament of York, in 1322; even the forty-eight representatives of Wales were called up, to serve the cause of Mortimer as they had then been made to swell the party of the Despensers. The writs had been issued first by young Edward at Bristol, on the 28th of October[1], in his father's name. They stated that the king would be, on the day named, December 15, absent from the kingdom, but that the business would be transacted before the queen and her son, as the guardian of the realm, by whom the writs were tested. After the great seal had been wrested from the king[2], new writs of more regular form had been drawn up, and on the 3rd of December the meeting was postponed to the 7th of January.

Proceedings of the parliament.

On that day the parliament met, the king being a prisoner at Kenilworth. But although the forms of the constitution were so far observed, the rest of the proceedings were as tumultuary as they were revolutionary. An oath was taken by the prelates and magnates to maintain the cause of the queen and her son[3]. Adam Orlton, the confidential agent of Mortimer, and the

Leicester, Thomas Wake, Henry de Beaumont, William la Zouche of Ashby, Robert of Montalt, Robert de Morle, and Robert de Wateville, with others, by assent of the whole 'communitas' of the kingdom elected Edward to be 'custos' in the name and by the authority of the king during his absence; Parl. Writs, II. i. 349.

[1] Parl. Writs, II. i. 350.

[2] On the 20th the bishop of Hereford was sent to demand the great seal from the king, who was then at Monmouth; he brought it on the 26th to the queen at Martley; on the 30th, at Cirencester, it was given to the bishop of Norwich; Foed. ii. 646; Parl. Writs, II. i. 349, 350. Stratford was made treasurer, but both he and the chancellor were superseded at the beginning of the new reign; Walsingham, i. 184. See p. 386.

[3] Parl. Writs, II. i. 354.

guiding spirit of the queen's party, took upon himself to lead the deliberations, an office which usually belonged to the chancellor. He declared that if Isabella should rejoin her husband she would be murdered by him, and begged the parliament to take a day to consider whether they would have father or son to be king. The next day he put the question; various opinions were stated, but in the midst of a noisy mob of Londoners few of the king's friends ventured to speak, and the voice of the assembly declared unmistakeably in favour of his son. The young Edward was led into Westminster Hall and presented with loud acclamations to the people[1]. Four bishops, William de Melton of York, John de Ross of Carlisle, Haymo Heath of Rochester[2], and Stephen Gravesend of London, were bold enough to protest. The wretched archbishop Reynolds cried out that the voice of the people was the voice of God. Among the lay lords none, so far as we know, had a word to say for Edward; but no doubt hatred of the Despensers, and fear of vengeance from one side or the other, stopped the mouths of many. The resolution thus irregularly taken was then put in due form. Six articles were drawn up by bishop Stratford, containing the reasons why young Edward should be crowned king[3]. First, the king was incompetent to govern; throughout his reign he had been led by evil counsellors, without troubling himself to distinguish good from evil or to remedy the evil when he was requested by the great and wise men of the realm. Secondly, he had persistently rejected good counsel, and had spent the whole of his time in unbecoming labours and occupations, neglecting the business of the kingdom. Thirdly, by

Orlton's declaration on the queen's behalf.

The younger Edward chosen king.

Six articles drawn by Stratford; justifying the deposition of Edward II.

[1] A careful account of the proceedings is given by W. Dene, the Rochester notary, Ang. Sac. i. 367. 'Vox populi vox Dei' seems to have been the archbishop's thesis; this maxim is ancient; see Alcuin, Epp. ed. Dümmler, p. 808; and Eadmer, Hist. Nov. lib. i. p. 29; it is quoted by William of Malmesbury, Gesta Pontificum (ed. Hamilton), p. 22; and in one of the lives of Becket, S. T. C. ii. 136. The bishop of Winchester added, 'cui caput infirmum, caetera membra dolent;' Orlton, 'Vae terrae cujus rex puer est;' Eccl. x. 17.

[2] W. Dene, p. 367. The bishop of Rochester however sang the Litany at the coronation; p. 368.

[3] See Orlton's answer to the appeal laid against him in 1334; in Twysden, Dec. Scriptt. c. 2765; Foed. ii. 650.

Charges against the king.

default of good government he had lost Scotland, Ireland, and Gascony. Fourthly, he had injured the church and imprisoned her ministers; and had imprisoned, exiled, disinherited, and put to shameful death many great and noble men of the land. Fifthly, he had broken his coronation oath, especially in the point of doing justice to all. Sixthly, he had ruined the realm and was himself incorrigible and without hope of amendment. The charges were taken as proved by common notoriety, but the queen's advisers thought it wise to obtain from the king a formal resignation rather than to furnish a dangerous precedent, and leave occasion for popular reaction. After two vain attempts to persuade Edward to face the parliament—the first made by two bishops [1] and the second by a joint committee of two earls, two barons, four knights, and four citizens chosen by the parliament—the three prelates who had had the chief hand in his humiliation, Lincoln, Hereford, and Winchester [2], with two earls, two barons, two abbots, and two judges, were sent to request his consent to his son's election. Edward yielded at once. Sir William Trussell, as proctor for the whole parliament, renounced the homage and fealties which the members had severally made to the king [3]; and Sir Thomas Blount, the steward of the household, broke his staff of office in token that his master had ceased to reign. This was done on the

Messages sent to him.

Renunciation of homage.

Completion of the deposition, Jan. 20, 1327.

[1] Parl. Writs, II. i. p. 354; the two were Winchester and Hereford, who brought their answer on Jan. 12; Ann. Lanerc. p. 257.

[2] Parl. Writs, II. i. p. 354; Galfr. le Baker, p. 27; Chr. Edw., ii. 313.

[3] Knighton, c. 2550; M. Malmesb. p. 244; Chr. Edw., ii. 290. The words of renunciation were as follows: 'Jeo William Trussell, procuratour des prelatez, contez et barons et altrez gentz en ma procuracye nomes, eyant al ceo playne et suffysant pouare, les homages et fealtez a vous Edward roy d'Engleterre, come al roy avant ces œures, de par lez ditz persones en ma procuracye nomes, rend et rebaylle sus a vous Edward et deliver et face quitez lez persones avantditz, en la meillour manere que lez et costome donnent, e face protestacion en non de eaux, quils ne voillent desormes estre en vostre fealte, ne en vostre lyance, ne cleyment de vous come de roy riens tenir, Encz vous tiegnent des horse priveye persone sanz nule maner de reale dignite.' The last commission contained twenty-four members, the bishops of Winchester and Hereford, the earls of Leicester and Warenne, the barons Ros and Courtenay, two abbots, two priors, two justices, two Dominicans, two Carmelites, two knights from the north of Trent, and two from the south, two citizens from London and two from the Cinque Ports; Ann. Lanerc. p. 258; cf. T. de la Moor, p. 600; Chr. Edw., ii. 313.

20th of January. Edward II survived his deposition for eight months; but his doom was sealed from the moment of his capture. So long as he lived none of his enemies could be safe; the nation was sure to awake to the fact that his faults, whatever they might have been, were no reason why they should submit to the rule of an adulterous Frenchwoman and her paramour. His death would rob the malcontents of a rallying point for revolt. He was murdered on the 21st of September, 1327. His son's reign was held to begin on the 25th of January.

Insecurity of the king's life.

His death, Sept. 1327.

The fate of Edward II suggests questions which are by no means easily answered; and the accusations brought against him by Stratford, although in themselves mere generalities on which no strictly legal proceedings could be based, probably contain the germ of the truth. Edward had neglected his royal work [1], he had never shown himself sensible of the dignity and importance, much less of the responsibility, of kingship. He had taken no pains to make himself popular, to diminish the unpopularity brought on him by the conduct of his servants, or by working for and in the face of his people to encourage the feeling of loyalty towards his own person. Except his few dangerous favourites he had had no friends, none whom he had tried to benefit; or if he had, as in the case of Reynolds, gone out of his way to promote a servant, he had chosen his men with marvellous imprudence. He had thrown off all the business of state upon his favourites, had listened to no complaints against them, and had allowed them to commit acts of illegal oppression which he himself had neither will nor energy to command. His vindictiveness, exaggerated probably by the queen and her friends, was in itself largely to be attributed to the elder Despenser, who no doubt regarded the death of earl Thomas as necessary to his own safety; but the death of

Edward's real misgovernment.

His neglect of his people.

His unwise choice of servants.

His indolence.

His vindictiveness.

[1] 'Ecce nunc rex noster Edwardus sex annis complete regnavit, nec aliquid laudabile vel dignum memoria hucusque patravit nisi quod regaliter nupsit et prolem elegantem regni heredem sibi suscitavit;' M. Malmesb. p. 135; Chr. Edw., ii. 191. Of Richard and John even their enemies allowed that they lived and reigned 'satis laboriose;' R. Coggesh. A.D. 1199, 1216.

the earl was not without legal justification, and its consequences were due not so much to his innocence as to the many and powerful interests that were wounded by it. But on the whole it must be said that the success of the revolution constitutes its justification. Edward could not have sunk so low as to fall a victim to a conspiracy contrived by his faithless wife and jealous kinsmen, if he had not alienated from himself every good and powerful influence in the realm. That his doom was unjust; that his punishment was, if we compare him with the general run of kings, altogether out of proportion to his offence; that, however much he may have brought it upon himself, it came from hands from which it ought not to have come, needs no argument. And if the moral justice of his fall be admitted, it is idle to question the legal justice of his deposition. A king who cannot make a stand against rebellion cannot expect justice either in form or in substance. The constitution had no rule or real precedent for discarding a worthless king. There was then no pretence of a formal trial; the accused was not heard in defence nor allowed to claim impunity by making promises or accepting new constitutional limitations. It is hard to say whence the parliament borrowed such few formalities as were really observed. True, the barons under John and Henry III had talked of changing the succession by renouncing the allegiance of the king and choosing another, and in the former case had actually done so; but they had never thought of extorting a resignation or setting the son in his father's stead. The undutiful sons of Henry II had rebelled with other pretexts and under widely different circumstances. John Stratford may have looked further back and read of his predecessor at Winchester declaring Stephen dethroned and choosing the empress in his place; but for anything like a real example in England recourse must be had to the Anglo-Saxon annals, which told how the ealdormen had set aside Ethelred the Unready, or how the North people renounced Edwy for his incompetency, and because, like Rehoboam, 'he forsook the counsel of the old men which they had given him, and consulted with the young men that were grown up with him and which stood

The revolution justified by its success.

Question of justice.

Question of procedure.

Questionable precedents.

Rehoboam the classical example.

before him[1].' The case of Edwy had some points in common with that of Edward II; but in the one the king was a boy of sixteen, in the other a man of forty-two.

Examples in Germany.

Outside England examples might be sought still farther back, in the days when the emperor Charles the Third was deserted by his people, as in mind and body incapable of reigning, or when the Merovingian puppets were set aside by Pipin. A very close resemblance may be traced between the articles of accusation against Edward II and those laid against the emperor Henry IV in 1076[2].

Case of Adolf of Nassau.

But it is possible that the deposition of Adolf of Nassau, king of the Romans, which took place in 1298, may have been present to Stratford's mind when he drew the articles. The electors who had chosen Adolf called together the people on the 23rd of June and proclaimed that the king had

[1] So the biographer of Dunstan says of Edwy, 'a brumali populo relinqueretur contemptus quoniam in commisso regimine insipienter egisset, sagaces vel sapientes odio vanitatis disperdens et ignaros quosque sibi consimiles studio dilectionis adsciscens,' p. 35; Osbern, p. 102: 'alter Roboam, despectis majoribus natu, puerorum consilia sectabatur;' ibid. 99; cf. Eadmer, pp. 188, 194. 'Latens odium, consilium juvenum, proprium lucrum destruit regnum;' Avesbury, ed. Hearne, p. 257. Archbishop Stratford in the great quarrel of 1341 brings up Rehoboam as a warning to Edward III; Foed. ii. 1143. See too Ann. Lanercost, p. 209.

[2] Lambert. Hersfeld, ed. Pertz, Scr. v. 252. The passage is long but significant: 'Replicabant ab tenero, ut aiunt, ungue omnem vitae regis institutionem, quibus probris, quibus flagitiis existimationem suam decusque imperii, vix tum adulta aetate, maculasset, quas injurias singulis, quas in commune omnibus, ubi primum pubertatis annos attigit, irrogasset: quod remotis a familiaritate sua principibus infimos homines et nullis majoribus ortos summis honoribus extulisset, et cum eis noctes perinde ac dies in deliberationibus insumens, ultimum si possit nobilitati exterminium machinaretur; quod barbaris gentibus vacatione data, in subditos sibi populos dedita opera ferrum distrinxisset et in eorum nece hostili crudelitate grassaretur; regnum quod a parentibus suis pacatissimum et bonis omnibus florentissimum accepit, quam foedum, quam despicabile, quam intestinis cladibus infestum cruentumque reddidisset; ecclesias et monasteria destructa, victualia servorum Dei versa esse in stipendia militum, studium religionis et rerum ecclesiasticarum transisse ad arma militaria, et ad munitiones exstruendas, non quibus vis et impetus barbarorum arceatur, sed quibus patriae tranquillitas eripiatur et liberae gentis cervicibus durissimae servitutis jugum imponatur; nullum usquam esse viduis et orphanis solatium, nullum oppressis et calumniam sustinentibus refugium, non legibus reverentiam, non moribus disciplinam, non ecclesiae auctoritatem suam, non reipublicae manere dignitatem suam; ita unius hominis temeritate sacra et profana, divina et humana, fasque nefasque confusa esse et implicita. Proinde tantarum calamitatum unicum ac singulare superesse remedium ut quanto ocyus, amoto eo, alius rex crearetur.'

Analogy between Adolf and Edward.

'rejected the counsels of the wise and acquiesced in those of the young, and never fulfilled the duties of a ruler. He had no wealth of his own nor friends who would help him faithfully.' Seeing these defects, and more than twenty others, they had asked, and, as they said, obtained, papal permission to absolve him from the dignity of reigning. Each elector had his own reason: one said, 'king Adolf is poor in money and friends; he is a fool; the kingdom under him will soon fail in wealth and honour;' another said, 'it is necessary that he should be deposed;' another proposed to choose the duke of Austria; another said, 'the counsel is sound, let it be done at once [1].' Among the more circumstantial charges were these: he had been useless and faithless to the interests of the empire, he had neglected Italy and the outlying provinces; he had failed to maintain the peace, and had allowed and encouraged private war; he had neglected good counsel, despised the clergy, contemned the nobles, and preferred mere knights in their place; and had served as a mercenary in the armies of Edward I of England [2]. With the very act which absolved him from the dignity of government was coupled the nomination of his successor.

But although this event must have been well known to the English lords, the analogy between the two cases may be merely accidental. Both serve to illustrate the truths that kings are not deposed until a rival is ready to take the vacant place, and that their sins are rather the justification than the cause of their rejection.

[1] Chron. Colmar, ap. Urstis. ii. 57, 59; Pertz, Scr. xvii. 263, 264: 'sapientum consilia sprevit, juvenum consiliis acquievit, et regenda minime terminavit; divitias per se non habuit, nec amicos qui eum vellent fideliter juvare.' 'Adolfus rex pauper est in rebus pariter et amicis; stultus est, regnum sub eo breviter deficiet in divitiis et honore.'

[2] Trithemius, Ann. Hirsaug. ed. Mabillon, ii. 69, A.D. 1298: 'Primam depositionis ejus causam principes eo in tempore assignabant quod imperio esset non solum inutilis sed etiam infidelis, propterea quod imperii coronam sperneret, et Italiam, Lombardiam, et alias nationes sive provincias imperii non curaret, sed regnum mancum et infirmum per suam negligentiam redderet;' secondly, he had caused civil wars; thirdly, he had multiplied diets and practised extortion; fourthly, 'quod principes regni per superbiam suam contemneret, nobiles sperneret, clericos despiceret, omnia regni negotia et maxime ardua non juxta consilia principum sed secundum proprii capitis judicium omnia disponeret;' fifthly, he had served under Edward I; and sixthly, had encouraged the robber knights.

If we ask how Edward came to be so entirely deserted, the answer is not hard to find. The Despensers had alienated all his friends; and, when the Despensers had fallen, the energy of his enemies left those who might have returned to his side no time to reunite around him. There were at least three parties in the baronage: one which hated the king and heartily sympathised with the queen and Mortimer, the party of which Orlton was the spokesman, and who were the agents in the murder of the king. A second party believed itself bound to avenge the death of Lancaster; and this included the earl Henry of Leicester his brother, and the northern lords. A third simply hated the Despensers, and were not likely, on constitutional grounds, to love the new rulers; but they had no time to think, no power, if they had the will, to save the king. The people in general were misled, for no pains had been spared to spread every sort of calumny against Edward; they were told that the pope absolved them from their allegiance, that the queen was an injured wife, the king an abandoned wretch, an idiot and a changeling. The citizens of London, foremost as usual in any work of aggression, had, by the murder of bishop Stapledon, bound themselves to the party of Mortimer. From the prelates alone some independent action might be expected; and no doubt archbishop Melton, and the three brave men who with him defied the threats of Mortimer and the cries of the London mob, had others who sympathised with them, but were disheartened by the cowardice of the archbishop of Canterbury. Reynolds, it is satisfactory to know, died of shame for the part that he had played. But Orlton, Burghersh, and Ayermin shared the triumph of their party, and Stratford reconciled himself, it would seem, to the patronage of the queen and her lover by the thought that the liberty of the church and people had grown stronger by the change of masters. Yet among these men, as the later events showed, there was little unity of purpose. Stratford, whose selfish fears were stronger than his gratitude, was somewhat of a statesman. He knew that he was unworthy of the king's confidence, and his consciousness of his danger stimulated his constitutional activity. Burghersh had the wrongs of his

Causes of the desertion of Edward.

Existing parties.

The people misled.

Violence of the Londoners.

Bad conduct of the bishops.

Excuse for Stratford and Burghersh;

none for Ayermin and Orlton.

uncle to avenge; otherwise he had little sympathy with the Lancastrians or with the defenders of the constitution. Ayermin as the queen's creature, and Orlton as Mortimer's confidant, were without such slender justification as might be furnished by the fears of Stratford or the vindictiveness of Burghersh. It was to Orlton in particular that the guilt of complicity with the king's murder was popularly attributed, although in so dark and cruel a transaction his own firm and persistent denial must be allowed to qualify the not unnatural suspicion[1]. These divisions were the result of the party divisions and court intrigues of the reign, and they run on into the history of Edward III, in which we shall see Stratford, the champion of the constitutional administration, matched against Burghersh as the spokesman of the court and Orlton the agent of the queen; in which the house of Lancaster emerges as the mainstay of right government, and another Pembroke attempts to maintain the court influence as against church and baronage; whilst the marriage of the heir of Mortimer to the great-granddaughter of Edward II carries the hereditary right to the crown into the family of his bitterest foe, and thus leads to the internecine struggle between York and Lancaster.

Continuity of factions in the next reign.

Administration of Isabella and Mortimer, 1327–1330.

256. Isabella and Mortimer retained for four years their ill-gotten power, veiled at first by some pretence of regard for the national will and for the causes under which Edward had fallen. The boy king was crowned on the 1st of February, 1327[2], taking the coronation oath in the same form as his father had done. On the 24th he had proclaimed his peace, and on the 29th re-issued the proclamation: the lord Edward, the late king, had, of his own good-will, and by common counsel and assent of the prelates, earls, barons, and other nobles, and of the commons of the realm, removed himself from the government and willed that it should devolve on his heir; by the same advice and consent the son had undertaken the task of ruling. The bishop of Ely as chancellor, and bishop Orlton as

The ministers.

[1] See Twysden's Scriptores, cc. 2763 sq.

[2] Foed. ii. 684. A. Murim. p. 51; his regnal years date from Jan. 25. See Knighton (ed. Lumby), i. 443.

treasurer, undertook the work of administration, and on the 3rd of February the young king met the parliament, which continued in session until the 9th of March. All that was done in it shows that, although the great seal and the treasury were secured by Mortimer's closest allies, the Lancastrian party was put prominently forward by the court as sharers with them in responsibility for the recent acts. The first measure was to appoint a standing council for the king, containing four bishops, four earls, and six barons; of these a bishop, an earl, and two barons were to be in constant attendance upon him[1]. In this council Henry of Lancaster held the first place; he knighted the young king, and under his nominal guardianship Edward III spent the first few months of the reign. Of the other members, Orlton only was in the confidence of the queen; archbishop Melton had been faithful to the last to Edward II; Reynolds and Stratford were indispensable, from their position and experience; the earls of Kent, Norfolk, and Warenne, were of royal blood; and the lords Wake, Percy, and Ros were all probably of the Lancastrian connexion. Sir Oliver Ingham, the last of the number, was an ally of Mortimer. As might be expected under such influence, the next act was to reverse the proceedings against earl Thomas, and thus qualify his brother to succeed to his great inheritance[2]. The petition of earl Henry for this act of justice was seconded by a long petition of the commons, 'la bone gent de la commune,' in which, not content with demanding the restoration of their friends and the enforcement of the sentence against the Despensers[3], they prayed for the canonisation of earl Thomas[4] and archbishop Winchelsey. A more practical measure was the statute founded on the remaining articles of the petition. This may be regarded,

The acts of the parliament of 1327.

The Council of government.

Reversal of the acts against earl Thomas;

and condemnation of the Despensers.

Legislative acts.

[1] Knighton, i. 454; Rot. Parl. ii. 52. The names are given in Leland, Coll. ii. 476, from a Peterhouse MS. Henry of Lancaster was 'in coronatione regis per procerum consensum regis custos deputatus;' Wals. i. 192; Hemingb. ii. 300; Knighton, i. 447.

[2] Rot. Parl. ii. 3, 5; Foed. ii. 684. Henry did not succeed to the earldom of Salisbury, which was claimed by the widow of his brother, and was afterwards given to William Montacute; but he had Lancaster, Leicester, Lincoln, and Derby.

[3] Rot. Parl. ii. 7; Statutes, i. 251.

[4] This proposal was revived from time to time, and it is even said by Walsingham to have been successful in 1390; ii. 195.

Legislation of 1327.

in one aspect, as a reward for the good service done by the several estates during the recent troubles, and, in another, as an instalment of the advantages which were to be gained by the commons during the new reign. Beginning[1] with the statement that the legislation was suggested by the petition of the commons and completed by the assent of the magnates, the king, in the spirit of the coronation oath, confirms the charters with their adjuncts, and renounces the right, so often abused, of seizing the temporalities of the bishops. Having thus propitiated the clergy, he proceeds to forbid the abuse of royal power in compelling military service, in the exaction of debts due to the crown, and of aids unfairly assessed; he confirms the liberties of boroughs, and reconstitutes the office of conservator of the peace. The twelfth clause substitutes a fine upon alienation of land held in chief of the king for the forfeiture which had been hitherto the penalty of alienating without licence. Other articles show that the administration of justice had been impeded by the officers who ought to have enforced it. The act is on the whole creditable both to the parliament and to the government; there is nothing servile in the position of the administration; although most of the petitions of the commons are granted, some are adjourned until the king comes of age, and some are refused downright. So far the reign begins with fair omens. The queen contented herself for the moment with an enormous settlement, which left to her son only a third of the crown lands to maintain his royal dignity.

Confirmation of the charters.

Petitions.

Campaign against the Scots.

Parliament at Lincoln.

The breach of the truce by the Scots, and the somewhat inglorious campaign which gave the young king his first taste of war, occupied the summer of 1327, and a parliament held in September, at Lincoln, furnished an aid of a twentieth to defray the expenses[2]. Previous to this the merchants had granted

[1] Statutes, i. 255.

[2] The parliament was summoned Aug. 7; it sat from Sept. 15 to Sept. 23; Lords' Report, i. 492. The writ for collecting the twentieth is dated Nov. 23; Rot. Parl. ii. 425. A scutage was levied the same year; Record Report, ii. App. p. 143. The convocation of Canterbury at Leicester, Nov. 4, and that of York, Oct. 12, granted a tenth, at the solicitation of the earl of Lancaster; Wilkins, Conc. ii. 538, 546; Wake, p. 279; Knighton, i. 445.

a loan of a mark on the sack and twenty shillings on the last, on the same pretext[1]. The young king was married to Philippa of Hainault on the 24th of January, 1328. Shortly after, in March, 1328, a peace was negotiated with Scotland[2], and the marriage of the heir of Robert Bruce with the king's sister, accompanied by the formal renunciation by Edward of his claims over Scotland, put a stop for a few years to the bloody struggle. For this arrangement it is probable that the queen and Mortimer were mainly responsible, but the interest which the Lancastrian lords had in obtaining peace for their northern estates, an interest which appears in the negotiations of the late reign and somewhat affected the policy of earl Thomas, prevented them from opposing it. This compact seems to have been the first thing that opened the eyes of the nation to the disgrace of enduring the queen's supremacy[3]. The greediness with which both Isabella and Mortimer laid hold on the forfeited lands of the Despensers showed that they were not exempt from the failing which had ruined the favourites. The murder of the late king was in common rumour laid to their charge; the council was unable to exercise any authority in consequence of their assumptions; and the government, newly formed as it was, showed signs of disruption. Orlton, in the summer of 1327, had been succeeded at the treasury by Burghersh, who, on the 12th of May 1328, received the great seal on the bishop of Ely's resignation[4]. Orlton further incurred the royal displeasure by obtaining for himself, whilst at Avignon, a papal provision to the see of Worcester[5], which the king had already filled up. On the death of Reynolds, which occurred two months after that of Edward II, an attempt was

Peace with Scotland, 1328.

Unpopularity of the queen and Mortimer.

Changes in the ministry.

[1] Customers' Inrolled Accounts, Rot. 1: on the information of Mr. Hubert Hall.

[2] March 1, 1328; Foed. ii. 730; Rot. Parl. ii. 442.

[3] Avesbury, p. 7, calls it 'pacem turpem;' cf. Walsingham, i. 192; A. Murimuth, p. 55. The Lanercost Chronicler describes the earnest desire of the northern counties for peace; p. 249; but ascribes the peace itself to the queen and Mortimer; p. 261.

[4] Foed. ii. 711, 743. Bishop Charlton of Hereford succeeded at the Treasury.

[5] Foed. ii. 726: he was forgiven and admitted to his temporalities March 5, 1328; Foed. ii. 733.

made to force Burghersh into the primacy, but this failed, and Simon Mepeham, who succeeded, was more of an ecclesiastic than a statesman. Stratford, the most powerful adviser of the constitutional party, was still excluded from office.

Disgust of the earl of Lancaster.

The earl of Lancaster was weary of his position: he had had no personal hatred to the late king, and was shocked at his cruel death; he was conscious that the government depended mainly on his support, and yet that Mortimer was using him for his own ends, and he was not allowed any intercourse with Edward. In the winter of 1328[1] he made an effort to throw off the yoke: he refused to attend a parliament held in October at Salisbury, and found himself supported by the earls of Kent and Norfolk, bishops Stratford and Gravesend, the lord Wake, and many others[2]. The avowed object of the rising was to deliver Edward from the hands of Mortimer, to restore the power of the council nominated at the coronation, and to bring to account the negotiators of the peace with the Scots[3]. The court took alarm, and Edward, at Mortimer's instigation, began to move about the country with an armed force. To stop this, Leicester, on the 17th of December, summoned his friends to London for deliberation[4]. Whilst they were, on the 2nd of January, making their preparations, Mortimer was acting, and, on the 4th of January, occupied the earl's town of Leicester, and ravaged his lands[5]. The earl encamped with his supporters at Bedford, where he expected to meet Mortimer, but, being deserted by Kent and Norfolk, he complied with the urgent advice of Mepeham, the new primate, and

The earl of Lancaster attempts to throw off the yoke of Mortimer in 1329.

[1] There were four parliaments in 1328: (1) at York, Feb. 7–March 5, in which the truce with the Scots was concluded; (2) at Northampton, April 24–May 14, in which the truce was confirmed, and the statute of Northampton passed; Statutes, i. 257; (3) at York, July 31–August 6; (4) at Salisbury, Oct. 16–31. The last was adjourned and sat at Westminster, Feb. 9–22, 1329; Foed. ii. 752, 756; Lords' Report, i. 492.

[2] The earl of Lancaster stopped at Winchester instead of going to Salisbury; A. Murimuth, p. 59. Nov. 11, Stratford was summoned before the king for leaving the parliament of Salisbury without permission; Foed. ii. 753.

[3] The articles of complaint are given by Barnes, p. 31, from a C.C.C. MS.

[4] W. Dene, Ang. Sac. i. 369.

[5] Knighton, i. 450; Chron. Edw. i. 342, 343.

made terms. Mortimer was not satisfied with the humiliation of his greatest competitor. The minor confederates had to save themselves by flight; heavier punishment was prepared for the greater offenders. The earl of Kent, persuaded, it was believed, by Mortimer's agents, that his brother was still alive, was drawn into a plot, which Mortimer was pleased to regard as treasonable, for a restoration. He showed him no mercy. In a parliament which met at Winchester on the 11th of March, 1330, he arrested him, had him tried by his peers, and beheaded on the 19th[1]. Lancaster saw that he must be the next victim. He determined to force the young king to emancipate himself. Edward was already chafing under the restraint; the earl opened his eyes to the unparalleled insolence of Mortimer, who in his prosperity was copying the demeanour of Gaveston and the Despensers. In the following October Edward, at Nottingham, arrested Mortimer[2], and brought him up to London, where a parliament met on the 26th of November. A heavy list of charges was laid against him: he had set aside the council of regency, was guilty of the murder of Edward II, had used violence in the parliament at Salisbury, and led the king against the earl of Lancaster as an enemy, had conspired for the death of the earl of Kent, had procured gifts of crown lands, had contrived to raise a force illegally, had summoned service for Gascony, caused discord between the king and queen, had taken the king's treasure, had appropriated £20,000 paid

Mortimer contrives the death of the earl of Kent, Mar. 1330.

Fall of Mortimer, Oct. 1330.

Charges against him.

[1] 'Absque communi consensu;' Knighton, i. 454; Ann. Lanerc. p. 265; Avesbury, p. 284; A. Murimuth, p. 60 sq. The parliament was summoned Jan. 25, 1330, and sat from March 11 to March 23; Lords' Report, i. 492. Edward reported his uncle's execution to the pope March 24; Foed. ii. 783. Mortimer confessed before his death that the earl was innocent; Rot. Parl. ii. 33; but the archbishop of York, the bishop of London, and others, after the death of Mortimer, took out pardons for their complicity with the earl of Kent; ibid. 54. Cf. Foed. ii. 802; Rot. Parl. ii. 443.

[2] Notice of the arrest of Mortimer, Sir Oliver Ingham, and Sir Simon Bereford was given to the sheriffs, Oct. 22; Foed. ii. 799. The parliament called Oct. 23, 1330, sat Nov. 26–Dec. 9; Lords' Report, i. 492. The record of the charges against Mortimer and the murderers of Edward II is in Rot. Parl. ii. 52 sq., 255 sq. Cf. Knighton, i. 454; A. Murimuth, pp. 66, 67. The statute passed in this parliament renewed the law of 28 Edward I on purveyance, ordered annual parliaments, and renewed the statute of Lincoln 9 Edward II, about the qualifications of sheriffs; Statutes, i. 263 sq.

by the Scots, had acted as if he were king, had exercised cruelties in Ireland, and had intended to destroy the king's friends. The unhappy man was condemned by the lords without a hearing and hanged on the 29th of November. The queen was compelled to surrender the possessions which on one plea or another she had obtained, and put on an allowance of three thousand pounds a year. On the 28th of November Burghersh was removed from the chancery; Stratford succeeded him [1], and the archbishop of York returned to the treasury; William Montacute, the king's confidant [2] in the attack on Mortimer, was made earl of Salisbury. From this time Edward ruled as well as reigned.

His death, Nov. 1330.

Change of ministers.

General character of the reign of Edward III.

257. His first few years were a period of quiet constitutional progress, and in this respect were a fair specimen of the general tenour of the reign. The constitutional side of the national life is not illustrated by the career of Edward in nearly so strong a light as the military and social sides. But, as it is scarcely necessary to observe, at different periods of national growth not merely social institutions, but wars, commerce, literature, sometimes even art, give colour and form to the external life. There are periods at which the history of its wars is the true history of the people, for they are the discipline of the national experience. And this is very much the case with the reign of Edward III. If the glories and sufferings, and the direct results of these glories and sufferings, be taken out of the picture, little remains but a dull background of administrative business: and yet in that dull background may be discerned the changes that connect two of the most critical scenes of English history, the tragedies of Edward II and Richard II. A reign of fifty years must moreover contain more than one crisis; and the growth of a nation during so long a period must supply some points of contrast at the be-

[1] Nov. 28; Foed. ii. 800. Robert Wodehouse, archdeacon of Richmond and Chancellor of the Exchequer, presided at the treasury between the resignation of Charlton, Sept. 16, and the appointment of Melton on the 28th of November.

[2] Besides Montacute, three Bohuns, Sir Robert Ufford, afterwards earl of Suffolk, the lords Stafford, Clinton, and Neville of Hornby assisted; Leland, Coll. ed. Hearne, i. 477; Barnes, p. 47; Rot. Parl. ii. 56.

ginning and the end. But although this is true, and it is further true that towards the end of the reign we come into view of new and powerful influences which alter the complexion of later history, and warn us that we are passing from medieval to modern life, the general features of the period do not require detailed description. If due regard be given to the point of growth which England had reached under Edward I and Edward II, the interest of the reign of Edward III is scarcely proportioned to its length. If on the other hand the interest of the more modern developments be allowed to outweigh that of the earlier growth and continuity of our institutions, if modern history be regarded as beginning with the distincter appearance of modern forms of thought and government, the reign of Edward III requires, as a starting-point, a minute study involving an examination of much that we have already explored. In the present work we have regarded the history from the former point of view; and we continue to look forward, taking note of the new influences as they arise, and leaving the older ones, when they have done their work, to the domain of archaeology.

Character of the reign.

Edward III was not a statesman, although he possessed some qualifications which might have made him a successful one. He was a warrior; ambitious, unscrupulous, selfish, extravagant, and ostentatious. His obligations as a king sat very lightly on him. He felt himself bound by no special duty either to maintain the theory of royal supremacy or to follow a policy which would benefit his people. Like Richard I he valued England primarily as a source of supplies[1], and he saw no risk in parting with prerogatives which his grandfather would never have resigned. Had he been without foreign ambitions he might have risen to the dignity of a tyrant or sunk to the level of a voluptuary. But he had great ambition and an energy for which that ambition found ample employment. If on the one side the diversion of his energy to foreign

Character of Edward III.

His energy.

[1] Yet he says, 'sur toutes autres terres et pays si ad il plus tendrement au coer sa terre d'Engleterre, quele luy ad este . . . plus delitable, honeste et profitable qe nul autre.' See the Chancellor's speech in 1366; Rot. Parl. ii. 289.

wars was to the benefit of his people, on the other it was productive of an enormous amount of suffering. The general history of the reign is thus full of strong contrasts. The glory and the growth of the nation were dearly bought by blood, treasure, and agony of many sorts. The long war which began under Edward placed England in the forefront of Christendom; it gave her a new consciousness of unity and importance, and exercised, even while it exhausted, her powers. It enabled her leading men to secure, one by one, steps in advance which were never retraced, and to win concessions from Edward which he was unable or did not care to estimate at their true value. Hence whilst England owes no gratitude to the king for patriotism, sagacity, or industry, she owes very much to the reign.

Results on England of Edward's wars.

Reasons of his historical reputation.

Much however of the glory of the reign, on which later historians loved to dwell, was due to retrospect, and to a retrospect taken through the medium of Froissart's narrative. Edward was the last of the great kings who governed England with a safe and undisputed title, the patriarch of the great houses which divided and desolated the land for a century; and it had not yet become clear that the present evils, which caused men to look back upon his age as an age of gold, were all results of his foolish policy and selfish designs. The writers of his own country and date, whilst they recognise his greatness as a warrior, describe the state of his kingdom in language which conveys a very different impression from that which is derived from the reading of Froissart. A king whose people fly from his approach [1], a king overwhelmed with debt, worn out with luxury, the puppet of opposing factions, such as Edward in his latter years became, is a very different thing from the gentle, gay, and splendid ideal king of chivalry.

[1] Archbishop Islip writes, 'O scandalum tibi regi et toti populo Anglicano quod talia accidunt in tuo adventu; Fy, fy, fy, heu, heu, heu, quod hujusmodi fieri permittuntur cum quasi per universum orbem talia de te praedicantur . . . Nec mirum quod lamentationes et suspiria fiunt in adventu tuo . . . Erubescere enim potest tota gens Anglicana habere regem in cujus adventu populus contristatur communiter et in recessu suo laetetur;' Speculum Regis, cc. 3, 4; MS. Bodl. 624. Similar language, addressed to Edward II, is given in M. Malmesb. p. 172; Chron. Edw. ii. 244.

The early years of the reign.

For several years after the fall of Mortimer the country was fairly governed. Edward's ambition, although since 1328 he had entertained the idea of claiming France in right of his mother, was still fixed on the reduction of Scotland; and the parliaments supplied him with money in moderation. Occasionally some petition of the commons betrays some social uneasiness; the abuses of purveyance, the malpractices of officials, the royal claims to exact tallage[1] and to extend the customs on merchandise, had survived the stringent legislation of the Ordinances and of the statutes founded upon them; and now and then a favourable answer is given to the request for redress, although it takes the form of a promise to amend the process of the executive rather than of distinct legislative enactment. But the country was growing rich and could afford to be liberal, and Edward had not yet either felt the jealousy of power on his own part or provoked the same feeling in his parliaments. He was willing to ask their advice in 1331[2] as to the conduct of his quarrel with France, and in 1332[3] as to the proposed crusade. Nor is the request addressed, as might be expected, to the magnates only; the knights of the shire are especially mentioned as deliberating apart on these and the like questions. The definite and final arrangement of parliament in two houses must be referred to this period and to the fact that such deliberations had become a reality[4]. It was not now merely to determine the amount

Edward accepts the theory of parliamentary institutions.

1 Edward ordered the collection of a fourteenth of moveables, and ninth of revenue by way of tallage, June 25, 1332; Foed. ii. 840; Rot. Parl. ii. 446; but recalled the order in the next parliament; Rot. Parl. ii. 66. In 1333 he raised a subsidy on his sister's marriage, by separate applications, admitting no excuse; Foed. ii. 852, 853. See on this point § 275, below.

2 The parliament of 1331 sat at Westminster Sept. 30–Oct. 9; Lords' Report, i. 492; Rot. Parl. ii. 60; Statutes, i. 265.

3 Three parliaments were called in 1332; they sat March 16–21, and Sept. 9–12 at Westminster; and Dec. 2–11 at York; Rot. Parl. ii. 64–68. The second granted a fifteenth and tenth; Foed. ii. 845; Rot. Parl. ii. 66, 447; Knighton, i. 461. The clergy were not asked for money between 1329 and 1332, the pope having granted the king a tenth for four years; Wake, p. 282; Foed. ii. 786, to be divided between king and pope.

4 In 1331 the chancellor asked whether the estates would prefer war or negotiation; they chose the latter; Rot. Parl. ii. 61; the prelates, earls, barons, and other magnates deliberated 'uniement et chescun par lui severalment.' In the first parliament of 1332 the prelates and proctors

Growth of parliamentary machinery. of a money grant that the several estates acted freely and deliberated independently. The general consultative voice that had belonged to the witenagemot, to the royal council of magnates, and to the assemblies of tenants-in-chief, would appear to have been now recognised as belonging to the whole body of parliament and to each of its members.

War with Scotland, 1332-1335. Scotland occupied the attention and gave scope for the warlike energy of the king from 1332 to 1335 [1]. It was the assistance which Philip of Valois lent to the Scots that finally determined him to engage in the great war on which his reputation rests.

Relations with France, 1328-1338. In 1328, on the death of Charles IV, he had asserted his right to succeed him, a right which could be sustained only by a series of assumptions parallel with those put forward by Lewis in 1216 to the throne of England. But by doing homage to his rival in 1329 he had really withdrawn the claim; although that withdrawal might be renounced as a measure taken under the pressure of Mortimer and Isabella. **Division of the guilt of the war.** The breach of the peace came from Philip who, not content with protracting a series of irritating and unmeaning negotiations about old quarrels, had conceived the notion of using the Scots as a thorn in the side of England and of winning Gascony by battles fought on British ground. **Philip began it.** After continuing in spite of remonstrance to supply the Scots with ships and men, and disregarding the entreaties of the pope that he would make

sat by themselves, and the earls, barons, and other magnates by themselves; the resolutions of the earls, barons, and magnates were read before the king, prelates, knights and 'gentz du commun,' and agreed to. In the September parliament the earls, barons, and other magnates sat together; the prelates by themselves, and the knights of the shire by themselves; Rot. Parl. ii. 66, 67. In 1341 the lords and commons sat as two houses; ibid. p. 127.

[1] The following is the list of the parliaments for these years:—

1333, Jan. 20–26, at York; an adjourned session of the parliament of December, 1332; Rot. Parl. ii. 68, 69.

1334, Feb. 21–March 2, at York; Rot. Parl. ii. 376.

Sept. 19–23, at Westminster; which granted a fifteenth and tenth; Knighton, i. 471; Foed. ii. 895; Rot. Parl. ii. 447; Record Rep. ii. 146.

In 1334 the convocation of Canterbury, on Sept. 26, and that of York, on Oct. 24, granted a tenth; Wake, p. 284; Wilk. Conc. ii. 576–578.

1335, May 26–June 3, at York; where a grant of hoblers and archers was made by the counties, which was redeemed by money payments; Foed. ii. 911.

peace for the sake of Christendom and the crusade, he availed himself of the pretext that Edward was promoting the cause of Robert of Artois, declared his determination to help the Scots[1], and proceeded to invade Gascony. Philip thus made the war inevitable; Edward by assuming the title of king of France made the quarrel irreconcileable. Edward showed considerable sagacity in preparing for the struggle. He contrived to obtain not merely the consent but the hearty sympathy of his people. He saw that, just as Philip could use Scotland, he himself might use the jealous neighbours by whom Philip was surrounded: Flanders especially might be turned to account, for there the mercantile communities were at war with the feudal lords. The count of Flanders was an ally of Philip, the merchants were in close connexion with the merchants of England, whose support the king courted for more reasons than one. Lewis of Bavaria and William of Hainault were his brothers-in-law, and allies might be looked for in Spain, whose princes were willing enough to retain the English in Guienne as a barrier between themselves and France. Brittany too, the rulers of which, since the Norman Conquest, had taken their place as lords of Richmond among the great feudatories of the English crown, might be made again a useful ally.

Edward made it irreconcileable.

Prudence of Edward in undertaking the war.

Edward took time to form his alliances and to raise funds. The records of the next few years are full of letters of negotiation with foreign powers. The parliaments[2] showed themselves

His preparations 1328–1338.

[1] August 24, 1336; Foed. ii. 944.

[2] The parliaments of 1336, 1337, and 1338 were held:—

1336, March 11–20, at Westminster; one tenth and one fifteenth were granted; the Canterbury clergy granting their tenth in parliament; Wake, p. 285; Record Report, ii. app. p. 147. The clergy of York granted two tenths May 6; Wilk. Conc. ii. 584.

Sept. 23–26, at Nottingham; one tenth and one fifteenth were granted; Record Report, ii. app. p. 147.

1337, Feb. 9 and March 3, at Westminster.

Sept. 26–Oct. 4, at Westminster; a tenth and fifteenth for three years were granted; Record Report, ii. app. 148; A. Murimuth, p. 82.

1338, Feb. 3–14, at Westminster; one half of the wool was granted; Foed. ii. 1022; Record Rep., ii. app. 150; Reg. Pal. iv. 226; A. Murim. p. 84.

July 26–Aug. 2, at Northampton; four merchants were summoned from each county to meet the council at the same time; Foed. ii. 1051. See A. Murimuth, p. 86; Knighton, ed. Twysden, c. 2571.

In 1336, besides the tenth granted in parliament, the clergy of Canter-

He obtains the sympathy of the nation,

ready to strain the resources of the country to the utmost, and even to share the responsibility for the war. Edward in 1337 laid before the nation through the sheriffs[1] the detailed efforts which he had made for peace, and in 1338 declared his expedition to be made by the assent of the lords, but at the earnest request of the commons[2]. The parliament, at Westminster in March and at Nottingham in September 1336, granted successively two fifteenths from the barons and knights and two tenths from the towns; two tenths were also voted by the clergy[3]. In 1337 the barons and knights gave a fifteenth and the towns and clergy a tenth for three years. The imposts on wool had now reached such importance that the merchants again seemed likely to furnish the realm with a new estate; and Edward, justified by the part which Flanders occupied in his plan of operations, revived his grandfather's expedient of dealing with the merchants collectively apart from the parliament. He began to summon representative merchants to wait upon the council; in May 1336 London and twenty-one other cities were directed to send four merchants each to Oxford; in June 105 were summoned by name to Northampton; and in September at Nottingham thirty-seven were ordered to meet the parliament. It need hardly be wondered that the result of these and the like deliberations was to increase the revenue from wool, to extend monopolies, and enlarge the privileges of trade; but the king required the advice of the merchants frequently as financiers, who, in the absence of the Jews and when foreign bankers were deservedly unpopular, might bring their experience to bear on the manipulation and outlay of the revenue. Anyhow the votes of the parliament bear evidence of their influence. In September 1336 was granted a custom of forty shillings on the sack of wool exported by denizens and

And large grants of money, 1336.

Imposts on wool.

Influence of the merchants on the form of taxation.

Votes of aid in wool, 1336.

bury, in convocation at Leicester, Sept. 30, and the clergy of York at Nottingham on the 23rd, granted a tenth; Wake, p. 285. In 1337, the clergy of Canterbury, Sept. 30, and the clergy of York, Nov. 13, granted a tenth for three years; ibid. 287; Wals. i. 222; A. Murimuth, p. 82; Wilkins, Conc. ii. 624.

[1] Foed. ii. 989, 990, and again in 1340; ibid. 1109.

[2] Foed. ii. 1015.

[3] Knighton, c. 2568.

three pounds from aliens[1]; in March 1337 a statute forbade the importation of foreign cloth and the exportation of wool, preparatory to the imposition of an additional custom[2]; but allowed foreign workmen to settle in the country and offered them special privileges. In 1338[3] the parliament gave the king half the wool of the realm, amounting to 20,000 sacks, and in 1339[4] the vote of the barons took the form of the tenth sheaf, the tenth fleece, and the tenth lamb: in 1340 the commons offered an aid of 30,000 sacks of wool. At a later period the same influence appears in the revival and regulation of the staples. Votes of 1337 and the following years.

Another permanent result of these preparations was the revival of the fleet and of the measures for the defence of the coast which had been taken by Edward I. Edward II had asserted his claim to the title of lord of the English seas[5], and the first fruit of the labour, so lasting and all important in its effects for England, was the victory won by Edward himself at Sluys on the 24th of June, 1340. Growth of the navy under Edward III.

The opening events of the war were not encouraging, and the enthusiasm of the nation was exhausted long before any success was obtained. The first expedition served only to show the king the narrowness of his resources and the apathy of his allies. He sailed on the 12th of July, 1338[6], and returned on the 21st of First expedition, 1338–1340.

[1] Knighton, c. 2568. The grant of custom is not given in the Rolls, but an order forbidding export is in the Foed. ii. 943, dated Aug. 12; and the Nottingham parliament no doubt enacted the custom as a supplementary measure. See below, § 277.

[2] Statutes, i. 280; A. Murim. p. 81; below, § 277.

[3] Foed. ii. 1022, 1049, 1051, 1054. The wool was ordered to Antwerp, Aug. 7, 1338. 20,000 sacks were to be delivered, and the king in consequence issued some ordinances, July 12, 1338, one of which ordered the election of sheriffs by their own counties; Foed. ii. 1049. The prelates in parliament joined in the grant, and the two convocations, Oct. 1, granted another tenth; Wake, p. 287; Record Report, II. App. ii. 150. Cf. A. Murimuth, pp. 84, 86; Reg. Palat. iii. 222; Wilk. Conc. ii. 625, 629.

[4] In 1339 the parliament was called for Jan. 14 and held Feb. 3–17, at Westminster; and Oct. 13–28, at Westminster.

[5] The Flemish envoys in 1322 had acknowledged, 'ipse est dominus dicti maris;' Rot. Pat. 14 Edw. II. p. 2. m. 26 d.; Edward revived the claim: 'Progenitores nostri reges Angliae domini maris Anglicani circumquaque exstiterint;' Rot. Scot. 10 Edward III. m. 16, quoted in Selden, Mare Clausum, Opp. ii. 1400, 1376.

[6] Foed. ii. 1050.

February, 1340; his chief exploit was the assumption of the name and arms of king of France[1]; and he had incurred debt to the amount of £300,000. His son Edward, duke of Cornwall, represented him during his absence with the title of custos or guardian and called the parliaments in his name.

The parliament makes conditions before granting money, Oct. 1339.

It was at the parliament of October 1339 that the first symptoms appeared of a disposition to make conditions before consenting to a grant. The whole assembly allowed that such a grant was necessary, but the magnates, while offering the tenth sheaf, fleece, and lamb, payable in two years, expressed a wish that the maletote, or additional customs imposed in 1336 and 1337, might cease, that the guardianship of tenants-in-chief might be given to the next blood-relation, and measures might be taken to prevent the mesne lords from being cheated of their rights of wardship[2]. The commons went further; they admitted that the king deserved a liberal aid, but doubted whether without consulting their constituents they could venture to make one; they prayed therefore that two knights girt with swords might be summoned from each shire to the next parliament, to represent the commons, and that no sheriff or other royal officer should be eligible. They in the meanwhile would do their best to prevail on their constituents to be liberal[3]. They added six points on which they required redress, one concerning the maletote, and others touching the grant of amnesty for offences, arrears of debts and fines, and a release from the customary aids and prises. The demand for a new election was acceded to, and the new parliament called for the 20th of January, 1340[4].

Caution of the Commons.

Their demands.

[1] As early as Oct. 7, 1337, Edward used the title of king of France, but it is not found in any documents between that date and the 26th of January, 1340, when also he began to use the double regnal year in dating letters, and to bear the arms of France; Nicolas, Chronology of History, p. 318. On the 8th of February, 1340, he issued a charter of liberties to the French as their king; Foed. ii. 1109, 1111. The pope, March 5, wrote to dissuade him from using the title; ibid. 1117.

[2] Rot. Parl. ii. 104; Foed. ii. 1098.

[3] Rot. Parl. ii. 105.

[4] The three parliaments of 1340 sat from Jan. 20 to Feb. 19; from March 29 and April 19 to May 10; and from July 12 to July 26; each time at Westminster. The July session was held to determine the way in which the grant of the Lent parliament could be best laid out; Rot.

At this session, in which the lords renewed their offer of the tenth sheaf, fleece, and lamb, an offer was made by the commons of 30,000 sacks of wool conditional on the king's acceptance of a schedule of articles presented at the time; and in any case they offered 2500 sacks either as an instalment of the larger gift or as a free gift if their conditions were not accepted [1]. The articles of complaint were regarded by the officers of state as important enough to require the king's personal consideration, and he in consequence returned to England and met a new parliament attended by a large body of merchants, on the 29th of March. His personal solicitations proved effective. Instead of a tenth, a ninth sheaf, fleece, and lamb were granted by the prelates, barons, and knights of the shires for two years: the towns granted a ninth of goods; for the rest of the nation who had no wool and yet did not come into the class of town population, a gift of a fifteenth was added: and besides all this a custom of forty shillings on each sack of wool, on each three hundred woolfells, and every last of leather [2]. As a condition of the grant the king accepted the petitions of the commons and ordered them to be referred to a committee of judges, prelates, and barons, to whom were added twelve knights and six citizens and burgesses chosen by the commons. This body was to examine the articles and to throw into the form of a statute such of them as were to become law; the rest, which were of a temporary character, being left to the king and council. Upon these petitions were founded the four statutes of the 14th year of Edward III. The first of these [3] establishes the points demanded in 1339, promises a cessation of the maletote, abolishes presentment of Englishry, forbids the sheriffs to continue more than one year in office, and restores the appointment to the Exchequer, thus reversing an order for the election of sheriffs in the county court which had been issued in 1338 and

Parliament of January, 1340.

The king returns and holds a new parliament in March.

Large grants.

Consideration of petitions.

Four statutes of 1340.

Parl. ii. 117 sq. See Foed. ii. 988. The convocation of Canterbury, Jan. 27, and that of York, Feb. 2, granted a tenth, the latter for two years; Wake, p. 288; Reg. Palat. iv. 241; Wilkins, Conc. ii. 654.

[1] Rot. Parl. ii. 107 sq.

[2] Rot. Parl. ii. 112; Statutes, i. 291; Hemingb. ii. 354; A. Murim. p. 93.

[3] Statutes, i. 281 sq.

1339[1]. It further attempts to remedy the evils of the decaying local jurisdictions, the hundred and wapentake courts which were let at ferm or held in fee; it limits the abuses of purveyance and extends the functions of the judges at Nisi Prius. The second statute[2] is of still greater importance and may perhaps be regarded as the most distinct step of progress taken in the reign. It orders not only that the present subsidy shall not be made an example for future imposts, but that no charge or aid shall henceforth be made but by the common assent of the prelates, earls, barons, and other great men and the commons of the realm of England and that in parliament. Here the king accords that abolition of unauthorised tallages which had been forced on his notice in the 6th year of his reign[3], and which he had then avoided by promising to impose them no more except in accordance with the custom of his predecessors. This act may then be regarded as the supplement to the confirmation of the Charters, the real act 'de tallagio non concedendo,' and the surrender of the privilege of taxing demesne lands which Edward I had retained as not expressly forbidden by the act of 1297. A third statute[4] declares that the assumption of the title of king of France shall never be held to imply the subjection of the English to the French crown; and the fourth[5], which was conceded at the request of the clergy, defends them against the abuses of purveyance, of the royal right of presentation to livings belonging to vacant sees and wards of the crown, and of waste during vacancies.

Abolition of the royal right of tallage, 1340.

Third and fourth statutes.

Battle of Sluys, June 24, 1340.

Provided with money by these concessions, Edward left England again in June, won the battle of Sluys, and in September concluded a truce with Philip of Valois. On his return, in November, he brought about by his impatience the second great ministerial crisis of the reign.

Administration of the Stratfords.

258. The age of Edward III produced no really great minister; and this fact has no doubt added to the exaggerated belief in the king's administrative ability. Since 1330 he had depended chiefly on the two Stratfords, John, who as bishop of

[1] Foed. ii. 1049, 1090. [2] Statutes, i. 289 sq. [3] Above, p. 395.
[4] Statutes, i. 292. [5] Ibid. i. 292 sq.; Foed. ii. 1121.

Winchester had drawn the indictment against Edward II, and who in 1333 became archbishop of Canterbury, and Robert his brother and archdeacon, who became in 1337 bishop of Chichester. The brothers had held the great seal alternately, and with two short interruptions, since the fall of Mortimer and the dismissal of bishop Burghersh. The archbishop had taken the office for the third time in April 1340, and in June had made way for his brother, now chancellor for the second time. Bishop Orlton had quitted the field of secular preferment and devoted himself to the attainment of ecclesiastical promotion. Having in 1327 forced himself into the see of Worcester, in 1333 he obtained, in spite of the king's opposition and on the recommendation of the king of France, the rich see of Winchester. On the latter occasion Edward showed some spirit, and an appeal was brought against the bishop for his share in the revolution of 1326[1]: the bishop defended himself successfully, but probably determined that it would be safer for him henceforth to avoid the responsibilities of ministerial life. Burghersh, after being out of office for four years, had been made treasurer in 1334 but superseded in 1337. John Stratford however, as archbishop, chancellor, and president of the royal council, was supreme in the treasury as well as in the chancery. Both brothers were honest if not brilliant administrators; they had risen from a comparatively humble rank, and, in the struggles in which they had taken so active a part, had made enemies. The archbishop politically was the head of the Lancastrian or constitutional party. Burghersh, on the other hand, was the head or chief counsellor of the court party, and with him Orlton was in close alliance; his antagonism to Stratford was perhaps chiefly a personal rivalry, although there are some indications that the old alliance between Pembroke and Badlesmere was continued in their representatives, and Lawrence Hastings, the nephew and successor of Aymer of Valence, had married a daughter of Mortimer.

The Stratfords, 1330–1340.

Retirement of Orlton.

Edward attempts to punish him, 1333–1334.

Stratford leads the Lancaster party,

Burghersh the court.

[1] The proceedings taken against him in 1323 were annulled in the first parliament of Edward III; Rot. Parl. ii. 427. His defence in 1334 is given in Twysden, Decem Scriptores, c. 2763.

Difficulties.

Edward's difficulties in obtaining money, his lack of success in the war, and possibly Stratford's opposition to its continuance[1], gave the archbishop's rivals their opportunity. They were helped by a strong anti-clerical party, which, owing to the ill-regulated and extravagant luxury of the court, strongly resented the interference of Stratford as a reformer of manners.

Edward's advisers, 1340.

He returns from France suddenly and removes the ministers and judges, Nov. 1340.

Prompted by these advisers[2] Edward, who had been obliged by want of supplies to retire from the siege of Tournay, returned hastily to England, unexpectedly landed at the Tower on the 30th of November, and on the following day removed from office[3] the chancellor bishop Stratford of Chichester, and the treasurer bishop Northburgh of Lichfield. The judicial body fared worse; Richard Willoughby, who had until lately been the chief justice of the Bench, John Stonor, chief justice of the Common Pleas, and William Shareshull, a judge of the same court, together with the chief clerks of the Chancery, and some of the most eminent merchants, William and Richard de la Pole, and with them the lord Wake, were arrested and imprisoned. The archbishop who was at Charing, hearing of the arrest of the judges, betook himself to his palace at Canterbury as to a sanctuary. A curious controversy followed. Stratford had bound himself to the merchants of Louvain for the payment of the king's debt to them, and they at Edward's instigation insisted that he should be carried in person to Brabant[4] as security. The king on the 2nd of December summoned him to court; he sent an excuse which the king disregarded. The

Controversy between the king and the archbishop.

[1] According to Avesbury, Stratford had resigned the Great Seal owing to his opposition to Edward's voyage in June, 1340; p. 311. He received on the 21st of June an assignment, £3333 6*s.* 8*d.*, as wages for work done in the king's service abroad, having on the 20th resigned the seal, on the ground of health; Foed. ii. 1126. The old seal was broken, and the new one given to his brother, the bishop of Chichester; ibid. 1129.

[2] 'Quidam de . . . regis secretariis . . . archiepiscopo, qui dicti domini regis patricius solebat quasi ab omnibus nominari, plus quam decuit invidentes;' Avesb. p. 324. The bishop of Lincoln and Sir T. (Geoffrey) le Scrope are mentioned by Birchington as the chief advisers of the attack; Ang. Sac. i. 21.

[3] Avesbury, p. 324; Foed. ii. 1141; Birchington, p. 20.

[4] The earl of Derby had been left in Flanders in prison for Edward's debts; Foed. ii. 1143; and Edward had described himself in 1340 as bound to return to Brussels, 'et demorer y come prisoun' until he could pay his debts; Rot. Parl. ii. 112.

archbishop then replied in a course of sermons, in one of which, on the anniversary of S. Thomas the Martyr of Canterbury, he compared himself to the Saint, and justified the comparison by a series of excommunications directed generally against the breakers of the Great Charter. A few days later (Jan. 1, 1341) he wrote in strong terms to the king on the unwarranted and illegal arrests, pointing him to the example of his father, threatening him with the fate of Rehoboam, and appealing to the judgment of his peers[1]. On January 28 he wrote to the new chancellor that, as the conditions on which the clerical grant was made had not been fulfilled, he prayed him to stay the collection[2]: he wrote the next day to the bishops to forbid it, and a day later to excommunicate offenders. Edward rejoined in a sort of pamphlet addressed to the bishops and chapters of the province of Canterbury, and called a 'libellus famosus,' dated Feb. 10[3]. In this he declared that the archbishop had been to him as a broken reed; he had disappointed him of the money granted by the parliament in March, and, by leaving him practically without funds, was answerable for the failure of the expedition which had begun so auspiciously. He had been made a scorn to friends and foes alike; and so, acting on good advice, he had determined on a searching investigation as to what had become of the money. Hence the arrest of the clerks, and the attempts to draw the archbishop out of his sanctuary. Now the contumacious prelate had declared that except in full parliament[4] he would not meet his king or speak to him. The rest of the letter, which is very disgraceful to Edward, is a tissue of violent abuse, in which the archbishop is made answerable for all the gifts by which the crown has been impoverished, and for the rash designs which the king has entertained since the beginning of his reign[5]. On the 18th of

The archbishop's measures of defence and remonstrance, Jan. 1341.

The *libellus famosus*, Feb. 1341.

Charges of the king against Stratford.

1 'Nous esteroms en toutz pointz a jugement de nos peeres salve toutz fois l'estat de seint eglise de nous et de nostre ordre, sicome nous avoms escript einz ces heures;' Jan. 1, 1341; Foed. ii. 1143; Hemingb. ii. 363.

2 Hemingb. ii. 368; Wilk. Conc. ii. 659, 660.

3 Hemingb. ii. 380; Foed. ii. 1147; Ang. Sac. i. 23.

4 Letters of safe conduct were issued Jan. 26; Foed. ii. 1146.

5 The custom of discussing public affairs in these long letters was coming into use on the continent as well as in England, in the struggle between

February, William Kildesby the keeper of the privy seal, and one of Stratford's most persevering foes, appeared at Canterbury with the Brabant merchants, who publicly summoned the archbishop to go to Flanders as security for the king's debts. Stratford replied to this in a sermon on Ash Wednesday. In answer however to the king he wrote an elaborate letter:—he was not in office when the claims on France were first urged; he was not answerable for the king's difficulties; he had not received or detained the king's money; the sum which was to be raised by the recent grant was pledged to the king's creditors before the grant was made; and he had had no share in the lavish administration by which the crown was reduced to poverty. But he had his own rights; and, saving his estate and order, he was ready to make answer before the king, the prelates, lords and peers, to every charge brought against him[1]. The king replied in a weak and abusive letter, reiterating the general charges, but adducing no facts in proof of his statement. This letter is dated on the 31st of March[2]; on the 3rd of that month the king had summoned a parliament to meet on the 23rd of April; and on the 14th he had written his account of the matter to the pope[3]. In the meanwhile on the 4th of December bishop Burghersh had died; and on the 14th Edward had committed the Great Seal to Sir Robert Bourchier, the first layman who undertook the office of Chancellor, and the Treasury to Sir Robert Parning, the chief justice of the King's Bench.

Stratford's answer, Mar. 1341.

He demands trial by his peers.

Parliament summoned.

A Lay Chancellor.

Parliament, April 23, 1341.

On the 23rd of April the parliament opened[4], and the usual appointments were made of persons to receive the petitions; but the dispatch of business was postponed to the next day. The archbishop, on arriving at the door of Westminster Hall,

Lewis of Bavaria and the pope. The word pamphlet may be used as equivalent to *libellus*, on the authority of Richard de Bury, who was for a short time chancellor to Edward III; 'sed revera libros non libras maluimus codicesque plus dileximus quam florenos, ac *panfletos* exiguos phaleratis praetulimus palfridis;' Philobiblion, c. 8. *Libellus famosus* is however a recognised legal term.

[1] Wilkins, Conc. ii. 663, &c.

[2] Foed. ii. 1154; Wilkins, Conc. ii. 674.

[3] Foed. ii. 1152.

[4] Rot. Parl. ii. 126. The writs of expenses were issued on the 18th of May; Lords' Report, i. 493; but the business of parliament was not concluded until May 26; Rot. Parl. ii. 134.

was met by the king's chamberlain, Sir John Darcy, and the steward of the household, Ralph Lord Stafford, and ordered to present himself in the Court of Exchequer to hear the charges made against him. After an attempt to evade the order he obeyed, and, having heard the charges, demanded time for deliberation. He then entered the Painted Chamber where the parliament was to meet, and found there only a few bishops, whom he addressed, telling them of his purpose to clear himself in full parliament. As he was doing this the chancellor adjourned the session to the following day. Edward however would not meet his injured friend; Stratford insisted on taking his own place, and the business was impeded from day to day. On the 26th the parliament was informed that the king purposed to continue the war, and that means must be taken for collecting the second year's produce of the last grant: the debates which arose thereon were adjourned from day to day until the 7th of May, when the king appeared in person. During the whole time the archbishop had been struggling to maintain his position and right, and the barons watched the contest with sympathetic interest. On the 26th[1] of April he had gone to the Exchequer and answered the complaints, thus absenting himself from the parliament on the day when the session really began; and on the 27th, when he arrived at the Hall, he was ordered to attend again at the Exchequer[2]. This he refused to do, and made his way to the Painted Chamber where the bishops were sitting, and where the king was expected. Again Edward avoided meeting him, and sent Orlton[3] and Bourchier to urge him to submit. Orlton took the opportunity of denying that he was the author of the *libellus*. The archbishop received his excuse without replying. On the following day the chamberlain and other knights attacked him with violent abuse as he entered the Painted Chamber[4]; and he replied with the words and gestures of

The archbishop in the Exchequer.

Edward avoids meeting him.

Parliament opened. April 26, 1341.

Stratford's perseverance.

[1] Rot. Parl. ii. 127. [2] Birchington, pp. 38, 39.

[3] Birchington, p. 39. Orlton was throughout the spokesman of the king, and was in that capacity convicted of lying; p. 40.

[4] The servants respectfully forbade him to enter; he replied 'Amici mei, dominus meus rex me Johannem archiepiscopum ad hoc parliamentum

his model, the martyr Becket. At length he forced himself into the chamber and proposed terms of reconciliation, the king retiring before him. The next day, Sunday, was spent by the king's agents in an endeavour to excite the citizens of London against him; on the Monday articles of accusation were laid before the commons. On the Tuesday, May 1, he went again to parliament, and offered to clear himself; and on the 3rd of May[1] a committee of twelve lords was chosen to advise the king on the general question whether the peers were liable to be tried out of parliament. These lords, although, perhaps as a matter of policy, they refused to hear the archbishop's statement, reported on the following Monday that on no account should peers, whether ministers or not, be brought to trial, lose their possessions, be arrested, imprisoned, outlawed or forfeited, or be bound to answer or judged, except in full parliament and before their peers[2]. Accordingly, on the 7th of May, when the king arrived, the archbishop found that, having the parliament on his side, he could afford to be humble, and Edward, aware that unless he temporised he would get no money, determined to be gracious. A formal reconciliation followed; the archbishop prayed that he might answer before the parliament, and the king graciously acceded[3]. And here the matter rested; for not only had Stratford won a personal victory, but the peers, acting at his instigation, had secured for their order a real privilege, which the events of the last reign, and of the early years of the present, had shown to be necessary. But the struggle which Stratford had so stoutly maintained determined the parliament to make still further demands. In answer to

Popular excitement.

Accusations in parliament.

Report of the lords on the trial of peers, May, 1341.

Reconciliation of the king and archbishop.

Further demands of the parliament.

per breve suum vocavit, et ego major post regem, primam vocem habere debens, jura ecclesiae meae Cantuariensis vendico, et ideo ingressum istius camerae peto.' Then the lords attacked him, and a good deal of abuse and cursing followed; Birchington, p. 39.

[1] Rot. Parl. ii. 127.

[2] 'Est avis as pieres de la terre, que touz les piers de la terre, officer ou autre, par cause de lour office, ne par nul autre cause, ne deivent estre menez en juggement, ne perdre lour temporaltez, terres, tenementz, biens ne chatelx, n'estrè arestuz, ne emprisonez, outlagez, ne forsjuggez, ne ne deivent respoundre, n'estre juggez, fors que en pleyn parlement et devant les piers ou le roi se fait partie;' Rot. Parl. ii. 127.

[3] Birchington, p. 40; Rot. Parl. ii. 127.

the king's request for advice as to the collection of the second year of the ninth, each estate presented a bill of conditions; the lords demanded a statute by which the privilege just asserted should be confirmed[1]; the clergy petitioned for the observance of their exemption from the jurisdiction of the lay courts, for the confirmation of the charters and an oath to observe them, for the release of imprisoned clerks, and for the restriction of the functions of justices of the peace[2]. The commons asked for the enforcement of the charters, for the imposition of an oath binding the officers of state and judges to keep the laws, the great charter and other statutes, and for the release of old debts due to the crown. The lords and commons further joined in a demand that commissioners should be appointed to audit the accounts of officers who had received money on the king's behalf; that an ordinance lately issued at Northampton for the arrest of reputed criminals, which had been perverted to the purpose of oppression, should be annulled; that the chancellor and other great officers and judges should be appointed by the king in parliament and sworn to obey the law; and that the statute passed when the ninth sheaf was granted should be held good in every point. The king found that he had put into the hands of the estates a weapon, the use of which he could not control. They declined to accept his first answers as being unsatisfactory, and he was obliged to state them more distinctly. He replied to the clergy with promises and professions of good intentions; he consented to confirm the privilege of the peers; he even accorded the petition of the commons. The two chief points, the examination of accounts, and the nomination of ministers, are distinctly granted; the auditors are to be elected in parliament; and on a ministerial vacancy the king will take counsel with his lords and counsellors as to the choice of a successor, who, when named, shall be sworn in parliament. At each parliament the ministers are to resign their offices into the king's hands, and to be compelled to answer all complaints[3].

Demands of the commons.

An audit of accounts demanded, May, 1341.

Concession of the king.

The proceedings of the parliament of 1341 are of very great

[1] Rot. Parl. ii. 127. [2] Ibid. ii. 129, 130. [3] Ibid. ii. 128, 130.

Importance of the parliament of 1341.

significance: they not only prove the determination of the country not to be governed by irresponsible officials, or by royal tyranny, but they show us the consolidated national council struggling for and winning privileges which just a century earlier the two elder estates had claimed from Henry III; they show the commons asserting, and the lords allowing them, an equal share in the common demand of right and control; and they very distinctly mark the acquisition by the third estate of its full share of parliamentary power. And as to the great question of the relations between the king and the parliament, it was now made impossible for the royal power to crush, as Henry III had crushed Hubert de Burgh, a minister who possessed the confidence of the nation. The regular audit, in parliament, of ministerial work and official accounts, which was now demanded, was an assertion that it is to the nation, not to the king only, that the ministers are accountable.

Ministers accountable to the nation.

Edward repudiates the concessions, Oct. 1341.

The great advantages, however, thus apparently won, were practically withheld by the king. Under an appearance of gracious magnanimity or careless generosity, he conceded all the privileges which his people demanded, and then by a clever manœuvre, a piece of atrocious duplicity, he nullified the concession. The articles demanded in the petitions, made a condition of the grant, and accorded in the royal answers, had to be turned into a statute, and that statute he confirmed and sealed [1]. But his officers protested: the chancellor, treasurer, and some of the judges declared that they had not assented, and could not be bound to observe such points as were contrary to the laws and constitutions of the realm which they had sworn to keep [2]. Under the shadow of this protest Edward himself protested in private; he had gained his point, and did not hesitate to repudiate his word.

The continuance of the truce with France allowed the king to stay in England until October, 1342, but during all this time he did not venture to call a parliament. On the 1st of

[1] Statutes, i. 295; Rot. Parl. ii. 132; Wilkins, Conc. ii. 681.
[2] Rot. Parl. ii. 131.

October, 1341, he revoked, by letters close enrolled on the statute roll, the statutes which he had sealed in the previous May, and in consideration of which the ninth sheaf, fleece, and lamb had been collected. He had, he said, in order to avoid breaking up the parliament in confusion and so ruining his whole design, 'dissembled, as he was justified in doing, and allowed the pretended statute to be sealed for that time:' he had since taken counsel with certain earls, barons, and others, who agreed in thinking that acts done in prejudice of his royal prerogative were null; and therefore, although he was quite willing to observe all engagements made with his people by his predecessors, these statutes he revoked [1]. He did not even, like John or Henry III, wait for papal absolution, for he had taken no oath.

Edward annuls the statutes of 1341.

259. Two years passed without a parliament; and although, during the short visit paid by Edward to Brittany, in the winter of 1342 and 1343 [2], an attempt was made by the regent, his son Edward, to hold a parliament for the southern counties, the estates were not called together until the 28th of April, 1343. This parliament, in which the lords temporal and spiritual sat in one house and the representative members in another [3], did

Parliamentary history, 1343.

[1] 'Quia editioni dicti statuti praetensi numquam consensimus, sed, praemissis protestationibus de revocando dictum statutum si de facto procederet, ad evitandum pericula quae ex ipsius denegatione tunc timebantur provenire, cum dictum parliamentum alias fuisset sine expeditione aliqua in discordia dissolutum, et sic ardua nostra negotia fuissent, quod absit, verisimiliter in ruina, dissimulavimus sicut oportuit, et dictum praetensum statutum sigillari permisimus;' Statutes, i. 297; Foed. ii. 1177.

[2] Edward left England Oct. 4, 1342; Foed. ii. 1212; and returned March 2, 1343, having made a truce for three years; ibid. 1220. William Kildesby, the privy seal, who was the chief agent of Edward in his attack on the ministry in 1340, went on pilgrimage to Palestine in 1343, probably to get out of the way; ibid. 1220. The parliament for the counties *citra Trentam* was summoned for Oct. 16, the southern convocation for Oct. 5, and the northern convocation for Dec. 9, 1342; it is not certain that the lay assembly ever met; no returns are found; see Wake, p. 290. The York convocation granted a tenth on strict conditions; Wilk. Conc. ii. 712: and probably that of Canterbury did the same; Knighton, c. 2582.

[3] The parliament of 1343 met April 28, and sat until May 20. In it Edward created his eldest son Prince of Wales, May 12. The lords met in the White Chamber, the knights and commons in the Painted Chamber; Rot. Parl. ii. 136. After consultation apart the commons went to the White Chamber and made answer by sir William Trussell. Hallam

The parliament of 1343 rescinds the statutes of 1341.

little more than formally repeal the statutes which Edward had revoked in 1341, and approve the truce which he had made for three years with the French. Edward did not ask for money, but the petitions of the commons were as comprehensive as if he had done so; they certainly prove that the repeal of the statutes of 1341 must have been very reluctantly granted, and probably only to avoid acknowledging that the royal revocation had really invalidated them[1]. The third estate presented thirty-five articles, which included not only the usual formal requests for the maintenance of the charters and newer statutes, but a petition for the identical remedies provided in 1341, a remonstrance against a grant of forty shillings on the sack which had been made by the merchants without the consent of the commons[2], a prayer that statutes made by the lords and commons might not be repealed or defeated, and that the chancellor and justices might be chosen from among the peers or wise men of the realm[3]. There was a timid remonstrance also against royal extravagance, which recalls the troubled days of Edward II. But the chief point on which two at least of the three estates agreed was the necessity of restricting the papal claims

Petitions of the commons.

Legislation of 1343.

Petitions against papal interference.

inclines to place the final arrangement of the two houses much earlier; Middle Ages, iii. 38. See above, p. 395, note 4.

[1] Rot. Parl. ii. 139. Some of the articles, it is added, were so reasonable that the king and council agreed that they should be re-enacted; ibid. 139–141.

[2] Art. 5, Rot. Parl. ii. 140. The grant of the parliament of 1340 ended at Whitsuntide, 1341. On the 8th of July, 1342, 142 merchants met the council in London, and these perhaps made the new grant; Lords' Report, iv. 540. An ordinance was issued fixing the price of wool variously in various counties, May 20, 1343; Foed. ii. 1225; Rot. Parl. ii. 138. A. Murimuth adds that three marks and a half on the sack were granted in the parliament; p. 146. It is indeed ordered by the king and magnates that 'the old custom and subsidy be paid for the passage of the wool from Midsummer to Michaelmas and for three years following;' Rot. Parl. ii. 138. If the subsidy was 40*s*. and the old custom 6*s*. 8*d*., the statement of Murimuth is exact, and some parliamentary authority is thus given to the unpopular impost. There is an ordinance that every one who exports wool shall bring two marks weight of silver per sack into the country; and a recommendation from the 'lieges marchantz' that the staple should be re-established, and that the king should have a subsidy of 40*s*. on the sack; Rot. Parl. ii. 143. See below, § 277.

[3] Art. 9, Rot. Parl. ii. 140: 'quant as chaunceller et tresorer, le roi poet faire ses ministres tieux come lui plerra, et si come lui et ses auncestres ont fait en tut temps passez. Mes il plest a ly de faire tieux ses ministres qi soient bons et suffisantz pur lui et pur son peuple.'

to ecclesiastical patronage, which had vastly increased since the beginning of the century, and which, now that the pope was living within the borders of the kingdom of France and in close alliance with Philip, at once diverted large revenues into the hands of the king's enemies, and robbed the English nation of due spiritual superintendence. Little immediate benefit resulted from the deliberation[1]. The payment of the increased customs was ordered for three years. Three short articles on the reform and regulation of the coinage represent all the legislation that was incorporated in the statute-law[2]. The royal answers to the long petition are either assertions that the existing law is sufficient to meet the case in question, or that the king would take the matter into consideration, which was equivalent to delay, and became the established form of refusal. The remonstrance against papal provisions took the form of a humble petition to the pope on the model of that drawn up in 1307 at Carlisle[3]. Stratford had by this time fully made his peace with the king, and it was ordered that all the proceedings which had been taken against him in 1341 should be annulled[4]. But the clergy appear to have avoided committing themselves to the position taken up by the king and the lay estates towards the pope.

Result of the petition of 1343.

Annulment of the proceedings against Stratford, 1343.

The long period of war that followed the breach of the truce in 1344[5], affords little direct illustration of constitutional

Internal history during the war, 1344–1346.

[1] The petition to the king is in the Rot. Parl. ii. 144, 145. On the 18th of May a letter of remonstrance from the lay estates assembled in parliament was written to the pope; A. Murimuth, p. 149: and on the 20th ambassadors were accredited; ibid. p. 147. Cf. Hemingb. ii. 101 sq.

[2] Statutes, i. 299.

[3] On the 23rd of July Edward ordered the sheriffs to proclaim the prohibition, issued in consequence of the petition of the commons, against the papal agents and receivers of favours; Foed. ii. 1230: on the 10th of September he wrote to the pope against reservations and provisions; ibid. 1234: on the 20th of October he ordered all papal bulls to be seized at the ports; ibid. 1237. Further orders were issued after a council held Feb. 16, 1344: A. Murimuth, p. 157; cf. Knighton, c. 2583; and a long proclamation was issued Jan. 30; Foed. iii. 2; Reg. Palat. iv. 315.

[4] Rot. Parl. ii. 131, 132, 139.

[5] Edward declared war May 26, 1345; Foed. iii. 41; Hemingb. ii. 416: constituted his son Lionel guardian of the realm, sailed for Flanders July 1, returning July 26; ibid. 50, 52: he sailed again for France July 2, 1346; ibid. p. 85: the battle of Crecy was fought Aug. 26. Calais was besieged in September, 1346, and taken August 4, 1347. Edward returned to England Oct. 12, 1347; Foed. iii. 139.

history, although it no doubt stimulated the growth of elements which were afterwards to come into greater prominence. The first few years were marked by great internal prosperity as well as by brilliant successes abroad; the king was careful in his demands and the estates temperate in their conditions. Even the first visitation, in 1349 and 1350, of the great plague, which put a stop to the domestic prosperity of England for many years, did not interrupt the good understanding that subsisted between the king and the parliament. During these years the elder generation of politicians passed away. Henry of Lancaster and bishop Orlton died in 1345; Stratford in 1348. Neither the archbishop nor his brother took secular office again after 1340; but the king was not able long to dispense with the service of ecclesiastical ministers. Sir Robert Bourchier resigned the Great Seal on October 29, 1341, immediately after the king's revocation of the statutes; and after two lay-chancellors, Parning and Sadington, the office was again in 1343 placed in the hands of a clerical holder, John Ufford, dean of Lincoln, whom the king intended to make archbishop of Canterbury[1]. The Treasury was also in 1345 placed under the management of William of Edington, who became bishop of Winchester in 1346. Some significant points of detail belong to the intervening period. In the parliament of 1344[2] the lords agreed to follow the king to the war, the commons made a grant of two-fifteenths from the shires and two-tenths from the towns so as to guarantee a supply for two years[3], and the clergy granted a tenth for three years. And this plan met with so much favour

Changes of actors.

A clerical chancellor again appointed, 1343.

Grants of supplies for several years at a time.

[1] Parning became chancellor Oct. 29, 1341, and died Aug. 26, 1343; Sadington succeeded Sept. 29, 1343, and was superseded by Ufford Oct. 26, 1345; Foss, Tabulae Curiales, p. 22.

[2] The parliament of 1344 sat June 7–28; Lords' Report, i. 493; Rot. Parl. ii. 146: the convocation of Canterbury met May 31, that of York June 16; Wake, p. 291; Wilk. Conc. ii. 727. A statute for the relief of the clergy was passed by the king, by assent of the lords and commons, in which the clerical grant is specially mentioned as made by the prelates and proctors of the clergy; this statute is dated on the 8th of July. The grant seems to have been made in convocation, and reported to the king by the parliamentary proctors, which was no doubt the usual course. See however Wake's remarks on Atterbury's view of this; State of the Church, pp. 291 sq.

[3] Rot. Parl. ii. 148; Knighton, c. 2584.

that it was followed in 1346[1], and the grant extended to three years in 1348 and 1351. The king did not indeed content himself with this revenue: the frequent writs by which the merchants are summoned to confer with him imply that concessions of additional custom or free gifts of wool must from time to time have been demanded; in 1346 the knighting of the prince of Wales was made an occasion for the demand of a feudal aid; and, although that aid was itself contrary to the statute of 1340, it was collected at double the amount fixed by the statute of Westminster and without the consent of the commons[2]. On each occasion of a grant of money petitions were received and statutes founded on such of them as the king saw fit to allow. In 1344 the burdens laid on the counties by the commissions of array, the expenses of which fell upon them, form the ground of complaint[3], the legislation of 1327 having proved insufficient to remedy the evil. In 1346 the king's right to issue such commissions without the assent and grant of parliament is questioned[4]. The independent action of the clergy aroused the jealousy of the commons; in 1344 the latter prayed that no petition of the clergy that might prejudice the lords or the commons should be granted without full inquiry[5]. The clergy made conditions before granting money, and thus obtained the statute which provided that prelates should be exempt from trial by the justices in criminal cases, and that certain other interferences with ecclesiastical privilege should be abandoned. From the petitions of 1346[6] we learn that the great subsidy of

Negotiations of the king with the merchants for a grant of wool.

Complaints against commissions of array, 1344–1346.

Jealousy of the commons and clergy, 1344.

[1] There was no parliament in 1345. In 1346 there was a session, Sept. 11–20, at Westminster; Lords' Report, i. 493: an aid of two fifteenths for two years, if the war should last so long, was granted by the whole body of the commons; Rot. Parl. ii. 159; from the tenants-in-chief the king demanded an aid of 40*s.* on the fee for the knighting of his eldest son; ibid. p. 163; Knighton, c. 2592; Wake, p. 294. The clergy of Canterbury granted a tenth for two years, Oct. 16; Wilkins, Conc. ii. 728.

[2] 'Le renable eide que feust pardone par estatut l'an quatorzisme, dount chescun fee est chargez de 40*s.* saunz graunt de la Commune, ou par estatut le fee serroit chargez fors que de 20*s.*' This proves that the statute of 1340 was understood to apply to all aids whatever; Rot. Parl. ii. 200. The aid was fixed at 20*s.* by Stat. Westm. I; Statutes, i. 35.

[3] Rot. Parl. ii. 149, art. 3.

[4] Rot. Parl. ii. 160, art 1–3; Hallam, Middle Ages, iii. 45.

[5] Rot. Parl. ii. 149, art. 8; see below, § 294.

[6] Rot. Parl. ii. 159, art. 11; 161, art. 7; Hallam, Middle Ages, iii. 44.

Taxation of wool, 1346.

forty shillings on the sack of wool was still taken on the plea that it had been granted by the prelates and magnates. The retention by the alien priories of their estates in England is the ground of another representation, and the commons pray that lands acquired in mortmain since the taxation of pope Nicolas in 1291 may be duly rated[1].

Edward's statecraft after 1347.

On the king's return home in 1347 it became evident that the patience of the country was nearly exhausted. Men had discovered that although Edward would give good words they meant nothing; if he promised to give up a tax, he made arrangements with the merchants by which they shared with him the profit of transactions the cost of which fell upon the nation; if he asked advice it was merely that he might commit the advisers to a policy of which, whatever the advice might be, they must defray the expenses. They had seen in the bankruptcy of the Bardi and Peruzzi, Florentine merchants to whom the king owed 1,500,000 gold florins,—a catastrophe which plunged all Florence in distress[2],—an illustration of the credit which was to be given to Edward's professions of obligation, and a warning that, as the foreign supplies of money were thus cut off, the English must be prepared for more direct and immediate oppression. Notwithstanding all the king's engagements to deal justly with his people, on the 3rd of March, 1347[3], the regent held a council at which the commons were

Ruin of the Italian bankers, 1345.

Great loan of wool in 1347.

[1] In 1341 it was ordered that these lands should be taxed for the ninth with those of the laity; Rot. Parl. ii. 130. The prayer of the commons in 1346 was answered by the king's promise that they should be duly assessed with the rest of the church property; but this did not decide the question; see Rot. Parl. ii. 162, art. 19; 163, art. 33.

[2] J. Villani, Muratori, Scr. xiii. 819, 820, 934. In January, 1345, the Bardi failed; Edward owed them 900,000 gold florins; the Peruzzi also, to whom he owed 600,000; and then the Acciaiuoli, Bonaccursi, Cocchi, Antellesi, Corsini, and others. Cf. Rot. Parl. ii. 240.

[3] There was no parliament in 1347, but a small council was held at Westminster, March 3, which obtained from the merchants a loan (aprest) of 20,000 sacks of wool; Record Report, ii. app. 2, p. 164; Foed. iii. 116, 121, 122, 126, 131. In a letter to the bishops, chapters, and religious houses, dated April 8, the regent invites them to follow the example of the magnates who in the last council had granted an aid, 'grata consideratione singillatim,' and prays them by way of loan to give him an aid in wool: a very great assembly of merchants was held April 21; Lords' Report, iv. 563; cf. Knighton, c. 2592, 2595; Rot. Parl. ii. 166, art. 11. The convocation of York met Jan. 19, 1347.

not represented, in which a loan of 20,000 sacks was negotiated, and separate promises of aid made, while the merchants shortly after were persuaded to increase the customs on wool, wine, and merchandise. Worse things were feared. The apprehension appears strongly in the first parliament of 1348 when, in answer to his request for advice about the war, the commons replied that they were so ignorant and simple as not to be able to counsel the king touching the war or the needful preparations;—if he would excuse them, and make, with the advice of the great and wise men of the council, such arrangements as should seem good, the commons would assent to them and keep them firm and stable [1]. They then presented sixty-four petitions for redress of grievances, in which the commissions of array, the monopolies of wool and tin, and the unauthorised impost on manufactured cloth, indicate the belief that the king was evading the letter of his promises: the increase of the customs without the consent of the commons must be illegal. Edward's replies must have confirmed the suspicion of the commons: the profit on tin belonged, he said, to the prince, and every lord may make his profit of his own; as for the wool, the ordinance of the staple may be reviewed; as for the custom on cloth, the king has as much right to profit on wool manufactured at home as on wool exported [2]. Two months later, on the 31st of March, at another parliament which the king asked for money, the complaints are stated distinctly, and in much the same language as that addressed by the barons to Henry III. It was no light burden that the nation had had to bear; the aid for knighting the king's son, taken without the assent of the commons, contrary to the statute of 1340, and at double the customary rate; the tenths and fifteenths, the maintenance of forces raised by commissions of array, the subsidy on wool—£60,000 annually,—the 20,000 sacks to boot; the petty oppressions by which the agents of the wool merchants beat down the price of wool to the sellers and enhanced it to the buyers. Notwithstanding, if the king

The commons in 1348 begin to decline responsibility for the war.

Petitions in the parliament of Jan. 1348.

Edward's answers.

Renewed complaints, Apr. 1348.

[1] Rot. Parl. ii. 165. In 1348 parliaments sat from Jan. 14 to Feb. 12, and from March 31 to April 13; and there was a provincial council of Canterbury in October, but no grants made in it.

[2] Rot. Parl. ii. 165 sq.

Grant made on conditions.

would undertake that the money now to be granted should not be turned into wool, but be collected with due consideration, that the proceedings of the itinerant justices should be stopped, that the subsidy on wool should cease in three years and not be again granted by the merchants, and that no impost, tallage or charge should be laid on the commons by the Privy Council without their assent in parliament, that the 20,000 sacks should be restored, that no aid should be taken for the marriage of the king's daughter, and that when these petitions were answered the answers should remain on record and in force without change,—then they would grant a fifteenth and tenth for three years [1]. The king accepted the grant, and accorded most of the petitions, but no new statute was founded upon them, a fact which seems to prove that the oppressions complained of were recognised as illegal.

The Great Plague, 1349–1351.

The next parliament met in 1351; for three years [2] the terrible plague of 1349 interrupted all public business; the war was discontinued by a series of short truces until the year 1355; the legal and judicial work of the country ceased for two years [3].

The period of Edward's military greatness.

This was the culminating point of Edward's glory: in 1349 he completed the foundation of the order of the Garter, and in 1350 he was requested to accept the imperial crown; but the plunder of France had already produced extravagance and increase of luxury in all classes, and the pestilence marks the era from which the decline of prosperity begins [4].

Difficulty of estimating the results of the Plague of 1349.

The plague of 1349 [5], the first of the three great visitations which desolated Europe during the fourteenth century, produced in every country some marked social changes. The exact amount and character of these changes can only be estimated on a strict examination of the condition of the several

[1] Rot. Parl. ii. 200, 201; Knighton, c. 2596.

[2] Foed. iii. 180, 182. In 1349 a full parliament was called to meet on the 19th of January, but prorogued to April 28, and on the 10th of March superseded altogether; so that it never met; Lords' Report, p. 585. No attempt was made to hold a parliament in 1350, nor was any convocation held; Wake, p. 295.

[3] Knighton, c. 2596. Cf. Rot. Parl. ii. 225, 227.

[4] The spoils of France had produced general extravagance: see Knighton, c. 2597.

[5] May 31–Sept. 29; Nicolas, Chronology of History, p. 389.

countries before and after the plague, and a comparison of the particular results in each. Such a generalisation is far too wide to be attempted here; but it seems necessary to guard against conclusions drawn from partial and local premisses; the actual incidence of the plague being equal throughout the area of extension, in England, France, Italy, and Germany, the variety of effects that follow it must be referred not to the plague simply, but to the state of things which existed when the plague came and the liability of that state of things to be modified by its influence. If the population were thinned, and the land thrown out of cultivation in the several regions, in nearly the same proportion, the later differences must not be ascribed indiscriminately to this single agency. A neglect of this consideration has led to very different opinions of the effects of the Black Death, as this pestilence is called. One theory ascribes to it, as a cause, nearly all the social changes which took place in England down to the Reformation, the depopulation of towns, the relaxation of the bonds of moral and social law, the solution of the continuity of national development caused by a sort of disintegration in society generally. Another view would regard it as an example of the social law, according to which a period of pestilence and distress results in an expansion of national life and energy, and is followed by an increase, after a certain time, in national prosperity. Such different conclusions can only be accounted for by supposing the writers who hold them to take opposite views not only of the action of the plague itself, but of the periods that precede and follow it. It must be sufficient now to say that in England the effects of the plague are historically prominent chiefly among the lower classes of society. The population was diminished to an extent to which it is impossible now even to approximate, but which bewildered and appalled the writers of the time[1]; whole districts were thrown out of cultivation, whole parishes depopulated, the number of labourers was so much diminished that on the one hand the survivors demanded

The Great Plague.

Difference of opinions on the subject.

Variety of views on the Great Plague of 1349.

Diminution of the population.

[1] Professor Rogers thinks that 'it really destroyed not much less than half the population;' History of Prices, i. 60; and shows that it doubled the rate of wages; ibid. p. 265.

an extravagant rate of wages, and even combined to enforce it, whilst on the other hand the landowners[1] had to resort to every antiquated claim of service to get their estates cultivated at all; the whole system of farming was changed in consequence, the great landlords and the monastic corporations ceased to manage their estates by farming stewards, and after a short interval, during which the lands with the stock on them were let to the cultivator on short leases, the modern system of letting was introduced, and the permanent distinction between the farmer and the labourer established[2]. At the very beginning of the trouble the attempt made by the government to fix the rate of wages produced disaffection, which smouldered until, after many threatenings, it broke into flame in 1381. The plague moreover extended to the cattle. If we may believe the chroniclers, whose statements are scarcely borne out by the revenue returns, it swept away with the shepherds the flocks[3], on whose wool the king's resources depended. If this is approximately true it must have cut off one of the ways by which he had so long been able to raise money without the national consent and in transgression of the constitutional limits by which his power of direct taxation was defined.

Change in agricultural management.

Attempt to fix the rate of wages.

Cattle Plague.

Up to this point we see the commons claiming their due share of power, unflinching in their demands for the rights which, according to the theory of the constitution as enunciated by Edward I and Edward II, were theirs; asserting moreover the same sorts of claims as had under Henry III been asserted by the baronage, which then filled the place now occupied by the parliament of the three estates. They had obtained from the king more than once a formal recognition of their rights. But formal recognition was a very different thing from practical enforcement. In spite of the legislative right of parliament Edward had revoked a whole series of statutes; in spite of the

View of the position of the commons up to 1350.

Means which the king took to defeat their constitutional action.

[1] It is to be set against the apparent harshness of the legislation on labour that many of the lords, both great and small, remitted the rents of their tenants, and actually reduced the amount of service due from their villeins; Knighton, 2601.

[2] Rogers, History of Prices, vol. i. c. 28, pp. 667 sq.

[3] Knighton, c. 2599.

assent given to petitions of the estates, the petitions remained a dead letter; he had obtained from one great section of the nobles, who were sharing with him the excitements and spoils of war, such support as enabled him to govern without any real limitation of his power. As to taxation, the parliament found itself able to give but not to withhold; to make conditions but not to enforce them: a negotiation with the merchants enabled the king to increase at will the custom on wool; the merchants agreed to pay the maletote, but they secured the monopoly, and the difference in price came out of the pockets of the commons. The commissioners of array required the troops to be maintained at the cost of the counties or the townships which furnished them, and which were thus taxed directly without a shadow of assent. If the commons proved obdurate, a negotiation with the pope or with the prelates enabled the king to raise money by tax or by loan from the clergy. But the parliament knew that in such circumstances its only policy was to protest but to submit; redress could not be enforced so long as the king had so many ways of raising money, and Edward's personal influence was so great that any idea of peremptory refusal would have been chimerical. The parliament, especially the commons, had learned that they must bide their time.

Unconstitutional taxation.

The clergy too were in no good plight. A succession of politicians like Reynolds and Stratford, broken only for a few months by the pious Mepeham and the learned Bradwardine, occupied the see of Canterbury with no advantage to the spiritual or political condition of the church. Monastic vigour was extinct. The zeal of the friars had been spoiled by popular favour and increasing fame; the beneficed clergy were, like their rulers, generally mere secular men of business, accumulating enormous preferments, and leaving their duties to be done by ill-paid deputies. Jealousy was widely felt of the wealth and power of men who grasped at the emoluments of both orders, of the state as well as of the church. The younger sons of the great houses,—who since the Conquest had formed more than a fair proportion of the episcopate, but had hitherto, as a rule, redeemed their position by devotion to the interests

Review of the condition of the clergy up to 1350.

of the nation, like the Cantilupes and the Beks,—or the creatures of the court, who had earned royal favours by sedulous devotion, engrossed the richer sees, except where the popes were strong enough to promote a poor man for merit only. It was an acknowledged evil, and Edward III, in presenting Simon Mepeham to John XXII, declared that the indiscreet policy of the prelates had been one great cause of the evils of his father's reign[1]. Bishop Beaumont of Durham, the cousin of the kings of England and France, Burghersh of Lincoln, Berkeley and Grandison of Exeter, the Charltons of Hereford, Montacute of Worcester, the Beks at Durham, S. David's, Lincoln, and Norwich, continue the long list of noble bishops to the days of the Courtenays, the Spensers, and the Arundels. Three Stratfords, at once bishops of Canterbury, Chichester, and London, prove that the ministerial type of prelate, the succession of Roger of Salisbury, was still flourishing[2].

Increase in the number of noble prelates.

Relations with the papacy.

The condition of the papacy, now in exile at Avignon, removed the discipline, such as it was, by which the nobler popes had tried to remedy the evils of non-residence and plurality. The court at Avignon was even more venal than it had been at Rome; men obtained bulls which allowed them to hold twenty livings at once, and as many more as they could get. The coincidence of the Babylonish exile of the papacy with the period of war between England and France somewhat relieved the clergy from papal exactions; they were content to be passive whilst the parliament was insisting on the reform of abuses. Where Grosseteste had spoken boldly, even Stratford was silent or acquiescent. Of the two great iniquities of this part of the reign, the revocation of the statutes in 1341 and the loan of wool in 1347, the former was perpetrated under a lay, the

[1] Foed. ii. 727: 'Praeteritorum memoria, viscera dolore saucians et humilians oculos mentis nostrae, de strage videlicet nobilium ac aliis diris et asperis quae genitoris nostri temporibus irreparabiliter evenerunt, quae ex taciturnitate quorundam immo verius indiscreto regimine praelatorum creduntur verisimiliter contigisse,' &c.

[2] On archbishop Stratford's death Edward seized his property, just as Henry II would have done. 'Obiit Johannes Stratford . . . dux regis et ejus consiliarius principalis in vita sua, et ideo post mortem ipsius pro mercede sua omnia ejus bona confiscantur, possessiones et praedia destruuntur;' W. Dene, Ang. Sac. i. 375.

latter under a clerical ministry. The want of sympathy, a sympathy which those who felt it were afraid to express, helped still more to divide the laity from the clergy. Yet the clergy possessed almost entirely the great offices of government. Besides their separate constitutional position in convocation and as an estate of parliament, they formed a very large portion of the house of lords, and, possibly, were not precluded from sitting in the house of commons. The network of ecclesiastical jurisdictions brought into every household troublesome and unwholesome questionings, and the cost and burden of courts not less costly or burdensome than those of the forests or of the common law.

Jealousy felt by the laity of the position of the clergy.

What was the political feeling of the great classes of the people that do not yet come into the foreground of political life must be inferred from the state in which we find them when they do appear. The legislature seems to look on them only to bind them. The irritating burden of royal purveyance, a cruel engine of petty tyranny, had grown to enormous proportion in late years. Wherever the king or the court went,—and owing to the energy of Edward I and Edward III, and the restlessness of the intervening reign, the court was ubiquitous,—there went a crowd of purveyors, taking the provisions of the husbandman or demanding his services, and paying either at nominal prices or not at all. Every old woman trembled for her poultry, the archbishop in his palace trembled for his household and stud, until the king had gone by[1]. As ever, the extravagance of this ubiquitous court was a cause of scandal

Question of popular feeling and opinion.

Mischiefs of purveyance.

[1] 'Quid faciunt pauperes hospitia tenentes quibus potius foret dandum intuitu caritatis quam ab eis aliquid capiendum? Quando audiunt de tuo adventu tristantur et statim prae timore abscondunt aucas, gallinas, et cetera bona, vel alienant seu in esculentis et poculentis consumunt, ne ea amittant in tuo adventu . . . praecursores tuae curiae garciones et alii capiunt homines et equos laborantes circa agriculturam et animalia quae terram arant et semina portant ad agrum, ut laborent per duos vel tres dies in tuo servitio nihil pro labore percipientes . . . Nec mirum quod lamentationes, suspiria, fiunt in adventu tuo, quia in veritate, quae Deus est, dico propria persona mea, quandocunque audierim rumores de adventu tuo et audio unum cornu, totus contremisco sive fuerim in domo sive in capitulo sive in ecclesia vel in studio vel etiam in missa. Quando vero aliquis de tua familia pulsat ad portam tunc magis contremisco, sed quando ad ostium tunc multo magis,' &c. Simon Islip; MS. Bodl. 624. See § 279, below.

as well as suffering. The king's expenses were the cause of the national impoverishment; he paid no debts; his father's soul was still in purgatory because the undutiful son had not paid his debts; the money spent on his horses would have almost sustained his starving subjects; the great windfalls that came to him in the shape of escheats and legacies he lavished in endowing his favourites instead of saving the pockets of his people. The prerogative of purveyance acted on the lower people as the enrichment of Gaveston and the Despensers had on the barons: if the king would be careful and keep his own and live on his own means, there need be no trouble, for there need be no taxation. In this view, in which, with much ignorance of political economy, there was likewise much truth, Edward III was by no means a popular king or the king of a contented people. There was a great gulf between him and the body of the nation; and his reign from this time is anything but a brilliant period of history. Giving him and his ministers credit for all that even makes a claim for admiration, we find a lack of good faith, an absence of national sympathy, a selfishness that repels more than all else attracts. There is also a wretched level of character; none to be praised, none to be greatly blamed; no great virtue to put small vice and petty selfishness to shame. There are no great aspirations or great acts of endurance and devotion; even the name of honour loses its charm when we know it to be a synonym for a pseudo-chivalrous selfishness, untinged with pity, love, or true devotion. These virtues have run, along with the giants and enchanters, into the pages of romance.

Separation between the king and people.

General mediocrity of character.

Parliamentary history of the years that followed the plague, 1350–1361.

The parliamentary history of the years which followed the first visitation of the plague does not furnish much proof that in the general depression the commons were less on their guard, or the king more conscientious in demands or promises. During the years of peace the finance was arranged on the same plan as before[1]; in 1352 the parliament granted three

[1] The parliaments of these years sat as follows:—

1351, Feb. 9–March 1, the subsidy on wool was granted for two years; Rot. Parl. ii. 229; and the clergy, of Canterbury, May 2, and of York, May 18, granted a tenth for two years; Wake, p. 296.

fifteenths and tenths; in 1353 the subsidy on wool, woolfells, and leather, was continued by a great council for three years; and in 1355 a similar subsidy for six years was granted on the understanding that no other tax should be imposed during the period. Notwithstanding this proviso a fifteenth and tenth were again granted in 1357. War broke out again in 1355. From 1356 to 1362 the rolls of parliament are lost, and our information on parliamentary business derived from other sources is very scanty. The year 1360 is the date of the peace of Bretigny: in 1361 the second visitation of the plague began in August, and it lasted until May 1362.

Renewal of war.

Peace of Bretigny.

These years are marked by the rise of a jealous feeling between the commons and the royal council which at a later period had some important results. The number of temporal peers had already been very much reduced, and was gradually approaching the point of rapid decline which was consummated by the civil wars of the next century. The average number of barons summoned to a full parliament by Edward II was 74; the average of the reign of Edward III was 43. The royal council in its widest sense, the magnum concilium of the magnates, contained all these, and, as the baronage under Edward III, or at least during the thirty years which intervene between his earlier difficulties and his later ones, had no great internal

Jealousy between parliament and council.

Diminution of the baronage.

1352, Jan. 13–Feb. 11, and August 16–25 the clergy were not summoned; a fifteenth and tenth for three years were granted in the first parliament; Statutes, i. 327; Rot. Parl. ii. 242; Knighton, c. 2602; see p. 428.

1353, Sept. 23–Oct. 12; a great council without clergy; see p. 429; for the grant see Rot. Parl. ii. 252.

1354, April 28–May 20; a full parliament; this session annulled the proceedings against Mortimer and Arundel; Rot. Parl. ii. 255, 256.

1355, Nov. 24–Dec. 30; for the grant see Rot. Parl. ii. 265. The convocation of Canterbury met Nov. 16; that of York, Dec. 7.

In 1356 there was no parliament. The Canterbury convocation, May 23rd, granted two tenths, and that of York, June 3, one tenth.

1357, April 10–May 16; see Statutes, i. 352; Record Report, II. app. ii. p. 167. The grant was a fifteenth and tenth. By the Statute which contained the grant (31 Edw. III. 3. 1) the export of wool is allowed from May to the next Michaelmas on payment of 50s. on the sack and 300 woolfells and 100s. on the last; (Statutes, i. 351) as custom and subsidy; viz. the six years' subsidy of 1355. Convocation of Canterbury, Ap. 26; of York, May 29.

1358, Feb. 5–27; Lords' Report, i. 494.

divisions, but shared the employments of the court and devoted itself to the interests of the king, the task of defending national liberty fell chiefly on the commons. And this was no doubt one of the secondary causes of their growth in power and of their vehemence in self-assertion. Up to this point their jealousy had been provoked chiefly by the unjustifiable financial policy of the king. Whatever might be the remaining rights of the king and his council to make ordinances, or to provide by temporary legislation or by special negotiations, loans, or requisitions, for temporary emergencies, no doubt could exist after the acts of 1297 that they had no right to involve the nation in any general taxation or general pecuniary responsibility without common consent. Yet that had been done, both in the matter of the aids and in the manipulation of the wool; even after the constitutional principle for which the commons contended had been reiterated, the ministers had again and again eluded the application of it, and had copied the most exceptional expedients by which Edward I, at a time when the functions of the executive and the legislature were much less clearly distinguished, had tried to justify himself[1]. Thus in 1359 the king and council obtained from the merchants, probably on November 10, a grant of *6d.* in the pound on exports and imports, which was soon after commuted as to wine and wool, for two shillings on the tun and sack, and, after the truce with France, entirely remitted. In 1360, before a parliament was held, the king ordered a fifteenth and tenth, which had been granted by the commons in five provincial assemblies, to be collected; the parliament called for May 15 granted a like aid[2].

The commons assert their right more boldly.

Evasions of the ministers.

The success with which this had been done seems to have suggested the idea of legislating without the consent of the commons; it certainly suggested to the commons the suspicion that the lords of the council wished to do so. There was a difference between the cases in which the petitions laid before parliament required a statute to be drawn up with the assent of the lords and made perpetual, and those in which the

Legislation by ordinance and legislation by statute.

[1] Foed. ii. 459, 460, 465, 468, 500.
[2] Ibid. pp. 480, 495, 503. See below, p. 429.

petitioners might be satisfied with a charter or the letter of the king, which could be drawn up by the chancellor or in the council, and which needed no sanction of the collective parliament. This difference was better understood then than it is now, when private acts of parliament are so numerous, and orders in council are issued under powers conferred or recognised by parliament. On one occasion, when a doubt arose as to the form which the result of the deliberations should take, and they were asked whether they would proceed by way of ordinance or by statute, the former plan was preferred as giving more room for subsequent modification[1]. The royal ordinances had from the time of Edward I been allowed to have very much the same force as the statutes themselves. Edward's ordinance of the new customs, which was declared illegal by the Ordainers in his son's reign, was not strictly speaking an ordinance, but a charter. All his other legislative acts have the force of laws. Until the great enunciation of the right of parliament in 1322, it might be questioned whether the royal ordinances were not laws within the letter of the constitution, and the acquiescence of the parliaments might be reasonably construed as an admission that they were so. The fact that the answers to particular petitions varied the language of the petitions so as not to give what was asked, caused a natural misgiving; and the non-observance of the conditions on which money was granted must have suggested the wisdom of obtaining, so far as it could be obtained, the redress of complaints before offering the grant. But the first sign of the real importance of the point appears in the demand that certain matters provided for by the king in ordinances should be made perpetual by being embodied in statutes.

Statute and Ordinance.

There was a second reason for some jealousy on this point; for the estate of the clergy, although they declined to comply with the premunition which would have made them an integral

Position of the clerical estate in parliament.

[1] In 1363, Rot. Parl. ii. 280: 'et partant demanda de eux s'ils vouloient avoir les choses issint accordez mys par voie de ordinance ou de Statuyt; qi disoient que bon est mettre les choses par voie d'ordinance et nemye par estatut, au fin que si rien soit de amender puisse estre amende a preschien parlement.' See also Rot. Parl. ii. 113.

Statutes founded on petition of clergy.

part of the parliament, retained the right of petitioning, and the king could, and did now and then, publish a statute with the assent of the lords spiritual and temporal, to which the assent of the commons was not perhaps more necessary than the consent of the clergy was to the statutes passed at the petition of the commons. Against this usage, or the abuse of it, we have already seen the commons petitioning.

Attempts to legislate by ordinance in 1349.

An instance of the working of this jealousy occurs in the parliament of 1351. The council in 1349 had attempted to meet the difficulty caused by the want of labourers, whose numbers were seriously diminished by the plague, by an ordinance fixing the rate of wages [1]. This regulation, as was most probable in the circumstances, had remained a dead letter. At the petition of the commons it was now made more stringent, and enacted as a statute [2]. In 1352 a proposition was made that the commons, to save time and trouble, should delegate twenty-four or thirty of their members to confer with the king and council on public business; this proposal was not accepted, and the whole house presented itself [3]. In the August of the same year, a still more startling change was made. No money was to be asked, and therefore perhaps the innovation may not have been dangerous, and at the moment it may have been justified as a necessary expedient in the great diminution of the population and in the general impoverishment; but it was certainly remarkable. Instead of summoning the representatives of the inferior clergy and the commons in the usual way, the writs of July 1352 order the sheriffs to return one knight for each shire; the town representatives are called by writ addressed to the mayors and bailiffs of a small number of boroughs, who are required to return but one member [4]; and the inferior clergy are not summoned at all. Such an assembly, as long as it merely assisted the council, was no matter of offence, although its constitution was new; it was not, in fact, so dangerous as were the conferences of the merchants; that of

The commons refuse to delegate their powers to a committee in 1352.

Diminution in the number of members summoned, 1352.

[1] Statutes, i. 307; Foed. iii. 198; this was merely an ordinance published in June, 1349, by the king and council; Knighton, c. 2600.

[2] Rot. Parl. ii. 227, 233; Statutes, i. 311.

[3] Rot. Parl. ii. 237.

[4] Lords' Report, iv. 593.

1352 attempted no more. But in September 1353 another assembly of an equally irregular character met: the sheriffs returned but one knight, and the mayors and bailiffs of thirty-seven towns returned two members for each. And this body acted very much as a parliament[1]. It granted a triennial subsidy on wool. Its proceedings are recorded in the Rolls of Parliament as the acts of a great council[2]; but its definitive acts were not at first enrolled among the statutes. It was in fact a 'magnum concilium,' including a representation of the commons; except the beneficed clergy, who might be regarded as represented by the bishops, it contained all the elements which were necessary to a perfect parliament, but those elements were combined in different proportions, and collected by different processes. When then, in 1354, the parliament of the three estates met in its proper constitutional form, it was found that the commons, by their representatives in the great council, had petitioned that the ordinances passed therein should receive parliamentary sanction[3].

The diminished assembly not regarded as a parliament, 1353.

Its measures require parliamentary authorisation, 1354.

The plan of voting three years' supplies at once seems to have increased the number of occasional councils, whilst it rendered frequent parliaments less necessary; and these occasional councils were of very variable form. In 1358, for instance, about a third of the bishops are summoned, and more than a hundred lay lords and councillors[4]. In 1360, on the occasion of an array to meet a threatened French invasion, the nation was bidden to meet by its representatives at five different centres, fifteen counties at London, and sixteen others at Worcester, Taunton, Lincoln, and Leicester[5], and these assemblies granted a tenth and fifteenth, which afterwards received the authorisation of parliament. In 1361 a council on the affairs of Ireland was held at the Chancery in London, to which seven countesses and four baronesses who had estates in Ireland were summoned to attend by their proctors, with four earls and thirty barons, and

Increase in the number of councils, 1358–1361.

Ladies send proctors to council.

[1] Lords' Report, iv. 609; Rot. Parl. ii. 246, 252. [2] Rot. Parl. ii. 246.
[3] Rot. Parl. ii. 253, 254, 257. [4] Lords' Report, iv. 616.
[5] Foed. iii. 468; Lords' Report, iv. 619 sq. The summons was issued Feb. 10 for the five assemblies to be held on the 9th of March. The parliament which followed was called on the 3rd of April to meet May 15.

a similar assembly was held in the following year [1]. None of these experiments left any lasting mark on the constitution.

Dangerous character of these precedents.

It would be perhaps wrong to regard these exceptional assemblies as summoned with the definite intention of confining the work of the representative parliaments to taxation, and thus reducing them to the position which the States-General of France, deprived of legislative and consultative power, were now assuming. But it is not improbable that, as the country was heartily tired of war, and, in consequence of the plague, very little able to endure its present burdens, Edward would avoid every unnecessary occasion of meeting his subjects or hearing their wishes only to refuse or delay compliance. Of the general feeling with respect to the war, the parliament of April, 1354, gave unmistakeable evidence. After the petitions had been read and answered, Bartholomew Burghersh, the king's chamberlain, laid before the assembled lords and commons the negotiations now pending, and explained that there was a good hope of peace; the king, however, would do nothing definite without assent of lords and commons. The question was put, would the parliament consent to peace? The commons with one consent replied that whatever issue the king and the lords might please to take of the said treaty would be agreeable to them. 'Would you then,' asked the chamberlain, 'assent to a treaty of perpetual peace if one might have it?' And the commons responded one and all together, 'Yes, yes [2].' Possibly at this moment, Edward himself, wearied of the subterfuges and false excuses with which the French king was attempting to delude him, would have agreed to any reasonable terms of peace.

The country is tired of the war.

Parliament of 1354.

Legislation.

Some part of the legislative work of these years is very important, and indeed is the chief legislative mark of the reign. The first statute of Provisors [3] was passed in February, 1351; the first statute of *Praemunire*, declaring the forfeiture and outlawry of those who sued in foreign courts for matters cognisable in the king's courts, was an ordinance of 1353 [4];

Statutes of Provisors (1351) and Praemunire (1353) and Treasons (1352).

[1] April 11, 1361, and March 11, 1362; Lords' Report, iv. 627, 629.

[2] 'Les dites communes responderent entierement et uniement, Oil, oil;' Rot. Parl. ii. 262.

[3] Statutes, i. 316; Rot. Parl. ii. 228.

[4] Statutes, i. 329.

the statute of Treasons, the first law that defined that crime and its penalty, passed in 1352 [1]. The common work of the council in 1353 and the parliament in 1354 was the ordinance of the Staples; and in 1357 the king published an ordinance for the government of Ireland [2], which stands to that country in the same relation as the statute of Edward I stands to Wales. Edward II had ordered that annual parliaments should be held in Ireland; from this act the institution dates in a more complete form: there is a vague attempt to extend the good government of England to the sister island, but the general impression produced by the act is that Ireland was in a state of disturbance which Edward was utterly unable to remedy.

Ordinance of the Staples.

Legislation for Ireland.

The ordinance of the Staples however has considerable importance, both constitutionally and socially. The royal revenue no longer depended directly on the land; the contribution of a fraction of personal property had long been superseding the older forms of direct taxation levied on the carucate, the hide, or the knight's fee; and both were now being complemented by a definite share in the marketable produce of the country, the wool, the lead, and the tin, the staple commodities of England. The growing mercantile interest, although strengthened by the alliance with the Flemings, needed both protection and regulation; and the king and the parliament recognised in that need an opportunity of retaining hold on the commodities themselves. The system of the staple was, it would seem, a combination of the principle of the guild and of the royal privilege of establishing fairs and markets. The merchants of the staple had a monopoly of purchase and export; the towns of the staple were centres for the collection, trial, and assessment of the goods. The growth of the system must date from the reign of Edward I, who had bought the town of Antwerp from the duke of Brabant, and established there the foreign centre for the wool trade [3]. Under Edward II the merchants had their foreign staple first at Antwerp and afterwards at S. Omer, and home staples at several large towns, such as Newcastle, York, Lincoln, Winchester, Exeter, Bristol, and London. The ordinances of Edward II

Importance of the ordinance of the Staples, 1353-1354.

Growth of the Staples.

[1] Statutes, i. 320; Rot. Parl. ii. 239. [2] Statutes, i. 357. [3] Foed. ii. 206.

The Staple.

were confirmed by Edward III in his first parliament; but in 1328, by the statute of Northampton, the monopolies of the staple were abolished and trade set free as it had been under the provisions of the great charter. Public opinion seems to have varied as to the propriety of continuing the system, and perhaps may have been determined from time to time by the political relations with Flanders. The staples were restored, and again abolished in 1334; from 1344 onwards they are frequently discussed in parliaments and assemblies of the merchants: and by the statute of 1353[1] the system was consolidated: the number and place of the staples were fixed; the regular or ancient custom was declared, and the rights and privileges of the merchants were confirmed. The companies of merchants, if strangers, were, like the Jews of former times, under the king's special protection; like the officers of the forest they had their own customs and tribunals, with which neither the judges nor the king's servants could intermeddle. They formed in fact, as has been already observed, a subordinate estate of the realm, with which the kings could negotiate separately from the other communities, and to which it is probable that they would gladly have given a more formal recognition. The varying fortunes of the staples during the early years of Edward III perhaps evince some jealousy on the part of the parliament as to the status of the merchants who had been too ready to play into the king's hands; or else they may show the varying extent to which the mercantile body was represented in the parliament itself.

Privileges of the merchants.

Period of peace, 1360–1369.

The peace with France concluded at Bretigny in 1360 was kept until 1369, when, in consequence of the repudiation by Charles V of the articles of the treaty, Edward, on the 3rd of June, resumed the title of king of France which he had resigned, and renewed the war. In 1362 the supply for three years was provided by a grant of twenty shillings on the sack and 300 woolfells, and forty shillings on the last of leather; in 1365 by a subsidy of exactly double amount, the additional sums being required for the pacification of Ireland and Gascony; in 1368

Supplies during the peace.

[1] Statutes, i. 332. Cf. Rot. Parl. ii. 268, 287 sq., 318 sq.; iii. 203. For the later history of the Staple and its relations with Calais, see Hall's Customs Revenue, i. 29 sq., and the authorities given in the appendix.

the wants of the two coming years were met by a vote of 36*s.* 8*d.* on the sack and twelve score woolfells, and four pounds on the last[1]. The king's advisers during the period were chiefly prelates: bishop Thoresby of S. David's, who became archbishop of York in 1352, was chancellor from 1349 to 1356; bishop Edington of Winchester, from 1356 to 1363; Simon Langham, bishop of Ely, from 1363 to 1367, becoming archbishop of Canterbury in 1366; and William of Wykeham, bishop of Winchester, from 1367 to 1371. At the Treasury bishop Edington presided from 1344 to 1356, when he became chancellor; bishop Sheppey of Rochester from 1356 to 1360; Langham succeeded in 1360, and became chancellor in 1363; bishop Barnet of Worcester from 1363 to 1369; and Thomas Brantingham, afterwards bishop of Exeter, from 1369 to 1371. All these were men who, independently of their political position, did good work for the church; archbishop Thoresby's administration of the northern province was singularly able and successful; Edington and Wykeham were not only magnificent benefactors by the foundation of churches and colleges, but indefatigable workers, as their own diocesan records testify. The see of Canterbury from 1349 to 1366 was occupied by archbishop Islip, who was likewise a founder of schools and an earnest advocate of good government, and who foresaw as clearly as most men the days of danger which were coming, and which he could do so little to remedy.

Ministers during 1350–1370.

Thoresby and Islip.

[1] The parliaments of these years were:—

1360, May 15; in this a fifteenth and tenth were granted; Foed. iii. 503; the clergy of Canterbury had granted a tenth, Feb. 4; the York convocation met Feb. 12; Wake, p. 300.

1361, Jan. 24–Feb. 18; Statutes, i. 364–370.

1362, Oct. 13–Nov. 17; a subsidy on wool, woolfells, and leather was granted for three years; Rot. Parl. ii. 273; Statutes, i. 371–378.

1363, Oct. 6–Nov. 3; Statutes, i. 378–383; Rot. Parl. ii. 275–282. Convocation sat Dec. 2.

1365, Jan. 20–Feb. 28; a similar subsidy was granted for three years; Rot. Parl. ii. 285; Statutes, i. 383–387.

1366, May 4–12; Rot. Parl. ii. 288–292.

1368, May 1–21; the subsidy on wool for two years was granted; Rot. Parl. ii. 295; Statutes, i. 388–390.

1369, June 3–11; a similar subsidy (43*s.* 4*d.* and 80*s.*) was granted for three years from the following Michaelmas; Rot. Parl. ii. 300; and on the 21st of January, 1370, the clergy granted a tenth for three years. Cf. Statutes, i. 390–392; Wake, p. 301.

Legislation during the years 1360–1369.

Sumptuary law, 1363.

The legislation of this period of the reign is both curious and important. The parliament endeavoured by sumptuary laws, prescribing the minutiae of diet and dress, to prevent the further impoverishment of the country, already desolated by the plague and exhausted by the war[1]; attempts were made to bring the statute of labourers into operation by applying the fines which were to be raised under it to the relief of the charges on the commons[2]. The use of the English language in the courts of law was ordered in 1362, and the speech of the chancellor on opening parliament in 1363 was delivered in English, forming a precedent which was frequently although not regularly followed[3]. By the same act, although this was not petitioned for, it was ordered that records should be kept in Latin; and the use of French was thus excluded by law, although practice was in this instance much more powerful than statute, and French continued to be the legal language for some centuries. The use of English, however, in parliament, must have been a concession made for the convenience of the commons: the period is that of the rise of the newer English literature of the middle ages; both bishops like Thoresby and reformers like Wycliffe were pressing the use of the native tongue in sermons and offices of devotion. In the same parliament of 1362[4] a great boon long demanded was at last obtained; it was enacted that from henceforth no subsidy should be set on wool without the assent of parliament. This most important limitation of the royal power of taxation required to be renewed in 1371, but it serves as a mark of the growing tendency to deprive the crown, by very definite legislation, of its power of defying national sentiment and raising money by indirect evasions of the letter of the constitutional law. The same parliament struck a blow at the custom of purveyance[5]; the enactment was granted, as the statute says, by the will of the

English language in the courts of law, 1362.

The king forbidden to tax the wool, 1362 and 1371.

[1] Statutes, i. 380.

[2] Ibid. 375; Rot. Parl. ii. 228, &c., 273, &c.

[3] Statutes, i. 375; Rot. Parl. ii. 275, 283. The speech in 1365 was in English; in 1377 apparently in French; in 1381 Courtenay preached in English; Rot. Parl. ii. 283; iii. 3, 98.

[4] Statutes, i. 374, art. 11; Rot. Parl. ii. 271, 283.

[5] Statutes, i. 371, art. 2; Rot. Parl. ii. 270.

king himself, without motion of the great men or of the commons; but these words were possibly inserted in order to preclude the king from reversing the law as he had done in 1341; for the thing itself had been constantly made a matter of complaint, and the archbishop of Canterbury had but lately addressed to the king an impassioned letter of remonstrance on the subject. By this law the right of purveyance was to be exercised only on behalf of the king or queen; the hated name of purveyor was to be exchanged for that of buyer, and payments were to be made in ready money. The petitions of the commons, besides the points here touched on, and a prayer for annual parliaments, were devoted chiefly to complaints of the papal usurpations which the act of 1353 had failed to check. In 1365 was passed a new statute of praemunire, definitely aimed against the jurisdiction of the papal court[1], and in the following year the parliament, the bishops, lords, and commons, unanimously repudiated the burden of papal superiority which had been undertaken by John, and refused to pay the tribute of 1000 marks which had been long in arrear and had now ceased altogether[2]; even Peter's Pence, the ancient Romescot, which dated from the days of Offa and Ethelwulf, was withheld for a time[3].

He renounces the right of purveyance, 1362, except in behalf of the king and queen.

Anti-papal legislation, 1365.

Refusal of the papal tribute, 1366.

260. But important as these points are, these years have, if

[1] Statutes, i. 386; Rot. Parl. ii. 284. The editors of the Parl. Hist. (i. 316) state that Edward himself made the speech which led to this enactment; this is not mentioned in the Roll itself, which is the only authority.

[2] 'Lour disoit comment le roi avoit entendu qe le pape par force d'un fait quel il dit qe le roi Johan fesoit au pape, de lui faire homage pur le roialme d'Engleterre et la terre d'Irelande, et qe par cause du dit homage q'il deveroit paier chescun an perpetuelment mille marcs, est en volunte de faire proces devers le roi et son roialme pur le dit service et cens recoverir. De qoi le roi pria as ditz prelatz, ducs, countes et barons lour avys et bon conseil, et ce q'il en ferroit en cas qe le pape vorroit proceder devers lui ou son dit roialme pur celle cause. Et les prelatz requeroient au roi q'ils se purroient sur ce par eux soul aviser et respondre lendemain. Queux prelatz le dit lendemain adeprimes par eux mesmes, et puis les autres ducs, countes, barons, et grantz, respondirent et disoient qe le dit roi Johan ne nul autre purra mettre lui ne son roialme ne son poeple en tiele subjection saunz assent et accorde de eux. Et les communes sur ce demandez et avisez respondirent en mesme la manere;' Rot. Parl. ii. 290. The tribute was in arrear since 1333.

[3] Stow, Chron. p. 266; Barnes (from the C.C.C. MS.), p. 670. Cf. Rot. Parl. iii. 21.

Family settlement.

Provision for the Prince of Wales;

viewed in their results, a much greater historical significance. It is to them that we must refer the maturity of Edward's scheme for the settlement of his family, and the origin of the strifes that make up the history of the following century. His eldest son, Edward the Black Prince, created in 1336 duke of Cornwall and in 1343 prince of Wales, was married in 1361 to his cousin Johanna of Kent, the heiress of earl Edmund of Woodstock and granddaughter of Edward I. Lionel, the second surviving son, had been married in 1342 to the heiress of William de Burgh, earl of Ulster, who inherited from her grandmother a third of the great possessions of the earls of Gloucester and Hertford; he became duke of Clarence in 1362. John of Gaunt, the next son, had married in 1359 his kinswoman Blanche of Lancaster, who inherited four of the five earldoms of earl Thomas; to these John himself added the earldom of Richmond, and in 1362 he became duke of Lancaster. The subsequent marriages of Edmund Mortimer earl of March, great-grandson of the traitor, with the daughter of the duke of Clarence, and of the two co-heiresses of Bohun with Henry of Lancaster, son of John of Gaunt, and Thomas of Woodstock, the youngest son of Edward III, completed an arrangement which collected in the family of the king all the great inheritances of the land, and might have seemed likely to preclude for ever the revival of the territorial and political parties which had so nearly wrecked the fortunes of England in the reign of Edward II. The idea of this arrangement must have been long in coming to full growth or in finding its opportunity. None of the Norman sovereigns had ventured to provide in this way for son or brother. Henry II had laboured to the utmost to obtain foreign territory for his sons, but had only allowed one of them to marry at home, and had sent all his daughters abroad. Henry III had given the earldom of Cornwall to his brother, and that of Lancaster to his second son, and thus had begun to gather in the escheated fiefs, as he saw Louis IX doing in France. Edward I had shown by the marriages of his daughters to the earls of Gloucester and Hereford, and by the lawyerlike settlement by which he laid

for Lionel of Antwerp;

for John of Gaunt.

Accumulation of great fiefs in the royal family.

Growth of this policy.

hold on the Bigod inheritance, a clear perception of the fact that the English princes must henceforth be used to strengthen the power of the royal house at home as well as abroad; and even Edward II, by providing for his younger brothers with the earldoms of Kent and Norfolk, had acted on the same principle. Nothing however had yet been done which wore the appearance of a political scheme; and, if Edward III married his children with an eye to such a scheme, he acted with more craft than real wisdom. The fate of his father might have warned him of what was in store for his grandson. But there was much to make the prospect inviting: there was something gained moreover in the complete identification of the interest of the royal house with the welfare of England; the locust flights of foreigners need be feared no more; the baronial jealousy could not be so easily excited when the chiefs of the baronage were all so closely united in blood and in common interests; and the widespread territorial influences of the great inheritances might well be reckoned on as sufficient to guide, combine, or divide the commons. The bestowal of the title of duke[1], almost new in England, on John of Gaunt and Lionel of Antwerp, in 1362, seems to be the symbolical consummation of the new policy.

Advantages and impolicy of the scheme.

Had England been a united country, or had Edward's sons been unambitious and patriotic, the result might have been good. As it was, the policy was fatal. Lionel died in 1368, and, as the prince of Wales had then two sons alive, the chance which the heiress of Clarence had of inheriting or transmitting a right to the throne might be deemed small. But John of Gaunt was ambitious and unpopular, and to him the absence of the Black Prince in Aquitaine left open the place of chief counsellor to his father. Although John had acquired the Lancaster heritage, he had not taken up the Lancaster policy: he cared to propitiate neither the clergy nor the commons, but acted as the guide and leader of the court. Consequently his reputation was even worse than he deserved; when in January,

John of Gaunt gains supreme influence over his father, 1368–1377.

[1] Rot. Parl. ii. 273. The Black Prince had been made duke of Cornwall in 1336, and Henry of Lancaster duke of Lancaster in 1351. These were the only precedents.

1371, the prince of Wales returned to England in broken health, the prospect of a royal minority, with John of Gaunt as guardian, became alarming, and he was suspected of aspiring to the succession.

Unhappiness of Edward's later years, 1369–1377.

Until the death of queen Philippa in 1369 the family harmony had been unbroken. From that date nothing prospered with Edward. Unsuccessful in war, luxurious in peace, he seemed to be reversing the glories of his early years, and, as his victories grew fewer and his popularity diminished, political questions at home became more threatening. The same year 1369 saw the last fatal visitation of the great plague.

Dangers in the religious condition of England.

The religious condition of England at this moment was full of difficult questions. The church, since the days of S. Edmund and Grosseteste, when we saw the clergy frankly allied with the laity not only in the struggle for common liberty but in resistance to papal encroachments, had been subjected to an alternation of rulers not less different from one another than were the kings whom they had to counsel. The arbitrary rule of Boniface of Savoy,—now as a military chieftain leaving the church to herself or enriching himself with her spoils, now as an apostolic judge enforcing the rigour of the laws which he did not profess to obey,—a sort of rule which might account for any amount of degeneration,—had been succeeded by the strict ecclesiastical administration of three successive primates, enlightened, sincere, earnest and cultivated, but profoundly impressed with the belief that it was their duty to set the priesthood above the secular power.

Archbishops, 1273–1313.

Imperfect discipline.

Kilwardby, Peckham, and Winchelsey were men of piety and zeal, good preachers and self-denying men; but their point of view was that of the Roman, not, as Langton's had been, that of the English priesthood. In the spirit of Becket they had striven for privileges, the abuse of which they could not prevent. They had had allies in the anti-royal, the baronial, or as it afterwards became, the Lancaster party, which had other grounds of quarrel with the royal power and was glad to have in the clergy a link that secured the alliance of the people at large.

Archbishop Reynolds, 1313–1327

Archbishop Reynolds who followed was, as we have seen, a creature of the king: yet Reynolds was wise enough to see the clerical abuses against which Winchelsey had fought, and had fought in vain because he would not allow the privilege, which gave occasion for the abuses, to be limited by any hands but his own. The abuse of plurality, which left the spiritual care of the people to hirelings, or to the volunteer agency of the friars, who had their own ends to seek, and who, beginning perhaps from a higher standing-point than the secular clergy, rapidly sank into a much deeper degradation; the neglect of learning and discipline which allowed men utterly unqualified for spiritual work to enter into holy orders, and after they were ordained to return to secular employments, licenced to sin and sheltered from punishment by a character which no secular power must be allowed to touch; the impotency of the ecclesiastical tribunals which could not inflict condign punishment on clerical criminals, but would not allow them to be tried by laymen; all these were points which constitution after constitution, canon after canon, were directed to amend. Not only Reynolds but Mepeham and Stratford, and almost every primate to the time of the Reformation, strove earnestly against the abuses of the spiritual courts which were really alienating the nation from the church and from religion also. It may be questioned whether these attempts at reform would ever have been successful; as it was, the preaching of Wycliffe startled the rulers of the church into an attitude of rigid conservatism. Before the Wycliffe movement began there was a strong anti-clerical feeling, and a strong anti-clerical party in the court itself, which, jealous at once of the influence of the church in social life, and of the preponderant share of the clergy in the administration of government, was likely enough for its own ends to ally itself with religious discontent, whilst it steadily resisted moral or spiritual reformation. A curious tissue of Lollard influences at court appears during the rest of the reign in opposition to constitutional reform.

Pluralities.

Clerical abuses.

Mepeham and Stratford, 1328–1348. Attempts to reform the spiritual courts.

Anti-clerical party at court.

261. The history of the last seven years of this long reign exhibits a singular combination or rather confusion of political elements together with a great amount of political activity.

A.D. 1369–1377.

Parliament of 1369.

The year 1369 had been marked by a singular unanimity. The parliament had not only advised the king to resume, as he had already resolved to do, the title of king of France, but had granted an increased subsidy, in addition to the custom, on wool for three years; and the clergy, after being consulted first in diocesan synods and afterwards in the provincial convocations, supplemented the grant of the laity with a tenth for the same period[1]. This liberal supply obviated the necessity of calling a parliament in 1370: the attention of the nation was fixed on the war in Gascony. From Gascony the Black Prince returned in January, 1371, leaving John of Gaunt as commander in his place. The expenses of the continued war had outrun the supply of money, and the successes were scarcely sufficient to maintain the national enthusiasm. As might be expected in these circumstances, public indignation turned against the ministers.

Return of the Prince of Wales in 1371.

Parliament of 1371.

The parliament of 1371 met on the 24th of February in the Painted Chamber[2]; Edward himself was present, with William of Wykeham as chancellor, and bishop Brantingham of Exeter as treasurer. The chancellor opened the proceedings with a speech, in which he described the enormous preparations made by the king of France, and requested the advice and support of the parliament, in order to avert invasion and prevent the destruction of the English navy. After the formal business of the petitions, the deliberations began, and the consultation between the lords and commons lasted for more than a month. Of the details of the discussion we have no account, unless we may refer to this occasion an extract from a speech of one of the lords on the wealth and immunities of the clergy, which was preserved by Wycliffe. The occasion of the speech was a claim on the part of the '*religiosi* possessionati,' the monastic owners of property, to be excused from the payment of tenths and fifteenths to the crown; and the speech was made by 'a lord more skilful than the rest[3].' He argues however

Attack on the property of the clergy.

[1] Wilkins, Conc. iii. 82–84. See above, p. 433.
[2] Feb. 24–Mar. 29; Rot. Parl. ii. 303 sq.; Lords' Report, i. 494.
[3] 'Unum dominum peritiorem ceteris;' possibly lord le Scrope, as the description could scarcely apply to Pembroke. See Fasciculi Zizaniorum, pref. p. xxi, where Dr. Shirley refers the speech to this parliament.

against the '*clerici* possessionati' in general. In the speech the clergy are represented as an owl dressed in feathers which had been contributed by the other birds for her protection; on the approach of the hawk the birds reclaimed their gifts; the owl declined to restore them, and each took back his own by force. The application of this apologue was that the temporalities of the clergy should be resumed in time of war as common property of the kingdom. Whoever the speaker may have been, the sentiment of the speech recommended itself strongly to a party in the parliament, which retained the anti-clerical feeling that had been exhibited in 1340. This party was headed by John of Hastings, earl of Pembroke, who had been the king's intended son-in-law[1], a young man of twenty-four, grandson of Roger Mortimer and also the representative of the house of Valence. Pembroke was the spokesman of the court influence, and may possibly have been supported indirectly by John of Gaunt. He seems however to have availed himself of the growing spirit of religious disaffection, in order to overthrow the ministry. A formal address was made to the king in the name of the earls, barons, and commons of England, representing that the government of the realm had long been carried on by ecclesiastics whom it was impossible to bring to account; thus great mischief had befallen the state in times past, and greater still might happen; it would be well if it should please the king that for the future sufficient and able laymen should be chosen, and none other hold the office of chancellor, treasurer, clerk of the privy seal,

Apologue spoken in parliament.

The earl of Pembroke, in the parliament of 1371.

Proposal to remove clerical ministers.

[1] Pembroke had been betrothed to Margaret, daughter of Edward III, but she died before marriage, and he married a daughter of Sir Walter Manny. Edward calls him 'notre tres ame fitz;' Foed. iii. 941. In 1372 Pembroke was captured by the Spaniards. The chronicler regards this as a judgment; for first he was an adulterer; secondly, 'perniciosus quadam dementia et insania fatigatus jura et libertates ecclesiasticas in quodam parliamento delevisse ex animo affectavit;' thirdly, 'ipse protinus exagitatus nequitiae stimulo suasit regi suoque consilio ut viri ecclesiastici bellorum tempore gravius quam alii saeculares mulctarentur. Ista vero ultima summe dominis temporalibus placuerunt, quae deinceps quasi in consuetudinem licet nunquam gaudentes traxerunt, reputantes se in hoc magnum aliquid consecutos, si quandocunque sanctam ecclesiam novis impositionibus et tallagiis valeant onerare;' Walsing. i. 315; Cont. Murim. p. 212.

baron or controller of the exchequer, or any important post of the kind: if this might be done, the execution of the resolution might be left to the king, whose choice of servants it was not intended otherwise to fetter. The king replied that he would make such order as should seem to him to be best, with the advice of his council [1]. But he yielded the point, or perhaps may have instigated the movement. William of Wykeham, on the 24th of March [2], resigned the great seal, and bishop Brantingham, on the 27th, quitted the treasury. Their successors were appointed immediately: the new chancellor was Sir Robert Thorpe, master of Pembroke Hall, Cambridge, the favourite foundation of the house of Pembroke; the treasurer was Richard lord le Scrope of Bolton, the faithful and life-long adviser of John of Gaunt [3]. That the duke of Lancaster was actively interested in the attack upon the clerical ministers it would be difficult to prove; and the supposition has been too rashly made, by an anticipation of the later relations of John of Gaunt with Wycliffe, and his opposition to Wykeham. John of Gaunt was abroad at the moment, and probably had little interest in the religious views of Wycliffe, who no doubt sympathised with the attack. But he was probably willing to embarrass the minister, and allowed his own political party to support Pembroke. The result of the king's concession was a grant on the part of parliament, reported on the 28th of March, of a sum of £50,000, to be raised by a contribution of 22*s*. 3*d*. from each parish. There were, it was calculated, 40,000 parishes in England, and the larger were to help the smaller [4]. More than forty petitions of the commons had been presented; some were immediately answered, others reserved for further

The king consents.

A Lay Chancellor and Treasurer appointed.

Was John of Gaunt a party in this attack?

New form of taxation.

[1] Rot. Parl. ii. 304.

[2] Foed. iii. 911.

[3] Foss, Biogr. Jurid. pp. 602, 656.

[4] Rot. Parl. ii. 304. The computation of 40,000 parishes, like that of the 60,000 knights' fees (above, vol. i. p. 432), is a curious illustration of the absolute untrustworthiness of medieval figures, which, even when most circumstantially minute, cannot be accepted except where, as in the public accounts, vouchers can be quoted. Hearne, in his appendix to Avesbury, gives the following *minutiæ* from MS.: 'Nota quod in Anglia sunt ecclesiae parochiales, 46,822; item villae, 52,285; item episcopatus, 17; item feoda militum, 53,215; de quibus religiosi habent, 28,000;' p. 264; Higden, Polychr. i. c. 49, makes the parishes 45,002.

examination. A single statute was passed, the most important provision of which was the repetition of the law of 1362, that no impost should be laid on wool, other than the custom and subsidy granted to the king, without the assent of parliament[1].

Inexperience of the ministers.

The extraordinary ignorance displayed by the parliament, or by the new ministers, in reference to the money grant, showed that a sudden transfer of power into lay hands was not without its disadvantages. It was found necessary to call a great council in June, at Winchester, to complete and remedy the proceedings of March. Half of the representative members of the late parliament were recalled to meet the king and a few of the lords[2]. The chancellor reported that instead of 40,000 parishes there were less than 9000[3]; the charge of 22*s.* 3*d.* must be raised to 116*s.*, and even then all the church lands acquired since 1292 must be included among the contributors[4]. The change was at once allowed, the outstanding petitions were answered, and the assembly broke up.

Parliamentary vote supplemented by a great council, June, 1371.

[1] Statutes, i. 393; Foed. iii. 918; Rot. Parl. ii. 308.

[2] June 8, Rot. Parl. ii. 304: writs were directed to four bishops, four abbots, six earls, and seven barons; and the sheriffs were ordered to send up one of the representative members of each constituency, who had attended the last parliament, and who was named in the writ; Lords' Report, iv. 650.

[3] Stow, Chron. pp. 268, 269, gives the number of parishes in each county, and the amount of assessment. The total number was 8,600; the assessment £50,181 8*s.* Chester was not included.

[4] This charge on the lands acquired by the clergy and religious since the taxation of pope Nicolas in 1291 was not a novelty, as sometimes imagined. See above, p. 416, note 1. The question whether they should be taxed with the laity or with the clergy was however settled, so far as this grant was concerned, by the words of the parliament, 'fors pris en ceste grant la counte de Cestre et les terres et possessions de Seinte Eglise du roialme amortisez devant l'an XX le roi l'aiel et taxes ove la clergie a la disme;' Rot. Parl. ii. 304. As early as 1307 the form of taxation of the temporal grant excluded 'the proper goods of the clergy issuing from the temporalities annexed to their churches' because they were included in the clerical grant, assessed according to the taxation of the tenth (i.e. the taxation of pope Nicolas). But all property of the clergy of whatever kind, not included in that taxation of the tenth, is included in the temporal grant. In 1341 and 1346 the question had arisen (above, p. 416) but was not decided. It certainly would seem not impossible that these lands should now and then escape taxation altogether; and some such claim may have been made in the speech which is answered by Wycliffe's friend, as above. See Parl. Writs, II. i. 15; Chron. de Melsa, ii. 209, 240. In the first parliament of Richard II it was ordered that these lands should for the future be taxed with those of the laity; Rot. Parl. iii. 24. Cf. Rot. Parl. iii. 75, 134, 176, 276; Vit. Abb. S. Alb. iii. 36.

Large grants made by convocation, May, 1371.

The warning thus given to the clergy was not unheeded. The convocations were called together immediately. On the 28th of April the royal commissioners demanded a grant of the same amount as that voted by the parliament. On the 2nd of May the prince of Wales met the convocation of Canterbury in the parlour of the Savoy palace and received their promise to provide £50,000, if the province of York and the exempt and privileged clergy were made to join in the contribution[1]. The York convocation acquiesced in the following July; the northern province was to pay one-fifth of the sum.

Ministerial changes, 1372.

The personal influence of Pembroke did not last long. He was captured by the Spaniards at sea, on the 23rd of June, 1372; and on the 29th of the same month Sir Robert Thorpe, the chancellor, died, and was succeeded by Sir John Knyvett, chief justice of the king's bench. John of Gaunt returned to England; and the king himself made an ineffectual attempt to relieve la Rochelle, on which he spent, it was said, £900,000. Before he started he had called a parliament, to be held on the 13th of October before his grandchild Richard as regent; he returned however before the day appointed and issued another summons for November 3rd. Sir Guy Brian, who appeared as the king's spokesman, made no secret of the royal discomfiture, and laid first before the lords, and afterwards before the assembled estates, the great exigencies of his master in Aquitaine, which the prince of Wales had, on the 5th of October, surrendered to his father[2]. The parliament made a virtue of necessity. It was now the turn of the wool to be taxed: the heavy subsidy imposed in 1369 was renewed for two years, a fifteenth was granted for a single year, and the citizens and burghers, after the departure of the knights, continued for another year the custom of tunnage and poundage, two shillings on the tun of wine and sixpence in the pound on merchandise, which had

The king goes to war, but returns.

Parliament of November, 1372.

Heavy taxation.

[1] Wilkins, Conc. iii. 91. This was no doubt a heavy increase of taxation, and included small endowments which had hitherto escaped, 'sacerdotes stipendiarii secundum valorem quem perceperunt erant taxati; minuta etiam beneficia quae nunquam prius erant taxata ad complementum illius similiter erant taxata;' Cont. Murimuth, p. 210; Wals. i. 312; Wake, p. 302; Hody, Hist. Conv. pp. 218–221.

[2] Foed. iii. 974.

been granted the year before for the protection of the merchant navy[1]. This was done at the request of the prince of Wales, who applied to the wine and other merchandise the same unconstitutional mode of negotiation which had been forbidden in the case of the wool. Among the petitions of this parliament one only was turned into a statute, and it betrays somewhat of the same jealousy towards the lawyers as had been shown in 1371 towards the clergy. It was desired that henceforth 'gentz de ley,' lawyers practising in the king's courts, who made the parliament a mere convenience for transacting the affairs of their clients to the neglect of the public business, should no longer be eligible as knights of the shire; and that the sheriffs also should be disqualified during their term of office[2]. But although the 'gentz de seinte Eglise' may have inspired the attack on their rivals, the lawyers remained in possession of the great offices of state until the last year of the reign. Other petitions concern the enforcement of the statute of labourers, the annual appointment of sheriffs, the abuses of the chancery and the ecclesiastical courts, and the privileges of the merchants, which were naturally re-asserted every time that a grant on wool was made in parliament.

Lawyers not to be knights of the shire, 1372.

Other petitions.

In 1373 the same story is repeated, but this time the hero of the unsuccessful enterprise is John of Gaunt. He had made his grand expedition, had traversed great part of France, but found it ravaged before him, and failed to meet an enemy or obtain supplies. Having lost a great part of his army and nearly all his horses, he sent home for money, and the king called the parliament to provide it on the 21st of November[3]. The transactions show that, whatever might have been the minor jealousies of class or estate in former years, the commons

Parliament of November, 1373.

[1] The parliament sat Nov. 3–24; the grant is given, Rot. Parl. ii. 310. The Parliament Roll of 1371 which must have contained the previous grant of tunnage and poundage is imperfect; Rot. Parl. ii. 308; Hale, Concerning the Customs, p. 173; on the grant by the burghers, see Hallam, Middle Ages, iii. 47.

[2] Rot. Parl. ii. 310; Statutes, i. 394.

[3] It sat until Dec. 10; Lords' Report, i. 494; Rot. Parl. ii. 316: but on the 29th of November, after the grant was made, the king gave leave to depart to all who wished.

Parliament of November, 1373.

Demand for aid.

still trusted the lords and the lords were willing to do their best for the commons. On the 22nd the chancellor discharged his very disagreeable duty: the expedition of the duke of Lancaster had been most costly; advice and aid must be given, and, until that was done, the petitions of the parliament must stand over. The tone was too peremptory, and the demand for aid without reference to the petitions was an aggression that provoked reprisals. The commons, on the 24th, sent to the lords asking them to appoint a number of their body to confer with them. This is the first instance since the institution of representative parliaments of a practice which was soon to acquire great importance. The lords readily acquiesced, and sent the bishops of London, Winchester, and Bath, the earls of Arundel, March, and Salisbury, Sir Guy Brian, and Sir Henry le Scrope of Masham. Of these the bishop of London was Simon Sudbury, afterwards archbishop of Canterbury, the victim of the revolt of 1381; the bishop of Winchester was William of Wykeham, who was no doubt still smarting under his humiliation of 1371; and the bishop of Bath had been the chancellor of Aquitaine under the Black Prince; the earls of Salisbury and Arundel and Guy Brian were intimate friends and companions of the king; the earl of March, as husband of Philippa of Clarence, had his own apprehensions of John of Gaunt; and Henry le Scrope was an old north-country lord. The majority certainly, and the whole committee probably, was opposed to the influence of John of Gaunt. After five days' consultation the commons returned their answer: they would join in a grant of a fifteenth for two years, if the war should last so long; they renewed the subsidy on wool, the tunnage and poundage for the same period [1]; but they prayed that the money might be spent on the war and on that only, and that members of the parliament should not be collectors of the impost. The other petitions were of the usual sort; the papal assumptions in particular, which seemed more and more encroaching as new legislation was devised to meet them, were a subject of very loud complaint. The adjustment of the relations with the papacy had already been made the

Conference between the lords and commons.

Offer of the commons.

Negotiation with Rome.

[1] Rot. Parl. ii. 317.

subject of an embassy to the pope, and was referred to a great conference or congress of ambassadors, which was to be held at Bruges, in 1374. The clergy, in their convocations, voted a tenth immediately after the dismissal of the parliament [1]. No other assembly of the estates was summoned until the famous 'Good Parliament' of 1376.

Negotiations at Bruges, 1374–1375. The nation waited no doubt with great anxiety the result of the negotiations which were carried on at Bruges for a concordat with the pope, and, under the shadow of that transaction, for a permanent peace with France. The former series of debates, conducted on the side of England by bishop Gilbert of Bangor and the famous John Wycliffe, lasted from July 1374 to September 1375 [2]; the latter, during 1375, were guided by John of Gaunt, and he in the month of June concluded a truce for a year, which practically lasted during the remainder of the reign. The result of the negotiation with the pope, as usual, disappointed the country [3]; a small temporary concession was made by the

[1] Canterbury Dec. 17, 1373, and York Feb. 6, 1374; Wake, p. 303; Foed. iii. 993.

[2] The commission, given July 27, 1374, mentions that the bishop, with three others, had been already at work; Foed. iii. 1007. The truce between England and France for a year was concluded by John of Gaunt at Bruges, June 27, 1375; it was prolonged by him in conjunction with archbishop Sudbury and the earl of Cambridge, at Bruges, March 12, 1376 to April 1, 1377; ibid. 1048.

[3] Foed. iii. 1037; the pope's letters are dated Sept. 1, 1375. The king, however, on the 15th of February, 1377, when he gave up, on the occasion of his jubilee, the right of presentation to certain preferments which had fallen into his hands during vacancies, published six articles extracted verbally from the pope, in which he promised (1) to abstain from reservations, (2) to wait for free elections to bishoprics, (3) to act justly with reference to other elective dignities, (4) to be moderate in bestowing preferments on foreigners, (5) to relieve the clergy in the matter of first fruits, and (6), without committing himself absolutely for the future, to be circumspect in declaring provisions and expectatives. Possibly this is the real result of the Bruges negotiations. The sum of them is stated by Walsingham, i. 317: 'tandem concordatum est inter eos quod papa de cetero reservationibus beneficiorum minime uteretur et quod rex beneficia per "quare impedit" ulterius non conferret; sed de electionibus pro quibus ambassiatores anno praeterito fuerunt missi ad curiam Romanam, in isto tractatu nihil penitus erat tactum.' And this seems to agree fairly well with the articles just quoted. See Lewis's Wycliffe, pp. 32, 33; Barnes, pp. 864, 866. By the writ 'quare impedit' the king was accustomed, on the ground of wardships or of his right to the patronage of vacant churches, to usurp a good deal of preferment, and also to treat as vacant livings which had been filled up by the pope. See Rot. Parl. ii. 8; iii. 20, 86, 163.

Negotiations at Bruges.

court of Avignon, which virtually re-asserted the larger claim; and the pope, by confirming the appointments made by the king and annulling the rival appointments made by himself and by Urban V, strengthened instead of renouncing his former position. No relief was therefore to be expected from these irritating and oppressive interferences with English freedom. Public disaffection was on the increase; the king since the death of Philippa had fallen under the influence of Alice Perrers, one of the court ladies who had served the queen, and who now assumed the position of an influential minister. The administration fell into contempt, which was increased during the absence of the duke of Lancaster, and on his return took the form of open hostility. The summer of 1375 was exceedingly hot and dry; a dread of the return of the plague probably hindered the calling of a parliament; and the abeyance of the parliament increased popular misgivings. The cessation of taxation was itself an alarming sign, for a greater effort than had ever been made before would be needed to meet the deficit. The influence of the duke of Lancaster moreover, which was used to support the corrupt agency of the king's mistress, was felt to be a national disgrace.

Their futility.

Alice Perrers.

The *Good Parliament*, 1376.

262. The parliament of 1376 shares the character of the great councils of 1258 and 1297 only in the fact that it marked the climax of a long rising excitement. It asserted some sound principles without being a starting-point of new history. It afforded an important illustration of the increasing power of the commons, but, as an attempt at real reform and progress, it was a failure. It had been summoned originally for the 12th of February, but did not meet until the 28th of April[1]. On that day the king presented himself, but, as it was usual to wait for late comers, the proceedings were delayed until the morrow, when, in the Painted Chamber and in the king's presence, Knyvett the chancellor declared the occasion of the meeting. This was threefold, to provide for the internal peace of the

[1] Lords' Report, iv. 662; Rot. Parl. ii. 321: 'Parliamenti quod *Bonum* merito vocabatur;' Walsingham, i. 324. 'Commonly called the Good Parliament;' Stow, Chron. p. 271; Daniel (quoted by Barnes, p. 893), p. 257.

country, for defence against France, and for the continuance of the war. After the appointment of the Triers of petitions, the two houses separated, and, on the application by the commons to be assisted in their deliberations by the lords, twelve magnates were appointed to confer with them, as had been done in 1373. Four bishops were named, William Courtenay of London, Henry le Despenser of Norwich, Adam Houghton of St. David's, and Thomas Appleby of Carlisle; four earls, March, Warwick, Stafford and Suffolk; four barons, Henry Percy, Guy Brian, Henry le Scrope and Richard Stafford[1]. The leaders in this committee, bishop Courtenay and the earl of March, were more or less constitutional politicians, and might be trusted not to concede too much to the court party. Henry Percy also was supposed to be faithful to the rights of the commons. Adam Houghton may have leaned to the duke of Lancaster who afterwards made him chancellor; Warwick, as may be inferred from later history, was a mere self-seeking politician; Brian and Scrope were men of much official experience; none of the others were in any way remarkable. The strength however of the commons lay in the support of the prince of Wales[2], who, with the bishop of Winchester, probably concerted the attack upon the court, which was the most marked result of the deliberation. The parliament lasted until the 6th of July; large documentary illustrations of its proceedings are extant, but unfortunately no

Conference of lords and commons.

Joint committee.

The Prince of Wales supports the commons.

[1] Rot. Parl. ii. 322. Instead of the bishop of S. David's, the Chronicon Angliae (ed. Thompson) mentions the bishop of Rochester, Thomas Brinton, and instead of Henry le Scrope, Roger Beauchamp; the nomination of the bishops is said to have been made by the knights of the shire, who with them chose the four barons, and with their advice four earls; pp. 69, 70; Archaeologia, xxii. 212.

[2] The participation of the prince of Wales in the attack on the court was believed at the time; one of John of Gaunt's advisers said to him, 'domine, non latet vestram magnificentiam quibus et quantis auxiliis isti milites, non plebei sicut asseruistis, sed armipotentes et strenui, fulciuntur. Namque favorem obtinent dominorum et in primis domini Edwardi principis fratris vestri qui illis consilium impendit efficax et juvamen;' Chr. Ang. pp. 74, 75. 'Communes Angliae per dominum principem Walliae primogenitum regis, ut dicebatur, erant secretius animati;' ibid. App. p. 393; Cont. Murim. p. 222. The chief evidence of Wykeham's share in this is the fact that it was upon him first that the duke's vengeance fell; see Lowth, pp. 138 sq. The story that Wykeham had declared John of Gaunt to be a changeling is only a proof of the open enmity existing at this moment between the two. See Shirley, Fasc. Ziz. p. xxv.

chronological arrangement of those proceedings is possible, and we gather only a general impression as to the sequence of events. The death, however, of the Black Prince on the 8th of June serves as a middle point.

The discussions in the Good Parliament.

The debates, if debates they may be called, were of two sorts. The commons with their associated lords concerted their measures apart in the chapter-house at Westminster; the court faction under the duke of Lancaster sat, as a distinct contracting party, probably at the Savoy. The first measure of the commons was to elect a foreman or Speaker; their choice fell on Sir Peter de la Mare[1], one of the knights who represented Herefordshire, and steward of the earl of March: he at once laid before the council, of which the duke was president, a demand for an examination of the public accounts[2]. The speaker was charged to report to the king's representatives that the nation was willing to do their utmost to help their lord, but that they claimed some consideration; if the king had had good counsellors he must have been rich; it was certain that some of his counsellors had become wealthy and that the kingdom was impoverished for their aggrandisement; if he would do justice on the culprits the commons would undertake that without extraordinary aid from them he would have sufficient supply for all needs. The duke, who was aware that the popular excitement against him was very strong, adjourned the sitting to the next day, and then attempted to temporise[3]. The Speaker, however, having got the first word, persisted in his statement, and declared the precise causes of the national poverty to be the frauds on the staple, the usurious loans taken up by the king

Election of a speaker.

He represents the opinion of parliament to John of Gaunt,

and points out the chief offenders at court.

[1] He does not bear the title of speaker, which was given first to Sir Thomas Hungerford in 1377; but it is clear that, like Sir William Trussell (above, p. 411, note 3) and others, he fulfilled the duties of the office; and Walsingham (i. 321) and the St. Alban's Chronicon Angliae (ed. Thompson, p. 72) call him 'prolocutor;' cf. Cont. A. Murim. p. 219.

[2] Rot. Parl. ii. 322, 323; Chr. Angl. p. 73; Wals. i. 320, 321; Cont. Murim. pp. 218–220. John of Gaunt seems to have acted as representing the king 'Anglorum dominus incoronatus,' Chr. Angl. 74, note 1; either as head of the council or in the capacity of High Steward. He passes sentence, 'judiciali sententia,' on Latimer; ib. p. 86: but the language of the writer is inflated and too violent to be construed literally.

[3] Chr. Angl. pp. 74, 76.

from private persons, and the shameful financial transactions by which the courtiers bought up the king's debts from despairing creditors, and then obtained full payment at the treasury[1]. The chief offenders were pointed out, Richard Lyons the king's agent with the merchants, and William lord Latimer the king's chamberlain and privy councillor. Latimer had been guilty of every sort of malversation, he had bought up the king's debts, he had extorted enormous sums from the Bretons, had sold the castle of S. Sauveur to the enemy and prevented the succour of Becherel, and had intercepted a great proportion of the money which by way of fine ought to have reached the king's treasury. Richard Lyons had been his partner in some gigantic financial frauds; in one instance they had lent the king 20,000 marks and received £20,000 in payment; they had also forestalled the market at the several ports and raised the price of foreign imports throughout the kingdom, to their own profit but to the loss of the entire nation. The duke, appalled by the charges, was obliged to allow the accused, thus formally impeached, to be imprisoned by the award of the full parliament[2]. An attempt to bribe the king and the prince of Wales, to interfere in their favour, failed; the king, it is said, took the bribe with a jest, the prince refused it[3]. The lord Neville, John Neville of Raby, the steward of the royal household, by an attempt to intercede for Latimer exposed himself to an impeachment[4]. After a searching examination carried on both in full parliament and before the lords only, it was determined that the charges against Latimer were proved; the lords condemned him to imprisonment and fine at the king's pleasure, and at the request of the commons he was deprived of his office. On the 26th of May, however, Latimer was released on bail furnished by a large number of the lords[5]; and, although the duke was ultimately obliged to sentence him to imprisonment and forfeiture of his place[6], the attempt to bring him to justice failed. Richard Lyons was likewise condemned

Attack on Latimer and Lyons.

Impeachment.

Condemnation of Latimer.

Sentence on Lyons.

[1] Rot. Parl. ii. 323.
[2] Rot. Parl. ii. 323–325; Chr. Angl. pp. 76–79.
[3] Chr. Angl. pp. 79, 80.
[4] Ibid. p. 80; Rot. Parl. ii. 328, 329.
[5] Rot. Parl. ii. 326, 327.
[6] Chr. Angl. p. 86.

to imprisonment and forfeiture. Encouraged by their temporary success the commons next attacked Alice Perrers[1]; under a general ordinance against allowing women to practise in the courts of law, they obtained against her an award of banishment and forfeiture. Several other minor culprits were also visited with penalties[2]; Sir Richard Sturry, a Lollard courtier, was banished from the court, and the lord Neville, who had been one of the buyers of the royal debts, was made the subject of a special petition for removal[3].

Ordinance against Alice Perrers.

Death of the Black Prince, June 8, 1376.

No sooner was the death of the prince of Wales known, than the commons determined on still more trenchant measures. If John of Gaunt were really all that they believed him, it was high time that the safety of the heir-apparent should be secured, and that some provision should be made for the government which the king was no longer capable of conducting, and which could not be trusted to the duke. His proposition that the parliament should settle the question of succession in case of Richard's death was rejected by the commons[4]. They drew up a petition to the king that Richard of Bourdeaux the son and heir of the Black Prince might be brought before parliament that they might see him. This was done on the 25th of June[5]. They then proposed the election of an administrative council such as had been appointed in the reigns of Henry III and Edward II; a body of lords, ten or twelve in number, were to be appointed to 'enforce' the council: no great business was to be undertaken without the advice of all; six, four or even fewer should be competent to dispatch smaller matters, and six or four should be always in attendance on the king[6]. Before presenting this proposition to the king they determined to offer to renew the subsidy on wool granted in 1373 with an apology for not giving more. This was done at Eltham at the close of the session; there the king acceded to the proposed addition to

The parliament insist on seeing Richard of Bourdeaux.

Appointment of a standing council.

Nomination of the members.

[1] Rot. Parl. ii. 325; Vitae Abb. S. Alb. iii. 231.
[2] Rot. Parl. ii. 329.
[3] Rot. Parl. ii. 329; Chr. Angl. p. 87.
[4] Chr. Angl. pp. 92, 93.
[5] Rot. Parl. ii. 330.
[6] Rot. Parl. ii. 322. From the way in which the results of the parliament are stated on the Rolls it might be inferred that the proposals for the council were made before the impeachment; but the narrative of the chronicler is clear on the point; Chr. Ang. p. 101.

the council, with the proviso that the chancellor, treasurer, and privy seal should not be hampered in the discharge of their offices; and measures were at once taken for carrying the proposal into execution: nine of the members were named, the archbishop of Canterbury, Simon Sudbury, with the bishops of London and Winchester; the earls of Arundel, Stafford and March, the lords Percy, Brian and Beauchamp of Bletso[1]. The parliament, the longest probably that had ever yet sat, was dismissed on the 6th of July[2].

Petitions presented in the Good Parliament, 1376.

The impeachment of the great offenders, and the substitution of a new council, were however only a small part of the business of the Good Parliament. A hundred and forty petitions of various kinds were delivered and answered during the nine weeks of the session. And from these the general character of the assembled body may be gathered, more certainly perhaps than from their greater exploits performed under Peter de la Mare. Some of these petitions are of the normal kind: for the enforcement of the charters, the maintenance of the privileges of boroughs, the reform of the staple, and of the jurisdiction of the justices of the peace, the limitation of the term of office and powers of the sheriffs, the regulation of the courts of Steward and Marshal, and against the abuses of purveyance and of interference with the course of justice by royal writs; these read like an accumulation of all the grounds of complaint that have been urged since the beginning of the century. There is also a large number of local petitions. More significant, however, are the following: the commons pray that there may be annual parliaments[3], and that the knights of the shire may be chosen by common election from the better folk of the shires, and not merely nominated by the sheriff without due election; the king replies that the knights shall be elected by common assent of the whole county; the annual parliaments are already provided for by law. They ask that the sheriffs may be annually elected, and not appointed at the Exchequer; that

Petition for annual parliaments; orderly elections; election of sheriffs.

[1] Chr. Angl. pp. lxviii, 100.

[2] The convocation of Canterbury was called for June 23, and that of York for July 28; Wake, p. 304.

[3] No. 128; Rot. Parl. ii. 355.

also, the king replies, is settled by law. To the request that officers convicted of default or deceit may be permanently incapacitated from acting on the royal council, the king replies that he will act according to circumstances[1]. Thirteen petitions are devoted to the pope and the foreign clergy. The 57th and 58th pray for the enforcement of the statute of labourers; the 81st for the restriction of the right of common in towns; the 3rd for the limitation of the powers of chartered crafts; the 10th for the treatment of sturdy beggars. From these we may perhaps infer either that the burgher element in parliament was less influential than the knights, who throughout the history of this parliament are specially mentioned as acting for the commons, or else that the ruling power in the boroughs was engrossed by the higher classes whose sympathies were with the employer of labour and the landlord rather than with the labourer and artisan. The 133rd petition prays that those who by their 'demesne' authority, by their own unauthorised assumption, without assent of parliament, impose new taxation and so 'accroach to themselves royal power in points established in parliament,' may be condemned to penalties of life, limb, and forfeiture. To this obscure demand, which the king perhaps understood no better than we do at this day, the answer is, 'Let the common law run as has been accustomed;' possibly the complaint proves the inadequacy of administration, but the practice is as unlawful as it can be. Four of the petitions touch the ancient local courts; the 135th prays that hundreds and wapentakes may not be granted by patent; the 136th that the courts may be held publicly with proper notice and at the legal times; the 137th that view of frank-pledge may not be demanded at the three weeks' court; the 138th that the bailiffs may not amerce non-residents for non-attendance. All these points indicate a decay in the ancient system, which probably was giving way before the institution of justices of the peace. As a whole, the petitions prove that the government was ill-administered rather than that any resolute project for retarding the growth

Petitions on the subject of labour.

Petition against illegal usurpation.

Touching the ancient popular courts.

[1] No. 14; Rot. Parl. ii. 333.

of popular freedom was entertained by the administrators, a conclusion which our view of Edward's character as a politician would *à priori* incline us to accept. There was no strong repressive policy, no deliberate design of creating a despotism, no purpose of retaining unconstitutional expedients for government; but, on the other hand, there was no check on dishonesty and extortion among public servants, nor any determination to enforce the constitutional law: and some of the highest officers of the court, the closest friends and associates of the king, were among the chief offenders. And this may partially at least account for the position of John of Gaunt, who was now acting in opposition to the principles maintained by the great body of nobles, whom by all the force of territorial associations he was entitled to lead. He might to some extent divide the Lancastrian party in order to screen an abuse or protect an offender, whilst in anything like a conflict of principles, had he taken the side of prerogative, he must have been left alone. And so perhaps we may account for the result, the melancholy collapse that followed.

General impression derived from the petitions.

263. No sooner was the parliament dispersed than the duke declared the intention of the government to show no respect to its determinations. Exercising an amount of power which has never been exercised by any subject and rarely by any sovereign, he dismissed the additional members of the council, proclaimed that the Good Parliament was no parliament at all, recalled to court and office the impeached lords[1], and allowed Alice Perrers to return in spite of civil and ecclesiastical threats. She had sworn on the cross of Canterbury to obey the sentence[2], but archbishop Sudbury, whose duty it was, in case of her unauthorised return, to excommunicate her, was silent, overawed perhaps by the violence of the duke, or perhaps influenced to some extent by professional jealousy, for Courtenay and Wykeham had in the proceedings of the parliament taken the reins of the clerical party out of his hands. Not one of the petitions of the commons became a statute. Not content with thus braving the national will, the duke proceeded to take vengeance

John of Gaunt sets the parliament at defiance.

Alice Perrers recalled.

[1] Chr. Angl. pp. 102, 103.

[2] Chr. Angl. pp. 100, 104.

on the leaders; the earl of March was compelled to resign the office of marshal[1], which he had held since 1369; Peter de la Mare was summoned before the king's court and imprisoned[2]. In the Michaelmas term following William of Wykeham was called before Sir William Skipwith, one of the justices of the Common Pleas, upon an elaborately drawn charge of malversation; in November his temporalities were confiscated and himself forbidden to approach within twenty miles of the court[3]. Equal energy was shown in the attempt to divide the opposition: Henry Percy was induced, probably by the promise of the marshal's staff, to join the duke's party[4], and the temporalities of the see of Winchester were held out as a gift to the heir-apparent, Richard, a bribe no doubt for the neutrality of his personal adherents[5]. The king was persuaded to make his will, and name Lancaster and Latimer among the executors[6]. Other measures were left to be completed in the next parliament, which was called on the 1st of December, to meet on the 27th of January, 1377. This is the first occasion on which any definite signs are traceable of an attempt to influence the elections for a political purpose. No pains were spared by the duke to pack the new parliament, and he was successful[7]. To make matters still safer he changed the ministry on the eve of the meeting; on the 11th of January he removed the chancellor and treasurer and filled their places with two bishops; Adam Houghton of S. David's took the great seal, and Henry Wakefield of Worcester, one of the king's executors, took the treasury[8]; both perhaps already inclined to the court faction and now secured by promotion. The position of the duke was beset with difficulties. It was absolutely necessary that a liberal grant of money should be obtained from the parliament; the

Peter de la Mare imprisoned.

William of Wykeham accused of malversation.

John of Gaunt's measures, 1376.

Parliament, Jan. 27, 1377.

Change of ministers.

[1] Chr. Angl. p. 108.

[2] Chr. Angl. p. 105.

[3] The charges are given in full in the English Chronicle, printed in Chr. Angl. pp. lxxv, sq.; Foed. iv. 12. On the charges themselves, see Lowth's Life of Wykeham, pp. 94, 124. The order to seize the temporalities was given Nov. 17; Lowth, p. 124. The bishop was summoned for further hearing on the 20th of January; Foed. iii. 1069.

[4] Chr. Angl. p. 108; Percy was made marshal May 8; Foed. iii. 1078.

[5] Chron. Angl. p. 106; they were given March 15, 1377; Foed. iii. 1075.

[6] Oct. 7, 1376; Foed. iii. 1080.

[7] Chron. Angl. p. 112.

[8] Foed. iii. 1069.

country was still excited by the unsettled papal claims, and the attack on William of Wykeham had placed the clergy in strong opposition. This opposition the duke had no power to break up, and in consequence he called to his assistance, as a temporary expedient no doubt, the great John Wycliffe [1], whom he had known during the conferences at Bruges, and on whom he felt that he could rely as a stern opponent of the aggrandisement of the clergy and not less as an influential popular leader. Wycliffe, led away perhaps by his own sanguine spirit, and looking on Lancaster as the Puritans of Elizabeth's time looked on Leicester—perhaps as Luther looked on Philip of Hesse,—too readily allowed himself to be used by the unscrupulous politician. That Wycliffe believed John of Gaunt to be sincere in his support of his own peculiar views seems clear from the way in which he defends the proceedings which he took at a later period [2] with regard to the law of sanctuary. Apostolic poverty for the clergy was the idea which they had in common; it was recommended to the two by very different reasons. Even thus fortified, however, the duke found it necessary to be cautious.

Strength of the opposition.

The parliament met on the 27th of January, the convocation on the 2nd of February. The former opened with a sermon from the new chancellor, who has recorded it at length in the Rolls: the king had completed the fiftieth year of his reign, and had made his grandson prince of Wales; such joyous occasions called for fervent charity and liberal offerings: the application of the discourse was the immediate and urgent need of a grant of money to continue the war which the French under the shadow of the truce were preparing to renew [3]. The bishop was followed by the chamberlain, Sir Robert Ashton, who propounded news which it was not safe for an ecclesiastic to state, seeing that it touched the pope; after declaring the goodwill of the king and the realm towards the apostolic see, he promised to lay certain propositions before the parliament

The chancellor's speech in parliament, Jan. 1377.

The message of the chamberlain.

[1] On the 22nd of September, 1376, Alan of Barley was sent with a writ to Oxford to summon John Wycliffe to appear before the king's council; Devon, Issues of the Exchequer, p. 200.

[2] Shirley, Fasc. Ziz. pp. xxvi, xxxvi, xxxvii; see below, p. 467.

[3] Rot. Parl. ii. 361.

Parliament of 1377. Joint committee of lords and commons.

by which the controversy might be closed [1]. The estates then separated, and, on the application of the commons for a committee of lords to advise them, the bishops of Lincoln, Chichester, Hereford, and Salisbury, the earls of Arundel, Warwick, Salisbury, and Stafford, and the lords Percy, Ros, Fitz-walter, and Basset were appointed; the majority of these were adherents of the duke [2], and Sir Thomas Hungerford, his steward and one of the knights of the shire for Wilts, was chosen Speaker, 'vant-parlour' or 'commune parlour.' The discussion immediately arose upon the grant. The ministers placed four courses before the commons; they might offer either two tenths, or a shilling in the pound on merchandise, or a scutage of a pound on the knight's fee, or a tax of a groat on every hearth; the latter an entirely novel form of general taxation. The knights, before making their answer, as usual discussed grievances: a strong minority attempted to insist on the release of Peter de la Mare [3], but this was prevented by the duke, who had secured a majority of votes. The same majority enabled him to pass petitions for the restoration of lord Latimer, Alice Perrers, and others who had been impeached in the Good Parliament [4].

Four courses.

The knights demand the liberation of Peter de la Mare, but in vain.

Transactions in convocation.

Whilst this was being done in parliament, the convocation, which sat on the 3rd of February, was employed in discussing the wrongs of William of Wykeham [5]. He had not been summoned to parliament, but Courtenay, as dean of the province, had summoned him to convocation. He did not attend on the first days, probably obeying the royal order not to come near

[1] Possibly those mentioned above, p. 447, note 3.

[2] The Chronicon Angliae (p. 113) describes these lords as nominated by the duke from the number of his own personal friends, and seven of them had certainly been among the sureties for lord Latimer in the last parliament; Rot. Parl. ii. 326.

[3] Chr. Angl. p. 112. [4] Art. 58, 59 and 89; Rot. Parl. ii. 372, 374.

[5] The summons to parliament was issued Dec. 1; Lords' Report, iv. 670. The king's writ for convocation was issued Dec. 16; Wake, p. 304; and the archbishop's letters the next day; Wilkins, Conc. iii. 104. The summons to convocation was issued by the archbishop through the bishop of London, who would of course summon his friend unless specially forbidden. Wykeham received his summons; Lowth, p. 131. His absence was no doubt caused by the royal prohibition mentioned above, which he would not disobey until he had a special authorisation from the archbishop. This Sudbury would have avoided giving, but it was forced on him by Courtenay and the other bishops; Chr. Angl. p. 114.

the court. Courtenay, however, undertook to plead his cause, and, when the king's request for aid was announced, urged the clergy to give nothing until the bishop of Winchester was restored to his rights. So unanimous were they that the archbishop adjourned the debate and laid the matter before the king, who gave a general promise of redress. Wykeham then took his place in convocation[1]. But Courtenay was not satisfied: he proceeded to attack the duke through his new ally. Wycliffe was called before a committee of bishops at St. Paul's on the 19th of February, to answer the charges of the convocation, and appeared under the protection of John of Gaunt and Henry Percy[2]. An insult offered to Courtenay by the duke provoked the Londoners; in the riot that ensued the latter had to fly for his life, and, although the prosecution of Wycliffe was given up for the time, Courtenay secured a momentary victory. The Londoners, rightly connecting the cause of their bishop with that of Peter de la Mare, insisted that the latter should have a fair trial, and sent a deputation to Edward, which, notwithstanding the opposition of the duke, was admitted into the king's presence. Edward's gracious demeanour and ready promises had their usual effect[3]. The excitement was allayed; the majority in parliament proved all powerful. Already, on the 22nd of February, they had signified to the king their grant of a poll-tax of a groat a head, with the sole condition that two earls and two barons should be appointed as treasurers of the subsidy[4], and that a pardon on the occasion of the Jubilee should be granted, from which however the duke secured the exception of William of Wykeham[5]. The clergy, after long debate, yielded to the ignominious motive of fear, and agreed to a poll-tax on the seculars and regulars alike, in the same proportion as that granted by the parliament. They also presented their petitions, and, except to their intercession in favour of Wykeham, which was not answered at all, received a series of replies which showed that

The clergy take the part of Wykeham.

Attempt to prosecute Wycliffe, Feb. 19, 1377.

Interview of the king and the Londoners.

Grant of a poll-tax by both laity and clergy.

[1] Lowth, p. 132.
[2] Wals. i. 325; Chr. Angl. p. 118.
[3] Chr. Angl. pp. 126–128.
[4] Rot. Parl. ii. 364.
[5] Rot. Parl. ii. 365; Statutes, i. 397.

The work of the Good Parliament undone.

they had little favour to expect at present from the king, who was now too weak or too lazy to make an effort to save his faithful servant[1]. Thus entirely was the work of the Good Parliament undone.

Influence of the religious elements in these transactions.

It would be very rash to speak positively of the composition of the parties which produced this result. It is of course quite possible that the support of Wycliffe obtained for the duke some additional influence in the house of commons; archbishop Sudbury was supposed to be not disinclined to a reformation of the more prominent ecclesiastical abuses[2], and there may have been in the court, as there certainly was in the universities, a party of doctrinal reform. But that John of Gaunt, or the permanent court influence, which we have seen acting against Stratford in 1340 and against Wykeham in 1371, looked on Wycliffe and his teaching as anything but tools and weapons for the humiliation of the clergy, particularly of the prelates who sympathised with the constitutional opposition, it is very difficult to believe. John of Gaunt was a vicious man, and chose his spiritual advisers from among the friars[3], the very class most hostile to Wycliffe. Neither morally nor doctrinally, but politically only, and that almost by accident, was he likely to sympathise with Wycliffe. Wycliffe himself was a deep thinker and a popular teacher; but his logical system of politics, when it was applied to practice, turned out to be little else than socialism; and his religious system, unless its vital doctrines are understood to be thrown into the shade by its controversial tone, was unfortunately devoid of the true leaven of all religious success, sympathy and charity. But he

Improbability of any real sympathy between John of Gaunt and Wycliffe.

[1] Rot. Parl. ii. 373; Hody, Hist. Conv. p. 225.

[2] Chr. Angl. p. 117; where the bishops are spoken of as generally lukewarm, but the archbishop as negligent of his duty. Sudbury's contempt for plenary indulgences on account of pilgrimages was regarded as the cause of his terrible death; Ang. Sac. i. 49.

[3] Dr. Shirley has pointed out that the duke's confessors were friars; Fasc. Ziz. p. 26. One of these, Walter Disse, a Carmelite, had a commission to create fifty papal chaplains who paid for their promotion; the money thus raised was given to John of Gaunt to enable him to carry on his war in Spain as a crusade against the Clementists, the supporters of the rival pope; Vitae Abb. S. Alb. ii. 417. This was in 1386; but John's war in Spain was recognised as a crusade in 1382; Rot. Parl. iii. 134.

had not yet developed the dogmatic views which led to his condemnation as a heretic; and the moment that he did so the Lancaster party withdrew from his side[1], leaving him to the support of the few who held his doctrines and the many who were dazzled by his social theories. Still he may have had some power in parliament, and in the city of London he had a party which, although at this time overborne by Courtenay's popularity, in the following year saved him from imminent condemnation[2]. On the whole it is most probable that John of Gaunt, as a sanguine but not far-sighted tactician, obtained a momentary victory by allying the court party with the religious malcontents. Such was the last act of the reign of Edward III. The few petitions presented by the commons were turned into a statute. The parliament broke up on March 2. The king sank gradually into his last lethargy, and on the 21st of June, 1377, the crown of England again devolved on a minor. Richard II was eleven years old when he began to reign.

Wycliffe's party in London.

Death of Edward III.

Accession of Richard II, June 21, 1377.

The death of Edward III determined the crisis without to any great extent altering the relations of the parties. John of Gaunt at once lost the power which he had wielded as director of his father's council. Alice Perrers had not waited for the king's death to secure her retreat from court. The boy king was surrounded by the influences with which his father had tried to fortify him, and his advisers were men of the same kind as those who had led the debates of the Good Parliament. An entire reversal of the recent political transactions was naturally to be expected, and all parties were to some extent prepared for it. The last acts of Edward III, and the first acts of Richard, were alike conciliatory. William of Wykeham, bowing to the corruption of the court, had bought his peace through Alice Perrers[3]; Edward and Richard both

New influences at court.

Conciliatory policy.

Wykeham restored.

[1] Fasc. Ziz. p. 114.

[2] See p. 466, below.

[3] June 18; Foed. iii. 1079: this was granted against the wishes of John of Gaunt; Chr. Angl. pp. 136, 137. The earls of March, Arundel, and Warwick were Wykeham's sureties. On the 31st of July he had a full pardon and release from Richard, 'ex certa scientia nostra et avisamento et assensu carissimi avunculi nostri Johannis;' Foed. iv. 14; cf. Chr. Angl. pp. 150, lxxv sq.: and this was renewed by the advice of the parliament, Dec. 4; Foed. iv. 25; Rot. Parl. iii. 387 sq.

laboured to reconcile John of Gaunt with the Londoners[1]. The duke himself acted as if he wished once for all to dispel the suspicion that he had any designs hostile to his nephew, and at once accepted his altered position[2]. Even Peter de la Mare felt the benefit of the change, and was, by Richard's spontaneous act, immediately released from confinement[3]. These omens of good government were eagerly welcomed; the Londoners professed themselves devotedly attached to Richard, scarcely waiting for his grandfather's death before they offered their congratulations; and, when the question of a council of government, so necessary under the circumstances, arose, it was answered by the appointment of a body of men in which both the great parties were represented. The coronation took place on the 16th of July[4], and on the 17th a standing council was chosen by the king and the assembled magnates.

Peter de la Mare released.

Council of government, July 17, 1377.

This council was not exactly a council of regency: the king remained under his mother's care, and she, without any formal title, acted as guardian and chief of the court; the king's uncles, John duke of Lancaster, Edmund earl of Cambridge, and Thomas of Woodstock, who was made constable of England at the accession and earl of Buckingham at the coronation[5], were not among the elected councillors; and the earl of March, father of the presumptive heir, was too wise to claim any direct share in the administration. The duke of Lancaster carefully asserted the position which his territorial dignities gave him, and, as high steward of England, arranged the ceremonies of the coronation as if he were content with his constitutional

[1] Edward failed to make peace; Chr. Angl. pp. 131–134: Richard succeeded; ibid. pp. 147, 148.

[2] Whether from fear of being dismissed or from a desire to obtain credit for moderation, he retired from court immediately after the coronation, but according to the hostile chronicler he still pulled the strings of government; Chr. Angl. p. 164. Lord Percy resigned the marshal's staff; Chr. Angl. p. 165.

[3] Chr. Angl. p. 150.

[4] The form of coronation is given in the Foedera, iv. pp. 9, 10; Chr. Angl. pp. 153 sq.

[5] He is called earl of Buckingham in the patent of his appointment as constable, June 22; Foed. iv. 1; but on the day of coronation 'statum comitis suscepit;' ibid. p. 10. The same day Henry Percy was made earl of Northumberland, John Mowbray of Nottingham, and Guichard d'Angle of Huntingdon; Mon. Evesh. p. 1.

influence and desired no more. The council accordingly bears evidence of a compromise[1]: two bishops, two earls, two barons, two bannerets, and four knights bachelors, were chosen to aid the chancellor and treasurer: the bishops were Courtenay of London, the late antagonist of John of Gaunt, and Ralph Erghum of Salisbury, his ally; of the earls, Edmund of March and Richard of Arundel represented the opposite parties; the other members were the lords Latimer and Cobham, who were probably opposed in the same way; Roger Beauchamp and Richard Stafford, bannerets; John Knyvett, Ralph Ferrers, John Devereux, and Hugh Segrave, knights. Latimer, Beauchamp, and Knyvett had been executors of the late king. The fact that none of the executors of the Black Prince was chosen is perhaps a proof of the influence of Lancaster. The Great Seal remained in the hands of the bishop of S. David's, but bishop Brantingham immediately after the coronation replaced Wakefield as Treasurer.

A compromise.

Members of the council.

The task of the council was not easy: the collapse of the military power of England had seemed complete: the French were burning the towns on the southern coast. The excitement of the country, roused by the late events in parliament, had not subsided on the reconciliation of the leaders, and a supply of money was again needed. The relations of the government with both the papacy and the national church were uneasy, and, although Courtenay was a member of the council, Wycliffe was in favour with the princess of Wales, and was consulted occasionally on the question of the papal claims[2]. The parliament, which met on the 13th of October, was in consequence a long and busy one[3], and its transactions show a marked

Danger of the country.

Wycliffe consulted.

Parliament, Oct. 13, 1377.

[1] Rot. Parl. iii. 386; Foed. iv. 10. Erghum and Latimer were the two suspected agents of the duke, Courtenay and the earl of March the popular leaders; the rest, 'partim timore, partim obsequiis' were bound to John of Gaunt; Chr. Angl. p. 164. This seems an extreme statement. Ralph Ferrers was the leader of the outrage on the Westminster sanctuary; see below, p. 466; Mon. Evesh. p. 8; and was protected by John of Gaunt in 1381 under a charge of treason; Wals. i. 448. Cobham was punished by Richard in 1398 as an adherent of the appellants.

[2] See the 'Responsio Magistri Johannis Wyccliff ad dubium infra scriptum quaesitum ab eo per dominum regem Angliae Ricardum secundum et magnum suum consilium anno regni sui primo;' Fasc. Ziz. p. 258.

[3] Rot. Parl. iii. 3.

Parliament of Oct. 1377.

consciousness of power and a freedom of action on the part of the commons unexampled except in the Good Parliament. The exigencies of the time were explained in an opening speech by the archbishop of Canterbury, who by the urgency with which he insists on Richard's hereditary right, to the disparagement of his title by election, seems strangely to strike the key-note of the boy's maturer policy[1]. The receivers and triers of petitions were then appointed.

John of Gaunt disavows treasonable intentions.

The commons showed their pacific spirit by naming John of Gaunt as the first of the body of lords whose advice they requested[2], and the duke responded by a solemn disavowal of any hostile design towards his nephew, which both lords and commons received with acclamations of approval.

Peter de la Mare Speaker.

Having thus propitiated the one leader whom they had to fear, they chose Peter de la Mare as Speaker, and laid three proposals before the king.

Proposal to add elected members to the council.

The first was for the remodelling of the council by the appointment of eight new members[3], the second for the appointment of the personal attendants of the king, with a view to his proper education, and to the regulation of his household; the third for a due security that in future the measures passed in parliament should not be repealed without the consent of parliament. The king's reply was sufficiently gracious: the council should be remodelled; the acts of the parliament should be held good. The second demand was objected to by the lords, who were prepared to provide safeguards for the royal household without the stringent measures suggested by the commons.

Grant of money.

The royal request for money was met by a liberal grant of two tenths and two fifteenths[4], to be collected

[1] 'La noble grace que Dieu vous ad donez en sa persone la quelle vous est naturel et droiturel seigneur lige, come dit est, nemye par election ne par autre tielle collaterale voie, einz par droite succession de heritage; de quoy vous luy estez de nature moelt le pluis tenuz de luy amer perfitement, et humblement obbeir;' Rot. Parl. iii. 3. 'Jure hereditario ac etiam voto communi singulorum;' Knighton, c. 2630.

[2] The lords named were John of Gaunt, bishops Courtenay, Arundel, Brinton, and Appleby; the earls of March, Arundel, Warwick, and Angus; the lords Neville, Henry le Scrope, Richard le Scrope, and Richard Stafford; Rot. Parl. iii. 5.

[3] Rot. Parl. iii. 5. On this parliament see Hallam, Middle Ages, iii. 59.

[4] The convocation of Canterbury, called for Nov. 9, and that of York Dec. 1, granted two-tenths; Wake, pp. 307, 308. Although the convocations

immediately, on the condition that two treasurers should be named to superintend the due application of the proceeds. The king accordingly appointed William Walworth and John Philipot, two London merchants, as treasurers [1]; and nominated as his council for one year the bishops of London, Carlisle, and Salisbury, the earls of March and Stafford; Richard Stafford and Henry le Scrope, bannerets, and John Devereux and Hugh Segrave, bachelors [2]. Other petitions praying that during the king's minority the chancellor, treasurer, and other great officers of state might be chosen by the parliament, and that no one who had been attainted during the late reign might be admitted as a councillor, were also granted [3].

Appointment of treasurers of the subsidy.

Petition for the election of ministers.

The result was a clear victory for the commons; the informality of the recent proceedings was admitted; lord Latimer was excluded from the council, the accounts of the subsidy of 1376 were subjected to strict examination, and the control of the supplies was protected as well as it could be from the interference of the courtiers. The commons were dismissed with thanks on the 28th of November [4]. On the 22nd of December the lords reheard the case of Alice Perrers, who was compelled to submit to the sentence passed upon her in 1376 [5]. This was done at the request of the commons, who had presented to the lords in a separate schedule the points in which they desired their co-operation in order to secure the fulfilment of the king's promises [6].

Alice Perrers has to submit, Dec. 1377.

The expectations of the nation raised by this success were too sanguine. John of Gaunt, although he would condescend to temporise and even make some sacrifice to propitiate the men whom he could make useful, was not content with any secondary

John of Gaunt does not lay aside his ambitions, 1378.

granted the money, the clergy of both provinces were represented in the parliament, and presented a petition as 'les prelatz et la clergie de la province de Canterbirs et d'Everwyk;' Rot. Parl. iii. 25; cf. Wake, l. c.; Mon. Evesh. p. 4. The lay grant was to be collected before the 2nd of February, the clerical grant of Canterbury before March 1; and that of York, before the 20th of July.

[1] Rot. Parl. iii. 7.

[2] Rot. Parl. iii. 6; Chr. Angl. p. lxxi.

[3] Rot. Parl. iii. 16.

[4] Rot. Parl. iii. 29; the writs of expenses were issued Dec. 5; Lords' Report, i. 495.

[5] Rot. Parl. iii. 12; Chr. Angl. p. 171.

[6] Rot. Parl. iii. 14.

part in the management of the kingdom. Either directly or indirectly he aimed at the control of the council and treasury, and the command in war; the country at the moment could furnish no competitor, and he was suffered to show his incapacity in every department. For several years however he is the central figure in the history of England: and his intrigues and quarrels, perhaps scarcely worth the attempt to disentangle them, occupy a large part of the annals. The military proceedings of the year 1378 were dilatory, and the results inglorious. The quarrel between the duke and the Londoners assumed a new character and formidable dimensions. He insisted on taking the subsidy out of the hands of Walworth and Philipot[1]; he connived at the outrage committed on the two squires Hauley and Schakel, who had taken sanctuary at Westminster rather than surrender a Spanish prisoner whose ransom was coveted by the court[2]. The influence which he had gained by his recent moderation was lost to him, and the court suffered rather than gained by his adhesion. With the clergy he was on no better terms. The princess of Wales, at his instigation probably, had interfered to stay the proceedings again renewed under papal authority against Wycliffe, and in this she had been supported by the fickle Londoners, or by those factions among them which had been appeased by the duke or sympathised with the reformer. An attempt made by the bishops to try the reformer at Lambeth was foiled by this strange combination. There were two parties as usual in London; that opposed to the duke was headed by Philipot, a popular and able man, in close alliance with Courtenay; that favourable to him by John of Northampton, who was a follower of Wycliffe. We must suppose that by using the influence of the princess in Wycliffe's favour, instead of inter-

Violence attributed to him and his friends.

New proceedings against Wycliffe stopped by the Princess of Wales.

Parties in London.

[1] Chr. Angl. p. 194. In the parliament of 1378, however, it was asserted that every penny of the subsidy had been laid out by Philipot and Walworth; Rot. Parl. iii. 35: the commons found on inspection that £46,000 had been spent on fortresses, the maintenance of which did not properly fall to the charge 'de la commune,' in Normandy, Gascony, and Ireland; ibid. p. 36. The ministry answered that such fortresses were the barbicans of the kingdom.

[2] Wals. i. 375; Mon. Evesh. pp. 7, 8.

fering personally, the duke avoided provoking the hostile party which had risen to defend Courtenay in 1377.

Contest between John of Gaunt and bishop Courtenay.

Bishop Courtenay, obliged to yield in this point, did not spare the duke as one of the abettors of the breach of sanctuary at Westminster, and Lancaster attempted to retaliate by an attack on ecclesiastical privilege and a muttered threat of spoliation. At Gloucester, to which place he had brought the parliament in 1378 in order to escape the hostile interference of the citizens of London, he was foiled in this attack[1], and although he tried to sow discord between the lords and commons, prompting the former to refuse the request for advice and assistance which had been granted in the last three parliaments[2], the commons forced the king to consent that the account of the last subsidy should be laid before them[3]. The parliament sat from the 20th of October to the 16th of November, the business was left unfinished; bishop Houghton the chancellor resigned on the 29th of October in the middle of the session[4]; an increased grant of a subsidy on wool and merchandise proved altogether insufficient[5], and at another session held in April and May

Parliament at Gloucester in Oct. 1378.

Insufficiency of supplies.

[1] Rot. Parl. iii. 23. 'Nempe retulit fama vulgaris quod inaestimabili summa pecuniae decreverunt regnum multasse, ac etiam sanctam ecclesiam de pluribus possessionibus spoliasse, si fuisset suum propositum consecutus;' Wals. i. 380; Chr. Angl. p. 211; Mon. Evesh. pp. 9, 10. One object of attack was the privilege of sanctuary, and in this Wycliffe no doubt acted with the duke; see Fasc. Ziz. pp. xxxvi, xxxvii. The subject was discussed in the parliament in connexion with the case of Hauley and Schakel; Rot. Parl. iii. 37, 51; and the opinion of certain 'Mestres en theologie et doctors d'ambedeux lois,' as well as of the judges, was taken: that the privilege is available only where life or limb is in peril. In the next parliament a statute was passed to prevent fraudulent debtors from taking advantage of it; Statutes, ii. 12; Chr. Angl. p. 223; Wals. i. 391. The bishops during the session at Gloucester made an order reducing the salaries received by priests for private masses (Wilkins, Conc. iii. 135) to eight marks per annum, or four marks and victuals. Another important vote of this parliament was the recognition of Urban VI as the duly elected pope; Rot. Parl. iii. 48.

[2] Rot. Parl. iii. 36.

[3] Rot. Parl. iii. 36. Hallam, Middle Ages, iii. 59, 60.

[4] Foed. iv. 51. Houghton had to answer to the pope for acts of violence which he had committed as chancellor; ibid. 55.

[5] 43*s.* 4*d.* on the sack and £4 6*s.* 8*d.* on the last, besides the ancient custom of the half-mark on the sack and the mark on the last. This was the grant of 1376. In addition a mark on the sack and 240 woolfells, and two marks on the last, were now granted, with a poundage of 6*d.* for a year; Rot. Parl. iii. 37; Chr. Angl. p. 211.

Poll-tax imposed by the parliament of April, 1379.

1379[1] the demand for further supply was so urgent that the former grant in augmentation was annulled and a graduated poll-tax substituted by which every man according to his dignity was rated for a direct contribution. The duke of Lancaster was to pay ten marks, earls £4, barons and bannerets £2, and so on, down to the lowest rank, in which every person above the age of sixteen was to pay a groat[2]. The proceeds were to be strictly applied to the maintenance of the national defence. Over and above this, the subsidy on wool and merchandise, granted in 1376, was continued for a year, to begin from the following Michaelmas. The clergy in their convocations adopted the same intricate method of taxation[3], one result of which was to produce one of the most important records of the state of the population of England that was ever drawn up, the Poll-Tax Rolls of the year 1379. So great was the necessity of the moment that the ministers themselves offered to lay the accounts of the war expenses before the parliament. A commission accordingly was appointed to examine into the accounts of the subsidy of 1377, the general revenues of the crown, and the property left by the late king[4]. This committee contained archbishop Sudbury, bishops Courtenay and Brinton, the earls of March, Warwick, and Stafford, lord Latimer, Guy Brian or John Cobham, and Roger Beauchamp; it was a committee of inquiry only, but a step towards the executive commission which a few years later assumed the task of administering the government.

Supply of money in 1379.

Commission on the finances.

Failure of funds for the war.

No new and tentative expedient like the Poll-Tax was sufficient to meet the ever-increasing expenses of the war, and the method of taxation helped to increase the irritation produced by the constant demands. The produce of the new imposts fell so far below their computed amount as to prove that the financiers, now as in 1371, were calculating at haphazard. The subsidy granted at Gloucester produced only £6000, and the graduated

[1] The parliament of 1379 sat at Westminster April 25–May 27; Lords' Report, i. 495.

[2] Rot. Parl. iii. pp. 57, 58; Chr. Angl. p. 224; Wals. i. 392; Mon. Evesh. p. 11.

[3] The convocation of Canterbury sat May 9; that of York, April 29; Wake, State of the Church, p. 312.

[4] Rot. Parl. iii. 57.

poll-tax of 1379 not more than £22,000 [1]. Within eight months, during which no military successes had occurred to lighten the burden, Richard le Scrope, who had succeeded as chancellor in October 1378, had to explain to a new parliament that they must be prepared to make a still greater effort [2]. The commons listened incredulously: but they knew no more than the ministers the extent of the national resources or the way to use them. Such results they thought could only follow from the extravagance of the court and the incapacity or dishonesty of the council; if the council were dismissed and the chief officers of state and of the household, the Chancellor, Treasurer, Privy Seal, Chamberlain, and Steward, were elected in parliament, if moreover the retrenchment of the court expenses were placed in the hands of an elected committee, matters must surely improve [3]. Richard readily consented; the requisite commission was appointed [4]. The committee consisted of bishops Wykeham, Gilbert, and Brinton; the earls of Arundel, Warwick, and Stafford; lords Latimer, Brian, and John Montagu; Ralph Hastings, John Gildesburgh the Speaker, and Edwin Dalingrugge, knights: William Walworth and John Philipot, of London, and Thomas Gray, of York, citizens. The chancellor resigned the seal and archbishop Sudbury took it. The grant consequently made was of the old kind, a tenth and a half and a fifteenth and a half, with another year's subsidy on wool: and in offering it the commons prayed that the whole proceeds might be applied to the war in Brittany, and that for at least a year they might be spared the burden of attendance in parliament to be taxed [5]. The prayer was vain; the return to the older plan of taxation was no more successful than the new

New demands for money in the parliament, Jan.–Mar. 1380.

Commission to regulate the household.

Sudbury chancellor, Jan. 1380.

Grants of 1380.

[1] Rot. Parl. iii. 72, 73.

[2] The parliament sat from January 16 to March 3; Lords' Report, i. 495; Rot. Parl. iii. 71 sq. The Canterbury convocation held February 4 granted 16*d.* on the mark; Rec. Rep. ii. app. ii. p. 173. The York convocation sat April 4.

[3] Rot. Parl. iii. 73; Hallam, Middle Ages, iii. 62. In another petition the commons prayed that the officers established in the present parliament might remain in office until the next; Rot. Parl. iii. 82; cf. pp. 96, 147.

[4] Rot. Parl. iii. 73; Foed. iv. 84, 85. Sudbury became chancellor January 27, 1380, not July 4, 1379, as stated by Foss; Foed. iv. 75.

[5] Rot. Parl. iii. 75.

Parliament at Northampton. Nov. 1380.

method had been. In November at Northampton[1] the estates were called together again and the archbishop had as sad a tale to tell as his predecessor. The riots in Flanders had prevented any money being raised by the customs[2]; the king's jewels had been pledged and were on the point of being forfeited. What sum, the commons now asked, was required? The answer was, £160,000. This they declared to be outrageous and intolerable; the lords must devise the way in which it could be raised. The lords accepted the task and proposed three courses,—a graduated poll-tax, a poundage on merchandise, or a sum of fifteenths and tenths. The commons chose the first; £100,000 should be raised by poll-tax. The clergy, they declared, possessed a third of the land[3], they must undertake to pay a third of the sum: it might then be raised by poll-tax, varying in the case of individuals from sixty groats to three[4]. The subsidy on wool was to be continued. The clergy, who were well awake to the importance of the crisis, undertook to raise their quota; they replied to the demand, that they had never made their grant in parliament, but if the laity would charge themselves they would do their duty: they were probably anxious to avoid giving the party at court which listened to Wycliffe any opportunity of attacking them; they knew that they were on delicate ground; but besides this the leading prelates were now so

Consultation on supply.

The poll-tax of 1380.

Contribution of the clergy.

[1] November 5–December 6; Lords' Report, i. 495; Rot. Parl. iii. 88 sq.; Wals. i. 449.

[2] Rot. Parl. iii. 73, 88.

[3] 'Le clergie qui occupie la tierce partie del roialme feust mys a cinquante M. marz;' the whole sum being £100,000; Rot. Parl. iii. 90. The former calculations on the resources of the country are so very wide of the mark that no reliance can possibly be put on this estimate. See above, p. 442. The parliament of Carlisle in 1307 estimated the church lands at two thirds, 'deux parties;' Rot. Parl. i. 219. The convocation of Canterbury met on the 1st of December and agreed to the grant; and that of York acquiesced on the 10th of January; Wake, p. 312.

[4] 'De chescune laie persone du roialme . . . qui sunt passez l'age de xv ans, trois grotes, forspris les verrois mendinantz . . . sauvant toutes foitz que la levee se face en ordeinance et en forme que chescune laye persone soit chargez owelment selonc son afferant et en manere qu'ensuyt, c'est assavoir: que a la somme totale accomptez en chescune ville les suffisantz selonc leur afferant eident les meindres, issint que les pluis suffisantz ne paient oultre la somme de lx grotes pur lui et pur sa femme, et nulle persone meins q'un grot pur lui et pur sa femme;' Rot. Parl. iii. 20; Wals. i. 449; Chr. Angl. pp. 280, 281; Mon. Evesh. p. 22; Knighton, c. 2632.

closely united by interest and consanguinity with the lords that even their class privileges were waived in the prospect of coming and pressing trouble. And this was hard at hand. The poll-tax of 1380 gave occasion for the revolutionary rising of 1381.

The rising of the commons.

Origin and spread of the revolt of 1381.

264. The rising of the commons is one of the most portentous phenomena to be found in the whole of our history. The extent of the area over which it spread [1], the extraordinary rapidity with which intelligence and communication passed between the different sections of the revolt, the variety of cries and causes which combined to produce it, the mystery that pervades its organisation, its sudden collapse and its indirect permanent results, give it a singular importance both constitutionally and socially. North and south, east and west, it broke out within so short a space of time as makes it impossible to suppose it to have arisen, like an accidental conflagration, from mere ordinary contact of materials. In Yorkshire and Lancashire, Devon, Norfolk, Suffolk, Essex, and Kent, far more rapidly than the news could fly, the people rose. The unity of the rising was not produced by unity of purpose; it would seem as if all men who had or thought they had any grievance had banded together. In one quarter the Wycliffite or Lollard preachers had raised a cry against the clergy; in another the clergy themselves were foremost, complaining of the oppressions of the church [2].

Variety of causes and purposes.

[1] Norfolk, Suffolk, Cambridge, Essex, Hertford, Middlesex, Hants, Sussex, Kent, and Somerset; Rot. Parl. iii. 111 sq.; Huntingdon, Mon. Evesh. p. 36. Knighton describes the rising in Devonshire, c. 2639. For Kent, Devon, Cambridge, and Herts the presentments of the juries are extant; Arch. Cant. iii. 66. At Cambridge the townsfolk burned the charters of the University before May 1, 1381; the mayor and bailiffs seemed to have joined the revolt in June, or to have taken advantage of it to attack the colleges; Rot. Parl. iii. 206 sq. Besides the southern seats of rebellion Froissart (liv. ii. c. 76) mentions Lancashire, York, Lincoln, and Durham as ready to rise. Tumults took place at Beverley and Scarborough, which together with Canterbury, Cambridge, Bury St. Edmund's, and Bridgewater, are excepted in the general pardon; Rot. Parl. iii. 103, 118, 353; Oliver's Beverley, p. 146. York, Beverley, and Scarborough had to purchase pardons in 1382, but apparently for disorderly acts committed in September of that year; Rot. Parl. iii. 135, 396, 397.

[2] Several clergymen are excepted from the pardon; Rot. Parl. iii. 108. John Wrawe, the leader in Suffolk, was 'sceleratissimus presbyter;' Wals. ii. 1, 2; Chr. Angl. p. 320. John Ball is the most conspicuous; see below, p. 473, note 1. The mendicant friars were blamed; Chr. Angl. p. 312.

Obscurity as to the objects.

In Essex and Suffolk the labourers were exasperated by the burdens of villenage; in Kent, where villenage was unknown [1], they attacked the lawyers and burned the title-deeds of the landlords. In London, John of Gaunt was the peculiar object of attack [2]; the oath prescribed by the London rebels was to be faithful to king Richard and the commons, and to accept no king named John. In some parts of the country John of Gaunt was looked upon as the leading emancipator, the house of Lancaster was to free the villein and put an end to servitude: in Kent, during the investigation that followed the rising, one of the culprits named John Cote "acknowledged that pilgrims who had come out of the north, 'extra patriam del north,' to the town of Canterbury, related in the county of Kent that John, the duke of Lancaster, had made all his natives free in the different counties of England; whereupon the said malefactors wished to have sent messengers to the said duke if it were so. Then the said malefactors consented one and all to have sent to the said duke, and him, 'per realem potestatem suam,' to have made their lord and king of England [3]."

Mystery of John of Gaunt's relation to the revolt.

Obscurity as to the leaders.

The agents of the movement bore nicknames under which some believed that great historical titles were hidden, others that they were convenient and appropriate class names descriptive of the aggrieved artisan or labourer whose wrongs they were to vindicate. No common political motive can be alleged: but, just as in court or parliament, forgetful of the older and nobler war-cries [4], men were intriguing and combining for selfish ends, year by year altering their combinations and diversifying the object of their intrigues:—so the general

The revolt a result of general discontent.

[1] 'Il ad nul vylenage en Kent;' Yearbook, 30 Edw. I, p. 169. The cry was 'that no tenant should do service or custom to the lordships in Thanet;' Arch. Cantiana, iii. 72.

[2] See Mon. Evesh. p. 24; Wals. i. 455; cf. Rot. Parl. iii. 99. The letters issued by Richard after the suppression of the revolt, declaring his uncle's innocence, are in the Foedera, iv. 126; Knighton, c. 2640.

[3] Arch. Cant. iv. 76, 85. With this may be compared the references to the suspected complicity of John of Gaunt mentioned in the different MSS. of Froissart, liv. ii. c. 76.

[4] The evidence of Walsingham (ii. 12) and Gower (Vox Clamantis) as to the general decline in morality and religion seems to be proved by everything we know of the private and public history of the time.

discontent and trouble in the humbler classes, acting on many different and opposed materials, produced a rebellion with many causes and many consequences, having perhaps a common organisation, but not animated by any one principle except a wish to shake off the particular burden. Such was the material that afforded fuel to the flame. The organisation was created, it may be believed, by three causes; by the associations formed for the purpose of defeating the statutes of labourers, which, inoperative for useful purposes, had led the way to a regular and well-arranged resistance; by the preaching of the Lollard emissaries, who, imitating the friars and taking advantage of the popularity of Wycliffe's order of poor priests[1], were spreading through the country perverted social views in the guise of religion; and by the existence, throughout the land, of numbers of discharged soldiers and possibly of mechanics thrown out of employment by war and accustomed to hear of the risings of the Flemish and French communes against their masters.

Means of organisation.

Two main pretexts of revolt are easily distinguished. The first was the political grievance, the constant pressure of taxation, which by the poll-tax was brought home in its most irritating form to every household. Nothing had helped so much to maintain the national feeling against the papacy as the payment of Peter's pence, the penny from each hearth due for the Romescot. So the poll-tax interpreted to the individual, far more intelligibly than any political propaganda, the misdoings of the rulers. The appointment of the chancellor and the treasurer, the misdoings of the court, the mismanagement of the war, became home questions to every one who had his groat

Two main pretexts.

The poll-tax a political grievance.

[1] John Ball had begun his preaching as early as 1366, when archbishop Langham ordered him to be cited by the dean of Bocking; Wilkins, Conc. iii. 65: he had fallen previously under the animadversion of archbishop Islip, and on the 26th of April, 1381, was denounced as a heretic by Sudbury; ibid. 152, 153. He was captured at Coventry and brought to S. Alban's, where Tressilian, on the 13th of July, condemned him to death. Courtenay obtained a reprieve of two days, but he was hanged on the 15th. If the account of his doctrines given by Walsingham (ii. 13) is correct, they were a perversion and practical application of Wycliffe's theories, but probably bearing to the practical teaching of Wycliffe much the same relation as those of the Anabaptists did to Luther's. Cf. Political Poems (ed. Wright), i. 235.

This was the grievance of the revolutionary party among the rioters.

to pay. Such was the idea of the rebels who rose in Kent and in the immediate neighbourhood of the court; they were no Lollards; the archbishop of Canterbury, they knew, had discouraged pilgrimages, he could be no rightful successor of S. Thomas either as primate or chancellor, his murder was no martyrdom but a just revenge. This class of rioters was especially anxious to burn the sheriff's rolls, the estreats or rate rolls of the general taxation. Wat Tyler at Canterbury compelled the sheriff to surrender the rolls: and at Wye and in Thanet the rioters took and destroyed the rolls of the Green Wax, that is the estreats or rate book of the hundred [1]. Title-deeds proper seem to have been obnoxious to all sections; on the 16th of June the archbishop's custumal at Petham was burned [2]. Michael de la Pole in opening the parliament of 1383 [3] affirmed that 'the sheriffs, escheators, and collectors of subsidies and the like were the source and principal cause of the traitorous insurrection lately made by the commons.' Thus it was that men talked of taking the king into their own hands, of appointing ministers and sheriffs, and making new laws; and amongst them deeper thinkers tried to trace the intrigues and disguised agents of the great men. And of this class Jack Straw was one representative hero; his reported confession, too comprehensive to be veracious, disclosed the scheme that first the knights, squires, and gentlemen were to be killed; then the king was to be led about as the captain of the revolution until the country was all raised, when the lords were to be slain. The king, having served the purpose, was to be killed next, then all bishops, monks, canons, and rectors. 'When no one survived greater, stronger, or more knowing than ourselves, we should have made at our pleasure laws by which the subjects would be ruled. For we should have made Wat Tyler king in Kent and set up a separate king in every county.' These were the men behind whose backs, and in courage derived from their success, the robbers

Indignation against public servants.

Jack Straw's confession.

The men of Kent.

[1] Arch. Cantiana, iii. 77, 83, 86, 91.
[2] Ibid. p. 94; cf. pp. 82, 84; Rot. Parl. iii. 114, 116, 164; Wals. i. 455.
[3] Rot. Parl. iii. 150.

and incendiaries in Kent and the home counties made their profit and wreaked their local hatreds [1].

The other grievance was that of villenage and villein service. And this social trouble was not a simple grievance, a hardship which might have been solaced by abundant food and light labour. The burden of villenage in England had not been heavy even under the Norman rule, when the English ceorl had under the shadow of his master's contempt retained many of the material benefits of his earlier freedom. But the English ceorl had had slaves of his own, and the Norman lawyer steadily depressed the ceorl himself to the same level. The ceorl had his right in the common land of his township; his Latin name villanus had been a symbol of freedom, but his privileges were bound to the land, and when the Norman lord took the land he took the villein with it. Still the villein retained his customary rights, his house and land and rights of wood and hay; his lord's demesne depended for cultivation on his services, and he had in his lord's sense of self-interest the sort of protection that was shared by the horse and the ox. Law and custom, too, protected him in practice more than in theory. So villenage grew to be a base tenure, differing in degree rather than in kind from socage, and privileged as well as burdened; the breaking up of great estates diminished the demand for villein labour; money payments were substituted for service; the emancipation of the villein was regarded by the landlord as a relief from an unwelcome burden, it was encouraged by the clergy as an act of religious merit; and even the courts of law favoured in doubtful cases the presumption of liberty. The final definition of manors which

Villenage and customary service, the social grievance.

Condition of the villein.

[1] See Mon. Evesh. p. 31; Wals. ii. 9; Chr. Angl. p. 309. The speech put by Gower (Vox Clamantis, p. 46) into the mouth of the Jay (Wat Tyler) is as follows:—

> 'O servile genus miserorum quos sibi mundus
> Subdidit a longo tempore lege sua,
> Jam venit ecce dies qua rusticitas superabit
> Ingenuosque suis coget abire locis;
> Desinat omnis honor, pereat jus, nullaque virtus
> Quae prius exstiterat duret in orbe magis.
> Subdere quae dudum lex nos de jure solebat
> Cesset et ulterius curia nostra regat.'

Condition of the villein.

resulted from the statute Quia Emptores may itself have helped the villein; he was no longer in dread of the multiplication of middle men placed between himself and the chief lord, each trying to prove himself entitled to a share in the produce of the land and the profit of the villein's labour; whilst in the court rolls which recorded the fact of his villenage he knew he had the title-deeds of his little estate, and that the custom of the manor fettered the arbitrary will of the lord. Since that statute the villein's spirit may well have risen: it was by a mere legal form that he was described as less than free,—he was free to cultivate his land, to redeem his children, to find the best market for his labour. On this hopeful state of things the great pestilence fell like a season of blight, but worse than the pestilence was the statute of labourers. The pestilence, notwithstanding its present miseries, made labour scarce and held out the prospect of better wages [1]; the statute offered the labourer wages that it was worse than slavery to accept. The villeins ignored the statute, and the landlords fell back on their demesne rights over the villeins. The old rolls were searched, the pedigree of the labourer was tested like the pedigree of a peer [2], and there was a dread of worse

Effect of the plague and of the statute of labourers.

The demand of villein service.

[1] Gower's description of the hired labourers makes it clear that physical hardships had little to do with the rising: they will not engage themselves for fixed periods—

> 'Hi sunt qui cuiquam nolunt servire per annum,
> Hos vix si solo mense tenebit homo;'

or keep their engagements—

> 'Horum de mille vix est operarius ille,
> Qui tibi vult pacto factus inesse suo.'

They are very dainty;

> 'Omnes communes reprobat ipse cibos;
> Nil sibi cervisia tenuis vel cisera confert,
> Nec rediet tibi cras ni meliora paras.'

Cf. Rot. Parl. ii. 261. Professor Rogers has shown that the period of the revolt was one of great abundance; Hist. of Prices, i. 80. The Rolls of Parliament as well as the Yearbooks show the numerous obstacles which existed to the reclaiming of a villein; see Rot. Parl. ii. 192, 242, 279, 397, &c.

[2] See the proceedings on the rebellion of the villeins at Waghen against the abbey of Meaux in Yorkshire in 1360: 'ipsum Ricardum et praefatos Johannem et Thomam patres dictorum duorum Willelmorum nativos esse domini regis ut de manerio suo de Esyngtona asseruerunt, sic genealogiam suam deducentes;' Chr. Mels. iii. 134. Compare the references to the Rolls of Parliament given in the last note. On the earlier and legal con-

things coming. The irritation thus produced spread to the whole class, whether bond or free, that murmured at the obligations of tenure. The sokemen of the abbey, who were forced to grind their corn at the abbot's mill and waste their time in attendance at the abbot's court, took up the cry [1], and learned from the wandering Franciscan or the more enterprising Lollard preacher that priests ought by divine law to have no such property or dominion. The lawyers were little better than the priests; the title-deeds of the lord and the court-rolls of the manor were stored together, let both be burned and the land would belong to the cultivator [2].

Irritation produced by the right to service.

Between these two classes of malcontents there was much unity: the politically aggrieved mechanic of the town, the craftsman who was kept out of his rights by the merchant guild and brought to justice by the chartered court, who chafed under class jealousies and looked on his superiors as the agents of a corrupt government, was in many cases the kinsman of the oppressed or frightened villein, perhaps the son sent out

Connexion between town and country discontent.

dition of the villein class, see especially Vinogradoff, Villainage in England, Oxford, 1892.

[1] See the proceedings of the tenants of S. Alban's abbey and the burghers of S. Alban's, who were constantly at issue with the monastery on these points, illustrated by the Vitae Abbatum S. Albani, vol. ii. pp. 156 sq. These began as early as 1326, when the burghers demanded charters of emancipation, the right of electing members of parliament, common of land, wood, and fishery, hand mills, and the execution of writs without the interference of the bailiff of the liberty. In support of these rights they produced forged documents. The struggle went on for a very long time, and accounts for the attitude taken by the men of the town in 1381; it is quite a different grievance from the occasional reclamation of a villein, such as is recorded in the Vit. Abb. iii. 39, and in the case of Meaux quoted above. The plan adopted of obtaining an exemplification from Domesday and claiming rights by virtue of it was made a matter of petition in 1377 (Rot. Parl. iii. 21), and a statute was founded on the petition (1 Rich. II. c. 6; Statutes, ii. 2, 3). From this it appears further that there were confederacies of the villeins to threaten the lords, and to help one another in case of their services being demanded; 'et ount denoie as ministres des ditz seigneurs, de les destreindre pur les custumes et services susditz et son confedres et entre-alies de countrestere lour ditz seigneurs et lour ministres a fort mayn; et que chescun serra aidant a autre a quele heure q'ils soient destreinez par celle cause, et manacent les ministres lour ditz seigneurs de les tuer si les destreinont pur les custumes et services,' &c.

[2] The books and rolls burned by the villeins were the court rolls, which contained the account of the villenage; see Vit. Abb. S. Albani, iii. 308, 328, &c.; Wals. i. 455; Rot. Parl. iii. 116.

to seek his fortune, who had won emancipation by dwelling for a year and a day in a free borough. The discharged soldier, too, was as likely as not a villein come home from the war wounded and penniless, and yet having forfeited his right to maintenance on the land where he was born. Thus much there was to help the two largest classes of the malcontents to understand each other. Some traces of these influences, theoretical perhaps but not improbable or altogether speculative, may be found in the melancholy story of national disintegration which we can sketch now but faintly, so far as it bears special reference to our main subject.

The poll-tax the immediate cause of the rising.

The whole action of the revolt occupied little more than a fortnight. The parliament had ordered that of the poll-tax two-thirds should be paid on the 13th of January, the remainder at Whitsuntide. This had kept the southern counties in a state of alarm during the whole spring. Whitsunday fell on the 2nd of June; on the fifth the riot began at Dartford, and on the 10th the Kentish rioters, under Walter Tegheler of Essex[1] and John Hales of Malling, occupied Canterbury, released the prisoners in the castle, and compelled the sheriff of Kent to surrender the Estreat Rolls of the county, according to which the taxation was levied[2]; on the 11th they broke open Maidstone gaol[3] and released the prisoners; the main body having taken up their position on Blackheath, on the 12th they reached Southwark. The duke of Lancaster was on the Scottish border, the earl of Buckingham in Wales[4], the king in the Tower of London; the mob of London, who sym-

Rising in Kent, June, 1381.

The rioters reach Southwark.

[1] The following Tylers are mentioned:—(1) Walter Tyler of Essex; Arch. Cant. iii. 93. (2) Wat Tyler of Maidstone; Stow, Chr. p. 284; 'del countee de Kent;' Rot. Parl. iii. 175. (3) William Tegheler of Stone Street; Arch. Cant. iii. 91. (4) John Tyler of Dartford, whose revenge for the outrage on his daughter caused the outbreak there; Stow, Chron. p. 284; Higden, ix. 5. He is clearly a different person from Wat Tyler of Maidstone who is mentioned in the same page. (5) Simon Tyler of Cripplegate; Rot. Parl. iii. 112. The tilers appear to have been a specially unmanageable body of artisans: in 1362 there was a proclamation forbidding them to raise their prices in roofing; Vitae Abb. S. Alb. iii. 47; and the tilers of Beverley had a violent feud with the abbey of Meaux; Chr. de Melsa, iii. 149.

[2] Arch. Cant. iii. 76.

[3] Arch. Cant. iii. 74, 79 sq.

[4] Froissart, ii. 74; Stow, p. 285, says that Buckingham was in the Tower.

pathised with the avowed purposes of the rebels, refused to allow the city gates to be closed[1]. The following morning, after an attempt on the part of the leaders to obtain access to the king, the insurgents moved from Blackheath and entered the city. Later in the day they destroyed the Savoy, the palace of the duke of Lancaster[2], and burned Temple Bar and the house of the Knights Hospitallers in Clerkenwell. Their cry was against the duke of Lancaster and the ministers who held the king in durance, especially the archbishop, who was chancellor, and the prior of the Hospitallers, Sir Robert Hales, who had in the preceding February undertaken the office of treasurer.

The Londoners admit them.

The Savoy destroyed.

Whilst the Kentishmen were marching northwards, the men of Essex[3], who at Brentwood, Fobbing, and Corringham had before Whitsuntide refused to pay the poll-tax, were advancing from the east, and the villeins of the abbey of S. Alban's with the Hertfordshire rebels[4] from the north. Their cry was for the abolition of the services of tenure[5], the tolls and other imposts on buying and selling, for the emancipation of the native or born bondmen, and for the commutation of villein service for a rent of fourpence the acre. The villein rising was planned in Essex, and the men of Kent having their own grievances had adopted immediately the programme of their allies. On the evening of the 13th the Hertfordshire men bivouacked at Highbury, the body of the men of Essex at Mile

Rising in Essex

and Hertfordshire.

Claims of the Essex rebels.

[1] Mon. Evesh. p. 25; Wals. i. 456.

[2] Mon. Evesh. pp. 25, 26; Wals. i. 457.

[3] Wals. i. 454; Stow, Chron. p. 283; Eulog. iii. 351; the discontent in Essex caused by the poll-tax had begun some time before Whitsuntide.

[4] Wals. i. 458, 467.

[5] They demanded (1) the abolition of bondage 'et quod de cetero nullus foret nativus;' (2) a general pardon; (3) the abolition of tolls; (4) the commutation of villein services 'quod nulla acra terrae quae in bondagio vel servitio teneatur, altius quam ad quatuor denarios haberetur;' Mon. Evesh. p. 28. The demands are given in exactly the same words in Richard's patent for the revocation of the manumissions; Foed. iv. 126. After the death of Wat Tyler the Essex men, who thought that they deserved something for their moderation, urged 'ut essent in libertate pares dominis et quod non essent cogendi ad curias nisi tantummodo ad visum franciplegii bis in anno.' This time the king, who was at Waltham, answered with cruel firmness, 'rustici quidem fuistis et estis, et in bondagio permanebitis non ut hactenus sed incomparabiliter viliori;' Wals. ii. 18.

End; the Kentishmen, under Wat Tyler with some of the Essex leaders, occupied Tower Hill. Early in the morning of Friday the 14th the king rode to Mile End [1], and by promising to fulfil the wishes of the Essex villeins prevailed on them to return home [2]. As soon as he left the Tower the Kentish leaders [3] entered, and, after insulting the princess of Wales and running riot in the royal chambers, murdered the chancellor and treasurer; an Essex man beheaded the archbishop, but the Kentish leaders were aiding and abetting the common outrage and cruelty. If the king had been in the Tower he must have fallen into their hands, for the men of Kent took possession of his bedchamber; on his return from Mile End he took refuge at the Wardrobe [4]. Not much is said about spoliation, for, although the rioters were followed by the released criminals, who probably made their own market, the authority of their chosen leaders was respected, and these men knew that anything like general pillage would retard rather than promote the redress of their grievances [5]. On Saturday the 15th the king attempted to negotiate with the Kentish men at Smithfield; there Wat Tyler, elated by the success which he had obtained, or perhaps rendered desperate by the consciousness of yesterday's outrage, engaged in a personal

Richard persuades the Essex men to retire, by promising charters of manumission.

Murder of the chancellor and treasurer.

The king meets the rioters at Smithfield, June 15.

[1] Mon. Evesh. p. 27.

[2] Wals. i. 459; Chr. Angl. p. 294; Stow, p. 287; Froissart, ii. 75.

[3] Henry Blundel, Richard of Denne, Roger Baldwyn, Kentish men, were engaged in the murder of the archbishop; Arch. Cant. iii. 87, 88. John Sterling of Essex beheaded him; Wals. ii. 14. Bartholomew Carter and John Lewis entered the king's chamber; p. 91. The Kentish men persevered after the Essex men had gone home; Wals. i. 463. Richard Lyons, the merchant impeached in 1376, was one of the victims; Stow, p. 288. See too the poem on the death of Sudbury; Polit. Poems, i. 227.

[4] The same day the king was at the Wardrobe, where he gave the seal, which Sudbury had surrendered on the 12th, to the earl of Arundel; Foed. iv. 123. The Wardrobe was close to Baynard's Castle, near Blackfriars, the strongest position in the city after the Tower; see Froissart, liv. ii. cc. 75, 76. Froissart however places the princess's refuge at the Tower Royal or Queen's Wardrobe in the Vintry Ward, and makes the king stay there with her on the night of the 14th. On the Saturday before going to Smithfield Richard went to Westminster Abbey; Mon. Evesh. p. 28.

[5] They destroyed a good deal, but kept nothing for themselves, paid for what they wanted, and hanged thieves; but when they got wine they became more mischievous; Stow, p. 285; Gower, Vox Clamantis, p. 55: and there were many murders; ibid. pp. 62, 63.

altercation with Sir John Newnton, who was sent by the king to ascertain the wishes of the rioters. Sir William Walworth, the mayor, thinking the king in danger, struck down the captain of the revolt, and the king's servants dispatched him with their swords[1]. Richard's presence of mind saved himself and the state. He rode forward into the threatening host of bowmen declaring himself their king and captain, and before they parted delivered to them the charters of emancipation which they demanded[2], interfering at the same time to save them from the vengeance of the body of knights and men-at-arms whom the Londoners had at last sent into the field.

Wat Tyler killed.

Richard stays the revolt.

At Smithfield the head of the revolt was crushed, but in the meantime the more distant shires were in the utmost disorder; at Bury S. Edmund's the Suffolk bondmen rose on the 15th[3], and murdered the prior of the monastery and Sir John Cavendish chief justice of the King's Bench; there, as well as at S. Alban's, the monks were forced to surrender the charters[4] and part of the treasure of the house. In Norfolk, the bishop, at the head of an armed force, arrested the progress of the rebellion in the spirit of a soldier rather than a priest[5]. The news of the fall of Wat Tyler and of the king's concessions, however, travelled as rapidly as the signal for the outbreak. Before the 20th of June the revolt had ceased to be dangerous. But whilst the offenders, divided between hope and fear, awaited the issue of their victory, the government and the alarmed and injured landlords were taking measures to undo what had been done and to revenge their own wrongs. Sir Robert Tressilian, who was made chief justice on the 22nd, undertook to bring the law to bear on the rebels. The chancery and treasury were left for two months in the hands of the king's servants[6], no

Murder of Sir John Cavendish at Bury.

Short duration of the crisis.

[1] Mon. Evesh. p. 29; Wals. i. 465; Political Poems, i. 228.

[2] The charters of manumission are dated June 15: 'ab omni bondagio exuimus;' Wals. i. 466, 467. Other letters were extorted, by which the king ordered the abbot of S. Alban's to surrender his charters; Wals. i. 473; Chr. Angl. p. 299.

[3] Wals. ii. 1; Chr. Angl. p. 301.

[4] Wals. i. 473–479.

[5] Ibid. ii. 7, 8.

[6] The king on the fifteenth of June had closed the court of common pleas; and the great seal was held by temporary keepers until, on the 10th of August, Courtenay became chancellor; Foed. iv. 123.

leading man probably wishing to encounter the inevitable odium that must fall on the successors and avengers of Hales and Sudbury. On the 23rd Richard issued a proclamation to forbid unauthorised gatherings, and to declare that the duke of Lancaster had not by any treasonable designs merited the hostility of the Commons[1]. On the 30th he ordered a proclamation that all tenants of land, bond or free, should continue to perform their due and accustomed services[2]. On the 2nd of July he annulled the charters of manumission and pardon which had been issued on the 15th of June[3], and on the 18th he forbade the local courts to release their prisoners[4]. During the autumn these prisoners were tried and punished with a severity which is accounted for rather than excused by the alarm which they had given. Seven thousand persons are said to have perished in consequence of the revolt[5]. Further measures were reserved for the parliament, which was called on the 16th of July, met on the 3rd of November, and continued in session, broken only by a prorogation for Christmas, until the 25th of February, 1382. On the 10th of August, bishop Courtenay took the great seal and Sir Hugh Segrave became treasurer.

Measures of remedy and reprisal.

The parliament of 1381,

The parliament had no light task to perform; they set about it in no great hurry and in no good spirit. On the one hand they had to deal with the question of villenage; on the other with that of the general administration. Composed of members of the dominant classes, the two houses alike were unanimous on the former point. The whole doctrine and practice of tenure had been attacked, the right of the occupier to the free ownership of the land had been asserted; the lords, the knights, the prelates, the monastic corporations, recognised in the abolition

unanimous on the social question;

[1] Foed. iv. 125. Similar letters forbidding 'conventicula, congregationes seu levationes' were issued on the 3rd of July; cf. Wals. ii. 16, 17: 'conventicula' was the term in common use for unauthorised meetings for training in arms, such as had been frequent in the reign of Edward II.

[2] Foed. iv. 126: 'quod omnes et singuli tenentes, tam liberi quam nativi, opera, consuetudines, et servitia quae ipsi dominis suis facere debent . . . faciant.'

[3] Foed. iv. 126.

[4] Foed. iv. 128. On the 12th of September the king interfered to prevent the tyrannical conduct of the special commissioners who had been sent into the country to punish the malefactors; Foed. iv. 133.

[5] Mon. Evesh. p. 33; this includes the victims on both sides; see Higden, ix. 8, 9.

of feudal services a sentence of forfeiture passed upon themselves. But the political question was different: the rising had been occasioned by the misgovernment of the country, under the administration and influence of the very men against whom the commons in parliament had been struggling for many years. John of Gaunt and the court party were scarcely more popular in the house of commons than in the city of London; certainly the poll-tax was no more welcome to the men who voted it than to those who paid it; nor was there among them any disposition to underrate the misery of the country. Yet all the enormities of the revolt had been perpetrated by the political rabble; the villeins had been easily satisfied with the king's promises, and had withdrawn from London before Wat Tyler was crushed: it would be hard to punish the already disappointed rustics, and virtually to concede the change of administration which the political innovators had demanded. Such however was the course finally taken. On the 9th of November[1] the chancellor, now archbishop of Canterbury, opened parliament with an English sermon. On the 13th the treasurer, Sir Hugh Segrave, laid the king's proposals before the commons: the king, he said, had issued the charters of manumission under constraint; they were contrary to good faith and the law of the land, but he had acted for the best, and as a matter of policy his action had been successful; when the danger was over he had revoked the charters; if the prelates, lords, and commons wished that the bondmen should be enfranchised, and such was the report, the king was quite willing that it should be done by proper form of law[2]. All this was true: no theory of royal prerogative that had ever been broached in England could authorise the king to deprive the landowners of their due services; and the admission of such a principle now would have made it lawful for any king who was strong enough to dispossess, in favour of his own creatures, the whole

but divided on the political grievance.

Sympathy for the political discontent.

Yet the horrors had been perpetrated by the political rebels.

The parliament sacrifices the villeins, and agrees to the annulling of their charters.

[1] Rot. Parl. iii. 98: 'fist une bone collacion en Engleys.'

[2] Rot. Parl. iii. 99: 'qar il dit, si vous desirez d'enfranchiser et manumettre les ditz neifs de vòtre commune assent, come ce luy ad este reportez que aucuns de vous le desiront, le roi assentera ovesque vous a vostre priere.'

Parliament of 1381.

of the landed interest on which now, and for many ages to come, the maintenance of national law and the defence of the national existence depended. It is possible that the king and his chancellor wished so far to observe the agreement with the rustics as to introduce some amelioration into their condition, and that Courtenay's resignation of the great seal may have been connected with this. However this may have been, the petition that the king would make a wise and sufficient chancellor who would reform the chancery, shows that the archbishop did not at the moment command the confidence of the commons.

Resignation of the chancellor.

On the 18th he retired from the chancery [1], and his successor Richard le Scrope led the rest of the proceedings. After hearing a second time from him the great questions to be settled, the two houses declared that the king had done well to revoke the manumissions [2].

Discussion on supply.

The commons then conferred with the lords touching supplies. The recent attempts at direct taxation had been either futile or perilous; another tallage they dared not propose;

Reform of the household.

nevertheless they laid before the king a scheme for the reform of his household and administration, the abuses of which they declared to have been the cause of the revolt, and earnestly prayed for a general pardon for the severities committed in putting down the rebellion [3]. The ministers pleaded for, at least, the continuance of the subsidy on wool, and this, after much discussion, was granted for four years and a half [4].

[1] Rot. Parl. iii. 101. On the 30th Courtenay surrendered the seal; Foed. iv. 136: but the Rolls of Parliament speak of Scrope as 'lors novellement crees en Chanceller' on the 18th; Rot. Parl. iii. 100.

[2] 'Si bien prelatz et seigneurs temporels come les chivalers, citeins et burgeys, respondirent a une voice, que celle repell fuist bien faite. Adjoustant que tiele manumission ou franchise des neifs ne ne poast estre fait sans lour assent q'ont le greindre interesse; a quoy, ils n'assenterent unques de lour bone gree, n'autrement, ne jamais ne ferroient pur vivre et murrir touz en un jour;' Rot. Parl. iii. 100.

[3] Rot. Parl. iii. 100. They insist particularly on the poverty of the realm, 'si ad le roialme este en declyn a poverte cestes xvi ans et pluis sanz remedie purveuz;' ibid. iii. 102. One point was this: the king's confessor was charged to abstain from coming to the king's lodging and staying there except on the four principal feasts of the year. The commons had prayed that he might be removed from his office; Rot. Parl. iii. 101.

[4] Rot. Parl. iii. 104, 114; Wals. ii. 49. The subsidy expired at Christmas ensuing: it was prolonged to Candlemas (p. 104), and then for four years from Midsummer 1382 to Midsummer 1386.

A commission for the reform of the household, to begin with the person of the king himself, was elected, with John of Gaunt at its head. The young queen, whose marriage and coronation were celebrated in January 1382, had the honour of obtaining pardon for the insurgents[1]. And so the alarm of revolution passed away.

General pardon.

Result of the rising.

The results of the rising were of marked importance. Although the villeins had failed to obtain their charters, and had paid a heavy penalty for their temerity in revolting, they had struck a vital blow at villenage. The landlords gave up the practice of demanding base services: they let their lands to leasehold tenants, and accepted money payments in lieu of labour; they ceased to recall the emancipated labourer into serfdom, or to oppose his assertion of right in the courts of the manor and the county. Rising out of villenage the new freemen enlarged the class of yeomanry, and strengthened the cause of the commons in the country and in parliament; and from 1381 onwards rural society in England began to work into its later forms, to be modified chiefly, and perhaps only, by the law of settlement and the poor laws. Thus indirectly the balance of power among the three estates began to vary[2].

Improved condition of the agricultural labourer.

Effect produced on John of Gaunt.

A second result was that which was produced on the politics of the moment; John of Gaunt was changed almost as by miracle[3]. The hatred which the insurgents had so loudly declared against him crushed any hope, if he had ever entertained it, of succeeding or of supplanting his nephew; from henceforth he contented himself with a much less conspicuous place than he had hitherto taken, and before long ceased to interfere except as a peacemaker. For his ambition and love of rule he found a

[1] Rot. Parl. iii. 103; there is a long list of persons excepted from the pardon; ibid. pp. 111-113.

[2] On this see Professor Rogers, History of Prices, vol. i. pp. 80 sq. Some attempts were made to degrade the villeins in the subservient parliament of 1391. The commons petitioned that they might not be allowed to send their children 'a Escoles pur eux avancer par clergie;' and that the lords might reclaim them from the chartered boroughs: the king negatived the petitions; Rot. Parl. iii. 294, 296. The citizens of London in 1387 excluded all born bondmen from enjoying the liberties of the city; Liber Albus, i. 452.

[3] Wals. ii. 43; Knighton, c. 2642.

more convenient sphere in Gascony and Spain. The constitutional party, which he might have led, fell partly under the influence of his brother Thomas of Woodstock, and somewhat later under that of his son Henry, the duke himself being generally found ranged on the side of the king.

Richard remains in practical tutelage.

Richard himself had certainly shown in the crisis both address and craft; and it is somewhat strange that, after he had given such proof of his ability, he was content to remain for some years longer in tutelage. His father, at the age of sixteen, had held command at Crecy, and he himself was now a married man. But neither the court nor the country was in a condition to encourage any noble aspirations on his part. His tutors and early advisers had been chosen for their accomplishments and reputation rather than for their political character; the mind of the young king was cultivated, but his energies were not trained or exercised. He had been brought up in an atmosphere of luxury and refinement, kept back from public life rather than urged on into premature attempts to govern, and yet imbued with the highest notions of prerogative; perhaps both the dissipations of his maturer years, and the untoward line in which his mental activity developed when it freed itself from the early trammels, indicate an amount of mismanagement which can hardly be described as accidental or merely unfortunate. The court, which existed but for the sake of the king, nourished the king as if he were to exist for the sake of the court; and spoiled a prince whose life evinces not only many traits of nobility, but certain proofs of mental power.

Mismanagement of his training.

Richard's friends and advisers.

265. Richard was most unfortunate in his surroundings; in his two half-brothers the Hollands he had companions of the worst sort, violent, dissipated and cruel. Robert de Vere, Richard's personal friend and confidant, bears a strong resemblance in his character, as well as in his fortunes, to Piers Gaveston. Sir Simon Burley is said to have been a brave and accomplished man[1], but he was certainly not above the rest of the court in his idea of government. Michael de la Pole too,

[1] Rot. Parl. iii. 104. Arundel and Burley were rivals and enemies; Wals. ii. 156.

although a man of experience, capacity, and honesty, was not equal to the needs of the times. For the choice of Burley and de la Pole as his servants Richard, of course, is not responsible; the former was no doubt appointed by his father, and the latter was approved by the parliament of 1381, together with the earl of Arundel, as a counsellor to be in constant attendance on the king and as governor of his person. In his youngest uncle, Thomas of Woodstock, Richard had a daring rival for popularity, who undertook the part, declined by John of Gaunt, of leading the baronial opposition to the crown and court.

Burley and de la Pole.

His uncle Thomas a rival for popularity.

How much of the action of the following years was due to Richard himself, and how much was due to the princess of Wales and the Hollands[1], it is difficult to say. The king was more or less in tutelage still, a tutelage which the magnates were intent on prolonging, and which the court was constantly urging him to throw off. Capable of energetic and resolute action upon occasion, Richard was habitually idle, too conscious perhaps that when the occasion arose he would be able to meet it. The Hollands were willing that the tutelage should last so long as they could wield his power or reap the advantage of his inactivity. Burley and de Vere also used their influence to make him shake off the influence of the advisers whom the parliament had assigned to him, and they certainly impressed him with ideas of royalty quite incompatible with the actual current of political history.

Richard's advisers.

The war continued but languidly, broken by truces, and seeming year by year further removed from a determination: no laurels were won on either side until in 1387 the earl of Arundel captured a fleet of Flemings, French, and Spaniards, and secured thereby a popularity which ruined him. The expenses continued to be heavy, although the commons took every means to diminish them. In 1382[2], and again in

Continuance of the war.

[1] John Holland, made earl of Huntingdon in 1388, married Elizabeth, daughter of John of Gaunt; Thomas, earl of Kent, married Alice, daughter of Richard, earl of Arundel. The earl of Huntingdon was credited with the murder of the Carmelite who accused John of Gaunt in 1384, and he certainly killed the son of lord Stafford in 1385; Chr. Angl. pp. 359, 365.

[2] The parliaments of 1382 sat from May 7 to May 22; and from Oct. 6 to Oct. 24; Rot. Parl. iii. 122, 132. In the first, the question of the king's

Parliaments of 1382 and 1383.

1383[1], Richard, acting under the advice of a council of magnates, proposed to go to the war in person; the commons, after conference with the merchants, declared that it was impossible to give security for such a loan as would be required to meet the expense.

Crusade of Henry le Despenser.

Henry le Despenser, bishop of Norwich, had obtained from pope Urban a commission for a crusade in Flanders against the anti-pope, as John of Gaunt had for a crusade in Spain. The commons did not object to the bishop's expedition, as it would weaken the French, and they authorised the king to transfer to the bishop a tenth and fifteenth, granted in October 1382 for the war.

Parliament of October, 1383.

But when the bishop returned unsuccessful in the autumn of 1383 he was impeached in parliament by the king's direction, and his temporalities were seized for the payment of a fine to be determined by the king at his discretion: at the same time two half-tenths and half-fifteenths were grudgingly given by the commons, and two half-tenths by the clergy, one half being in each case unconditional, the other appropriated to the purpose of the war in case it should be prolonged. The same plan was followed in 1384[2]; the commons made no scruple of declaring that they desired peace, and bestowed very inadequate grants; but they would not recom-

expedition was discussed, tunnage and poundage granted for the protection of the coast, and a statute passed against heretic preachers. In the October parliament a tenth and fifteenth was granted, the proposal of the bishop of Norwich approved, and the statutes against the heretics repealed. The clerical grant this year was half a tenth; Wake, p. 314.

[1] The parliaments of 1383 sat from Feb. 23 to March 10; and from Oct. 26 to Nov. 26. In the first, the tenth and fifteenth was made over to the bishop of Norwich; in the autumn session he was called to account for it. The clergy granted a half-tenth in convocation in January, and two half-tenths in November; Wake, pp. 315, 316. See Rot. Parl. iii. 149, 151 sq.; Wals. ii. 84, 85, 109; Mon. Evesh. pp. 43, 44, 49; Eulog. iii. 357. It was in the February parliament that the king, having allowed the commons to elect nine lords to confer with them, declared that the right of nomination belonged to the crown; Hallam, Middle Ages, iii. 66; Rot. Parl. iii. 145. Notwithstanding this the commons chose their own advisers in 1384; ibid. p. 167.

[2] The parliaments of 1384 sat from April 29 to May 27 at Salisbury, and Nov. 12 to Dec. 24 at Westminster; Rot. Parl. iii. 166 sq., 184 sq.; Wals. ii. 112 sq.; Mon. Evesh. p. 50. The grant of half a tenth and fifteenth was made in the spring session, two tenths and fifteenths in November. One of these two tenths and fifteenths was remitted on the 15th of May, 1385; Rymer, viii. 471; Rot. Parl. iii. 398. The clergy gave a half-tenth in June, and two tenths in November; Wake, p. 317.

mend the king to resign the claims on France which could not be even asserted without war. The grants made by the commons in both 1383 and 1384 were made conditional upon similar grants to be obtained from the clergy [1], an assumption which called forth from the archbishop a formal protest against the attempt to bind the spirituality [2].

Truce made in 1384.

The truce which was concluded in January 1384, lasted until May 1385, and thus left the court at liberty for a quarrel.

Continued influence of John of Gaunt.

John of Gaunt had, as we have said, withdrawn from the somewhat threatening attitude which he had maintained at the beginning of the reign, and contented himself with the legitimate influence which he could exercise in council. That influence was still considerable enough to provoke the jealousy of his rivals and to awake alarm among his conscientious friends. In the summer of 1382 Richard le Scrope, the duke's friend and honest adviser, was compelled to resign the great seal in consequence of a remonstrance addressed by him to the king on the lavish grants that he was making [3]. Yet, when in the following year the duke was able to drive the bishop of London, Robert Braybrook, from the chancery [4], his successor

Michael de la Pole made Chancellor, 1383.

Michael de la Pole proved a more powerful enemy to the Lancaster influence. In the parliament of Salisbury, in April, 1384, an Irish friar denounced the duke as a traitor; the friar was committed to the charge of Sir John Holland and was soon afterwards murdered, tortured to death, as it was alleged, by the servants of the duke [5]. Thomas of Woodstock in violent wrath went so far as to threaten Richard himself as an abettor of the accusation [6]. The imprisonment of John of Northampton, the late mayor of London, who had been accused of sedition, and had appealed to the protection of the duke, helped to widen the breach [7]; and a quarrel which had been long proceeding

Quarrels at Court.

[1] Rot. Parl. iii. 151, 168.
[2] Dec. 17, 1384; Wake, App. p. 77.
[3] July 11; Walsingham, ii. 68–70; Foed. iv. 150; Higden, ix. 15.
[4] March 10; Foed. iv. 162; Foss, Biogr. Jur. p. 120.
[5] Chr. Angl. p. 359; Higden, ix. 35–40.
[6] Wals. ii. 112 sq.; Mon. Evesh. pp. 50, 51.
[7] Wals. ii. 116; Mon. Evesh. p. 49.

between the duke and the earl of Northumberland created further complications. Richard, under the influence of his private advisers, formed a design of arresting his uncle; he was summoned to appear before Sir Robert Tressilian, but refused. He declined moreover to attend, without an armed retinue, a council at Waltham at which he was informed that his death was compassed. In the end he shut himself up in Pomfret castle [1]. Shortly after however reconciliation was effected by the princess of Wales, whose death in August 1385 seems to have given the signal for the outbreak of political quarrels, which had perhaps been temporarily healed by her influence whilst she lived [2]. From this part of the struggle John of Gaunt withdrew; at Easter, 1386, he left England for Spain and did not return until November, 1389.

Danger of John of Gaunt.

Death of the Princess of Wales.

John of Gaunt goes to Spain.

Parliamentary proceedings in 1384.

The commons during these proceedings were called on for considerable grants. Two fifteenths were voted in November, 1384 [3], to be spent on the first expedition taken by the king in defence of the realm. One of these was spent on an expedition to Scotland, the only real military undertaking in which Richard ever took part, during which Sir John Holland killed the heir of the earl of Stafford, and thus compelled the king to banish him [4]. On the 6th of August, 1385, Thomas of Woodstock was made duke of Gloucester, Edmund of Langley duke of York, and Michael de la Pole earl of Suffolk; and the young earl of March was recognised as heir-presumptive to the crown [5]. In a parliament held in October the commons bestowed a tenth and a half and a fifteenth and a half, and renewed their grant of the subsidy on wool, which expired at the next Midsummer, for a year from August 1, 1386; the former grant they attempted, according to the Chroniclers, to make conditional on a contribution by the clergy as had been done in 1383 and 1384. The knights of the shire are said to have also proposed a confiscation of the temporalities of the clergy; but this design was frustrated by archbishop Courtenay,

Richard's expedition to Scotland in 1385.

Parliamentary business in 1385.

[1] Wals. ii. 126; Mon. Evesh. p. 57.
[2] Wals. ii. 130.
[3] See above, p. 488, note 2.
[4] Mon. Evesh. p. 63.
[5] Eulog. iii. 361.

and the king was made to declare that he would leave the church in a state as good as that in which he found it, or better[1]. Richard immediately afterwards conferred the title of marquess of Dublin on his friend Robert de Vere, and followed up the promotion, which had already exposed him to the indignation of the lords, by making him duke of Ireland. This was done during the session of the parliament in October 1386, with which the clearer and more dramatic action of the reign begins.

Vere made duke of Ireland, Oct. 1386.

Richard II was not, like Edward II, the victim of enmities which he provoked by his own perversity. Edward for the most part made his own difficulties, Richard inherited the great bulk of his. Richard again had a policy of his own, whilst Edward had none. Richard might possibly have stemmed the tide that overwhelmed his great grandfather; but that tide had now risen so high that he had scarcely any more chance than Edward had of resisting it. There can be little doubt that Richard had early begun to chafe under restraint, and that he saw his best policy to be not a perverse attempt to thwart his uncles and the political party that sustained them, but to raise up a counterpoise to them by promoting and enriching servants of his own. His choice of Michael de la Pole, an honourable warrior and an experienced administrator, a man sprung from the commons themselves, and apparently trusted by them, was a wise choice. In taking Robert de Vere for his companion and confidant he seemed to avoid the error of promoting an upstart; for the earls of Oxford, although not among the richest and mightiest, were among the most ancient, of the nobility, and no existing family held the title of earl by so long descent. But the lords were as jealous as ever; they would see in Vere a new Gaveston, and in Michael de la Pole a new Despenser, a deserter of the interests of his class. Thomas of Woodstock and Henry of

Contrast between Richard and Edward II.

Richard's choice of friends.

[1] The parliament of 1385 sat from Oct. 20 to Dec. 6; Rot. Parl. iii. 203; Record Report, ii. app. p. 117. Nothing is said in the rolls of the attempt to bind the clergy; perhaps the historian may have confounded this with the last parliament; see above, p. 488, note 2; Wals. ii. 139; Mon. Evesh. p. 67; cf. Malvern, in Higden, ix. p. 74.

Reconstitution of the baronial party under Gloucester and Derby, 1385–1387.

Derby, the son of John of Gaunt, had, with more craft than the duke of Lancaster, reformed the old baronial party, of which, as representing the interests of Bohun and Lancaster, they were the hereditary chiefs. Henry perhaps was already alienated from his cousin's interest by being excluded from the succession, which was now guaranteed to the young Mortimer. With them were Thomas Beauchamp earl of Warwick, whom the parliament in 1380 had appointed as governor to the king[1]; Thomas Mowbray earl of Nottingham, the heir of a long line of Mowbrays who had taken their part and paid their forfeit in all the constitutional struggles against the crown, and who also by the female side represented a younger branch of the royal house; and earl Richard of Arundel. These were until the close of the reign the leaders of a bitter and cruel opposition. They were strong, as the old Lancaster party had been, in the support of the clergy. Archbishop Courtenay had opposed John of Gaunt both as a favourer of heresy and as dangerous to the crown; by his boldness in reproving Richard himself he had incurred the boy's intense dislike, and had once been threatened with the punishment of a traitor[2]. Henry of Derby and Thomas of Gloucester avoided the Wycliffites, although they courted that section of the commons in which the strength of the Wycliffites was supposed to reside. But it would be wrong to attempt to determine within exact lines the extent and nature of the Lollard interest. It was strong in the court; in the country it gained by the unpopularity of the friars; among the bishops there was great reluctance to proceed to extremities with the heretics, and it was owing to the pressure of the religious orders, urging on the pope against the Wycliffites, that persecution, a new thing altogether in England[3], was set on foot. Wycliffe had been suffered to

Warwick,

Nottingham,

and Arundel.

Position of archbishop Courtenay.

The Wycliffites.

[1] Wals. i. 427, 428.

[2] Wals. ii. 128; Mon. Evesh. p. 58.

[3] It is doubtful whether any one had ever in England been capitally punished by law for heresy before this time. An Albigensian was burned during the Interdict, in the reign of John. The Chronicle of Meaux mentions (ii. 323) among the persecutions of the Minorites under John XXII that some of them were burned 'in quadam sylva,' in 1330; but the writer lived long after the time, and comprises England with Provence, Languedoc, northern Italy, Naples, and Burgundy, making the whole number burned in that year sixty-three.

die in peace at Lutterworth, and the prelates would probably, if left free to act, have confined themselves to repressing and repelling the attempts made to diminish their political power and wealth. Notwithstanding the repeated attacks, prompted by the Wycliffites, and made by the commons upon the clergy, Courtenay was faithful to the party with which the commons more and more closely identified themselves: with him was Thomas Arundel bishop of Ely, brother of the earl, a man whose later history shows him an equally bitter enemy of the king and of the heretics, and who was the guiding spirit of the revolution that closed the reign. William of Wykeham, now growing old, was on the same side. The king could reckon on the support of the archbishop of York, Alexander Neville, and some of the poorer prelates who had been promoted during the present reign, and who were more or less connected with the court, such as bishop Rushook of Chichester, who was the king's confessor. The elder bishops, who had risen by translations or by family influence, were chiefly in opposition.

Politics of the prelates.

Bishop Arundel.

The other bishops.

The country was not without real grievances. Each year had seen additions to the Statute book, as each parliament had been employed with numerous petitions. Yet none of the crying evils of the time had been redressed. The act of 1382 against heresy, by which it was ordered that, on certificate from the bishops, the chancellor should commission the sheriffs and others to compel the accused to satisfy the demands of the church, was repealed in the same year at the petition of the commons, as not having been passed with their assent[1]. It was perfectly true, as the act asserted, that the Lollards were engendering dissension and discord between divers estates of the realm. Between the two parliaments the representatives

Inactivity of the government.

[1] This statute was passed in the May session of 1382 (Statutes, ii. 25; see above, p. 487, note 2), and repealed in the October session of the same year, at the request of the commons: 'la quiel ne fuist unques assentu ne grante par les communes, mes ce que fuist parle de ce fuist sanz assent de lour; qe celui estatut soit annienti qar il n'estoit mie lour entent d'estre justifiez, ne obliger lour ne lour successours as prelats pluis que lours auncestres n'ont este en temps passez;' Rot. Parl. iii. 141; Wals. ii. 65, 66. The repeal is not entered among the statutes; see Hallam, Middle Ages, iii. 89.

Various causes of national division.

of the commons had been changed[1], the chancellor had also been changed, and the proceedings against Wycliffe, which were actually going on at the time and had been interrupted by an earthquake, had produced a recoil favourable to the heretics. The statutes against Roman aggressions were multiplied but disregarded, and, although the schism in the papacy continued, and was aggravated by national antipathies, the bishop of Rome drew his revenue and promoted his servants in England as he had done so long. But notwithstanding the many permanent lines of separation between class and class, interest and interest, estate and estate, the division of dynastic factions is the only one that seems powerfully to influence political life. The reputed Lollardy at court[2], the growing desire of the commons to weaken the power of the clergy, do not bring the court and the commons together. There is a general decline of the older forms of moral and religious sincerity. Richard was as unfit to restore the soundness and strength of the nation as he was unable to gain a real victory in the struggle of faction. But what the politicians wanted was not so much reform of abuses as the possession of power. The commons saw no diminution in the extravagance and luxury of the court, whoever might be chancellor, treasurer or counsellors. They saw the lords in opposition more careful to court them than the lords in power. Richard had disappointed them, for no prince however good could have given them what they desired in him. In the parliament of 1385 he had told them, when they requested an annual examination of the state of the household, that he would do it when he pleased; and to a petition for the declaration of the names of his officers for the year he had replied that he should change them when he pleased. Henry of Derby, although he was the son of John of Gaunt, became the darling of the Londoners; and Gloucester determined to

Decline of public morality.

Disappointment felt at Richard's behaviour.

[1] Forty-five names are common to the two parliaments.

[2] Three influential members of the council, Lewis Clifford, John Clanevow, and Richard Sturry were well known to be patrons of the Lollards; see Proceedings of Privy Council, i. 6; Walsingham, ii. 159, 216. And Sir John Montagu, brother of the earl of Salisbury, was a heretic himself. Sturry was one of the counsellors of Edward III removed by the Good Parliament; Chr. Angl. pp. 87, 377.

make a stroke for power as soon as his elder brother left the field open to him. He chose his first step craftily, and had his programme of reform ready to his hand. A charge of malversation would easily be believed, when so much malversation was known to exist, and the imputation so liberally made; it was by such charges that the kings had overwhelmed the ministers of whom they were tired: the dealings of Henry II with Becket, of Henry III with Hubert de Burgh, of Edward III with archbishop Stratford, and of John of Gaunt with Wykeham, formed precedents for the parliament when they in turn would impeach a minister. Such a charge would be fatal to Michael de la Pole.

Measures of the opposition.

266. The parliament of 1386 opened on the 1st of October, in the king's presence [1]. The chancellor, Michael de la Pole, according to custom, declared the cause of the summons: a great council, held at Oxford [2], had agreed that it was time for the king to cross the sea in person, and there were four good reasons; it was better for England to invade than to repel invasion; it was well that the king should show his good-will to take an active part in the national work; he had a right to the crown of France; he wanted to acquire honour and culture or knowledge of the world [3]. To secure these ends the parliament must grant money; the king for his part would redress all grievances. Four tenths and fifteenths, it was whispered, was the least that could be expected on so great an occasion [4], but whether the sum was imprudently mentioned by the chancellor, or the report was a part of the scheme for involving him in public odium, does not appear.

Parliament of 1386.

Heavy taxation needed.

[1] This parliament sat Oct. 1 to Nov. 28; Lords' Report, i. 495. Half a tenth and fifteenth was granted in the usual way, tunnage of 3*s*. and poundage of 1*s*. a continued subsidy on merchandise and wool, appropriated to the defence of the sea; and another half-tenth and fifteenth, if the commission of government to be appointed should find it necessary for the defence of the kingdom; Rot. Parl. iii. 220, 221; Knighton, c. 2686; Wals. ii. 150; Mon. Evesh. p. 76. The clerical grant of two half-tenths was made in convocation, Dec. 3; Wake, p. 318. The clergy of York declined to vote any money, and the parliament of 1388 petitioned the king to compel them; ibid. 319.

[2] 'Grant counseill,' Rot. Parl. iii. 215.

[3] 'Pour conquerre honour et humanite,' Rot. Parl. iii. 215.

[4] Knighton, c. 2681.

Parliament of 1386. Richard retires to Eltham. The parliament demands the dismissal of the ministers, and refuses to proceed to business.

The king retired after the opening of parliament to Eltham, perhaps in anticipation of the attack[1]; on the 13th of October the patent was sealed by which Robert de Vere was made duke of Ireland, and immediately the storm arose. Both houses signified to the king that the chancellor and the treasurer, the bishop of Durham, should be removed from their posts. This Richard refused: he bade the parliament mind its proper business, and declared that he would not at their request dismiss a servant of his kitchen[2]. The parliament replied that unless the king returned to Westminster and removed the chancellor they would not proceed to any other business. The king then proposed that forty members of the house of commons should be sent to confer with him at Eltham; this was rejected, and a rumour set abroad that Richard intended, if they were sent, to put them to death.

Declaration of Gloucester and Arundel.

In their stead the duke of Gloucester and bishop Arundel presented themselves with a message, declaring that there was an ancient statute by which the king was bound to hold a parliament once a year, at which, among other matters, they should discuss how the public burdens could most easily be borne; and by way of inference they stated their opinion that, as the parliament had to bear the burden, they had a right to inquire how and by whom their money was spent. There was, however, another statute according to which the parliament might break up, if the king without good cause absented himself for forty days[3].

Dispute with the king.

Richard replied that if this was a threat of rebellion he would seek advice from the king of France. The king of France, they answered, was his greatest enemy, and would advise him to his ruin. Then, returning to the point, they expatiated on the poverty of the country and referred that poverty to the misgovernment of the king's servants:

Statutes quoted against him.

nay there was another old statute, which not so long ago had been put in force, that if the king, from any

[1] Knighton, c. 2680. According to the Eulogium (iii. 359) he had attempted to dissolve the parliament.

[2] Knighton, c. 2681.

[3] Knighton, cc. 2681, 2682. See also, on the whole of this discussion, Hallam, Middle Ages, iii. 68 sq.

Parliament of 1386.

malignant design or foolish contumacy, or contempt, or wanton wilfulness, or in any irregular way, should alienate himself from his people, and should not be willing to be governed and regulated by the laws, statutes, and laudable ordinances of the realm with the wholesome advice of the lords and peers of the realm, but should headily and wantonly by his own mad counsels work out his own private purposes, it should then be lawful for them with the common assent and consent of the people of the realm to depose the king himself from the royal throne and elevate in his place some near kinsman of the royal line [1].

Threat of deposition.

Whether the envoys really believed themselves to be speaking the truth or no, the distinct references to the ancient laws, or more probably the warning of the fate of Edward II, alarmed Richard; he returned to the parliament; on the 24th of October the two ministers were removed [2]; bishop Arundel became chancellor, and the bishop of Hereford, John Gilbert, treasurer; and the earl of Suffolk was formally impeached by the commons. The charges against him were minute and definite [3]: he had (I) contrary to his oath accepted or purchased below their value great estates from the king; (II) he had not seen to the execution of the ordinances for the reform of the household by nine lords appointed [4] in the last par-

Richard returns to parliament.

Impeachment of the chancellor.

[1] 'Habent enim ex antiquo statuto et de facto non longe retroactis temporibus experienter, quod dolendum est, habito, si rex ex maligno consilio quocunque vel inepta contumacia, aut contemptu seu proterva voluntate singulari aut quovis modo irregulari, se alienaverit a populo suo, nec voluerit per jura regni et statuta et laudabiles ordinationes cum salubri consilio dominorum et procerum regni gubernari et regulari, sed capitose in suis insanis consiliis propriam voluntatem suam singularem proterve exercere, extunc licitum est eis cum communi assensu et consensu populi regni, ipsum regem de regali solio abrogare et propinquiorem aliquem de stirpe regia loco ejus in regali solio sublimare;' Knighton, c. 2683. It is needless to say that there was no such statute, but from the king's later action it is clear that both parties had in view the measures taken for the deposition of Edward II. It would seem from the Modus tenendi parliamentum (Select Charters, p. 510) that the king's absence from parliament was 'res dampnosa et periculosa.'

[2] Rymer, viii. 548.

[3] Rot. Parl. iii. 216; Knighton, c. 2684; cf. Wals. ii. 149.

[4] This commission is not given in the Rolls of the Parliament of 1385; but is possibly referred to in an imperfect article; iii. 214. The commons had however asked to know who should be the king's chief officers during the coming year, and been told that the king had sufficient officers at present, and would change them when he pleased; Rot. Parl. iii. 213. If the

Charges against Michael de la Pole.

liament; (III) he was responsible for the misapplication of the money then granted for the defence of the sea; (IV) he had fraudulently received the pension of a Limburg merchant long after it had been justly forfeited; and (V) had appropriated to himself the revenue of the master of S. Antony, which, as its owner was a schismatic, ought to have been paid to the king; (VI) as chancellor he had sealed charters contrary to the interest of the crown and to the law; and (VII) by his neglecting to relieve the town of Ghent, that town had been lost and with it money to the amount of 13,000 marks. Suffolk defended himself, and Richard le Scrope made a statement of his services and merits [1].

His defence.

Every point charged against him he either denied or explained; and, although the parliament replied and he rejoined in a way that seems on the record sufficiently convincing, his enemies were his judges. As for his services, he had, as Scrope said, served in war for thirty years, been captain of Calais, admiral, and ambassador. He was no upstart, but a man of inherited fortune, and in every capacity he had lived without dishonour or reproof. The dignity of earl the king had bestowed of his own accord, and the lands received with the title were only what was needed to maintain it.

The commons press the charges.

Notwithstanding this able defence, the commons insisted that he had broken his oath, and prayed for judgment against him on six out of seven of the counts. The discussion and terms of the judgment are rather confused; finally, the lords declared that on the second, third, and seventh heads, as his guilt was shared by others of the council, he should not be impeached alone; but, the rest being proved, the king was forced to condemn him to surrender all his acquisitions, save his earl's title and pension of £20, and to be imprisoned until he should pay a fine or ransom [2]. The guilt or innocence of de la Pole was however a matter of minor importance when he was once

He is sentenced as guilty.

commission be that referred to in the imperfect article the bishops of Winchester and Exeter were two of the lords nominated, and the object was to examine into the condition of the exchequer, the expenditure of £120,000, the case of the schismatics, and the king's debts. Cf. Rot. Parl. iii. 213, 217.

[1] Rot. Parl. iii. 216, 217. Cf. Hallam, Middle Ages, iii. 68.

[2] £20,000; Mon. Evesh. p. 75.

removed; and it may be variously estimated according as the circumstances are judged by the letter of the law, or by the ordinary practice of ministers. It is quite clear that in his administrative capacity he was equitably entitled to acquittal, and that it was not for the reasons alleged that his condemnation was demanded. This the result proved. The success of the Gloucester party encouraged them to a further imitation of the acts of the Good Parliament, and Richard, before he could obtain a subsidy which took the form of half a tenth, half a fifteenth, and an increase and continuance of the customs, was obliged to consent to the appointment of a commission of regency or council of reform. This body was to hold office for a year to regulate the royal household and the realm, to inquire into all sources of revenue, receipts, and expenditure, to examine and amend all defaults and misprisions whereby the king was injured or the law broken, and to hear and determine complaints not provided for by the law; all subjects were ordered to obey them to the extent of the commission, and none was to advise the king to revoke the commission under severe penalties. This commission was issued on the 19th of November, and embodied in a statute dated on the 1st of December[1]. The lords named were eleven in number: bishops Courtenay, Neville, Wykeham, and Brantingham, the abbot of Waltham, the dukes of Gloucester and York, the earl of Arundel, and the lords John of Cobham, Richard le Scrope, and John Devereux[2]. These were to act in conjunction with the new chancellor, treasurer, and privy seal[3].

It was a political condemnation.

A commission of reform is appointed to regulate the realm and household.

The commissioners.

Richard was blind to his own advantages, or he might have found in the technical character of the proceedings or in the personal composition of the council some sources of strength. Old statesmen like Wykeham and Scrope were not likely to allow extreme measures, and in Neville the king had a devoted

Richard's impatience.

[1] Statutes, ii. 39–43; Malvern (ed. Lumby, Higden, ix.), pp. 83–89.
[2] Rot. Parl. iii. 221; Knighton, cc. 2685, 2686 sq.
[3] The privy seal was John Waltham, afterwards bishop of Salisbury. The minutes of the first proceedings of the commission are printed in the Proceedings of the Privy Council, ed. Nicolas, i. 3: but they contain merely a list of articles of inquiry.

friend. But Richard was only twenty-one; the despotic and impatient impulses of royalty had been aroused in him, and he knew that, notwithstanding the mixed composition of the commission, the leading spirit in it was Gloucester. He set himself to thwart rather than to propitiate his temporary masters.

His protest in favour of his prerogative.

Before the close of the session he protested by word of mouth that for nothing done in the parliament should any prejudice arise to him or his crown, that the prerogative and liberties of his crown should be safely observed notwithstanding[1].

He forms a party against the commission, 1387.

Immediately afterwards he released Suffolk from prison without ransom, and called into his councils Sir Simon Burley, archbishop Neville, the duke of Ireland, Tressilian the chief justice, and Nicholas Brember, the head of his party in the city of London. With their advice he formed a deliberate scheme of policy[2]. He would have been fully justified, both by what he knew of Gloucester and by the examples of the reigns of Henry III and Edward II, in taking precautions in case the commission should decline to surrender its powers at the end of the term of office; but his elder advisers should have warned him that excessive and imprudent precaution might easily be interpreted as aggression. This was not done. The king and his friends made a rapid progress through the country, courting adherents and binding their partisans by strict obligations to support them.

He tries to raise forces, and tampers with the sheriffs.

They prepared to call on the sheriffs to raise the forces of the shires for the king's defence, and to influence the elections for the next parliament in his favour[3]; and not content with this, they brought together, first at Shrewsbury and afterwards at Nottingham, a body of judges to give an

[1] Rot. Parl. iii. 224.

[2] 'Commoverunt regem contra dominos susurrantes regem non in effectu esse regem sed nomine tenus, futurumque ut nihil sui juris existeret, domini tamen potestate gauderent;' Mon. Evesh. p. 77; cf. Wals. ii. 156; Hallam, Middle Ages, iii. 71.

[3] 'Vicecomites convenire fecit ut sciret quantam potentiam possent contrahere contra barones, et ut ipsi nullum militem de pago vel de schira permitterent eligi ad parliamentum nisi quem rex et ejus consilium elegissent. Ad quae vicecomites dixerunt quod communes faverent dominis, nec esse in potestate illorum ad hanc causam exercitum contrahendi; de militibus ad parliamentum eligendis dixerunt, communes velle tenere usitatas consuetudines, quae volunt ut a communibus milites eligantur;' Mon. Evesh. p. 85; Wals. ii. 161; Chron. Angl. p. 379; Malvern, p. 94.

opinion adverse to the legality of the commission of council. On the 25th of August, 1387, at Nottingham, five of the justices[1], under compulsion as they afterwards said, declared that the commission was unlawful, as being contrary to the prerogative of the crown, and that those who had procured it deserved capital punishment; that the direction of procedure in parliament belonged to the king; that the lords and commons had no power to remove the king's servants; that the person who had moved for the production of the statute by which Edward II was deposed, which was really the model on which the recent ordinance was framed, was a traitor, and that the sentence on Suffolk was revocable and erroneous. This opinion was attested by the archbishops of York and Dublin, the bishops of Durham, Bangor, and Chichester, the duke of Ireland, and the earl of Suffolk[2]. Even if Richard could at once have acted upon this declaration, it would have been imprudent to publish it; as matters stood it was equivalent to a declaration of war. It was followed by a rash attempt to arrest the earl of Arundel; this failed, and Gloucester, in the prospect of a continuance of power, was not slow in taking up the challenge in arms[3]. On the 10th of November Richard returned to London, and was received in great state by the mayor and citizens[4]. On the 12th, however, Gloucester, Warwick, and Arundel were reported to be approaching in full force. The archbishop of Canterbury, and lords Cobham, Lovel, and Devereux, appeared as negotiators: the council, they declared, was innocent of any attempt to injure the king; the five false advisers, Neville, Vere, de la Pole, Tressilian, and Brember, were the real traitors, and against these, on the 14th, Gloucester and his friends laid a deliberate charge of treason. Richard at first thought of resisting, and summoned the Londoners to his aid; but when he found them determined not to fight for him, and when the lord Basset,

He obtains from the judges an opinion adverse to the commission, Aug. 1387.

Alarm of war, Nov. 1387.

Gloucester charges the king's friends with treason.

[1] Mon. Evesh. p. 85; Knighton, cc. 2693, 2694; Wals. ii. 162; Malvern, pp. 98–102; Eulog. iii. 361.
[2] Rot. Parl. iii. 233, 234; Mon. Evesh. pp. 86–89; Knighton, cc. 2694 sq.
[3] Mon. Evesh. p. 90; Wals. ii. 163.
[4] Knighton, c. 2696; Malvern, p. 104.

the earl of Northumberland and others declared that they believed in the honesty of the council and refused to fight for the duke of Ireland[1], he was obliged to temporise. In Westminster Hall, on the 17th, he received the lords of the council graciously[2], accepted their excuses, and promised that in the next parliament his unfortunate advisers should be compelled to appear and give account of themselves. On the 20th the five culprits took to flight[3]. Suffolk and Neville escaped safely. Vere raised a force with which he endeavoured to join the king, but was defeated by the earl of Derby in Oxfordshire, and made his way to France. Tressilian found a temporary hiding-place, and only Brember was taken. On the 27th of December[4] Richard found himself obliged to receive the formal appeal, and at the bidding of the appellants to order the arrest of the remainder of his personal friends. Possibly he had not until then given up all hope of resistance; for in the writs of parliament issued on the 17th of December he had inserted a provision that the knights to be elected should be 'in debatis modernis magis indifferentes[5]:' but the defeat of the duke of Ireland settled the matter for the time; the king was obliged by another writ on the 1st of January to withdraw the order as contrary to the ancient form of election and the liberties of lords and commons, and to direct that the knights should be chosen without any such condition[6]. The day fixed was the 3rd of February, and then the parliament met[7].

Richard is obliged to submit, Nov. 17, 1387.

Appeal of treason against the king's friends, Dec. 1387.

Summons of the parliament of 1388.

Gloucester declares his innocence.

After the chancellor's speech, Gloucester on his knees disavowed all intention, such as had been imputed to him, of making himself king, and, when Richard had declared himself

[1] Knighton, c. 2698.
[2] Knighton, c. 2700; Wals. ii. 166; Malvern, p. 107.
[3] Knighton, c. 2701.
[4] Knighton, cc. 2704, 2705; Wals. ii. 171, 172, 173; Mon. Evesh. p. 100; Eulog. iii. 365; Malvern, pp. 113-118.
[5] Lords' Report, iv. 725.
[6] Lords' Report, iv. 727; Rot. Parl. iii. 400; Rymer, vii. 566.
[7] This parliament sat Feb. 3 to March 20, and April 11 to June 4; Lords' Report, i. 495; Knighton, c. 2706. Half a tenth and fifteenth was granted, with tunnage and poundage and custom on wool as in 1386; Rot. Parl. iii. 244. The Convocation of Canterbury, Feb. 26, granted half a tenth on the understanding that the York clergy did the same; Wake, pp. 319, 320.

satisfied of his uncle's good faith, the business of the session began[1]. The five appellant lords, Gloucester, Derby, Nottingham, Warwick, and Arundel brought forward thirty-nine charges against the five accused[2], some counts being common to all, some peculiar to individuals. They had conspired to rule the king for their own purposes, and had bound him by an unlawful oath to maintain them. They had withdrawn him from the society of his magnates, and had defeated all the measures taken by the parliament for his good. They had caused him to impoverish the crown by lavish gifts of land, jewels, money, and privileges. They had attempted to make Robert de Vere king of Ireland; they had carried off the king into distant parts of the realm, and had negotiated treasonably with the king of France. By the formation of secret leagues, the levying of forces, connivance with the military operations of the duke, and trying to influence the sheriffs in the elections, they had all alike proved their consciousness of guilt. They had incited the Londoners to resist in arms and to slay the lords and commons, and they had obtained from the judges a false opinion to justify them in treating the council of government as traitors. The bill of appeal was first presented to the judges, who declared it informal, whether tested by the common law of the realm or by the civil law. The lords thereupon announced that in matters of such high concern the rules of civil law could not be observed; the parliament was itself the supreme judge; it was not to be bound by the forms which guided inferior courts, that were merely the executors of the ancient laws and customs of the realm, and of the ordinances and establishments of parliament. In their supreme authority they determined, and the king allowed, that the appeal was well and sufficiently made and affirmed[3]. The names of the accused were then called;

Parliament of Feb. 1388. Declaration of the lords appellant.

Charges against Neville, Vere, de la Pole, Tressilian, and Brember.

The bill of appeal declared illegal.

The parliament overrules the opinion.

[1] Rot. Parl. iii. 228 sq.

[2] Rot. Parl. iii. 229 sq.; Knighton, cc. 2713–2726; Malvern, pp. 119–140.

[3] 'Que en si haute crime come est pretendu . . . la cause ne serra aillours deduc q'en parlement, ne par autre ley que ley et cours du parlement, et q'il appartient as seignurs du parlement et a lour franchise et libertee d'auncien custume du parlement, d'estre juges en tieux cas, et de tieux cas ajugger par assent du roi; et que ensi serra fait en cest cas par agarde du parlement, pur ce que le roialme d'Engleterre n'estoit devant ces heures,

Parliament of Feb. 1388. The four absent culprits first tried.

Suffolk, Vere, Neville, and Tressilian were absent, and against them the appellants pressed for an immediate sentence. The lords spiritual, after protesting their right as peers to take part in all proceedings of the house, withdrew from the trial in which, as a case of capital offence, the canons forbade them to take part; and the lords temporal examined the charges.

Sentence of condemnation, Feb. 13, 1388.

Fourteen of the counts were found to contain treason, and on all the accused were guilty[1]: Suffolk, Vere, and Tressilian were therefore condemned to be drawn and hanged; Neville

Brember and Tressilian executed.

to forfeit his temporalities and await further judgment. This sentence was published on the 13th of February; on the 17th Brember was tried, and on the 20th condemned and executed. Tressilian was captured during the trial, and hanged on the 19th[2].

Condemnation of the judges.

On the 2nd of March the judges who had given their opinion at Nottingham were impeached by the commons, and on the 6th found guilty by the lords. The sentence of death however was, at the request of the queen and bishops, commuted for perpetual exile in Ireland.

Impeachment of Burley and others.

On the 6th of March the bishop of Chichester, and on the 12th Sir Simon Burley, Sir John Beauchamp of Holt, Sir John Salisbury, and Sir James Berners were also impeached by the commons, on sixteen charges of treason similar to those on which the others had been condemned. They had a short respite. Parliament was adjourned for Easter from March 20 to April 22. As soon as proceedings were resumed they were found guilty and condemned.

They are executed.

The laymen were executed, Burley on the 5th of May, the other three on the 12th[3]. The earl of Derby and the duke of

ne a l'entent du roi notre dit seigneur et seigneurs du parlement unques ne serra, reule ne governe par la ley civill; et auxint lour entent n'est pas de reuler ou governer si haute cause come cest appell est, que ne serra aillours trie ne termine q'en parlement, come dit est, par cours, processe et ordre, use en ascune court ou place plus bas deinz mesme le roialme, queux courtes et places ne sont que executours d'aunciens leys et custumes du roialme et ordinances et establissementz de parlement; et feust avis au mesmes les seigneurs du parlement, par assent du roi notre dit seigneur, que cest appell feust fait et afferme bien et assetz deuement, et le process d'ycell bone et effectuel solonc les leys et cours de parlement, et pur tiel l'agarderont et ajuggeront;' Rot. Parl. iii. 236.

[1] Rot. Parl. iii. 237; Knighton, c. 2706.

[2] Knighton, c. 2726; cf. Wals. ii. 173 sq.; Mon. Evesh. p. 102.

[3] Wals. ii. 174; Malvern, p. 177.

York were very anxious to spare Burley, but were overruled by Gloucester and Arundel. For the disposal of the archbishop of York and the bishop of Chichester further measures were necessary. The circumstances of the case were laid before the pope, and Urban VI was not restrained by any scruples of conscience from allowing the powers of the church to be used for the humiliation of a political enemy. By an act of supreme power, in which the English church and nation acquiesced, he translated archbishop Neville to the see of S. Andrew's, and the bishop of Chichester to that of Triburna, or Kilmore, in Ireland. Scotland acknowledged the rival pope, and the translation of Neville was a mere mockery; he died serving a small cure in Flanders. The appointment to Triburna was simply banishment. So rapid was the action of the lords that on the 30th of April Thomas Arundel was nominated to succeed Neville at York, and thus much was completed before the parliament broke up. The session lasted until the 4th of June. On the 2nd the lords and commons granted a large subsidy on wool and other merchandise, out of which £20,000 was voted to the lords appellant [1]. Besides the formal registration of the acts and supplementary securities for the execution of the sentences of forfeiture, and for the protection of the appellants, no legislative work was undertaken. The 'merciless' parliament [2] sat for 122 days. Its acts fully establish its right to the title, and stamp with infamy the men who, whether their political aims were or were not salutary to the constitution, disgraced the cause by excessive and vindictive cruelty.

Summary translation of Neville and Rushook.

Arundel made archbishop of York.

Other acts of the *Merciless* parliament.

Gloucester and his allies retained their power for a year longer. During this time a parliament was held at Cambridge [3], in which some useful statutes were passed and further

Parliament at Cambridge, 1388.

[1] Rot. Parl. iii. 245.

[2] 'Parliamentum sine misericordia;' Knighton, c. 2701. The statute of this parliament is chiefly composed of the enactments against the favourites; five short clauses in addition limit the acceptance of gifts of the king, forbid the increase of custom on wool, and the issue of royal letters to disturb the execution of the law, and alter the law on justices of assize; Statutes, ii. 54, 55.

[3] Sept. 9 to Oct. 17, 1388; Lords' Report, i. 495; Malvern, pp. 189-198. A tenth and fifteenth was granted; Record Report, ii. app. 2, p. 178. The Convocation of Canterbury granted a tenth, Oct. 20; Wake, pp. 320, 321.

aid granted; and a truce was made with France for two years. The king continued in retirement, and the country at peace.

Richard declares himself of age, May 3, 1389.

On the 3rd of May, 1389, Richard took the kingdom by surprise. Entering the council, he asked to be told how old he was. He was three and twenty [1]. When this was acknowledged he announced that he was certainly of age, and intended no longer to submit to restraints which would be intolerable to the meanest of his subjects. Henceforth he would manage the affairs of the realm for himself, would choose his own counsellors, and be a king indeed. Following up his brave words by action, he demanded the great seal from Arundel, who at once surrendered it; bishop Gilbert resigned the treasury, and on the following day William of Wykeham and Thomas Brantingham returned to the posts of chancellor and treasurer. Some minor changes were made in the legal body, and the appellant lords were removed from the council. On the 8th of May the king issued letters to the sheriffs declaring that he had assumed the government [2]. The success of this bold stroke was as strange as its suddenness. According to the chronicler it was welcomed with general satisfaction [3]. Whether it was that the country was tired of the appellants, or that all fears were extinguished as to the restoration of the favourites, it is impossible to say. Richard however acted with astonishing moderation. Although he contrived to ameliorate the condition of his exiled friends, he made no effort to recall them or to avenge the dead. Suffolk died the same summer in France; Robert de Vere never returned to England; the exiled judges remained for eight years longer in Ireland. In September a negotiation was set on foot for the

Changes of ministers, May, 1389.

Moderation of the king.

The Statute of Cambridge forbids the sale of offices, confirms the previous legislation on labourers, artificers, and beggars; forbids children who have been kept at the plough till twelve to learn any craft or mystery; fixes six as the number of justices of the peace in each county, who are to hold their sessions quarterly; orders the slanderers of great men to be punished by the king's council, and puts provisors of benefices out of the king's protection; Statutes, ii. 55–60; Knighton, c. 2729; Wals. ii. 177; Mon. Evesh. p. 105.

[1] Knighton, c. 2735; Wals. ii. 181; Mon. Evesh. p. 108; Rymer, vii. 616; Malvern, pp. 210, 211.

[2] Rymer, vii. 618; Rot. Parl. iii. 404.

[3] 'Omnes Deum glorificaverunt qui sibi talem regem sapientem futurum providere curavit;' Knighton, c. 2736.

admission of the appellants to the king's favour. A violent dispute took place in the council on the 15th of October; Richard apparently wishing to buy over the earl of Nottingham with a large pension given him as Warden of Berwick, and the chancellor objecting to the expense[1]. In the following November, John of Gaunt returned home, and by a prompt use of his personal influence produced an apparent reconciliation among all parties[2]. For eight years Richard governed England as, to all appearance, a constitutional and popular king. **Reconciliation of the appellants.**

267. The truce with France, concluded in 1389, was continued by renewals for short periods until 1394, and then prolonged for four years, before the expiration of which the king, who lost his first wife in 1394, married a daughter of Charles VI, and arranged a truce for twenty-five years. The cessation of a war which had lasted already for half a century, intermitted only by truces, which were either periods of utter prostration or seasons of expensive preparation for fresh enterprises, is almost enough to account for the internal peace of England from 1388 to 1397[3]. Taxation was moderate and regular, although not unvaried from year to year: in 1391 a fifteenth and a half, and a tenth and a half; in 1392 two halves of a fifteenth and tenth; and in 1395 a fifteenth and tenth, were granted. The subsidy on wool and merchandise was continued through the **Public business from 1388 to 1397.** **Taxation, 1389–1395.**

[1] Proceedings of Privy Council, i. 11, 12.
[2] Wals. ii. 194, 195.
[3] The parliaments of these years sat as follows:—

In 1390 Jan. 17–March 2; Nov. 12–Dec. 3. A grant of the subsidy and tunnage and poundage for a year was made in the first session; in the second the vote was raised on the wool to 50*s.* and 53*s.* 4*d.* on the sack and 7½ and 8 marks on the last, for three years.

In 1391 Nov. 3–Dec. 2; Record Reports, ii. p. 178.

In 1392 a parliament summoned to York for the 14th of October was adjourned on September 8, and never met.

In 1393 Jan. 20–Feb. 10, at Winchester; Rot. Parl. iii. 300 sq.

In 1394 Jan. 27–March 6. Tunnage and poundage were granted; Rot. Parl. iii. 314.

In 1395 Jan. 27–Feb. 15; Rot. Parl. iii. 330.

The Convocations of the same period were these:—(1) In 1391, April 17, the clergy of Canterbury granted a subsidy to the pope. (2) The clergy of Canterbury, Dec. 9, and those of York, Dec. 4, granted a half-tenth. (3) In 1393 the clergy of Canterbury, March 3, and of York, March 17, granted three half-tenths. (4) In 1394 the clergy of Canterbury, May 21, and of York, March 1, granted a tenth. (5) In 1395 the clergy of Canterbury, Feb. 5, and of York, Feb. 9, granted a tenth; Wake, pp. 321–324.

whole time: after a grant of a single year in 1390, it was renewed at an increased rate, which bespeaks continued prosperity[1], for three years; in 1393 for the same term; and in 1397 the custom on wool was given for five years. The variations of taxation imply some irregularity in the sessions of parliament; no parliament was held in 1389; the estates met twice in 1390, in January and November; and in November 1391; the next session was in January 1393, and in the same month the parliament met in 1394 and 1395. Most of these were long sessions, varying from three weeks to three months, and a considerable amount of business was transacted in each. The ministerial changes were not great, and the ministers themselves seem to have enjoyed the confidence of the parliament, and the apparent approval of the king. In the first parliament of 1390 the chancellor, treasurer, and councillors resigned their offices, and prayed that if they had done any wrong it might be laid against them before the parliament. The lords spiritual and temporal and the commons declared that they had no fault to find, and they all resumed their offices[2]. In September 1391[3] archbishop Arundel succeeded Wykeham as chancellor, and remained in office until 1396, when he succeeded Courtenay at Canterbury, and consequently resigned the seal to Edmund Stafford, bishop of Exeter; at the treasury bishop Brantingham presided from May to August 1389; bishop Gilbert of S. David's from August 1389 to May 1391; and John Waltham, bishop of Salisbury, from May 1391 to September 1395, when Roger Walden was appointed. Under the advice of his experienced counsellors Richard took some very important steps in legislation. Almost every year of the reign is marked by its own statute, but the acts of this portion of it are of great significance. First in historical prominence comes the statute of Provisors, passed in 1390[4], which re-enacted the memorable

Sessions of parliament.

The ministers offer to resign in 1390.

Arundel chancellor, 1391–1396.

Legislation of the period: on Provisors,

[1] Wals. ii. 196. [2] Rot. Parl. iii. 258. [3] Rymer, vii. 707.
[4] Statutes, ii. 61, 70. See also Rymer, vii. 673. The bishops protested against the infringement of the papal right by this statute; Rot. Parl. iii. 264; Wals. ii. 198; and in consequence of a papal remonstrance some relaxation of this statute was permitted in the next parliament; Wals. ii. 203; Mon. Evesh. p. 123. See also Malvern, pp. 221–234, 248–258, 262.

statute of 1351, with additional safeguards against Roman usurpation. The ordinance against maintenance[1], that is the undertaking to promote other men's quarrels and causes in the courts of justice by unauthorised persons, especially such as make a trade out of the political influence of their lords, includes a prohibition of the old custom of giving 'livery of company,' the retaining of large retinues, which supplied, for the sake of pomp, the place of the old feudal court and following. This also was issued in 1390. In the second parliament of that year the number of justices of the peace was enlarged from six to eight in each shire, and the staple reformed. In 1391 the provisions of the statute of mortmain were interpreted to forbid the contrivance of granting enfeoffment to laymen to the uses of religious houses, and the acquisition of land by perpetual corporations such as guilds and fraternities[2]; and the private courts of landlords were forbidden to try cases concerning freehold. The petitions of the commons that villeins might not be allowed to acquire lands, to send their children to the schools 'to advance them by means of clergy' or scholarship[3], for fear of their increasing the power of the clergy and defeating the rights of the lords, were rejected by the king in this parliament. In 1393 the great statute of Praemunire imposed forfeiture of goods as the penalty for obtaining bulls or other instruments at Rome[4]. The legislation of 1394 is chiefly mercantile, and most of the other statutes contain provisions for improving or confirming the laws which had been made in the time of Edward III for the benefit of trade[5].

mainten-ance, livery, justices of the peace, mortmain, and Praemunire.

Mercantile legislation.

Period of compromise.

This interposition of a period of eight years of peace between two epochs of terrible civil discord is very remarkable. A certain amount of good government was indispensable to its continuance, and for this Richard appeared to be honestly labouring. His efforts were seconded by a somewhat subservient parliament. In the winter session of 1390 and again in 1391 it was declared, on the petition of the lords and commons,

[1] Statutes, ii. 74 sq.; Wals. ii. 195, 196; Mon. Evesh. p. 121.
[2] Statutes, ii. 79; Mon. Evesh. p. 123; Knighton, c. 2738.
[3] Rot. Parl. iii. 294.
[4] Statutes, ii. 84, 85, sq.
[5] Statutes, ii. 87 sq.

Declaration on prerogative. that the king's prerogative was unaffected by the legislation of his reign or those of his progenitors, even of Edward II himself; and this article, which is a renunciation of political opposition, must have been one condition of the promotion of the Arundels[1]. The king showed no vindictiveness: the ministers of the time were chosen from among the men who had been most hostile to the favourites. **Mixed composition of the council.** The composition of the council was not one-sided; Arundel, Nottingham, Derby, and the duke of Gloucester himself, were restored to their places in it before December 1389[2]; and in March 1390 the king agreed to a body of rules for the management of the council-business which show that it must have been the threat of compulsion, or the advice of really dangerous counsellors, that had prevented him from accepting the commission of 1386[3]. **Difficulty of judging of Richard's character.** It is indeed possible that Richard dissembled; that he forced himself to associate with men whom he hated, in the hope that the time would come for him to destroy them in detail: but such a theory is extremely improbable; he was young, impulsive, and at no period of his life capable of self-restraint in small matters. It is perhaps more conceivable that in his earlier difficulties he was, as his opponents said, the scarcely

[1] In 1390 Richard had made fresh provision for the dukes of York and Gloucester, which may account for the petitions from both lords and commons, 'que la regalie et prerogative de notre dit seigneur le roi et de sa corone soient tout dis sauvez et gardez;' Rot. Parl. iii. 278, 279. The petition of 1391 is more full, and proceeds from the commons: 'En ycest parlement le second jour de Decembre, les communes prierent overtement en plein parlement que notre seigneur le roi soit et estoise aussi frank en sa regalie liberte et dignite roiale en son temps, come ascuns de ses nobles progenitours jadys rois l'Engleterre furent en lour temps; nient contresteant ascun estatut ou ordinance fait devant ces heures a contraire, et mesment en temps le roi Edward II, qui gist a Gloucestre. Et que si ascun estatut fuist fait en temps le dit roi Edward, en derogation de la liberte et franchise de la corone, qu'ils soit annulle et de null force. Et puis toutz les prelatz et seigneurs temporels prierent en mesme le manere. Et sur ce notre dit seigneur le roi mercia les ditz seigneurs et communes de la grant tendresse et affection q'ils avoient a la salvation de son honour et de son estat. Et a cause que lour ditz prieres et requestes luy semblerent honestes et resonables, il l'agrea et assenta pleinement a ycelles;' Rot. Parl. iii. 286.

[2] Privy Council Proceedings, i. 17.

[3] Ibid. i. 18. One clause forbids all gifts by the king without the consent of the dukes of Lancaster, York, and Gloucester, and the chancellor, or two of them.

voluntary tool of abler men, with whom, although he had a boyish affection for them, he had not as yet any political sympathy. It could scarcely have been dissimulation that led him to promote Thomas Arundel to the almost impregnable position of the primacy, and to trust the earl his brother with supreme military command. We may conclude that Richard had accepted the determination of the country to be governed by the Arundels or by ministers of their principles, and thought it better to share his power with them than to be treated as a prisoner or an infant. He lived then as a constitutional king, and did his best: if he loved pleasure and ease, he had to deal with ministers who would meddle little with his self-indulgence provided that it did not interfere with their popularity. Another reason for tranquillity is found in the fact that, during great part of the time, John of Gaunt, who had reformed his life and was growing wiser with years, was present in England: he seems to have exercised great power over the dukes of Gloucester and York, the latter of whom was a mere idle man of pleasure; the earl of Derby, his son, found scope for his energies by engaging in the crusade of the military orders in north-eastern Europe and afterwards made a pilgrimage to Jerusalem, returning by way of Italy, Bohemia, and Germany. The influence of the queen Anne of Bohemia may also, as was believed at the time, have led Richard to cultivate the arts of peace. His one great enterprise, the expedition to Ireland which occupied a great part of 1394 and 1395, was undertaken after her death.

General tranquillity.

Pacific influences.

Expedition to Ireland.

Yet these years did not pass without considerable difficulties. The Lollards were increasing in number and in political courage and weight; and the leaders of the church had no easy task in combining the confidence of the commons in parliament with the repression of heresy. The abortive attempt at legislation made in 1382 had emboldened the heretics, and the bishops, who were engaged in a struggle on one hand with Rome and on the other with Avignon, were in no haste to promote extreme measures against their religious critics, who generally recanted when ecclesiastical pressure was applied. Pastoral

Growth of Lollardy.

Insufficient measures of repression.

The Lollards.

exhortations and inhibitions were freely issued; Richard in March 1388, whilst the commission of government was in full power[1], had ordered heretical books to be collected and brought before the council[2]; a great inquiry made by the archbishop at Leicester in 1389 ended in the absolution of the guilty Lollards[3]. In the meanwhile the doctrinal views of the party spread; they counted among their friends some influential knights, and some courtiers in whose eyes the political power of the bishops was their greatest sin. To the assistance of these men we must ascribe the fact that in the parliament held by the duke of York, during Richard's absence in Ireland, was presented a bill of twelve articles containing the conclusions of the Lollards against the church of England[4]. These articles are based upon or clothed in the language of Wycliffe, and enlarge upon the decay of charity, the invalidity of holy orders without personal grace, the celibacy of the clergy, the idolatry of the mass, the use of exorcisms and benedictions of salt, bread, clothes, and the like, the secular employments of clergymen, the multiplication of chantries in which prayer is made for particular dead people, pilgrimages and image worship, auricular confession, war and capital punishments, vows of chastity, and unnecessary trades. Notwithstanding the curious confusion of ideas which pervades this manifesto, the movement appeared so important that the king on his return enforced an oath of abjuration on the suspected favourers of

Bill of the Lollards delivered in parliament.

[1] See Wilkins, Conc. iii. 191.

[2] On the death of Urban VI the earl of Northumberland advised the king not to obey any new pope until he had conferred with the lords and people on the subject; and the king through Sir Lewis Clifford and the privy seal agreed to abstain from all correspondence with Rome for the time; Privy Council Proceedings, i. 14; cf. Rymer, vii. 686. Possibly there was an idea of closing the schism; but it must be remembered that Wycliffe was as bitter against the antipope as the most rigid of the papal party were. The bishops are very severely handled by the chroniclers for not defending their flocks against the wolves; only bishop le Despenser of Norwich threatened persecution; Wals. ii. 189. The design of closing the schism was revived by Charles VI in 1395; Knighton, c. 2763.

[3] Wilkins, Conc. iii. 208 sq.

[4] Wilkins, Conc. iii. 221 sq.; Ann. Ricardi, pp. 174 sq.; Fasc. Ziz. pp. 360-369.

heresy. But the religious quarrel was soon lost sight of in the renewed political troubles [1].

268. These were due to a change in Richard's behaviour, which, whether it were a change of policy or a change of character, seems to have begun to show itself early in 1394. The earl of Arundel had quarrelled with the duke of Lancaster. On the 2nd of March, 1390, Richard had made his uncle duke of Aquitaine for life, reserving only his liege homage to himself as king of France, and thus alienating the duchy from the English crown for the time [2]. The duke moreover is said to have demanded in the parliament of 1394 that his son should be recognised as heir to the crown, as representing Edmund of Lancaster, who was falsely stated to be the elder brother of Edward I [3]. Both these matters served to revive the national dislike to John of Gaunt, of which Arundel willingly became the spokesman. And there were private grudges besides. The duke had in 1393 been engaged in putting down a revolt in Cheshire, at which he suspected that the earl was conniving; and with this he taxed Arundel in parliament [4]. Arundel, on the other hand, complained in parliament that the king allowed too much power and showed too much favour to the duke of Lancaster [5], condescending even to wear the collar and livery of his uncle: he objected strongly to the bestowal of Aquitaine on the duke and to the continuance of the truce with France. Richard replied forcibly in defence of his uncle; and Arundel had to beg pardon, which was granted by charter. The affair seemed to have ended here; but on the occasion of the queen's funeral Richard, conceiving that the procession had been kept waiting by Arundel, lost his temper and struck him with so much violence as to draw blood, and so, in ecclesiastical language, polluted the church of Westminster [6]. This was a bad omen, for there was an old prophecy that the divine vengeance for the death of S. Thomas of Canterbury would be

Change in Richard's behaviour.

Quarrel of Lancaster and the earl of Arundel.

Richard strikes Arundel.

Outrage in Westminster Abbey, 1394.

[1] Wilkins, Conc. iii. 225; Wals. ii. 216; Ann. Ricardi, pp. 173, 183.
[2] Rot. Parl. iii. 263; Rymer, vii. 659.
[3] Eulog. iii. 369.
[4] Ann. Ricardi, pp. 162, 166; Wals. ii. 214.
[5] Rot. Parl. iii. 313.
[6] Ann. Ricardi, p. 169; Wals. ii. 215. Arundel was sent to the Tower August 3; Rymer, vii. 784; but liberated on the 10th; ibid. 785.

deferred only until Westminster Abbey was polluted with human blood. But the quarrel went no further at the time; the earl did not, in spite of the outrage and a week's imprisonment in the Tower, cease from attendance at the council; and the promotion of his brother to the see of Canterbury must be regarded as a sign that the breach was healed. The death of the queen had removed one good influence about Richard; the same year the dukes of Lancaster and York lost their wives, who were sisters, and the countess of Derby, who was also sister-in-law to Gloucester, died. The domestic relations of the royal house were largely modified by this; John of Gaunt now married Catherine Swinford, the mother of several of his children, and obtained for them recognition as members of the royal family. Richard in 1396 married a second wife, a daughter of Charles VI; and, although the new queen was a child, the influx of French manners introduced by her attendants, and the increase of pomp and extravagance at court which ensued, tended to augment the dangerous symptoms [1]. From the very moment of the marriage Richard's policy as well as his character seems to have changed: whether it was that the sight of continental royalty, even in so deplorable a state as that into which it had fallen under Charles VI, wrought in him, as long afterwards in James V of Scotland, an irresistible craving for absolute power, or that his mind, already unsettled, was losing its balance altogether. He was led to believe that he was about to be chosen emperor in the place of his drunken brother-in-law Wenzel [2]. He began to borrow money, as Edward II had done, from every person or community that had money to lend, and to raise it in every other exceptional and unconstitutional way. He filled the court, it

Death of the queen and the duchesses, 1394.

Richard's second marriage, 1396.

His visit to France.

[1] 300,000 marks were spent on the visit to France; Ann. Ricardi, p. 194; Wals. ii. 222.

[2] Ann. Ricardi, p. 199: 'Unum certe scitur quod ab illo tempore cepit tyrannizare, populum aporiare, grandes summas pecuniae mutuari,' &c. As early as 1392 Richard had begun to borrow; in that year the Londoners refused to lend him a thousand pounds, and a long quarrel followed, in which Gloucester supplanted the king in their favour; Wals. ii. 207–211; Knighton, c. 2745; Eulog. iii. 368; Political Poems, i. 282 sq. His loans in 1397 were very great; Wals. ii. 222, 223.

was said, with bishops and ladies, two very certain signs of French influence, neither being probably of the best sort. The cry of the excessive influence of John of Gaunt was revived, and involved the king in his uncle's unpopularity; John of Gaunt had negotiated the French marriage, which was in itself unpopular; he had obtained the cession of Aquitaine as a principality for himself, to the disinheritance of the crown of England. In the Beauforts too, the duke's newly legitimised family, Gloucester saw another obstacle between himself and the crown which he coveted, and he began, or was believed to have begun, to renew the schemes which he had suspended since 1389.

Extravagance at court.

The year 1397 began with omens unfavourable to peace. The parliament, which met on the 22nd of January and sat until the 12th of February [1], showed itself sufficiently obsequious. It accepted the legitimation of the Beauforts, which Richard declared himself to have enacted as 'entier emperour de son roialme;' and granted to the king tunnage and poundage for three years, and the custom on wool for five years to come. But a bill was laid before the commons, accepted by them and exhibited to the lords, which contained a bold attack on the administration, and, in fact, on the king himself. In this four points were noted [2]; the sheriffs and escheators were not, as the law directed, persons of sufficient means, and were continued in office for more than a year; the marches of Scotland were insufficiently defended; the abuses of livery and maintenance were very prevalent; last and worst was the condition of the royal household: a multitude of bishops possessing lordships were maintained by the king with their retinues, and a great number of ladies and their attendants lived in the king's lodgings and at his cost. Richard heard of this, and on the 2nd of February sent for the lords [3]; the question of the sheriffs he said might be argued; his opinion was that hew as

Parliament of January, 1397.

Bill of complaints.

Richard's answer to the bill.

[1] Lords' Report, i. 496; Rot. Parl. iii. 337. The Convocation of Canterbury met Feb. 19, that of York Feb. 26, and granted a half-tenth; Wake, p. 324.

[2] Rot. Parl. iii. 340. The sums paid to the bishops and others for their attendance at court were an important item in the accounts of Edward III; see Household Ordinances, p. 9.

[3] Rot. Parl. iii. 338, 339; 407, 408.

more likely to be wisely, boldly and honestly served by men who had more time to learn their duties, and who felt in their hold of office strong enough to defy mere local influences. The defence of the marches must be considered. The question of livery he did not discuss; but the fourth article was most offensive: he was king of England by lineal right of inheritance and determined to maintain the rights and liberties of his crown; he was grieved that the commons who were his lieges should 'misprise and take on themselves any ordinance or governance of the person of the king or his hostel or of any persons of estate whom he might be pleased to have in his company.' By his direction[1] the lords were to inform the commons of the offence that they had given, and the duke of Lancaster was charged to obtain from the Speaker the name of the member who had brought forward the last article. The commons, through their Speaker Sir John Bussy, gave up the name of Sir Thomas Haxey[2], a prebendary of Southwell and an agent of the earl of Nottingham: his bill was laid before the king, and was found to contain a prayer that the bishops might dwell on their estates and not at court, both for the relief of the king and for the 'help and salvation of their subjects;' and that consideration might be given to the fact that the pope during the preceding year had exacted from the clergy of the province of Canterbury a tax of fourpence in the pound[3],

He demands the name of the proposer.

[1] Compare the action of Edward I in the case of Keighley; above, p. 158.

[2] There is a full account of Haxey in Raine's Fabric Rolls of York Minster, pp. 203–206. He was no doubt a clergyman, canon of Lichfield, Lincoln, Howden, Southwell, and afterwards of York, Ripon, and Salisbury, but, as his name does not appear in any return of the elections to this parliament, it must be supposed that he was a proctor of the clergy in attendance under the praemunientes clause, and therefore, according to the rehearsal of convocation in 1547, 'adjoined and associate with the lower House of Parliament;' Burnet, Hist. Ref. ii. 47, App. p. 117. Sir Thomas Haxey and Sir William Bagot were appointed attorneys or proxies for the earl of Nottingham for a year, Oct. 3, 1396; Rymer, vii. 844; cf. Christian's Blackstone, i. 173, n. 27. But as Nottingham was himself present in the parliament, Haxey could not have been acting as his proxy; Rot. Parl. iii. 343. He was also in 1418 Treasurer of York, and his tomb is still in the minster.

[3] This grant is ascribed to the influence of archbishop Courtenay, who died July 31, 1396. See Ann. Ricardi, p. 116: Wals. ii. 218.

contrary to the prerogative of the crown and the rights of the clergy and commons[1]. The commons in the humblest manner entreated the king to excuse them for their part in the matter: they had no wish to offend the king; the cognisance of such matters as the number of lords and ladies at court they knew appertained not to them but to the king himself and his ordinance. The lords declared that any one who stirred up the commons to demand such a reform ought to be treated as a traitor[2]. Richard accepted the apology, but Haxey was adjudged in parliament to die as a traitor. Archbishop Arundel saved him by claiming him as a clergyman, and he was shortly after pardoned.

Apology of the commons.

Haxey, the proposer of the bill, pardoned.

Withdrawal of Gloucester and Arundel from court.

This occurrence contributed no doubt to increase the king's excitement, and when the earls of Arundel and Gloucester withdrew, as they shortly did, from the court, after a personal altercation with him, in which his uncle reproached him for his indolence[3], he determined to forestall any designs which they might have against him. The old Gloucester party of opposition was broken up already: the earl of Derby was at court, obedient to his father and on good terms with his cousin; Nottingham was governor of Calais and in favour; he had moreover quarrelled with Warwick about his Welsh estates[4]. But Gloucester, Arundel and Warwick, were supposed to be acting together. And Richard was informed by Nottingham that at Arundel they had formed a formidable conspiracy against him. He determined to anticipate them, and invited them to a royal banquet on the 8th of July[5]. Gloucester made the excuse of

[1] Haxey's bill is given in full in Richard's pardon, which was granted on the 27th of May; Rot. Parl. iii. 407, 408.

[2] 'Per dominos dicti parliamenti per assensum nostrum adjudicatum fuit et declaratum quod si aliquis, cujuscunque status seu conditionis fuerit, moverit vel excitaverit communes parliamenti aut aliquam aliam personam, ad faciendum remedium sive reformationem alicujus rei quae tangit nostram personam, vel nostrum regimen aut regalitatem nostram, teneretur et teneatur pro proditore;' Rot. Pat. 20 Rich. II; Rot. Parl. iii. 408.

[3] Mon. Evesh. p. 129; Chron. de la Trahison, p. 4. The surrender of Brest to the duke of Brittany, and of Cherbourg to the king of Navarre, with the return of the garrisons, caused the reproach; see Privy Council Proceedings, i. 93.

[4] Lands in Gower: this is one of the many minute coincidences of the fall of Richard II with that of Edward II. See above, p. 362.

[5] Ann. Ricardi, ed. Riley, p. 201; Mon. Evesh. p. 129.

ill-health, Arundel sent no excuse at all; only Warwick attended, and he was arrested. The order for the arrest was given by the advice of the earls of Rutland, Kent, Huntingdon, Nottingham, Somerset, and Salisbury, Thomas le Despenser and the under-chamberlain, William le Scrope: this was declared by Richard in giving notice of the arrest, July 15, to the sheriffs[1]. Whether the absence of Gloucester and Arundel saved them from arrest, or so alarmed the king that he hastily determined to arrest Warwick, is uncertain: Richard's violence however really justified their caution. A few hours afterwards, Arundel having, as his brother declared, obtained from Richard a promise that he should suffer no bodily harm, surrendered, and the same night[2] the king, with his half-brother the earl of Huntingdon, the earl of Kent his nephew, Rutland his cousin, and Nottingham, went down to Pleshy and seized the duke of Gloucester, who was forthwith sent in custody to Calais. Having done this, Richard prepared to meet his parliament, the writs for which were issued on the 18th of July[3]. At a gathering of his partisans at Nottingham it was arranged on the 5th of August[4] that the prisoners should be appealed of treason, for the acts done in 1387 and 1388, by the eight lords on whose advice Richard had acted in ordering the arrest. Of these Nottingham, himself one of the former appellants, was the chief; the earls of Rutland and Somerset were sons of the dukes of York and Lancaster, the earls of Kent and Huntingdon were nephew and brother of the king; the earl of Salisbury, the lord le Despenser and Sir William le Scrope were the most trusted of his personal friends[5]. For fear of a popular rising, an army was levied in Cheshire and other royalist counties. The parliament, which was elected under the king's undisguised influence, met at Westminster on the 17th of September.

Richard arrests Warwick.

Arundel surrenders.

Gloucester arrested.

Measures for a new appeal.

Parliament, Sept. 17, 1397.

The king's proceedings in this parliament[6] show that, how-

[1] Rymer, viii. 7; cf. Ann. Ricardi, p. 206.

[2] Ann. Ricardi, pp. 202, 203; Chronique de la Trahison, pp. 6–9; where however dates are hopelessly confused.

[3] Lords' Report, iv. 758, 759.

[4] Ann. Ricardi, p. 207; Rot. Parl. iii. 374.

[5] Ann. Ricardi, p. 207.

[6] Rot. Parl. iii. 347 sq.; Ann. Ricardi, p. 208; Chron. de la Trahison, pp. 9 sq.; Chron. Ad. Usk (ed. Thompson), pp. 9 sq.

ever we may be inclined to account for the temerity of his design by mental excitement or passion, every step of the great constitutional change which he contemplated was carefully taken, with cautious reference to precedent and respect to the formal rights of the estates. The king's agents in the house of commons were Sir John Bussy the speaker, Sir Henry Green, and Sir William Bagot [1]. The chancellor declared in his opening speech that the cause of summons was to establish the king in his rights and to consult on the revocation of all measures by which those rights were diminished. On the second day the speaker on behalf of the commons prayed that the estate of the clergy might appoint a proctor to act in their stead in the trials for treason, that the proceedings might not hereafter be annulled, as had occurred sometimes, by reason of their absence or abstention [2]. This was done; Sir Thomas Percy was chosen, and on the third day the business began. After obtaining from the prelates an admission that statutes and charters issued on compulsion might be revoked [3], the king, with the assent of the lords spiritual and temporal and the proctors of the clergy, and at the request of the commons, repealed the statute or commission of 1386 and the pardons issued in 1388 and 1394 to Gloucester, Arundel, and Warwick [4]. They therefore were now responsible for all their early offences. On the 20th the commons impeached the archbishop of Canterbury [5], and on the 25th he was

Elaborate preparations made by Richard.

Proposal to revoke measures prejudicial to the king's rights.

Sir Thomas Percy made proctor for the clergy.

Repeal of the pardons of the appellants of 1388.

Impeachment of the archbishop.

[1] Ann. Ricardi, p. 20; Pol. Poems, i. 363–366, 367. The two parliaments of 1397 contain 47 names in common.

[2] Rot. Parl. iii. 348: 'Les prelatz et le clergie ferroient un procuratour, avec poair sufficeant pur consenter en lour noun as toutz choses et ordenances a justifiers en cest present parlement . . .' The nomination was made by the lords spiritual, and declared by the two archbishops in the name of the prelates and clergy of the two provinces 'jure ecclesiarum nostrarum et temporalium earundem habentes jus interessendi in singulis parliamentis domini nostri regis,' &c. The king refused to allow the words 'salvis ecclesiae sanctae privilegiis et libertatibus quibuscunque;' Ann. Ric. p. 212. The continuator of the Eulogium complains that the parliament acted 'non secundum legem Angliae sed secundum civilia jura;' iii. 173.

[3] Archbishop Arundel alone denied this; Ann. Ricardi, p. 211.

[4] Rot. Parl. iii. 350; Eulog. iii. 376.

[5] Rot. Parl. iii. 351. The archbishop was warned by the king through the bishop of Carlisle not to appear again; Mon. Evesh. p. 134. See also Ann. Ric. p. 213; Ad. Usk, pp. 10, 11

sentenced to banishment. On the 21st the appellants laid their accusation in due form before the lords; the earl of Arundel was accused first; he answered the charges with more passion than discretion, giving the lie to the duke of Lancaster and the earl of Derby, insisting on the validity of his pardon, and declaring that the house of commons was packed: 'the faithful commons of the realm are not here[1].' Richard reminded him how himself and the queen had interceded in vain for Burley; John of Gaunt, as high steward, declared the verdict and the barbarous sentence, which the king commuted for simple beheading, and the sentence was executed the same day. Gloucester was next attacked, but he was not forthcoming. On the 24th it was declared that Gloucester was dead at Calais. Before his death he had confessed his treason, and death did not save him from the sentence[2]. On the 28th Warwick was tried. Unlike Arundel, he confessed his crime, and named Gloucester as the chief leader of the conspiracy. He was condemned to perpetual imprisonment[3]. These were the chief victims; orders were given for the arrest of the lord Cobham and Sir Thomas Mortimer. The parliament moreover defined the four articles of treason to be, to compass and purpose the king's death or his deposition, or the surrender of the liege homage due to him, and to levy war against him[4]. The usual precautions were taken to secure that the sentences should not be revoked, and declarations of innocence were made in favour of the other members of the commission of 1386, and of the earls of Nottingham and Derby the remaining two of the appellants.

Trial of the earl of Arundel.

Gloucester accused in his absence.

His death.

Trial of Warwick.

Definition of treason.

It is impossible not to pity the fate of Arundel and Gloucester, condemned practically without a hearing for offences committed ten years before; but they had shed the first blood,

[1] Mon. Evesh. pp. 136–138; Rot. Parl. iii. 377; Ann. Ricardi, pp. 214, 215; Eulog. iii. 375; Ad. Usk, pp. 12, 13.

[2] Rot. Parl. iii. 378; Rymer, viii. 16. The blame of Gloucester's death or murder was laid on the king. It is not clear that he was murdered; if he was, the guilt must be shared between Richard and the earl of Nottingham.

[3] Rot. Parl. iii. 379; Ann. Ricardi, pp. 219, 220; Mon. Evesh. p. 140.

[4] Statutes, ii. 98; Rot. Parl. iii. 351; Mon. Evesh. p. 143.

and they reaped as they had sown. On the 29th of September the lords who had lent themselves to Richard's design received as their reward a step in the ranks of peerage. The earl of Derby was made duke of Hereford, the earl of Rutland duke of Aumâle, the two Hollands dukes of Surrey and Exeter, the earl of Nottingham duke of Norfolk, the earl of Somerset marquess of Dorset, le Despenser earl of Gloucester, Neville earl of Westmoreland, Sir Thomas Percy earl of Worcester, and Sir William le Scrope earl of Wiltshire [1]. The same day the parliament was adjourned to Shrewsbury, for the 28th of January; and on the 30th, after a solemn oath taken in the name of the three estates before the shrine of S. Edward, for the maintenance of the acts of the session, the members departed. The oath bound them to sustain in every way the statutes, establishments, ordinances, and judgments made in the present parliament, not to contravene any of them, and not to repeal, reverse, annul them, or suffer them to be so repealed, 'a vivre et murer; sauvant au roy sa regalie et liberte et le droit de sa corone;' this oath was in future to be taken before the lords had livery of their lands, and to be enforced with excommunication [2]. In the interval between the two sessions the pope was requested to confirm the acts of the parliament and to relieve the king from the claims of archbishop Arundel. Boniface IX showed himself as obsequious as Urban VI had been, and followed his example. Arundel was translated to S. Andrew's as Neville had been in 1388, and the king's treasurer, Roger Walden, was appointed in his place [3].

Reward of the king's supporters.

Creation of dukes and earls.

Oaths taken to maintain the acts of the Parliament.

Translation of archbishop Arundel.

The parliament of Shrewsbury met on the 28th of January, 1398, and, although it sat only four days [4], it made Richard to

Parliament of Shrewsbury, Jan. 28, 1398.

[1] Rot. Parl. iii. 355. [2] Ibid. 352, 355; Eulog. iii. 377.

[3] Walden's bull of provision and every monument of his primacy were destroyed by Arundel after his restoration to the see of Canterbury; he bound himself, however, for the customary payments to the Apostolic Chamber, Nov. 8; Brady, Episcopal Succession, i. 1; he received his temporalities on the 21st of January, and his pall on the 17th of February from William of Wykeham; see Rymer, viii. 31; Lowth's Wykeham, p. 268. He held a convocation March 2, 1398, which granted a tenth and a half-tenth; that of York having on October 10 granted a half-tenth; Wake, pp. 326, 327.

[4] Rot. Parl. iii. 356 sq.

all intents and purposes an absolute monarch. The whole of the acts of the parliament of February, 1388, were, at the joint prayer of the new appellants and the commons, declared null, and the persons prejudiced by those acts were restored to all their rights; as a meet pendant to this the old statutes against the Despensers were repealed, and the new earl of Gloucester entered on his short-lived honours. The duke of Hereford received a new pardon; even Alice Perrers on her own petition had a promise of redress; and, finally, a general amnesty was issued. On the 31st the commons, by the assent of the lords spiritual and temporal, granted to the king a tenth and a fifteenth and half a tenth and fifteenth for the coming year and a half; but what was far more than this, and more than had ever been granted to any English king, the subsidy on wool, woolfells, and leather was granted for the term of the king's life[1].

Grant of customs for the king's life.

The powers of parliament delegated to a committee.

The last act of this suicidal parliament was to delegate their authority to eighteen members chosen from the whole body: ten lords temporal, of whom six were to be a quorum, two earls as proctors for the clergy, and six members of the house of Commons, three or four to be a quorum. This committee was empowered to examine, answer, and plainly determine not only all the petitions before the parliament and the matters contained in the same, but all other matters moved in the presence of the king, and 'all the dependences of those not determined,' as they should think best, by their good advice and discretion in this behalf, by authority of the said parliament[2]. For the former part of their commission, the determination of petitions already

[1] Rot. Parl. iii. 368. The grant on the wool is at the former rate with an addition of half a mark from aliens.

[2] 'De examiner, respondre et pleinement terminer si bien toutz les ditz petitions et les matiers comprisez en ycelles, come toutes autres matiers et choses moevez en presence du roy, et toutes les dependences d'icelles nient determinez, solonc ceo que meulx lour semblera par lour bon advys et discretion en celle partie, par auctorite du parlement;' Rot. Parl. iii. 368; cf. pp. 360, 369. On the statute roll, where the commission is quoted, the words are 'de examiner respoundre et pleinement terminer toutz les ditz peticions et les matiers contenuz en ycelles come leur meulx semblera,' &c.; Statutes, ii. 107. Richard was accused of falsifying the record: 'Rex fecit rotulos parliamenti pro voto suo mutari et deleri, contra effectum concessionis praedictae;' Rot. Parl. iii. 418; Ann. Ricardi, p. 222.

before the parliament, there was a precedent in the events of 1388[1], when on the petition of the commons a body of lords had been assigned to dispatch such business after the close of parliament. For the latter and larger function, there was no precedent in English history unless the parliamentary constitution of 1258 be regarded as such; and the nearest parallel in foreign states was the appointment in Scotland of Lords of Articles, who were commissioned to hold parliament for the three estates, a practice which had been in use since the year 1367. The committee, whatever may have been the secret of its origin, consisted of the dukes of Lancaster, York, Aumâle, Surrey, and Exeter, the marquess of Dorset, the earls of March, Salisbury, Northumberland, and Gloucester for the lords, the earls of Worcester and Wiltshire for the clergy, and John Bussy, Henry Green, John Russell, Richard Chelmswyk, Robert Teye, and John Golafre for the commons. All these were men whom the king believed to be devoted to his interests, and whom he had spared no pains to attach to himself. He held therefore his parliament in his own hand; he had obtained a revenue for life; he had procured from the estates a solemn recognition of the undiminished and indefeasible power of his prerogative, and from the pope, it was alleged, a confirmation of the acts of the

Precedent for this course.

Composition of the committee.

Completeness of the king's victory.

The extent of the concession is described by Gower:—

'Perprius obtentum semper sibi parliamentum,
Per loca conservat, in quo mala quaeque reservat;
Est ubi persona regis residente corona
Corpus praesenti, stat ibi vis parliamenti;
Sic ubicumque sedet praesentia regia laedet,
Quod nullus scivit sceleris quae facta subivit;'

and more intelligibly in prose, 'Nota qualiter rex subtili fraude concessum sibi obtinuit quod ubicumque sedere vellet cum certis personis sibi assignatis perprius inceptum continuare posset parliamentum;' Vox Clamantis, p. 410: cf. Eulog. iii. 377, 378.

[1] A precedent had been set in 1388 for the treatment of petitions which remained unanswered at the close of parliament, by a committee assigned: 'A notre seigneur le roi et son sage conseil supplient tous les seigneurs et communes de son roiaume d'Engleterre, qu'il soit ordeigne en cest present parlement, que toutes les billes especiales qui sont ou seront donez en cest parlement, qui ne purront estre endossez ou responduz devant le departir du parlement pour brieftee du temps, soient endose et responduz bien toust en apres par certeins seigneurs a ce assignez, et yce fait soit tenuz si forcible et si valable et de mesme l'effeit come autres billes en parlement et come cy faite en pleyn parlement et ensi soit fait en touz autres parlemenz en temps a venir;' Rot. Parl. iii. 256.

parliament. He had punished his enemies, and in the deposition of the archbishop had shown that there was no one strong enough to claim immunity from his supreme authority and influence. All this had been done apparently with the unanimous consent and ostensibly at the petition of the parliament, and it had been done, as compared with the work of the appellants, at very slight cost of blood. Whether the result was obtained by long waiting for an opportunity, by labour, and self-restraint and patience, combined with unscrupulous craft and unflinching promptitude of action, or whether it was, like the cunning of a madman, a violent and reckless attempt to surprise the unwary nation, conceived by an excited brain and executed without regard to the certainty of a reaction and retribution, it is hard to say. Neither documentary record, nor the evidence of writers, who both at the time and since the time have treated the whole series of phenomena with no pretence of impartiality, enables us to form a satisfactory conclusion. Richard fared ill at the hands of the historians who wrote under the influence of the house of Lancaster, and he left no posterity that could desire to rehabilitate him. His personal character is throughout the reign a problem; in the earlier years because it is almost impossible to detect his independent action, and in the later ones because of its surprising inconsistencies; and both earlier and later because where we can read it it seems so hard to reconcile with the recorded impression of his own contemporaries. Such as he was, however, he made himself absolute.

Richard's manipulation of the parliament.

Historical difficulties.

Significance of the crisis.

Richard's grand stroke of policy, viewed apart from the question of punishing Gloucester and Arundel, has a remarkable significance. It was a resolute attempt not to evade but to destroy the limitations which for nearly two centuries the nation, first through the baronage alone and latterly through the united parliament, had been labouring to impose upon the king. Like Henry III and Edward I, believing in the rules of casuistry which the age accepted, he refused to regard himself as bound by promises which he had given on compulsion; but he went much further, and stated in its broadest form, and obtained the consent of the nation to the statement, that his

Richard aimed at absolutism to be acknowledged by the nation.

royal power was supreme. He condescended to no petty illegalities, but struck at once at the root of constitutional government. And notwithstanding the comparative moderation of his rule during the eight years of civil peace, it is clear that he maintained in theory as well as in practice the principle on which he afterwards acted. No king urged so strongly the right of hereditary succession; no king maintained so openly the extreme theory of prerogative[1]. The countless references to the 'regalie,' in the parliamentary records of the reign, prove that Richard was educated in, and determined to realise, the highest doctrine of prerogative. He challenged the determination of his people in the most open way. Strangely enough, the challenge was accepted and the issue decided by men who worked out the result almost unconsciously. The boldness of Richard's assumptions was equalled by the obsequiousness of the parliament.

Richard's high theory of royal authority.

Only one little cloud was on the horizon,—the quarrel between Hereford and Norfolk, the two chief survivors of the appellants, the representatives of the two great names, Bohun and Bigod, which had always been found hitherto on the same side in the struggles of the constitution. Both had deserted the cause which they had so ardently maintained, and possibly a common consciousness of wrong-doing may have inspired them with mutual distrust. As they were riding between Brentford and London, in December 1397, words passed between them which were reported to the king. Hereford, by the king's order, laid the statement before the parliament. He told his story at full length: the duke of Norfolk had said that the king intended to destroy both Henry and his father; Hereford alleged the pardon which had just before been granted; Norfolk replied that the king was not to be believed on his oath. This was done on the 30th of January, 1398[2]; and after the par-

Quarrel between the dukes of Hereford and Norfolk.

[1] On the history of his deposition there is a remarkable poem, 'Richard the Redeless,' written most probably by Langland, the author of the Vision of Piers Plowman, in Political Poems, i. 368–417; and, ed. Skeat, 1886, pp. 603–628.

[2] Rot. Parl. iii. 382. Cf. Mon. Evesh. p. 145; Chronique de la Trahison, pp. 12 sq.; Eulog. iii. 379.

liament at Shrewsbury the two dukes met in Richard's presence at Oswestry, on the 23rd of February. There Norfolk gave Hereford the lie: the quarrel was then referred by the committee of parliament, which met on the 19th of March at Bristol[1], to a court of chivalry at Windsor, which determined on the 28th of April that it should be decided by combat at Coventry on the 16th of September. This decision Richard forbade, and thinking it perhaps a favourable opportunity for ridding himself of both, compelled them to swear to absent themselves from England—Hereford for ten years and Norfolk for life. They obeyed the award, which was confirmed by the committee of parliament, and Norfolk died a few months after. In January, 1399, John of Gaunt died, and, although the duke of Hereford had had special leave to appoint a proxy to receive his inheritance, Richard, still acting with the committee of parliament, on the 18th of March[2] annulled the letters patent by which that leave was given, took possession of the Lancaster estates, and thus threw into open enmity the man who but for the existence of the earl of March would have been his presumptive heir. Hereford, seeing himself thus treated, conceived himself freed from his oath, and, although he had bound himself by another oath to hold no communication with the exiled archbishop Arundel[3], at once opened negotiations with him. Arundel was no more inclined than the duke to content himself with his humiliation. He had visited the pope at Florence, and obtained from him a confession that he had never in his life repented so bitterly for anything as for his deposition of the archbishop[4];

Their quarrel discussed before the king.

Banishment of the two dukes.

Death of John of Gaunt.

Richard takes possession of his estates.

Negotiation between Arundel and Hereford.

[1] Rot. Parl. iii. 383. The story is very differently given in the Chronique de la Trahison, in which everything is made to turn on the history of Brest, Cherbourg, and Calais.

[2] Rot. Parl. iii. 372. See Rymer, viii. 49, 51. [3] Rot. Parl. iii. 383.

[4] 'Littera Thomae Arundel archiepiscopi missa ad conventum Cantuariensem et subscripta manu propria, ex Paradiso terrestri prope Florentiam quando erat in exilio: Cum in Romanam curiam pervenissem favorem reperi penes dominum nostrum summum pontificem sacrumque collegium cardinalium quantum nunquam cogitare potui vel speravi. Siquidem vero inter alia verbum apostolicum erat, se nullius rei quam post assumptionem suam fecerat tantam poenitentiam concepisse, quantam ex dispositione quam de me fecerat sapiebat; de rebus enim meis ut spero longe melius quam credatur a malevolis disponetur;' MS. Reg. Eccl. Cantuar. Printed in full in Literae Cantuarienses, ii. 70 sq.

he had found that at the papal court no obstacle to his restoration would be raised, and, calculating securely on an opportunity which Richard sooner or later was certain to give, he waited his time. The opportunity was given when Henry, the heir of Lancaster, was disinherited; and, when Richard left England to pay a long visit to Ireland, the time was come.

Richard goes to Ireland.

Landing of Henry of Lancaster.

Richard went to Ireland at the end of May, 1399 [1], leaving his uncle Edmund duke of York as regent. Henry landed in Yorkshire on the 4th of July, and the external features of the revolution in 1326 at once repeated themselves. Again the cause is the wrong done to Lancaster, again the invader marches westward, and as his prospect of success increases his pretensions expand; again the northern lords, now especially the Percies and the Nevilles, throw in their lot with him; again the king is wanting at the crisis, and when he is found has lost all nerve and power to meet it [2]; and again Bristol is the point aimed at by the invaders, and its capture marked by the shedding of noble blood. On the 27th of July the regent himself joined Henry [3]. Archbishop Arundel returned and began forthwith to act as chancellor. Bristol was taken, and on the 29th of July the earl of Wiltshire, with Bussy and Green, underwent the fate of Hugh le Despenser. Meanwhile Richard had landed in Wales. He saw at once that all was over, and made no attempt to stem the tide of desertion and ingratitude. After a conference held at Conway with the earl of Northumberland and archbishop Arundel, in which he offered to resign the crown [4], he joined the duke of

Success of the invasion.

Return of Arundel.

Richard lands and submits.

[1] May 29; Chron. de la Trahison, p. 28.

[2] Ann. Ricardi, p. 246. Bishop le Despenser of Norwich, Sir William Elmham, Walter Boterley, Laurence Drew, and John Golafre alone resisted. See Appendix E to the Chronique de la Trahison, p. 292; Mon. Evesh. p. 153.

[3] At Berkeley; Mon. Evesh. p. 152.

[4] On the 17th the king was visited by archbishop Arundel at Conway, and on the 19th he met the duke of Lancaster at Flint; Chron. de la Trahison, pp. 46 sq.; Ann. Ricardi, p. 249; Mon. Evesh. pp. 150 sq.; Eulog. iii. 382. Adam of Usk places the meeting at Conway on the 14th; p. 27. Richard demanded on his surrender assurance of safety for the dukes of Exeter, Aumâle, and Surrey, the earls of Salisbury and Gloucester, Thomas Merks bishop of Carlisle, and the clerk Maudelyn.

Lancaster at Flint, and went with him to Chester, whence on the 2nd of September he was brought to London. On the 19th of August the writs for a parliament to be held on the 30th of September were issued from Chester; the first writ being addressed to Arundel as archbishop, and attested by the king himself and the council. In the interval means were taken to make all secure, and Richard was placed in the Tower of London. The question was debated whether the throne should be vacated by resignation or by deposition; and it was determined that both expedients should be adopted. A committee of doctors and bishops was appointed to draw up articles of deposition and a statement of the claims of the successor. They fulfilled their charge with zeal; the articles were carefully elaborated, and a form of resignation was prepared for Richard's acceptance. Edmund of York, who on this one occasion comes forward as a politician, has the credit of proposing a plan which, under these complicated contrivances, should save the forms of the constitution. He proposed that before the parliament met the king should execute a formal act of resignation. Archbishop Arundel's objection, that in that case the parliament as soon as it met would be dissolved by the act of resignation, was met by the preparation of new writs to be issued on the day on which the resignation was declared, summoning the parliament to meet six days later[1]. Before the second summons was to come into force the revolution was accomplished.

Parliament summoned.

Plan of proceedings.

Double summons of parliament.

269. Richard executed the deed of resignation on the 29th of September[2]. Northumberland and Arundel had received his promise at Conway; Northumberland now demanded that he should fulfil it. He asked that Arundel and Lancaster should be summoned to his presence, and when they appeared he read a written form in which he absolved all his people from the oaths of fealty and homage and all other bonds of

Richard resigns.

Formal renunciation of the crown.

[1] Lords' Report, iv. 768. These writs must have been prepared in a great hurry, for one of them is addressed to Henry himself as duke of Lancaster: 'Rex carissimo consanguineo suo.'

[2] Ann. Ricardi, pp. 252, 253 sq.; Mon. Evesh. pp. 157 sq.; Twysden, cc. 2744 sq.; Wals. ii. 235 sq.

allegiance, royalty, and lordship by which they were bound to him, as touching his person; he renounced in the most explicit terms every claim to royalty in every form, saving the rights of his successors; he declared himself altogether insufficient and useless, and for his notorious deserts not unworthy to be deposed; and these concessions he swore not to contravene or impugn, signing the document with his own hand. He added that, if it were in his power to choose, the duke of Lancaster should succeed him; but, as the choice of a successor did not depend upon him, he made Scrope archbishop of York and John Trevenant bishop of Hereford his proctors, to present this form of cession to the assembled estates, and placed his royal signet on the duke's finger.

Richard's resignation.

He appoints proctors to present his resignation to the parliament.

On the morrow the parliament met in the great Hall at Westminster[1]. The duke of Lancaster was in his place; the throne was prepared but vacant. The archbishop of York delivered the deed of cession, which was read in Latin and English. The question was then put, should the resignation be accepted? Archbishop Arundel first, then the estates and the people present, declared assent. It was then determined to read in form the articles of objection against Richard, on the ground of which he had declared himself worthy of deposition. These had been drawn up by the committee of doctors and bishops, who had sat at Westminster during the last week to determine whether there were reasonable grounds for such an extreme proceeding[2]. First the coronation oath was recited; thirty-three counts of accusation followed, in

The resignation accepted, Sept. 30.

Articles of accusation against Richard.

[1] Rot. Parl. iii. 416 sq.; Ann. Ricardi, pp. 257 sq.

[2] Adam of Usk, the chronicler who tells us this, was himself a member of the commission: 'Item per certos doctores, episcopos et alios, quorum praesentium notator unus extiterat, deponendi regem Ricardum et Henricum Lancastriae ducem subrogandi materia, et qualiter et ex quibus causis, juridice committebatur disputanda. Per quos determinatum fuit quod perjuria, sacrilegia, sodomitica, subditorum exinanitio, populi in servitutem reductio, vecordia et ad regendum imbecillitas, quibus rex Ricardus notorie fuit confectus, per capitulum "Ad Apostolicae" (extr. *de re judicata* in Sexto) cum ibi notatis, deponendi Ricardum causae fuerant sufficientes; et licet cedere paratus fuerat, tamen ob causas praemissas ipsum fore deponendum cleri et populi auctoritate, ob quam causam tunc vocabantur, pro majori securitate fuit determinatum;' p. 29.

which the wrong-doings of the reign were circumstantially recounted. The first seven concern the old quarrel, the royalist 'conventiculum' or plot of 1387, the tampering with the judges, the revolt of Robert de Vere, the revocation of the pardons of the appellants, and the preliminary and consequent acts of violence and injustice. Others declare Richard's injustice and faithlessness to Henry of Lancaster and archbishop Arundel; (9) he had forbidden any one to intercede for the duke, (11) he had illegally exiled him, and (12) had deprived him of his inheritance; the archbishop (30) had been sentenced to exile and (33) had been shamelessly deceived by the king with promises of safety at the very moment that he was plotting his humiliation. Shameless dissimulation practised generally (25) and especially towards the duke of Gloucester (32), whom he had solemnly sworn not to injure, is the burden of two distinct articles. The recent violent infractions of the constitution are enumerated: the delegation of the powers of the parliament to a committee of the estates, the interpolation of the record of parliament, and the fraudulent use of that (8) delegation to engross the entire authority in his own hands, (17) the procuring of a petition of the commons for the assertion of the prerogative, (28) the imposition of the oaths to sustain the acts of the parliaments of 1397 and 1398, the (19) tampering with elections by nominating the knights whom the sheriffs were to return in order to secure himself a revenue for life, and (10) the degradation of the realm by applying to the pope for a confirmation of those acts[1]. The old constitutional grievances reappear; Richard had (15) alienated the crown estates, and exacted unlawful taxes and purveyances; he had (13) interfered in the appointment of sheriffs, (18) had allowed them to remain more than a year in office, and had (20) imposed on them a new oath binding them to arrest any who

His action in 1387.

His injustice to Lancaster and Arundel.

His treatment of Gloucester.

His infractions of the constitution.

The old abuses of prerogative.

[1] 'Item quamvis corona regni Angliae et jura ejusdem coronae, ipsumque regnum, fuerint ab omni tempore retroacto adeo libera quod dominus summus pontifex nec aliquis alius extra regnum ipsum se intromittere debeat de eisdem, tamen praefatus rex ad roborationem statutorum suorum erroneorum supplicavit domino papae quod statuta in ultimo parliamento suo ordinata confirmaret;' Rot. Parl. iii. 419.

should speak evil of his royal person; he had used the courts of the household (27) for purposes of oppression, had (29) checked the ecclesiastical courts by prohibitions, and had (23) by personal violence tried to constrain the action of the judges. His pecuniary transactions were indefensible; he had (21) extorted money from seventeen whole shires for pretended pardons[1]; (14) he had not repaid loans made in dependence on his most solemn promises; he had (22) compelled the religious houses to furnish him with horses, carriages, and money for his visit to Ireland; and (24) had carried off thither the jewels of the crown. His rash words were the ground of other charges: he had said (16) that his laws were in his own mouth and often in his own breast, and that he alone could change and frame the laws of the kingdom; and (26) that the life of every liegeman, his lands, tenements, goods, and chattels lay at his royal will without sentence of forfeiture; and he had acted upon the saying. Not content with overthrowing the laws during his life, and binding his people by oath to acquiescence, he had tried to secure the same result after his death[2], (31) by leaving in his will the whole residue of his estate to his successor with the proviso that, if the statutes of 1397 were not kept, it should go to four of his friends, who were to reserve five or six thousand marks for the maintenance of those iniquitous acts[3].

Richard's illegal taxation.

His claim to make laws; his assertion that the goods of his subjects were his own.

The directions in his will.

This long list of charges having been read, the estates voted that they formed a sufficient ground[4] for deposing the king, and appointed seven commissioners to execute the sentence.

The parliament proceeds to depose him.

[1] This was done in 1399 after Easter; the sums so raised were called 'le Plesaunce;' Ann. Ricardi, p. 235; Wals. ii. 230. The monk of Evesham places it at Michaelmas, 1398; p. 147. See too Eulog. iii. 378.

[2] His will is printed in Rymer, viii. 75–77.

[3] The monk of Evesham points the moral, which is indeed unmistakeable, 'Qui gladio percutit, gladio peribit;' he adds the usual reference to Rehoboam, 'quia spreto antiquorum procerum consilio juvenibus adhaerebat;' p. 169. See above, p. 383.

[4] Rot. Parl. iii. 422: 'videbatur omnibus statibus illis superinde singillatim ac etiam communiter interrogatis, quod illae causae criminum et defectuum erant satis sufficientes et notoriae ad deponendum eundem regem . . . omnes status praedicti unanimiter consenserunt ut ex abundanti ad depositionem dicti regis procederetur.'

Sentence pronounced, Sept. 30, 1399.

One of these, bishop Trevor of S. Asaph, in the name of the rest[1] read a written sentence, pronouncing Richard to be useless, incompetent, altogether insufficient and unworthy, and therefore deposing him from all royal dignity and honour. The same commissioners were chosen to bear to Richard the renunciation of homage and fealty, and the definitive sentence of deposition.

Henry claims the crown.

Then Henry of Lancaster rose and stood forward; signing himself with the cross on his forehead and breast, he claimed in an English speech[2] the kingdom of England and the crown as descended in the right line of descent from Henry III, and as sent by God to recover his right when 'the realm was in point to be undone for default of governance and undoing of the good laws.' The whole assembly assented at once to the proposal that the duke should reign over them. Archbishop Arundel led him by the right hand to the throne, and then, assisted by Scrope, archbishop of York, seated him upon it. Thus the revolution was accomplished.

The claim as the heir of Lancaster.

In the form of words used on these great critical occasions there is often something that strikes the mind as conveying more than the speaker could have conceived. So it is with the claim of Henry of Lancaster to the throne of Henry III. To him it probably was merely an expedient, which his hearers were not likely to criticise, to avoid the mention of Edward III or Richard, whose direct heir he could not declare himself to be, so long as the line of Lionel of Clarence existed: and he may have thus chosen to countenance that false rumour which his followers had spread abroad, that Edward I had supplanted Edmund of Lancaster who was, they said, the elder brother, and the rightful heir of Henry III[3]. Henry by his mother repre-

False statement.

[1] The seven were the bishop of S. Asaph, the abbot of Glastonbury, the earl of Gloucester, Thomas lord Berkeley, Sir Thomas Erpingham, Sir Thomas Gray, and Sir William Thirning. Gloucester (le Despenser) was one of the men for whose safety Richard had specially treated when he surrendered.

[2] Rot. Parl. iii. 423; Ann. Ricardi, p. 281; Twysden, c. 2760.

[3] See above, p. 513. We learn from Adam of Usk (Chron. p. 29) that the committee of doctors, bishops, and others which sat to determine the question of Henry's right to the throne, discussed the pretended claim of

sented that line of Lancaster; so that, even if John of Gaunt had been a changeling, his title of Lancaster could not have been impugned. But although this was a mere fabrication, and Henry's possible appeal to it an act unworthy of a king, it was true that as the heir of Lancaster, and by taking up the principles for which Thomas of Lancaster was believed to have contended, he made good his claim. The name of the martyr of Pomfret had been revived, and made a watchword with the faithful commons: his canonisation had been again broached, and his shrine had streamed forth with fresh blood. The end was now accomplished; and his heir had entered on the inheritance of his murderer. The forces trained and concentrated for the purpose of freeing the realm from a tyranny of royalty, scarcely more hateful than the tyranny of oligarchy which would have superseded it, were at last employed and found sufficient to bring in, with a new dynasty, a theory and practice of government not indeed new, but disentangled from much that was old and pernicious. Henry IV, coming to the throne as he did, made the validity of a parliamentary title indispensable to royalty; and Richard II, in vacating the throne, withdrew the theory, on which he had tried to act and by which he had been wrecked, of the supremacy of prerogative.

Vindication of the principles attributed to Thomas of Lancaster.

The political party founded by earl Thomas brings in the Lancastrian dynasty.

There can be little doubt that the proceedings of 1394 and 1398 were the real causes of Richard's ruin; and that the personal wrongs of Lancaster were subsidiary only, although they furnished the opportunity and instrument of the overthrow. Later events proved that the sway of Lancaster was not by itself welcome. Only the certainty that Richard was insupportable could have created the unanimous consent that he should be rejected. He had resolutely, and without subterfuge or palliation, challenged the constitution. Although the issue was deferred for a few months, the nation accepted it as soon as a

The personal wrongs of Henry gave the opportunity for the revolution.

the house of Lancaster. According to the statement of the earl of Northumberland preserved by Hardyng (Chr. p. 352), this claim was on the 21st of September rejected by the council, but was notwithstanding asserted by Henry on the 30th. See however below, vol. iii. p. 11.

Richard was not friendless. leader appeared, and the struggle was over in a moment. Yet Richard had many friends; there was not in his fall the bitterness that is so distinct a feature in the fall of Edward II. Henry was not at this period of his life, what perhaps the hazardous character of his success made him, a bitter or cruel man. He had interfered in 1388 to save sir Simon Burley, he would now perhaps have been content to be duke of Lancaster if Richard would have suffered him. And the darkness that hangs over Richard's end does not conclusively condemn his successor. But, unless we are to believe one curious story of a parliamentary discussion, not one friend said a word for Richard; although many died afterwards for his sake, none spoke for him at the time. Northumberland and Scrope presently paid with their blood the penalty of resisting Henry IV, yet for the moment both had accepted him rather than Richard. **Speech attributed to bishop Merks.** One advocate, bishop Merks of Carlisle, whom the chroniclers describe as a boon companion of the king, is said upon foreign testimony to have spoken in his favour before the excited parliament, and he certainly lost his see immediately after, probably in consequence of his attachment to the king[1]. But this exception, if admitted, rather proves than disproves the general unanimity. Richard fell, not unpitied or undeserving of pity, but without help and without remedy.

Richard II as compared with Edward II. 270. It is usual to compare Richard II with Edward II, but it is perhaps more germane to our subject to view him side by side with Edward III, the magnanimous, chivalrous king who had left him heir to difficulties which he could not overcome and a theory of government which could never be realised. Edward II had no kingly aspirations, Richard had a very lofty idea of his dignity, a very distinct theory of the powers, of the

[1] The speech is given in the Chronique de la Trahison, pp. 70, 71. There is nothing intrinsically improbable in it, but the Chronique contains so much else that is at variance with our other authorities that it cannot be relied on at all. It is almost impossible that the speech should have been delivered in parliament; if there is any truth at all in the story, it must have been made in one of the preliminary consultations. See below, vol. iii. p. 10. Merks was translated after the accession of Henry from Carlisle to an island in the Archipelago, but he died rector of Todenham in Gloucestershire.

functions, and of the duties of royalty. It is true that they were both stay-at-home kings in an age which would tolerate royal authority only in the person of a warrior; but while Edward from idleness or indisposition for war stopped abruptly in the career which his father had marked out for him, when all chances were in his favour and one successful campaign might have given him peace throughout his reign, Richard during the time that he was his own master was bound by truces which honour forbade him to break, and if he had broken them would have had to contend with the opposition of a parliament always ready to agree that he should go to war, but never willing to furnish the means of waging war with a fair hope of victory. The legislation again of the reign of Richard is marked by real policy and intelligible purpose: Edward II can scarcely be said to have legislated at all: everything that is distinctive in the statutes of his reign was forced upon him by the opposition. Nor, singularly parallel as the circumstances of the deposition in the two cases were, can we overlook the essential difference, that the one was the last act of a drama the interest of which depends on mere personal questions, the other the decision of a great struggle, a pitched battle between absolute government and the cause of national right. The reign of Edward III was the period in which the forces gathered. The magnificence of an extravagant court, the shifty, untrustworthy statecraft of an unprincipled, lighthearted king, living for his own ends and recking not of what came after him, careless of popular sorrows unless they were forced upon him as national grievances, careless of royal obligation save when he was compelled to recognise it as giving him a claim for pecuniary support,—these formed the influences under which Richard was educated; and the restrictions of his early years caused him to give an exaggerated value to the theory which these influences had inculcated. Richard cannot be said to have been the victim of his grandfather's state policy, because he himself gave to the causes that destroyed him both their provocation and their opportunity; but he reduced to form and attempted to realise in their most definite form the principles upon which his grandfather had

Difference of their characters and circumstances.

Comparison of the two crises.

Relation of Richard II to Edward III.

Edward III and Richard II.

acted. Edward III was a great warrior and conqueror, the master of his own house and liable to no personal jealousies or rivalries in his own dominion; Richard was a peaceful king, thwarted at every turn of his reign by ambitious kinsmen. But Edward was content with the substance of power, Richard aimed at the recognition of a theory of despotism, and, as has so often happened both before and since, the assertion of principles brought on their maintainer a much severer doom than befell the popular autocrat who had practised them, however little he was loved or trusted.

CHAPTER XVII.

ROYAL PREROGATIVE AND PARLIAMENTARY AUTHORITY.

271. Questions of the existence of a political scheme.—272. The burden borne by the knights of the shire.—273. Antagonistic growth of royal assumption and popular claims.—274. The king should live of his own.—275. Limitation of his right of tallage.—276. Limitation of his right to exact custom.—277. Origin and growth of the Customs.—278. The king's power of borrowing, and system of loans.—279. Limitation of the right of Purveyance.—280. Limitation of the abuse of commissions of array.—281. Coinage.—282. Estimate of the king's revenue.—283. Attempts to limit the household expenses.—284. Restraints on the alienation of crown lands.—285. Compulsory economy at court.—286. Parliamentary checks on ministers; oaths, election, and account.—287. Appropriation of supplies.—288. Audit of accounts.—289. Restraint on the king's power of legislation.—290. Treatment of petitions.—291. Suspension of Statutes.—292. Legislation by ordinance.—293. Right of initiation, debate, and consent.—294. General power of deliberation exercised by the commons.—295. Interference with justice forbidden.—296. The king's power in the constitution of parliament.—297. Minor prerogatives.—298. Influence of the period on the character of the nation.

271. THE material elements of constitutional life are inherent in the nation itself, in its primitive institutions and early history. The regulative and formative influences have proceeded mainly from the authority of the kings, the great organisers of the Norman and early Plantagenet lines. The impulse and character of constitutional progress have been the result of the struggles of what may be termed the constitutional opposition.

Material, formal, and progressive elements of constitutional life.

It is so much easier, in discussing the causes and stages of a political contest, to generalise from the results than to trace the growth of the principles maintained by the actors, that the historian is in some danger of substituting his own formulated conclusions for the programme of the leaders, and of giving them credit for a far more definite scheme and more conscious

Scheme of progress.

Difficulty of detecting any definite scheme of constitutional progress.

political sagacity than they would ever have claimed for themselves. This is especially true with regard to the period which we have just traversed, a period of violent faction struggles, graced by no heroes or unselfish statesmen, yet at its close marked by very significant results. It is true, more or less, of the whole of our early history; the march of constitutional progress is so steady and definite as to suggest everywhere the idea that it was guided by some great creative genius or some great directive tradition. Yet it is scarcely ever possible to distinguish the creative genius; it is impossible to assign the work to any single mind or series of minds, and scarcely easier to trace the growth of the guiding tradition in any one of the particulars which it embodies. As in the training of human life, so in national history, opportunity is as powerful as purpose; and the new prospects, that open as the nation advances in political consciousness and culture, reveal occasions and modes of progress which, as soon as they are tried, are found to be more exactly the course for which earlier training has prepared it than any plan that might have been consciously formed.

How far were the actors in the drama conscious of their part?

As this is clear upon any reading of history, it must be allowed that some generalisation from results is indispensable: without it we could never reach the principles that underlie the varied progress, and history would be reduced to a mere chapter of accidents. But the questions remain unanswered how far the men who wrought out the great results knew what they were doing; had they a regular plan? was that plan the conception of any one brain? who were the depositaries of the tradition? had the tradition any accepted formula? The history of political design is not less interesting than the registration of results. We have seen that the great champions of the thirteenth century directed their efforts to the attainment of an ideal which they failed to realise, and that the overt struggles of the fourteenth century had their source and object in factious aims and factious divisions; that in the former the constitution grew rather according to the spirit of the liberators than on the lines which they had tried to trace; and in the latter its development was due to the conviction, common to all factions, that the nation in parliament was a convenient arbiter, if not the ultimate judge of their quarrels. There is this difference between the two: the former witnessed a real growth of national life, the latter a recognition of formal principles of government—principles which all parties recognised, or pretended, when it was convenient, to recognise. The thirteenth century had the spirit without the letter of the constitutional programme; the fourteenth had the letter with little of the spirit. Many of the principles that appear in the programme of the fourteenth existed in the minds of the heroes of the thirteenth: the idea of limiting royal power by parliaments, of controlling royal expenditure, of binding royal officials, of directing royal policy, was in the mind of the barons who worked with Simon de Montfort; very little of the spirit of the deliverer was in Thomas of Lancaster or Thomas of Woodstock. The peculiar work of Edward I had introduced into the national life the elements that gave form and attitude to political principle. By completing the constitution of parliament he perfected the instrument which had been wanting to Simon de Montfort; by completing administrative machinery he gave a tangible and visible reality to the system for the control of which the king and the parliament were henceforward to struggle. The effect of this on the design of the constitution was to substitute for the negative restrictions, by which the Provisions of Oxford had limited the royal authority, the directive principles which guided the national advance in the following century; and thus to set clearly before men's minds royal prerogative on the one hand and constitutional government on the other. Thus distinctly presented, the political formula was less dependent than it had been before upon individual championship; but it was more liable to be abused for personal and party ends.

Contrast between the thirteenth and fourteenth centuries.

The spirit and the letter.

Place of Edward I between the two.

Important bearing of his reign on constitutional consciousness.

272. If we ask who were the men or the classes of men who believed in as well as took advantage of the formula, now made intelligible and practical, the whole history of the fourteenth century supplies a harmonious answer. It was not men like Thomas of Lancaster; he used it because it had already

The battle of the commons fought by the knights of the shire.

Historical prominence of the knights.

become an influence which he could employ for his own purposes. It was not the clerical body generally, for they, although they supplied many supporters and workers, were hampered by their relations to the papacy, and were now losing that intimate sympathy with the nation which had given them their great position in the days of Langton. It was not the town communities, in which, beyond an occasional local tumult, the history of the age finds little to record; nor the great merchants who, for good or for evil, are found chiefly on the side of that royal authority which seemed to furnish the most certain guarantees of mercantile security and privilege. Both historical evidence and the nature of the case lead to the conviction that the victory of the constitution was won by the knights of the shires [1]; they were the leaders of parliamentary debate; they were the link between the good peers and the good towns; they were the indestructible element of the house of commons; they were the representatives of those local divisions of the realm which were coeval with the historical existence of the people of England, and the interests of which were most directly attacked by the abuses of royal prerogative. The history bears evidence of their weakness as well as of their strength, their shortcomings as well as their deserts; the manipulation of the county courts by the sheriffs could change the policy of parliament from year to year; the interest of the landowner predominates every now and then over the rights of the labourer and artisan. Yet on the whole there is a striking uniformity and continuity in the policy of the knights; even the packed parliaments are not without courage to remonstrate, and, when uninfluenced by leaders of faction, their voice is invariably on the side of freedom. They are very distinctly the depositaries of the constitutional tradition; and this fact is one of the most distinctive features of our political history, as compared with most other nations in which representative institutions have been tried with less success.

273. The growth of constitutional life is stimulated by the

[1] 'It is pretty manifest that the knights, though doubtless with some support from the representatives of towns, sustained the chief brunt of battle against the crown;' Hallam, Middle Ages, iii. 118.

growth of royal assumption. Royal prerogative during this century is put upon its defence and compelled to formulate its claims, reserving however a salvo of its own indefeasible omnipotence that will enable it to justify any amount of statecraft. If popular claims are now and then outrageously aggressive, it must be confessed that the history of prerogative is one long story of assumption and evasion: every concession is made an opportunity for asserting pretensions that may cover new usurpations, and the acceptance of such a concession is craftily turned into an assumed acquiescence in the supreme right which might withhold as easily as it gives. The history of the national growth is thus inseparable from the history of the royal prerogative, in the widest sense of that undefinable term; and for every assertion of national right there is a counter assertion of royal autocracy. On the one side every advantage gained by the parliament is regarded as one of a very limited number of privileges; on the other every concession made by the crown is made out of an unlimited and unimpaired potentiality of sovereignty. Thus it sometimes strikes the student that the theory and practice of the constitution vary inversely, and that royalty becomes in theory more absolute as in practice it is limited more and more by the national will: as the jealousy of parliamentary or ministerial interference becomes more distinctly felt, the claims of the king are asserted more loudly; the indefinite margin of his prerogative is extended more indefinitely as restraint increases; the sense of restraint compels the exaggeration of all royal attributes. The theory of sovereignty held by Henry III is far more definite than that of Henry II, and that of Richard II than that of Edward I.

Antagonistic growth of prerogative.

Mutual action of prerogative and popular pretension.

The principles of constitutional growth, as enunciated by the party opposed to royal assumption, may be arranged under a small number of heads; and the counter principles of prerogative may be ranged side by side with them; it being always understood that the prerogative is not limited by these assertions, but still possesses an inexhaustible treasury of evasion. That the king should 'live of his own,' supporting royal state and ordinary national administrative machinery out of

Programme of constitutional development.

Principles of the constitutional party.

ordinary revenue; that the laws should not be changed without the national consent; that the great charter should be kept inviolate and inviolable, not merely in the letter, but as a pregnant source of rights and principles; that the king's ministers are accountable to the nation for their disposal of national contributions, and for their general good behaviour; that grievances should be redressed before the money granted becomes payable; that the king should act by the counsel of his parliament, should not go to war, or attempt any great enterprise without its consent; and, if he withdrew himself from its advice and influence, should be constrained to do his duty;—such were some of the fundamental convictions of the national party.

Principles of the supporters of prerogative.

That the nation must provide for the royal necessities irrespective of the king's good behaviour, that the most binding part of the royal oath was to secure the indefeasibility of the king's authority, that the king being the supreme landowner had a heritable right over the kingdom, corresponding with that of the private landowner over his own estate; that as supreme lawgiver he could dispense with the observance of a statute, suspend its operation, pardon the offenders against it, alter its wording and annul it altogether; that in fact he might do everything but what he was bound not to do, and even repudiate any obligation which he conceived to militate against his theory of sovereign right;—such were the principles in which Richard II was educated, or such was his reading of the lessons taught by the reign of his grandfather.

The theory of prerogative must be judged by history.

Yet royal prerogative was not in its origin a figment of theorists. It grew out of certain conditions of the national life, some of which existed before the Norman Conquest, others were the products of that great change, and others resulted from the peculiar course of the reigns of Henry II and his descendants. The general results of the history of the fourteenth century may be best arranged with reference to this consideration. We must look at the original basis of each great claim made on behalf of the crown, the design adopted for its remedy and the steps by which this remedy was obtained; but, we must remember always that beyond the definite claims there extends the region of undefined prerogative, which exists in theory without doing harm to any but the kings themselves, but which, the moment they attempt to act upon it, involves suffering to the nation and certain if not speedy retribution to the rulers.

The king should live of his own.

274. The principle that the king should live of his own[1] had a double application: the sovereign who could dispense with taxation could dispense likewise with advice and co-operation; if his income were so large that he could conveniently live within it, his administration must be so strong as to override all opposition; if his economy were compulsory, his power would be strictly confined within limits, whether territorial or constitutional, which would make him, what many of the continental sovereigns had become in the decay of feudality, only the first among the many almost equal potentates who nominally acknowledged him as lord. The former alternative would have left him free to become a despot; the latter, although perhaps it was the ideal of a party among the feudal lords of the thirteenth century, was made impossible by circumstances, by the personal character and policy of nearly all the Plantagenet kings, by the absolute necessity of a consolidated and united national executive for purposes of aggression and defence, and by the existence in the nation itself of a spirit which would probably have preferred even a despotic monarch to the rule of a territorial oligarchy. No king of the race of Plantagenet ever attempted to make his expenditure tally with his ordinary income, and no patriotic statesman dreamed of dispensing altogether with the taxation, which gave to the nation an unvarying hold on the king whether he were good or bad. But the adjustment and limitation of taxation, the securing of the nation against the hardships which could not but follow from the impoverishment of the crown, and the enforcing of honest dealing in the raising and expenditure of money, formed a body of constitutional questions

Difficulties in the way of enforcement.

The source of constitutional struggles.

[1] The words of the 4th Ordinance of 1311, Statutes, i. 158, constantly recurring; e.g. 'Que notre seigneur le roi vive de soen;' Rot. Parl. 6 Edw. III. vol. ii. p. 166; 'viver deinz les revenues de votre roialme;' ibid. iii. 139.

the answer of which had to be worked out in the political struggles of two centuries.

Legislation of *Magna Carta* on taxation.

The great charter had seemed to give a firm basis on which a structure of limited monarchy might be raised, in the rule that the king might not impose any general tax without the consent of the nation, expressed by the common council of the tenants-in-chief; but that article had been allowed to drop out of the charter at its successive confirmations; and the real restraint of the taxing power of the crown was imposed by other means. The honesty of the early ministers of Henry III, and the weakness of his own personal administration, had made it impossible for him to act without the national consent; and under Edward I the power of consent was lodged in the hands of a parliament far more national in its character than the 'commune consilium' of the charter. Yet even the 'confirmatio cartarum' had left some loopholes which the king was far too astute to overlook, and which the barons must have known to be dangerous when they compelled him to renounce the general salvo in 1299 [1]. These were too tempting even for the good faith of Edward I; and his son and grandson took ample advantage both of the laxity of the law and of the precedents which he had created. One of the results of the reign of Richard II was the final closing of the more obvious ways of evading the constitutional restrictions; but the entire prevention of financial over-reaching on the part of the crown was not attained for many centuries; and successive generations of administrators developed a series of expedients which from age to age gave new name and form to the old evil.

Incompleteness of the limitations on the royal power of taxing.

Division of the subject.

The financial evasions of the period now before us may be referred to the head of direct taxation, customs, and the incurring of royal or national debt; closely connected with these as engines of oppression are the abuses of the royal right to purveyance, to pressed service of men and material, and to the ordering of commissions of array. The origin, the abuse, and the remedying of the abuse, of these devices, form an interesting portion of our national history, and as such they

[1] See above, p. 155.

have been noticed as they arose in the foregoing pages. A brief recapitulation of the main points is however necessary from the higher ground which we have now reached.

275. The right of the king to tallage his demesnes, whether cities, boroughs, or rural townships, was not abolished by the 'confirmatio cartarum' in terms so distinct as to leave no room for evasion. The word 'tallagium' was not used in the document itself, and the 'aides, mises et prises,' which were renounced, were in the king's view the contributions raised from the kingdom generally without lawful consent, not the exactions made by demesne right from the crown lands[1]. It might be pleaded on Edward's behalf that in that act he intended only to renounce that general and sovereign power of taxing the commons which he had attempted to exercise in 1297, and which was one cause of the rising to which he was compelled to yield; not to surrender the ordinary right which as a landlord he possessed over his demesne, or over those communities which had purchased the right of being called his demesne in order to avoid more irksome obligations[2]. And

The right to tallage demesne.

[1] This is not the view of Hallam, who argues as if the act 'de tallagio' were the authentic form of the concession, and as if the king had never tallaged any lands except demesne lands, so that only this right was now renounced. He thinks then that the right of tallage was expressly surrendered, and accuses the three Edwards of acting illegally in exacting it; Middle Ages, iii. 43. Unconstitutional the exaction certainly was, but not contrary to the letter of the law. He writes too as if he thought that these tallages were common, whereas there is but one instance in each reign. But Hallam's view of Edward I was, as he allows, influenced by that of Hume.

[2] The ancient demesne of the crown contributed to general taxation, together with the towns, in a larger proportion than the counties; paying a tenth, for instance, when the knights of the shires voted a fifteenth. Hence it was of some importance to the little country towns which enjoyed no particular privileges, to be taxed 'cum communitate comitatus,' and not with the towns; and even London itself did not despise the privilege, which it obtained by special charter from Edward III and Richard II; Liber Albus, i. 147, 167, 168. In the 19th of Edward II the men of Sevenhampton, Stratton, and Heyworth, in Wiltshire, proved to the king that, as they were not tenants in ancient demesne by Domesday, they ought not to be tallaged; Madox, Firma Burgi, p. 6. This record proves that Edward I and Edward II thought themselves justified in tallaging ancient demesne only. A very large portion of the boroughs were however in ancient demesne, and the sheriffs and judges probably gave the king the benefit of the doubt in all doubtful cases, e.g. 'in carta dicti prioris non fit aliqua mentio de tallagio; videtur consultius esse pro statu domini

Tallage of Edward I in 1304.

probably this view was shared by the magnates. When then, on the 6th of February, 1304, Edward ordered a tallage to be collected from his cities, boroughs, and lands in demesne, assessed, according to the historian, at a sixth of moveables, it is by no means clear that he acted in contravention of the letter of the law. From the extant rolls of this tallage it is clear that demesne only was tallaged[1]. In the parliament of 1305 no complaint was made against the measure, but the king, at the petition of the archbishops, bishops, prelates, earls, barons, and other good men of the land, granted them leave to tallage the ancient demesne that was in their hands as he had tallaged his own demesne[2]. The circumstances of the case are obscure; the accounts of Edward II show that in 1303 a scutage for the Scottish war was due, for which no parliamentary authority is producible, but against which no complaint was made. Possibly the tallage of 1304 was a supplementary measure to the scutage of 1303, both of them being the result of some deliberation, the history of which is lost.

Tallage of Edward II in 1312.

This tallage however of Edward I was an unfortunate precedent. In the sixth year of Edward II the example was followed; on the 16th of December, 1312, the very day on which the letters of safe-conduct were issued to the earl of Lancaster after Gaveston's murder, the king published an order for the collection of a fifteenth of moveables and a tenth of rent in his cities, boroughs, and demesne lands. The fact that the ordinances of 1311 had made no provision against such a tax, and that the writs for collection, which were issued on the last day of a parliament[3], make no mention of the authorisation of

regis in hac parte quod supradicti tenentes dicti prioris remaneant onerati versus dominum regem;' Madox, Firma, p. 248. The represented towns of course paid the larger rate in all cases, unless, like London, they could obtain special exception. Thus then the obligation to pay tallage, or the value of corporate privilege which was coincident with it, was the foundation of the difference of rate between the towns and the counties; and this may to some extent account for the general dislike of the small towns to send members to parliament.

[1] Hemingb. ii. 233; Rot. Parl. i. 266; Record Report, ii. app. ii. 139, 141. See too Morant, Hist. Colchester, p. 47.

[2] 'Antiqua dominica unde sunt in tenancia desicut rex dominica sua talliavit;' Rot. Parl. i. 161, 162; above, p. 163.

[3] Parl. Writs, II. ii. 59, 60, 61, 83–85; Liber Albus, i. 428.

the parliament, points to the conclusion that the tallage was not regarded as unlawful. But the lesson of the ordinances had already begun its work: the citizens of London and the burghers of Bristol resisted the impost. The latter, who refused to pay because some of their fellows were imprisoned in the Tower of London, were engaged in an internal quarrel which left them very much at the king's mercy; the former however made a firm stand. They granted that the king might at his will tallage his demesnes, cities, and boroughs, but they maintained that the citizens of London were not to be so tallaged, appealing to the clause of Magna Carta which guaranteed to them their ancient privileges. The chancellor had stated that the tallage was imposed by the king in the right of his crown, a distinct assertion of prerogative which the citizens did not contradict, and against which they would have cited the 'confirmatio cartarum,' if that act had been understood to apply to their case. Neither party however was in a position to take extreme measures, and the citizens by two loans, one of £1000 and one of £400, purchased a respite until the parliament of 1315; the loans were to be allowed in the collection of the next general aid, and the tallage was thus merged in the twentieth granted in the next parliament. Many other towns procured exemption[1] on the ground that they were not of ancient demesne; the scheme no doubt proved unprofitable, and no other tax of the kind was attempted during the remainder of the reign. Edward III however, in 1332, revived the impost in exactly the same form. The letters for the collection were issued on the 25th of June[2]; the parliament, which met on the 9th of September, immediately took up the matter, and the king, in accepting a grant of a fifteenth and tenth, recalled the commissions for the tallage, promising that henceforth he would levy such tallages only as had been done in the time of his ancestors and as he had a right to do[3]. This

It is resisted by London and Bristol.

Resistance of the Londoners to tallage in 1312.

Tallage under Edward III in 1332.

[1] Madox, Firma Burgi, pp. 6 sq., 248.

[2] Foed. ii. 840.

[3] 'Le roi a la requeste des ditz prelatz, countes, barouns, et les chivalers des countes, en esement de son dit poeple, ad grante que les commissions nadgaires faites a ceux qui sont assignez de asseer taillage en les cités, burghs, et demeynes par toute Engleterre soient de tot repellez quant a

was probably the last occasion on which this ancient form of exaction was employed[1]. The second statute of 1340[2] contained a clause providing that the nation should be 'no more charged or grieved to make any common aid or sustain charge, except by the common assent of the prelates, earls, barons, and other magnates and commons of the realm, and that in parliament.' Of the scope of this enactment there can be no doubt; it must have been intended to cover every species of tax not authorised by parliament, and, although in other points Edward systematically defied it, it seems to have had the effect of abolishing the royal prerogative of tallaging demesne. But public confidence was not yet assured; in 1348 the commons made it one condition of their grant that no tallage or similar exaction should be imposed by the Privy Council[3]. In 1352 the king declared that it was not his intention or that of the lords that tallage should be again imposed[4], but the petition of the parliament in 1377[5], almost in the words of the statute of 1340, was answered by Edward with a promise that only a great necessity should induce him to disregard it. Another ancient impost was now becoming obsolete. The scutages so frequent under John and Henry III had ceased to be remunerative. The few taxes of the kind raised by Edward I seem to have been collected almost as an after-thought, or by a recurrence to the old idea of scutage as commutation for personal service. The scutage for the Welsh war of 1282, for instance, appears in the accounts of 1288, and the scutages of the 28th, 31st, and 34th years of the reign appear so late in the reign of Edward II as to seem nothing better than a lame expedient

Abolition of the power of tallage.

Scutages become obsolete.

ore; et que sur ce briefs soient mandez en due forme et que pur temps a venir il ne ferra asseer tiel taillage fors que en manere come ad este fait en temps de ses autres auncestres et come il devera par reson;' Rot. Parl. ii. 66.

[1] See Hallam, Middle Ages, iii. 112, 113, where the beginning of Edward III's reign is fixed as the point of time when tenants in ancient demesne were confounded with ordinary burgesses; and, in fact, if the rating of tenths and fifteenths, settled in the 8th of Edward III, were, as is asserted, the final assessment of that impost, followed on all subsequent occasions, there would be no object in maintaining the distinction. See below, § 282.

[2] Statutes, i. 290.

[3] Rot. Parl. ii. 201.

[4] Rot. Parl. ii. 238.

[5] Rot. Parl. ii. 365.

for pecuniary exaction [1]. Yet it occasionally emerges again as a tax payable when the king went to war in person; as so due it was remitted by Richard II after his Scottish expedition in 1385; and henceforth it sinks into insignificance [2]. The three customary aids however continued to be collected, although the nation expected them to be abolished by the statute of 1340. In 1346 Edward, on the occasion of the knighthood of the Black Prince, levied the aid in an unconstitutional way and in illegal amount, not however without a strong remonstrance from the parliament [3].

Continuance of the three customary aids.

276. The disappearance of these ancient taxes is not to be attributed either to the opposition of the parliament or to the good faith of the king so much as to the fact that they were being superseded by other methods of exaction, which were at once more productive and more easily manipulated, the subsidies on moveables and the customs on import and export. In the former no new exercise of prerogative was possible; the tallage, in fact, which we have just examined, was simply an unauthorised exaction on moveables, which disappears with the feudal obligations of demesne. The history of the customs is more interesting and important.

The newer forms of taxation.

The forty-first article of the great charter empowered all merchants to transact their business freely within the kingdom without any 'maletote' or unjust exaction, but subject to certain ancient and right customs, except in the time of war, when the merchants of the hostile nation were disqualified. The mention of a maletote seems to show that such an impost was not unusual, and the ancient and right customs were sufficiently well ascertained [4]. The principal taxable commodities were of

Freedom of trade established by *Magna Carta*.

[1] Rot. Parl. i. 292; Parl. Writs, II. i. 442 sq. So also the scutage for 4 Edw. II collected in 1319; Parl. Writs, II. i. 517. The counties were amerced by Edward II in 1321 for not sending their force to Cirencester; Parl. Writs, II. i. 543.

[2] Rot. Parl. iii. 213. In 1377 a tax of a pound on the knight's fee was proposed and rejected; above, p. 458. According to Coke no scutage was levied after the eighth year of Edward II; the impost was expressly abolished by statute 12 Charles II; Blackstone, Comm. ii. 75.

[3] Above, p. 415.

[4] Mr. Hubert Hall, in the History of the Customs Revenue of England (1885), has offered a very probable and tempting theory of the origin of

Ancient and right customs or prises.

three sorts: wine, wool, and general merchandise [1]. On wine there was, besides an ancient custom of eightpence on the tun in the nature of a port-due, a royal right of 'prise, *recta prisa*,' or taking from each wine-ship, containing above ten and below twenty casks, one cask, and from every ship containing above twenty casks, two casks and no more, one before and one behind the mast, on the payment, for the king, 'at his price,' which seems to have averaged twenty shillings for each cask [2]. The customs on general merchandise were collected in the shape of a fifteenth or other sum levied very much as a toll or licence to trade [3]. The wool was especially liable to be arrested and redeemed from the king's hands by a ransom, for which even the name maletote is too mild a term. Great irregularity prevailed in the whole management of the customs until the accession of Edward I: the merchants, except where they were secured by royal charter or by the strength of their own confederations, lying very much at the mercy of the king's servants, and the prices of their commodities being enormously enhanced by the risk of trading. The wine trade was probably the most secure in consequence of the necessity of keeping Gascony in good temper. The negotiations of Henry III with the merchants have been already noted.

Edward I regulates the customs.

The vote of the parliament of 1275 [4], which gave to Edward I a custom of half a mark on the sack and 300 woolfells [5], and a

the customs in their English form, tracing it to (1) an ancient royal right or pre-emption (on a system of purveyance), (2) the royal power of restraint of trade, and (3) to the official supervision of the Ports in connexion with the administration of the Exchequer. In addition perhaps to these may be alleged the immemorial restraints on, or profits from, commerce which belongs to the historical idea of sovereignty in all reigns and ages. Mr. Hall has corrected in detail many misunderstandings on the subject, and has kindly enabled me to make several amendments in the brief summary contained in this work.

[1] To these may be added as subsidiary staple commodities, minerals and provisions which seldom come into constitutional controversy, and wax and cloth which are more important as subjects of treatment by charter and statute; Hall, p. 5.

[2] If the ship contained less than 20 casks, the prisage was one; but it never rose above two. Madox, Hist. Exch. p. 525; Hale, on the Customs, printed in Hargrave's Tracts, i. 116 sq.; Liber Albus, i. 247, 248.

[3] Madox, Hist. Exch. p. 529 sq.

[4] Above, pp. 113, 200, 256; Hale, Customs, pp. 147, 154.

[5] The number was reduced to 240 in 1368. See above, p. 433; Hall, Customs Duties, ii. 204.

mark on the last of leather, is the legal and historical foundation of the custom on wool. It was levied on all exports, and became at once an important part of the ordinary revenue, not as a maletote and therefore not transgressing the terms of the great charter. In the summer of 1294, under the immediate pressure of a war with France, the king obtained the consent of the merchants to a great increase of the custom; the rate on the sack of broken wool was raised to five marks, other wool paid three marks on the sack, the woolfells passed at three marks for the 300, and leather at ten marks on the last [1]. The rate was reduced the same year, probably in consequence of a parliamentary remonstrance, the wool and woolfells paying three marks and the leather five. The seizure of the wool in 1297 [2] was clearly an exceptional measure, like the prohibition of export under Edward III, adopted probably to secure an immediate payment of the custom, for the rate fixed in 1294 is mentioned in the 'confirmatio cartarum' as the regular impost which, with all similar maletotes, the king promises to release; on the abolition of the maletotes the custom fell to the rate fixed in 1275.

Origin of the customs on wool: grant in 1275.

Increase in 1294 by the merchants.

Seizure of wool in 1297.

277. The exigencies of the year 1303 suggested to the king a new method of dealing with the wool, as well as with other merchandise; and, by a grant of large privileges to the foreign merchants, he obtained from them the promise to pay, among other duties, a sum of forty pence on the sack, the same on 300 woolfells, and half a mark on the last, in addition to the ancient

Imposition of custom on foreign merchants by the 'Carta mercatoria.'

[1] Above, p. 131. 'Custumam anno xxii mercatores regni in subsidium guerrae, quam rex pro recuperatione Vasconiae contra Gallicos intendebat, de lanis et coriis exeuntibus regnum regi gratanter concesserunt, videlicet de quolibet sacco lanae fractae quinque marcas, de quolibet sacco alterius lanae vel pellium lanutarum tres marcas, de quolibet lasto coriorum decem [B. Cotton, p. 246, reads *quinque*] marcas; quod quidem subsidium rex postmodum gratiose mitigavit, videlicet concessit xv° die Novembris eodem anno xxii° finiente, incipiente xxiii°, quod omnes mercatores tam regni quam aliunde, mercatoribus regni Franciae duntaxat exceptis, . . . regi de quolibet lasto tam lanae fractae quam alterius et etiam pellium lanutarum tres marcas, de quolibet lasto coriorum ducendorum ad easdem partes quinque marcas persolverent, a 29° Julii anno xxii° Edw. I et usque festum sancti Michaelis tunc proxime sequentem, et ab eodem festo usque festum natalis Domini anno xxv° incipiente;' Account of 28 Edw. I; cited by Hale, p. 135.

[2] Above, p. 139.

custom. In this act, which was no doubt negotiated between the royal council and the merchants, and which took the form, not of statute or ordinance, but of royal charter[1], the king avoided a direct transgression of the 'confirmatio cartarum'; the persons who undertook to pay were aliens, and not included among the classes to whom the 'confirmatio' was granted, and the impost was purchased by some very substantial concessions on the king's part. But although the money came through the foreign merchants, it was really drawn from the king's own subjects; the price of imports was enhanced, the price of exports was lowered by it. Accordingly the English burghers, assembled at York the same year, refused to join in the bargain, and Edward did not attempt to coerce them. The increment fixed in 1303 was known as the 'nova' or 'parva custuma,' in opposition to the 'custuma antiqua sive magna' of 1275, and its history from this point is shared by the other custom duties which had a somewhat different origin.

'Parva custuma' on wool.

Customs on wine and other merchandise under the 'Carta mercatoria' of 1303.

The customs paid by the foreign merchants affected, as has been mentioned, not only exports of wool, but cloth exported or imported, wine and all other commodities, on which the king had by ancient prescription a right of prise, regulated only by separate arrangement with the several bodies of foreign traders, each of which had its agency at the great ports. The charter of 1303[2] commuted the prises exacted from foreign merchants and reduced the irregularities of these imposts to a fixed scale; cloth, imported or exported, was charged at two shillings, eighteen pence, and one shilling on the piece, according to its quality; imported wine paid, besides the ancient custom, two shillings on the cask in lieu of prisage, and all other imports threepence on the pound sterling of value; the same sum of threepence in the pound was levied on all goods and money exported; with these was accorded the increment on wool just described. The opposition of the English merchants, who had refused to agree to a similar scale of payments[3], continued

[1] Above, pp. 164, 200, 256; Hale, p. 157; Foed. ii. 747.
[2] Hale, pp. 157 sq.; Foed. ii. 747.
[3] The Prisage of wine is the exaction of the two casks, the Butlerage

to be manifested[1]; although they were not contrary to the 'confirmatio,' they contravened the article of the Great Charter which secured the freedom of trade, and were the subject of a petition presented by the parliament in 1309[2]. In reply to that petition Edward II suspended the collection of the new customs on wine and merchandise[3], to see, as he said, whether prices were really affected by them; after a year's trial he determined to reimpose them, but after the lapse of another year, they were, together with the new customs on wool and leather, declared illegal by the ordainers, and ceased to be collected in October 1311. During the whole time of the rule of the Ordinances the new customs were in abeyance; the new increment of 1317 was of the nature of a loan, not an unauthorised general impost[4]; when Edward had gained his great victory in 1322 he restored the new customs, and for one year added an increment on wool, doubling the whole custom payable by denizens and charging aliens double of that[5]. The customs regulated by the Carta Mercatoria were confirmed by Edward III in 1328[6], and became from that time a part of the ordinary income of the crown, receiving legal sanction in the Statute of Staples in 1353[7]. The later variations of tariff are beyond the scope of our inquiries.

Petitions against the new customs.

Suspended by the ordainers.

Restored by Edward II.

Become a part of the ordinary revenue.

is the new custom prescribed in the Carta Mercatoria of 1303; Hall, ii. 108.

[1] In 1309, June 27, Edward appointed the Friscobaldi to receive the new customs from the foreign merchants, and from the native merchants who were willing to pay them; Parl. Writs, II. ii. 20. Two months after this they were suspended.

[2] Rot. Parl. i. 443; above, p. 338.

[3] Above, p. 340, note 1. The additional custom on wool continued to be collected; Parl. Writs, II. ii. 25.

[4] Above, p. 358. See Parl. Writs, II. ii. 116–121; it was a heavy sum, on cloth, 6*s*. 8*d*., 4*s*., and 13*s*. 4*d*., according to value and dye; 5*s*. on the tun of wine, and 2*s*. on the pound of value; on wool, woolfells, and leather 10*s*.

[5] Parl. Writs, II. ii. 193, 229. The impost of 3*d*. in the pound on the German merchants, by Edward I, is petitioned against in 1339; Rot. Parl. ii. 46.

[6] Foed. ii. 747, 748.

[7] Statutes, i. 333. The custom paid by aliens according to this statute is ten shillings on the sack and 300 woolfells, and twenty shillings on the last (art. i.); the poundage (3*d*. in the pound sterling) is authorised by the 26th article, p. 342; cf. Hale, p. 161. The substitution of 240 for 300 in calculating the woolfells begins in 1368; above, p. 433.

Character of this struggle.

These details are sufficient to show that up to the accession of Edward III the regulation of the customs was quietly contested between the crown and the nation; the latter pleading the terms of the charter and the authority of the Ordainers, the former acting on the prerogative right and issuing regulations in council.

Use of the staples.

The contest continues during a great part of the reign, especially with regard to wool, the institution of the staples making this source of income peculiarly easy to be tampered with.

Unconstitutional taxation of wool by Edward III, through his dealings with the merchants.

As early as July 1327 Edward obtained as a loan from the merchants the concession of a double custom on wool and an increase of fifty per cent. on leather; and this duty was collected till the following Michaelmas, in some cases still later [1]. This was done of course under the guidance of the queen and Mortimer. In 1332, the year that witnessed the king's unsuccessful attempt to tallage demesne, he issued an ordinance for the collection of a subsidy on the wool of denizens, at the rate of half a mark on the sack and 300 woolfells, and a pound on the last. This was done by the advice of the magnates, and was recalled the next year [2]. In 1333 the merchants granted ten shillings on the sack and woolfells and a pound on the last, but this also was regarded as illegal and superseded by royal ordinance [3]. The history of these attempts is not illustrated by the Rolls of the Parliament, so that it is impossible to say how far the issue or withdrawal of the order received the national sanction. The national enthusiasm for the war however put a more formidable weapon in the king's hands. In August 1336 the export of wool was forbidden by royal letters, and the parliament which met in the following month at Nottingham granted a subsidy of two pounds on the sack from denizens, three pounds from aliens [4].

Variety of negotiations.

In 1337 the process was reversed; in March the export of wool was forbidden by statute until the king and council should determine how it was to be dealt with [5], and the king and council thus authorised imposed a custom of two pounds on the sack and woolfells, and three on the last, doubling

[1] Inrolled Accounts; rot. i.

[2] June 30, 1333; Hale, p. 162.

[3] Sept. 21, 1334; Hale, p. 163.

[4] See above, pp. 398, 399; cf. Rot. Parl. ii. 122, 143.

[5] Statutes, i. 280.

the charge in the case of aliens [1]. This exaction, although imposed under the shadow of parliamentary authority, had distinctly the character of a maletote, and as such the estates in 1339 petitioned against it, praying that it might be abolished by statute; the commons added that, so far as they were informed, it had been imposed without assent given either by them or by the lords [2]. The popular excitement had risen so high in consequence that a revolt was threatened, and the king had been compelled in 1338 to use the mediation of the archbishop to prevent a rising [3]. The financial measures of 1339 and 1340 resulted, as we have seen [4], in a grant of the tenth fleece, sheaf and lamb in the former year, and of the ninth in the latter. In consideration of the urgency of the case, the king having consented to abolish the maletote, the parliament granted an additional subsidy of forty shillings on the sack, the 300 woolfells and the last [5]. This was intended to continue for a year and a half [6], but on the expiration of the term was continued by agreement with the merchants, and again became matter of petition in 1343 [7]. To the petition the king replied that as the price of wool was now fixed by statute it could not be affected by the maletote, and the increased rate was continued for three years longer with parliamentary authority. In 1345 the whole of the customs, with the exception of the tax on wine, were farmed by twelve English merchants for £50,000 yearly, the king reserving the residue of the 30,000 sacks lately granted, amounting to 4000 sacks; the contract was for three years [8]. In 1346 the commons again [9] petitioned for the removal of the impost, but it was already pledged to the payment of the king's obligation to the merchant contractors. This contract however appears to have been abruptly terminated at the end of the second year. The process is repeated each time the

Petitions against the maletote.

Grants renewed by arrangement with the merchants, against the will of parliament.

[1] Hale, p. 263.
[2] Rot. Parl. ii. 104, 105; above, p. 400.
[3] Hale, p. 163; Foed. ii. 1025.
[4] Above, pp. 401–402.
[5] Stat. 14 Edw. III. st. 2, c. 4; vol. i. p. 291.
[6] Rot. Parl. ii. 114; Stat. 14 Edw. III. st. 1, c. 21; vol. i. p. 289.
[7] Rot. Parl. ii. 138, 140.
[8] The authority for this is an account in the Customers' enrolled accounts, found by Mr. Hall.
[9] Rot. Parl. ii. 161.

impost expires; the merchants continue the grant and the parliament renew the authorisation, notwithstanding the petitions against it[1]. The commons apparently consent to the renewal instead of insisting on their remedy, knowing that if they did not the king and council would collect it in virtue of their bargain with the merchants. The dates of these renewals have been given in the last chapter. On several of these occasions the king undertook that it should be done no more, and that after the expiration of the present grant the old rate should be restored. The statute of 1340 was appealed to as the time from which the innovation was forbidden[2]. The exaction, although felt to be heavy, was agreed to by the parliament as a matter of necessity, the commons clearly thinking that, if their right to impose it were now fully recognised, their claim to withdraw it could not be resisted when the time came. The result proved their wisdom; Edward would never refuse to grant a perpetual privilege in return for a momentary advantage; so without any critical struggle the principle was yielded in 1340; but as in the case of the tallage, the commons did not trust the king; in 1348 they insisted that the merchants should not again make grants on the wool. Finally in 1362 and again in 1371 it was enacted by statute that neither the merchants nor any other body should henceforth set any subsidy or charge upon wool without the consent of the parliament[3]. The wearisome contest, so long continued for the maintenance of this branch of prerogative, comes thus to an end.

The commons have to submit.

Unauthorised customs made illegal in 1362 and 1371.

Origin of tunnage and poundage.

The process by which denizens as well as aliens became subject to custom on wine and merchandise is in exact analogy with the history of the wool. In 1308 Edward II persuaded

[1] 'Certeinz marchantz par confederacie faite entre eux, en coverte et coloure manere de usure, bargainez ove le roi, et cheviz sur meismes les biens a trop grant damage de lui et grant empoverissement de son poeple;' Rot. Parl. ii. 170.

[2] Rot. Parl. ii. 365. In 1377, 'ne nul imposition mys sur les leynes, pealx lanutz, quirs, si non le aunciene coustume . . . tant soulement, solonc l'estatut fait l'an de votre roialme quatorzisme;' to this the king replies, 'il y a estatut ent fait quele le roi voet q'il estoise en sa force.'

[3] Statutes, i 374, 393; Rot. Parl. ii. 308.

a considerable number of English merchants to buy off the right of prise by paying two shillings a tun on wine[1]; but the great majority continued their refusal to commute although they lost largely by the rise of prices during the wars with France. In 1347 however, the council under Lionel of Antwerp imposed a tax of two shillings on the tun and sixpence in the pound by agreement with the merchants[2]. This was continued from term to term by similar negotiations: the same rate was granted by the representatives of the towns under the influence of the Black Prince in 1372[3], and in 1373 it was formerly granted in parliament for two years; from that time, under the name of tunnage and poundage, with some variations of rate[4], it became a regular parliamentary grant[5]. The exactions on manufactured cloth exported, after a short struggle on the king's part, were also subjected to the control of parliament. The new customs on exported cloth, for which English merchants were rated considerably less than aliens, were finally limited to a scale which continued for centuries, while cloth which was not exported was liable to a small subsidy in the nature of excise when exposed for sale[6].

Importance of these details.

The history of the customs illustrates the pertinacity of the commons as well as the evasive policy of the supporters of prerogative; and it has a constitutional importance altogether out of proportion to its interest among the more picturesque objects of history. If the king had not been induced or compelled finally to surrender his claim, and to abide both in letter and spirit by the terms of the 'confirmatio cartarum,' it would have been in his power either by allying himself with the

[1] Parl. Writs, II. ii. 18.

[2] Rot. Parl. ii. 166, cf. p. 229; above, p. 416; Sinclair, Hist. of Revenue, i. 122.

[3] Above, p. 444; Rot. Parl. ii. 310.

[4] The tunnage from the 10th of Richard II to the end of the reign is 3*s.*, and the poundage 12*d.*; and, except for a few years under Henry IV, these were the regular rates.

[5] Above, p. 446; Rot. Parl. ii. 317; Hale, p. 173.

[6] The customs on exported cloth and on panni venales respectively are an important feature in this branch of the revenue. The rate on the latter was 14*d.* for denizens, 19*d.* for aliens per piece. (Hall.)

magnates entirely to crush the trade and independent spirit of the towns, or by allying himself with the merchants to tax the body of the nation at his discretion. The commons showed, by their determination to make no difference between direct and indirect taxation, a much more distinct perception of the circumstances than appears in other parts of their policy. The king might be requested to live of his own, and so far they would relax the hold which royal necessities might give them over him; but, if he could not live of his own, they would neither allow him to sacrifice one half of the nation to the other, nor purchase a relief from direct imposts by conniving at unfair manipulation of indirect taxation. No attempt at unauthorised taxation of merchandise was made after the accession of Richard II, at least during the middle ages.

No difference to be made between direct and indirect taxation.

The king's power of borrowing money.

278. The financial science of the fourteenth century had devised no scheme for avoiding a national debt; nor indeed was the idea of national debt in its barest form presented to it. The king was both in theory and practice the financier of the nation; all its expenditure was entered in the king's accounts; the outlay on the army and navy was registered in the rolls of the Wardrobe of Edward I; and if the king had to provide security for a loan he did it upon his own personal credit, by pledging his jewels, or the customs, or occasionally the persons of his friends for the payment. The system of borrowing, from both foreigners and denizens, had been largely developed by Henry III, whose engagement of the credit of the kingdom to the pope was a stroke of financial genius that rebounded with overwhelming force against himself and nearly cost him his crown. It was however only one example of a systematic practice.

The Jews as a source of Revenue.

Throughout his reign, and onwards to the year 1290, the Jews afforded the most convenient means of raising money. This was done frequently, as had been usual under the earlier kings, by directly taxing them; they were exempted from the general taxation of the country to be tallaged by themselves; for the Jews, like the forests, were the special property of the king[1], and, as a property worth careful cultivation, they had peculiar privileges and a very dangerous protection; like the foreign merchants they had their own tribunals, a legal and financial organisation of their own, which, whilst it gave them security against popular dislike, enabled the king at any moment to lay hand upon their money. Not being, like the natives, liable to the ecclesiastical penalties for usury, the Jews were able to trade freely in money, and their profits, if they bore any proportion to their risks, must have been extremely large. As a result they were disliked by the people at large and heavily taxed by the crown. Henry II in 1187 exacted a fourth part of the chattels of the Jews; John in 1210 took 66,000 marks by way of ransom; Henry III in the form of tallage exacted at various periods sums varying between 10,000 and 60,000 marks, and in the year 1230 took a third of their chattels; in 1255 he assigned over the whole body of the Jews to earl Richard as a security for a loan. The enormous sums raised by way of fine and amercement show how largely they must have engrossed the available capital of the country[2]. As the profits of the Jewish money trade came out of the pockets of the king's native subjects, and as their hazardous position made them somewhat audacious speculators and at the same time ready tools of oppression, the better sense of the country coincided with the religious prejudice in urging their banishment. S. Lewis in 1252 expelled them from France; in England, Simon de Montfort persecuted them. Grosseteste advised their banishment for the relief of the English whom they oppressed, but he declared that the guilt of their usury was shared by the princes who favoured them, and he did not spare the highest persons in the realm in his animadversions[3]. The condition of the Jews

Condition of the Jews in England.

Exactions from them.

Their exile demanded.

[1] By the statute 'De la Jeuerie,' Statutes, i. 221, 222, of the reign of Edward I, every Jew over twelve years old paid threepence annually at Easter, 'de taillage au roy ky serf il est;' and every one over seven years old wore a yellow badge, 'en fourme de deus tables joyntes.' According to Sinclair, i. 107, quoting Stevens, p. 79, the tallage in the third year of Edward I was threepence a head, in the fourth year fourpence. The statute probably belongs to the year 1275. See Madox, Exch. p. 177, note r. On the earlier history see Jacobs, Jews of Angevin England.

[2] Madox, Hist. Exch. pp. 150–178.

[3] He writes to the countess of Winchester thus: 'Intimatum namque

was felt to be discreditable to the nation; the queen Eleanor of Provence was their steady enemy, and her son Edward I shared her antipathy. An early statute of his reign[1] forbade usury with special reference to the Jews, and in 1290 they were banished. This act of course was an exercise of considerable self-denial on the part of the crown, and the drain of money which resulted was no doubt one cause of Edward's pecuniary difficulties which occurred in 1294; but the expulsion was felt as a great relief by the nation at large, and it cut off one of the most convenient means by which the king could indirectly tax his people. It does not appear, however, that Edward himself had to any great extent used the Jews as his bankers.

Usury forbidden.

Banishment of the Jews.

The employment of foreign bankers.

The employment of foreign bankers for the purpose of raising money by loan, anticipating revenue, or collecting taxes, had been usual under Henry III, and possibly had begun as early as the reign of John, who had constantly furnished his envoys at Rome with letters of credit for the large sums which they required for travelling expenses and bribes. It is unnecessary for our present purpose to trace these negotiations further back; but the extent of the foreign dominions of Henry II, and the adventurous policy of Richard I, had opened England to the foreign speculators, and laid the foundation for a system of international banking[2]. Under Henry III, however, the system had expanded, one chief cause being the exactions of the court of Rome, which involved the maintenance of a body of collectors and exchangers. Like the Jews, these money dealers lent themselves to the oppressions of the alien favourites; and the Caorsini and their fellows shared the popular hatred with the Poictevins and Savoyards, whose agents they frequently were. From the

Expansion of the system under Henry III.

est mihi quod Judaeos quos dominus Leircestriensis de municipio suo expulit, ne Christianos in eodem manentes amplius usuris immisericorditer opprimerent, vestra disposuit excellentia super terram vestram recolligere. . . . Principes quoque, qui de usuris quas Judaei a Christianis extorserunt aliquid accipiunt, de rapina vivunt, et sanguinem eorum quos tueri deberent sine misericordia comedunt, bibunt et induunt;' Epistt. ed. Luard, pp. 33, 36.

[1] Usury was forbidden them by the statute 'de la Jeuerie;' Statutes, i. 221.; cf. Madox, p. 177; Pike, Hist. of Crime, i. 462 sq.

[2] On the whole of this subject see Mr. Bond's valuable article and collection of documents in the 28th volume of the Archaeologia.

beginning of the reign of Edward I we find the Italian bankers regularly engaged in the royal service. Edward was encumbered with his father's debts, and his own initiatory expenses were increased by the cost of his crusade and his long detention in France in 1274. His first financial measure, the introduction of the great custom on wool, was carried out with the assistance of the Lucca bankers, who acted as receivers of the customs from 1276 to 1292 [1]. The new source of income was in fact pledged to them before it became due. In 1280 merchants of Lucca and Oudenarde received the fifteenth granted by the estates [2]. Ten different companies of Florentine and Lucchese merchants were engaged in the wool transactions of 1294 [3]. In 1304 the Friscobaldi of Florence were employed to receive the new customs granted by the foreign merchants, and throughout the reign of Edward II the Friscobaldi and Bardi shared the king's unpopularity. The national records of these two reigns are filled with notices of payments made on account of sums bestowed by way of indemnity for loss incurred in the royal service. Under Edward III these notices are rarer, partly because that king negotiated more easily with Flemish and English merchants, but chiefly perhaps because he did not pay his debts. The bankruptcy of the Florentine bankers in 1345 went a long way towards closing this way of procuring money, and must have damaged the credit of Edward all over the continent; in 1352 the commons complained that the Lombard merchants had suddenly quitted the country with their money, and without paying their debts [4]. The Flemish merchants however showed more astuteness than the Italians; they obtained from Edward III and his great lords tangible security for their debts; the crown of England and the royal jewels were more than once pawned [5]. The earl of Derby was detained in prison for the debts of Edward III, as Aymer de Valence had been for those of Edward II; the merchants of Brabant in 1340 insisted, according to the story, on arresting the arch-

Italian bankers employed by Edward I.

The Friscobaldi.

Flemish merchants.

[1] Hale, p. 154; Parl. Writs, i. 381; Madox, Hist. Exch. pp. 536, 537.
[2] Bond, p. 280. [3] Ibid. pp. 284, 285. [4] Rot. Parl. ii. 240.
[5] Foed. ii. 1213, 1229; iii. 7, 12.

bishop of Canterbury as surety for payment[1]; and the king himself declared that he was detained very much like a prisoner at Brussels. The English merchants, who succeeded to the ungrateful task of satisfying the king's necessities, fared no better than the aliens; the commons in 1382 told the king that 'utter destruction' had been the common fate of those who, like William de la Pole, Walter Chiryton and others, had negotiated the king's loans[2].

Loans from princes and popes.

These negotiations were not confined to professional agents: the princes of the Netherlands were ready and able to lend, the great feudatories of the French crown were among the royal creditors, and more than one of the popes lent to the king not only the credit of his name but sums of money told down, the payment of which was secured by a charge on the revenue of royal estates.

The nation was expected to pay, and paid.

All these transactions have one common element: to whomsoever the king became indebted the nation was the ultimate paymaster; either the parliament was asked for additional grants which could not be refused, or the treasury became insolvent, all the ordinary revenue being devoted to pay the creditors, and the administration of the country itself was carried on by means of tallies. The great mischief that would have arisen from repudiation compelled the parliaments to submit, but this necessity called forth more strongly than before the determination to examine into royal economies and especially into the application of the national contributions.

Loans from the prelates, towns, and monasteries.

Besides these, however, moneys were largely borrowed from individuals and communities at home. We have seen Henry III personally canvassing his prelates and barons for contributions of the kind. The special negotiations with the several communities for grants of money may even under Edward I have taken the form of loan, but after the concessions of 1297 they could take no other. If it was necessary for any reason to anticipate the revenue, the clergy or the towns could be compelled to lend. Thus in 1311[3] Edward II borrowed largely

[1] Above, p. 404.

[2] Rot. Parl. iii. 123.

[3] In 1311 Edward II obtained a subsidy from certain 'fideles' and

from the towns and monasteries; in 1313 he borrowed nearly ten thousand pounds from the bishops, chapters, and religious houses, to be repaid out of the next grant made in parliament or in convocation; in 1314, 1315, and 1316 similar sums were raised in this way [1], and the plan was followed by Edward III and Richard II. As the money was already paid, the lenders, when they met in council, had really no alternative but to release the king from repayment. The raising of money by a vote of the clerical estate in convocation does not seem to have been considered as a breach of the letter of the 'Confirmatio Cartarum.' Yet it appears, at first sight, more distinctly in contravention of that act than the exaction of tallage and custom. Nor can it be asserted that the grants made in convocation were reported in parliament, so that they became in that way a part of the parliamentary grant; that was occasionally done, just as occasionally the grant was made by the clerical proctors in parliament; but generally the clergy met at a different time and place from the parliament; they were very jealous of any attempt made by the parliament to control or even to suggest the amount of their vote, and they declined as much as they could to accept the character of a secular court even for the most secular part of national business. The idea that the clerical aids were free gifts made by the clergy out of their liberality to the king's needs, or for national defence, was probably found so convenient that no one insisted on maintaining the letter of the law; on the one hand it saved the clergy from the penalties of disobedience to the canon law as expressed in the bull of Boniface VIII; on the other it

Loans to Edward II to be repaid from the taxes.

Votes of money in Convocation.

'probi homines' of Norfolk and Suffolk, for which he issued letters undertaking that the payment should not prejudice them; Parl. Writs, II. ii. 34. This may have been of the nature of a loan; and the instructions given to the townsmen of Oxford, Canterbury, &c., and to the religious houses of the neighbourhood, to listen to what Ingelard de Warle should tell them on the king's behalf (ibid. p. 31) probably referred to a similar negotiation, either for men or money; see below, p. 569. Other loans were raised from towns; Parl. Writs, II. ii. 35, 36.

[1] For the loans of 1313 see Parl. Writs, II. ii. 64 sq.; for those of 1314, ibid. pp. 78 sq.; for those of 1315, ibid. pp. 87 sq., 97 sq.; for those of Edward III, Foed. ii. 1040, 1064, 1107, 1116, 1206, 1214, iii. 68, 233, &c., &c.; and for the attempts of Richard II, Rot. Parl. iii. 62, 64, 82, &c.

enabled the king to dispense with or to diminish the pressure of parliamentary negotiation; nor did the laity in parliament ever propose to relieve the clergy if they were willing to give. As the clergy moreover paid in common with the towns the higher rate of contribution on their estimated revenue they really gave little occasion for jealousy. The value of taxable property during the fourteenth century did not vary very much; the annual sum of £20,000 which was the amount of a clerical tenth was a very important item in a royal revenue which did not perhaps ordinarily exceed £80,000; it was easily collected, and paid, if not willingly, at least unresistingly. The clergy however were, as we have seen, not less alive than were the laity to the opportunity of making their own conditions and of securing some check on the application of their grants.

Importance of the clerical grant.

The right of purveyance.

279. Next in importance to the unconstitutional practice of raising money by tallage, custom, and loan, without the co-operation of parliament, may be ranked the prerogative right of purveyance [1], and its accompanying demands of service to be paid for at the lowest rate and at the purchaser's convenience,—often not to be paid for at all. There can be little doubt that this practice, which was general throughout Europe, was a very old privilege of the crown, that, wherever the court moved or the king had an establishment, he and his servants had a recognised right to buy provisions at the lowest rate, to compel the owners to sell, and to pay at their own time. It was not like the *feorm-fultum* of the Anglo-Saxon kings or the *firma* recorded in Domesday, a fixed charge on distinct estates and communities, but rather akin to the ancient right of *fodrum* or *annona militaris* exercised by the Frankish kings, who when engaged in an expedition took victuals and provender for their horses, or to the procurations levied by prelates on visitation [2]. It had also much in common

[1] Hallam, Middle Ages, iii. 148.

[2] The right of purveyance implied payment, and is thus distinguished from the procurations; see Waitz, Deutsche Verfassungs-geschichte, iv. 14. But except in the matter of payment it is almost identical with the *fodrum*, which had its analogies in Anglo-Saxon institutions. Of such a

with the prerogative of prise exercised on the owners of wine and other merchandise for the relief of the king's necessities, which prerogative very probably grew out of a still more primitive form of purveyance[1]. The early history of the practice in England is obscure; the abuse of it may have been of comparatively late origin, or its early traces may be lost in the general oppressions, so that it comes to light only when men begin to formulate their grounds of complaint. Archbishop Islip, whose letter on the subject addressed to Edward III has been already quoted[2], refers the initiation of the abuse to Edward II and his courtiers; forty years before he wrote, it had, he says, begun to be burdensome[3]; and, as he became archbishop in 1349, the traditionary era coincides with the parliament of 1309, in which purveyance was the first subject of complaint. It had however been touched by legislation much earlier, in the great charter of 1215, in the provisions of 1258, in the dictum of Kenilworth in 1266, and in the statute of Westminster in 1275. In Magna Carta we find that the right was claimed by the constables of the royal castles[4], who are forbidden to exact it; the statute of Westminster, in its first clause, limits and provides a remedy for the common abuse. It was not expressly renounced in the confirmation of the charters[5], but legislation was again attempted in the second of the *Articuli super Cartas* of 1300. According to the rehearsal

Archbishop Islip's letter.

Early legislation on the subject of purveyance.

kind was the custom of billeting the king's servants, his hawks and hounds, on the religious houses, which is often mentioned in the charters.

[1] See above, p. 549, note 4.

[2] Above, pp. 394, 423.

[3] 'Illud enim maledictum praerogativum tuae curiae, videlicet capere res aliquas pro minori pretio quam venditor velit dare, coram Deo est dampnabile. Sed modo est tantum induratum et usitatum in tua curia et tempore patris tui et avi tui, quod jam duravit per XL annos et sic tibi videtur praescriptum illud maledictum praerogativum;' Speculum Regis, c. 4.

[4] Articles 28–31.

[5] In 1297, on the 26th of August, immediately after the king had sailed (above, p. 145), the judges at the Guildhall proclaimed on behalf of the king and his son, that for the future no prise should be taken of bread, beer, meat, fish, carts, horses, corn, or anything else, by land or by water, in the city or without, without the consent of the owner. This was before the Charters were formally confirmed, and may have been a special boon to the Londoners; Lib. Cust. p. 72.

Restraint imposed in 1300.

of this statute the king and his servants wherever they went took the goods of clerks and laymen without payment, or paying much less than the value; it is ordered that henceforth such purveyance shall be made only for the king's house, that it shall not be taken without agreement with the owner, in due proportion to the needs of the house and for due payments; the taking of undue purveyance is punishable with dismissal and imprisonment, and, if done without warrant, is to be treated as felony. Notwithstanding this enactment, and the demand for its execution, made in the parliament of Lincoln in 1301, in 1309 purveyance is the first of the gravamina presented to parliament, and, by a promise that the law should be enforced, Edward obtained a grant of a twenty-fifth[1]. But the following year the complaints were renewed in the petition which led to the appointment of the ordainers[2]: the state had been so much impoverished by the king's follies that he had no means of maintaining his household but by extortions which his servants practised on the goods of Holy Church and of the poor people without paying anything, contrary to the great charter. The practice was forbidden by the tenth of the Ordinances[3], and Edward, when he revoked the Ordinances, confirmed the statute made in 1300 by his father[4]. No legislation however seems to have been strong enough to check it; it fills the petitions addressed to the parliament; not only the king but his sons and servants everywhere claim the right; it is the frequent theme of the chroniclers; and it is the subject of ten statutes in the reign of Edward III, by the last of which, passed in 1362, the king declares that of his own will he abolishes both the name and the practice itself; only for the personal wants of the king and queen is purveyance in future to be suffered, and the hateful name of purveyors is changed for that of buyers[5]. It is probable that this statute really effected a reform; legislation however, though less frequently

Petitions in 1309, and 1310.

Forbidden by the Ordinances; and in the revocation in 1322.

Legislation of 1362.

[1] Writs for the trial of officers who had acted dishonestly in regard to prisage were issued Dec. 18, 1309; Parl. Writs, II. ii. 24.

[2] Liber Custumarum, p. 199; above, p. 340.

[3] Above, p. 346.

[4] Rot. Parl. i. 456.

[5] Statutes, i. 371.

required, was occasionally called for; in the times of civil war purveyance was revived as a terrible instrument of oppression, and was not finally abolished until Charles II resigned it along with the other antiquated rights of the crown.

Exaction of labour in connexion with purveyance.

The prerogative of purveyance included, besides the right of pre-emption of victuals, the compulsory use of horses and carts and even the enforcement of personal labour[1]. In the midst of ploughing or harvest the husbandman was liable to be called on to work, and to lend his horses for the service of the court, or of any servant of the king who had sufficient personal influence to enable him to use the king's name. It is difficult to conceive an idea of any custom which could make royalty more unpopular, for it brought the most irritating details of despotic sovereignty to bear upon the humblest subject. Nor can the maintenance of such a right be defended as a matter of policy or expediency; it might be advisable, under the pressure of circumstances, in case of a hurried march or on great occasions of ceremony, that the king's household should be protected against the extortion of high prices for the necessaries of life; but the systematic use of what at the best should only have been an occasional expedient betrays either a deliberate purpose of oppression or a neglect of the welfare of the people which was as imprudent as it was criminal.

A great cause of unpopularity.

The abuse of purveyance accounts for the national hatred of Edward II, and for the failure of Edward III to conciliate the affection of the people, and helps us to understand why even Edward I was not a popular king. But it was unconstitutional as well as unwise. The goods and services extorted by the king's servants were paid for, if they were paid for at all, with tallies, on the production of which the unfortunate

[1] See above, p. 423, note 1. 'Item aliquando contingit quod aliqui de familia tua volunt habere homines, equos et carectas in una parochia; illi de parochia conveniunt cum eis pro dimidia marca vel plus vel minus ut possint domi remanere et non laborare in tuo servitio; die sequenti veniunt alii de familia tua et capiunt homines equos et carectas in eadem parochia, quamvis illi qui dederunt dimidium marcae crediderunt securitium habuisse; et ideo cave tibi!' Islip, Spec. Reg. c. 3. One of the charges against William Longchamp in 1190 was that he exacted the service of horses from the monasteries; see Ben. Pet. ii. 106. The impressment of carts and horses is forbidden by the 30th article of the Charter of 1215; Select Charters, p. 300.

owner, at the next taxing, was relieved to the amount of his claims. He was therefore taxed beforehand not only against his will but in the most vexatious way.

Supplies levied on the countries.

280. Nor did the abuse end here; not only individuals but whole counties were harassed by the same means: on one occasion the sheriff is ordered to furnish supplies, beef, pork, corn, for the coronation festival or for the meeting of parliament; on another he is directed to levy a supply of corn to victual the army[1]; the supply is to be allowed from the issues of the shires or in the collection of the next aid. Enforced labour at the king's wages is extended even to military service; the commission of array becomes little else than a purveyance of soldiers, arms, and provisions, and the ancient duty and institution of training under the assize of arms is confounded, in popular belief and in the system of ministerial oppression, with the hateful work of impressment. The commission of array affords a good instance of the growth of a distinct abuse from a gradual confusion of rights and duties into a tyrannical and unconstitutional exaction,—a growth so gradual that it is almost impossible to say when and where the unconstitutional element comes in. The duty of every man to arm himself for the purpose of defence and for the maintenance of the public peace, a duty which in the form of the fyrd lay upon every landowner, and under the assize of arms and statute of Winchester on the whole 'communa liberorum;' the duty of the sheriff to examine into the efficiency of equipment as a part of the available strength of the shire;

Commissions of Array.

Growth of the system of Commissions.

[1] These instances are in close analogy with the annona militaris or fodrum; above, p. 564. In 1301 the sheriffs are ordered to furnish corn to be paid for out of the fifteenth; Parl. Writs, i. 402; in 1306 purveyance of corn for the army seems to be allowed to the sheriffs in passing their accounts; ibid. p. 374. So in 1297 supplies of meat were levied; above, p. 139. Under Edward II in 1307 the sheriffs are ordered to pay for the provisions taken for the coronation, out of the funds in their hands, 'absque injuria cuiquam inferenda, propter quod si super illo clamor ad nos perveniat, nos ad te punitione gravissima capiemus;' Foed. ii. 26. In 1312, 1313, and 1314, purveyance is ordered for the meeting of parliament, the payments to be made at the Exchequer; Parl. Writs, II. ii. 54, 55, 63 sq., 82 sq. In 1330 the counties of Dorset and Somerset complain of the purveyance of corn and bacon taken by the sheriff; Rot. Parl. ii. 40. In 1339 commissions of purveyance were issued and hastily recalled; ibid. ii. 106. The petitions on the subject are very numerous; purveyance for Calais is a matter of complaint in 1351 and 1352; ibid. ii. 227, 240.

the right of the king to accept a contingent from each community to be maintained by the contributions of those who were left at home, an acceptance which has been welcomed by the nation as a relief from general obligation: such duties and rights were of indisputable antiquity and legality. The right of the king to demand the service of labourers and machinists at fair wages was a part of the system of purveyance, and the impressment adopted by Edward I was probably a reform rather than an abuse of that right. Yet out of the combination of these three, the assize of arms, the custom of furnishing a quota, and the royal right of impressment, sprang the unconstitutional commission of array. This existed in full force only in the worst times of the reigns of Edward II and Edward III, but in its origin it dates much farther back, even to the days when William Rufus could call out the fyrd and rob the men of the money with which their counties had supplied them for travelling expenses. Nor was the practice of making a grant of men, like a grant of money, altogether strange to the *commune concilium*; Henry III had accepted a grant of one labourer from each township to work the engines at the siege of Bedford. What the council could grant, the king could take without a grant; the same king could impress by one writ all the carpenters of a whole county. Such expedients were however under Henry III only a part of the general policy of administration; after Edward I had infused the spirit of law and order they became exceptional, and, as an exception to his general system, the demand of service in arms from the whole nation at home and abroad caused the loud complaints of his subjects in 1297; only as exceptional can it be justified on the plea of necessity. No such plea could be alleged under Edward II. Edward I moreover had always paid the wages of his forced levies; under Edward II the counties and even the townships were called upon to pay them; they were required to provide arms not prescribed by the statute of Winchester, to pay the wages of the men outside of their own area, and even outside of the kingdom itself. In 1311[1], whilst the

Grants of men in council.

Payment of wages.

[1] May 20: 'hominibus illis peditibus vadia sua pro septem septimanis sumptibus dictarum villarum ministrari;' possibly this was done by a

Edward II tries to levy a force at the cost of townships.

ordainers were employed in drawing up the Ordinances, Edward II, without consulting parliament, applied to the several counties for the grant of an armed man from each township to be paid for seven weeks at the expense of the township; on consulting the barons however, and perhaps after a remonstrance from them, he withdrew the request. In 1314, after the battle of Bannockburn, commissions of array were issued for the election of soldiers to be paid by the townships[1], and in 1315 a full armament according to the statute of Winchester was ordered; all men capable of bearing arms were to prepare themselves for forty days' service[2]; and there was a similar levy in 1316[3]. It seems to have made little difference whether the king was acting with or against the authority of the Ordinances. On two occasions, in 1316[4] and 1322[5], the parliament granted a vote of men to be provided by the communities of the shires, when the towns made a grant of money; but each time, in a subsequent assembly of the knights of the shire, the grant of men was commuted for a contribution in money. But if the parliament could authoritatively make such a grant, the king could ask it as a favour of the communities without consulting parliament. In 1318[6] he requested the citizens of London and other large towns to furnish armed men at their own cost, undertaking that it should not prejudice them in future; in 1322[7] both before and after the battle of Boroughbridge he made the same request and took money in commutation. In 1324 however the king, or the Despensers in his name, ventured without consulting parliament

Votes in parliament to the same effect.

Grants of men commuted for money.

separate negotiation with the county courts similar to that by which Edward was raising money at the time; see above, p. 562. He wrote on the same day to the earl of Lancaster and other great lords, asking their consent to the aid; but on the 5th of July the commissions were withdrawn and the money spent was repaid; Parl. Writs, II. i. 408, 414.

[1] Parl. Writs, II. i. 431. [2] Ibid. 457. [3] Ibid. 479.

[4] The service required in 1316 was for sixty days; it was redeemed by a grant of a sixteenth; see above, p. 356; Parl. Writs, II. i. 157, 464; Sinclair, Hist. of Revenue, i. 119.

[5] The service in 1322 was for forty days; Parl. Writs, II. i. 573; ii. 186.

[6] Parl. Writs, II. i. 505, 510.

[7] Parl. Writs, II. i. 556, 557, 566. Even after the parliamentary grant of 1322 Edward continued his 'earnest requests' for additional grants of men from the towns; ibid. 579; and for increased force, the wages of which he would pay; ibid. 578, 597.

to demand a similar aid: on the 6th of August, in alarm at the threat of invasion, Edward issued letters patent in which he declared that the array of arms under the statute of Winchester was unsuitable and insufficient for national defence, and that therefore 'de consilio nostro' it was ordained that in each county a certain number of men should be equipped with sufficient armour at the expense of the county[1]. This 'purveyance of armour' tempted the avarice of the king's servants, and the demand was shortly afterwards considerably reduced, the conduct of the purveyors being subjected to severe scrutiny[2]. The failure of the expedient in 1311 and 1314, and its commutation even when fortified with parliamentary authority in 1316 and 1322, show that it was viewed with repulsion and alarm. The principle on which it rested was called in question by the first parliament of Edward III. A petition was presented that the 'gentz de commune' might not be distrained to arm themselves at their own cost contrary to the statute of Winchester, or to serve beyond the limits of their counties except at the king's cost[3]. This was established by statute in a modified form, and it was enacted that except in case of invasion it should not be done[4]. Another petition states the abuse of the commissions of array: such commissions had been issued to certain persons in the several counties to array men-at-arms and to pay them and convey them to Scotland or Gascony at the cost of the commons, arrayers and conveyers, without receiving anything from the king: whereat

Purveyance of armour in 1324.

Dislike of the system.

Statutes passed under Edward III.

[1] Parl. Writs, II. i. 668: 'considerantes etiam quod dictum statutum tempore domini Edwardi quondam regis Angliae patris nostri pro conservatione pacis, tempore pacis etiam, periculo extero non ingruente, ordinatum fuit, et quod pro prompta defensione nostra et dicti regni contra subitos et inopinatos aggressus dicti regis (Franciae) praeter formas proclamationis et statuti praedictorum majorem et fortiorem potentiam aliorum hominum peditum armatorum oportet necessario nos habere, de consilio nostro . . . ordinavimus.' The particular sorts of armour are then prescribed; the armour is to be kept in the towns until the levies are ready, and after the campaign it is to be carefully preserved and used for training under a new form to be afterwards issued.

[2] On the 19th of November (Parl. Writs, II. i. 677) the king ordered that the purveyance of haubergeons and plate armour should cease, but that the men required should be armed with aketons, bacinets, gauntlets, and other infantry arms.

[3] Rot. Parl. ii. 10, art. 9.

[4] Statutes, i. 255; 1 Edw. III. st. 2, c. 5.

the commons, the arrayers and the conveyers, were greatly aggrieved: the king's answer recorded in the statute was that it should be done so no more[1]. One of the charges brought against Mortimer in 1330 was that he had obtained from the knights at the parliament of Winchester a grant of men to serve in Gascony at the cost of the townships[2]. No sooner however was the pressure of war felt than the practice was resorted to again. In 1339 the men provided for the Scottish war were directed by the parliament to be paid by their counties until they reached the frontier, and from thence onwards by the king[3]. The statute of 1327 was contravened, by competent authority perhaps, but without being repealed. As a natural consequence the king regarded himself as freed from his obligation. In 1344 and 1346 the commons urged loudly the breach of faith involved in this: notwithstanding their liberal grants and the king's equally liberal promises, there were issued from day to day commissions to array all over England men-at-arms, hobelours, and archers; the weapons were charged to the commons; victuals were levied from the commons without any payment, and the horses of the king and prince were in several places lodged at the heavy cost of the commons. Edward in reply urged the authority of parliament, the necessity of the case, and the existence of a remedy in case of oppression[4]. Warned by this answer the commons in the next parliament declined to advise the king as to the maintenance of the war and petitioned again; the king promised redress 'sauvee totefoiz la prerogative[5].' The commissions take

Practice resumed

Persistence of the commons in petitioning against it.

Arguments in answer.

[1] Rot. Parl. ii. 8; 'ensement pur ceo que commissiouns sunt este mandez as certeinz persones del ditz countes de araier gentz d'armes et a paier, de eux mener in Escoce, et en Gascoyne, as custages de la commune et des araiours et menours, sauntz rien prendre de roy, dount la commune et les araiours et menours ount est greve grantment; dount ils prient remedie, issint que quant le roy envoit ses commissiouns pur choses que luy touchent, que la execucion ceo face a custages le roy, et que nul ne soit destreint de aler en Escoce ne en Gascoyne, nule part hors de realme, ne de autre service faire que a ses tenementz ne devient de droit a faire.' 'Quant al point tochante la commission des arraiours et des menours des gentz, il semble au conseil, qe mes ne soit fait;' ibid. p. 11. It was ordered by statute; 1 Edw. III. st. 2, c. 7; Statutes, i. 256.

[2] Rot. Parl. ii. 52.

[3] Rot. Parl. ii. 110.

[4] Rot. Parl. ii. 159, 160. See above, p. 415.

[5] Rot. Parl. ii. 165, 166; petition 16. See also Rot. Parl. ii. 170, 171.

their place with the maletote and purveyance among the standing grievances; and the remedy is equally long in coming. In 1352 it was prayed that no one who was not bound by his tenure should be compelled to furnish armed men, unless by common assent and grant made in parliament[1]. The petition was granted and incorporated in a statute[2], which was confirmed in the fourth year of Henry IV[3]. Neither royal promise nor legislation however was sufficiently powerful to restrain abuses, although during the latter years of Edward III and the comparatively peaceful reign of Richard the complaints are less loud than before.

Legislation of 1352.

Insufficiency of legislation to restrain the abuse.

281. Besides the contrivances just enumerated, by which the royal prerogative enabled the king, indirectly or directly, contrary to the law and spirit of the constitution, to tax his subjects, there were other means of doing the same thing in a more circuitous way: the management of the coinage for instance, which was on the continent a most fertile expedient of tyranny. This is a matter of considerable interest, but its history does not furnish data sufficiently distinct to be calculated along with the more direct means of oppression. We have noted the early severities of Henry I against the fraudulent moneyers, the accusation of connivance brought against Stephen, the changes of coinage under Henry II. That king has the credit of restoring the silver coinage to its standard of purity, which, except in the latter years of Henry VIII and in the reign of Edward VI, was never afterwards impaired. Under Henry III and Edward I the introduction of foreign coin and the mutilation of the English currency shook the national confidence, and the edicts of the latter king as well as those of Edward II seem to have been insufficient to restore it. The parliament of 1307[4] however, by authorising the existing currency, asserted the right of the nation to ascertain the purity of the coinage; in the thirtieth of the Ordinances the king is forbidden to make an exchange or alteration of the currency except by the common counsel of the baronage and in

Minor sources of income.

Profits on coinage.

Coinage regulated by parliament.

[1] Petition 13; Rot. Parl. ii. 239.
[2] Statutes, i. 328.
[3] Statutes, ii. 137.
[4] Above, p. 330, note 1.

parliament[1]; and frequent legislation in the course of the century shows that the right was maintained so far as the legislature could bind the executive power. None of the kings however need be suspected of conniving at any direct abuse in this matter[2].

Difficulty of estimating the royal income.

282. It would greatly assist us in forming a judgment as to the amount of justification or excuse that could be alleged on behalf of the kings in their exercise of prerogative, if we could calculate what the amount of their regular income really was; and probably materials are in existence which might furnish the laborious student with trustworthy conclusions on the point. But the labour of working through these materials would be stupendous, and the results of such investigation can scarcely be looked for in this generation.

Existing materials.

We have however several detached volumes of accounts and occasional estimates which on particular items leave little to be desired. The royal income from the crown lands, escheats, and ordinary revenue, is the most difficult to calculate because of its perpetual variations. The produce of the customs has been estimated with some approach to exactness[3]; the grants from the clergy can be exactly determined; and the Rolls of Parliament contain several estimates, not always to be relied on, of the amount of the lay grants. In the Wardrobe Accounts and Issue Rolls of the Exchequer we have records of expenditure, the usefulness of which is diminished by the fact that we cannot separate ordinary from occasional outlay and must therefore leave a very large margin in all conclusions. The general statements of contemporary historians are, it is believed, utterly unworthy of credit; they are estimates founded on the merest gossip of the times, and in many instances the results of calculations that seem in the last degree chimerical: in common with all medieval generalisations as to numbers, they partake of the primitive indis-

[1] Statutes, i. 165.

[2] See Ruding, Annals of the Coinage, i. 17, 18. The petitions on the subjects are very numerous, but the abuses are owing to the currency of foreign coins, or to the want of a new issue of English silver; the old money was clipped, not debased.

[3] A large quantity of new data on this subject, so far as concerns the port of London, is furnished by Mr. Hall in his Appendix to the History of the Customs Revenue, ii. 201–273.

tinctness which has been remarked in the Homeric computations, and are in singular contrast with the scrupulous accuracy in matters of names and dates which the most critical judgment will not refuse to acknowledge in the annalists of this period.

The Wardrobe Account of the year 1300 certifies the amount of royal receipts and expenditure during that year: the sum of receipts is £58,155 16*s.* 2*d.*; the sum of expenditure £64,105 0*s.* 5*d.*[1] This was a year of active but not costly hostilities with Scotland, and was not marked by any extraordinary taxation. The account seems to be very exact, but no doubt some margin must be allowed for the supplies received in kind from the royal estates.

Accounts of the year 1300.

The Issue Roll of the year 1370 exhibits an expenditure of £155,715 12*s.* 1½*d.*[2], and that of 1346 is described as containing an account of £154,139 17*s.* 5*d.*[3] Both of these were years of great military preparation and extravagant expenditure; taxation also was extremely heavy. The estimated expenditure of Edward III between July 20, 1338, and May 25, 1340, a period of unexampled outlay, was £337,104 9*s.* 4*d.*[4] The Wardrobe Accounts of Edward II vary in a most extraordinary manner; the expenditure of 1316–1317 is £61,032 9*s.* 11¾*d.*; that of 1317–1318 is £36,866 16*s.* 3½*d.*; and that of 1320–1321 is £45,343 11*s.* 11¾*d.*[5] The variation may be accounted for probably by the fact that, whilst in the first of these years the kingdom was comparatively peaceful and under the management of the council of the ordainers, it was in a very disturbed state during the second in consequence of the war between the earls of Warenne and Lancaster, and in the third

Accounts of 1370 and 1346.

Estimate of 1338–1340.

Accounts of Edward II.

[1] Wardrobe Account, or Liber Quotidianus Contrarotulatoris Garderobae; ed. Topham, 1787; pp. 15, 360.

[2] Issue Roll of Thomas de Brantingham, bishop of Exeter, for the forty-fourth year of Edward III. The sum of the first half of the year is given in the roll itself, £78,516 13*s.* 8½*d.*; the second half, which I have added up, amounts to £77,198 18*s.* 5*d.*, but I cannot certify its exact accuracy.

[3] Forster on the Customs, Intr. p. 31; quoted by Sinclair, i. 128. Forster found the sum recorded on the Pell or Issue Roll of the year. A summary of the Issue Rolls of the reign of Edward III is given by Sir James H. Ramsay in the Antiquary, vol. i. pp. 158, 159. He estimates the total legitimate revenue of the crown in the middle of the reign at £110,000.

[4] Ordinances and Regulations of the Household (ed. Soc. Antiq. 1790), pp. 3–12.

[5] Archaeologia, xxvi. pp. 318, 319; from an article by Mr. T. Stapleton.

owing to the attack on the Despensers. The revenue was probably collected with some difficulty and the accounts ill kept.

Later estimates.

Of the income of Richard II we have no accessible computation, but that of Henry IV, Henry V, and Henry VI has been carefully estimated, and may be referred to now so far as it illustrates that of the earlier reigns, although there is great difficulty in bringing the results of research into exact comparison with the calculations of historians, either of the time or later. Recent investigations furnish the following averages for the two reigns. Henry IV[1] had from the old crown revenues and his own estates an income of £32,300 gross, £22,600 net, from the customs £45,000 net, and from the taxes and other incidents £38,660 net; altogether £106,260. The income of Henry V calculated in the same way averaged £115,299[2]. With these figures before us, it is not easy to reconcile with probability the varied estimates which, both at the time and since, have been formed as to the revenues of the kingdom in the fourteenth century. Comparing them however with the earlier calculations[3], we may perhaps infer that the sum of £65,000 may be taken to represent the ordinary revenue in time of peace, and that of £155,000 the expenditure in time of war, when the nation was exerting itself to the utmost. The variations of prices and fluctuations in the value of the current coinage during the century and a half to which these figures belong cannot be exactly estimated, but the like variations affect all the accounts from year to year, and the differences at the beginning and

Amount of revenue in time of war and peace.

[1] Sir J. Sinclair, Hist. Rev. i. 144, makes the income of Henry IV £48,000.

[2] To realise the discrepancy of calculation we have to compare Sir John Sinclair's figures with those of Sir James Ramsay (Lancaster and York, i. 155, 316 sq.). The revenue of the ninth year of Henry V consists of the customs and subsidies on wool, merchandise, tunnage, and poundage, amounting to £40,687 19*s.* 9¼*d.*; the casual revenue paid at the exchequer £15,066 11*s.* 1*d.*; altogether £55,754 10*s.* 10¼*d.* To these Sir John Sinclair adds the sum of the revenue derived from the other estates of the king, the duchies of Cornwall, Lancaster, Aquitaine, &c., making the whole £76,643 1*s.* 8¾*d.*; Hist. Rev. i. 47.

[3] The gross income of the crown, exclusive of the customs and subsidies on wool, &c., was in 1433 £34,224 10*s.* 8½*d.*; which was reduced by establishment charges and the like to £8,990 17*s.* 6*d.*, exclusive of the duchy of Lancaster. The customs and subsidies on an average of three years amounted to £30,722 5*s.* 7¾*d.* See Rot. Parl. iv. 433; Sinclair, i. 153.

end of a century are not greater or more determinate than those which mark the beginning and end of a decade. Any calculation must be accepted subject to these variations, which necessarily affect its exact accuracy, but which it is, if not impossible, exceedingly difficult, to adjust.

Difference between ordinary and extra-ordinary expenditure.

If these figures be accepted as an approximation to the truth, the difference between ordinary and extraordinary expenditure would seem to be from £90,000 to £100,000, which sum would represent the contributions of the country at large, including the vote of additional customs and subsidies from clergy and laity. And a rough computation of the sums derived from these sources leads to the same conclusion. The greatest variation is found in the sums raised by the imposts on wool. The regular or ancient custom of half a mark on the sack ought to be accounted in the ordinary revenue, but it may be used as a basis for calculating the extraordinary contribution. The 'magna custuma'[1] during the reign of Edward I produced about £10,000 a year; when, then, in 1294 that king demanded five marks on the sack, the exaction, if it had been collected, would have amounted to £100,000 in addition. As however five marks was not far from being the full value of the wool, and as the exaction was on the whole a failure, the sum of £80,000 may be perhaps an extravagant estimate. In 1338 a grant of half the wool of the country was reckoned at 20,000 sacks[2]; a subsidy then of 45*s.* on the sack would produce £90,000, and a grant of 43*s.* 4*d.* would produce £86,666 13*s.* 4*d.*; if on the other hand the vote of 30,000 sacks granted in 1340[3] be regarded as

Produce of the 'magna custuma.'

Various estimates of the subsidy of wool.

[1] Hale, p. 154, gives the following data for the 'Magna Custuma':—

						£	*s.*	*d.*
'A festo S. Dunstani anno	7	ad idem festum	anno	8	Edw. I	8,108	13	5
	8	,,	,,	9	,,	8,688	19	3
	9	,,	,,	10	,,	8,694	19	3
	10	,,	,,	11	,,	10,271	13	3
	11	,,	,,	12	,,	9,098	7	0
	12	,,	,,	13	,,	8,094	13	6
	14	,,	,,	15	,,	8,023	6	10
	15	,,	,,	16	,,	8,860	6	1
	16	,,	,,	17	,,	9,974	6	1

In 1421 the whole customs on wool produced £6,414 10*s.* $3\frac{1}{4}d.$; Rymer, x. 113. The produce of the customs on wool in the 9th of Henry VI was £7,780 3*s.* 1*d.*; in the 10th, £6,996 16*s.* $0\frac{3}{4}d.$; in the 11th, £6,048 0*s.* 8*d.*; Rot. Parl. iv. 435; Hale, p. 154. [2] Above, p. 399. [3] Above, p. 401.

indicating the taxable amount more truly, the revenue from it would amount to £65,000. In 1348 the annual subsidy of wool was valued at £60,000[1]. Again, the vote of the tenth fleece, sheaf, and lamb, given in 1339[2], was estimated by reference to the spiritual revenue of the church, as valued for the papal taxation in 1291; it was in fact the tithe of the kingdom; the spiritual revenue under that taxation amounted in the gross to about £135,000, including however all the glebe-lands of the parish churches and the estimated income from offerings, which must be calculated at at least a third of the sum. Neither the grant of the tenth fleece nor that of the ninth, which was conceded in 1340, produced anything like the amount of the taxation of 1291, and this principle of assessment was therefore given up, but we may infer from these circumstances that it had been calculated to bring in about £100,000, a sum considerably in advance of that as yet arising from the increased custom or subsidy of wool.

Greatest amount raised.

An exact account of the revenue from wool in the twenty-eighth year of Edward III furnishes the following data: the sacks exported were 44,470 and a fraction (custom, £14,824 2*s.* 10¼*d.*); the woolfells, 539,893 (custom, £611 4*s.* 10¾*d.*); the lasts, 56 and nine hides (custom, £36 18*s.* 0¼*d.*). The total of the Great Custom was £15,472 5*s.* 9¼*d.*; of the subsidy, £89,083 9*s.* 7½*d.*, and of the new custom, £7,299 3*s.* 11*d.* The new custom and subsidy on cloth amounted to £353 13*s.* 10¼*d.*, and the sum total is £112,284 12*s.* 11¼*d.* It appears however from a comparison with the returns of the accounts on wool in other years of the reign, that this sum is very largely beyond any possible average[3]. It is however a

[1] Rot. Parl. ii. 200.

[2] Above, p. 399. The editors of the Nonae Rolls, i.e. the account of the ninth sheaf, fleece, and lamb granted in 1340, remark that the commissioners in 1340 'were to consider the ninth of corn, wool, and lambs in 1340 worth as much in a parish as the tenth of corn, wool, and lambs, and all other titheable commodities and the glebe lands were, when the valuation was made of them in 1292.' The commons in 1410 state that the subsidy and custom on wool in 1390–1391 amounted to £160,000; Rot. Parl. iii. 625: this seems impossible.

[3] Other figures are given in the Parliamentary History; see also Misselden's Circle of Commerce (1633), pp. 119, 120.

curious fact that within six years of the devastation of the great plague such an amount could be reached [1].

Lastly, we may infer from the general tenour of the financial statements on the Rolls of Parliament that the sum which under the greatest pressure the country was expected to furnish in the way of subsidy, was about £120,000. The parliaments of Richard II declared that to raise £160,000 [2] was altogether beyond their power, and that of 1380 reckoned the grant of 100,000 marks as a fair contribution from the laity; but in both cases these are ex parte statements and the resources of the country must have been underrated.

Produce of tenths and fifteenths.

Of the produce of a vote of tenths and fifteenths we have no computation after the reign of Henry III that is trustworthy [3]; but as the amount of the clerical grant was commonly estimated at a third of the whole subsidy, and as the clerical tenth amounted to a little less than £20,000, we arrive at the sum of £60,000 as an approximation to the total sum. From the eighth year of Edward III, the lay assessment of this impost took a settled form [4]; the several districts were permanently rated at the amount paid in that year, particular incidence being determined by the local authorities. The produce of the lay tenth and fifteenth was in the fifteenth century about £37,000: and the clerical tenth had likewise much depreciated. Under Edward III, however, the computation of £60,000 for

Tenths and fifteenths.

[1] Mr. Hubert Hall has furnished me with the following sums of the gross proceeds of the customs (wine not included) every fifth year of the reign, all the ports included: anno 5°, 1331, £16,004; anno 10°, £9,954; anno 15°, £40,365; anno 20°, £50,000; anno 25°, £50,361; [anno 28°, £112,272;] anno 30°, £66,830; anno 35°, £65,265; anno 40°, £76,027; anno 45°, £74,387; anno 49°, £64,870.

[2] See above, p. 470.

[3] In 1224 a fifteenth produced £57,838 13*s*. 6*d*.; in 1233 a fortieth produced £16,475 0*s*. 9*d*.; in 1237 a thirtieth produced £22,594 2*s*. 1*d*.; Liber Ruber Scaccarii; Hunter, Three Catalogues, p. 22. The English envoys at Lyons in 1245 estimated the whole revenue of Henry III at less than £40,000; and Matthew Paris in 1252 says that the 'reditus regis merus' was less than a third of 70,000 marks; M. Paris, iv. 443; v. 335. In 1337 the men of Ledbury estimated the subsidy of wool as double, and the men of Weobley as treble the amount of the fifteenths; but these are local valuations.

[4] Coke, 4 Inst. p. 34; Brady, Boroughs, p. 39; Blackstone, Comm. i. 308; Madox, Firma Burgi, pp. 110 sq. Illustrations of the amounts will be found below in Vol. III.

the whole is not perhaps excessive. A single tenth and fifteenth seldom proved sufficient for a year when the subsidy on wool was not granted; a fifteenth and a half and a tenth and a half would produce £90,000, which is a little more than the calculated subsidy on wool. The variations of the budgets during those years of Edward III in which the greatest pressure was felt, would thus seem to have been caused rather by a wish to avoid alarming the people with the prospect of fixed and regular imposts than by any desire or indeed any possibility of altering the incidence of taxation.

Revenue of the clergy.

The revenue of the clergy, including such portions of the property of the bishops as were not taxed with the property of the laity, amounted, spirituals and temporals together, to £210,644 9*s.* 9*d.*[1], under the taxation of 1291; heavy deductions have to be made on account of the devastation of the northern province by the Scots, which compelled a new taxation in 1318, and which reduced the entire sum to £191,903 2*s.* 5¼*d.*

Taxation of the clergy.

On this valuation all the grants of the clergy in parliament and convocation were based, the lands acquired since 1291 being after some discussion in parliament taxed with those of the laity[2]. When Edward I in 1294 took a moiety of this, or £105,000[3], the exaction bore to the sum usually demanded about the same proportion as the tax on wool bore to the usual custom, but the demand was fully paid by the clergy, whilst the wool to a great extent escaped. In 1371 the clergy voted a sum equal to that granted by the laity, £50,000[4]; and in 1380 half as much as the lay grant, 50,000 marks[5].

[1] These figures are given subject to correction by competent authority. They are the result of a painful calculation from the *Taxatio* itself. In the province of Canterbury the sum of spirituals is £107,567 10*s.* 5½*d.*; that of temporals £61,453 5*s.* 5¼*d.* The spirituals of York come to £28,098 2*s.* 7¾*d.*, and the temporals to £13,525 11*s.* 2½*d.*; but these sums were reduced under the New Taxation in the reign of Edward II to £16,905 15*s.* 4½*d.*, and £5,976 11*s.* 2*d.* respectively. The property of the bishops included in the general account of temporalities amounted to £16,826 1*s.* 8½*d.* Sir James Ramsay estimates the average of the clerical tenths, under Henry IV at £11,600 and under Henry V at £16,250; Lancaster and York, i. pp. 160, 321. In 1497 the lay tenth had sunk to £30,000, and the clerical to £10,000.

[2] See above, pp. 416, 443.

[3] Above, p. 130.

[4] Above, p. 443.

[5] Rot. Parl. iii. 90; above, p. 470. A petition of the year 1346 that

SUMMARY OF ECCLESIASTICAL TAXATION UNDER THE VALUATION OF POPE NICHOLAS, A.D. 1291.

	Spirituals.			Temporals.			Total.			Temporals of Bishops included in col. 2.		
	£	*s.*	*d.*	£	*s.*	*d.*	£	*s.*	*d.*	£	*s.*	*d.*
Canterbury ...	4,773	6	4	4,108	12	6¾	8,881	18	10¾	1,355	8	1
Rochester......	1,838	10	0	554	19	2	2,393	9	2	143	12	3
London.........	5,283	8	3	4,907	11	0¼	10,190	19	3¼	1,000	0	0
Lincoln.........	28,840	9	4	13,535	3	9½	42,375	13	1½	1,000	0	0
Norwich	15,607	2	5	7,905	12	8½	23,512	15	1½	666	13	4
Chichester ...	4,708	16	8	2,095	15	8	6,804	12	4	462	4	7¾
Exeter	4,601	15	5¼	1,398	2	9½	5,999	18	2¾	461	18	4¾
Hereford	3,848	17	10¾	2,135	4	2	5,984	2	0¾	449	1	5
Salisbury	7,914	11	10½	6,310	8	0¼	14,224	19	10¾	529	19	5
Bath and Wells	4,109	2	8	2,395	5	5	6,504	8	1	541	13	11
Winchester ...	6,585	8	0	5,689	14	7¾	12,275	2	7¾	2,977	15	10
Worcester ...	4,816	9	6	2,506	14	3	7,323	3	9	485	12	8
Lichfield	6,369	7	0	2,260	2	10¾	8,629	9	10¾	349	2	10
Ely	2,945	0	0	3,843	3	8½	6,788	3	8½	2,000	0	0
S. David's......	2,138	15	0	563	10	9	2,702	5	9	104	17	0
Llandaff	1,154	14	8	922	17	8	2,077	12	4	93	9	8
S. Asaph	1,332	18	9	157	17	1	1,490	15	10	22	2	10
Bangor	698	16	8	162	9	1½	861	5	9½	56	1	10
York	18,816	13	6½	8,718	9	11	27,535	3	5½	1,333	6	8
Durham	6,723	19	3¼	4,193	5	6	10,917	4	9¼	2,666	13	4
Carlisle.........	2,557	9	10	613	15	9½	3,171	5	7½	126	7	7
	135,665	13	1¼	74,978	16	7¾	210,644	9	9	16,826	1	8½
New Taxation.												
York...........	15,229	15	8½	4,953	17	10	20,183	13	6½	666	13	4
Durham	1,281	0	8	936	13	4	2,217	14	0	666	13	4
Carlisle.........	394	19	0	86	0	0	480	19	0	20	0	0
New Tax ...	16,905	15	4½	5,976	11	2	22,882	6	6½			
Old Tax ...	28,098	2	7¾	13,525	11	2½	41,623	13	10¼			
	11,192	7	3¼	7,549	0	0½	18,741	7	3¾			

Taxation of 1291, total..............	210,644	9	9
Reduction of Taxation	18,741	7	3¾
	£191,903	2	5¼

To face Vol. II, p. 580.

The fact then that their assessment had been made once for all, whilst that of the laity was re-adjusted from year to year, did not, as might be supposed, enable the clergy to elude taxation. They had no inducement to conceal their wealth, the record of which was in the king's keeping; and if at any time their grants failed to produce a sum proportionate to that given by the laity, the matter was at once re-adjusted by raising the rate of the tax instead of re-assessing individuals.

General estimate. From these data we may conclude that when the king would live of his own, and in time of peace, he had a revenue of about £65,000; that for a national object, or for a popular king, grants would be readily obtained to the amount of £80,000; and that under great pressure and by bringing every source of income at once into account, as much as £120,000 might be raised, in addition to the ordinary revenue.

Ordinary revenue. The ordinary revenue is however what was meant by the king's own; a sum of about £65,000, of which about £10,000 proceeded from the customs; these, with the other proceeds of the exchequer, the ferms of the counties, and other sources of ancient revenue, which had amounted to £50,000 [1] under Richard I, were received at the exchequer to nearly the same amount under Edward I [2]; casual windfalls in the shape of escheats and small profits on coinage and the like brought in about £10,000 [3], and the revenue of the next year was generally anticipated in some small degree until a general grant wiped away the king's debts.

Estimate of outlay. Obscure as these calculations of income now seem, the calculations of expenditure are much more difficult, and the student of to-day shares the bewildered sensations of the taxpayer of the fourteenth century as he approaches them. Certain records of outlay we possess, but they are very imperfect and

the fifteenths might be collected 'saunz rien encrestre' seems to show that the commons wished to avoid new valuations; Rot. Parl. ii. 161.

[1] Bened. Petr. ii. pref. p. xcix; where I have made the sum £48,781; a later calculation brings it up to £51,679 7*s*. 9*d*.

[2] Wardrobe Account, p. 1: 'Summa totalis receptae per scaccarium anno praesenti 28°, £49,048 19*s*. 10*d*.'

[3] Wardrobe Account, p. 15: 'Summa totalis receptae praeter scaccarium £9,106 16*s*. 2½*d*.'

irregular, and no doubt were known to be so when the nation both in and out of parliament was clamouring in vain for an audit of the royal accounts; the blame of all extravagance was thrown upon the royal household; and no wonder, when the whole accounts of army, navy, and judicial establishments appeared in the computus of the wardrobe along with the expenses of the royal table, jewel chests, and nursery. The Wardrobe Account of the 28th of Edward I assigns the several items of expenditure thus: Alms, £1,166 14*s.* 6*d.*[1]; necessaries, horses bought, messengers, wages, and shoes, £3,249 16*s.* 2*d.*[2]; victualling, stores, and provisions for the royal castles, £18,638 1*s.* 8*d.*[3]; the maintenance of the royal stud, £4,386 4*s.* 5*d.*[4]; the wages of military officers, artillerymen, infantry, and mariners, £9,796 9*s.* 2½*d.*[5]; the proper expenses of the wardrobe, including the purchases made for the queen and the chancery, £15,575 18*s.* 5½*d.*[6]; the difference between the sum of the Wardrobe Account and the entire outlay of the king, £10,946 5*s.* 4*d.*, is put down to the expense of the household and probably accounted for in another roll[7]. Far the largest portion of the expenditure is however seen to be devoted to the public service, considerably more than half being assigned to the garrisons and to the payment of the troops. The household expenses, properly so called, form a minor item. On this head we have some other data. The roll of the household expenses of the 44th year of Henry III exhibits an outlay of £7,500[8], but this was at the time at which his freedom was very much limited by the government established under the Provisions of Oxford; in 1255 he is found complaining that he had to allow his eldest son more than 15,000 marks[9]. In the first year of Edward I the household expenses from Easter to August amount to £4,086 0*s.* 4½*d.*; and in the 21st year the expenditure of his son Edward for the year is £3,896 7*s.* 6½*d.*[10]

Expenses of Edward I.

Wardrobe and Household accounts.

[1] Wardrobe Account, p. 47.
[2] Ibid. p. 100.
[3] Ibid. p. 154.
[4] Ibid. p. 187.
[5] Ibid. pp. 210, 240, 270, 279.
[6] Ibid. p. 360.
[7] Ibid. p. 360.
[8] Devon, Preface to Pell Roll of Edw. III, p. xvii.
[9] Sinclair, History of the Revenue, i. 103; M. Paris, v. 488; Hume, ii. 57.
[10] Devon, Preface to the Pell Roll of 44 Edw. III, pp. xvi, xvii.

The household expenditure of Henry IV is said to have varied between £10,000 and £16,000 annually, but on a minute calculation is estimated at an average of £36,400[1]. Like Edward III he had a large family and establishment, and the expenditure of his magnificent grandfather can scarcely be computed at less.

283. These figures do not make it at all easier to understand the constant irritation caused by the expenses of the household, so long as those expenses are regarded as mere personal extravagance. The largest of the estimated sums could scarcely be considered enormous for a court which was expected by the nation to be at least as splendid as the courts of the great continental kings, at a time too when the king had no private revenue; for from the Conquest until the accession of Henry IV the king's estate was simply the estate of the crown, his foreign dominions being a cause of expense rather than a source of revenue. We may safely conclude that the murmurs against the prodigality of the kings were produced rather by the fact that they failed to make the ordinary revenue meet the ordinary expenditure, and that the nation having no way of auditing either receipts or outlay readily laid hold of the expenses of the court as the cause of increased taxation. It was the greediness of the courtiers, as they thought, which brought the evil of purveyance to every man's door, which increased general taxation, and threw on the several communities, in the shape of provisions of men, arms, and victuals, the maintenance of the public burdens. To some extent the instinct was a true one; the maintenance of an enormous household and stud[2], for which provisions were collected at the lowest possible prices, just when the nation was suffering from bad harvests or plague and famine, shows an absence

Household expenses.

Want of a proper audit.

Popular feeling on the expense of the household.

[1] £10,000 in 1404; £16,000 anno 11 Henry IV; Sincl. i. 144, from Noy, p. 5; see Rot. Parl. iii. 528. Ramsay, i. 156, makes the average, exclusive of the Wardrobe, £24,000; but the older authorities are irreconcileable.

[2] The number of horses kept at the king's expense is one important item in archbishop Islip's remonstrance; the cost of a horse is calculated at £6 1*s.* 4*d.* per annum; Speculum Regis, c. 8. The great cost of the stud appears also from the Wardrobe Accounts; and the exercise of the right of purveyance for horses is a frequent matter of complaint; Rot. Parl. ii. 169, 229, 270.

National discontent at the royal expenses

of the proper feeling which the king should have had for his people, and condemns such a king as Edward III. A little self-denial might have proved at least a wish to show sympathy; to maintain the splendour of the court during the prevalence of the plague was a folly as well as a sin. But the complaints are far louder against Edward II and Richard II than against Edward III. In their case we see how necessary it was for a powerful king to be a warrior. Their inactivity may have spared the pockets of the people, but the lightness of taxation did not make them popular. From anything that appears, the English would rather have been heavily taxed for war than see the king spend his time in hunting and feasting at his own cost. True, when the burden of war became intolerable, they wished for peace. Possibly the sins of the warrior kings were visited on the next generation who tried in vain to pay their debts and were called to account for everything they spent, every friend they promoted, every minister they trusted. But it remains a most puzzling fact that the household outlay of the sovereign was the point which, in some measure from the minority of Henry III, and more distinctly from the accession of Edward II, formed the subject of national outcry and discontent. It was the easiest point to attack; it was also the most difficult to defend, and the hardest so to reform as to make it defensible. To make the king a mere stipendiary officer, or to place over him, as over an infant or lunatic, a commission for the management of his income, presented insurmountable difficulties under the actual conditions as well as on the theory of royalty.

Attempt to limit the king's power of giving.

284. The most plausible means of making and keeping the king rich enough to pay his own way was doubtless to prevent him from alienating the property of the crown; and the attempts to secure this object come into historical importance earlier than the direct restraints on expenditure. The outcry against foreign favourites, which had been raised at intervals ever since the Conquest, was the first expression of this feeling. The crown was very rich; so the nation was fully persuaded. The Conqueror had had an enormous income, William Rufus

and Henry I had maintained and increased it. Stephen had begun the process of impoverishment, from which the crown had never recovered. His supporters, it is said, had been endowed out of crown revenue, royal demesne had been lavished on natives and aliens. Henry II had resumed, or tried to resume, what Stephen had alienated, and had been economical in private as well as in public, but Richard sold all that he could sell, and John wasted all that he could waste. The early years of Henry III were spent in attempts made by his ministers to restore the equilibrium of the administration; again there had been a resumption of alienated estates and a contraction of expenses. But Henry, when he came of age, was as lavish as his father had been, and the crown was poorer than ever. And now there was less excuse than before, for the great families of the Conquest were dying out; the vast escheats that fell to the king might have sufficed for the expenses of government, but instead of keeping them in his own hands he lavished them on his foreign friends and kinsmen. It may be questioned whether, if the administration had been sound and economical, the king could have attempted to enrich himself by retaining the great fiefs, as the duchy of Lancaster, and to some extent the earldoms of Cornwall and Chester, were afterwards retained. The barons would have probably been jealous of any attempt to alter the balance existing between the crown and their own body. Owing to this feeling, which, when the crown was adequately endowed, was a just one, the early emperors had been expected at their election to divest themselves of such fiefs as they had held before. But on the other hand there was an equally well-founded jealousy of a king who heaped upon his own sons and brothers all the fiefs that escheated during his reign, just as against a bishop who reserved all preferment for his own nephews. In Germany the king of the Romans was forced on his election to swear that he would not alienate the property of the crown, and the like promise appears in one form of the English coronation oath[1]. The barons were amply justified in urging on Henry III the banishment of the aliens and the recovery of royal demesne;

Lavish bestowal of escheated lands.

Resumptions of royal demesne.

[1] See above, p. 108.

at the beginning of the reign they had compelled him to make proper provision for his brother, at the end of the reign they begrudged every acre that he bestowed on his sons[1]. In a penitential proclamation issued in 1271 he declared that he would retain all escheats for the payment of his debts[2]. The bestowal of the earldom of Cornwall on Piers Gaveston by Edward II was offensive, not merely as the promotion of an insolent favourite, but as a piece of impolitic extravagance. The national instinct was aroused by it; when the barons got the upper hand their first act was to limit the royal power of giving; the third article of the Ordinances directed that no gift of land, franchise, escheat, wardship, marriage or bailiwick should be made to any one without consent of the ordainers[3]; the clergy, in 1315, granted their money on condition that all grants made during the reign should be resumed[4]. The same principle was maintained under Richard II; Edward III in this, as in many other points, had been either crafty enough to evade, or strong enough to break down, the rule; but by promoting his friends and kinsmen in the presence, and with the approval of, parliament, he had made the nation sharers in his imprudence. Yet in 1343 the commons petitioned that he would not part with the property of the crown; and Archbishop Islip urged in vain that he should pay his debts before he alienated his escheats[5]. Edward III had gone a long way towards building up a new nobility; the Montacutes, Percies, Latimers, Nevilles, and other great houses of the later baronage, owed their promotion to his policy or bounty. These adopted the prejudices or principles of the elder baronage. What Edward had done for them Richard attempted to do for Michael de la Pole and Robert de Vere, and was as speedily arrested in his design, as if he had really hoped to supplant them by his new creations. Again the cry was raised against alienation; a stringent oath against the acceptance of gifts was imposed on the ministers; and the friends of the king were sacrificed on

Policy of Edward III.

The later baronage.

[1] See above, p. 42. [2] Foed. i. 488; see p. 587 below.
[3] Statutes, i. 158; see above, p. 345.
[4] Parl. Writs, II. ii. 92; see above, p. 355.
[5] Rot. Parl. ii. 141; Speculum Regis, cc. 7, 8.

the ground that contrary to oath and public policy they had received such gifts [1]. The principle was not conceded when the struggle ended in the king's destruction.

285. Still less effective were the attempts made to limit the expenses of the household by direct rules. In this object the nation had help from the practice of some at least of the kings. The expenditure of the court had been regulated by Henry II in the curious ordinance which prescribes the allowances of the great officers of state and servants of the kitchen in the same page [2]. Henry III had been seized with qualms of conscience more than once, and had reduced his expenditure very materially. In 1250 he had cut down the luxuries and amusements of the court, diminished his charities, and even reduced the number of lights in his chapel; the historian remarks that his economy verged on avarice; he paid his debts and plundered the Jews [3]. In 1271, when on recovery from sickness he had taken a new vow of crusade, he had made over the whole revenue to his council for the payment of his debts, reserving to himself only six score pounds to give away before he should start for Palestine [4]. The orderly accounts of Edward I, so often quoted above, show that he was careful although not parsimonious. But Edward II could not be trusted to manage his own. Accordingly with his reign began the attempts of the barons, in and out of parliament, to direct the administration of the household. The Ordinances of 1311 were based on a proposition for the regulation of the household; the ordainers were empowered 'ordener l'estat de nostre hostel et de nostre realme [5];' and in 1315 the king was put on an allowance of ten pounds a day [6], scarcely as much as he had when he was a boy. In 1318, on the reconciliation of Lancaster, another commission of reform was appointed [7]. The repeal of the Ordinances left Edward free to hasten his own fall; and no limit was attempted during the reign of Edward III, until in the Good Parliament the elected counsellors were directed to attempt the general amendment of

Enforced economy of the court.

Commissions to reform the king's household.

Under Edward II,

[1] Rot. Parl. iii. 15, 16, 115, 213, &c.
[2] See above, vol. i. p. 345.
[3] See above, p. 67.
[4] Foed. i. 488.
[5] Foed. ii. 105; Liber Custumarum, pp. 198, 199.
[6] Above, p. 355.
[7] Above, p. 360.

and Richard II.

the administration. Although this project was abandoned when John of Gaunt recovered his power, it was revived immediately on the accession of Richard II. Year after year we have seen commissions appointed in parliament to make the reforms needed, and the constant renewal of the commissions shows that the reforms were not made. When the king had at last emancipated himself from tutelage, he gave free reins to his prodigality. The bill of Thomas Haxey, in which the expenses of the ladies and bishops about the court were complained of, touched only a portion of the evil. Popular rumour alleged that not less than 10,000 people were daily entertained at the king's expense, and although this is incredible, and even a tithe of the number must have been in excess of the truth, the evil was not imaginary. The court was extravagant; it was also unpopular; its unpopularity made prodigality a greater sin. Richard's fall initiated a long reign of economical administration; Henry IV, although his general expenditure was very large, and his son and grandson, avoided offence in this respect, but the restraint was imposed by policy rather than by necessity. The parliament had claimed and exercised the right of interference, but it had likewise become apparent that no such restrictions as they had sought to impose on Edward II and Richard II were applicable to a strong king; that the extravagance of the court was really only a minor cause of public distress, a colourable ground of complaint against an otherwise intolerable administration; and that such abuses were only a part of a wider system of misgovernment, the correction of which demanded other more stringent and less petty contrivances.

Haxey's bill.

Responsibility of ministers insisted on.

286. The idea of controlling expenditure and securing the redress of all administrative abuses by maintaining a hold upon the king's ministers, and even upon the king himself, appears in our history, as soon as the nation begins to assert its constitutional rights, in the executory clauses of the great charter. Three methods of attaining the end proposed recommended themselves at different times: these are analogous, in the case of the ministers, to the different methods by which, under various systems, the nation has attempted to restrain the exercise of

Three ways of doing it.

royal power: the rule of election, the tie of the coronation oath, and the threats of deposition; and they are liable to the same abuses. The scheme of limiting the irresponsible power of the king by the election of the great officers of state in parliament has been already referred to, as one of the results of the long minority of Henry III[1]. It was in close analogy with the practice of election to bishoprics and abbacies, and to the theory of royal election itself. When, in 1244 and several succeeding years, the barons claimed the right of choosing the justiciar, chancellor and treasurer, they probably intended that the most capable man should be chosen, and that his appointment should be, if not for life, at least revocable only by the consent of the nation in parliament. The king saw more clearly perhaps than the barons that his power thus limited would be a burden rather than a dignity, and that no king worthy of the name could consent to be deprived of all freedom of action. Henry III pertinaciously resisted the proposal, and it was never even made to Edward I, although in one instance he was requested to dismiss an unpopular treasurer[2]. Revived under Edward II, in the thirteenth and following articles of the Ordinances, and exercised by the ordainers when they were in power[3], it was defeated or dropped under Edward III; in 1341 the commons demanded that a fresh nomination of ministers should be made in every parliament; Edward agreed, but repudiated the concession. It was naturally enough again brought forward in the minority of Richard II. The commons petitioned in his first parliament, that the chancellor, treasurer, chief justices and chief baron, the steward and treasurer of the household, the chamberlain, privy seal, and wardens of the forests on each side of the Trent, might be appointed in parliament; and the petition was granted and embodied in an ordinance for the period of the king's minority[4]. In 1380 the commons again urged that the five principal ministers, the chancellor, treasurer, privy seal, chamberlain and steward of the household, should be elected in parliament, and that the five chosen in the present

Claim to elect ministers.

Petitions on the subject.

[1] See above, pp. 41, 64 sq.

[2] See above, p. 156.

[3] See above, pp. 346, 349, 360.

[4] Rot. Parl. iii. 16.

parliament might not be removed before the next session; the king replied by reference to the ordinance made in 1377[1]. In 1381 they prayed that the king would appoint as chancellor the most sufficient person he could find, whether spiritual or temporal[2]; in 1383 that he would employ sage, honest, and discreet counsellors[3]; and in 1385 he had to decline summarily to name the officers whom he intended to employ 'for the comfort of the commons[4].' But it may be questioned whether under the most favourable circumstances the right claimed was really exercised; the commons seem generally to have been satisfied when the king announced his nomination in parliament, and to have approved it without question. The appointments made by Edward II in opposition to the ordainers, when he removed their nominees and appointed his own, were acts of declared hostility, and equivalent to a declaration of independence. The ultimate failure of a pretension, maintained on every opportunity for a century and a half, would seem to prove that, however in theory it may have been compatible with the idea of a limited monarchy, it was found practically impossible to maintain it; the personal influence of the king would overbear the authority of any ordinary minister, and the minister who could overawe the king would be too dangerous for the peace of the realm. The privy council records of Richard II show that even with ministers of his own selection the king did not always get his own way.

Failure of the pretension.

Attempts to bind the ministers by oaths.

A second expedient was tried in the oath of office, an attempt to bind the conscience of the minister which belongs especially to the age of clerical officials. The forms of oath prescribed by the Provisions of Oxford illustrate this method[5], but there is no reason to suppose that it was then first adopted. The oath of the sheriffs and of the king's counsellors is probably much more ancient, and the king's own oath much older still. The system is open to the obvious objection which lies against all such obligations, that they are not requisite to bind a good minister or strong enough to bind a bad one; but they had

[1] Rot. Parl. iii. 82.
[2] Rot. Parl. iii. 101.
[3] Rot. Parl. iii. 147.
[4] Rot. Parl. iii. 213.
[5] Above, p. 80.

a certain directive force, and in ages in which the reception of money-gifts, whether as bribes or thank-offerings, was common and little opposed to the moral sense of the time, it was an advantage that the public servants should know that they could not without breach of faith use their official position for the purpose of avarice or self-aggrandisement. But when we find the best of our kings believing themselves relieved from the obligation of an oath by absolution, we can scarcely think that such a bond was likely to secure good faith in a minister trained in ministerial habits, ill paid for his services, and anxious to make his position a stepping-stone to higher and safer preferment. It is seldom that the oath of the minister appears as an effective pledge: the lay ministers of Edward III in 1341[1] allowed their master to make use of their sworn obligation to invalidate the legislation of parliament and to enable him to excuse his own repudiation of his word. Generally the oath only appears as an item among the charges against a fallen or falling minister, against whom perjury seems a convenient allegation[2].

Futility of the device.

The third method was rather an expedient for punishment and warning than a scheme for enforcing ministerial good behaviour; it was the calling of the public servant to account for his conduct whilst in office. In this point the parliament reaped the benefit of the experience of the kings; and did it easily, for, as the whole of the administrative system of the government sprang out of the economic action of the Norman court, a strict routine of account and acquittance had been immemorially maintained. The annual audits of the Exchequer had produced the utmost minuteness in the public accounts, such as have been quoted as illustrating the financial condition of England under Edward I. Minute book-keeping however does not secure official honesty, as the Norman kings were well aware; the sale of the great offices of state, common under Henry I and tolerated even under Henry II shows that the

Annual audit in the Exchequer.

How this was affected by the sale of offices.

[1] Above, p. 410.

[2] On the oaths demanded from ministers, see Rot. Parl. ii. 128, for the year 1341; ibid. 132, for 1343; and under Richard II, ibid. iii. 115, etc., etc.

kings were determined that their ministers should have a considerable stake in their own good conduct; a chancellor who had paid £10,000 for the seals was not likely to forfeit them for the sake of a petty malversation which many rivals would be ready to detect. On the other hand the kings possessed, in the custom of mulcting a discharged official,—a custom which was not peculiar to the Oriental monarchies,—an expedient which could be applied to more than one purpose. Henry II had used the accounts of the Chancery as one of the means by which he revenged himself on Becket. Richard I had compelled his father's servants to repurchase their offices, and the greatest of them, Ranulf Glanvill, he had forced to ransom himself with an enormous fine. The minister who had worn out the king's patience, or had restrained his arbitrary will, could be treated in the same way. Hubert de Burgh had been a good servant to Henry III, but the king could not resist the temptation to plunder him. Edward I again seems to have considered that the judges whom he displaced in 1290 were rehabilitated by the payment of a fine, a fact which shows that the line was not very sharply drawn between the lawful and unlawful profits of office. Edward II revenged himself on Walter Langton, Edward III vented his irritation on the Stratfords, John of Gaunt attacked William of Wykeham with much the same weapons; and in each case the minister assailed neither incurred deep disgrace nor precluded himself from a return to favour.

The mulcting or 'ransoming' of ministers.

Disgraced ministers restored on payment of fines.

Such examples taught the nation the first lessons of the doctrine of ministerial responsibility. Great as were the offences of Edward II, Stapledon the treasurer and Baldock the chancellor were the more immediate and direct objects of national indignation; they were scarcely less hated than the Despensers, and shared their fate. The Kentish rioters or revolutionists of 1381 avenged their wrongs on the chancellor and treasurer, even whilst they administered to the Londoners generally the oath of fealty to king Richard and the commons. But it is in the transactions of the Good Parliament that this principle first takes its constitutional form; kings and barons had used it as a cloak of their vindictive or aggressive hostility, the commons

The ministers of Edward II held accountable by the people.

The victims of 1381.

first applied it to the remedy of public evils. The impeachment of lord Latimer, lord Neville, Richard Lyons, Alice Perrers, and the rest of the dishonest courtiers of Edward III, is thus a most significant historical landmark. The cases of Latimer and Neville are the most important, for they, as chamberlain and steward, filled two of the chief offices of the household; but the association of the other agents and courtiers in their condemnation shows that the commons were already prepared to apply the newly found weapon in a still more trenchant way, not merely to secure official honesty but to remedy all public abuses even when and where they touched the person of the king, and moreover to secure that public servants once found guilty of dishonest conduct should not be employed again[1]. As the grand jury of the nation, the sworn recognitors of national rights and grievances, they thus entered on the most painful but not the least needful of their functions. The impeachment of Michael de la Pole in 1386 and of Sir Simon Burley and his companions in 1388 was the work of the commons. It is to be distinguished carefully from the proceedings of the lords appellant, which were indefensible on moral or political grounds; for there the guilt of the accused was not proved, and the form of proceeding against them was not sanctioned by either law or equity. But the lesson which it conveyed was full of instruction and warning. The condemnation of Michael de la Pole especially showed that the great officers of state must henceforth regard themselves as responsible to the nation, not to the king only. The condemnation of the favourites proved that no devotion to the person of the king could justify the subject in disobeying the law of the land, or even in disregarding the principles of the constitution as they were now asserting themselves. The cruelty and vindictiveness of these prosecutions must be charged against the lords appellant who prompted the commons to institute them: the commons however were taught their own strength even by its misuse. And still more terribly was the lesson impressed upon them when Richard's hour of vengeance came, and they were employed to impeach archbishop Arundel,

Impeachments by the Commons in 1376.

Impeachments in 1386 and 1388.

Importance of these as precedents.

[1] See Rot. Parl. ii. 333, 355; iii. 160, 249.

ostensibly for his conduct as chancellor and for his participation in the cruelties of which their predecessors in the house of commons had been the willing instruments, but really that they might in alliance with the king complete the reprisals due for the work in which they had shared with the appellants. The dangerous facility with which the power of impeachment might be wielded seems to have daunted the advocates of national right; the commons as an estate of the realm joyfully acquiesced in the change of dynasty, but, by subsequently protesting that the judgments of parliament belonged to the king and lords only, they attempted to avoid responsibility for the judicial proceedings taken against the unhappy Richard.

The question of expenditure undertaken by the parliament.

287. If the king could not be made 'to live of his own,' and no hold which the nation could obtain over his ministers could secure honesty and economy in administration, it would seem a necessary inference that the national council should take into its own hands the expenditure of the grants by which it was obliged to supplement the royal income. The functions of the legislature and the executive were not yet so clearly distinguished as to preclude the attempt: the consent of the nation was indeed necessary for taxation, but the king was the supreme judge of his own necessities; he was still the supreme administrator in practice as well as in theory, an administrator who must be trusted whether or no he were worthy, and whom it was impossible to bring to a strict account. The men who had not hesitated to claim a right to interfere with the household expenditure, were not likely to be restrained by any theoretical scruples from interference with the outlay of money which they themselves had contributed. In this, as in so many other ways, the barons of the thirteenth century set the example to the commons of the fourteenth. Strangely enough the first idea of the kind came from the king's ministers. From the beginning of the reign of Henry III we have seen the special grants of the parliament entrusted for collection and custody to officers specially appointed for the purpose; frequently the form of taxation, including provision for the custody as well as the assessment of the grant, is issued by the advice

Proposal in 1237 that special officers should take charge of the grant.

and consent of the national council, and the audit withdrawn from the ordinary view of the court of Exchequer, where the king might be supposed to have too much influence [1]. In 1237 William of Raleigh, as the king's minister, proposed that the national council should not only draw up the form of taxation but elect a committee in whose hands the money collected should be deposited, and by whom it should be expended [2]. Although on that occasion the barons do not seem to have realised the importance of the concession, they are found a few years later complaining that no account had been rendered of this very grant, and intimating a suspicion that the proceeds were in the king's hands at the time that he was asking for more [3]. In 1244 the scheme of reform contained a proposal for the election of three or four counsellors, one part of whose work would be to secure the proper expenditure of the aids [4]. Throughout the baronial struggle the attempt was made to take out of the king's hands the power of expending public money. The time was not ripe for this. Edward I was too strong for any such restriction. Under Edward II the attempt to impose it was but one part of a project which took all real power out of the king's hands; the proposal enforced in 1310 and 1311, that all the proceeds of the taxes and customs should be brought into the Exchequer [5], shows that the court had become a sort of national court of audit; but its efficiency depended too much on the power or good-will of the king to be trusted implicitly, and the hold which the ordainers kept upon it superseded rather than restricted the king's authority. From the time however at which the wars of Edward III began to be burdensome, the parliament showed a strong wish both to determine the way in which the grants should be applied, and to secure an efficient audit of accounts by the appointment of responsible treasurers for each subsidy. The first of these points the king readily yielded: the ministers were accustomed, at the opening of parliament, to declare the special need

Proposal to elect treasurers.

Order for all taxes to be brought into the Exchequer.

Increased desire for an audit under Edward III.

[1] Select Charters, pp. 352, 361, 366; and pp. 38, 289, above.
[2] Above, p. 54. [3] Above, p. 60. [4] Above, p. 64.
[5] Above, pp. 344, 345.

of the moment, and, although the form frequently degenerated into mere verbiage, the hearers seem to have understood it as a recognition of their right to discriminate. Sometimes then the subsidy of the year is given for the defence of the coast, sometimes to enable the king to maintain his quarrel with his adversary of France, sometimes for the restoration of the navy, sometimes for the defence of Gascony; in 1346 and 1348 the money raised from the northern counties is applied to the defence against the Scots[1]; in 1353 the whole grant is appropriated to the prosecution of the war[2]; in 1346, 1373, and 1380, the continuance of the aid is made contingent on the continuance of the war. In 1380 the commons prayed that the aid might be spent on the defence of the kingdom, especially in the reinforcement of the earl of Buckingham's army in Brittany: the king replied that it should be spent for this purpose subject to the advice of the council and the lords[3]. In 1390 the custom on wool was appropriated partly to the expenses of the king, partly to the war, in a way which anticipates the modern distinction between the civil list and public expenditure[4].

Appropriation of grants.

Audit of accounts attempted.

288. The efficient audit of the accounts was a much more difficult point, and it was not finally secured so long as Edward III lived. In 1340, however, William de la Pole was required by a committee of lords and commons to render an account of his receipts[5], and in 1341 the demand was dis-

[1] Rot. Parl. ii. 161, art. 15; 202, art. 7.

[2] 'Que les subsides a ore grantez, ensemblement ove les quinzismes et dismes qui sont a lever soient sauvement gardez sanz estre despendues ou mys en autre oeps nul fors que tant soulement en la maintenance de ses guerres solonc sa bone disposition;' Rot. Parl. ii. 252; cf. pp. 160, 317; and see below, p. 598, note 5.

[3] Rot. Parl. iii. 90, 93, 94.

[4] 'Concessum est autem regi in hoc parliamento, ut habeat de quolibet sacco lanae xl. solidos, de quibus xls. decem applicarentur in praesenti regis usibus, et xxx. servarentur in futurum in manibus thesaurariorum constituendorum per parliamentum non expendendi nisi cum werrae necessitas instare videretur. Similiter rex habebit de libra sex denarios, quatuor servandos ad usum praefatum per dictos thesaurarios et duos jam percipiendos et expendendos ad voluntatem regis;' Wals. ii. 196. The same plan was adopted under Henry IV in 1404; Annales Henrici IV (ed. Riley), pp. 379, 380. In 1327 the petition that no minister might be replaced in office until he had rendered a final account was summarily negatived; Rot. Parl. ii. 9, 11.

[5] Rot. Parl. ii. 114.

tinctly made by both lords and commons, that certain persons should be appointed by commission to audit the accounts of those who had received the subsidy of wool and other aids granted to the king, and likewise of those who had received and expended his money on both sides of the sea since the beginning of the war; all the accounts to be enrolled in chancery as had been aforetime the custom[1]. The king yielded the point, as we have seen; undertook that the accounts should be presented for audit to lords elected in parliament, assisted by the treasurer and chief baron of the Exchequer. Whether the promise was better kept than the other engagements entered into at this parliament, we cannot distinctly discover: notwithstanding many just grounds of complaint, this particular point does not again come into prominence until the last year of the reign, when in the Good Parliament Peter de la Mare demanded an audit of accounts. In the last parliament of Edward III the commons petitioned that two earls and two barons might be appointed as treasurers to secure the proper expenditure of the subsidy[2]. Immediately on the accession of Richard II, when the difficult position of John of Gaunt and the prevailing mistrust of the court seemed to give an opportunity, the claim, which had been frustrated in 1376, was again made[3]. In the grant of aid made in October 1377 the lords and commons prayed that certain sufficient persons might be assigned on the part of the king to be treasurers or guardians of the money raised, 'to such effect that that money might be applied entirely to the expenses of the war and no part of it in any other way[4].' William Walworth and John Philipot were accordingly appointed, and swore in parliament to perform their duty loyally, and to give account of receipt and issue according to a form to be devised by the king and his council. The expedient was not altogether successful. John of Gaunt was suspected and openly accused of getting the money out of the hands of the treasurers for his own purposes, and when, at the next parliament,

Election of auditors.

Audit demanded in 1376 and 1377.

Failure of the experiment.

[1] Above, p. 409; Rot. Parl. ii. 128, 130.
[2] Rot. Parl. ii. 364.
[3] Above, p. 465.
[4] Rot. Parl. iii. 7.

the commons, through Sir James Pickering their Speaker, demanded the account, the chancellor, Sir Richard le Scrope, demurred. Yielding however to the urgency of the commons, he laid the statement before them and they proceeded to examine and criticise it. The result was the bestowal of another grant with a humble prayer that it might be spent on the defence and salvation of the country and on nothing else, and that certain sufficient persons might be assigned as treasurers [1]. The warning thus given was taken: in the parliament of 1379 the king without being asked ordered the accounts of the subsidy to be presented by the treasurers [2]; and among the petitions of the commons appears a prayer that the treasurers of the war may be discharged of their office and the treasurer of the king of England appointed to receive all the money and all the grants to be made henceforth for war, as had been usual aforetime [3]; and this was followed up in 1381, when the commons proposed and the king directed a searching reform of the whole procedure of the Exchequer [4]. The particular point is again, as in the reign of Edward II, merged in the general mass of constitutional difficulties which fill the rest of the reign of Richard, but it furnished an example to the following parliaments, and from thenceforward, except during times of civil discord, treasurers of the subsidies were regularly appointed, to account at the next parliament for both receipts and issues [5]. The commons had thus secured

The principle is yielded in 1379.

Regular appointment of treasurers of the war.

[1] Rot. Parl. iii. 35, 36.
[2] Rot. Parl. iii. 56, 57.
[3] Rot. Parl. iii. 66, art. 27.
[4] Rot. Parl. iii. 118, 119.
[5] In 1382 tunnage and poundage were granted for two years, 'issint toutes voies que les deniers ent provenantz soient entierment appliez sur la salve garde de la meer, et nulle part aillours. Et a la requeste de la commune le roi voet que Mons[r]. Johan Philipot, Chivaler, soit resceivour et gardein de les deniers,' &c.; Rot. Parl. iii. 124. The same year in October the grant of a tenth and fifteenth was made 'entierment sur le defens du roialme;' ibid. 134. In 1383 the fifteenth is to be delivered to the admirals for the safe keeping of the sea; ibid. p. 151. In 1385 the receivers of the fifteenth were appointed in parliament, and ordered to pay nothing except by warrant from the king, and under the supervision of two lords appointed as supervisors; ibid. 204, 213; for the neglect of this order the chancellor was called to account in 1386; see above, p. 498. In 1390 a treasurer and controller were appointed; Rot. Parl. iii. 262, 263.

the right which the barons in 1237 had failed to understand, and they had advanced a very important step towards a direct control of one branch of administration as well as towards the enforcing of ministerial responsibility. This point is however interesting in connexion with the subject of general politics, rather than as one of the details of financial administration.

Great importance of the financial limitation thus set.

289. The command of the national purse was the point on which the claims of the nation and the prerogative of the king came most frequently into collision both directly and indirectly; the demand that the king should live of his own was the most summary and comprehensive of the watchwords by which the constitutional struggle was guided, and the ingenuity of successive kings and ministers was tasked to the utmost in contriving evasions of a rule which recommended itself to the common sense of the nation. But it must not be supposed that either the nation or its leaders, when once awakened, looked with less jealousy on the royal pretensions to legislate, to resist all reforms of administrative procedure, to interfere with the ordinary process of law, or to determine by the fiat of the king alone the course of national policy. On these points perhaps they had an easier victory, because the special struggles turned generally on the question of money; but though easier it was not the less valuable. There is indeed this distinction, that whilst some of the kings set a higher value than others on these powers and on the prerogatives that were connected with them, money was indispensable to all. The admission of the right of parliament to legislate, to inquire into abuses, and to share in the guidance of national policy, was practically purchased by the money granted to Edward I and Edward III; although Edward I had a just theory of national unity, and Edward III exercised little more political foresight than prompted him to seek the acquiescence of the nation in his own schemes. It has been well said that although the English people have never been slow to shed their blood in defence of liberty, most of the limitations by which at different times they have succeeded in binding the

The royal pretensions to legislate, to administer and to determine public policy.

The share of Parliament in these points vindicated.

Purchase of liberties and rights.

royal power have been purchased with money[1]; many of them by stipulated payments, in the offering and accepting of which neither party saw anything to be ashamed of. The confirmation of the charters in 1225 by Henry III contains a straightforward admission of the fact: 'for this concession and for the gift of these liberties and those contained in the charter of the forests, the archbishops, bishops, abbots, priors, earls, barons, knights, freeholders and all men of the realm granted us a fifteenth part of all their moveable goods[2].' The charter of the national liberties was in fact drawn up just like the charter of a privileged town. In 1297 Edward I in equally plain terms recognised the price which he had taken for renewal of the charter of his father[3]. In 1301 at Lincoln the barons on behalf of the whole community told the king that if their demands were granted they would increase their gift from a twentieth to a fifteenth[4]; in 1310 they told Edward II that they had by the gift of a twentieth purchased relief from prises and other grievances[5]; in 1339 the king informed the commons, by way of inducing them to be liberal, that the chancellor was empowered to grant some favours to the nation in general, 'as grantz et as petitz de la commune;' to which they replied in the next session that if their conditions were not fulfilled they would not be bound to grant the aid[6]. The rehearsal, in the statutes of 1340 and later

Bargain and sale of privilege.

[1] Hallam, Middle Ages, iii. 162.

[2] 'Pro hac autem concessione . . . dederunt nobis quintam decimam partem omnium mobilium suorum;' Select Charters, p. 354.

[3] 'Quintam partem omnium bonorum suorum mobilium . . . concesserint pro confirmatione Magnae Cartae;' Parl. Writs, i. 53.

[4] 'Le pueple du reaume ensi ke totes les choses suzdites se facent e seent establement afermez e accompliz ly grante le xvme en luy del xxme einz ces houres graunte, issint ke tote les choses suzdites entre sy e la Seint Michel prochein suant se facent, autrement que rien ne seit levee;' Parl. Writs, i. 105.

[5] 'La communaute de vostre terre vous donerent le vintisme dener de lour biens, en ayde de vostre guerre de Escoce, e le vintisme quint pur estre deporte des prises et grevances;' Lib. Cust. p. 199. Similar expressions are found in the reign of Edward III; see for example, Rot. Parl. ii. 273.

[6] 'Furent monstrez ascunes lettres patentes par les queles monseigneur l'ercevesque avoit poair de granter ascunes graces as grantz et as petitz de la commune;' Rot. Parl. ii. 104; cf. p. 107.

years, of the conditions on which the money grants of those years were bestowed, shows that the idea was familiar. It furnished in fact a practical solution of difficult questions which in theory were insoluble. The king had rights as lord of his people, the people had rights as freemen and as the estates of the realm which the king personified: the definition of the rights of each, in theory most difficult, became practically easy when it was reduced to a question of bargain and sale.

Purchase of privileges.

As year by year the royal necessities became greater, more complete provision was made for the declaration of the national demands. The presentation of gravamina was made an invariable preliminary to the discussion of a grant, the redress of grievances was the condition of the grant, and the actual remedy, the execution of the conditions, the fulfilment of the promises, the actual delivery of the purchased right, became the point on which the crisis of constitutional progress turned. Except in cases of great and just irritation, an aid was never refused. When it was made conditional on redress of grievances the royal promise was almost necessarily accepted as conclusive on the one side; the money was paid, the promise might or might not be kept. Especially where the grievance was caused by maladministration rather than by the fault of the law, it was impossible to exact the remedy before the price was paid. Even under Henry IV the claim made by the commons, that the petitions should be answered before the subsidy was granted, was refused as contrary to the practice of parliament. Thus the only security for redress was the power of refusing money when it was next asked, a power which might again be met by insincere promises or by obstinate persistence in misgovernment which would ultimately lead to civil war. The idea of making supply depend upon the actual redress could only be realised under a system of government for which the nations of Europe were not yet prepared, under that system of limited monarchy secured by ministerial responsibility, towards which England at least was feeling her way.

Presentation of gravamina.

Promises of redress.

The demand of redress before supply.

Offer of the king to receive petitions.

290. It was under Edward III that it became a regular form at the opening of parliament for the chancellor to declare the king's willingness to hear the petitions of his people[1]: all who had grievances were to bring them to the foot of the throne that the king with the advice of his council or of the lords might redress them; but the machinery for receiving and considering such petitions as came from private individuals or separate communities was perfected, as we have seen, by Edward I. Petitions however for the redress of national grievances run back to earlier precedents, and these became, almost immediately on the completion of the parliamentary system in 1295, the most important part of the work of the session. The articles of the barons of 1215, the petition of 1258, the bill of articles presented at Lincoln in 1301, the petitions of 1309 and 1310, were the precedents for the long lists of petitions, sometimes offered by the estates together or in pairs, but most frequently by the commons alone. These petitions fill the greatest part of the Rolls of Parliament; they include all personal and political complaints, they form the basis of the conditions of money grants, and of nearly all administrative and statutory reforms. They are however still petitions, prayers for something which the king will, on consultation with the lords or with the council, give or withhold, and on which his answer is definitive, whether he gives it as the supreme legislator or as the supreme administrator, by reference to the courts of law, or by an ordinance framed to meet the particular case brought before him, or by the making of a new law.

Precedents of petitions offered in behalf of the community.

Multitude of petitions presented.

Machinery for judicial action on petitions.

The first of these cases, the reference of petitions addressed to the king, to the special tribunal to which they should be submitted, need not be further discussed at this point[2]. It has, as has been pointed out in an earlier chapter, a bearing on

[1] For example in 1352: 'Que s'ils avoient nulles petitions des grevances faites a commune poeple, ou pur amendement de la ley, les baillassent avant en parlement: et aussint fut dit a les prelatz et seigneurs que chescun entendreit entour le triere des petitions des singuleres persones, es places ou ils furent assignez;' Rot. Parl. ii. 237; cf. ii. 309; iii. 56, 71 sq.

[2] See above, pp. 275–277.

the history of the judicature, the development of the chancery, and the jurisdiction of the king in council; but, except when the commons take an opportunity of reminding the king of the incompleteness of the arrangements for hearing petitions, or when they suggest improvements in the proceedings, it does not much concern parliamentary history: although the commons make it a part of their business to see that the private petitions are duly considered, the judicial power of the lords is not shared by the commons nor is action upon the petitions which require judicial redress ever made a condition of a money grant.

Legislation on petitions, by statute or ordinance.

The other two cases are directly and supremely important. Whether the king redresses grievances by ordinance or by statute he is really acting as a legislator[1]. Although in one case he acts with the advice of his council and in the other by the counsel and consent of the estates of the realm, the enacting power is his: no advice or consent of parliament can make a statute without him; even if the law is his superior, and he has sworn to maintain the law which his people shall have chosen, there is no constitutional machinery which compels him to obey the law or to observe his oath.

Office of the king.

More particularly, he is the framer of the law which the advice or consent of the nation have urged or assisted him to make; he turns the petitions of the commons into statutes or satisfies them by ordinance; he interprets the petitions and interprets the statutes formed upon them. By his power too of making ordinances in council he claims the power not only to supply the imperfections of the statute law, but to suspend its general operation, to make particular exceptions to its application, to abolish it altogether where it is contrary to his prerogative right. Many of these powers and claims are so intimately bound up with the accepted theory of legislation that they cannot be disentangled without great difficulty, and in some points the struggle necessarily ends in a compromise.

Legislation based on petition of the estates.

Nearly the whole of the legislation of the fourteenth century is based upon the petitions of parliament. Some important

[1] See below, pp. 615, sq.

developments of administrative process grew out of the constructive legislation of Edward I, and were embodied in acts of parliament as well as in ordinances; but a comparison of the Rolls of Parliament with the Statute Book proves that the great bulk of the new laws were initiated by the estates and chiefly by the commons. Hence the importance of the right of petition and of freedom of speech in the declaration of gravamina, asserted by the invaluable precedents of 1301 and 1309. As the petitions of the commons were urged in connexion with the discussion of money grants, it was very difficult to refuse them peremptorily without losing the chance of a grant. They were also, it may be fairly allowed, stated almost invariably in reasonable and respectful language. Thus, although, when it was necessary to refuse them, the refusal is frequently stated very distinctly; in most cases it was advisable either to agree or to pretend to agree, or, if not, to declare that the matter in question should be duly considered; the form 'le roi s'avisera' did not certainly in its original use involve a downright rejection. But the king's consent to the prayer of a petition did not turn it into a statute; it might be forgotten in the hurry of business, or in the interval between two parliaments; and, as the house of commons seldom consisted of the same members two years together, it might thus drop out of sight altogether, or it might purposely be left incomplete. If it were turned into a statute, the statute might contain provisions which were not contained in the petition and which robbed the concession of its true value; or, if it were honestly drawn up, it might contain no provisions for execution and so remain a dead letter. And when formally drawn, sealed, and enrolled, it was liable to be suspended either generally or in particular cases by the will of the king, possibly, as was the case in 1341, to be revoked altogether. The constant complaints, recorded in the petitions on the Rolls of Parliament, show that resort was had to each of these means of evading the fulfilment of the royal promises even when the grants of money were made conditional upon their performance; and the examination of these evasions is

Petition gives the power of initiation.

Chances of defeat after the petition is answered.

Evasions of the answers.

not the least valuable of the many lessons which the history of the prerogative affords.

The first point to be won was the right to insist on clear and formal answers to the petitions: and this was itself a common subject of petition: in several of the parliaments of Edward III, for instance in 1332[1], the proceedings of the session were so much hurried that there was no time to discuss the petitions, and the king was requested to summon another parliament. In 1373 the king urged that the question of supplies should be settled before the petitions were entertained; the commons met the demand with a prayer that they should be heard at once[2]. Occasionally the delay was so suspicious that it had to be directly met with a proposition such as was made in 1383[3], that the parliament should not break up until the business of the petitions had been completed. If the answer thus extorted were not satisfactory, means must be taken to make it so: in 1341, when the king had answered the petitions, the lords and commons were advised that 'the said answers were not so full and sufficient as the occasion required,' and the clergy were likewise informed that they were not 'so pleasant as reason demanded.' The several estates accordingly asked to have the answers in writing; they were then discussed and modified[4]. If the answers were satisfactory, it was necessary next to make them secure; to this end were addressed the petitions that the answers should be reduced into form and sealed before the parliament separated; thus in 1344 and 1362 the commons prayed that the petitions might be examined and redress ordered before the end of the parliament 'pur salvetee du poeple[5];' in 1352 that all the reasonable petitions of their estate might be granted, confirmed and sealed before the departure of the parliament[6]; and in 1379 the same request was made with an additional prayer that a statute might be made to the same effect; the king granted the first point, but said nothing about the statute, and no such statute was enacted[7].

The Commons insist on clear and formal answers.

Petitions answered at once.

[1] Rot. Parl. ii. 65–68. [2] Rot. Parl. ii. 316, 318.
[3] Rot. Parl. iii. 147. [4] Rot. Parl. ii. 129, 130, 133.
[5] Rot. Parl. ii. 149, 272. [6] Rot. Parl. ii. 238. [7] Rot. Parl. iii. 61.

As a rule however this was the practice: either the petitions were answered at once, or the private and less important were left to the council, or once or twice perhaps, as in 1388, were deferred to be settled by a committee which remained at work after the parliament broke up [1].

Petitions altered in the process of being turned into statutes.

A more damaging charge than that of delaying the answers to petitions is involved in the complaint that the purport of the answers was changed during the process of transmutation into statute. To avoid this the commons petitioned from time to time that the statutes or ordinances of reform should be read before the house previously to being ingrossed or sealed. Thus in 1341 it was made one of the conditions of a grant, that the petitions showed by the great men and the commons should be affirmed according as they were granted by the king, by statute, charter, or patent [2]; in 1344 the commons prayed that the petitions might be viewed and examined by the magnates and other persons assigned [3]; in 1347 the commons prayed that all the petitions presented by their body for the common profit and amendment of mischiefs might be answered and endorsed in parliament before the commons, that they might know the endorsements and have remedy thereon according to the ordinance of parliament [4]; in 1348 they asked that the petitions to be introduced in the present session might be heard by a committee of prelates, lords, and judges, in the presence of four or six members of the commons, so that they might be reasonably answered in the present parliament, and, when they were answered in full, the answers might remain in force without being changed [5]. In 1377 it was necessary to maintain that the petitions themselves should be read before the lords and commons, that they might be debated amicably and in good faith and reason, and so determined [6]: and in the same parliament the

Attempts of the commons to prevent this.

[1] In 1344 the commons petitioned 'que vous pleise ordener par assent des prelatz et grantz certeynes gentz qui voillent demorer tan que les petitions mys avant en parlement soient terminez avant lour departir, issint qe la commune ne soit saunz remedie;' Rot. Parl. ii. 149. See also p. 524 above, and compare the proceedings in 1371; Rot. Parl. ii. 304.

[2] Rot. Parl. ii. 133; Statutes, i. 298.

[3] Rot. Parl. ii. 149, 150.

[4] Rot. Parl. ii. 165.

[5] Rot. Parl. ii. 201.

[6] Rot. Parl. iii. 14.

commons demanded that, as the petitions to which Edward III in the last parliament but one had replied 'le roi le veut' ought to be made into statutes, the ordinances framed on these petitions should be read and rehearsed before them with a view to such enactment[1]; in 1381 they demanded that the ordinance for the royal household, made in consequence of their petition, might be laid before them that they might know the persons and manner of the said ordinance before it was ingrossed and confirmed[2]; in 1385, as in 1341, it was made one of the conditions of a grant, that the points contained in certain special bills should be endorsed in the same manner as they had been granted by the king[3]. Many expedients were adopted to insure this; in 1327 it was proposed that the points conceded by the king should be put in writing, sealed and delivered to the knights of the shire to be published in their counties[4]; in 1339 the commons prayed the king to show them what security he would give them for the performance of their demands[5]; in 1340 a joint committee of the lords and commons was named to embody in a statute the points of petition which were to be made perpetual, those which were of temporary importance being published as ordinances in letters patent[6]; in 1341 the prayer was that the petitions of the magnates and of the commons be affirmed accordingly as they had been granted by the king, the perpetual points in statutes, the temporary ones in letters patent or charters[7]; and in 1344 the conditions of the money grant were embodied in letters patent 'pur reconforter le poeple,' and so enrolled on the statute roll[8]. This form of record recommended itself to the clergy also; they demanded that their grant and the conditions on which it was made should be recorded in a charter[9].

Demands of the commons for the honest handling of their granted petitions.

We have not, it is true, any clear instances[10] in which unfair

[1] Rot. Parl. iii. 17. [2] Rot. Parl. iii. 102. [3] Rot. Parl. iii. 204.
[4] Rot. Parl. ii. 10. [5] Rot. Parl. ii. 105. [6] Rot. Parl. ii. 113.
[7] Rot. Parl. ii. 133. [8] Rot. Parl. ii. 150. [9] Rot. Parl. ii. 152.

[10] One instance, quoted by Ruffhead in his preface to the statutes, is this. In 1362 the commons petitioned against the use of French in the courts of law; the king answered the petition with an assent that legal proceedings should be henceforth in English; but when this answer became

Variation of petitions.

Introduction of saving clauses.

manipulation of the petitions was detected and corrected, but the prayers of the petitions here enumerated can scarcely admit of other interpretation; unless some such attempts had been made, such perpetual misgivings would not have arisen. There was no doubt a strong temptation, in case of any promise wrung by compulsion from the king, to insert in the enactment which embodied it a saving clause, which would rob it of much of its value. The mischief wrought by these saving clauses was duly appreciated. By a 'salvo ordine meo,' or 'saving the rights of the church,' the great prelates of the twelfth century had tried to escape from the obligations under which royal urgency had placed them [1], and had perpetuated if they had not originated the struggles between the crown and the clergy. Henry II, himself an adept in diplomatic craft, had been provoked beyond endurance by the use of this weapon in the hands of Becket. Edward I had in vain attempted in 1299 [2] to loosen the bonds in which his own promise had involved him, by the insertion of a proviso of the kind; and again in 1300 [3] the articles additional to the charters had contained an ample reservation of the rights of his prerogative. The instances, however, given above, which are found scattered through the whole records of the century, show that the weak point of the position of the commons was their attitude of petition. The remedy for this was the adoption of a new form of initiation; the form of bill was substituted for that of petition; the statute was brought forward in the shape which it was intended ultimately to take, and every modification in the original draught passed under the

Remedy for this abuse, the introduction of *Bills* in the form of statutes.

a statute, it contained a provision that the records should be kept in Latin. This however is scarcely an instance in point. See Rot. Parl. ii. 273; Statutes, i. 375; Ruffhead, i. pref. p. xv.

[1] 'Nam sicut nostri majores formulas juris suspectissimas habebant in jure, sic rex semper in verbis archiepiscopi, conscientiam habentis purissimam, quasdam clausulas causabatur, scilicet nunc "salvo ordine meo," nunc "salvo honore Dei," nunc "salva fide Dei;"' R. de Diceto, i. 339.

[2] Above, p. 155.

[3] 'En totes les choses desusdites et chescune de eles, voet le rei e entent, il e soen consail et touz ceus qui a cest ordenement furent, que le droit et la seignurie de sa coroune savez lui soient par tout;' Art. super Cartas, Stat. i. 141. The importance of this clause came into discussion in the debates on the Petition of Rights in 1628, and is especially treated in Glanvill's speech printed in Rushworth's Collections, vol. i. p. 374.

eyes of the promoters[1]. This change took place about the end of the reign of Henry VI. Henry V had been obliged to reply to a petition, in which the commons had insisted that no statutes should be enacted without their consent, that from henceforth nothing should 'be enacted to the petitions of his commune that be contrarie of their asking, whereby they should be bound without their assent[2].' This concession involves, it is true, the larger question of the position of the commons in legislation, but it amounts to a confession of the evil for the remedy of which so many prayers had been addressed in vain.

Undertaking of Henry V with regard to petitions.

The frequent disregard of petitions ostensibly granted, but not embodied in statutes, is proved by the constant repetition of the same requests in successive parliaments, such for instance as the complaints about purveyance and the unconstitutional dealings with the customs, which we have already detailed. The difficulty of securing the execution of those which had become statutes is shown by the constant recurrence of petitions that the laws in general, and particular statutes, may be enforced: even the fundamental statutes of the constitution, the great charter, and the charter of the forests, are not executed in a way that satisfies the commons, and the prayer is repeated so often as to show that little reliance was placed on the most solemn promises for the proper administration of the most solemn laws[3]. It became a rule during the reign of Edward III for the first petition on the roll to contain a prayer for the observance of the great charter, and this may have been to some extent a mere formality. But the repeated complaints of the inefficiency of particular statutes are not capable of being so explained. Two examples may suffice: in 1355 the commons pray specially that the statute of the staple, the statute of 1340 on sheriffs, the statute of purveyance, the statute of weights and measures, and the statute of Westminster the First, may be kept; in each case the king assents[4]. The annual appointment

Petitions for the enforcing of statutes actually passed.

General Petition.

Petition for particular statutes to be observed.

[1] Ruffhead, Statutes, i. pref. p. xv: the form being 'quaedam petitio exhibita fuit in hoc parliamento formam actus in se continens.'
[2] Rot. Parl. iv. 22; Hallam, iii. 91.
[3] See for example, Rot. Parl. ii. 139, 163, 165, 203, 227.
[4] Rot. Parl. ii. 265, 266.

of sheriffs, which was enacted by statute in 1340, is a constantly recurring subject of petitions of this sort. It would seem that the king tacitly overruled the operation of the act and prolonged the period of office as and when he pleased; the answer to the petition generally is affirmative, but Edward III in granting it made a curious reservation which seems equivalent to a refusal: in case a good sheriff should be found, his commission might be renewed and he himself sworn afresh[1]. Richard II in 1384 deigned to argue the point with the commons: it was inexpedient, they were told, that the king should be forbidden to reappoint a man who had for a year discharged loyally his duty to both king and people[2]. In 1383 he had consented that commissions granting a longer tenure of the sheriffdom should be repealed, saving always to the king his prerogative in this case and in all others[3]; but now he declared simply that he would do what should seem best for his own profit and that of the people. He stated his reasons still more fully in 1397[4].

Argument of the king on the statutes touching sheriffs.

Interference of the king with the execution of statutes.

291. If it were within the terms of the king's prerogative not merely to allow a statute to become inefficient for want of administrative industry, but actually to override an enactment like that fixing the duration of the sheriff's term of office, it was clearly not forbidden him to interfere by direct and active measures with the observance of laws which he disliked. It is unnecessary to remark further on the cases of financial illegality in which the plain terms of statutes were transgressed, and which have been already noticed. These infractions of the constitution cannot be palliated by showing that an equal straining of prerogative was admitted in other departments, but the examples that prove the latter show that finance was not the only branch of administration

[1] Rot. Parl. ii. 168. A very similar answer was given in 1334; ibid. p. 376; cf. Rot. Parl. iii. 44.

[2] 'Le responce du chanceller fuist tiell, q'il serroit trop prejudiciel au roi et a sa corone d'estre ensi restreint, que, quant un Viscont s'ad bien et loialment porte en son office au roi et au poeple par un an, que le roi par avys de son conseill ne purroit re-eslir et faire tiell bon officier Viscont pur l'an ensuant. Et pur ce le roi voet faire en tiell cas come meulsz semblera pur profit de lui et de son poeple;' Rot. Parl. iii. 201.

[3] Rot. Parl. iii. 159.

[4] Rot. Parl. iii. 339.

in which the line between legislative and executive machinery was very faintly drawn. The case of a king revoking a statute properly passed, sealed, and published, as Edward III did in 1341, is happily unique[1]; that most arbitrary proceeding must have been at the time regarded as shameful, and was long remembered as a warning. Edward himself, by procuring the repeal of the obnoxious clauses, in the parliament of 1343, acknowledged the illegality of his own conduct. The only event which can be compared with this is the summary annulment by John of Gaunt of the measures of the Good Parliament, an act which the commons in the first parliament of Richard II remarked on in general but unmistakeable terms of censure[2]; but the resolutions of the Good Parliament had not taken the form of statute, and so far as they were judicial might be set aside by the exercise of the royal prerogative of mercy. The royal power however of suspending the operation of a statute was not so determinately proscribed. The suspension of the constitutional clauses of the charter of Runnymede, which William Marshall, acting as regent, omitted in the reissue of the charter of liberties in 1216, shows that under certain circumstances such a power was regarded as necessary; and the assumption by Edward I, in 1297, of the attitude of a dictator, was excused, as it is partly justified, by the exigency of the moment. There are not however many instances in which so dangerous a weapon was resorted to[3].

Revocation of statutes in 1341.

John of Gaunt annuls the acts of the Good Parliament.

Suspension of the execution of statutes.

[1] Above, p. 410.

[2] 'Item que la commune loy et auxint les especialx loys, estatutz et ordinances de la terre, faitz devant ces heures, pur commune profit et bone governance du roialme, lour feussent entierement tenuz, ratifiez et confermez, et que par ycelles ils fussent droiturelement governez; qar la commune soy ent ad sentuz moelt grevez cea en ariere que ce ne lour ad my este fait toutes partz einz qe par maistrie et singulertees d'aucuns entour le roy, qui Dieux assoille, ont este plusours de la dite commune malmesnez . . . Requerante as seigneurs du parlement, que quan que y feust ordenez en ce parlement, ne fust repellez sanz parlement;' Rot. Parl. iii. 6. Here the commons themselves added the saving clause, 'salvant en toutes choses la regalie et dignitee nostre seigneur le roi avaunt dit, a la quelle les communes ne veullient que par lours demandes chose prejudiciele y fust faite par aucune voie;' ibid.

[3] In 1385 Richard II suspended the execution of the act of 1384, touching justices and barons of the Exchequer, until it could be explained by parliament; Rot. Parl. iii. 210: but this suspension was itself enrolled as

The most significant are those in which the king was acting diplomatically and trying to satisfy at once the pope and the parliament. Thus in 1307 Edward I, almost as soon as he had passed the statute of Carlisle, which ordered that no money raised by the taxation of ecclesiastical property should be carried beyond sea, was compelled by the urgent entreaty of the papal envoy to suspend the operation of the law in favour of the pope: in letters patent he announced to his people that he had allowed the papal agents to execute their office, to collect the firstfruits of vacant benefices, and to send them to the pope by way of exchange through the merchants, notwithstanding the prohibitions enacted in parliament[1]. The whole history of the statute of provisors is one long story of similar tactics, a compromise between the statute law and the religious obedience which was thought due to the apostolic see; by regarding the transgression of the law simply as an infraction of the royal right of patronage, to be condoned by the royal licence, the royal administration virtually conceded all that the popes demanded; the persons promoted by the popes renounced all words prejudicial to the royal authority which occurred in the bulls of appointment, and when the king wished to promote a servant he availed himself of the papal machinery to evade the rights of the cathedral chapters. This compromise was viewed with great dislike by the parliaments; in 1391 the knights of the shire threw out a proposal to repeal the statute of provisors, which had lately been made more rigorous, although the proposal was supported by the king and the duke of Lancaster; but they allowed the king until the next parliament to overrule the operation of the statute[2].

Edward I suspends the operation of the statute of Carlisle.

Exceptions from the statute of provisors.

Evasion of the statute of provisors.

part of a statute, so that it is really a case of initiation by the king, not of arbitrary suspension; Statutes, ii. 38.

[1] Rot. Parl. i. 222; above, p. 163.

[2] 'Fait a remembrier touchant l'estatut de provisours, que les communes pur la grant affiance qu'ils ont en la persone nostre seigneur le roy et en son tres excellent sen, et en la grant tendresse qu'il ad a sa corone et les droitz d'icelle, et auxint en les nobles et hautes discretions des seigneurs, s'assenterent en plein parlement que nostre dit seigneur le roy par advys et assent des ditz seigneurs purra faire tielle soefferance tochant le dit

Petitions against grants of pardon and protection.

The more common plan of dispensing by special licence with the operation of a statute, in the way of pardons and grants of impunity, was less dangerous to the constitution and less clearly opposed to the theory of the monarchy as accepted in the middle ages. Yet against the lavish exercise of this prerogative the commons are found remonstrating from time to time in tones sufficiently peremptory. The power was restricted by the statute of Northampton passed in 1328; but in 1330 and 1347 the king was told that the facilities for obtaining pardons were so great that murders and all sorts of felonies were committed without restraint; the commons in the latter year prayed that no such pardons might be issued without consent of parliament, and the king, in his answer, undertook that no such charters should thenceforth be issued unless for the honour and profit of himself and his people[1]. A similar petition was presented in 1351[2], and instances might be multiplied which would seem to show that this evil was not merely an abuse of the royal attribute of mercy or a defeat of the ordinary processes of justice, but a regularly systematised perversion of prerogative, by the manipulation of which the great people of the realm, whether as maintainers or otherwise, attempted to secure for their retainers, and those who could purchase their support, an exemption from the operation of the law. Even thus viewed however it belongs rather to the subject of judicature than to legislation.

The king undertakes to use them moderately.

Contrivances for the repeal of statutes.

These were the direct ways of thwarting the legal enactments to which the king had given an unwilling consent. Indirectly the same end was obtained by means which, if not less distinctly unconstitutional, were less distinctly illegal; that is, by obtaining petitions for the reversal of recent legislation, or by influencing the election in order to obtain a subservient majority. For both of these devices the short duration

estatut come luy semblera resonable et profitable tan qu'al proschein parlement, par issint que le dit estatut ne soit repellez en null article d'icell;' Rot. Parl. iii. 285; cf. pp. 301, 317, 340; Walsingham, ii. 203.

[1] Statutes, i. 264; Rot. Parl. ii. 172. See also pp. 242, 253; iii. 268, &c.

[2] Rot. Parl. ii. 229.

of the parliaments afforded great facilities; and under Edward III and Richard II both were adopted. In 1377 for instance the awards of the Good Parliament were annulled on the petition of a packed house of commons[1]. In 1351 the commons prayed that no statute might be changed in consequence of a bill presented by any single person[2]; in 1348 that for no bill delivered in this parliament in the name of the commons or of any one else might the answers already given to their petitions be altered[3]. The king in the former case asked an explanation of the request, but in the latter he replied more at length: 'Already the king had by advice of the magnates replied to the petitions of the commons touching the law of the land, that the laws had and used in times past, and the process thereon formerly used, could not be changed without making a new statute on the matter, which the king neither then nor since had for certain causes been able to undertake; but as soon as he could undertake it he would take the great men and the wise men of the council and would ordain upon these articles and others touching the amendment of the law, by their advice and counsel, in such manner that reason and equity should be done to all his lieges and subjects and to each one of them.' This answer is in full accord with the policy of the king; it is a plausible profession of good intentions, but an evasive answer to the question put to him.

Evasive answer of the king.

292. The theory that the laws were made or enacted by the king with the consent of the lords and at the petition of the commons implies of course that without the consent of the king no statute could be enacted at all: and, so far as the rolls of parliament show, no proposed legislation except the ordinances of 1311 reached the stage at which it took the form of statute without having been approved by the king. The legislation of the ordainers was altogether exceptional. As a rule, it was the petition not the drafted statute which received the royal consent or was refused it. Hence the king retained

The king's power of answering petitions otherwise than by granting or rejecting them.

[1] Above, p. 458.

[2] Rot. Parl. ii. 230; art. 29.

[3] Ibid. ii. 203.

considerable power of discussing the subject of petition before giving his final answer, and many of the recorded answers furnish the reasons for granting, modifying or refusing the request made. These cases of course differ widely from the examples given above, in which, after the prayer was granted, the language of the statute was made to express something else. But, although they illustrate very remarkably the political history of the period at which they occur, they need not here be considered as instances of the king's admitted power or prerogative in legislation, and the examples which we have already given are enough to show the danger of abuse to which the accepted theory was liable. Two further points may however be summarily noticed in this place, rather as completing our survey of the subject than as directly connected with the history of prerogative: these are the king's power of issuing ordinances, and the exact position occupied by the separate estates in parliamentary legislation.

Distinction between statutes and ordinances.

The difficulty of determining the essential difference between a statute and an ordinance has been already remarked more than once. Many attempts have been made to furnish a definition which would be applicable to the ordinance at all periods of its use, but most frequently it is described by enumerating the points in which it differs from a statute [1]: the statute is a law or an amendment of law, enacted by the king in parliament, and enrolled on the statute roll, not to be altered, repealed, or suspended without the authority of the parliament, and valid in all particulars until it has been so revoked; the ordinance is a regulation made by the king, by himself, or in his council or with the advice of his council, promulgated in letters patent or in charter, and liable to be recalled by the same authority [2]. Moreover the statute claims perpetuity; it pretends to the sacred character of law, and

Recognised distinctions.

[1] See Hallam, Middle Ages, iii. 49, 50.

[2] In 1373 the commons complained that the clergy had ignored an ordinance, made in the recent great council at Winchester, touching tithe of underwood, because it had not been made a statute: 'les persones de seint Eglise, entendantz qe cel ordinance ne restreint mye lour aunciene accrochement, surmettantz qe ceo ne fust mye afferme pur estatut;' Rot. Parl. ii. 319.

is not supposed to have been admitted to the statute roll except in the full belief that it is established for ever. The ordinance is rather a tentative act which, if it be insufficient to secure its object or if it operate mischievously, may be easily recalled, and, if it be successful, may by a subsequent act be made a statute. But these generalisations do not cover all the instances of the use of ordinance. The fundamental distinction appears to lie far deeper than anything here stated, while in actual use the statute and the ordinance come more closely together. The statute is primarily a legislative act, the ordinance is primarily an executive one; the statute stands to the ordinance in the same relation as the law of the Twelve Tables stands to the prætor's edict; the enacting process incorporates the statute into the body of the national law, the royal notification of the ordinance simply asserts that the process enunciated in the ordinance will be observed from henceforth. But although thus distinguished in origin, they have practically very much in common: the assizes of Henry II, viewed in their relation to the common law of the nation, are ordinances, although they have received the assent of the magnates; their subject matter is the same, the perpetuity of their operation is the same, and in time they themselves become a part of the common law. Magna Carta is in its form an ordinance rather than a statute, but it becomes one of the fundamental laws of the realm almost immediately after its promulgation. Throughout the thirteenth century, during which the functions of the legislative were being only very gradually separated from those of the executive, the king still regarded himself as sovereign lawgiver as well as sovereign administrator. Hence even under Edward I the ordinance is scarcely distinguishable from the statute, and several of the laws which were afterwards implicitly accepted, as statutes of his enacting, were really ordinances,—ordinances which, like the Extravagants of the popes or the *Novellæ* of the Byzantine emperors, only required to be formally incorporated with the Corpus juris, to become laws to all intents and purposes. When however, in consequence of Edward's consoli-

Primary distinction.

Reason for the confusion between them.

Statutes and ordinances under Edward I.

dating and defining work, the functions of the parliament as sharing sovereign legislative power gained recognition, and the province of the executive both in taxation and legislation was more clearly ascertained, it was not possible at once to disentangle the action of the king in his two capacities; matters which might have well been treated by ordinance, such as the banishment of the Despensers, were established by statute, and matters which were worthy of statutable enactment were left to the ordinance. Nor was this indistinctness solely due to the double function of the king; the magnates also as members of the royal council, or a large proportion of them, had double duties as well; and thus, although the form of statute differed from that of ordinance, the two were now and then issued by the same powers and occupied the same ground. Hence even in the parliament itself little fundamental difference was recognised: the ordinances of the great council of 1353 were not allowed to be enrolled as statutes until they had received fresh authority from the parliament of 1354; but on the other hand the answers to the petitions in 1340 were divided into two classes[1], to be embodied respectively in statutes and ordinances, the latter as well as the former being published with the full authority of the parliament, but not regarded as perpetual or incorporated with the statute law.

Confusion between the two.

As, however, the growth of the constitution in the reign of Edward III cleared up very considerably what was obscure in the relations of the crown and parliament, as the ordaining power of the crown in council became distinguishable by very definite marks from the enacting power of the crown in parliament, and as further the jealousy between the crown and

The obscurity cleared up in the reign of Edward III.

[1] 'Lesqueux Ercevesque, Evesques, et les autres ensi assignez, oies et tries les ditz requestes, par commune assent et accord de touz firent mettre en estatut les pointz et les articles qui sont perpetuel. Le quel nostre seignur le roi, par assent des touz en dit parlement esteantz, comanda de engrosser et ensealer et fermement garder par tut le roialme d'Engleterre, et lequel estatut comence, "A l'honur de Dieu," &c. Et sur les pointz et articles qui ne sont mye perpetuels einz pur un temps, si ad nostre seignur le roi, par assent des grantz et communes, fait faire et ensealer ses lettres patentes qui commencent en ceste manere, "Edward, &c. Sachetz que come prelatz, countes,"' &c.; Rot. Parl. ii. 113; cf. p. 280, quoted above, p. 427.

Jealousy felt of the ordaining power of the council.

parliament increased, the maintenance and extension of the ordaining power became with the supporters of high prerogative a leading principle, and the curbing of that ordaining power became to the constitutional party a point to be consistently aimed at. It had long been found that the form of charter or letters patent was capable of being used to defeat, rather than to openly contravene, the operation of a law which limited the power of the crown. The Charter granted by Edward I to the foreign merchants was an ordinance which evaded the intention of the Confirmatio Cartarum; and, as we have seen in our brief summary of the history of the Customs, the precedent was followed as long as the kings were strong enough to enforce compliance. With the reign of Richard II this dishonest policy was largely extended: the chronicles complain that whatever good acts the parliaments passed were invalidated by the king and his council[1]. That this was done in the overt way in which in 1341 and 1377 Edward III and John of Gaunt had repudiated constitutional right, we have no evidence. There is however a petition of the commons, presented in 1390, in which they pray that the chancellor and the council may not, after the close of parliament, make any ordinance contrary to the common law or the ancient customs of the land and the statutes aforetime ordained or to be ordained in the present parliament: the king replies that what had hitherto been done should be done still, saving the prerogative of the king[2]. This petition and the answer seem to cover the whole grievance. The commons define and the king claims the abused prerogative: and the saving words dictated by Richard, 'issint que la regalie du roi soit sauve,' embody the principle, which in the condemning charges brought against him in 1399 he was declared to have maintained, that the laws were in the mouth and breast of the king,

Petition in 1390.

Claim of prerogative.

[1] It is said of the parliament of 1382, 'multa sunt et alia quae statuta sunt ibidem. Sed quid juvant statuta parliamentorum cum penitus expost nullum sortiantur effectum? Rex nempe cum privato consilio cuncta vel mutare vel delere solebat quae in parliamentis antehabitis tota regni non solum Communitas sed et ipsa nobilitas statuebat;' Wals. ii. 48; Chr. Angl. p. 333.

[2] Rot. Parl. iii. 266.

and that he by himself could change and frame the laws of the kingdom[1].

Right of the executive to act in unforeseen emergencies.

The subject, as it is needless to debate here, has its own difficulties, which are not peculiar to any stage or form of government. The executive power in the state must have certain powers to act in cases for which legislation has not provided, and modern legislation has not got beyond the expedient of investing the executive with authority to meet such critical occasions. The crown is able on several matters to legislate by orders in council at the present day, but by a deputed not a prerogative power; but there are conceivable occasions on which, during an interval of parliament, the ministers of the crown might be called upon to act provisionally with such authority as would require an act of indemnity to justify it. The idea of regulating the ordaining power of the crown by recognising it within certain limits was in embryo in the fourteenth century[2], but it appears distinctly in the rules laid down in 1391 and 1394 for the 'sufferances' or exceptions which the king was allowed to make from the operations of the statute of provisors. The statute of proclamations passed in 1539[3], the 'lex regia' of English history, which gave to the proclamations of Henry VIII the force of laws, is one of the most curious phenomena of our constitutional life: for it employs the legislative machinery which by centuries of careful and cautious policy the parliament had perfected in its own hands, to authorise a proceeding which was a virtual resignation of the essential character of parliament as a legislative body; the legislative power won for the parliament from

Parliament authorises the king to make ordinances in particular cases.

Statute of proclamations.

[1] Above, p. 531.

[2] In 1337 the export of wool was forbidden by statute 'until by the king and his council it be thereof otherwise provided;' Statutes, i. 280: that is, the king and council were empowered to settle the terms on which the wool should be set free; see above, p. 554. In 1385 similar power was given to settle the staples by ordinance: 'ordinatum est de assensu parliamenti et plenius concordatum quod stapula teneatur in Anglia: sed in quibus erit locis, et quando incipiet, ac de modo et forma regiminis et gubernationis ejusdem, ordinabitur postmodum per consilium domini regis, auctoritate parliamenti: et quod id quod per dictum consilium in hac parte fuerit ordinatum, virtutem parliamenti habeat et vigorem;' Rot. Parl. iii. 204.

[3] 31 Henry VIII, c. 8.

the king was used to authorise the king to legislate without a parliament.

How the king and estates shared the work of legislation.

293. The second point referred to above as necessary to complete our view of this subject is the part taken by the several factors employed in legislation; the king, the parliament, and the separate estates of parliament; the powers of initiation, consultation, consent, and enactment, as they are modified during the course of the fourteenth century, and illustrated by the documentary evidence already adduced in relation to other parts of the subject. And it is by no means the least of the constitutional results of the century, that, whereas at the beginning almost all legislation is originated by the king, at the close of it the petitions of the commons seem almost to engross the power of initiation.

Initiative power of the king and council.

The fact that the king and council could at any time initiate legislation in parliament is of course beyond question; and there can be little doubt that until the reign of Edward II almost all modifications of the existing laws were formally introduced by the king, and, where the consent of the parliament was deemed necessary, were laid before the assembled estates for the purpose of consultation. The barons in their controversy with the same king alleged that England was not governed by written law but by ancient customs, which when they were insufficient he was bound to amend and reduce to certainty by the advice of the magnates and on the complaint of the people[1]. This implies a most distinct assertion of the royal duty and responsibility; the 'querimonia vulgi' was a not less powerful weapon than the 'quas vulgus elegerit' of the coronation oath.

The royal right of initiating reform in legislation.

The enacting clause of the statute of 1362 on purveyance is perhaps the best instance of the continuity of the king's right of initiation: 'for the grievous complaint which hath been made of purveyors,' 'the king of his own will, without motion of the great men or commons, hath granted and ordained in ease of his people[2]' that the abuses shall cease. The clause however is prefaced by a statement that the king is legislating at the

[1] See above, p. 353, note 3.
[2] Statutes, i. 371; Rot. Parl. ii. 270. See above, pp. 434, 435.

petition of the commons and by the assent of the magnates, and his claim to initiate is stated rather as an additional sanction to the act than as a special feature of the process of legislation.

The magnates had a right of initiation.

That a similar power of introducing new laws belonged to the great council of the nation before the completion of the parliamentary system is equally unquestioned. Not to adduce again the articles of Runnymede or the petitions of 1258, we may quote as a sufficient proof the proposal made by the bishops in the council of Merton in 1236: 'all the bishops asked the magnates to consent that children born before marriage should be legitimate as well as they that be born after marriage, as touching succession of inheritance, because the church holds such for legitimate: and all the earls and barons with one voice answered that they would not change the laws of England which have been hitherto used and approved[1].' Here it is clear that the bishops had introduced a proposal for a new law.

Examples.

The statute 'Quia emptores' was passed 'ad instantiam magnatum[2],' as was also the statute 'de malefactoribus' in 1293[3]. The *articuli super cartas* in 1300 were enacted at the request of the prelates, earls, and barons[4]. Throughout the fourteenth century petitions presented by the magnates either by themselves or in conjunction with the commons are sufficiently frequent to show that the right was not allowed to remain unexercised[5]. The fact that such origination is not mentioned in the wording of the statutes may be accounted for on the grounds that the commons almost invariably included in their petitions the points demanded by the magnates, and thus the petition of the latter was merged in the more general statement of counsel and consent.

Statute framed on the petition of the magnates.

A single instance will suffice: in 1341 the lords petitioned for a declaration that the peers of the land should not be tried except in parliament: that declaration was embodied in a statute enacted 'by the assent of the prelates, earls, barons, and other great men, and of all the commonalty of the realm of

[1] Statutes, i. 4.

[2] Statutes, i. 106.

[3] Statutes, i. 111.

[4] Statutes, i. 136.

[5] In 1339 the magnates petitioned alone on the subject of wardship and the rights of lords of manors; Rot. Parl. ii. 104: in 1341 the lords and commons petitioned together; ibid. 118.

England[1],' a form sufficiently exceptional to prove that legislation on the petition of the magnates was less usual than legislation on petition of the commons.

Petitions of the whole parliament.

The bills of articles presented by the barons, on behalf of the whole community of the realm, to Edward I at Lincoln in 1301[2], and the petitions of 1309[3] and 1310[4] were rather petitions of the parliament than petitions of the commons: but they were important precedents for the separate action of the third estate. The statute of Stamford, the result of the petitions of 1309, mentions more than once the supplications of the commonalty as the moving cause of the legislation[5]; in 1320 again the supplication of the commonalty is referred to in the preamble to the statute of Westminster the Fourth[6]. It is however the second statute of 1327 that introduces the form which was afterwards generally adopted, of specifying the petition of the commons in contradistinction to the assent of the magnates[7]; and thus the right of initiation is distinctly and unmistakeably recognised. This form continues to be generally used until the twenty-third year of Henry VI, when the words 'by authority of parliament' were added; from the first year of Henry VII the mention of petition is dropped and the older form of assent substituted, a change which was probably connected with the adoption of the form of an act or draughted statute in preference to that of petition.

Petitions of the commonalty.

Initiation by the clergy.

The power of initiation by petition belonged to the estate of the clergy assembled in parliament; and upon their representations statutes were occasionally founded, the enacting words of which imply the co-operation of the lords and commons by way of assent: thus in 1344, on the grant made by the prelates and proctors of the clergy, and, as we know from the rolls of parlia-

Statute of 1344 founded on a petition of the clergy.

[1] Statutes, i. 295.

[2] Parl. Writs, i. 104: 'Billa praelatorum et procerum regni liberata domino regi ex parte totius communitatis in parliamento Lincolniae.'

[3] Rot. Parl. i. 443: 'Les articles souz escritz furent baillez a nostre seigneur le roy par la communalte de son roialme a son parlement.'

[4] Lib. Cust. p. 199: 'Ceo est la petition des Prelats, contes et barons.'

[5] Statutes, i. 154–156.

[6] Statutes, i. 180.

[7] Statutes, i. 253.

ment, as the result of their petition, the king, by assent of the magnates and of all the commonalty, does of his good grace grant the privileges demanded[1]. As the right of petition belonged to every subject it is scarcely necessary to adduce these illustrations of the practice; legislation however, properly so called, does not seem to have ever followed on the petition of private individuals[2].

Right of discussion in parliament.

The right of debating on the subjects which were either laid by the king before the parliaments, or introduced by means of petition, was recognised in the widest way as belonging to each of the estates separately and to all together: there seems indeed to have been no restriction as to the intercourse of the two houses or individual members; the king's directions at the opening of parliament that the several estates, or portions of them, should deliberate apart being simply a recommendation or direction for the speedy dispatch of business.

Communication between the lords and commons.

Late in the reign of Edward III, long after the final arrangement of the two houses, we have seen a custom arising by which a number of the lords, either selected by their own house or chosen by the commons, were assigned to confer with the whole body of the commons on the answer to be given to the king's request for money[3]; but long before this, and in fact almost as soon as the parliament definitely divided into two houses, it is clear that the closest communication existed between the two. The commons were expected, after debating on the questions laid before them, to report their opinion to the lords[4]; the lords and

[1] Statutes, i. 302; Rot. Parl. ii. 150.

[2] The statute 'de Vasto' of 1292 is enacted by the king in full parliament in consequence of a private lawsuit exhibited to the king; but the enactment is made for the decision of a point on which the judges were disagreed, and the initiation of the legislation comes from the king in council; Statutes, i. 109.

[3] In 1373; see above, p. 446.

[4] In 1347 they are expressly directed to do this; Rot. Parl. ii. 165; in 1348 they are ordered to report to the king and his council; in 1351 to report to the king on a day fixed; in 1352 to report by means of a chosen committee; Rot. Parl. ii. 200, 226, 237. In the last year the lords sent their advice to the commons; in 1362 the knights were examined before the lords; in 1368 the two houses had full deliberation together; Rot. Parl. ii. 269, 295; and in 1376 the king directed them to report to one another on each point; ibid. p. 322.

Freedom of intercourse between the lords and commons. commons in 1341 joined in petitions[1], and in every case of a money grant not only conference but agreement must have been the rule. The attempt made by Richard II in 1383[2] to nominate the committee of lords who were to confer with the commons was the only occasion on which the king tried to disturb this right of consultation; but on one or two occasions the lords by adopting a sullen tone towards the commons endangered the free exercise of it; in 1378 for instance they objected to a conference of select lords with the house of commons as a novelty introduced of late years, and stated that the proper and usual plan was for both houses to depute a small number of their members to discuss matters quietly together, after which each of the two committees reported to its own house[3]. In 1381 they declared, in answer to a request from the commons to know the mind of the prelates, barons, and judges separately, that the practice of parliament was that the commons should lay their advice before the lords and not the lords before the commons[4].

Communication of the clergy with the commons. The consultative voice belonging to the estate of clergy would seem to have been equally free, but the traces of it are more rare, partly because of the uncertainty of the attendance of the proctors of the clergy under the præmunientes clause, partly because that voice when exercised at all would generally be exercised by the bishops, and it is difficult to distinguish between their action as members of the house of lords and as the leaders of the clerical estate.

Haxey's case. If we suppose Thomas Haxey, the famous petitioner of 1397, to have been a clerical proctor, his history affords a proof, not only of the session of the estate of clergy in that parliament, but of its actual co-operation and consultation

[1] See above, p. 622. [2] See above, p. 488, note 1.
[3] Rot. Parl. iii. 36.
[4] Rot. Parl. iii. 100: 'Et priast outre la dite commune que les prelatz par eux mesmes, les grantz seigneurs temporelx par eux mesmes, les chivalers par eux mesmes, les justices par eux et touz autres estatz singulerement fussent chargez de treter et communer sur ceste lour charge, et que lour advis fust reportez a la commune, a fyn que bon remede fust ordenez. A quoi fust dit et responduz, qe le roi ad fait charger les seigneurs et autres sages de communer et treter diligeaument sur les dites matires, mais l'anciene custume et forme de parlement a este tout dys, que la commune reporteroit leur advis sur les matires a eux donez au roi nostre seigneur et as seigneurs du parlement primerement, et non pas e contra.'

with the house of commons. Such association of the two representative bodies was, in the sixteenth century, believed to have been customary at the time, then long past, when the clerical proctors had attended; but this is not quite clear[1]. We shall however find reason to believe that the proceedings of parliament in the fourteenth century were not bound by any very strict rules. The 'Modus tenendi parliamentum,' which, although it does not describe anything that ever existed, may be regarded as exhibiting the popular idea of parliament at the close of the fourteenth century, gives a rule for settling disputed questions between the several estates of parliament: the steward, constable, and marshall or two of them are to choose five-and-twenty members from the whole body, two bishops, three clerical proctors, two earls and three barons, five knights of the shire, and five citizens and burghers; these twenty-five are to reduce their number either by pairing off or by electing a smaller number among themselves, and the process is to be repeated until the representation of the whole parliament is lodged in the hands of a committee that finds itself unanimous[2]. There is no instance on the rolls of parliament in which this plan was followed, but the method adopted in 1397, when the clerical estate delegated its functions to a single proctor, and in 1398, when the committee to which the parliament delegated its full powers was chosen in something like the same proportion from the several estates, may show that such an expedient may have recommended itself to the statesmen of the day.

Account given in the 'Modus tenendi parliamentum.'

Committee of the whole parliament.

The question of assent is of greater importance, but is also more clear. The theory of Edward I, that that which touches all should be approved of all, was borne out by his own practice and by the proceedings of his son's reign. The statutes of Edward II are almost invariably declared to be enacted with the assent of prelates, barons, and whole community, which in this collocation can scarcely be understood to mean anything but the commons. The mention of the petition of the commons,

Right of assent belonging to the several estates.

[1] See above, p. 516, and vol. iii. § 432.

[2] Select Charters, p. 506. Prynne (4th Inst. p. 5) regards this rule as a misreading of the Statute 14 Edward III. st. 1. c. 5.

Assent to legislation.

which is introduced under Edward III, does not merely describe a lower position taken up by the third estate, but must be regarded a fortiori as implying assent;—that for which they have prayed they can hardly need to assent to;—it would further seem proved by the fact that in the statutes of the clergy, which were not passed at the petition of the commons, the assent of the commons is declared as it had been under Edward II[1]. It may however be questioned whether the assent of the commons was necessary to such statutes framed on the petitions of the clergy, whether the assent of the clerical estate was necessary to statutes framed on petition of the commons, and whether there was not some jealousy felt by the commons of any legislation that was not founded on their own petitions.

Two subordinate questions.

Was the assent of the commons necessary to statutes passed on petition of the clergy?

The first of these points has been referred to already; and it cannot be very certainly decided[2]. If Edward I, as his practice seems to show, regarded the enacting power as belonging to the crown advised by the magnates, it is very possible that he looked on the other two estates as being in somewhat the same position with respect to himself and the lords, and required the assent of each in those measures only which concerned them separately. But if this were the case, the practice had as early as 1307 outgrown the theory, for the statute of Carlisle[3], which closely concerns the clergy, does not express the consent even of the prelates, and was passed, no doubt, without their overt cooperation, which might have exposed them to excommunication. It is not however surprising that, when the commons under Edward III contented themselves with the title of petitioners, the clergy should imagine themselves entitled to the same rights, or that the kings should favour an assumption that tended to exalt their own claims to legislate. Thus, although in 1340, 1344, and 1352 the statutes passed at the petition of the clergy received the assent of the commons[4], it seems

Statutes passed on petition of the clergy, by assent of lords and commons.

[1] Statutes, i. 293, 302.
[2] Above, p. 259.
[3] Statutes, i. 150–152.
[4] The statute of 1340 is enacted at the request of the prelates and clergy 'par accord et assent des ditz peres et de toutz autres somons et esteantz en notre dit parlement;' Statutes, i. 293; Rot. Parl. ii. 113. The statute of 1344 is in the form of a charter granted 'par assent des grantz et des

almost certain that from time to time statutes or ordinances were passed by the king at their request without such assent. The 'articuli cleri' of 1316, which were the answers of the king and council to certain questions propounded by the clerical estate in parliament, were enrolled as a statute without having received the consent of the commons[1]. In some instances the results of the deliberations of convocation, in the form of canons and constitutions, would require royal assent, or a promise to abstain from interference, before the church could demand the aid of the secular arm in their execution or repel the prohibitions of the civil courts; in such cases it might well be questioned whether the enactments would come before parliament at all, and the letters of warning addressed by Edward I to the ecclesiastical councils of his reign, forbidding them to attempt any measure prejudicial to the crown or kingdom, show that some suspicions of their aggressive character were felt at that time.

Statutes passed on petition of the clergy.

In 1344 the commons petition that no 'petition made by the clergy to the disadvantage or damage of the magnates or commons should be granted without being examined by the king and his council, so that it might hold good without damage to the lords and commons.' This somewhat self-contradictory request seems certainly to imply that such legislation had been allowed, and that the commons did not at the moment see their way to resist it by declaring that no such statute should be enacted without their consent. But after all it is not quite clear that the petition refers to statutes at all, and not rather to ordinances, for which the assent of the commons was not required[2]. In the parliament of 1377, however, it was definitely

The commons petition that petitions of the clergy may not be granted without examination.

communes;' Statutes, i. 302. That of 1352 is 'de l'assent de son dit parlement;' ibid. i. 325.

[1] Statutes, i. 175, 176. The questions were presented in the parliament of Lincoln in January; the answers were given, after a clerical grant of money, at York in the following November.

[2] The petition of 1344 may have had a general application, but the particular circumstances under which it was presented were these: in 1343 archbishop Stratford in a council of bishops issued a series of constitutions, by one of which ecclesiastical censures were decreed against all who detained tithe of underwood or 'sylva caedua.' The commons immediately seized on this as a grievance, petitioned as stated in the text, and further prayed that prohibitions might issue in cases where suits for tithe of wood

demanded that neither statute nor ordinance should without the consent of the commons be framed on a petition of the clergy: the clergy refused to be bound by statutes made without their consent, the commons would not be bound by constitutions which the clergy made for their own profit. The king answered by a request for more definite information, which was equivalent to delay; and the commons afterwards took the matter into their own hands[1]. The statute of 1382 against the heretic preachers, which was repealed in the next parliament at the petition of the commons, as having been made without their consent, forms one clause of a statute which declares itself to have been made by the king, the prelates, lords and commons in parliament[2]. It may or may not have received the assent of the commons, but it bears no certain evidence of having been framed on a petition of the clergy, nor do the commons allege that it has. It almost certainly was suggested by the bishops, whose functions it was intended to amplify, but there is nothing to connect it specially with the parliamentary estate of the clergy, nor was the dread of heresy at all peculiar to that body.

Statute of 1382 against heretic preachers.

The consent of the estate of clergy not required for legislation.

That the consent of the estate of clergy was necessary to legislation approved by the lords and commons has never been maintained as a principle, or even as a fact of constitutional government. It is therefore sufficient to cite the declaration of the statute of York in 1322, in which no mention is made of the clergy among the estates of parliament whose consent is necessary for the establishment of any measure touching the king and the realm[3]. If there had been any intention on the

were instituted; Rot. Parl. ii. 149. In 1347 they accused the clergy of claiming tithe of timber under the same constitution, and the bishops denied the charge; Rot. Parl. ii. 170: but it was renewed in 1352; ibid. 241. In 1371 a statute was passed at the request of the commons forbidding the clergy to demand tithe for wood of more than twenty years' growth; Statutes, i. 393; Rot. Parl. ii. 301; but the clergy persisted in regarding this as an ordinance and as not binding: and there can be little doubt that the petition of 1377 had this point in view. The question of tithe of underwood occupies far more space in the Rolls of Parliament than that of heresy.

[1] Rot. Parl. ii. 368.

[2] Statutes, ii. 23, 26; Rot. Parl. ii. 124.

[3] Statutes, i. 189; see above, p. 369.

part of Edward I to make the clerical estate a permanent check on the commons, that intention was defeated by the abstention of the clergy themselves, their dislike to attend in obedience to a secular summons, and their determination to vote their taxes in convocation. But it seems to have been regarded as a piece of necessary caution that in critical cases their right to participate in the action of parliament should not be overlooked. On more than one occasion, as in 1321, their presence is insisted on, in order that the proceedings of parliament may not be subsequently annulled on the ground of their absence; and the delegation of their powers to Sir Thomas Percy in the parliament of 1397 and to the earl of Wiltshire in 1398, shows that Richard II carefully avoided even the chance of any such flaw invalidating his proceedings. Yet the protests of the clergy must now and then have defeated proposed legislation. In 1380 the prelates and clergy protested against the extension of the functions of the justices of the peace: the king declared that he would persist in doing justice, but the resolution did not become a statute [1]. Sometimes their protests were formal; in 1351, probably, they withheld their assent to the statute of Provisors; at all events it contains no statement of the assent of the prelates [2]; and in 1365, in particular reference to the statute of Praemunire, they declared that they would not assent to anything that might injure the church of England [3]. A similar protest was made by the two archbishops in the name of the clergy in 1390 [4], and in 1393 archbishop Courtenay put on record a schedule of explanatory protests intended to avoid offending the pope, whilst he supported the national legislation against his usurpations [5]. These protests can be scarcely regarded as more than diplomatic subterfuges: in each case the law is enacted in spite of them.

Abstention of the clergy from parliament.

Their presence required.

Protests of the clergy.

Protests by the prelates.

The jealousy of the commons with regard to any statute which was initiated by any other means than by their petition was not unreasonable, if we consider the attitude of the king in council, and the legislative powers claimed for the magnates

Reasonable jealousy of the commons about legislation.

[1] Rot. Parl. iii. 83. [2] Statutes, i. 317. [3] Rot. Parl. ii. 285.
[4] Rot. Parl. iii. 264. [5] Ibid. 304.

and clergy. The illustrations already given of the manipulation of petitions prove that there was ground enough for apprehension, and the case of the repealed statute of 1382 just referred to is strictly in point here. Strange to say, the same influence which had obtained the passing of that statute prevented the record of its repeal from being entered on the Statute Roll. Possibly the lords refused their consent to the petition; at any rate the repeal was inoperative.

Dissent of the lords defeats legislation.

We have not yet reached the point at which recorded discussions in parliament enable us to say how the dissent of the lords to a petition of the commons or the dissent of the commons to a proposal of the lords was expressed: so far as we have gone it was announced by the king in his answer to the petitions. Where the lords had refused to consent the king states the fact and the reasons of the refusal. Such for instance is the case in 1377, when the commons had proposed special measures for the education of the boy king, to which the lords demurred, thinking that all that was needed could be done in other ways[1]. From similar examples it would appear that, although the lords and commons had ample opportunities of conference, their conclusions were stated to the king separately. But it is in many instances impossible to distinguish whether the lords are acting as a portion of the royal council or as an estate of the realm: sometimes they join in the prayer of the commons, sometimes they join in the answers of the king[2].

The lords oppose a proposal of the commons.

Importance of the point now examined.

In following up the points that have arisen touching the legislative rights of the commons we may seem to have wandered far from the main question of the chapter, the contest between prerogative and parliamentary authority. The digression is however not foreign to the purpose; the period has two great characteristic features, the growth of the power of the commons, and the growth of the pretensions of pre-

[1] Above, p. 464.

[2] See, for example, Rot. Parl. ii. 130; and cf. Rot. Parl. ii. 152: 'au queux fu respondu par notre seigneur le roi et par les grantz en dit parlement.'

rogative. Whatever conduces to the former is also a check on the latter; and every vindication of the rights of parliament is a limitation of the claims of prerogative. Thus viewed, each of the several steps by which the commons claimed and obtained their right takes away from the crown a weapon of aggression or cuts off a means of evasion: and the full recognition of the right of initiating, consulting on and assenting to or dissenting from legislation, destroys the king's power of managing the powers and functions of council, and of indirectly affecting the balance of power among the estates, so as to keep in his own hands the virtual direction of legislation. When all is done he possesses, in his right to say 'le roi le veut' or 'le roi s'avisera,' more power than can be wisely entrusted to an irresponsible officer.

The decisive power of the king in legislation.

General deliberation.

294. The ninth article of the ordinances of 1311 prescribed that 'the king henceforth shall not go out of his realm nor undertake against any one deed of war without the common assent of his baronage, and that in parliament[1].' This claim, made on behalf of the baronage, was exercised, from the beginning of the reign of Edward III, and more or less efficiently from the date of the ordinances themselves, by the whole body of the parliament. The importance of the point thus claimed would seem to be one of the results of the loss of Normandy and Anjou by John. That king, so long as he stood, as his brother and father had stood, at the head of a body of vassals whose interests on the continent were almost identical with his own, had had no need to consult his baronage or ask permission of his people before making an expedition to France: when he did consult the 'commune consilium' on such questions it was simply with a view to taxation or the collection of forces. His own will seems to have been supreme as to the making of war or peace: he persisted or pretended to persist in his preparations for his expedition of 1205[2] in spite of the most earnest entreaties of the archbishop, his chief constitutional adviser; and in the later years of his reign the barons, who could not disobey his summons to arms, could fetter his action

Claim of the parliament to decide on peace and war.

[1] Statutes, i. 159.

[2] M. Paris, ii. 490.

only by refusing to follow him to Aquitaine, a refusal which he construed as rebellion. Under Henry III it was very different; he could not have stirred a step without the baronage, and accordingly in his few expeditions he acted with the advice and support of the parliament. He carried the semblance of consultation still further; for if we are to believe the London annalists, he not only took but asked leave of the citizens of the capital before starting on his journeys. In Easter week, 1232, at S. Paul's Cross, he asked leave to cross over to Gascony; the same form was observed in 1253, 1259, and 1262[1], and would almost seem to have been a customary ceremony in which the citizens of London represented the community of the realm. The acceptance of the Sicilian crown for his son Edmund, an act to which the magnates, if they had been duly consulted, could not be supposed to have assented, was a rash and fatal assumption of prerogative on Henry's part which brought its own punishment and afforded a warning to his successors. Edward I engaged in no war without obtaining both advice and substantial aid from his parliaments, and, when the barons in 1297 refused to go to Flanders at his command, they sought their justification in technical points of law[2], not in the statement that the war had been begun without their consent.

Henry III asked advice on these subjects.

Edward I discussed peace and war in parliament.

The ordinance of 1311.

The language of the ordinance of 1311 seems then unnecessarily stringent if it be understood as limiting an exercise of arbitrary power on this point. Read in connexion with the weak and halting policy of Edward II, it seems almost an insult to limit the military power of a king, one of whose great faults was his neglect of the pursuits of war. If it were not intended as a declaration of public policy, in which case it assumes, much more than the other ordinances, the character of a political principle, it must have been meant to prevent Edward from raising forces, on the pretext of foreign war, which might be used to crush the hostile baronage at home.

[1] Liber de Antt. Legg. p. 9, 'petiit licentiam'; p. 19, 'cepit licentiam'; cf. pp. 42, 50, where 'capere licentiam' may merely mean 'to take leave.'
[2] See above, p. 137.

However this may have been, both during the domination of the ordainers and during his own short periods of independent rule, the subject was kept before the king's eyes. In 1314 the earls refused to follow him to Bannockburn because the expedition had not been arranged in parliament[1]; in 1319 he had to announce the day of muster as fixed by assent of the magnates in parliament[2]; he asked by letter their consent to the issue of commissions of array[3], and in the latter years of his reign the contemplated expedition to France was the chief object for which he tried to bring the parliaments together. Although during this reign the commons as well as the magnates, when they were called on to furnish money, arms, and men, had opportunity of showing willingness or unwillingness to join in the wars, the complete recognition of their right to advise, a right which they were somewhat reluctant to assume, belongs to the reign of Edward III.

Refusal of the earls to go to Scotland without order of parliament.

From the very first transactions of this reign the commons were appealed to as having a voice in questions of war and peace. Isabella and Mortimer were anxious to fortify their foreign policy with the consent of the commons; and, when Edward himself started on his great military career, he started with the conviction, which every subsequent year of his life must have deepened, that he could sustain his armaments and his credit only by drawing the nation into full and sympathetic complicity with his aims. In 1328 it was with the counsel and consent of the prelates and 'proceres,' earls, barons, and commons that Edward resigned his claims on Scotland[4]; in 1332 the lords by themselves, and the knights of the shire by themselves, debated on the existing relations with Scotland and Ireland, and joined in recommending that the king should continue in the north watching the Scots, but not quitting the realm[5]. From the beginning of the French war onwards, to enumerate the several occasions on which the commons were distinctly asked for advice would be to recapitulate a great part of the history discussed in the last chapter. We have

Advice of the commons asked on war and peace.

[1] See above, p. 354. [2] See Parl. Writs, I. ii. 518, 519.
[3] Above, p. 570. [4] Rot. Parl. ii. 442. [5] Rot. Parl. ii. 66, 67.

The importance of this in the reign of Edward III.

there seen how their zeal kept pace with the king's successes, how in his necessities they welcomed the opportunity of making conditions before they granted money, how when the war flagged they inclined to throw the responsibility of continuing it upon the lords, and how when they were thoroughly wearied they made no scruple of declaring themselves unanimously desirous of peace [1]. But on the whole they seem to have been awake to the king's policy, and to have been very cautious in admitting that peace and war were within their province at all. And the same feeling appears in the following reign; in 1380 the commons petitioned against the plurality of wars [2]; from time to time we have seen them vigorously endeavouring to limit, direct, and audit the expenditure on the wars, and even attempting to draw distinctions between the national and royal interests in the maintenance of the fortresses of Gascony and Brittany. But when the question is put barely before them they avoid committing themselves. In 1382 they declared that it was for the king and the lords to determine whether he should go in person to the war or undertake any great expedition [3]; but by their reluctance to provide funds they showed conclusively that their wish was, not perhaps that the king should waste his youth in idleness, but that he should not gain experience and military education at their cost. In 1384, when consulted on the negotiations for peace, they replied that they could not, in the sight of existing dangers, advise the king either way; it seemed to them that the king might and should act in this behalf as it should seem best to his noble lordship, as concerning a matter which was his own proper inheritance that by right of royal lineage had descended to his noble person, and not as appertaining to the kingdom or crown of England [4]. Such a response, implying that Richard

Under Richard II.

The commons are cautious in accepting the place of counsellors.

[1] In 1339 the commons declare that they are not bound to give advice on matters of which they have no knowledge; Rot. Parl. ii. 105: in 1348 they say much the same; ibid. ii. 165. See above, pp. 400, 417.

[2] Rot. Parl. iii. 93.

[3] Rot. Parl. iii. 145: 'ne l'ordinance de son voiage, ou de nul autre grant viage a faire soleit ne doit appertenir a la commune einz au roi mesmes et as seigneurs du roialme.'

[4] Rot. Parl. iii. 170, 171.

should enforce his claims on France without the assistance of England, provoked a sharp rejoinder; the commons were charged on the part of the king to declare on the spot their choice of war or peace; there was, he told them, no middle course, for the French would agree to truces only on terms most favourable to themselves. They answered that they wished for peace, but were not able to understand clearly the terms on which peace was possible, and that they did not think that the English conquests in France should be held under the king of France in the same way as the royal inheritance in Gascony was held. The king, having told them that peace could not be made on such terms, asked them how 'if the said commons were king of the realm, or in the state in which the king is,' they would act under the circumstances. They answered that, as the magnates had said that if they were in the position of the king they would choose peace, so they, the commons, protesting that they should not henceforth be charged as counsellors in this case, nor be understood to advise either one way or the other, agreed to return the answer which the prelates and magnates had given; 'such answer and no other they give to their liege lord.' Under these circumstances, had the occasion ever arisen for the commons to demand a peremptory voice in the determination of peace or war, they might have been silenced by their own confession.

Richard II forces them to answer directly.

Caution of the commons.

So far then the king could in this point have made no claim on the part of his prerogative, which the commons could have contested. As it was, however, no such assertion was necessary, and the dangerous exercise of sovereign power in this department consisted in unwarranted acts of executive tyranny, the raising of provisions and munitions by way of purveyance, and the levying of forces by commissions of array, both which subjects we have already examined. The commons preferred, in questions of peace and war, an indirect to a direct control over the king's actions; the king would have preferred more substantial power with a less complete acknowledgment of his absolute right to determine national policy. Royal prerogative

The royal usurpations in this matter were indirect.

Attitude of king and parliament.

and parliamentary control seem to change places. The king is eager to recognise the authority that he may secure a hold on the purse of the commons; the commons, as soon as they feel confident in the possession of the purse, do not hesitate to repudiate the character of advisers, and leave to the king the sole responsibility for enterprises which they know that he cannot undertake alone. Hence the interchange of compliments, the flattering recognition of the prerogative power and personal wisdom of the prince, the condescending acknowledgment that in all matters of so high concern the prince must have the advice of his faithful commons.

Advice asked on the public peace.

Participation of the commons in the review of judicial matters.

295. The speeches of the chancellors at the opening of parliament very frequently contained, besides a request for advice on war or peace and a petition for money, a demand of counsel from the several estates of the realm on the best means of securing the public peace[1]; and it is in this clause, coupled with the general offer to receive petitions and gravamina, that the fullest recognition is found of the right of the commons to review the administrative system, and recommend executive reforms as well as new statutes. They were thus justified in pressing on the king's notice the misconduct of the sheriffs, their continuance in office for more than a year contrary to the statutes, the evils which attended the unsettled jurisdiction of the justices of the peace, the abuses of the Exchequer, the usurpations of the courts of the steward and marshall, and in general those mischiefs which arose from the interference with the ordinary course of justice by the exercise of royal prerogative. Thus the commons, although not pretending to be a court of law, attempted to keep under review the general administration of justice, and to compel the king to observe the promises of the coronation oath and the emphatic declaration of the great charter. No words of that famous document were better known or more frequently brought forward than the fortieth clause, 'nulli vendemus, nulli negabimus aut differemus

The great charter a watchword in matters of justice.

[1] For example, see Rot. Parl. ii. 103: 'furent trois causes purposes, dount la primere fu, que chescun grant et petit endroit soi penseroit la manere coment la pees deinz le roialme purroit mieutz et se deveroit plus seurement estre gardee.' Cf. ibid. pp. 136, 142, 161, 166.

rectum et justitiam[1];' and none probably were more necessarily pressed on the unwilling ear of the dishonest or negligent administrator. The frequent petitions of the commons on this point show the prevalence of the abuses and the determination of the nation not to rest until they were abated. The sale of writs in chancery was made a matter of complaint in 1334, 1352, 1354, 1371, 1376, and 1381; the words of the great charter being in each case quoted against the king[2]: the complaints are variously answered; in 1334 and 1352 the king charges the chancellor to be gracious; in 1371 he is directed to be reasonable; but in each case the answer implies that the royal right to exact heavy fees cannot be touched; 'the profit of the king that has customarily been given aforetime for writs of grace cannot be taken away,' is the reply of Edward III in 1352[3]: 'our lord the king does not intend,' says Richard II, 'to divest himself of so great an advantage, which has been continually in use in chancery as well before as after the making of the said charter, in the time of all his noble progenitors who have been kings of England[4].' The prescriptive right thus pleaded in the king's favour as the source of equity could not be allowed in the case of the clearer infractions of common right, even when they proceeded from the highest authority. In 1351 begins a series of petitions against the usurped jurisdiction of the council; the commons pray that no man be put to answer for his freehold, or for anything touching life or limb, fine or ransom[5], before the council of the king or any minister whatsoever, save by the process of law thereinbefore used. The king replies that the law shall be kept, and no man shall be bound to answer for his freehold but by process of law; as for cases touching life and limb, contempt or excess, it shall be done as was customary. The next year, 1352, the complaint is stated more definitely; the petitioners appeal to the thirty-ninth article of the charter, and insist that except on indictment or presentment of a jury no man shall be ousted

Profits on writs.

Royal answers.

Petitions against the jurisdiction of the privy council.

[1] E.g. Rot. Parl. ii. 313, iii. 116, and the passages referred to below.
[2] Rot. Parl. ii. 241, 261, 305, 376.
[3] Rot. Parl. ii. 241.
[4] Rot. Parl. iii. 116.
[5] Rot. Parl. ii. 228.

Petitions against the jurisdiction of the council.

of his freehold by petition to the king or council; the king grants the request[1]. Ten years after, in 1362 and 1363, the complaint is renewed; false accusations have been laid against divers persons before the king himself; the commons pray that such false accusers may be forced to find security to prosecute their charges, or incur the punishment of false accusers, that no one may be taken or imprisoned contrary to the great charter; the petition is granted, and the answer incorporated in a statute[2]. The royal council was the tribunal before which these false suggestions were made, and before which the accused were summoned to appear: the punishment of the accusers did not tend to limit the powers of the council; in 1368 the prayer is again presented and granted, but, like all administrative abuses, it was not remedied by the mere promise of redress[3]; and as the council grew in power the hope of redress was further delayed.

The jurisdiction of council a prerogative right.

In 1390 Richard included this jurisdiction of the council among the rights of the prerogative: the commons prayed that no one might be summoned by the writ 'quibusdam certis de causis' or other such writ before the chancellor or the council to answer in any case in which a remedy was given by the common law; the king 'is willing to save his prerogative as his progenitors have done before him[4].' It is scarcely a matter of wonder that with such a system of prevarication in the highest quarters there should be oppression wherever oppression was possible.

Mischief of this in times of disorder.

In the disorder of the times there are traces of attempts made on the part of the great lords to revive the feudal jurisdictions which had been limited by Henry II, and to entertain in their courts suits which were entirely beyond their competence. The complaint made to Edward III in 1376, against those who accroached royal power by new impositions[5], may possibly be explained in this way; but under Richard II the evil is manifest. In 1391 the commons grievously complained that the king's subjects were caused to come before the councils of

[1] Rot. Parl. ii. 239.
[2] Rot. Parl. ii. 270, 280, 283; Statutes, i. 382, 384.
[3] Rot. Parl. ii. 295: cf. also the petitions in 1377; ibid. iii. 21: in 1378; ibid. iii. 44: and in 1394; ibid. 323.
[4] Rot. Parl. iii. 267.
[5] Above, p. 454.

divers lords and ladies to answer for their freeholds, and other things real and personal, contrary to the king's right and the common law[1]: a remedy was granted by statute[2], but in 1393 the complaint was renewed and the king had to promise that the statute should be kept[3]. It is not improbable that the foundation of the great palatine jurisdiction of the duke of Lancaster may have afforded an inviting example for this species of abuse.

Private jurisdictions.

Courts of the king's officers.

Such prerogative or prescriptive right as could be claimed for the jurisdiction of the royal council, within lawful limits, might also be pleaded for the courts of the steward, the constable, the marshall, and other half private, half public tribunals, which had survived the enactments of the great charter, and which, throughout the whole period before us, were felt as a great grievance. The necessity of maintaining these courts for certain specific purposes, and the instinctive policy, inherent in such institutions, of extending their jurisdiction wherever it was possible, together with the vitality fostered by the possessors of the vested interests, gave them a long-continued existence. The Articuli super Cartas in 1300 had defined their jurisdiction[4]: notwithstanding much intermediate legislation, they were found in 1390 to be drawing to themselves cases of contracts, covenants, debts, and other actions pleadable at common law. The king again defines the sphere of their work, but even here he draws in the question of prerogative; the jurisdiction of the constable of Dover touches the king's inheritance; before doing anything there he will inquire into the ancient custom and frame his remedy thereupon[5].

Innumerable petitions on matters of judicature.

It would be vain to attempt, even by giving single examples, to illustrate all the plans suggested by the indefatigable commons to meet the abuses prevalent in the administration of justice, very many of which were quite unconnected with the doctrine of prerogative, except that, where the king gave a precedent of illegality and defended it by his prerogative right, he was sure to find imitators. Justice was delayed, not only in

[1] Rot. Parl. iii. 285. [2] Statutes, ii. 82. [3] Rot. Parl. iii. 305.

[4] Statutes, i. 138, art. 3: for petitions on the subject, see Rot. Parl. ii. 140, 201, 228, 240, 336, 368; iii. 65, 202.

[5] Rot. Parl. iii. 265, 267.

compliance with royal writ, contrary to the charter, but by the solicitations of great men, lords and ladies, who maintained the causes not merely of their own bona fide dependents, but of all who were rich enough to make it worth their while[1]. The evil of maintenance was apparently too strong for the statutes; the very judges of the land condescended to accept fees and robes from the great lords[2], as the king out of compliment wore the livery of the duke of Lancaster. The justices of assize were allowed to act in their own counties, in which they were so closely allied with the magnates that abuses prevailed of which it was not honest or decent to speak particularly: that especial mischief was abolished by statute in 1384[3]. The inefficacy of appeals was a crying evil; the judges heard appeals against their own decisions. The choice of the justices of assize was a frequent matter of discussion, and the functions as well as the nomination of the justices of the peace was a subject both of petition and statute, of peculiar interest to the knights of the shire, who were, as we have remarked, the most energetic part of the parliament[4]. Enough, however, has been said on this point to illustrate the question before us, the unwillingness of the king to grant a single prayer that might be interpreted as limiting his 'regalie[5],' and the determination of the commons to control the power which they believed themselves competent to regulate, and fully justified in restricting where restriction was necessary.

Evil of maintenance and livery.

Claims of the commons to regulate the choice of justices.

It is curious perhaps that the house of commons, whilst it thus attempted, and exercised in an indirect way, a control over every department of justice, should not have taken upon

[1] See the petitions against maintenance; e.g. Rot. Parl. ii. 10, 62, 166, 201, 228, 368.

[2] Rot. Parl. iii. 200.

[3] Rot. Parl. ii. 334; iii. 139, 200; Statutes, ii. 36.

[4] In 1363 the commons petitioned for power to elect justices of labourers and artisans and guardians of the peace, but the king directed them to nominate fit persons out of whom he would choose; Rot. Parl. ii. 277. The same proposal was made in the Good Parliament; ibid. 333.

[5] The constant allegation of the *regalie* appears in the very first years of Richard II, and continues throughout the reign. Many instances have been already given; see also Rot. Parl. iii. 15, 71, 73, 99, 267, 268, 279, 286, 321, 347.

itself to act judicially, but have left to the house of lords the task of trying both the causes and the persons that were amenable to no common-law tribunal. If they ever were tempted to act as judges it must have been during the period before us, when the arrangement in the two houses was still new and when many members of the lower house might fairly have considered themselves to be the peers of the magnates, who were distinguished only by the special summons. The king or the influential minister—Edward II at York in 1322, Mortimer at Winchester in 1330, or Edward III in the destruction of Mortimer—would perhaps have welcomed the assistance of the commons in judgment as well as in legislation. But it was a happy thing on the whole that the commons preferred the part of accuser to that of judge, and were content to accept the award of the magnates against the objects of their indignation. The events of the closing years of Richard's reign show that the third estate, notwithstanding its general character of patriotic independence, was only too susceptible of royal manipulation; that the right of impeachment was a weapon which might be turned two ways. The fact that most of the great malefactors on whom the power of impeachment was exercised were magnates, gave them as a matter of course the right to be tried by their peers, and the lords, new in their judicial work, thought it necessary in 1330 to disavow any intention of trying any who were not their peers[1]. But the commons wisely chose their attitude on the occasion of the deposition of Richard, and declared that they were not and had not acted as judges[2]. The fact that they had in 1384 heard the complaint of John Cavendish against Michael de la Pole, and the other occasions on which the petitions of individuals were laid before them, show how nearly they were willing to undertake the functions of a court of law[3].

Possibility that the house of commons might become a court of justice.

The commons content themselves with the power of impeachment.

They decline to be judges.

[1] Rot. Parl. ii. 53, 54: they had tried Sir Simon Bereford, John Maltravers, Thomas Gurney, and William de Ocle for the murder of Edward II. Thomas Berkeley was tried by a jury of knights in the parliament; ibid. p. 57.

[2] Rot. Parl. iii. 427.

[3] Rot. Parl. iii. 168: 'un Johan Cavendish de Londres pessoner soi pleignast en ce parlement, primerement devant la commune d'Engleterre

Confusion between legislative and executive functions.

The indistinctness of the line drawn between the executive and legislative powers in the kingdom, and between the executive and legislative functions of the king, accounts to some extent, not indeed for the theoretical assumptions of high prerogative, but certainly for the difficulty of securing in the hands of the parliament proper control over the administration.

It explains the attitude of the more despotic kings.

Nor is the indistinctness all on one side. A king who inherited traditions of despotism, or who like Richard II had formed a definite plan of absolute sovereignty, saw little difference between the enacting and enforcing of a law, between the exaction and the outlay of a pecuniary impost, between the raising and the command of an army: he inherited his crown from kings, many of whom had exercised all these powers with little restraint from the counsel or consent or dissent of their parliaments. With the barons of the thirteenth century and the parliaments of the fourteenth it was the substance of power, not the theoretical limitation of executive functions, that was the object of contention. The claims made in 1258 for the direct election of the king's council and ministers, the resuscitation of the same projects in 1311 and 1386, were nearly as much opposed to the ultimate idea of the constitution as were the abuses of power which they were intended to rectify.

Intrusions of the parliament into executive matters.

When the parliament under the leadership of the barons proceeded to make regulations for the household, to fix the days and places of muster, to determine beforehand the times for their own sessions, to nominate justices of the peace and other subordinate ministers of justice, they were clearly intruding into the province of the executive. That their designs were beneficial to the nation, that their attempts even when frustrated conduced to the growth of liberty, that they were dictated by a true sense of national sympathy, is far more than enough to acquit them of presumption in the eyes of the posterity which they so largely benefited. But the same facts did not present themselves in the same light to the kings who

en lour assemble en presence d'autres prelatz et seigneurs temporels illoeques lors esteantz, et puis apres devant touz les prelatz et seigneurs esteantz en ce parlement.' The chancellor answered the complaint first before the lords, then before the lords and commons together.

had in the person of Richard II perfected the idea of territorial monarchy. And this must be allowed to mitigate in some degree the censure that is visited on those sovereigns who were the most ardent maintainers of prerogative. They had inherited their crown with duties to both predecessors and successors: they were none of them, unless it was Edward II, men of mean ability, or consciously regardless of their duties towards their people: they looked on the realm too much as a property to be managed, not indeed without regard to the welfare of the inhabitants, but with the ultimate end and aim of benefiting its owner; a family perhaps, but one in which the patria potestas was the supreme rule,—a rule to which there was no check, against which there was no appeal. The constitutional historian has not to acquit or condemn, but he must recognise the truth of circumstances in which entire acquittal and entire condemnation alike would be unjust.

Some excuse for the high theory of prerogative.

Equitable judgment necessary.

296. In no part of the constitutional fabric was more authority left to the king, and in none was less interference attempted by the parliament, than in the constitution of the parliament itself. It would almost seem as if the edifice crowned by Edward I in 1295 was already deemed too sacred to be rashly touched. The king retained the right of summoning the estates whenever and wherever he chose; he could, without consulting the magnates, add such persons as he pleased to the permanent number of peers, and he might, no doubt, with very little trouble and with no sacrifice of popularity, have increased or diminished the number of members of the house of commons by dealing with the sheriffs. On these three points occasional contests turned, but they scarcely ever, as was the case in later reigns, came into the foreground as leading constitutional questions.

Power of the king in the constitution of parliament.

The frequent session of parliament was felt by the nation at large far more as a burden than as a privilege; the counties and boroughs alike murmured at the cost of representation; the borough representatives in the lower house and the monastic members of the upper house avoided attending whenever they could; and frequent parliaments were generally

Sentiment of the king and the nation as to frequent sessions of parliament.

Frequent parliaments unpopular.

regarded as synonymous with frequent taxation. On the other hand the more active politicians saw in the regular session of the estates the most trustworthy check upon the arbitrary power of the king, who was thus obliged to hear the complaints of the people, and might, if they dealt judiciously in the matter of money, be obliged to redress their grievances. With the king the feeling was reversed in each case; as a means of raising money, he might have welcomed frequent and regular sessions; as a time for compulsory legislation and involuntary receiving of advice, he must have been inclined to call them as seldom as possible. Accordingly when political feeling was high, there was a demand for annual parliaments; when the king's necessities were great and the sympathy of the nation inert or exhausted, there was a manifest reluctance to attend parliament at all. Thus in 1258 the barons under the Provisions of Oxford directed the calling of three parliaments every year, and Edward I observed the rule so far as it involved annual sessions for judicial purposes; but neither of these precedents applied exactly to the parliaments when completely constituted. Three times in the year was clearly too often for the country to be called on to send representatives either to legislate or to tax. The completion of the parliamentary constitution having rendered the necessity less pressing, the latter years of Edward I and the early years of Edward II saw these assemblies called only on urgent occasions, and this no doubt, as well as the wish to imitate the barons of 1258, led the lords ordainers[1] of 1311 to direct annual parliaments; the same question arose in 1330[2] and 1362, and in both those years it was ordered by statute that parliaments should be held once a year and oftener if necessary[3]. The same demand was made in the Good Parliament and was answered by a reference to existing statutes[4]. The question and answer were repeated in the first parliament of Richard II[5],

Three parliaments in the year.

Annual parliaments, ordered by the ordainers, and by statute.

[1] Statutes, i. 165, art. 29. [2] Statutes, i. 265.

[3] Statutes, i. 374: on the subject of annual parliaments, see especially the article by Mr. Allen in the 28th volume of the Edinburgh Review, no. 55, pp. 126 sq.

[4] Rot. Parl. ii. 355, art. 186. [5] Rot. Parl. iii. 23, art. 54.

and in 1378 the chancellor in his opening speech referred to the rule now established as one of the causes of the summons of parliament[1]. In 1388 the commons even went so far as to fix by petition the time for summoning the next parliament[2]. Examples of a contrary feeling may be found: thus in 1380 both lords and commons petition that they may not be called together for another year[3]. Other instances show that the need of money occasionally influenced the king more strongly than the fear of receiving unwelcome advice; in 1328 four parliaments were held, in 1340 three, and in some of the later years of Edward III and of the early years of Richard II the estates were called together twice within a period of twelve months. In those years again for which supplies had been provided by biennial or triennial grants made beforehand no parliament was called at all. The result was to leave matters very much as they were; annual parliaments were the rule; it was only in unquiet times that the commons found it necessary or advisable to insist on the observance of the rule; but when they found Richard II proposing to dispense altogether with parliament and reduce the assembly of the estates to a permanent committee, they were at once roused to the enormity of the offence against their rights.

Annual Parliaments.

Irregularity of sessions accounted for.

The determination of the place of parliament and of the length of the session rested with the king. Occasionally the place was fixed with a view of avoiding the interference of the London mob with the freedom of debate; Winchester and Salisbury were chosen by Mortimer, and Gloucester by John of Gaunt for this reason; most of the deviations from the rule of meeting at Westminster were however caused by the Welsh and Scottish wars. The power of prorogation either before or after the day of meeting rested with the king, and, although in a vast majority of instances the parliaments were newly summoned and the representative members chosen afresh for each session, the few exceptional cases of prorogation are

Place of session fixed by the king.

Power of prorogation.

[1] Rot. Parl. iii. 32.

[2] Rot. Parl. iii. 246.

[3] Rot. Parl. iii. 75: 'en priantz a nostre seignur le roi que nul parlement soit tenuz deinz le dit roialme pur pluis charger sa poevre commune par entre cy et le dit feste de S. Michael proschein venant en un an.'

sufficient to prove that the royal right was exercised without hesitation and without producing any irritation[1]. Occasionally as in 1339 the commons expressed a wish for a new election[2], being unwilling perhaps to extend their delegated powers to purposes which were not contemplated when they were first chosen. Neither king nor parliament liked long sessions; the king would gladly dispense with the attendance of his advisers as soon as money was granted; and the advisers were eager to depart as soon as their petitions were answered. In 1386, on the occasion of the impeachment of Michael de la Pole, it is doubtful whether the parliament resisted the king's intention to dismiss them or compelled him, by a threat of dissolution, to attend against his will. But generally it seems to have been more difficult to keep the members together than to shorten, for any reason, the duration of the session.

New election asked for.

Long sessions disliked.

The king exercised without any direct check the power of adding to the numbers of the house of lords by special summons, in virtue of which the recipient took his seat as a hereditary counsellor. Edward III however introduced the custom of creating great dignities of peerage, earldoms and dukedoms, in parliament and with the consent of that body. By doing this he probably hoped to avoid the odium which his father had incurred in the promotion of Gaveston, and to obtain parliamentary authorisation for the gifts of land or other provision, made out of the property at his disposal, for the maintenance of the new dignity. Thus in 1328 at the Salisbury parliament he made three earls, those of Cornwall, March, and Ormond[3]; in the parliament held in February, 1337, he made seven earls[4], three by the definite advice and four with the counsel and consent of parliament, one of whom, William Montacute earl of Salisbury, had some years before received a considerable endowment at the request of the parliament as a reward for his

Creation of earls by advice and consent of the parliament.

[1] The principal cases of prorogation up to this point were in 1311, above, p. 347; in 1328, p. 390; in 1333, p. 396; in 1381, p. 482; in 1388, p. 504, and in 1397–8, p. 521. Mr. Allen (Edinb. Rev. xxviii. 135–137) gives some other instances which are not prorogations; e.g. the great council at Winchester in 1371, and the supplementary sessions at Lincoln in the reign of Edward II.

[2] Above, p. 400. [3] A. Murimuth, p. 58. [4] Ibid. p. 81.

assistance rendered to the king against Mortimer[1]. The promotions made by Richard II were likewise announced or made in parliament, although not always with a statement of counsel or consent. But this practice did not extend to simple baronies, which continued to be created by the act of summons until in 1387 Richard created Sir John Beauchamp of Holt, lord Beauchamp and baron of Kidderminster by letters patent[2]. These examples therefore do not affect the general truth of the proposition that the determination of the numbers of the house of lords practically rested with the king, controlled, and that very inadequately, by the attempts made in parliament to prevent him from alienating the estates of the crown by the gift of which his new nobility would be provided for. As has been already observed, the number of barons summoned during the fourteenth century gradually decreased: the new creations or new summonses did not really fill up the vacancies caused by the extinction of great families or the accumulation of their baronies in the hands of individual magnates. The institution of dukedoms and marquessates by Edward III and Richard II,

Creation of a baron by patent.

Power of the king in forming the house of lords.

New titles.

[1] Rot. Parl. ii. 56: William Montacute was made earl of Salisbury by the request of parliament; Henry of Lancaster earl of Derby, and Hugh of Audley earl of Gloucester 'de diffinito dicti parliamenti nostri consilio;' Lords' Report, vol. v. pp. 27, 31, 32: William Clinton earl of Huntingdon, ibid. p. 28; William Bohun earl of Northampton, ibid. p. 30; Robert Ufford earl of Suffolk, ibid. p. 31; by the counsel and consent of parliament. So also the marquess of Juliers in 1340 was made earl of Cambridge; the king's eldest son was created prince of Wales by advice of parliament; Ralph Stafford earl of Stafford, and Henry duke of Lancaster in 1351, were promoted with the consent of the lords. Richard II did not uniformly follow his grandfather's precedents; but it was occasionally done down to the year 1414; see Sir Harry Nicolas on the proceedings in the case of the earldom of Devon, app. ix. p. clxxviii. In 1425, the law was distinctly laid down: 'quod hujusmodi creatio ducum sive comitum, aut aliarum dignitatum, ad solum regem pertinet et non ad parliamentum;' Rot. Parl. iv. 274.

[2] 'Sciatis quod pro bonis et gratuitis serviciis quae dilectus et fidelis miles noster Johannes de Beauchamp de Holt senescallus hospitii nostri nobis impendit, ac loco per ipsum tempore coronationis nostrae hucusque nobis impenso, et quem pro nobis tenere poterit in futuro in nostris consiliis et parliamentis, necnon pro nobili et fideli genere unde descendit, ac pro suis magnificis sensu et circumspectione, ipsum Johannem in unum parium ac baronum regni nostri Angliae praefecimus; volentes quod idem Johannes et heredes masculi de corpore suo exeuntes statum baronis optineant ac domini de Beauchamp et barones de Kydermynster nuncupentur;' Lords' Report, v. 81. The example was not followed until 1433.

and the creation of viscounts by Henry VI, increased the splendour of the house of lords and perhaps contributed to set it wider apart from the body of Englishmen, but did not in any way strengthen either the royal power or the actual importance of the baronage. It was copied from the customs of France and the empire, and may even have produced, in the multiplication of petty jealousies and personal assumptions, evils which, however rife abroad, had not yet penetrated deep into English society.

No attempt to alter the numerical proportion of the house of commons.

Number of the knights of the shire unvaried.

No attempt seems to have been made during the first century of its existence to alter the numerical proportions of the house of commons, either on the part of the king or on the part of parliament. The number of counties being fixed, and the number of representatives from each being determined by a custom older than the constitution of parliament itself, there was no colourable pretext on any account to vary it. The exceptional assemblies of 1352, 1353, and 1371, to which one representative was summoned from each county, were not regarded as full and proper parliaments, but as great councils only, the action of which required subsequent ratification from the proper assembly of the estates.

Variation in the number of borough members.

The number of town representatives might no doubt easily have been tampered with. Summoned as they were by the general writ addressed to the sheriff, and not individually specified in that writ, the towns might, either by the indulgence or by the political agency of the sheriff, have been deprived of the right or allowed to escape the burden of representation. That this was to some extent allowed, would seem to be proved by the statute of 1382, which forbids the sheriff to be negligent in making his returns, or to leave out of them any cities or boroughs that were bound and of old time were wont to come to the parliament[1]. But the borough element of parliament was, during the greatest part of the fourteenth century, of very secondary importance; the action of the town representatives is scarcely ever mentioned apart from that of the knights of the shire, and seldom noted in conjunction with it; it is only from the subservient and illiberal

[1] Statutes, ii. 25; Rot. Parl. iii. 124.

action of Richard's later parliaments that we can infer that they occupied a somewhat more influential place at the close of the reign than at the beginning; and it would seem to have been scarcely worth while for either the royal or the anti-royal party to have attempted important action through their means.

Attempts to influence the elections.

It was not then by altering the balance of numbers in the house of commons that the rival parties, in the infancy of representative institutions, attempted to increase their own power; but by the far more simple plan of influencing the elections and, if the use of the term is not premature, by modifying or trying to modify the franchise. The former seems to have been the policy of the king, who could deal immediately with the sheriffs or could overawe the county court by an armed force; the latter was attempted on one occasion at least by the opposition. In 1377 John of Gaunt procured the return of a body of knights of the shire which enabled him to reverse the acts of the parliament of 1376[1]; in 1387 Richard by directing the sheriffs to return knights who had not taken part in the recent quarrels, 'magis indifferentes in modernis debatis,' was held to have interfered unconstitutionally with the rights of the commons[2]; and the parliament of 1397 was elected and assembled under intimidation[3]. The despairing cry of the earl of Arundel when put on his trial, 'The faithful commons are not here,' and his persistent declaration that the house of commons did not express the real sense of the country, can bear no other interpretation. It was moreover one of the charges on which the judicial sentence against Richard was founded that 'although by statute and the custom of his realm, at the convoking of every parliament, his people in every county ought to be free to choose and depute

The king employs the sheriffs to return his candidates.

Alleged against Richard II.

[1] Chron. Angl. p. 122: 'Milites vero comitatus, quos dux pro arbitrio surrogaverat; nam omnes qui in ultimo parliamento steterant procuravit pro viribus amoveri, ita quod non fuerunt ex illis in hoc parliamento praeter duodecim, quos dux amovere non potuit, eo quod comitatus de quibus electi fuerant alios eligere noluerunt.' As a matter of fact only sixteen members of the parliament of 1376 were returned in 1377; nine knights and seven burgesses; Returns, pp. 193–197.

[2] See above, p. 502.

[3] Ann. Ricardi, p. 209: 'Militibus parliamenti qui non fuerunt electi per communitatem, prout mos exigit, sed per regiam voluntatem.' Cf. Political Poems, ed. Wright, i. 413.

Richard's scheme of regulating the elections.

knights for such counties to be present in parliament and exhibit their grievances and to prosecute for remedies thereupon as it should seem to them expedient; the king, in order that he might in his parliaments obtain more freely effect for his arbitrary will, frequently directed his mandates to the sheriffs directing them to return to his parliaments certain persons named by the king himself as knights of the shires; which knights, being favourable to the king, he was able to induce, sometimes by various threats and terrors, sometimes by gifts, to consent to things which were prejudicial to the realm and very burdensome to the people, especially the grant of the custom of wool for the king's life[1].' The charge was no doubt true, and the evil practice itself may have been an integral part of Richard's deliberate attempt on the national liberties.

Attempts made by the commons to alter the mode of election.

The commons, however jealous of the king's interference with the elections, were not themselves disposed to acquiesce in the unsatisfactory condition of the electoral body,—the county court, which was peculiarly amenable to manipulation, not only by the king but by the great lords of the shire. The petition presented in 1376 might tell two ways: in it the commons prayed that the knights of the shire for these parliaments might be chosen by common election from the best people of the counties, and not certified by the sheriff alone without due election, on certain penalties[2]; it might mean that the mixed crowd of the county courts was unfit to choose a good representative, or that the sheriff took advantage of the unruly character of the gathering, sometimes perhaps to return the members without show of election, sometimes to interpret the will of the electors in favour of his own candidate. Instances were not unknown in which the sheriff returned his own knights when the county had elected others[3]. The attempt made by the commons in 1372[4] to prevent the election of lawyers as knights of the shire is another illustration of the wish to purge the assembly of a class of mem-

[1] Above, p. 530; Rot. Parl. iii. 420.

[2] Rot. Parl. ii. 355.

[3] In 1319 the sheriff of Devon returned members not elected by the commons of the county, and Matthew Crauthorne, who had been duly elected, petitioned against the return; Parl. Writs, II. ii. App. p. 138.

[4] Rot. Parl. ii. 310; Statutes, i. 395.

bers who were supposed to be more devoted to private gain than to public good[1]. On both occasions the king refused the petition, deciding in favour of the liberty of the constituencies on the ground of custom. Whether the liberty or the custom was in reality so important an object in the royal mind as the retention of the power exercised by the government through the sheriffs in the county court, the events of the reign of Richard enable us to decide.

The king refuses to alter the custom.

297. It is unnecessary to discuss the further points of royal prerogative in this place. Numerous as they are, they are not matters in which the crown came into conflict either with the parliament when full grown or with that constitutional spirit which was the life-breath of parliamentary growth. We have examined in detail the struggle between prerogative, in the sense of undefined royal authority, and parliamentary control, under the three chief heads of taxation, legislation, and executive functions, in council, courts of justice and military affairs. The minor points, to which properly belongs the definition of prerogative, as 'that which is law in respect to the king which is not law in respect to the subject,' are matters of privilege rather than of authority. Some of these points touch tenure, as the peculiar rights and customs enumerated in the apocryphal statute *de Praerogativa Regis*[2]; such are the right of wardship, marriage and dower of the heirs of tenants-in-chief, the restraints on alienation of lands held in chief and serjeanties, the presentation to vacant churches after lapse, the custody of the lands of lunatics and idiots, the right to wreck, whales and sturgeons, the escheats of the land falling by descent to aliens, and other like customs. These are more or less distinctly

Technical points of prerogative.

Statute *de Praerogativa Regis.*

[1] In 1330 Edward III had been obliged to order that more care should be taken in the county elections: 'pur ce que avant ces heures acuns des chivalers, que sunt venuz as parlementz pur les communautes des countes, ount este gentz de coveigne et maintenours de fauses quereles, et n'ount mie soeffret que les bones gentz poient monstrer les grevaunces du comun people, ne les choses que deussent aver este redresses en parlement a grant damage de nous et de nostre people, vous mandoms et chargeoms que vous facez eslire par commun assent de vostre countee deux des plus leaux et plus suffisauns chivalers ou serjauntz a meisme le countee, qui soient mie suspecionous de male conveigne,' &c.; Rot. Parl. ii. 443.

[2] Statutes, i. 226. Pollock and Maitland, i. 316.

Powers of the king with reference to trade, and to the clergy.

defined by law or prescription. Of another class, those concerning trade, such as have up to our present point a practical importance, have been noted in connexion with our discussion on the revenue; others, such as the power of creating monopolies, have an importance which lies far ahead of the present inquiry. The special prerogatives of the king with regard to the church and clergy will call for some notice in another part of our work.

The revolution of 1399 not a final determination of the whole question.

The examination however of the former points, so far as it has gone, leads to the same conclusions as those which are drawn from the direct and continuous narrative of the history of the fourteenth century. The struggle between royal prerogative and parliamentary authority does not work out its own issue in the fate of Richard II; the decision is taken for the moment on a side issue,—the wrongs of Henry of Lancaster; the judicial condemnation of Richard is a statement not of the actual causes of his deposition, but of the offences by which such a measure was justified. Prematurely Richard had challenged the rights of the nation, and the victory of the nation was premature. The royal position was founded on assumptions that had not even prescription in their favour; the victory of the house of Lancaster was won by the maintenance of rights which were claimed rather than established. The growth of the commons, and of the parliament itself in that constitution of which the commons were becoming the strongest part, must not be estimated by the rights which they had actually secured, but by those which they were strong enough to claim, and wise enough to appreciate. If the course of history had run otherwise, England might possibly have been spared three centuries of political difficulties; for the most superficial reading of history is sufficient to show that the series of events which form the crises of the Great Rebellion and the Revolution might link themselves on to the theory of Richard II as readily as to that of James I. In that case we might have seen the forces of liberty growing by regular stages as the pretensions of tyranny took higher and higher flights, until the struggle was fought out in favour of a nation uneducated and untrained for the use of the rights that fell to it, or in favour of a king who should know

The discipline of three centuries more was required for a successful issue of the struggle.

no limit to the aspirations of his ambition or to the exercise of his revenge. The failure of the house of Lancaster, the tyranny of the house of York, the statecraft of Henry VII, the apparent extinction of the constitution under the dictatorship of Henry VIII, the political resurrection under Elizabeth, were all needed to prepare and equip England to cope successfully with the principles of Richard II, masked under legal, religious, philosophical embellishments in the theory of the Stewarts. Hence it is that in our short enumeration of the points at issue we are obliged to rest content with recording the claims of parliament rather than to pursue them to their absolute vindication: they were claimed under Edward III, they were won during the Rebellion, at the Restoration, or at the Revolution: some of them were never won at all in the sense in which they were first claimed; parliament does not at the present day elect the ministers, or obtain the royal assent to bills before granting supplies; but the practical responsibility of the ministers is not the less assured, and the crown cannot choose ministers unacceptable to the parliament, with the slightest probability of their continuing in office. If the development of the ministerial system had been the only point gained by the delay of the crisis for three centuries, from 1399 to 1688, England might perhaps have been content to accept the responsibility of becoming a republic in the fifteenth century. Had that been the case, the whole history of the nation, perhaps of Europe also, would have been changed in a way of which we can hardly conceive. Certainly the close of the fourteenth century was a moment at which monarchy might seem to be in extremis, France owning the rule of a madman, Germany nominally subject to a drunkard,—the victim, the tyrant, and the laughing-stock of his subjects,—and the apostolic see itself in dispute between two rival successions of popes. That the result was different may be attributed, for one at least out of several reasons, to the fact that the nations were not yet ready for self-government.

Progress of parliamentary institutions to be calculated by claims rather than by vindication.

298. The fourteenth century had other aspects besides that in which we have here viewed it, aspects which seem paradoxical until they are viewed in connexion with the general course of

Other aspects of the fourteenth century.

human history, in which the ebb and flow of the life of nations is seen to depend on higher laws, more general purposes, the guidance of a Higher Hand. Viewed as a period of constitutional growth it has much to attract the sympathies and to interest the student who is content laboriously to trace out the links of causes and results. In literary history likewise it has a very distinct and significant place; and it is scarcely second to any age in its importance as a time of germination in religious history. In these aspects it might seem to furnish sufficient and more than sufficient matters of attractive disquisition. Yet it is on the whole unattractive, and in England especially so: the political heroes are, as we have seen, men who for some cause or other seem neither to demand nor to deserve admiration; the literature with few exceptions owes its interest either to purely philological causes or to its connexion with a state of society and thought which repels more than it attracts; the religious history read impartially is chilling and unedifying; its literature on both sides is a compound of elaborate dialectics and indiscriminate invective, alike devoid of high spiritual aspirations and of definite human sympathies. The national character, although it must be allowed to have grown into strength, has not grown into a knowledge how to use its strength. The political bloodshed of the fourteenth century is the prelude to the internecine warfare of the fifteenth: personal vindictiveness becomes, far more than it has ever yet been, a characteristic of political history. Public and private morality seem to fall lower and lower: at court splendid extravagance and coarse indulgence are seen hand in hand; John of Gaunt, the first lord of the land, claims the crown of Castille in the right of his wife, and lives in adultery with one of her ladies; he is looked up to as the protector of a religious party, one of whose special claims to support lies in its assertion of a pure morality; his son, Henry Beaufort, soon to become a bishop, a crusader, and by and by a cardinal, is the father of an illegitimate daughter, whose mother is sister to the earl of Arundel and the archbishop of Canterbury. If we look lower down we are tempted to question whether the growth of reli-

Its character is generally unattractive.

Decline in moral power.

Impressions made by the literature of the time.

gious thought and literary facility has as yet done more good or harm. Neither the lamentations nor the confessions of Gower, nor the sterner parables of Langland, nor the brighter pictures of Chaucer, nor the tracts and sermons of Wycliffe, reveal to us anything that shows the national character to be growing in the more precious qualities of truthfulness and tenderness. There is much misery and much indignation; much luxury and little sympathy. The lighter stories of Chaucer recall the novels of Boccaccio, not merely in their borrowed plot but in the tone which runs through them; vice taken for granted, revelry and indulgence accepted as the enjoyment and charm of life; if it be intended as satire it is a satire too far removed from sympathy for that which is better, too much impregnated with the spirit of that which it would deride. Edward III, celebrating his great feast on the institution of the order of the Garter in the midst of the Black Death, seems a typical illustration of this side of the life of the century. The disintegration of the older forms of society has been noted already as accounting for much of the political history of a period which notwithstanding is fruitful in result. There is no unity of public interest, no singleness of political aim, no heroism of self-sacrifice. The baronage is divided against itself, one part maintaining the popular liberties but retarding their progress by bitter personal antipathies, the other maintaining royal autocracy, and although less guilty as aggressors still more guilty by way of revenge. The clergy are neither intelligent enough to guide education nor strong enough to repress heresy; the heretics have neither skill to defend nor courage to die for their doctrines; the universities are ready to maintain liberty but not powerful enough to lead public opinion; the best prelates, even such as Courtenay and Wykeham, are conservative rather than progressive in their religious policy, and the lower type, which is represented by Arundel, seems to combine political liberality with religious intolerance in a way that resembles, though with different aspect and attitude, the policy of the later puritans.

Prevalence of luxury and misery.

General disintegration.

Decline in the clergy.

The transition is scarcely less marked in the region of art; in architecture the unmeaning symmetry of the Perpendicular style

Changes in architecture and writing.

is an outgrowth but a decline from the graceful and affluent diversity of the Decorated. The change in the penmanship is analogous; the writing of the fourteenth century is coarse and blurred compared with the exquisite elegance of the thirteenth, and yet even that is preferable to the vulgar neatness and deceptive regularity of the fifteenth. The chain of historical writers becomes slighter and slighter until it ceases altogether, except so far as the continuators of the Polychronicon preserve a broken and unimpressive series of isolated facts.

Decline of history.

These things are not to be explained by theories.

It may seem strange that the training of the thirteenth century, the examples of the patriot barons, the policy of the constitutional king, organiser and legislator, should have had so lame results; that, whilst constitutionally the age is one of progress, morally it should be one of decline, and intellectually one of blossom rather than fruit. But the historian has not yet arisen who can account on the principles of progress, or of reaction, or of alternation, for the tides in the affairs of men. How it was we can read in the pages of the annalists, the poets, the theologians: how it became so we can but guess; why it was suffered we can only understand when we see it overruled for good. It may be that the glories of the thirteenth century conceal the working of internal evils which are not new, but come into stronger relief when the brighter aspects fade away; and that the change of characters from Edward I to Edward II, Edward III and Richard II, does but take away the light that has dazzled the eye of the historian, and so reveals the hollowness and meanness that may have existed all along. It may be that the strength, the tension, the aspirations of the earlier produced the weakness, the relaxation, the grovelling degradation of the later. But it is perhaps still too early to draw a confident conclusion. Weak as is the fourteenth century, the fifteenth is weaker still; more futile, more bloody, more immoral; yet out of it emerges, in spite of all, the truer and brighter day, the season of more general conscious life, higher longings, more forbearing, more sympathetic, purer, riper liberty.

INDEX.

END OF VOL. II.